Foreign Policy

Additional endorsements for *Foreign Policy 2e*

'The editors have mobilized an outstanding group of scholars and practitioners to explore through literature reviews and case studies how theories of international relations, such as realism, liberalism, and constructivism, can help us to understand foreign policy behaviour. They also demonstrate how the choice of analytical level—the states system, national and organizational characteristics, and personality traits—affect the explanations that emerge. The original studies are sensitive to the role of non-state actors in accounting for foreign policy choices, and they also include important examples of middle powers' influence in certain global issue areas. The editors' theoretical vision of the project assures readers of a comprehensive and enduring effort. This volume is an authoritative last word in the field of foreign policy analysis.'

K. J. Holsti, University Killam Professor, Emeritus, University of British Columbia

'A unique and indispensable resource. Its coverage is remarkably comprehensive and provides a judicious blend of theory and illustration. The theoretical chapters are clear and accessible, and the case materials and topical chapters offer a rich array of pedagogical possibilities. Like *The Globalisation of World Politics*, this book deserves to be widely adopted.'

Stephen M. Walt, Harvard University

'The editors have filled a long-neglected gap by producing a volume that authoritatively covers the state of the art in the study of foreign policy. The book looks set to become a definitive text for the teaching and study of foreign policy.'

Richard G. Whitman, University of Kent

'The book combines old and new perspectives with discerning care. In-depth explorations of empirical examples present a geographically diverse set of cases for teaching. Highly recommended.'

Olav F. Knudsen, Swedish Institute of International Affairs

Foreign Policy

Theories, Actors, Cases

SECOND EDITION

Edited by

Steve Smith

Amelia Hadfield

Tim Dunne

OXFORD
UNIVERSITY PRESS

OXFORD
UNIVERSITY PRESS

Great Clarendon Street, Oxford OX2 6DP,
United Kingdom

Oxford University Press is a department of the University of Oxford.
It furthers the University's objective of excellence in research, scholarship,
and education by publishing worldwide. Oxford is a registered trade mark of
Oxford University Press in the UK and in certain other countries

© Oxford University Press 2012

The moral rights of the authors have been asserted

First Edition published 2008

Impression: 5

British Library Cataloguing in Publication Data

Data available

Library of Congress Cataloging in Publication Data

Data available

ISBN 978-0-19-959623-2

Printed in Great Britain by
Ashford Colour Press Ltd, Gosport, Hampshire

Links to third party websites are provided by Oxford in good faith and
for information only. Oxford disclaims any responsibillty for the materials
contained in any third party website referenced in this work.

Foreword

JAMES N. ROSENAU

My contribution to the analysis of foreign policy began on a blackboard. I was prompted to clarify for students what variables were central to probing the dynamics of foreign policy. The result was an eight-column matrix that listed the relative importance of five key variables in eight types of countries (Rosenau 1966). That matrix still informs my teaching and research. It also implicitly underlies more than a few of the chapters in this volume. Needless to say, I am honoured that this volume takes note of my contribution to the field.

I called the eight-column matrix and the description of it a 'pre-theory of foreign policy'. It provoked sufficient interest among colleagues around the country to convene a series of conferences that explored various facets of the pre-theory, which in turn led to the publication of a collection of essays prepared for the conferences (Rosenau 1974). This collaboration among some 20 scholars who had developed a keen interest in comparing foreign policies gave rise to the founding of the Inter-University Comparative Foreign Policy (ICFP) project. The members of ICFP remained in continual contact for some six years, thus demonstrating that like-minded colleagues can pool their resources and sustain collaboration across some 10 universities during a period of diminishing support for comparative and quantitative research.

The matrix was impelled by the milieu of the field at that time. It was a period in which comparison was very much in vogue and it seemed to me that foreign policy phenomena were as subject to comparative analysis as any other political process. Indeed, I still find it remarkable that no previous analyst had undertaken a comparative enquiry of when, how, and why different countries undertook to link themselves to the international system in the ways that they did.

In retrospect, it seems clear that the original pre-theory sparked wide interest not only because it stressed the need for comparative analysis, but for several other reasons that also underlay the enthusiasm for the ICFP. First, the pre-theory offered a means for analysing the conduct of foreign policy in previous years as well as anticipating future developments in a country's external behaviour. Second, as stressed below, it provided a means for bringing foreign and domestic policy together under the same analytical umbrella. Third, it highlighted the virtues of case studies as a basis for comparing, analysing, and interpreting foreign policy phenomena. All of these central characteristics of the field are fully represented in the chapters that comprise this volume.

Much progress has occurred in the field since the founding of the ICFP. The very fact that it is now comfortably regarded as a 'field' is in itself indicative of how securely it has been established. This is not to say, however, that the field is easily mastered. On the contrary, several of its key aspects pose difficult analytical problems. If politics is conceived as processes of trying to control the actions and attitudes of other actors in the more remote environment, a formulation I have always considered sound and worthy of applying to empirical materials (Rosenau 1963), it follows that analysis must focus on a wide range of phenomena—from individuals and their orientations to the groups and institutions that form the bases of societies,

Some possible sources of fragmegration at four levels of aggregation

Levels of aggregation → Sources of fragmegration ↓	MICRO	MACRO	MACRO–MACRO	MICRO–MACRO
Skill Revolution	expands people's horizons on a global scale; sensitizes them to the relevance of distant events; facilitates a reversion to local concerns	enlarges the capacity of government agencies to think 'out of the box', seize opportunities, and analyse challenges	multiplies quantity and enhances quality of links among states; solidifies their alliances and enmities	constrains policy making through increased capacity of individuals to know when, where, and how to engage in collective action
Authority Crises	redirect loyalties; encourage individuals to replace traditional criteria of legitimacy with performance criteria	weaken ability of both governments and other organizations to frame and implement policies	enlarge the competence of some IGOs and NGOs; encourage diplomatic wariness in negotiations	facilitate the capacity of publics to press and/or paralyse their governments, the WTO, and other organizations
Bifurcation of Global Structures	adds to role conflicts, divides loyalties, and foments tensions among individuals; orients people toward local spheres of authority	facilitates formation of new spheres of authority and consolidation of existing spheres in the multicentric world	generates institutional arrangements for cooperation on major global issues such as trade, human rights, the environment, etc.	empowers transnational advocacy groups and special interests to pursue influence through diverse channels
Organizational Explosion	facilitates multiple identities, subgroupism, and affiliation with transnational networks	increases capacity of opposition groups to form and press for altered policies; divides publics from their elites	renders the global stage ever more transnational and dense with non-governmental actors	contributes to the pluralism and dispersion of authority; heightens the probability of authority crises
Mobility Upheaval	stimulates imaginations and provides more extensive contacts with foreign cultures; heightens salience of the outsider	enlarges the size and relevance of subcultures, diasporas, and ethnic conflicts as people seek new opportunities abroad	heightens need for international cooperation to control the flow of drugs, money, immigrants, and terrorists	increases movement across borders that lessens capacity of governments to control national boundaries

Microelectronic Technologies	enable like-minded people to be in touch with each other anywhere in the world	empower governments to mobilize support; render their secrets vulnerable to spying	accelerate diplomatic processes; facilitate electronic surveillance and intelligence work	constrain governments by enabling opposition groups to mobilize more effectively
Weakening of Territoriality, States, and Sovereignty	undermines national loyalties and increases distrust of governments and other institutions	adds to the porosity of national boundaries and the difficulty of framing national policies	increases need for interstate cooperation on global issues; lessens control over cascading events	lessens confidence in governments; renders nationwide consensus difficult to achieve and maintain
Globalization of National Economies	swells ranks of consumers; promotes uniform tastes; heightens concerns for jobs	complicates tasks of state governments vis-à-vis markets; promotes business alliances	intensifies trade and investment conflicts; generates incentives for building global financial institutions	increases efforts to protect local cultures and industries; facilitates vigour of protest movements

economies, and polities. Put succinctly, little of human behaviour falls outside the scope of the analysis of foreign policy phenomena.

More important than its vast scope, however, this formulation is not easily subjected to analysis. One not only needs to be familiar with the dynamics whereby states interact with each other, but the internal processes whereby foreign policies are formed also need to be probed. To ignore these processes by classifying them as 'domestic', and thus as outside the analyst's concerns, would be to omit central features of the behaviour one wants to investigate. Students of domestic phenomena may be able to hold foreign inputs constant, but the same cannot be said about the phenomena that culminate in foreign policies. Inevitably the student of a country's foreign policy must also be concerned with its internal affairs. Put differently, he or she must be a student of sociology and psychology as well as political science, economics, and history. No less important, they should have some knowledge of the problems inherent in comparative enquiry. The methodologies of the field are as salient, as are the substantive problems that countries face in linking themselves to the international system.

In short, foreign policy phenomena are inordinately complex. They encompass inputs that can give rise to a variety of outputs, with a slight variation in one of the inputs having sizeable consequences for the outputs they foster. Thus the causal processes are not easily traced. They can be highly elusive when their variation spans, as it usually does, a wide range of inputs that may vary from *time1* to *time2*. Nor can the complexities be assumed away. They are too central to the dynamics of foreign policy to ignore or bypass. One has no choice but to allow for them and trace their consequences across diverse situations. Such a procedure facilitates cogent analysis even as it risks drawing a less than complete picture.

The main characteristics of foreign policy—and the requirements they impose on analysts of the subject—are fully observable in the ensuing chapters. Their authors demonstrate a keen sensitivity to the problems of the field and the rewards for analysing them. They understand the need for theory as well as empirical analysis of how any country conducts itself in the international community. More than that, this understanding includes a grasp of how the analysis must be varied to accommodate different approaches to the field.

In order to cope with the enormous variety of phenomena that may be relevant to the study of foreign policy one has to select some of them as important and dismiss others as trivial in so far as one's enquiry is concerned. This process of selection is what being theoretical means. More accurately, the selected phenomena have to be examined in relation to each other, as interactive, and the theoretician needs to grasp the dynamics of the interactive processes as well as the domestic variables of the country of concern. Constructing incisive theoretical perspectives is not easy, however. The process of explicating causal dynamics can be very frustrating as well as very complicated. It is fairly easy to have a general sense of the phenomena that underlie the foreign policy behaviour of interest, but it is quite another thing to transform one's general understanding into concrete, testable, and relevant hypotheses. Put differently, specifying the dependent variables—the outcomes of a foreign policy input—is readily conceived, but identifying and operationalizing the independent variables that foster alterations in the dependent variable serves to challenge one's grasp of the field. Everything can seem relevant as an independent variable, but the analyst has to be selective and focus on those dynamics that account for most of the variance conceived to be relevant to the analysis. There is no need to account for 100% of the variance, as some of it may be due to chance factors that cannot readily be anticipated, but even accounting for, say, 90% can be difficult. Not only do analysts need to calculate the relative importance of the different factors, but they also have to have some idea of how they interact with each other.

Consider, for example, the distinction between large and small countries. To differentiate between the two, one has to have some sense of how a country's size affects its conduct in the international arena. Are small countries more aggressive abroad because of their limitations? Do their foreign policies avoid confrontation because of an imbalance between the resources at their disposal and those of the adversaries they contemplate taking on abroad? Are their decision-making processes, in effect, paralysed by the relative size of their potential adversaries? Such questions are not easily answered at first glance. And they become even more difficult if one has to assess the amount of the variance involved.

However, many analysts have not been deterred by the problems encountered in estimating variances. They know that such estimates are essentially arbitrary, as few have a perspective founded on clear-cut notions of the range within which the causal potency of a variable is specified. Nor are matters helped by stressing the relevance of a finding—'other things being equal'. Usually other things are not equal, so that clustering them together as if they were equal can be misleading.

How, then, to proceed? If the available conceptual equipment cannot generate reliable hypotheses, and if a *ceteris paribus* (i.e. all things being equal) context has limited utility, how does the analyst confront the task of framing and probing meaningful insights? The answer lies in maintaining a focus on the potential rather than the pitfalls of comparative analysis. Even if the underpinnings of a country's foreign policy are ambiguous, one can nonetheless proceed to examine what appear to be the main sources of the ambiguity, noting throughout the factors that may undermine the analysis. To focus on the obstacles to an enquiry is to ensure that the enquiry will fall short of what can be gleaned from the empirical materials at hand.

The best technique for moving ahead is that of specifying what independent variables seem especially relevant to the phenomena to be explained even as one acknowledges that the sum of the variance they account for may fall short of 100%. Such an acknowledgement is not so much a statement of fact as it is a noting of the limits that confine the analysis. Furthermore, even if only 80% or 90% of the variance is accounted for, such findings are likely to be valuable despite the fact that they fall short of a full explanation. The goal is not to account for all the variability, but to explain enough of it to enlarge our understanding of the key dynamics at work in the examined situation. Foreign policy phenomena are too complex to aspire to a full accounting of all the dynamics at work in a situation. It is enough to compare them carefully and draw conclusions about the central tendencies they depict. A close reading of the ensuing chapters demonstrates that proceeding in this way can yield deep and important insights into the diverse ways societies interact with their external environments.

While most of the relevant independent variables are amply assessed throughout the foreign policy literature, two are less widely cited and thus can usefully be elaborated here. One involves what I call the skill revolution and the other is the organizational explosion. Each accounts for a sufficient proportion of the variance to warrant amplification and together they significantly shape the conduct of any country's foreign policy.

The skill revolution

Considerable evidence is available to demonstrate that people everywhere, in every country and community throughout the world, are increasingly able to trace distant events through a series of interactions back into their own homes or pocketbooks. The skill revolution is understood to consist of three main dimensions: the analytical, the emotional, and the imaginative. The first of these involves an intellectual talent, an expanding ability to link the course of events to the observer's personal situation. Facilitated by the internet and many other technological innovations, people are ever more able to construct scenarios that depict how situations in the arenas of world politics impact on their lives and well-being (Rosenau, 2003: Chapter 10). The expansion of skills is presumed to occur through adding new scenarios to those people employed in order to perceive and assess the situations of interest to them. The emotional dimension of the skill revolution focuses on the way people feel about situations—to judge them as good or bad, welcoming or threatening—capacities that have also expanded as a consequence of a world that is shrinking and impinging ever more closely on their daily lives. The imaginative dimension depicts the capacity of people to envision alternative futures, lifestyles, and circumstances for themselves, their families, and their cherished organizations.

The materials for wide-ranging imaginative musings are abundantly available in all parts of the world. They include global television, soap operas, letters from relatives working as maids in Hong Kong, cousins who find employment in Saudi Arabia, and children who marry foreign spouses. The learning embedded in messages sent home is less directly experiential for the recipients than are the encounters reported by their authors, but nevertheless it can be a major contributor to the more worldly skills of those who do not travel. It may even be that the letters and phone calls from relatives abroad can be as much a window on the norms and practices of distant places as those offered on the television screen. These stimuli are especially relevant for peoples in developing countries whose circumstances previously limited contacts with other cultures and alternative lifestyles. Indeed, from the perspective of those who have long been hemmed in by the realities of life on or below the poverty line, the freeing up of their imaginative capacities is among the most powerful forces at work in the world today.

The organizational explosion

Hardly less so than the population explosion, recent years have witnessed a veritable explosion in the number of voluntary associations that have crowded onto the global stage. In all parts of the world and at every level of community, people—ordinary folk as well as elites and activists— are coming together to concert their efforts on behalf of shared needs and goals. Exact statistics on the extent of this pattern do not exist (largely because so much of it occurs at local levels and goes unreported), but few would argue with the propositions that the pace at which new associations are formed and old ones enlarged is startling, so much so that to call it an explosion is almost to understate the scale of growth. It has been calculated, for example, that in 1979 Indonesia had only a single independent environmental organization, whereas in 1999 there were more than 2000 linked to an environmental network based in Jakarta (Bornstein 1999).

The social media explosion

Since the first edition of this book was published, we have, of course, witnessed the major changes represented by the Arab Spring of 2011, which have further blurred the distinctions between domestic and international politics, and further illustrate the interconnectedness of all politics on the planet. This sees its most extreme example in the role of social media in previously seemingly closed societies. The visions of Iranian protestors, or Syrian activists, organizing their protests by Twitter and Facebook show only too clearly that governments can no longer control information flows. Such control was only ever partial, but the new social media fundamentally breach the old walls of the state. In this sense, the rise of social media represents a third revolution.

* * * *

Integrating the skill revolution, the organizational explosion, and the political consequences of the social media revolution into the analysis of the dynamics that shape foreign policy is not an easy task. Not to do so, however, would be to greatly distort the analysis. Clearly, what countries do abroad is highly dependent on the skills and attitudes shared amongst their populations at home. Taken together, the three variables account for a great deal of the variance from one country to another and from one point in time to another.

Editors' postscript

As we were finishing the editing of this new edition, word came through that Jim Rosenau had passed away (he died on 9 September 2011, aged 86, after suffering a stroke). This upset all three editors for a variety of reasons, some personal and some professional. Jim was one of the most significant scholars working in foreign policy, and was one of the subject's founding fathers. His influence on foreign policy analysis was not only through his published works, but also through the personal encouragement he gave to generations of students and scholars. Jim only gave up teaching at George Washington University in 2009, and still started each class by asking students to read out headlines from the *New York Times* and then asking them 'What is this an instance of?', and how it related to ideas they had covered in the course. His daughter, Margaret, said in one obituary that 'he was in love with teaching and in love with the academic world'. The editors of this book—particularly Steve Smith who had a close academic and personal relationship with him going back to 1980—experienced his personal kindness and, like countless other academics in the field, we owe Jim a massive debt for his always stimulating and stretching thinking about foreign policy analysis and international relations. Jim was a true scholar, a wonderful intellect, and an exceptionally kind man. We would simply like to mark his passing by dedicating this new edition to him.

October 2011

Guided tour of textbook features

This text is enriched with a range of learning tools to help you navigate the text material and reinforce your knowledge of foreign policy. This guided tour shows you how to get the most out of your textbook package.

Reader's guide

The aim of this chapter is to explore the concept of national security is a familiar concept in foreign policy, it i tially contested concept. This chapter introduces stude conceptions of national security, beginning with the tra of national security that has had a significant influence International Relations and foreign policy makers. The overview of the field of security studies. The chapter con cal controversy about the meaning of national security t debate on grand strategy.

Reader's guides

Reader's guides at the beginning of every chapter set the scene for upcoming themes and issues to be discussed and indicate the scope of coverage within each chapter topic.

BOX 10.1 Competing conceptions of national security

'A nation has security when it does not have to sacrifice its legitimate interes challenged, to maintain them by war.' (Lippmann 1943: 51)

'Any feminist definition of security must therefore include the elimination including violence prod uced by gender relations of domination and subord

'National security is the preservation of a way of life. . . . It includes freedor coercion, freedom from internal subversion and freedom from the erosion c and social values which are essential to the quality of life.' (Canadian Nation Buzan 1991: 17)

'National security is about the protection of core values, that is, the identif adoption of policies to protect core values.' (Leffler 2004a: 131)

'National security is the ability of a nation to protect its internal values f

Learning boxes

A number of topics benefit from further explanation or exploration in a way that does not disrupt the flow of the main text. Throughout the book boxes provide you with extra information on particular topics to complement your understanding of the main chapter text.

Questions

1. What does Wolfers mean when he writes that natior
2. How does realist theory contribute to the primacy of
3. How do the three S's of realism account for the prim
4. What is the relationship between the theory of realis
5. During the Cold War, how did scholars conceive of national security?
6. What is the meaning of national security?

Questions

A set of carefully devised questions has been provided to help you assess your comprehension of core themes and may also be used as the basis of seminar discussion and coursework.

Further reading

Baldwin, D. (1985), *Economic Statecraft* (Princeton, NJ:
An authoritative study of economic statecraft from the pe
systematically comparing economic with other instrume

Cortright, D. and Lopez, G. (2002), *Smart Sanctions: Tar*
Rowman & Littlefield).
A systematic examination of negative economic sanctio

Doxey, M. (1996), *International Sanctions in Contempo*
MacMillan).

Further reading

To take your learning further, reading lists have been
provided as a guide to find out more about the issues
raised within each chapter topic and to help you locate
the key academic literature in the field.

Glossary

Acquis communautaire: EU terminology for the
entire body of European law, including all the
treaties, regulations, and directives passed by European
institutions.

Active learning: active learning exercises put the
student in the centre of the learning process. Listening
to a lecture and simply taking notes is a passive learning

Aggressiv
structure o
to maximiz
pursuit of l
competitio

Analogica
ogies. Use

Glossary terms

Key terms are emboldened in the text and are defined
in a glossary at the end of the book to aid you in exam
revision.

Guided tour of the Online Resource Centre

The Online Resource Centre that accompanies this book provides students and lecturers with ready-to-use teaching and learning materials.

www.oxfordtextbooks.co.uk/orc/smith_foreign2e/

For Lecturers

These resources are password protected, but access is available to anyone using the book in their teaching. Please contact your local sales representative.

Reader's guide

The rise of China as a leading Asian power puts it on a collision course with another regional superpower. Increasingly, the two states are engaged in bitter territorial waters, national defence, natural resources, and most crucially, over in historical understandings of Japan's actions during the Second World Japanese relations can be analysed from various angles, but a Constructivist focusing on how Tokyo perceives Beijing as an antagonist enables us to appreciate and how—these conflicts have emerged and become entrenched into the cau that we see today. This case study therefore approaches the emer manifestation of vituperative bilateral relations from the Japanese perspe particular attention to the role of identity in Japanese foreign policy; but analytical thrust can also be used to study the Chinese side of the story as w

Case studies

Steven Lamy draws out the key themes from the case study chapters in the book and suggests potential teaching topics. Three additional case studies have been provided for use in teaching.

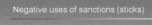

PowerPoint slides

A suite of customizable PowerPoint slides has been included for use in lectures. Arranged by chapter, the slides may also be used as handouts in class.

For students

Timeline

A timeline has been provided so that you can find out about the different periods in the evolution of foreign policy analysis.

Web links

Additional annotated web links.

Flashcard glossary

A series of interactive flashcards containing key terms and concepts has been provided to test your understanding of terminology.

Acknowledgements

All three editors are teachers of foreign policy. Steve Smith first taught foreign policy analysis in the mid-1980s while a young lecturer at the University of East Anglia. Tim Dunne, who was in Steve's class in 1987–1988, taught comparative foreign policy at the University of Exeter, and currently teaches and writes about decision-making in relation to intervention at the School of Political Science and International Studies at the University of Queensland. Amelia Hadfield first taught foreign policy analysis at the University of Kent, Canterbury, and continues to research and teach FPA at the Vrije Universiteit Brussel.

The aim of the first edition was to gather into a single text the waterfront of themes that ought to feature on a foreign policy course. The second edition continues that same goal, with new and revised chapters written by first-rate scholars and instructors whose ability to communicate their ideas via the research-led teaching of foreign policy analysis is clearly revealed in the pages that follow. The second edition is nothing if not genuinely international. Spanning time zones from Exeter, Brisbane, and Brussels, the editors continued working with each other to steer the text through the various stages, as well as collaborating with a talented line-up of contributors who quite literally are drawn from the corners of the globe.

During the long journey to publication, we could not have wished for a better and more supportive commissioning editor than Kirsty Reade at OUP. Kirsty helped to ensure that the second edition incorporated new ideas and changes but retained the authenticity and pedagogic value of the first. Amelia's two research interns, Dusan Radivojevic and Nika Jurcova, have also provided ready assistance to key aspects of the text.

We set out to assemble a book that could serve as an ideal resource for bringing courses on foreign policy to life. If readers and instructors use it to debate and contest the great foreign policy issues of our day, then the book will have made its mark. If readers and instructors do this *and* draw on the major theories and concepts informing the study of foreign policy, then we will have achieved more than we could have reasonably expected.

We are all three indebted to the work of Jim Rosenau in different ways. He graciously wrote the Foreword to the first edition. When we first came up with the idea of asking Jim, we thought it was a long shot. Within minutes of sending the invitation, we had an enthusiastic reply that suggested all kinds of possible ways of opening *Foreign Policy: Theories, Actors, Cases*. Such energy and creativity has marked out Jim's contribution to a field which, more than any other writer and thinker, he has shaped and defined.

As readers will note at the end of the Foreword, Jim sadly passed away before seeing the completed second edition. Jim has educated countless students, written pioneering books and articles, and consistently sought to make foreign policy a theoretically informed field. Therefore we think it is fitting to dedicate this book to him.

Steve Smith, University of Exeter, UK
Amelia Hadfield, Vrije Universiteit Brussel, Belgium
Tim Dunne, University of Queensland, Australia
October 2011

Contents in brief

SECTION THREE Foreign Policy Case Studies

Detailed contents

SECTION THREE Foreign Policy Case Studies

Notes on contributors

Lisbeth Aggestam is a lecturer in Politics and International Relations at the University of Bath, UK. She has written extensively on European foreign policy and was the guest editor of a special issue of *International Affairs* (2008) that examined the EU's global role from ethical perspectives. Her forthcoming book is a comparative foreign policy analysis of Britain, France, and Germany, entitled *European Foreign Policy and the Quest for a Global Role* (London: Routledge, 2012).

Graham Allison is Director of the Belfer Center for Science and International Affairs and Douglas Dillon Professor of Government at Harvard's John F. Kennedy School of Government. Dr Allison has served as Special Advisor to the Secretary of Defense under President Reagan and as Assistant Secretary of Defense for Policy and Plans under President Clinton, where he coordinated Department of Defense strategy and policy towards Russia, Ukraine, and the other states of the former Soviet Union. Dr Allison's first book, *Essence of Decision: Explaining the Cuban Missile Crisis* (1971), was released in an updated and revised second edition in 1999 and ranks among the all-time bestsellers in Political Science, with more than 450,000 copies in print.

Lloyd Axworthy is President and Vice-Chancellor of the University of Winnipeg. In 2010 he was elected International President of the World Federalist Movement–Institute for Global Policy. He is the former director of the Liu Institute for Global Issues at the University of British Columbia (2000–2004) and was a Member of Parliament for over twenty years, serving as Canada's Foreign Minister from 1996 to 2000. He is the author of *Navigating a New World: Canada's Global Future* (2003).

Michael Barnett is University Professor of International Affairs and Political Science at the George Washington University. His most recent book is *Empire of Humanity: A History of Humanitarianism* (2011).

Elisabetta Brighi is Teaching Fellow in International Security at University College London and Visiting Lecturer in International Relations at Middlesex University. Her articles have been published in *Government and Opposition*, *Geopolitics*, and *Rivista di Scienza Politica*, amongst other journals. She has also co-edited the volume *Pragmatism in International Relations* (Routledge, 2009) and, most recently, a collection of essays entitled *Il Mediterraneo nelle Relazioni Internazionali* (Vita e Pensiero, 2010) with Fabio Petito. A fully trained photographer, she is based in London.

Walter Carlsnaes is Senior Professor of Political Science in the Department of Government, Uppsala University, and was until very recently also Adjunct Professor at the Norwegian Institute of International Affairs. He was founding editor of the *European Journal of International Relations* (1995–2000), and has published three monographs and eight co-edited volumes, including the *Handbook of International Relations* (2002; 2nd edn 2012), *International Encyclopedia of Political Science* (2011) and a five-volume reference set on *Foreign Policy Analysis* (2011). His main research interests are in foreign policy analysis, international relations theory and the philosophy of social science, EU external relations, and Swedish and South African foreign and security policy.

Michael W. Doyle is the Harold Brown Professor of International Affairs, Law, and Political Science at Columbia University. In 2009 he was elected to the American Philosophical Society and received the Charles Merriam Award of the American Political Science Association (APSA). In 2011 he received APSA's Hubert H. Humphrey Award in recognition of notable public service by a political scientist. His publications include *Striking First: Preemption and Prevention in International Conflict* (Princeton University Press, 2008), *Ways of War and Peace* (W.W. Norton) and *Empires* (Cornell University Press). From 2001 to 2003, he served as Assistant Secretary-General and Special Adviser to United Nations Secretary-General Kofi Annan and he is a Chair of the United Nations Democracy Fund Advisory Board.

Tim Dunne is Professor of International Relations in the School of Political Science and International Studies, and Research Director at the Asia-Pacific Centre for the Responsibility to Protect, University of Queensland. He has written and edited ten books, which include *Terror in our Time* co-authored with Ken Booth. He is currently an editor of the *European Journal of International Relations* and from 2012 he will serve on the governing council of the International Studies Association (ISA). He is also President of the ISA Asia and the Pacific regional section.

Trine Flockhart is Senior Researcher at the Danish Institute for International Studies (DIIS). Before joining DIIS she was Associate Professor at universities in Australia, Denmark, and Britain. In her current position in a policy research institute she works with policy-relevant issues related to NATO and the EU, whilst also maintaining an interest in constructivist theorizing. Her policy work is available at http://www.diis.dk/sw57548.asp and her most recent research publications can be found in *Journal of Common Market Studies* (2010) and *Perspectives on European Politics and Society* (2011).

Rosemary Foot is Professor of International Relations and John Swire Senior Research Fellow in the International Relations of East Asia at St Antony's College, University of Oxford. Her monograph publications of relevance to this chapter include *Rights Beyond Borders: Tthe Global Community and the Struggle over Human Rights in China* (Oxford University Press, 2000) and (with Andrew Walter) *China, the United States and Global Order* (Cambridge University Press, 2011).

Amelia Hadfield is Professor of European Affairs at the Vrije Universiteit Brussel (VUB) where she teaches and researches on European foreign and public policy and foreign policy analysis as well as directing the EuroMaster programme. She is also a Senior Research Fellow at the Institute for European Studies (IES), Brussels, where she directs the Educational Development Unit (EDU). Her special area of interest is EU energy security issues as they relate to Russia, the Mediterranean, and the EU's neighbourhood. She is also an Associate Fellow of the Energy, Environment and Development Programme (EEDP) at Chatham House. Her recent publications include *International History and International Relations* (with Andrew Williams and Simon Rofe, 2012), *British Foreign Policy, National Identity and Neoclassical Realism* (2010) and 'EU–Russia Energy Relations: Aggregation and Aggravation', *Journal of Contemporary European Studies* (2008).

Lene Hansen is Professor of International Relations in the Department of Political Science, University of Copenhagen. She is the author of *Security as Practice: Discourse Analysis and the Bosnian War* (Routledge, 2006), co-author with Barry Buzan of *The Evolution of International Security Studies* (Cambridge University Press, 2009), and the co-editor with Ole Wæver of *European Integration and National Identity: The Challenge of the Nordic States* (Routledge, 2002). She is currently an editor of the *European Journal of International Relations*.

Christopher Hill FBA is the Sir Patrick Sheehy Professor of International Relations in the Department of Politics and International Studies at the University of Cambridge. He is the author of *The Changing Politics of Foreign Policy* (Palgrave, 2003) and most recently (edited with Reuben Wong) *National and European Foreign Policies: Towards Europeanization* (Routledge, 2011).

Valerie M. Hudson is Professor and George H.W. Bush Chair in the Bush School of Government and Public Service at Texas A&M University, teaching in the masters of international affairs programme. She is editor or co-editor of *Political Psychology and Foreign Policy, Culture and Foreign Policy, Artificial Intelligence and International Politics*, and *The Limits of State Autonomy*, and is author of *Foreign Policy Analysis: Classic and Contemporary Theory*. She is a past president of the Foreign Policy Analysis Section of the International Studies Association, and is on the editorial board of *Foreign Policy Analysis*.

Yuen Foong Khong is Professor of International Relations at and a Fellow of Nuffield College, Oxford University. He is the author of *Analogies at War* (Princeton) and (with Neil MacFarlane) *Human Security and the UN: A Critical History* (Indiana). He is currently working on a book project on *International Politics: The Rules of the Game*.

Steven L. Lamy is Professor of International Relations at the University of Southern California and Vice Dean for Academic Affairs in the Dornsife College of Letters, Arts and Sciences. His areas of research and teaching are foreign policy analysis and international relations theory. His current work is funded by a Luce Grant on religion and international relations.

Matt McDonald is Senior Lecturer, International Relations at the School of Political Science and International Studies at The University of Queensland. His research interests are in the area of international security and foreign policy. His research focuses on critical theoretical approaches to security and their application to environmental change, Australian foreign and security policy, the War on Terror, and security dynamics in the Asia–Pacific. He is the author of *Security, the Environment and Emancipation* (Routledge, 2011) and editor (with Anthony Burke) of *Critical Security in the Asia–Pacific* (Manchester University Press, 2007).

Michael Mastanduno is the Nelson Rockefeller Professor of Government and Dean of the Faculty of Arts and Sciences at Dartmouth College, Hanover, New Hampshire, USA. He has written widely on economic statecraft, international political economy, and international relations theory.

Amrita Narlikar is Reader in International Political Economy at the Department of Politics and International Studies, University of Cambridge. She is also Director of the Centre for Rising Powers and an Official Fellow of Darwin College, Cambridge. Her single-authored books are *International Trade and Developing Countries: Bargaining Coalitions in the GATT & WTO*, (Routledge, 2003), *The World Trade Organization: A Very Short Introduction* (Oxford University Press, 2005), and *New Powers: How to Become One and How to Manage Them* (Hurst, 2010). Her edited books include the forthcoming collection (with Martin Daunton and Robert Stern) *The Oxford Handbook on the World Trade Organization* (Oxford University Press).

Piers Robinson is Senior Lecturer in International Politics, Department of Politics, University of Manchester. He researches the relationship between communications and world politics. His book *The CNN Effect: The Myth of News, Foreign Policy and Intervention'* (Routledge, 2002) analyses the relationship between news media, US foreign policy, and humanitarian crises. In the last five years he has been leading a major ESRC project exploring media coverage of the 2003 Iraq invasion. This project has led to a series of publications culminating in the book *Pockets of Resistance: British News Media Theory and the 2003 Invasion of Iraq* (co-authored with Peter Goddard, Katy Parry, Craig Murray, and Philip M. Taylor) (Manchester University Press, 2010).

James N. Rosenau (25 November 1924–9 September 2011) Prior to his death, Professor Rosenau held the distinguished rank of University Professor of International Affairs at The George Washington University, an honour reserved for the few scholar–teachers whose recognition in the academic community transcends the usual disciplinary boundaries. Professor Rosenau had held a Guggenheim Foundation Fellowship and was a former president of the International Studies Association. He was also the author of some 140 articles and author or editor of more than forty books, including *Turbulence in World Politics: A Theory of Change and Continuity* (1990). *Governance Without Government: Order and Change in World Politics* (1992), *Information Technologies and Global Politics: The Changing Scope of Power and Governance* (2002), *Along the Domestic–Foreign Frontier: Exploring Governance in a Turbulent World* (1997), *Distance Proximities: Dynamics Beyond Globalization* (2003), and *The Study of World Politics* (two volumes, 2006).

Brian C. Schmidt is Associate Professor in the Department of Political Science at Carleton University, Canada. He is the author of *The Political Discourse of Anarchy: A Disciplinary History* *of International Relations* (SUNY, 1998) and *Imperialism and Internationalism in the Discipline of International Relations*, co-edited with David Long (SUNY, 2005).

Steve Smith is Vice-Chancellor of the University of Exeter. From 2009 to 2011 he was President of Universities UK (the representative body of all UK universities). He has previously served as Chair of the 1994 Group of research-intensive universities in the UK. From 1992 to 2002 he was Professor of International Politics at the University of Wales Aberystwyth. From June 2007 until May 2010, he led for higher education on the Prime Minister's National Council of Excellence in Education. He has honorary degrees/fellowships from Jilin University in China, Southampton University, the University of the West of England, Aberystwyth University, and the University of Wales Institute, Cardiff. He is the author/editor of sixteen books, most recently *International Relations Theories*, co-edited with Tim Dunne and Milja Kurki (Oxford University Press, 2007) and over 100 academic papers and chapters in international journals and edited collections. He was knighted in the Queen's Birthday Honours List in June 2011.

Gareth Stansfield is Professor of Middle East Politics and Director of the Institute of Arab and Islamic Studies at the University of Exeter. He is the author of *Iraq: People, History, Politics* (Polity Press, 2007), and was the guest editor of the November 2010 special edition of *International Affairs* which focused on 'Post-American Iraq'. His current research focuses on counter-insurgency and stabilization strategies in post-conflict states. He is an Associate Fellow of the Middle East and North Africa Programme at Chatham House.

Janice Gross Stein is the Belzberg Professor of Conflict Management in the Department of Political Science and the Director of the Munk School of Global Affairs at the University of Toronto. She is an Honorary Foreign Member of the American Academy of Arts and Sciences and a Member of the Royal Society and the Order of Canada. Her most recent book is *Diplomacy in the Digital Age* (2011).

Arlene B. Tickner is Professor of International Relations in the Political Science Department at the Universidad de los Andes, Bogotá, Colombia. Her main areas of research include Latin American and Colombian foreign policy, United States policy towards the region, Western hemisphere and Andean security, and the sociology of knowledge in the field of international relations. Her most recent book in this area, co-edited by David L. Blaney, is Thinking International Relations Differently (Routledge, 2012).

William C. Wohlforth is the Daniel Webster Professor at Dartmouth College, where he teaches in the Department of Government. His most recent books are *International Relations Theory and the Consequences of Unipolarity* (2011), coedited with G. John Ikenberry and Michael Mastanduno, *World Out of Balance: International Relations Theory and the Challenge of American Primacy* (2008), co-authored with Stephen Brooks, and *The Balance of Power in World History* (2007), co-edited with Stuart Kaufman and Richard Little. He has published numerous articles on international and strategic affairs, including 'Reshaping the World Order', *Foreign Affairs* (2009), 'American Primacy in Perspective', *Foreign Affairs* (2002), and 'Unipolarity, Status Competition, and Great Power War', *World Politics* (2009). Recent publications on realism include 'Gilpinian Realism and International Relations', *International Relations* (2012), and 'No One Loves a Realist Explanation: The Cold War's End Revisited', *International Politics* (2011).

Introduction

STEVE SMITH, AMELIA HADFIELD, AND TIM DUNNE

Chapter contents

One of the great pleasures of teaching foreign policy theory is that it must always be grounded in empirical examples: the theory is of little interest unless one can utilize it in specific case studies. The second edition of this book, like the first, builds on that assumption, and our explicit view as editors is that we want theoretical chapters to illuminate case studies, and case studies that are themselves theoretically informed. That, we believe, makes the subject genuinely fascinating, and, as you will see in the chapters that follow, also raises some of the most problematic questions in the social sciences. Courses on foreign policy have, in the experience of the editors, always been popular with both undergraduate and postgraduate students, and since the first edition claim an increasingly central place in both political science and area studies degree courses. Of particular appeal for students is that the study of foreign policy pushes them to think about why x did z, whether he/she made the right choice, and what might have been the costs/ benefits of the alternatives. Foreign policy as a field of study challenges students and scholars alike both to explain the broad structure of international relations and to understand the specific challenges facing key policy makers, and then judge whether—in light of the context—they did the right thing (and for whom?). The second edition has a variety of new chapters that strengthen the theories reviewed in Section 1—its extensive case studies found in Section 3. Echoing the rationale of the first edition, the case studies represent a deliberate choice of the editorial team, designed to encourage both students and instructors to get as close as they can to state practice, and to ask themselves the endlessly fascinating questions about both the reasons for action and the wisdom of those choices with the benefit of hindsight.

To be clear at the outset, we do not believe that case studies can be 'simply' factual, since what that means in effect is that the theoretical assumptions that guide the analysis of the factual material are merely hidden from view. Consider a seemingly empirical question such as 'Why did the United States refuse to support the proposal, made by the Palestinian President Mahmoud Abbas in September 2011, that Palestine should become a full member of the United Nations?' At first sight it would seem that such a question supposes a variety of fairly obvious answers, but further reflection soon raises some serious issues, all of which can only be dealt with by either an explicit, or more likely an implicit, theoretical position. What exactly do we mean by the USA—President Obama? The Cabinet? Congress? The American people?

US businesses? The State Department? The US media? The country that is the dominant military power in the world and possesses a right of veto in the UN Security Council? What do we mean by the term 'refused'? President Obama made it clear that any question about Palestinian membership of the UN had to be seen as part of a wider process of change in the Middle East, so it was not simply a refusal, and was instead linked to guarantees for Israel's security. Was President Obama's stance thus genuinely reflective of US strategic interests in the Middle East, reflective of changing views as to the implementation of a two-state solution, or more to do with internal political considerations, such as the power of the pro-Israel lobby and the next round of American elections? Put like this, such questions may strike readers as exercises in idle academic speculation, but in fact they are not. Answering key questions about the central actors, inputs, and outputs of foreign policy decisions means placing oneself within a particular view of what foreign policy is, who makes it, and how we judge its implementation. Answers to such questions are found first in the realm of theory, and only subsequently in case studies.

In this Introduction we do not need to give an overview of the history of foreign policy theory, since this is expertly dealt with in Valerie Hudson's opening chapter. However, we do want to do three things: first, to say something about the contemporary relevance of the study of foreign policy; second, to look at some definitional issues concerning the study of foreign policy; finally, to discuss the updated organization of the second edition so that lecturers and students alike can understand how we intend it to work as a text.

The contemporary relevance of foreign policy

There are two ways in which foreign policy is of relevance to the study of world politics. The first relates to the agenda of world politics after 9/11 and the renewal of interest in foreign policy *per se*. The second relates more closely to an academic dialogue between the literatures on foreign policy and International Relations (IR). Both of these points are elaborated upon below.

For much of the preceding twenty years, the dominant discussions in the discipline of international relations were about the structure of the international system: why bipolarity had declined, and the nature of its replacement—a unipolar system or a drift towards multipolarity? But the events of 9/11 changed this, primarily because they focused attention both on the centrality of decisions taken by states and other independent actors, and on reasons why the US and UK intelligence services turned out not to be fit for purpose. Moving from the attacks on the World Trade Center to the response, it is evident that the burgeoning literature on the USA's role in the world draws on, and is relevant to, the study of foreign policy (e.g. Walt 2006).

Readers might immediately think that foreign policy has no role in discussing the behaviour of an actor such as al-Qaeda. For us, foreign policy, although usually linked to the behaviour of a state, can apply to other actors. Thus it is perfectly possible to speak of companies, regional governments, and non-state actors having foreign policies. A classical definition is provided by Walter Carlsnaes, for whom foreign policy entails 'those actions which, expressed in the form of explicitly stated goals, commitments and/or directives, and pursued by governmental representatives acting on behalf of their sovereign communities, are directed towards objectives, conditions and actors—both governmental and non-governmental—which they want to affect and which lie beyond their territorial legitimacy' (Carlsnaes 2002: 335). A broader definition, which many contributors to the book concur with, is given by Christopher Hill, who defines foreign policy as 'the sum of official external relations conducted by an independent actor (usually a state) in international relations' (Hill 2003: 3).

For many IR scholars, the processes of globalization and interdependence that had gained pace in the 1990s undermined the state as an actor, thereby making a focus on the foreign policy of states less central to explanations of international relations than during the rest of the post Second World War period. Yet, as other scholars argued, globalization and interdependence did not lead to the demise of the state; instead they made it both more constrained and more central. More constrained because there were an increasing number of restrictions on the freedom of the state to act as it might wish; globalization created a web of interdependence that undermined the state's ability to control its own fate. But the state was also more central than ever, simply because populations continued to look to the state to mitigate the effects of globalization, and yet now they do so over a significantly increased range of policies than ever before (from inward investment to climate change). Thus globalization and interdependence have not withered away the importance of statecraft, but have made it more complicated. A good example here is the 'blowback' effect of foreign policy decisions on domestic constituencies—for example, critics of the Bush administration argue that the dangers of the grand strategy to eliminate terrorist threats could generate greater insecurity both for the USA and the wider international order. This links to our earlier comment about the applicability of the notion of foreign policy to actors other than the state. We are now more inclined to see 'foreign policy' as something that a variety of actors do, from influential social movements on the one hand to regional actors like the European Union on the other. These actors have foreign policies, and consequently they have a high impact on other states and organizations.

A second area where foreign policy is of growing relevance is in terms of its innovative contribution to how we understand the behaviour of international actors. Whereas the analysis of foreign policy has traditionally focused on the state as the central foreign policy actor, it has not meant accepting the core assumptions of realism. Just as the international system can be studied according to various theoretical frameworks, the same can be said of foreign policy. Indeed, one of the drivers for the book was to join up theoretical work on foreign policy with wider currents in IR and, to a lesser extent, in the discipline of politics. Examples of the re-integration of IR theory with foreign policy concerns are evident in the opening section of the book in which leading theorists outline the relevance to foreign policy of the three main IR theories: realism, liberalism, and constructivism. In other chapters of the book, authors apply some of the more radical accounts of international relations, for example drawing on insights from post-structuralism and the literature on the power of discourse. What this tells us is that there is not one approach to foreign policy but many. Finally, foreign policy is an almost perfect subject for examining in detail the fundamental debates within the social sciences, most significantly the debate on the relative importance of structures and agency, and the debate on whether we should seek to explain or to understand foreign policy behaviour.

Foreign policy theory: disciplinary groundings

We need to state from the outset that underpinning *Foreign Policy: Theories, Actors, Cases* is the belief that the study of foreign policy ought not to be regarded as an independent intellectual domain. This is an important issue, since for most of the period since the end of the

Second World War there has been a flourishing approach known as Foreign Policy Analysis (FPA). Valerie Hudson's chapter is a comprehensive overview of the history of FPA, and thus we do not need to discuss it at length here. However, we do need to say why we do not want to restrict the coverage of this book to FPA.

FPA developed in the 1950s, and for the next thirty years it was a vibrant research community in IR. As Hudson notes, there were three main themes, each focused around a paradigmatic book. First there was the focus on foreign policy policy making, inspired by the work of Snyder, Bruck, and Sapin in the 1950s, and then by the literature on bureaucratic and organizational politics in the 1960s and 1970s (notably the work of Allison and Halperin). Second, there was a focus on the psychological dimension of foreign policy making, inspired by the work of Kenneth Boulding and Harold and Margaret Spout in the 1950s, by Alexander George and Michael Brecher in the 1960s, and by Irving Janis in the 1970s. Third, there was the attempt to develop a theory of comparative foreign policy (CFP), inspired by Jim Rosenau's work on the relationship between genotypes of states and the sources of their foreign policy in the 1960s. FPA sought to develop middle-range theories, that is to say theories that were not general accounts of all foreign policy behaviour but instead were accounts of either the foreign policies of some types of states or foreign policy in specific situations (such as crises).

By the late 1980s, FPA began to fall out of fashion. Hudson discusses the reasons for this, but clearly one of the main ones was the failure of the CFP project to develop a robust theoretical framework. But if CFP was unsuccessful, the other two main strands of FPA—the work on psychological processes and on policy making—had built up robust and powerful accounts of foreign policy. Therefore to treat FPA as the only approach to the study of foreign policy would limit our discussions, and of course would link our volume to a specific approach to the study of foreign policy that was at its most influential and productive in the 1960s and 1970s. In short, reducing the study of foreign policy to be only FPA-related is inaccurate, since many more theories are involved than those covered by FPA, and would also focus on a specific approach that has declined in the last twenty years. The vast literature on the USA's role in the world after 9/11 has connected with significant FPA themes, such as bureaucratic politics and groupthink, while not at the same time remaining inside the sub-field of FPA.

We believe that the dynamics of foreign policy are found in a wide range of IR works. Indeed, the objects of foreign policy inquiry necessitate an engagement with a host of social science fields, and a number of sub-fields (including comparative politics and public policy, as well as IR). In terms of its links to the wider social sciences in general, the study of foreign policy requires an engagement both with the literature on policy making in social psychology, and with rational-actor models of policy making that originated in economic interpretations of the policy process. With regard to the political science literature, much depends on how it is defined. As an aspect of state behaviour, foreign policy represents the policy making and unit behaviour involved in inter-state relations. Therefore it can be distinguished as a form of public policy from domestic affairs. Conceptually, foreign policy links into much of the literature of public policy, with the notable difference that its targets are (usually) actors outside the domestic process.

Within this context of interdisciplinarity, we nevertheless believe that there is a special relationship between foreign policy and IR. Rather like a distant cousin, FPA is often still referred to as an IR sub-field. As we noted above, it has always had a rather uneasy location between public policy, comparative policy, realism, and psychology, as well as a host of other interdisciplinary contributions. While IR yields a host of approaches exploring (if not always engaging with) the tenets of state behaviour, it is rarely deployed to discuss key aspects of FPA. This is odd, because both sides are effectively talking about the same thing; both are interested in understanding the input and output of state behaviour, and from a conceptual standpoint both attempt to judge which particular methodology is best to understand, explain, or even predict state behaviour and its underlying motives. Where they sometimes differ is in relation to both the level of analysis and the units of analysis.

To an extent, this connection has always been both organizationally and intellectually strong. Organizationally, FPA has been a standing group of the International Studies Association (ISA) for over thirty-five years; in recent years, this connection has been further enhanced by the creation of a new ISA journal on foreign policy. Intellectually, the entire history of IR has witnessed a constant debate within the main theories in terms of whether they were theories of the international system or theories of foreign policy. This was most famously discussed in David Singer's seminal article on 'The Level of Analysis Problem in International Relations' (Singer 1961), in which he noted that the two main levels at which we could analyse IR were the state and the systems levels; each had their strengths and weaknesses, but crucially each introduced biases into their explanations (for example, by respectively overestimating and underestimating the differences between states as actors). A similar discussion has been a constant theme in the work of Kenneth Waltz, who in *Man the State, and War* (Waltz 1959) saw accounts of war being developed on three levels: human nature, the type of state, and the structure of the international system. The latter two of these became the alternative choices for explanation in his ground-breaking *Theory of International Politics* (Waltz 1979). More recently, there has been the development of a new and dynamic interplay between IR and what would previously have been termed FPA. A good example here is Christopher Hill's outstanding textbook *The Changing Politics of Foreign Policy* (Hill 2003) which draws heavily on ideas and concepts found in writers associated with the theory of international society, such as Hedley Bull and R.J. Vincent.

The final issue concerning disciplinary grounding relates to foreign policy theory and the recent more radical accounts of IR. By and large, most critical theorists have avoided the study of foreign policy because it implies a normative commitment to the values and interests of particular states or of sovereign actors *per se*, exceptions being David Campbell (1989, 1992) and Henrik Larsen (1997). However, we believe that taking states seriously is not the same as privileging state actors as the 'normal' or 'proper' unit of international political analysis. In short, we do not believe that such a focus entails committing the error of state-centrism. Studying state behaviour, an unavoidable dimension of foreign policy, does not make one a statist.

Colin Hay's work on critical political analysis (Hay 2002) has been neatly adapted to apply to foreign policy by Paul Williams (2005: 5–7). Following him, we consider that there are five relevant features of critical political analysis in the building of a non-statist foreign policy.

- Critical foreign policy should be empirical without being empiricist; this is to say that analysis should look at actual case studies and evidence, but within an explicit theoretical and normative commitment. Empiricism implies that the analysis is in some way 'neutral' and that the evidence is not tainted by the theoretical and normative lenses through which these 'facts' rather than others are seen as the ones to use.

- Both structure and agency need to be brought into consideration. This is one of the most contentious debates within the humanities and social sciences, but at its base is the concern that, as Hollis and Smith (1991) put it, in the social world there are always at least two stories to tell. Thus we can either explain state behaviour as the result of the structure of the international system, or see it as the outcome of policy making within the state. Hay (and Williams) stress that both agency and structure are involved in foreign policy, with decisions being made (agency) but always within a set of constraints (structure).

- A critical approach to foreign policy accepts a broad view of politics and avoids the danger of seeing politics as only involved at the governmental level. Instead, states find themselves in a context in which their actions are being shaped by non-governmental organizations (NGOs) on the inside and transnational norms/social movements on the outside. Therefore critical accounts of foreign policy move beyond the interrelationships between governmental bodies and factions to look at a wider definition of the political realm, specifically looking at the role of individuals and groups in terms of who wins and who loses from foreign policy decisions.

- Studying foreign policy critically also means confronting important theoretical issues to do with knowledge and reality. On the one hand, knowledge is constitutive in that ideas/beliefs/discourses shape and constitute the world in which policy makers find themselves; on the other hand, care must be taken to avoid accepting the leaders' rationale as the *cause* of a particular action. All critically inclined scholars search for gaps between words and deeds—moreover, such discrepancies allow academics to hold leaders accountable to the claims and benchmarks contained in policy statements and commitments.

- The study of critical foreign policy recognizes the contingency of the political process. Decision-makers find themselves operating within parameters which constrain their freedom, but equally they do make decisions. Thus a critical approach accepts that things could always have been different—foreign policy is never simply the realm of necessity.

To Hay's five points, we would add a sixth.

- Being critical does not entail assuming bad faith about leaders and their reasons. Responses to events often mean that there are no good or right choices, and responsible scholarship needs to recognize the costs of non-decisions as well as the price of decisive actions. For example, during the Cuban Missile Crisis in October 1962, President Kennedy made the controversial decision to set up a quarantine around Cuba. This risked escalation of the crisis but, as he noted at the time, doing nothing was not an option. Similarly, in the case of the diplomacy over Iraq in 2002–2003, it is very easy to believe that every move in the diplomatic game was part of a grand strategic plan. Saddam Hussein could have done far more to persuade the world that he was serious about disarmament; likewise, Britain could have delayed—or possibly derailed entirely—the US desire for a punitive war. Decisions by leaders matter; and quite often alternative policy responses were available to them but they chose not to advance them. In realizing that foreign policy is a realm of decisions and actions, albeit under conditions of constraint and uncertainty, we should remember not to treat historical outcomes as though they were a given. In the words of former US Secretary of State Madeleine Albright: 'History happens forwards but is written backwards'.

Taken together, we believe that a critical approach to foreign policy offers significant potential for looking at foreign policy within a wider notion of politics than has traditionally been the case within FPA. As a framework for thinking about foreign policy, the notion of a critical approach as outlined in the preceding six points offers significant advantages over the limited perspectives represented by FPA. In sum, all theories of IR make assumptions about state behaviour. The relationship between them and the study of foreign policy is absolutely unavoidable. Levering FPA artificially into various social science pigeonholes is not a good idea. Better is an analysis of the *broad* dynamics of foreign policy, and the *specific* findings of the subfield of FPA, in which both are subjected to the scrutiny of a limited number of prevailing IR viewpoints.

Organization of the second edition

As Valerie Hudson makes clear in her opening chapter, since the 1950s FPA has sought answers to inter-state relations by looking at the three levels involved in foreign policy: *individuals* (psychological/sociological studies), *groups* (group-based analyses), and *states* themselves (comparative foreign policy). This three-level analysis is very much the organizing theme of this book. Beginning with Hudson's own appraisal of the ups and downs of FPA, the text reviews the role of individuals, groups, and states using both FPA perspectives (Stein and Robinson) and broad IR perspectives (Hill and Carlsnaes).

What this text adds, and indeed is its key rationale, is an appreciation of the role of IR theory in shedding light on the dynamics of state-to-state activity. FPA has of course ventured out onto the high seas of middle-range theory with Rosenau as the first captain of theories that 'mediated between grand principles and the complexity of reality'. Vast amounts of cross-disciplinary data have been produced from the latter side of this equation. As Hudson points out, whilst this data has been of significant benefit in generating new views on what constitutes a proper analysis of foreign policy in the American, British, and European schools, an impasse as to the right methods and tools has of late created something of a 'methodological impasse' which, if not resolved, could further widen already divergent approaches. Analyses of 'grand principles' has also lacked the benefit of a close association with the explicit axioms available principally from IR. Carlsnaes reminds us that realism itself is capable of linking axioms to variables, thanks to Morthenthau's work on translating 'the maxims of nineteenth-century European diplomatic practice into more general laws of an American social science' (Guzzini 1998: 1). Realist, liberal, constructivist, and post-structural tenets can all shed equally robust explanations on the external behaviour of sovereign states.

While the second edition, like the first, does not attempt to produce a new type of middle-range theory, it continues to engage with IR theory as the conceptual underpinning of the key actors, structures, motives for action, and modes of implementation of foreign policy. The text is just as focused as the first edition on fleshing out a clearer idea of the grand principles at work in foreign policy both as a form of state behaviour and as an intellectual field, and its main source for this remains IR theory. As such, the following chapters retain a keen appreciation for the individual and group-based analyses of FPA, but they are equally determined to shed light on the inter-state dynamics of which foreign policy is ultimately comprised. Therefore the uniqueness of the text lies in the advice first given by the late James Rosenau, namely to provide a robust integrated analysis 'at several levels of analysis—from individual leaders to the international system—in understanding foreign policy'.

The role of the IR perspectives presented in the text is not merely to warm them over FPA. The point is to generate conceptual pay-offs to students, analysts, and practitioners. Our contributors do this by illustrating the complementarity between individual, state, and structural dynamics of IR, and those same levels of analysis found in FPA. As a result, the textbook is something of an exercise in bridge-building. Narrowing the gap between FPA and IR should ultimately bestow IR with a greater appreciation of the multilevel and multicausal dynamics (so comprehensively studied in FPA by Snyder and others), whilst granting FPA a clearer idea of 'grand principles'—in other words, finding appropriate connective tissue for both sides, as well as keeping both the *conceptual* and *practical* sides of foreign policy as clearly balanced as possible.

We have asked the contributors to the book not to assume that students have necessarily taken an 'introduction to international relations' course. Therefore part of the rationale for opening with accounts of four dominant IR perspectives is to ensure that students have a grasp of realist, liberal, constructivist, and post-structural understandings of actors, interests, commitments, and outputs. The second edition adds to the original conceptual lenses by adding a new chapter on discourse analysis, all designed to shed light on the wider dynamics of state behaviour and the specific tenets of FPA. Here, realism is reviewed again by Wohlforth not merely as the progenitor of the state, but as the conceptual foundation of statecraft, revealing more clearly the links between anarchy, survival, the national interest, and national security, as further illustrated by Schmidt. As evidenced by many of our case studies, the realist canon is alive and well and is working in the many ministries of foreign affairs.

Liberalism is again explored for its ability to produce a more sophisticated overview of individuals, states, and structures. As Doyle points out, liberalism needs to be understood both as a foreign policy attitude and as a conceptual tool with which to deconstruct foreign policy actions, shedding light on how individuals, ideas, and ideals (human rights, liberty, and democracy) connect to social forces (capitalism, markets) and political institutions (democracy, representation) which in turn directly affects foreign relations.

Constructivism takes further steps to open the black box of the state, permitting an in-depth overview of the myriad forces of power, influence, and interest. Flockhart demonstrates that constructivism possesses the capacity to understand how alliances, such as NATO, adapt in response to new contexts. Together, she and Carlsnaes illustrate the potential of an IR–FP interface in their examination of individual policy making, the role of bureaucracies and organizations (as first explored by Allison), and the activities of international society. This is magnified at the international level where, as Barnett, Axworthy, Dunne, and Hadfield explore, key norms are beginning to operate as a compass by which to guide foreign policies relative to national and international goals. Robinson's chapter on the discursive effect of the media's influence on foreign policy is a necessary complement to these ideas. The new chapter on discourse analysis by Hansen rounds out Section 1 not only by bringing the spectrum of IR up to date, but also persuasively arguing in favour of the need to systematically deconstruct the textual artefacts of foreign policy (e.g. speeches, statements, primary documents) to grasp more clearly the nature of what is said, and what is left unsaid.

Arguably, IR approaches are helpful in testing the veracity of the assumptions that exist in the tripartite approaches of FPA. At the same time, a theory-based approach in no way pushes FPA back to seeing the role of the state as a 'metaphysical abstraction'. The realist, liberal, constructivist, and post-structural viewpoints espoused here shed light on the myriad dynamics of state power and the motives behind state action; they do not resort to abstractions. The evidence is found first in our four thematic chapters in which the realist, liberal, constructivist, and post-structuralist approaches are used to explain a series of related foreign policy choices covering national security, economic statecraft, and normative foreign policy, respectively. The same IR–FP interface is found in each of the case studies: Khong and Dunne tangle with national security from the perspective of US neoconservatism and British foreign policy on Iraq, respectively, Narlikar with economic foreign policy, Hadfield with the overlap between national security and national resources, and Axworthy, Foot, and Aggestam with the role of norms changing the foreign policy perspectives of Canada, China, and the European Union, respectively. Reflecting a world of emerging powers and regions, Stansfield examines the role of culture affecting the Arab–Israeli peace process, whilst the new chapters by McDonald and Tickner examine climate change in relation to Australian foreign and security policy, and the role of Brazil and Latin America in international political analysis, respectively.

In summary, we think that there are six main features of this book. First, as we hope we have made clear in this Introduction, our aim is to bridge the literature on FPA with wider theoretical insights from IR. Second, and related, contributions to the book demonstrate that there is no single approach to explaining and understanding foreign policy: it is a varied field that reaches out to many disciplines and draws on diverse theoretical groundings. Third, the book seeks to build knowledge about foreign policy on the basis of empirically informed theory and theoretically informed cases. Fourth, we have attempted to include studies on all three core focal points of FPA as identified by Hudson (group policy making, psychology, and state-level explanations). Fifth, this collection does not confine our thinking about foreign policy to the state; instead, most of our contributors concur that many other types of organizations and actors are capable of constructing and pursuing foreign policies, and therefore we assume that the kinds of account discussed in this book will be applicable to these other types of actors. Sixth, we have opened up for reflection the possibility of a critical account of foreign policy—one which draws on a wider notion of politics explicitly guided by progressive norms, and where policy makers are seen as having choices, albeit ones to be made within powerful internal and external structures.

We hope that readers will find this a helpful and clear guide to thinking about foreign policy. The study of foreign policy is entering an exciting period of renewal, and we trust that the theories, concepts, and case studies dealt with in this book will serve as a valuable road-map which can help make sense of the choices and dilemmas facing actors trying to reach their foreign policy goals.

Foreign Policy Analysis: Theoretical and Historical Perspectives

The history and evolution of foreign policy analysis

VALERIE M. HUDSON

Chapter contents

 Reader's guide

This chapter traces the evolution of Foreign Policy Analysis (FPA) as a subfield of International Relations (IR) from its beginnings in the 1950s through its classical period until 1993; it then sketches the research agenda of contemporary FPA, which is represented by the other chapters in this volume. Three paradigmatic works, by Richard Snyder and colleagues, James Rosenau, and Harold and Margaret Sprout, laid the foundation of this subfield. In turn, these works created three main threads of research in FPA, focusing on the decision making of small/large groups, comparative foreign policy, and psychological/sociological explanations of foreign policy. These three primary areas of research have waxed and waned in importance to the subfield over the years. Current FPA scholarship explores linkages between these literatures, seeking both greater cross-level integration of explanation and new methodologies more appropriate to cross-level analysis.[1]

Introduction: three paradigmatic works

What are the origins of **foreign policy analysis** (FPA)? In one sense, FPA-style work—that is, scholarship whose theoretical ground is human decision makers, acting singly or within groups—has been around as long as there have been historians and others who have sought to understand why national governments have made the choices they did regarding inter-state relations. (See Box 1.1). But FPA-style work within the field of International Relations *per se* is best dated back to the late 1950s and early 1960s.

Three paradigmatic works arguably built the foundation of FPA.

- *Decision Making as an Approach to the Study of International Politics by Richard C. Snyder, H.W. Bruck, and Burton Sapin (1954: see also Snyder et al. 1963; reprinted in 2002).*

BOX 1.1 Key definitions

FOREIGN POLICY The strategy or approach chosen by the national government to achieve its goals in its relations with external entities. This includes decisions to do nothing.

FOREIGN POLICY BEHAVIOUR The observable artefacts of foreign policy—specific actions and words used to influence others in the realm of foreign policy; may include the categorization of such behaviour, such as along conflict-cooperation continua, which categorizations could be used to construct data including event data. FPB may include behaviour that was accidental or unintended by the government, and in addition decisions to do nothing may not leave any behavioural artefact. Thus there is slippage between the concept of foreign policy and the concept of foreign policy behaviour.

FOREIGN POLICY ANALYSIS The subfield of international relations that seeks to explain foreign policy, or, alternatively, foreign policy behaviour, with reference to the theoretical ground of human decision makers, acting singly and in groups. The subfield has several hallmarks:

- a commitment to look below the nation-state level of analysis to actor-specific information;
- a commitment to build actor-specific theory as the interface between actor-general theory and the complexity of the real world;
- a commitment to pursue multicausal explanations spanning multiple levels of analysis;
- a commitment to utilize theory and findings from across the spectrum of social science;
- a commitment to viewing the process of foreign policy decision making as important as the output thereof.

ACTOR-GENERAL THEORY Theory that explains the behaviour of actors in general, such as game theory.

ACTOR-SPECIFIC THEORY Theory that explains the behaviour of specific actors, such as FPA theory. This type of theory may be generalizable, but under specific scope conditions for applicability. Actor-specific theory is a form of middle-range theory, in that it is more generalizable than insights derived from case studies but, on the other hand, has more severe scope conditions constraining its generalizability than actor-general theory. However, given its nature, actor-specific theory allows for richer explanation and even prediction of the foreign policy behaviour of particular entities than does actor-general theory.

- 'Pre-theories and Theories of Foreign Policy' by James N. Rosenau (a book chapter written in 1964 and published in Farrell 1966).
- *Man–Milieu Relationship Hypotheses in the Context of International Politics* by Harold and Margaret Sprout (1956: expanded and revised in article form in 1957) and their 1965 book *The Ecological Perspective on Human Affairs with Special Reference to International Politics*). (See Box 1.2.)

The work of Richard Snyder and his colleagues inspired researchers to look below the nation-state level of analysis to the players involved:

> We adhere to the nation-state as the fundamental level of analysis, yet we have discarded the state as a metaphysical abstraction. By emphasizing decision making as a central focus we have provided a way of organizing the determinants of action around those officials who act for the political society. Decision makers are viewed as operating in dual-aspect setting so that apparently unrelated internal and external factors become related in the actions of the decision makers. Hitherto, precise ways of relating domestic factors have not been adequately developed. (Snyder *et al.* 1954: 53)

BOX 1.2 Three paradigmatic works of foreign policy analysis

Richard Snyder	James Rosenau	Harold and Margaret Sprout
Decision making as an Approach to the Study of International Politics by Richard C. Snyder, H.W. Bruck, and Burton Sapin (1954: see also Snyder *et al.* 1963; reprinted in 2002).	'Pre-theories and Theories of Foreign Policy' by James N. Rosenau (a book chapter written in 1964 and published in Farrell 1966).	*Man–Milieu Relationship Hypotheses in the Context of International Politics* by Harold and Margaret Sprout (1956: expanded and revised in article form in 1957 and their 1965 book *The Ecological Perspective on Human Affairs with Special Reference to International Politics*).
Contributed a focus on the decision-making *process* itself as part of the explanation, rather than just foreign policy outputs	Development of actor-specific *theory* that would lead to the development of generalizable propositions at the level of middle-range theory	Foreign policy can only be explained with reference to the psycho-milieu (the psychological, situational, political, and social *contexts*) of the individuals involved in decision making

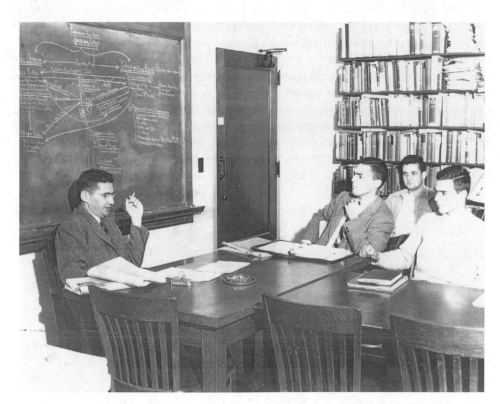

Richard Snyder leading a foreign policy seminar.

Source: © Princeton University Library. Princeton University Archives, Department of Rare Books and Special Collections, Princeton University Library.

In taking this approach, Snyder and his colleagues bequeathed to FPA its characteristic emphasis on **foreign policy *decision making*** (FPDM) as versus foreign policy *outcomes*. Decision making was best viewed as 'organizational behaviour', by which the basic determinants would be spheres of competence of the actors involved, communication and information flow; and motivations of the various players. Desirable explanations would thus be both multicausal and interdisciplinary.

As explored in the Foreword, James Rosenau's pre-theorizing encouraged scholars to systematically and scientifically tease out cross-nationally applicable generalizations about nation-state behaviour. As Rosenau put it,

> To identify factors is not to trace their influence. To understand processes that affect external behavior is not to explain how and why they are operative under certain circumstances and not under others. To recognize that foreign policy is shaped by internal as well as external factors is not to comprehend how the two intermix or to indicate the conditions under which one predominates over the other. . . . Foreign policy analysis lacks comprehensive systems of testable generalizations. . . . Foreign policy analysis is devoid of general theory. (Rosenau 1966: 98–9)

General testable theory was needed, and the intent of Rosenau's article was to point in the direction it lay. However, the general theory Rosenau advocates is not the grand theory of Cold War IR: the metaphor Rosenau used in this work is instructive in this regard—FPA researchers should emulate Gregor Mendel, the father of modern genetics, who was able to discern genotype from phenotype in plants through careful observation and comparison. Are there genotypes of nation-states, knowledge of which would confer explanatory and predictive power on our models of foreign policy interaction? What Rosenau was encouraging was the development of **middle-range theory**—theory that mediated between grand principles and the complexity of reality. At the time Rosenau wrote this article, he felt that the best way to uncover such mid-range generalizations was through aggregate statistical exploration and confirmation. Rosenau also underscored the need to integrate information at several levels of analysis—from individual leaders to the international system—in understanding foreign policy. As with Snyder, the best explanations would be multilevel and multicausal, integrating information from a variety of social science knowledge systems.

James Rosenau, pioneer of foreign policy analysis.

Harold and Margaret Sprout contributed to the formation of the field by suggesting that understanding foreign policy outputs, which they associated with the analysis of power capabilities within an interstate system, without reference to foreign policy undertakings, which they associated with strategies, decisions, and intentions, was misguided: 'Explanations of achievement and estimations of capabilities for achievement invariably and necessarily presuppose antecedent undertakings or assumptions regarding undertakings. Unless there is an undertaking, there can be no achievement—and nothing to explain or estimate' (1965: 225). To explain undertakings, one needs to look at the *psycho-milieu* of the individuals and groups making the foreign policy decision. The **psycho-milieu** is the international and operational environment or context as it is perceived and interpreted by these decision makers. Incongruities between the perceived and the real operational environments can occur, leading to less than satisfactory choices in foreign policy. The sources of these incongruities were diverse, requiring once again multicausal explanations drawing from a variety of fields. Even in these early years, the Sprouts saw a clear difference between foreign policy analysis and what we have called actor-general theory:

> Instead of drawing conclusions regarding an individual's *probable* motivations and purposes, his environmental knowledge, and his intellectual processes linking purposes and knowledge, on the basis of *assumptions* as to the way people are likely on the average to behave in a given social context, the cognitive behavioralist—be he narrative historian or systematic social scientist—undertakes to find out as precisely as possible how specific persons actually did perceive and respond in particular contingencies. (Sprout and Sprout 1965: 118)

The message of these three works was powerful in its appeal to certain scholars: the particularities of the human beings making national foreign policy were vitally important to understanding foreign policy choice. Such particularities should not remain as undigested idiosyncracies (as in traditional single-country studies), but rather be incorporated as instances of larger categories of variation in the process of cross-national middle-range theory-building. Multiple levels of analysis, ranging from the most micro to the most macro, should ideally be integrated in the service of such theory. The stores of knowledge of all the social sciences must be drawn upon in this endeavour. The process of foreign policy making was at least as important, if not more important, than foreign policy as an output. The substance of this message was and continues to be the 'hard core' of FPA. (See Box 1.3.)

The second wave of theorizing built upon the foundational paradigmatic works. Between 1974 and 1993 FPA developed a number of parallel research pathways. (See Box 1.4.)

Other parts of the message were more temporally bounded. As we shall see, certain methodological stances that perhaps seemed self-evident in the early 1960s would not stand the test of time. These would engender troubling paradoxes, which would plague the field and lead to a temporary decline in some areas in the mid to late 1980s until they were satisfactorily resolved. Despite these paradoxes, the first bloom of FPA, lasting from the late 1960s to the aforementioned decline, was a time of great intellectual effort and excitement.

Classic FPA scholarship (1954–1993)

The energy and enthusiasm of the first generation of work in FPA (1954–1973) was tremendous. Great strides in conceptualization, along with parallel efforts in data collection and methodological experimentation, were the contributions of this time period. The second

Harold and Margaret Sprout who emphasized the psychological milieu of individual and group decision making.

Source: © Priceton University Library. Princeton University Archives, Department of Rare Books and Special Collections, Princeton University Library.

BOX 1.3 Primary levels of analysis in FPA

Cognitive processes Cognition, learning, heuristic fallacies, emotion, etc.

Leader personality and orientation Operational codes, motivations, psychobiography, etc.

Small-group dynamics Groupthink, newgroup, coalitions, etc.

Interface of leader personality with small-group composition

Organization process Incremental learning, standard operating procedures, implementation issues, etc.

Bureaucratic politics Turf, morale, budget, influence, inter-agency group politics, etc.

Culture and foreign policy Identity and nationalism, heroic histories, role theory, etc.

Domestic political contestation Regime type, media, political interest groups, organized party contestation and electoral politics, etc.

National attributes and foreign policy Geography, resources, economic factors, etc.

System effects on foreign policy Anarchy, distribution of power, regional balances of power, etc.

---

generation of work from about 1974 to 1993 expressly built upon those foundations. Though it is always difficult to set the boundaries of a field of thought, the overview which follows includes a representative sampling of classic works in the first and second generation which both examined how the 'specifics' of nations lead to differences in foreign policy choice/behaviour, and put forward propositions in this regard that at least have the potential to be generalizable and applicable cross-nationally.

BOX 1.4 Classical foreign policy analysis—the second generation

Small-group decision making

Refers to the process and structure of groups making foreign policy decisions. The groups that were studied ranged in size from very small groups to large organizations and bureaucracies. Insights from social psychology were incorporated into FPA. It was discovered that the motivation to maintain group consensus and personal accpetance by the group could result in a deterioration of decision-making quality.

Organizational process and bureaucratic politics

Researchers began to study the influence of organization process and bureaucratic politics on foreign policy decision making. Organizations and bureaucracies put their own survival at the top of their list of priorities; often they will seek to increase their relative strength. It was found that the ulterior objectives of foreign policy decision 'players' influenced their decision making.

Comparative foreign policy

The subfield of comparative foreign policy (CFP) developed as a response to James Rosenau's challenge to build a cross-national and multilevel theory of foreign policy. Foreign policy *behaviour*, as disparate as warfare, treaty making, or diplomacy—these events could be compared and aggregated. Data was collected on a variety of possible explanatory factors to determine patterns by which these independent variables were correlated. Researchers hoped to emerge with a grand unified theory of foreign policy behaviour applicable to all nations and time periods. The empirical results were less than the protagonists had hoped.

Psychological influences on foreign policy decision making

Increasing attention was directed to the *mind* of the foreign policy decision maker. Under certain stressful conditions, individual characteristics would become crucial in understanding how decisions are made. Also, the problem of misperception was identified, with potential disastrous consequences in relation to questions of war and peace.

Societal milieux

The societal context also came to the fore. Researchers examined how far national attributes, such as culture, history, geography, economics, political institutions, military power, ideology, and demographics, determined policy making. The nature of regime type also rose in prominence, particularly with the realization that democracies tended not to fight with one another.

Group decision making

Snyder and colleagues had emphasized the process and structure of groups making foreign policy decisions (Snyder extended his work with case studies in collaboration with Glenn Paige; see Snyder and Paige 1958; Paige 1959; Paige 1968). Numerous scholars echoed this theme in their work, which ranged from the study of foreign policy making in very small groups to the study of foreign policy making in very large organizations and bureaucracies.

Small group dynamics

Some of the most theoretically long-lived work produced during this period centred on the consequences of making foreign policy decisions in small groups. Social psychologists had explored the unique dynamics of such a decision setting before, but never in relation to foreign policy decision making, where the stakes might be much higher. The most important work is that of Irving Janis, whose seminal *Victims of Groupthink* almost single-handedly began this research tradition. In that volume, and using studies drawn specifically from the realm of foreign policy, Janis shows convincingly that the motivation to maintain group consensus and personal acceptance by the group can cause deterioration of decision-making quality. The empirical research of Leana (1975), Semmel (1982), Semmel and Minix (1979), Tetlock (1979), and others extended this research using aggregate analysis of experimental data as well as case studies. **Groupthink** becomes one of several possible outcomes in the work of C.F. Hermann (1978). Hermann categorizes groups along several dimensions (size, role of leader, rules for decision, autonomy of group participants), and is able to make general predictions about the likely outcome of deliberations in each type of group.

The work of the second wave moved 'beyond groupthink' to both refine and extend our understanding of small-group processes. Representative work includes Herek *et al.* (1987, 1989), McCauley (1989), Ripley (1989), Stewart *et al.* (1989), Hart (1990), Gaenslen (1992), and Hart *et al.* (1997).

The second wave also brought with it a new research issue. How does a group come to understand, represent, and frame a given foreign policy situation? Works include those by George Breslauer, Charles F. Hermann, Donald Sylvan, Philip Tetlock, and James Voss (Vertzberger 1990; Breslauer and Tetlock 1991; Voss *et al.* 1991; Billings and Hermann 1994). Turning to efforts by individual scholars, we will highlight the work of Khong (1992) and Boynton (1991).

Boynton wishes to understand how human agents in groups come to agreement on the nature of a foreign policy situation. In his 1991 paper (cited above), he uses the official record of Congressional Committee hearings to investigate how committee members make sense of current events and policies. By viewing the questions and responses in the hearing as an unfolding narrative, Boynton is able to chart how 'meaning' crystallizes for each committee member, and how they attempt to share that meaning with other members and with those who are testifying. Boynton posits the concept of 'interpretive triple' as a way to understand how connections between facts are made through plausible interpretation—in effect, ascertaining which interpretations are plausible within the social context created by the hearings.

Khong's 1992 book, *Analogies at War*, has a similar aim but with a different focus: the use of analogies to guide **problem framing** by foreign policy makers. In this particular work, Khong demonstrates how the use of conflicting analogies to frame the problem of Vietnam led to conceptual difficulties in group reasoning about policy options. The 'Korea' analogy gained ascendance in framing the Vietnam problem, without sufficient attention being paid to the incongruities between the two sets of circumstances.

Organizational process and bureaucratic politics

This first period also saw the emergence of a strong research agenda that examined the influence of organizational process and bureaucratic politics on foreign policy decision making. The foundations of this approach can be traced back to Weber's *The Theory of Social and*

Economic Organizations (from the 1920s). First-period research showed how 'rational' foreign policy making can be upended by the attempt to work with and through large organized governmental groups. Organizations and bureaucracies put their own survival at the top of their list of priorities, and this survival is measured by relative influence *vis à vis* other organizations ('turf'), by the organization's budget, and by the morale of its personnel. The organization will jealously guard and seek to increase its turf and strength, as well as to preserve undiluted what it feels to be its 'essence' or 'mission'. Large organizations also develop **standard operating procedures** (SOPs) which, while allowing them to react reflexively despite their inherent unwieldiness, permit little flexibility or creativity. These SOPs may be the undoing of more innovative solutions of decision makers operating at levels higher than the organization, but there is little alternative to the implementation of policy by bureaucracy. The interface between objectives and implementation is directly met at this point, and there may be substantial slippage between the two because of the incompatibility of the players' perspectives.

Although the articulation of this research agenda can be found in works such as Huntington (1960), Schilling *et al.* (1962), Hilsman (1967), and Neustadt (1970), probably the most cited works are Allison (1971) and Halperin (1974) (additional works co-authored by Halperin include Allison and Halperin (1972) and Halperin and Kanter (1973)). In his famous *Essence of Decision*, Graham Allison offers three cuts at explaining one episode in foreign policy—the Cuban Missile Crisis of 1962. Investigating both the US and the Soviet sides of this case, Allison shows that the unitary rational-actor model of foreign policy making does not suffice to explain the curiosities of the crisis. Offering two additional models as successive 'cuts' at explanation, the Organizational Process Model and the Bureaucratic Politics Model (one of intra-organizational factors, and one of inter-organizational factors), allows Allison to explain more fully what transpired. His use of three levels of analysis also points to the desire to integrate rather than segregate explanations at different levels.

Halperin's book *Bureaucratic Politics and Foreign Policy* (1974) is an extremely detailed amalgam of generalizations about bureaucratic behaviour, accompanied by unforgettable examples from American defence policy making of the Eisenhower, Kennedy, and Johnson years. It should be noted that bureaucratic politics research gained impetus from the Vietnam War ongoing during this period, because the war was seen by the public as defence policy run amok due, in part, to bureaucratic imperatives (e.g. Krasner 1971).

Comparative foreign policy

Those who took up James Rosenau's challenge to build a cross-national and multilevel theory of foreign policy and subject that theory to rigorous aggregate empirical testing created the subfield known as **comparative foreign policy** (CFP). It is in CFP that we see most directly the legacy of scientism/behaviouralism in FPA's genealogy. Foreign policy could not be studied in aggregate—foreign policy *behaviour* could. Searching for an analogue to the 'vote' as the fundamental explanandum in behaviouralist American political studies, CFPers proposed the foreign policy **event**—the tangible artefact of the influence attempt that is foreign policy, alternatively viewed as 'who does what to whom, how' in international affairs. Events could be compared along behavioural dimensions, such as whether positive or negative effect was being displayed, or what instruments of statecraft (diplomatic, military, economics, etc.) were used in the influence attempt, or what level of commitment of resources was evident. Behaviour as disparate as a war, a treaty, or a state visit could now be compared *and aggregated* in a theoretically meaningful fashion.

This conceptualization of the dependent variable was essential to the theory-building enterprise in CFP. To uncover law-like generalizations, one would have to conduct empirical testing across nations and across time; case studies were not an efficient methodology from this standpoint. However, with the conceptual breakthrough of the 'event', it was now possible to collect data on a variety of possible explanatory factors and determine (by analysing the variance in the event's behavioural dimensions) the patterns by which these independent variables were correlated with foreign policy behaviour (see McGowan and Shapiro 1973). Indeed, to talk to some scholars involved in CFP research, it seemed that their goal was nothing less than a GUT (grand unified theory) of all foreign policy behaviour for all nations for all time. Some set of master equations would link all the relevant variables, independent and dependent, together, and when applied to massive databases providing values for these variables, would yield R-squares approaching 1.0. Although the goal was perhaps naive in its ambition, the sheer size of the task called forth immense efforts in theory building, data collection, and methodological innovation that have few parallels in IR.

Events data

The collection of **events data** was funded to a significant degree by the US government. Andriole and Hopple (1981) estimate that the government (primarily Defense Advanced Research Projects Agency and the National Science Foundation) provided over $5 million for the development of events datasets during the time period 1967–1981. Generally speaking, the collection effort went like this: students were employed to comb through newspapers, chronologies, and other sources for foreign policy events, which they would then code according to rules listed in their coding manuals, have their coding periodically checked for intercoder reliability, and finally punch their codings up on computer cards. For example, if we wanted to code an event such as 'The USA invaded Afghanistan', we would code a date (DDM-MYYYY), the actor (USA), the subject (Afghanistan), and some code or series of codes that would indicate 'invasion'. A series of codes might work like this: the code for invasion might be '317', the '3' indicating that this was a hostile act, the '1' indicating it was a military act, and the '7' indicating in more specific fashion invasion. Many other variables could also be coded; for example, we might code that the United Nations facilitated the act by sponsoring a Security Council Resolution, we might link in previous events such as Mullah Omar's refusal to turn in Osama bin Laden, and so forth. Events data sets, then, contain thousands or even millions of lines of code, each of which is a foreign policy 'event'.

The acronyms of some of these events data projects live on: some because the data are still being collected (e.g. Gerner *et al.* 1994) (some collection is funded by the DDIR (Data Development for International Research) Project of the NSF), and others because the data are still useful as a testing ground for hypotheses—WEIS (the World Event/Interaction Survey), COP-DAB (the Conflict and Peace Data Bank), CREON (Comparative Research on the Events of Nations), and so forth. The Kansas Event Data System (KEDS) is more of a second-wave effort, in that the Kansas team has developed machine coding of events, leading to much more reliable and capacious data collection and coding than was possible in the first wave of events data (Schrodt 1995).

Integrated explanations

In contrast to the other two types of FPA scholarship being discussed, CFP research aimed explicitly at *integrated multilevel* explanations. The four most ambitious of these projects were those of Brecher (1972) and his associates in the IBA Project (Wilkenfeld *et al.* 1980), DON (Rummel 1972, 1977), CREON (East *et al.* 1978; Callahan *et al.* 1982), and Harold Guetzkow's INS (Guetzkow 1963). Independent variables at several levels of analysis were linked by theoretical propositions (sometimes instantiated in statistical or mathematical equations) to properties or types of foreign policy behaviour. At least three of the four attempted to confirm or disconfirm the propositions by aggregate empirical testing. Unfortunately, the fact that the empirical results were not all that had been hoped for ushered in a period of disenchantment with all things CFP, as we shall see in a later section.

The psychological and societal milieux of foreign policy decision making

The mind of a foreign policy maker is not a *tabula rasa*: it contains complex and intricately related information and patterns, such as beliefs, attitudes, values, experiences, emotions, traits, style, memory, national, and self-conceptions. Each decision maker's mind is a microcosm of the variety possible in a given society. Culture, history, geography, economics, political institutions, ideology, demographics, and innumerable other factors shape the societal context in which the decision maker operates. The Sprouts (1956, 1957, 1965) referred to these as the milieu of decision making, and scholarly efforts to explore that milieu were both innovative and impressive during this first period. Michael Brecher's work cited above (Brecher 1972) belongs in this genotype as well. Brecher's *The Foreign Policy System of Israel* explores that nation's psycho-cultural environment and its effects on Israel's foreign policy. Unlike Brecher's integrative approach to the psycho-social milieu, most works in this genotype examined either the psychological aspects of FPDM, or its broader societal aspects.

Individual characteristics

Would there be a distinct field of foreign policy analysis without this most micro of all explanatory levels? Arguably not. It is in the cognition and information processing of an actual human agent that all the explanatory levels of FPA are in reality integrated. What sets FPA apart from more mainstream IR is this insistence that, as Hermann and Kegley put it, '[a] compelling explanation (of foreign policy) cannot treat the decider exogenously' (1994: 4).

Political psychology can assist us in understanding the decider. Under certain conditions— high stress, high uncertainty, dominant position of the head of state in FPDM—the personal characteristics of the individual will become crucial in understanding foreign policy choice.

The work of Harold Lasswell on political leadership was a significant influence on many early pioneers of political psychology with reference to foreign policy (see Lasswell, 1930, 1948). Joseph de Rivera's *The Psychological Dimension of Foreign Policy* (1968) is an excellent survey and integration of early attempts to apply psychological and social psychological theory to foreign policy cases. Another early effort at a systematic study of leader personality effects is the concept of **operational code**, an idea originating with Leites (1951), and refined and extended by one of the most important figures in this area of research—Alexander George (1969). Defining an operational code involves identifying the core political beliefs of the leader about the inevitability of conflict in the world, the leader's estimation of his or her own power to change events, and so forth, as well as an exploration of the preferred means and style of pursuing goals (see also O. Holsti 1977; Johnson 1977; Walker 1977). It should be noted that George's influence on the field is by no means confined to his work on operational codes; he has offered useful suggestions on methodological issues (see George on process tracing (George 1979), on the demerits of abstract theorizing versus **actor-specific theory** (George and Smoke 1974; George 1993), and on the need to bridge the gap between theory and practice in foreign policy (George 1993, 1994).

The work of Margaret G. Hermann is likewise an attempt to typologize leaders with specific reference to foreign policy dispositions. A psychologist by training, she was also involved in a CFP project (CREON). However, the core of her research is leaders' personal characteristics (Hermann 1970, 1978). Using a modified operational code framework in conjunction with content analysis, she is able to compare and contrast leaders' beliefs, motivations, decisional styles, and interpersonal styles. Furthermore, Hermann integrates this information into a more holistic picture of the leader, who may belong to one of six distinct 'foreign policy orientations'. Orientation allows her to make more specific projections about a leader's behaviour in a variety of circumstances. In the second wave of research, scholars began to explicitly compare and contrast the findings of different personality assessment schemes (Winter *et al.* 1991; Singer and Hudson 1992; Snare 1992; see also Winter 1973; Post 1990).

The role of perceptions and images in foreign policy was a very important research agenda in this first generation of FPA. The work of both Robert Jervis and Richard Cottam deserves special mention here. Jervis's *Perception and Misperception in International Politics* (1976) and Cottam's *Foreign Policy Motivation: A General Theory and a Case Study* (1977) both explicate the potentially grave consequences of misperception in foreign policy situations by exploring its roots. Deterrence strategies can fail catastrophically if misperception of the other's intentions or motivations occur (see also the stimulus-response models of Holsti *et al.* (1968)). Like Janis, Halperin, and others, the work of Jervis and Cottam is consciously prescriptive: both include advice and suggestions for policy makers. Work in the late 1980s continuing this tradition included scholarship by Janice Gross Stein, Richard Ned Lebow, Ole Holsti, Alexander George, Deborah Welch Larson, Betty Glad, and Stephen Walt (as well as Jervis *et al.* 1985; Larson 1985, 1993; M. Cottam 1986; Glad 1989; George and Smoke 1989; O. Holsti 1989; Lebow and Stein 1990; Walt 1992). An excellent example of work in this period is that of Richard Herrmann (1985, 1986, 1993), who developed a typology of stereotypical images with reference to Soviet perceptions (the other as 'child', as 'degenerate', etc.) and began to extend his analysis to the images held by other nations, including American and Islamic images.

The work on cognitive constraints was informed by the work of scholars in other fields, including that of Herbert Simon (1985) on bounded rationality, Heuer (1999, but written between 1978 and 1986) on cognitive bias, and Kahneman *et al.* (1982) on heuristic error. Many other important cognitive and psychological studies which appeared during the 1970s and early 1980s dealt with a diversity of factors: motivations of leaders (Barber 1972; Winter 1973; Etheredge 1978), cognitive maps, scripts, and schemas (Shapiro and Bonham 1973; Axelrod 1976, Carbonell 1978), cognitive style (Suedfeld and Tetlock 1977); life experience of leaders (Stewart 1977), and others. Good edited collections of the time include Hermann (1977) and Falkowski (1979).

National and societal characteristics

Kal Holsti's (1970) elucidation of **national role conception** spans both the psychological and the social milieu. With this concept, Holsti seeks to capture how a nation views itself and its role in the international arena. Operationally, Holsti turns to elite perceptions of national role, arguing that these perceptions are arguably more salient to foreign policy choice. Perception of national role is also influenced by societal character, a product of the nation's socialization process. Differences here can lead to differences in national behaviour as well (e.g. Broderson 1961; Hess 1963; Merelman 1969; Renshon 1977; Bobrow *et al.* 1979). The methodology of national role conception was continued in the 1980s by Walker (1987) and others (Wish 1980; Cottam and Shih 1992; Shih 1993).

The study of culture as an independent variable affecting foreign policy was just beginning to be redeveloped near the end of the 1980s after petering out in the 1960s (Almond and Verba 1963; Pye and Verba 1965). Culture might have an effect on cognition (Motokawa 1989); it might have ramifications for structuration of institutions such as bureaucracies (Sampson 1987). Conflict resolution techniques might be different for different cultures as well (Cushman and King 1985; Pye 1986; Gaenslen 1989). Indeed, the very processes of policy making might be stamped by one's cultural heritage and socialization (Holland 1984; Etheredge 1985; Lampton 1986; Merelman 1986; Leung 1987; Banerjee 1991; Voss and Dorsey 1992).

The study of the role of societal groups in foreign policy making can be seen as an outgrowth of the more advanced study of societal groups in American domestic politics. Sometimes an individual scholar used theory developed for the American case to explore the more diverse universe of the international system. For example, Robert Dahl's volume, *Regimes and Oppositions* (1973), provided the key theoretical concepts necessary to analyse the relationship between domestic political pressure by societal groups and foreign policy choice by the government. Other more country- and region-specific case studies were also developed: see Deutsch *et al.* (1967), Hellman (1969), Dallin (1969), Chittick (1970), Hughes (1978), and Ogata (1977), among others. In the late 1980s, a **new wave** of thinking began to explore the limits of state autonomy in relation to other societal groups in the course of policy making. The work of Putnam (1988) on the **two-level game** of foreign and domestic policy was paradigmatic for establishing the major questions of this research subfield. Other excellent work includes Evans *et al.* (1985), Hagan (1987), Levy (1988), Lamborn and Mumme (1989), Levy and Vakili (1989), and Mastanduno *et al.* (1989). A **second wave** of research in this area can be seen in the work of Kaarbo (1993), Skidmore and Hudson (1993), and Van

Belle (1993) (see also Bueno de Mesquita and Lalman (1992) for an interesting combination of game theory and FPA to understand domestic political imperatives and their effect on foreign policy).

The second-wave work of Joe Hagan deserves special note. He has compiled an extensive database on the fragmentation and vulnerability of political regimes, with special reference to executive/legislative structures (Hagan 1993). The set includes 94 regimes for 38 nations over a 10-year period. His purpose is to explore the effects of political opposition on foreign policy choice. Using aggregate statistical analysis, Hagan is able to show, for example, that the internal fragmentation of a regime has substantially less effect on foreign policy behaviour than military or party opposition to the regime.

Domestic political imperatives could also be ascertained by probing elite and mass opinion (again, piggy-backing onto the sophisticated voter-attitude studies of American politics). Though usually confined to studies of democratic nations (especially America, where survey research results were abundant), these analyses were used to investigate the limits of the so-called Almond–Lippman consensus—that is, that public opinion is incoherent and lacking unity on foreign policy issues, and thus that public opinion does not have a large impact on the nation's conduct of foreign policy (see Bailey 1948; Almond 1950; Lippman 1955; Campbell *et al.* 1964; Converse 1964; Lipset 1966). Opinion data collected during the Vietnam War period appears to have served as a catalyst to re-examine this question. Caspary (1970) and Achen (1975) found more stability in American public opinion concerning foreign policy and international involvement than their predecessors. Mueller (1973) used the Vietnam War to show that although the public may change their opinions on international issues, they do so for rational reasons. Holsti and Rosenau (1979) and Mandelbaum and Schneider (1979) used survey data to identify recognizable ideological positions to which the public subscribes on foreign policy issues. A large amount of research was undertaken to show that public and elite opinion does affect governmental foreign policy decision making (see Cantril 1967; Verba *et al.* 1967; Graber 1968; Verba and Brody 1970; Hughes 1978; Yankelovich 1979; Beal and Hinckley 1984).

The study of the effect of national attributes (size, wealth, political accountability, economic system, etc.) on foreign policy was certainly, in a theoretical sense, in the Sprout genotype, but was carried out by scholars and with methods more to be placed in the Rosenau genotype (if you exclude pre-Rosenau writers such as Lenin). The propensity to be involved in war was usually the foreign policy dependent variable of choice in this work (see Rummel 1972, 1977, 1979; Kean and McGowan 1973; East and Hermann 1974; East 1978; Salmore and Salmore 1978; for a more holistic treatment, see Korany 1986).

The questions raised by these theorists are fascinating. Are large nations more likely to go to war than small nations? Are rich nations more likely to go to war than poor ones? Are authoritarian regimes more bellicose than democracies? Statistical manipulation of aggregate data, at best a blunt instrument, was unable to uncover any lawlike generalizations on this score (though for an interesting and hard-to-classify treatment of the multilevel causes and effects of war, see Beer (1981)). Political economy research on the effects of economic structures and conditions on foreign policy choice are fairly rare: the 'culture' of IPE and the 'culture' of FPA did not mix well, for reasons explored below. However, the works of Neil Richardson and Charles Kegley (e.g. Richardson and Kegley 1980) and Peter Katzenstein (e.g. Katzenstein 1985) are notable as exceptions to this generalization.

However, in the second-wave years, one notable exception to all the analysis of the previous years burst forth upon the scene—democratic peace theory. Democracies, it was noted, tend not to fight one another, though they fight non-democratic countries as often as other non-democracies do. This appeared to be an example of how a difference in polity type produced a difference in foreign policy behaviour (Russett 1993a,b). This has been a particularly interesting bridging question for FPA and IR (and is examined further in Chapter Three). Why do democracies not fight one another? Here we find more abstract theorists of war (Merritt and Zinnes 1991; Morgan 1992; Bremer 1993; Dixon 1993; Ray 1993; Maoz and Russett 1993) wrestling with a question that leads them into FPA waters and into conversation with FPA scholars (Hagan 1994; Hermann and Kegley 1995).

Finally, if it is possible to see the international system as part of the psycho-social milieu in which foreign policy decision making takes place, then the work of much of mainstream IR at this time can be seen as contributing to the Foreign Policy Analysis research agenda. The effects of system type, as elucidated by Kaplan (1957, 1972), may depend on the number of poles in the system, the distribution of power among poles, and the rules of the system game that permit its maintenance. This structure may then determine to a large extent the range of permissible foreign policy behaviour of nations. The work of Waltz was extremely influential in its description of the effects of an anarchical world system on the behaviour of its member states (see also Hoffmann 1961; Rosecrance 1963; Singer *et al.* 1972). FPA seemed not to emphasize this type of explanation, primarily because the variation in behaviour during the time when a certain system is maintained cannot be explained by reference to system structure because the structure has not changed. Explanation of that variation must be found at lower levels of analysis, where variation in the explanations can be identified. Here, then, is one of several sources for the notable lack of integration between actor-general systems theory in IR and FPA.

FPA self-reflection in the late 1970s and 1980s

A period of critical self-reflection in FPA began in the late 1970s and continued until the mid-1980s. The effects were felt unevenly across FPA, with CFP being affected the most; it is here that we see the most pruning, both theoretical and methodological, which will be discussed later. In decision-making studies there was a period of rather slow growth because of methodological considerations. The information requirements for conducting a high-quality group or bureaucratic analysis of a foreign policy choice are tremendous. If one were not part of the group or bureaucracy in question, detailed accounts of what transpired, preferably from a variety of primary source viewpoints, would be necessary. Because of security considerations in foreign policy, such information is not usually available for many years (e.g. until declassified). The question facing decision-making scholars became: Is it possible to be theoretically and policy relevant if one is relegated to doing case studies of events twenty years or more old? If so, how? If not, how is it possible to manoeuvre around the high data requirements to say something meaningful about more recent events? (See P. Anderson 1987.) Scholars wrestling with this issue came up with two basic responses: (a) patterns in group/bureaucratic processes can be isolated through historical case studies, on the basis of which both general predictions of and general recommendations for present-day foreign policy decision making can be made; (b) innovative at-a-distance indicators of closed group/bureaucracy process can be developed, which allow for more specific explanation/prediction of resultant foreign policy choice.

FPA work at the psychological level actually expanded during this time period, but work at the societal level arguably contracted on some research fronts. The reason for this bifurcation in the genotype was methodological: psychology provided ready-made and effective tools for the study of political psychology, but political science did not offer the foreign policy analyst the same advantage. To understand how the broader socio-cultural-political context within a nation-state contributes to its governmental policy making (whether domestic or foreign) is, perforce, the domain of comparative politics. It is hopefully not controversial to aver that the theories and methods of comparative politics in this period were not quite as highly developed as those of psychology. The attempt to graft 'scientific' statistical analyses of variance onto the underdeveloped theory of comparative politics of the 1970s and 1980s was a failure. More successful were efforts to spin existing comparative politics work on a particular nation to the cause of explaining factors that contribute to that nation's foreign policy—for example, borrowing techniques from American politics (such as public opinion surveys) to study domestic political imperatives in the USA on foreign policy issues. Still missing were the conceptual and methodological tools necessary to push past the artificial barrier between comparative politics and international relations that stymied theory development. One of the greatest leaps forward in the present period of FPA is the innovative work begun on conceptualizing the 'two-level game' (Putnam 1988).

As mentioned, CFP dwindled in the 1980s. Indeed, the very term 'comparative foreign policy' began to sound quaint and naive. Membership of the Comparative Foreign Policy Section of the International Studies Association plummeted. Public vivisections took place, while Rosenau-genotype-style scholarship became scarce. Both sympathetic and unsympathetic criticism abounded (e.g. Ashley 1976, 1987; Munton 1976; East 1978; Kegley 1980; Caporaso *et al.* 1987; Hermann and Peacock 1987; Smith 1987). At one point, in exasperation, Kegley (1980: 12), himself a CFPer, chides, 'CFP risks being labelled a cult of methodological flagellomaniacs'.

This searing criticism and self-criticism revealed a number of inconsistencies in the CFP approach, which needed to be sorted out before any progress could be contemplated. The stumbling blocks included the following:

1. *You can't have your parsimony and eat it, too.* The tension between the desire of some CFPers for a hard-science-like grand unified theory and the assumption that micro-level detail is necessary if one really wants to explain and predict foreign policy behaviour became unbearable. Rosenau's 'Pre-theories' article (Rosenau 1966), when reviewed from this vantage point, sets the genotype up for an inevitable dilemma about parsimony. To what should we aspire: richly detailed, comprehensively researched micro-analyses of a few cases, or conceptually abstract, parsimonious statistico-mathematical renderings of thousands of events? One can see the problem in desiring richly detailed, comprehensively researched micro-analyses of thousands of events: a lifetime would be over before a theorist had collected enough data to do the first big 'run'! But many CFPers rejected the case study approach as unscientific and too much like the soft anecdotal research of the 'traditionalists' (Kegley 1980).

CFPers wanted to be behaviouralists and to be scientific, and a hallmark of this was aggregate empirical testing of cross-nationally applicable generalizations across large values of *N*. At the same time, they were fiercely committed to unpacking the black box of decision making, so the detail of their explanans grew, and with it their rejection of knee-jerk idealization of parsimony. Push had to come to shove at some point: CFP methods demanded parsimony in theory; CFP theory demanded nuance and detail in method.

2. *To quantify or not to quantify?* A corollary of large-*N*-size testing is the need for more precise measurement of data; indeed, quantification of variables is essential to linear regression and correlation techniques, as well as to mathematical manipulations such as differential equations. However, the independent variables of CFP included such non-quantifiables as perception, memory, emotion, culture, history, etc., all placed in a dynamic and evolving stream of human action and reaction that might not be adequately captured by arithmetic-based relationships. To leave such non-quantifiable explanatory variables out seems to defeat the very purpose of micro-analysis; to leave them in by forcing the data into quasi-interval level pigeonholes seems to do violence to the substance that CFP sought to capture. CFPers began to ask whether their methods were aiding them in achieving their theoretical goals or preventing them from ever achieving those goals.

3. *A final inconsistency centred in policy relevance.* As mentioned earlier, CFP had received a large amount of money from the government to create events data sets. CFP researchers successfully argued that such an investment would yield information of use to foreign policy makers. Specifically, events data would be used to set up early warning systems that would alert policy makers to crises in the making around the world (as if they do not also read the same sources from which events data come!).

Computerized decision aids and analysis packages with telltale acronyms began to appear— EWAMS (Early Warning and Monitoring System); CASCON (Computer-Aided Systems for Handling Information on Local Conflicts); CACIS (Computer-Aided Conflict Information System); XAIDS (Crisis Management Executive Decision Aids) (see Andriole and Hopple 1981). Unfortunately, these could never live up to their promise: the collected events could be had from other sources and so were nothing without the theory to explain and predict their occurrence. The methodological paradoxes explicated above resulted in theory that was stuck, by and large, at the level of globally applicable but specifically vacuous bivariate generalizations such as that 'large nations participate more in international interactions than small nations' (see McGowan and Shapiro 1973). Again, CFP found itself pulled in two opposed directions: Was the research goal to say something predictive about a specific nation at a specific time in a specific set of circumstances (which would be highly policy relevant, but which might closely resemble the output of a traditional country expert)? Or was the goal a grand unified theory (which would not be very policy relevant, but which would qualify you as a scientist and a generalist)? Attempts to accomplish both with the same research led to products that were unsatisfactory in a scholarly as well as a policy sense.

Hindsight is always 20/20; it does seem clear in retrospect that change was necessary. Left behind were (1) the aim of a grand unified theory, and (2) the methodological straitjacket imposed by the requirement of aggregate empirical testing. In 1980, Kegley spoke of the need to come down from the rarified air of grand theory to middle-range theory, and to capture more of the particular:

> To succeed partially is not to fail completely. . . . Goals (should be) downgraded to better fit capacities. . . . This prescribes reduction in the level of generality sought, so that more contextually-qualified, circumstantially bounded, and temporally/spatially-specified propositions are tested. More of the peculiar, unique, and particular can be captured at a reduced level of abstraction and generality. (Kegley 1980: 12, 19)

To be fair, this was arguably Rosenau's original aim, and the CFP community had to reach a consensus to return to its founding vision. The conference on New Directions in the Study of Foreign Policy, held at Ohio State University in May 1985, probably represents a finalization of these changes for the CFP group (see the resulting volume, Hermann *et al.* 1987; see also Gerner 1992).

Conclusion: contemporary FPA's research agenda

As FPA was being liberated from its inconsistencies in the late 1980s, the world was being liberated from the chess match of the Cold War. This was a felicitous coincidence for FPA, and was an added source of vigour for its research agenda. The significance of this temporal coincidence can be understood by remembering what types of IR theory were in ascendance at the time: neorealist systems structure theory and rational choice modelling. Indeed, the dominance was so overwhelming that on taking an IR theory course during this time, one would think these two were the *summum bonum* of all thinking in international relations (at least in the USA). This state of affairs was natural for American thinkers: America was one of two poles of power in the Cold War international system. A bipolar quasi-zero-sum rivalry lends itself relatively well to abstract actor-general analysis focused primarily on the macro-constraints imposed by the system. Furthermore, **actor-general theory** was more practical for scholars during the Cold War, because so little was known of the black box of the closed Soviet, Chinese, and Eastern Bloc foreign policy decision making bodies.

However, when the bipolar system collapsed with the fall of the Soviet bloc regimes, an important theoretical discovery was made: *it is impossible to explain or predict system change on the basis of system-level variables alone.* Along the same lines, in a period of great uncertainty and flux, lack of empirically grounded inputs to rational choice equations is deadly in terms of the usefulness of such analysis. Our intuitive understanding of the collapse involves variables more to be found in FPA: the personalities of Gorbachev, Havel, and Walesa; the activities of transnational groups such as the Lutheran Church and the Green Movement; the struggles between various domestic political players, such as the military, the Communist Party, the bureaucrats, etc.; the role of economics and societal needs in sparking the desire for change, etc. With the fall of the Iron Curtain, the need for an 'actor-specific' complement to mainstream IR theory became stark in its clarity.

FPA in the post Cold War era retains the distinctive theoretical commitments that demarcated at its inception. Included among these are:

- *a commitment to look below the nation-state level of analysis to actor-specific information;*

- a commitment to build middle-range theory as the interface between actor-general theory and the complexity of the real world;
- a commitment to pursue multicausal explanations spanning multiple levels of analysis;
- a commitment to utilize theory and findings from across the spectrum of social science;
- a commitment to viewing the process of foreign policy decision making as important as the output thereof.

Nevertheless, FPA has evolved in the sophistication of the questions asked, and in the means of answering those questions. Indeed, FPA's ability to ask new questions is perhaps more promising in relation to its future theoretical potential than any other indicator. Einstein and Infeld (1938) commented that, '(t)he formulation of a problem is often more essential than its solution which may be merely a matter of ¼ skill. To raise new questions, new possibilities, to regard old problems from a new angle, requires creative imagination and works real advance in science'.

In order to see this advance, let us examine some of the new questions that have evolved from the old. As a detailed overview of FPA scholarship from 1993 to the present can be found in Hudson (2005, 2007), let us now turn to the micro-levels of analysis and then move toward macro-levels.

New questions

When studying the effects of **individual leaders** on foreign policy decision making, the key question is whether we can extend our understanding of how a leader's personality affects foreign policy through determining its effect on choice of advisors, preference for issues, preference for certain group processes, and so forth? Moreover, can we integrate different analytical schemes for analysing leader personality and its effects? What are the ramifications of new breakthroughs in **neuroscience** for FPA? How do various leader personality types shape the structure and process of groups serving them?

At the **group level**, we must then ask how problems are actually recognized by the group? How are situations 'framed' and 'represented'? How are options developed? How does a group come to share an interpretation of the situation? How does a group change an established interpretation? How does a group learn? How is the group's potential for creativity enhanced or dampened? How does group memory affect group action? How do groups become players in the 'two-level game'? How are group structure and process a function of societal culture?

At the level of **society and political competition**, we explore whether we can uncover the societal sources of change in shared perceptions? For example, how do attitudes of leaders and publics change as context changes? Can national role conception be re-configured to serve as the theoretical interface between a society and the individual members of that society who come to lead it and make its foreign policy decisions? Can we specify the effect on foreign policy of domestic political competition? Can we complete the theoretical circle and specify the effects on domestic politics of the implementation of a certain foreign policy choice? How can we discern culture's influence on foreign policy? Does type of political system impact on foreign policy? What is the effect of systemic change on foreign policy?

Methodologically speaking, there are just as many key questions to be considered. These include: Can events data be re-conceptualized to be of use to contemporary FPA? Can FPA utilize methods created to simulate human decision making as a means of integrating complex non-quantifiable data? Can we think of non-arithmetic ways to relate variables? Can rational choice models be altered to accommodate actor-specific idiosyncracies with regard to utility, choice mechanisms, and choice constraints? Can we create models that will allow us to use as inputs the actor-specific knowledge generated by country/region experts? When is the detail of actor-specifics necessary, and when is actor-general theory sufficient to explain and project FPDM? How could one instantiate a model of the 'two-level game'? Can discursive analysis or interpretivism be used to introduce the dynamics of evolving understanding in FPDM?

An Atlantic divide?

While there are new efforts to both catalogue and promote the analytical study of foreign policy in the Global South (Brummer 2011; Giacalone 2011; Zhang 2011), at this point such study is predominantly of Atlantic origins. This raises the question of whether there are important differences in the way such studies are conducted in the USA compared with European countries, to which an affirmative answer can be given. In a recent overview of such differences (Hadfield and Hudson 2011), the authors point out several distinctions between FPA (American) and what they term AFP (the analysis of foreign policy, European). This issue is of interest to the readers of this volume, for about half of its authors are American and about half are European.

Hadfield and Hudson note a greater emphasis on cognitively oriented theories in FPA than in AFP, as well as the more frequent use of quantitative methods by Americans and historical process-tracing by Europeans. They also note a clear preference for the use of American cases by American scholars, which, while not unexpected and also understandable, also bears predictable consequences for theory-building. For example, Zhang (2011) finds that in the Chinese case, being 'ideological' and being 'practical' are not oxymoronic terms, whereas in American-inspired theory, such personality orientations are seen as precluding one another. Hadfield and Hudson also note a greater sense of community among American FPA scholars, which they attribute to the small number of graduate programmes training FPA scholars in that country; they are all likely to know one another within one or two degrees of separation. Turning to the European context, there are almost no graduate programmes that emphasize FPA/AFP, and so as yet scholars have not been able to create a critical social mass that is the prerequisite for an epistemic community. Finally, Hadfield and Hudson suggest that AFP is far more theoretically inclusive than FPA has been to date, embracing not only actor-specific theories, but also grand theory and constructivist approaches. For example, one is not likely to see a reference to the work of Roy Bhaskar in American FPA literature, while such a reference might be very likely in AFP work.

New attempts to bridge IR and FPA

Also fairly recent in origin are sustained organized attempts to bridge the divide between FPA and IR. The two that we will mention in this section are neoclassical realism (exemplified by Lobell *et al.* 2009) and behavioural IR (exemplified by Walker *et al.* 2011; see also Mintz 2007).

Neoclassical realism attempts to cross the divide from the IR side to the FPA side, while behavioural IR is moving in the opposite direction.

Neoclassical realism is premised on the understanding that 'unit-level variables constrain or facilitate the ability of all types of states—great powers as well as lesser states—to respond to systemic imperatives' (Lobell *et al.* 2009: 4). While the power distribution within a system may bound grand strategy, the implementation of this strategy through decisions by foreign policy executives concerning threat assessment, risk, and mobilization of domestic resources, including public support, simply cannot be inferred from the 'grand' level. Historical process-tracing is the preferred methodology of this school.

Behavioral IR, on the other hand, takes as its touchstone the field of 'behavioural economics', associated with the work of such scholars as Richard Thaler. Walker and his co-authors define the approach as 'a social-psychological analysis of world politics, which emplys a general systems theory [i.e. role theory—ed.] to unify the understanding of actors, actions, and relations that constitute foreign policy and international relations' (Walker *et al.* 2011: 5). In other words, behavioural IR seeks to integrate the external world of events with the internal world of beliefs by examining strategic moves within dyads. The operational codes of the two actors are deciphered by quantitative content analysis of leader texts, and then a theory of strategic game moves (TOM) is employed to determine (at an abstract level) the next move that each actor in the dyad will take and how their game will resolve over sequential moves. The use of a game-theoretic logic informed by unit-level characteristics is an interesting amalgam of actor-general and actor-specific theorizing which, like neoclassical realism, attempts to bridge the divide between FPA and IR. Noteworthy, however, is the fact that neoclassical realism and behavioural IR—research programmes with the very same bridging goal—are working in such divergent methodological traditions that one wonders if they could possibly communicate with one another. But that is a topic for the future.

These are all exciting new questions, issues, and approaches to be exploring. Doubtless some of you will be involved in this work. It is a wonderful time to become engaged in FPA—a time of new horizons.

 Key points

- Foreign policy analysis takes as its theoretical ground the human decision makers, acting singly and in groups, who make foreign policy.

- Three paradigmatic works laid the foundation of FPA—Richard Snyder and colleagues on decision making, James Rosenau on comparative foreign policy, and Harold and Margaret Sprout on the psycho-social milieu of foreign policy decision making.

- Several emphases, corresponding to levels of analysis in FPA, began to emerge from this foundation, including work on small/large groups, events data, political psychology of leaders, cultural effects on foreign policy, the effects of domestic political contestation on FPDM, and the influence of national attributes and systemic characteristics on FPB.

- FPA retains its emphases on actor-specific theory, multicausal explanations, interdisciplinarity, and the explanations of foreign policy processes, as well as foreign policy outcomes.

- Current FPA scholarship explores linkages between the levels of FPA analysis, and combines that with a search for new methodologies that are more appropriate for actor-specific theoretical investigation.

Questions

1. What are the key hallmarks of FPA?
2. What is the difference between foreign policy and foreign policy behaviour?
3. What are the primary levels of analysis examined in FPA?
4. What did Richard Snyder and his colleagues contribute to FPA's foundations?
5. What did James Rosenau contribute to FPA's foundations?
6. What did Harold and Margaret Sprout contribute to FPA's foundations?
7. What is events data and how is it used in FPA?
8. What is comparative foreign policy (CFP)?
9. Why did FPA enter a period of self-reflection in the late 1970s and early 1980s, and what was the result?
10. What kinds of questions are being asked in FPA research today? How effective and/or necessary are 'bridging techniques' between IR and FPA?

 Further reading

Caporaso, J.A., Hermann, C.F., and Kegley, C.W. (1987), 'The Comparative Study of Foreign Policy: Perspectives on the Future', *International Studies Notes*, 13: 32–46.
This is an interesting piece, from a historical point of view, as it attempts to engage international political economy (IPE) with FPA.

Garrison, J. (ed.) (2003), 'Foreign Policy Analysis in 20/20', *International Studies Review*, 5: 156–163.
This special issue of *ISR* features a variety of FPA scholars discussing the future prospects of FPA as a field of study.

Gerner, D.J. (1992), 'Foreign Policy Analysis: Exhilarating Eclecticism, Intriguing Enigmas', *International Studies Notes*, 18(4).
Gerner's piece is an excellent summary of FPA scholarship up until the end of the Cold War.

Hudson, V.M. (2007), *Foreign Policy Analysis: Classic and Contemporary Theory* **(New York: Rowman and Littlefield).**
This textbook not only covers the history of FPA, but also seven levels of analysis, as well as a discussion of integrative efforts in the field.

Neack, L., Hey J.A., and Haney, P.J. (1995), *Foreign Policy Analysis: Continuity and Change in Its Second Generation* **(Englewood Cliffs, NJ: Prentice Hall).**
This edited volume served as a textbook in many FPA classes from 1995 to 2005, and includes chapters on nearly all levels of analysis, as well as subjects such as events data.

 Visit the Online Resource Centre that accompanies this book for more information:
www.oxfordtextbooks.co.uk/orc/smith_foreign/

2 Realism and foreign policy

WILLIAM C. WOHLFORTH

Chapter contents

 Reader's guide

This chapter shows how familiarity with realist theory improves Foreign Policy Analysis (FPA). The main challenge is to exploit two features of realism that are often in tension with each other: its firm grounding in centuries of real foreign policy practice, and its aspiration to create powerful general theories that help to simplify and explain the international setting in which foreign policy takes place. The chapter identifies a branch of realist theory—neoclassical realism—which bridges the gap between these two aspects of the realist tradition and thus is most useful for the analysis of foreign policy. The following key questions are addressed.

● What is realism?

● How is it applied to the analysis and practice of foreign policy?

● What are the main pitfalls in applying realist theories to FPA?

● What is a useful set of guidelines for avoiding those pitfalls and using realist insights to sharpen the analysis of foreign policy?

Introduction

Realism is the foundational school of thought about international politics around which all others are oriented. It follows that any foreign policy analyst who wishes to make use of International Relations (IR) theory must understand realism. Fortunately, this is not difficult to do. As this chapter demonstrates, the realist school can be understood as a body of theories and related arguments that flow from a very small set of basic assumptions about how the world works. Used with sensitivity in their application to the complexity and uncertainty of the real political world, realist theories can substantially sharpen the analysis of foreign policy.

To apply realism to FPA, one has to bridge the gap that divides highly general, 'top-down' theory from the 'inside-out' analysis of specific cases. Realism itself embodies this tension, reflecting the desire to be both realistic (i.e. grounded in actual foreign policy practice) and theoretical (i.e. aspiring to general timeless knowledge). Realists seek to distil the accumulated wisdom of generations of foreign policy practitioners into general theories of IR. Realism's basic conceptual foundations are derived from the close observation of lived politics. But in seeking to construct and apply a reality-based theory, realists constantly face the challenge of cycling between the nuanced subtleties of real foreign policy situations and the razor-sharp assumptions and deductions of theory.

In this chapter, I show that realism's promise for the analysis of foreign policy stems from its twin commitments to particular and general knowledge, and that most of the pitfalls of applying realism derive from a failure to get this balance right. I outline an approach to realist theory designed to connect the insights of general theory to the details and uncertainty of analysing specific foreign policy situations. This approach reflects a sustained effort on the part of a new generation of scholars to gain the analytical benefits of realist theory without falling prey to its potentially misleading over-generalization. To understand this new approach, however, one first needs to know what realism is, how it has developed over the years, and how the general theories that have developed as part of the realist canon have been used to analyse foreign policy.

What is realism?

Realism is a school of thought based on three core assumptions about how the world works.[1]

- **Groupism** Humans face one another mainly as members of groups. To survive at anything above subsistence level, people need the cohesion provided by group solidarity, yet that very same in-group cohesion generates the potential for conflict with other groups. Today the most important human groups are nation-states, and the most important source of in-group cohesion is nationalism. For convenience, I shall use the term 'states' henceforth. However, it is important to stress that realism makes no assumption about the nature of the polity. It may apply to any social setting where groups interact.

- **Egoism** Self-interest ultimately drives political behaviour. Although certain conditions can facilitate altruistic behaviour, egoism is rooted in human nature. When push comes to shove and ultimate trade-offs between collective and self-interest must be confronted, egoism tends to trump altruism. As the classic realist adage has it, 'Inhumanity is just humanity under pressure'.

- **Power-centrism** Power is the fundamental feature of politics. Once past the hunter–gatherer stage, human affairs are always marked by great inequalities of power in both senses of that term: social influence or **control** (some groups and individuals always have an outsized influence on politics) and **resources** (some groups and individuals are always disproportionately endowed with the material wherewithal to get what they want). Key to politics in any area is the interaction between social and material power, an interaction that unfolds in the shadow of the potential use of material power to coerce. As Kenneth

Waltz put it, 'The web of social and political life is spun out of inclinations and incentives, deterrent threats and punishments. Eliminate the latter two, and the ordering of society depends entirely on the former—a utopian thought impractical this side of Eden' (Waltz 1979: 186).

If one believes the world generally works by these rules, then many important consequences follow for how one thinks about international politics: that the main groups with which people identify—be they tribes, city-states, empires, or nation-states—will exert a major influence on human affairs; that the group's collective interest, however defined, will be central to its politics; that necessity as the group interest defines it will trump any putatively universal morality and ethics; and thus that humankind is unlikely ever to wholly transcend power politics through the progressive power of reason.

This way of thinking about IR leads immediately to an identifiably realist approach to foreign policy: an orientation towards the most powerful groups (i.e. the most resource rich and influential) at any given time (today this means major powers like the USA or China); a scepticism towards professed aims of foreign policy other than the state interest; a tendency to question the ability of any state's foreign policy to transcend power politics; and a penchant for looking beyond rhetoric to the power realities that realists expect nearly always underlie policy. These precepts represent a simple realist checklist for FPA: look for where the power is, what the group interests are, and the role power relationships play in reconciling clashing interests.

Certain types of thinkers tend to share similar bets about how the world works. Critics like to say that the kind of person most likely to accept the core realist assumptions is a congenital pessimist and cynic. Realists counter that these assumptions are simply realistic—based on the dispassionate observation of human affairs the way they are, as opposed to the way we might wish them to be. There is a degree of truth to both views, and they add up to produce a unity of realist thought stretching from Thucydides to Machiavelli, Weber, Carr, Morgenthau, and Waltz. Even though the thinkers indelibly associated with realism are a highly diverse lot, and even though their ideas often contradict each other, the threads of those three core assumptions tie them all together into a coherent intellectual school. Reading any of the writings of any of these thinkers concerning the foreign policies of their day, one immediately discerns the unmistakably realist approach to foreign policy I identified above.

To be sure, realism is more than academic theory. It is also a tradition of statecraft that tends to reflect these same basic assumptions. But the focus here is on the use of scholarly theory to inform the analysis of foreign policy. For that purpose, it is important to be clear about how scholars transform the basic assumptions about the world into theories. And that demands clarity about what we mean by the word 'theory'. Confusingly, scholars use 'theory' to refer to three distinct things: realism itself (a large and complex school of thought), subschools within realism such as **neorealism** (smaller but still complex schools of thought fitting within the realist tradition), and specific realist theories like the **balance of power**, the **security dilemma**, or the **offence–defence balance** (all propositions about patterns of relations among states or pressures facing a particular state). In this chapter, I keep these things clear, reserving the term 'theory' for specific propositions or arguments. These distinctions are not academic quibbles. The foreign policy analyst may well be sceptical of realism in general but still find specific realist theories very helpful indeed.

The development of realist theories

Trademark realist theories all proceed from realism's three core assumptions of groupism, egoism, and power-centrism. The first and most general of all these theories, and the one from which most others proceed, can be stated simply: if human affairs are indeed character- ized by groupism, egoism, and power-centrism, then politics is likely to be conflictual unless there is some central authority to enforce order. When no authority which can enforce agree- ments exists —a condition theorists call **anarchy**—any state can resort to force to get what it wants. Even if a state can be fairly sure that no other state will take up arms today, there is no guarantee against the possibility that one might do so tomorrow. Because no state can rule out this prospect, states tend to arm themselves against this contingency. With all states thus armed, politics takes on a different cast. Disputes that would be easy to settle if states could rely on some higher authority to enforce an agreement can escalate to war in the absence of such authority. Therefore the classic realist theoretical argument is that anarchy renders the security of states problematic and potentially conflictual, and is a key underlying cause of war.

To move from this very general argument about the potential importance of power and conflict in IR to any real foreign policy situation requires three steps: a knowledge of theoreti- cal schools within realism, familiarity with specific realist theories, and, perhaps most impor- tant, clarity about how theories, assumptions, and conditions are related.

Theoretical schools within realism

The development of realist thought can be seen as a series of refinements, amendments, qualifications, and extensions of the basic argument. For simplicity, scholars often lump to- gether all realist thought from Thucydides to the middle years of the Cold War as **classical realism**. They describe distinctions within the massive classical realist canon by reference to individual thinkers. The classical realists all sought to translate the distilled wisdom of genera- tions of practitioners and analysts into very general theories. However, they were not always clear about when their theories applied to specific situations as opposed to general patterns. This ambiguity in the classical realist writings led to endless debates about what was actually being claimed for any particular theory.

As interest in the scientific approach to the study of politics grew (especially in the USA), Kenneth Waltz sought to revivify realist thinking by translating some core realist ideas into a deductive top-down theoretical framework that eventually came to be called neorealism. Waltz (1959) held that the classical realists' powerful insights into the workings of interna- tional politics were weakened by their failure to distinguish clearly among arguments about human nature, the internal attributes of states, and the overall system of states. His *Theory of International Politics* (Waltz 1979) brought together and clarified many earlier realist ideas about how the features of the overall system of states affect the ways states interact. He re- stated in the clearest form yet the classic argument about how the mere existence of groups in anarchy can lead to powerful competitive pressure and war—regardless of what the inter- nal politics of those groups might be like.

The advent of neorealism caused scholars to think much harder and more clearly about the underlying forces that drive IR. Realists discovered that, depending on how they thought about the core assumptions and what they saw as the most reasonable expectations about real-world conditions, neorealism could lead to very different predictions. Written in a highly abstract manner, Waltz's neorealism ignored important variations in IR, including geography and technology. Depending on how one conceptualized those factors, the exact same neorealist ideas could generate widely disparate implications about the dynamics of inter-state politics. Out of this realization were borne two new theoretical subschools, each of which built on the basic insights of neorealism.

Defensive realists reasoned that under very common conditions the war-causing potential of anarchy is attenuated. Proceeding from the core realist assumption about groupism, these theorists argued that the stronger group identity is—as in the modern era of nationalism—the harder it is to conquer and subjugate other groups. And the harder conquest is, the more secure all states can be. Similarly, technology may make conquest hard—for example, it is hard to contemplate the conquest of states that have the capacity to strike back with nuclear weapons. Thus, even accepting all of Waltz's arguments about how difficult it is to be secure in an anarchic world, under these kinds of conditions states could still be expected to find ways of defending themselves without threatening others, or could otherwise signal their peaceful intentions, resulting in an international system with more built-in potential for peace than many realists previously thought. The result was to push analysts to look inside states for the domestic/ideational causes of war and peace.

Offensive realists, by contrast, were more persuaded by the conflict-generating structural potential of anarchy itself. They reasoned that, with no authority to enforce agreements, states could never be certain that any peace-causing condition today would remain operative in the future. Even if conquest may seem hard today owing to geography, technology, or group identity, there is no guarantee against the prospect that another state will develop some fiendish device for overcoming these barriers. Given this uncertainty, states can rarely be confident of their security and must always view other states' increases in power with suspicion. As a result, states are often tempted to expand or otherwise strengthen themselves, and/or weaken others, in order to survive over the long haul. The result is to reinforce the classic realist argument about the competitive nature of life under anarchy, regardless of the internal properties of states.

As clear and elegant as neorealism and its immediate outgrowths were, it remained unclear just how relevant they were to any given foreign policy problem. So focused were realists on defining the single best and most universal formulation of their theory that it began to seem as if the development of realism had taken a completely different path from the analysis of foreign policy. Waltz (1996) himself argued famously that 'international politics is *not* foreign policy', implying that theory development and FPA had become two distinct endeavours with little connection to each other.

Neoclassical realism is a subschool within realism that seeks to rectify this imbalance between the general and the particular. It accepts from neorealism and its descendants the basic utility of thinking theoretically about the international system as distinct from the internal properties of states (Rose 1998). However, having carefully specified their assessment of the international conditions particular states face, neoclassical realists go on to factor in specific features of a given situation to generate more complete explanations of foreign policy. They seek to recapture the grounding in the gritty details of foreign policy that marked classical realism, while also benefiting from the rigorous theorizing that typified neorealism.

Neoclassical realists are not driven by the dream of creating a single universal theory of international politics. For them, the question is: Which realist school (if any) is most useful for analysing issues of foreign policy at a given place and time? To some extent, the choice of theory is a contextual issue. For example, offensive realism provides a powerful shorthand portrayal of the incentives and constraints faced by states in parts of Europe for long stretches of the eighteenth to twentieth centuries. In other periods, and for some groups of states in Europe, defensive realism arguably provides a more accurate model of the international setting. And many analysts hold that in today's EU anarchy is sufficiently attenuated that neither is much use.

The degree to which a theoretical picture of the international system really applies is a matter of judgement, based on the analyst's reading of the context. Neoclassical realists remain agnostic over which theoretical proposition may apply; they bring to bear those theories that are arguably relevant. However, while they are agnostic over *which* theory or theoretical school may apply, they agree that theory helps strengthen analysis. From the perspective of realism, a basic set of questions constantly recurs in FPA. To what degree is state X's policy a response to external pressures and incentives as opposed to internally generated? If a new party were to come to power, how much would the policy change? Would state X respond more favourably to incentives or threats? To answer these questions, one has to imagine what *any* state would do in X's position. The key contribution of neorealism and its offshoot subschools of offensive and defensive realism is rigorous thinking about exactly these questions. For neoclassical realists, theoretical structures like offensive and defensive realism are not always and everywhere true or false. Rather, they make it easier to perform the key mental experiments that lie at the core of FPA by helping analysts frame their assessments of the external constraints and incentives states face.

This, I shall argue, is the approach most likely to exploit the benefits of realism for the analysis of foreign policy while avoiding the potential pitfalls. To see why this is so, it is necessary to be familiar with more specific realist theories, and to be aware of how theories actually relate to specific situations.

Theories within realism

Theoretical subschools do not capture realism's full diversity. Equally important are specific theories about the fundamental constraints and incentives that shape foreign policy. A knowledge of realist theories prompts one to ask questions about foreign policy one would not otherwise ask, to look for patterns that would not otherwise seem relevant, and to see commonalities through time and so help distinguish the mundane from the remarkable.

Arguably the best-known theoretical proposition about IR is balance of power theory. Given the basic problem that under anarchy any state can resort to force to get what it wants, it follows that states are likely to guard against the possibility that one state might amass the wherewithal to compel all the others to do its will and even possibly eliminate them. The theory posits that states will check dangerous concentrations of power by building up their own capabilities ('internal balancing') or aggregating their capabilities with other states in alliances ('external balancing'). Because states are always looking to the future to anticipate possible problems, balancing may occur even before any one state or alliance has gained an obvious power edge. Thus, Britain and France fought the Russian Empire in the Crimea in the middle of the nineteenth century less because they saw an immediate challenge to their position than because they reasoned that, if unchecked, Russian power might some day be a threat to them. However wise or unwise it may have been, the thinking in London and Paris at that time strikes many historians as entirely consistent with the expectations of balance of power theory.

Balance of threat theory adds complexity to this picture. As its name implies, this theory predicts that states will balance against threats. Threat, in turn, is driven by a combination of three key variables: aggregate capabilities (i.e. a state's overall military and economic potential), geography, and perceptions of aggressive intentions. If one state becomes especially powerful, and if its location and behaviour feed threat perceptions on the part of other states, then balancing strategies will come to dominate their foreign policies. Thus the USA began both external and internal balancing after the end of the Second World War even though the Soviet Union remained decidedly inferior in most categories of power. Ultimately, the Western alliance overwhelmed the Soviet-led alliance on nearly every dimension. Balance of threat theory holds that it was the *location* of Soviet power in the heart of Europe, as well as the threat inherent in its secretive government and perceived aggressiveness, that produced this outcome.

Hegemonic stability theory builds on the observation that powerful states tend to seek dominance over all or parts of any international system, thus fostering some degree of hierarchy within the overall systemic anarchy. It seeks to explain how cooperation can emerge among major powers and how international orders, comprising rules, norms, and institutions, emerge and are sustained. The theory's core prediction is that any international order is stable only to the degree that the relations of authority within it are sustained by the underlying distribution of power. According to this theory, the current 'globalization' order is sustained by US power and is likely to come undone as challengers like China gain strength.

Power transition theory is a subset of hegemonic stability that seeks to explain how orders break down into war. Building from the premises of hegemonic stability theory, it deduces that dominant states will prefer to retain leadership, that the preference of lesser states for contesting that leadership will tend to strengthen as they become stronger relative to the dominant state, and that this clash is likely to come to the fore as the capabilities of the two sides approach parity. Applied to the current context, the theory posits that the stronger China becomes, the more likely it is to become dissatisfied with the US-led global order. It predicts that a war, or at least a Cold War style rivalry, between the USA and China will become likely unless China's growth slows down or Washington finds a way to accommodate Beijing's preferences.

Assumptions, conditions, and theories

The chief challenge for FPA is: How do we know whether one of these theoretical subschools or specific theories applies to a specific foreign policy issue? The answer lies in being clear about how the various parts of any theory fit together. Recall the general argument I spelled out about how anarchy fosters conflict. This contains three components: the three **assumptions** of groupism, egoism, and power-centrism; a postulated **scope condition** (anarchy); and a very general **theory** (given those assumptions, politics in anarchy is conflictual). Many realists and critics of realism confuse these three things. For example, many assert that anarchy or conflict are assumptions that define realism. This is wrong, and leads to major analytical mistakes on the part of scholars both favourably and unfavourably disposed towards realism.

Realists do not *assume* anarchy. Rather, they create theories about what happens in anarchical settings. Realists do not *assume* that inter-state interaction will be conflictual. Rather, realism contains theories that identify the conditions under which inter-state interactions are likely to be conflictual. Thus, two common ways in which analysts can go astray when applying realism to foreign policy are apparent.

The first error is to confuse assumptions with scope conditions. If you think that anarchy is a core assumption about international politics, then you are likely to think that realist theories which highlight anarchy apply equally strongly to all states everywhere. But in practice anarchy is variable. The ability of states to rely on some authority to enforce agreements is a matter of degree. For example, great powers sometimes seek to enforce order among nearby small states. For those smaller states, anarchy is attenuated. On some set of issues, those states might reasonably expect the local great power to enforce agreements. Therefore realist theories that highlight anarchy would not apply particularly strongly to those states on that set of issues. Thus, for example, the USA in Central America, the EU in the Balkans, and perhaps Russia in Central Asia may all perform this anarchy-attenuating role (albeit in very different ways). The only way to know where and to what degree anarchy is attenuated is to acquire in-depth knowledge about specific states—just what foreign policy analysts are supposed to do.

The second kind of error is to confuse assumptions with predictions. If you mistakenly think that conflict is a core assumption of realism, you might well conclude that whenever states are nice to each other, realist theories must not apply. But this is not necessarily so. Because realist theories explain war, they also explain peace. For realists, peace results when the key causes of war are absent. Thus the amity you might observe among some group of states may be a result of the attenuation of anarchy among them caused by a local order-providing great power. Or amity among one group of states may arise from their shared need to oppose another state or group. In either case, realist theories predict that the absence of conflict is contingent on a particular configuration of power and that conflict might return when that configuration changes. (See Figure 2.1.)

The upshot is that realist theories can be powerful tools in FPA, but applying them is harder than it might seem. The trick is to recognize the contingent nature of all theories. The question of whether a theory applies to a given case is hard to answer, and often requires precisely the kind of deep local knowledge analysts of foreign policy tend to possess. Neoclassical realism, I have suggested, best captures this delicate combination between the general and the particular. So far, I have made this case at a very general level. It becomes much clearer when we examine actual realist analysis of foreign policy.

Realist analysis of foreign policy

While the analysis of foreign policy might begin with theory, it should never end there. To generate explanations of foreign policy, one must combine the general and timeless causes theories identify with the particulars of a given situation. As I have stressed, realism is the school of thought arguably most firmly grounded in real foreign policy practice while also most committed to creating highly general theories. How have realists reconciled these potentially contradictory commitments?

Propositions commonly seen as definitive 'assumption of Realism'	Actual relation to three core assumptions
'States are main actors'	Current manifestation of the groupism assumption
'Universal moral principals do not apply to states'	Predictions/arguments derived from three assumptions
'States calculate interest in terms of power'	
'Scepticism toward international law and institutions'	
'International politics is essentially conflictual'	
'Humankind cannot transcend conflict through the progressive power of reason'	
'Primacy of balance of power politics'	
'International system is anarchic'	Scope conditions
'Uncertainty'	
'The utility of force'	
'Politics not a function of ethics; reasons of state trump ethics'	Implication of egoism
'State interest is survival'	Implication of groupism
'Realists assume tendency to evil'	Mis-stated implication of egoism

Figure 2.1 Many propositions thought to be definitive of realism are actually derivative of the three core assumptions.

Practitioners' realist foreign policy approaches

Examples are easy to find. Frequently one encounters the explicit or implicit use of realist theory balanced with in-depth case-specific knowledge in the analysis of real policy makers.

In 1900, the Russian Minister of War, Prince Kuropatkin, wrote a comprehensive report for Tsar Alexander II on the strategic situation. It provided three important assessments, all of which were controversial at the time but in hindsight appear prescient, given the fate that we now know would soon befall the Russian Empire: that Russia was a satisfied power needing no further expansion for any of its core interests; that any expansion would only frighten other states, causing them to build up their own forces or ally against St Petersburg; and that, given its own power and that of its potential enemies, Russia could ill afford any such confrontation and needed to do all it could to reduce tensions with other major powers. Focusing on the relative power of states and the ever-present potential for conflict, Kuropatkin's analysis built on all the core realist assumptions. Most importantly, the report recognized that, whatever its universal validity as a general portrayal of international politics, in 1900 balance of power theory was working against Russia. In today's terms, the report relies on balance of threat theory and the general assessment of the security dilemma found in defensive realism.

The brilliance of Kuropatkin's analysis was its sophisticated recognition that even though Russia was weak, it could still seem strong and threatening to others, causing them to take countermeasures that could end up making Russia even less secure. This report was, historian William Fuller (1992: 379) notes, 'a masterly effort and inspires admiration'.

In 1907 a British diplomat, Sir Eyre Crowe, wrote a memorandum for the government outlining the need for a thoroughgoing reorientation of Britain's foreign policy. At its core was a dispassionate analysis of the Empire's overall power position and the fundamental challenges presented by the rise of Germany. Crowe used balance of power theory to explain why Britain had to concentrate its dwindling resources on the problem of containing German power. The memorandum brought together the typical realist emphasis on systemic power concerns with a detailed examination of German domestic politics, statecraft, and intentions.

In 1946, George Kennan, the US Ambassador to the Soviet Union, drafted one of the most famous memoranda of modern times, the 'long telegram', urging Washington to adopt a policy of containing Soviet power. He argued that the Soviet Union was in a position that threatened the global balance of power and that the country was internally disposed to continue expanding unless it met a powerful counterweight. Once again we see the general realist precepts (a dispassionate analysis of Soviet, US, and British capabilities and of the fundamental importance of the world's key power centres, a penchant for discounting the universalistic rhetoric on both sides, a focus on narrow group interest and the potential for conflict), a very general timeless theory (again, the balance of power), *and* an in-depth and insightful analysis of domestic Soviet politics.

In the early 1970s, President Richard Nixon and his Secretary of State Henry Kissinger engineered a reorientation of US foreign policy. Underlying this shift was Kissinger's hardheaded analysis of the relative decline in US power against the backdrop of the increasing power of the USA's own allies in Europe and Asia, as well as that of their main rival, the Soviet Union, and many other regional states. The chief argument of this study was that in view of its weakened power position, Washington should do less by itself, work to get allies and partners to shoulder more of the burden of containing Soviet power, reduce the number of potential enemies by reaching out to China, and attenuate the rivalry with the Soviet Union by pursuing a relaxation of tensions known in diplomatic parlance as détente.

These examples are all from foreign policy practitioners steeped in the realist intellectual tradition. They share the trademark realist emphasis on a dispassionate analysis of the relative power positions of groups in anarchy and the ubiquity of power politics. Their realism becomes clearer when compared with what others were saying at the time. In each case, these analysts confronted competing analyses that did not share the basic realist features noted above. The historian Fuller observed that Kuropatkin's report was 'the first occasion in Russian history in which a statesman had tried to commit to paper a synoptic vision of Russia's political and military strategies in the past, present, and future'. Crowe's memorandum met with a sceptical response from the Liberal cabinet of the day, and both Kennan's and Kissinger's mode of thinking struck many of their fellow countrymen as somehow un-American.

These practitioners deployed arguments that would later develop into rigorous academic theories like the security dilemma or balance of threat theory. But they are also based on a deep familiarity with specific players involved in each situation, their history, culture, and collective mindsets. Needless to say, this balance between theory and case is just what today's neoclassical realists seek to recapture. (See Box 2.1.)

BOX 2.1 **Russia and America play the E.H. Carr flip-flop**

'Morality is the product of power', E.H. Carr wrote in his realist classic *The Twenty Years' Crisis*. He meant that standards of right and wrong tend to be defined by the powerful in ways that further their narrow group interest. Carr effortlessly cited case after case of principles flip-flopping in response to changing relations of power and interest. It is just as easy to find cases today. In 1999, NATO bombed Serbia to force it to cease its violent suppression of an independence movement in its province of Kosovo. Russia protested strongly, claiming that the intervention violated the principle of sovereignty enshrined in the UN Charter, and, moreover, that it was illegal because it was neither taken in self defence nor authorized by the UN Security Council. NATO defended the action as a response to a humanitarian crisis and a threat to regional security.

Nine years later, Russia invaded its neighbour Georgia, ostensibly to force it to cease its violent suppression of separatists in the Georgian provinces of South Ossetia and Abkhazia. Now, NATO countries protested this violation of Georgia's sovereignty, citing the very same principles that Russia had touted in the Kosovo case. Russia's response? Its diplomats literally repeated to the Western powers the very same arguments that NATO had used nine years earlier concerning Kosovo. Had these governments really changed their views on the principle of sovereignty? Hardly. Different constellations of power and interest called forth different justifying principles.

Scholars' realist foreign policy approaches

Academic analysts of foreign policy frequently reach for realist theories to inform their critical studies. Hans Morgenthau, the most renowned US realist scholar of the mid-twentieth century, periodically used realist ideas to inform trenchant critiques of his government's foreign policy. He argued that waging a cold war against all states led by communist parties, no matter what the differences among them, only multiplied US enemies and commitments. The analyses (see Box 2.2) made just as the USA was gearing up for a major and ultimately disastrous military commitment to Vietnam show many hallmarks of realist FPA.

Let us consider another example in detail. In the late 1980s, the Cold War had defined international politics for over a generation and it seemed set to endure far into the future. But there was a new actor on the scene. The Soviet leader, Mikhail Gorbachev, had inaugurated a new diplomatic strategy that entailed making concessions on key outstanding issues dividing the Soviet Union from the USA and its allies. At the same time, Gorbachev espoused a new set of foreign policy principles called 'new political thinking' that called for transcending conflict and building a new world order. Most foreign policy analysts in the USA discounted the new thinking as an attempt to hoodwink the Western powers into making dangerous concessions, and held that real change in Moscow's course would be strictly limited. A small minority took the ideas seriously, contending that major changes were possible, provided that the West reciprocated Gorbachev's concessions.

Into this debate came an article whose title said it all: 'Gorbachev's Foreign Policy: Diplomacy of Decline?' The author, Stephen Sestanovich, proceeded from the core realist assumptions to suggest that group interest and power (not the global visions of new thinking) are the key to politics. This led him to look at the underlying power position of the Soviet Union, which was arguably declining. Against the majority position, he held that the new Soviet policy was serious precisely because it was a response to power shifts. Against the minority

> **BOX 2.2 Morgenthau on US Cold War foreign policy and Vietnam**
>
> From *New York Times Magazine*, 18 April 1965:
>
> It is ironic that this simple juxtaposition of 'Communism' and 'free world' was erected by John Foster Dulles's crusading moralism into the guiding principle of American foreign policy at a time when the national Communism of Yugoslavia, the neutralism of the third world and the incipient split between the Soviet Union and China were rendering that juxtaposition invalid.
>
> Today, it is belaboring the obvious to say that we are faced not with one monolithic Communism whose uniform hostility must be countered with equally uniform hostility, but with a number of different Communisms whose hostility, determined by different national interests, varies. In fact, the USA encounters today less hostility from Tito, who is a Communist, than from de Gaulle, who is not.
>
> We can today distinguish four different types of Communism in view of the kind and degree of hostility to the USA they represent: a Communism identified with the Soviet Union—e.g. Poland; a Communism identified with China—e.g. Albania; a Communism that straddles the fence between the Soviet Union and China—e.g. Rumania; and independent Communism—e.g. Yugoslavia. Each of these Communisms must be dealt with in terms of the bearing its foreign policy has upon the interests of the USA in a concrete instance.
>
> It would, of course, be absurd to suggest that the officials responsible for the conduct of American foreign policy are unaware of these distinctions and of the demands they make for discriminating subtlety. Yet it is an obvious fact of experience that these officials are incapable of living up to these demands when they deal with Vietnam.
>
> Thus they maneuver themselves into a position which is anti-revolutionary *per se* and which requires military opposition to revolution wherever it is found in Asia, regardless of how it affects the interests— and how susceptible it is to the power—of the USA. There is a historic precedent for this kind of policy: Metternich's military opposition to liberalism after the Napoleonic Wars, which collapsed in 1848. For better or for worse, we live again in an age of revolution. It is the task of statesmanship not to oppose what cannot be opposed without a chance of success, but to bend it to one's own interests.
>
> From *Meet the Press* May 16 1965:
>
> Q.: Professor, do you think because we may not be able to stop them [the Chinese], is that a good reaon for not trying if they are dangerous and they want to get the whole world under their thumb?
>
> Morgenthau: This is the best reason in the world. If you look at the problem of politics in general, you realize that politics is the art of the possible. There are certain things that you would like to do but you can't do because you haven't got the means to do them.

position, he contended that the new thinking ideas were not important in themselves, but rather reflected the attempt to put the best face on a concessionary policy of appeasement driven by decline. He observed that states tend to generate ideas for transcending conflict just when they see that they lack the power to carry on the struggle. Sestanovich realized that declining states do in fact have other options. For example, realist thinking also emphasizes that a declining power can use force to try to rescue its position. It was only by combining the general theory with his detailed knowledge of the Cold War and Soviet politics that he could be reasonably confident that Moscow would choose appeasement over war.

As things turned out, Sestanovich was right about many things. Remember: the policy debate was over whether the new Soviet course was serious and whether the West had to move towards Gorbachev's new thinking and reciprocate his concessions in order to attenuate the Cold War rivalry. As it happened, US policy makers never accepted new thinking and never reciprocated Gorbachev's major concessions, yet the Soviet Union continued to back away from its Cold War positions and the rivalry was ended on Western terms. And although scholars continue to debate its relative importance, there is no question that decline was a major driving force behind Soviet foreign policy during the Cold War's endgame.

One issue on which Sestanovich was less than clear was whether Gorbachev actually believed his new thinking rhetoric. The diplomacy may well have been a response to decline, and the ideas may have been rationalizations for the tough decisions Gorbachev had to make, but nonetheless they may have been sincerely believed. This brings us to the Soviet side of the story. In Moscow, at exactly this time, there was a group of Russian realist analysts. Looking at them is instructive, because realist analysis had been forbidden in the Soviet Union for many decades. All FPA had formally to adhere to the official ideology of Marxism–Leninism. As Soviet society began to loosen up, Russian analysts were able to express realist ideas openly for the first time in decades.

By 1988, young Russian realist analysts felt emboldened enough to publish careful critiques of official Soviet policy.[2] Their studies are instantly recognizable as belonging to the same (classical realist) tradition as Kuropatkin, Crowe, Kennan, and Kissinger. Conducting the familiar realist assessment of relative power trends, these analysts agreed with Sestanovich that Soviet foreign policy had to respond to decline by making concessions to ease the burdens of empire. However, they criticized Gorbachev's new thinking for obscuring rather than clarifying the tough trade-offs facing Moscow. In their view, the grand visionary ideas were delaying tough decisions, particularly regarding Germany. Pre-emptive concessions on that issue, they argued, would allow Moscow to get ahead of the curve, gain control of the agenda, and buy time for critical domestic reforms. Given what occurred in the two years after these analyses were published—Moscow's total loss of its alliance system and ultimately the collapse of the Soviet Union itself—they look prescient indeed.

Recent examples of scholars' realist FPA include the opposition of many self-proclaimed realists to the US invasion of Iraq in 2002–2003 and NATO's intervention in Libya in 2011, and, more generally, opposition to unqualified support for Israel. As the USA and many if its key allies entered a prolonged economic slump after the financial crisis of 2008, placing intense strains on military and foreign affairs budgets, realists began arguing strongly for the need to pare down security commitments and move to a more restrained posture in world affairs. The details are different, but the thrust is redolent of Morgenthau's arguments four decades earlier—that an overly idealistic definition of US interest ran the risk of multiplying enemies and expanding commitments beyond the country's means.

Using realism in analysing foreign policy

Guidelines

To illustrate the potential analytical power of realism, I have selected examples in which analysts struck an ideal balance between realism's aspiration to general theory and its equally strong commitment to grounding in foreign policy practice. While they show that realism can inform the analysis of foreign policy, they do not tell us how this occurs. Despite the apparent overlap between realist principles and the dynamics of foreign policy, realist theories do not necessarily guarantee a clear and accurate analysis of foreign policy. It is all too easy to find examples of analyses reliant on realist theories that do not read so well in retrospect. Examining some of these less successful examples helps to clarify the potential pitfalls of realism as a guide to foreign policy.

Example 1: The never-ending Cold War

The most renowned realist theorist of the last generation, Kenneth Waltz, proclaimed in 1988 that the Cold War was 'firmly rooted in the structure of postwar international politics and will last as long as that structure endures' (Waltz, in Rotberg 1988: 52). No one reading that article would have expected the Cold War structure to come crashing down in the next few years. The contrast with Sestanovich's article and the analysis by the Russian realists noted above is instructive. The chief difference is that those analyses were deeply immersed in the analysis of Soviet foreign policy. They were acutely aware that the bipolar structure was the product of the ability of the two superpowers to sustain it, and that the depths of Soviet decline placed a question mark over the stability of the Cold War order. They did not question Waltz's theory linking bipolarity to the Cold War; rather, their case-specific knowledge led them to question whether the theory's initial conditions—two relatively equally matched superpowers—would remain in place. To his credit, Waltz understood this as well, having posed the question of whether the Soviet Union could long keep up its side of the Cold War. But the passage just cited is an example of reasoning from theory to a case without using case detail to interrogate the theory. It exemplifies the pitfalls of applying a theory without due regard to whether its scope conditions are actually present.

Example 2: Major power war in 1990s Europe

The following year, another highly influential realist scholar, John J. Mearsheimer, argued that his brand of offensive realism predicted that the end of the Cold War would lead to a more war-prone Europe. As such, 'the West has an interest in maintaining the Cold War order, and hence has an interest in maintaining the Cold War confrontation', meaning, of course, that Western powers should support 'the continued existence of a powerful Soviet Union with substantial military forces in Eastern Europe' (Mearsheimer 1990: 125). Needless to say, policy makers did not heed this advice. Similar to the above case, one problem with this application of realist theory to a specific foreign policy situation was that the Soviet Union was losing the material wherewithal to maintain a massive troop presence in Central Europe. Hence, even setting aside the willingness of Central European publics to tolerate the Soviet presence, it was unclear that Moscow could afford to sustain it. More importantly, Mearsheimer did not question whether the scope conditions of polarity theory really applied. The theory that **multipolarity** (an international system shaped by the power of three or more major states) is more prone to war than **bipolarity** (an international system shaped by the power of two major states, or superpowers) may well be right, but it is not clear whether it applied to a region like Europe in which a powerful outside actor, the USA, maintained a strong security presence. Hence, even in terms of a spare realist theory that ignores the EU and new domestic politics and identities, it was doubtful that Mearsheimer's analysis applied to that case.

Example 3: Anti-US counterbalancing in the 1990s

Waltz and other realists began to argue that, with the end of the Cold War, a new multipolar balance of power order would re-emerge in which other major powers would counterbalance the USA. They held that overly provocative US policies such as the expansion of NATO to former Soviet allies in Central Europe would push Russia and other major powers into an anti-US alliance. Again, policy makers in Washington and Europe chose to ignore this advice. NATO expansion occurred, accompanied by a highly active and interventionist US foreign policy. No traditional counterbalancing occurred. As in the other cases, there are plenty of non-realist theories that might account for this outcome. However, more to the point here, this appears to be another case of applying a theory to a situation without due regard to whether its scope conditions are actually present. Realists' predictions of counterbalancing and the accompanying policy analysis were based on balance of power theory, but it became increasingly clear that that theory's scope conditions did not apply to the 1990s USA (Wohlforth 1999) in a condition of **unipolarity**. The theory predicts reactions to a *rising* hegemonic power, not responses to a power whose hegemony is already firmly established. All the centuries of theory, practice, and lore about the balance of power may well be right, but they simply did not apply to the case at hand. Belatedly recognizing this, realists began developing a new theory of **soft balancing** to explain constraint actions against a dominant power in a unipolar setting (see Pape 2005).

Avoiding pitfalls

Assessing the veracity of FPA from the comfortable vantage of hindsight is hard to do fairly. The point is not to play the 'Gotcha!' game against individual scholars—all scholars have mixed records of prognostication and policy assessment—but to understand where specific discussions of foreign policy might have gone astray in their particular application of realism.

Realist theories clearly generate widely disparate implications for foreign policy, some of which may illuminate while others may be perceived as flat wrong. How does one increase the likelihood that realist theories will help rather than hinder FPA? The key is a knowledgeable use of these theories. Knowing how to use these theories requires careful thought about how precisely they are related to realism's own core assumptions, scope conditions, and expected outcomes as well as to the real-world foreign policy scenarios to which they are applied. As illustrated above, in the simple confusion of scope conditions with assumptions, analysts of foreign policy may try to apply realist theories to international settings where they are profoundly misleading (Figure 2.2).

The two major lessons for avoiding erroneous or inaccurate foreign policy analyses are to know the specifics of the foreign policy case at hand and to pay close attention to the scope conditions that may connect it more generally to key realist precepts. Theories, especially realism, are sometimes assumed to be universal—applying always and everywhere without alteration. In reality, as Fig. 2.2 suggests, theories and even subschools within realism apply in very different conditions. Only by knowing the details of a given foreign policy issue can one determine whether the circumstances under analysis truly correspond to the known parameters of a given theory. Applying these lessons is much harder to do than it seems, for it requires deep familiarity with both general theory and the specifics of the foreign policy case, as well as a continual mental back-and-forth check between the case and the theory.

Theory or Subschool	Main theorist	What it explains	Scope conditions
Offensive realism	Mearsheimer	Expansionism/war	Security is scarce; offence/defence cannot be distinguished; technology/geography favour offence
Defensive realism	Jervis, Glaser	Over-expansionism; cooperation	Security is plentiful; offence/defence distinguishable; technology/geography favour defence
Balance of power	Waltz	Alliances, military build-ups, militarized rivalries	One great power rising to potential hegemony/predominance
Balance of threat	Walt	Alliances, military build-ups, militarized rivalries	One great power rising to potential hegemony/predominance whose geographical location, military posture, and overall behaviour engender threat perceptions
Soft balancing	Pape	Subtle constraint actions vs. unipole	One great power too strong to be balanced: unipolarity
Hegemonic stability	Gilpin	Cooperation; institution-norm construction; 'order'	One great power predominant in system or region
Power Transition	Organski, Gilpin	War	Capabilities of a rising challenger approaching parity with dominant hegemon

Figure 2.2 Theories and scope conditions

Conclusion: hedgehogs, foxes, and analysing foreign policy

Aside from the admonition to study both realist theories and the specifics of contemporary foreign policy problems—and the unhelpful warning that this is in fact quite hard to do—what other concrete lessons can be taken away? Analysts, frequently academics themselves, make mistakes by failing to recognize the contingent nature of theory; whether a theory applies to a given situation depends on the degree to which its scope conditions are actually present. However, one can be very critical of academic realist theory and yet still find realism very useful in FPA. Indeed, most decent practitioners will tell you that this is exactly how they approach FPA.

Ironically, academic realists can be their own worst enemies when it comes to FPA. Theo-rists face two incentives to treat their theories as universal as opposed to contingent. First, to clarify their theories they need pure and clean conceptual building blocks. In other words, they strive to put the basic ideas out of which their theories are built in the clearest possible way so that the basic logic at work is clear for all to see. The notion of 'anarchy' is an example. Theorists require a clear understanding of anarchy in order to construct a co-herent theory of what international politics in an anarchical setting looks like. Scholars mainly interested in building theory are thus very resistant to understanding anarchy as I have discussed it here—as a matter of degree. Hence, realist scholars squabble over whether the logic of anarchy spelled out in defensive or offensive realism is universally valid. Foreign policy analysts, by contrast, must be sensitive to the fact that anarchy in the real world is a variable, not a constant. In order to know how strongly realist theories apply, one needs to know to what degree anarchy might be attenuated. As I have noted, anarchy can be attenu-ated for purely 'realist' reasons, as in a regional order created by a local hegemon. Or, of course, it may be attenuated for reasons not identified in realist theory, as in the institu-tions-based order of the EU. In either case, realist theories about the conflict-generating potential of anarchy do not apply particularly strongly. As scholars move from theory to the real world, they sometimes fail to adjust their pure conception of anarchy to the messy reality they confront.

Second, theorists operate in a competitive scholarly world, where theories and schools of thought are often seen to be competing against others. Adjustments to the theory—recogni-tion of its contingent nature—may be seized upon by intellectual rivals as admissions of the theory's weakness or irrelevance. Realism is the fulcrum of these academic debates. Most other schools of thought and theories are written in one way or anyother as a response to realism. Perhaps responding in turn, realist scholars sometimes seem very reluctant to ac-knowledge the contingent nature of their theories. Analysts of foreign policy, by contrast, generally have no reason to increase competition between theories. To understand foreign policy dilemmas from as many angles as possible, such analysts naturally gravitate towards the idea that theories are complementary rather than competitive.

Over half a century ago, the philosopher Isaiah Berlin wrote an essay that built on a line among the fragments of the Greek poet Archilochus which says: 'The fox knows many things, but the hedgehog knows one big thing.' Berlin argued that:

> . . . taken figuratively, the words can be made to yield a sense in which they mark one of the deepest differences which divide writers and thinkers, and, it may be, human beings in general. For there exists a great chasm between those, on one side, who relate everything to a single central vision, one system less or more coherent or articulate, in terms of which they understand, think and feel—a single, universal, organizing principle in terms of which alone all that they are and say has significance—and, on the other side, those who pursue many ends, often unrelated and even contradictory, connected, if at all, only in some *de facto* way, for some psychological or physiological cause, related by no moral or aesthetic principle; these last lead lives, perform acts, and entertain ideas that are centrifugal rather than centripetal, their thought is scattered or diffused, moving on many levels, seizing upon the essence of a vast variety of experiences and objects for what they are in themselves, with-out consciously or unconsciously, seeking to fit them into, or exclude them from, any one unchanging, all-embracing, sometimes self-contradictory and incomplete, at times fanatical, unitary inner vision.

Academic theorists tend to be hedgehogs, not foxes. Berlin (1992) suggested that foxes will be better at practical tasks like FPA. There is more than intuition to support this conclusion; practitioners themselves argue that they have to be foxes. As explored in Chapter Six, we have the results of a twenty-five year long research project that tracked experts' real analytical and forecasting acumen. The result? Foxes systematically outperform hedgehogs (Tetlock 2006).

The implication is that analysts should not be dogmatic realists—or anti-realists. They should know theories without becoming overly committed to any one. And nothing in the realist approach makes one inevitably a hedgehog. On the contrary, many realist scholars and analysts are foxes. Fox-like FPA involving a constant dialogue between case expertise and general theory is possible. All the examples cited above are cases in point. As explored above, a whole scholarly approach is devoted to putting these ideas into practice. After neorealism gave birth to defensive and offensive realism, a new subschool came into its own. Neoclassical realism is, simply put, realist theory for the foreign policy analyst. While this proliferation of realisms causes some physics-envying purists to quip about a 'declining research programme', it is only a boon to FPA.

Examples of work by neoclassical realists can be found in 'Further reading'. All have in common sensitivity to realist core insights and an appreciation of how neorealism can aid in the mental experiments that lie at the core of FPA, but they lack dogmatic attachment to one theory or the other. All are masters, not slaves, of theory. But neorealists, too, can avoid the pitfalls of hegdehogism. Consider the case of the US neorealists' opposition to the Bush administration's foreign policy, especially the Iraq war. There is no doubt that realists were the most visible IR scholars opposing the march to war. Yet the analysis behind their policy prescription was quintessentially fox-like. It did not flow directly from neorealist theory, but rather from a careful analysis of the situation informed generally by realist ideas.

In a sense, these scholars seek to do what classical realists like Hans Morgenthau or George Kennan did when they analysed foreign policy, or what analysts like Stephen Sestanovich did in his study of Soviet policy under Gorbachev, but to do so with a more self-conscious attention to the interaction between general theories and specific cases. For that purpose, specific realist theories are in many ways more important than the more general schools of thought.

 ## Key points

- Realism is the foundational approach to IR theory, and other approaches are mainly responses to it, so those who wish to use IR theory in FPA must be knowledgeable about realism.

- Realism is a diverse intellectual approach that combines a general school of thought about IR, with subschools like neorealism, and specific theories like the security dilemma or the balance of power.

- All this diversity can be understood as derived from three basic assumptions: groupism, egoism, and power-centrism.

- Knowledge of realism as a general school of thought sharpens FPA by inculcating basic realist analytical precepts (which themselves reflect centuries of diplomatic practice) as well as helping us understand other theoretical approaches in IR.

- Realism is at once committed to deep grounding in real foreign policy practice and to the construction of highly general theories.

- While they often seem as if they are universal in scope, realist theories and subschools are conditional; different theories apply in different strengths depending on circumstances.

- Most pitfalls in applying realism to FPA have to do with getting the balance wrong—uncritically using theory without sufficient cross-checking with detailed knowledge about the foreign policy situation under scrutiny.

- When we get the balance right—as today's neoclassical realists seek to do—the result is a powerful tool of FPA, as demonstrated by prescient realist analysis of decisions on US policy ranging from Vietnam to Iraq.

 ## Questions

1. According to this chapter, how is realism defined?
2. What are the key components of realism?
3. What are the main hallmarks of realist FPA?
4. Name a recent example, not mentioned in the text, of realist FPA?
5. What is the main mistake people make when applying realist theory to FPA?
6. What is the most important distinction to keep in mind when applying realist theory to FPA?

 ## Further reading

Donnelly, J. (2000), *Realism and International Relations* (Cambridge: Cambridge University Press). The best general introduction to realism.

International Security (2005), 30: 1–140. This presents a useful set of articles proposing and debating the new theory of 'soft balancing' against the USA.

Rose, G. (1998), 'Neoclassical Realism and Theories of Foreign Policy', *World Politics,* 51: 144–72. An excellent article reviewing several examples of neoclassical realist foreign policy analysis.

Vasquez, J. A., and Elman C. (eds) (2003), *Realism and the Balancing of Power: A New Debate* (Saddle River, NJ: Prentice-Hall). This is an excellent compendium on balance of power theory and balance of threat theory.

Wivel, A. (2005), 'Explaining Why State X Made a Certain Move Last Tuesday: The Promise and Limitations of Realist Foreign Policy Analysis', *Journal of International Relations and Development,* 8: 355–80. This article presents a useful and more critical view of realism and FPA.

Visit the Online Resource Centre that accompanies this book for more information: **www.oxfordtextbooks.co.uk/orc/smith_foreign/**

Liberalism and foreign policy

MICHAEL W. DOYLE

Chapter contents

 Reader's guide

For more than two centuries, liberal countries have tended to maintain peaceful relations with each other. Liberal democracies are each other's natural allies. They tend to respect and accommodate other democratic countries and negotiate rather than escalate disputes. This provides a positive incentive to try to preserve and expand the liberal zone of peace. And that is the fundamental postulate of liberal foreign policy. But liberalism has also proved to be a dangerous guide to foreign policy, often exacerbating tensions with non-liberal states. Expanding liberalism can sometimes provoke danger and war. This chapter thus addresses a large and perplexing foreign policy question central to all democracies: Can the liberal peace be effectively preserved and expanded without provoking unnecessary danger and inflicting unnecessary harm? The chapter also addresses how scholars have analysed liberalism's effects, distinguishing three key interpretations of liberal foreign policy: individualist, commercial, and republican.[1]

Introduction

Liberalism contributes to the understanding of foreign policy by highlighting how individuals and the ideas and ideals they espouse (such as human rights, liberty, and democracy), social forces (capitalism, markets), and political institutions (democracy, representation) can have direct effects on foreign relations. It contrasts with the assumptions of structural realists regarding the determinative role of system structure (unipolar, bipolar, or multipolar) and the consequent assumption of state homogeneity (rational, material, and unitary actors). By opening the box of state action and allowing for the effects of varying ideas, interests, and institutions, liberalism complicates the study of international politics. But it also produces better predictions of foreign policy behaviour and incorporates modern conceptions of ethical foreign policy (Doyle 1997). This chapter begins by defining what scholars have meant by liberalism, describes the major features of liberal foreign relations, and then shows how the three schools of liberal foreign policy analysis have connected liberal principles and institutions to foreign policy outcomes. It concludes with reflections on preserving and expanding the zone of liberal peace—while avoiding war with the wider non-liberal world.

Liberalism

Liberalism is identified with an essential principle—the importance of the freedom of the individual. Above all, this is a belief in the importance of moral freedom—of the right to be treated and a duty to treat others as ethical subjects, and not as objects or means only. A concern for this principle generates rights and institutions.

The challenge within liberalism is how to reconcile the three sets of liberal rights (see Box 3.1). The right to private property, for example, can conflict with equality of opportunity, and both rights can be violated by democratic legislation. The liberal tradition has evolved two high roads to individual freedom and social order: one is **laissez-faire** or 'neo-conservative' liberalism, and the other is **social welfare** or social democratic (or in US terms 'liberal') liberalism. Both reconcile these conflicting rights (though in differing ways) by successfully organizing free individuals into a political order.

The political order *combining* laissez-faire and social welfare liberals is marked by a shared commitment to four institutions.[2] First, citizens possess juridical equality and other civic rights such as freedom of religion and the press. Second, the effective sovereigns of the state are representative legislatures deriving their authority from the consent of the electorate and exercising their authority free from all restraint apart from the requirement that basic civic rights be preserved.[3] Most pertinently for the impact of liberalism on foreign affairs, the state is subject to neither the external authority of other states nor the internal authority of

BOX 3.1 The foundations of liberalism

A commitment to a threefold set of rights forms the foundation of liberalism. Liberalism calls for freedom from arbitrary authority, often called 'negative freedom', which includes freedom of conscience, a free press and free speech, equality under the law, and the right to hold, and therefore to exchange, property without fear of arbitrary seizure. Liberalism also calls for those rights necessary to protect and promote the capacity and opportunity for freedom—the 'positive freedoms'. Thus such social and economic rights as equality of opportunity in education and rights to health care and employment, necessary for effective self-expression and participation, are among liberal rights (Berlin 1969). A third liberal right, democratic participation or representation, is necessary to guarantee the other two. To ensure that morally autonomous individuals remain free in those areas of social action where public authority is needed, public legislation has to express the will of the citizens making laws for their own community.

special prerogatives held, for example, by monarchs or military castes over foreign policy. Third, the economy rests on the recognition of the rights of private property, including the ownership of means of production. Property is justified as a stimulus to productivity and a limit on the monopoly of state authority. The institution of private property excludes state socialism or state capitalism, but it need not exclude market socialism or various forms of the mixed economy. Fourth, economic decisions are predominantly shaped by the forces of supply and demand, domestically and internationally, and are free from strict control by bureaucracies.

In order to protect the opportunity of the citizen to exercise freedom, laissez-faire liberalism has leaned towards a highly constrained role for the state and a much wider role for private property and the market. In pursuit of the same goal of freedom, welfare liberalism reverses its approach, and instead has expanded the role of the state and constricted the role of the market.[4] However, both perspectives accept the four institutional requirements and as a result contrast markedly with the monarchical regimes, military dictatorships, and single-party governments, including communist dictatorships, with which they have shared the political governance of the modern world. Not even overwhelmingly liberal countries are purely liberal. Liberal principles and institutions sometimes vie with autocratic or racist rivals for the allegiance of the public (Skowronek 2006). There are also domestic variations within liberal regimes. For example, Switzerland was liberal only in certain cantons; the US was liberal only north of the Mason–Dixon Line until 1865, when it became liberal throughout. These lists also exclude ancient 'republics', since none appear to fit modern liberal criteria of individualism (Holmes 1979).

The domestic successes of liberalism have never been more apparent. Never have so many people been included in, and accepted the domestic hegemony of, the liberal order; never have so many of the world's leading states been liberal, whether as republics or as constitutional monarchies. Indeed, the success of liberalism as an answer to the problem of masterless men in modern society is reflected in the growth in the number of liberal regimes from the handful of semi-liberal regimes that existed in the first half of the nineteenth century (e.g. Britain, France, and the USA) to more than 100 that exist today. But we should not be complacent about the domestic affairs of liberal states. Significant practical problems endure: enhancing citizen participation in large democracies, distributing 'positional goods' (for example, prestigious jobs), controlling bureaucracy, reducing unemployment, paying for a growing demand for social services, reducing inflation, and achieving large-scale restructuring of industries in response to growing foreign competition (Hirsch 1977). While these domestic problems have been widely explored, they are by no means solved. Liberalism's foreign record is more obscure and warrants greater consideration.

Liberal foreign relations

The historical record of liberal international relations includes incentives for a separate zone of peace among liberal states, but also, unfortunately, for imprudent aggression against non-liberals and complaisance in vital matters of security and economic cooperation.

The liberal zone of peace

The first and most important of the effects of liberalism on the foreign relations of liberal states is the establishment of a peace among them.[5] Medieval and early modern Europe served as the cockpit of warring states, with France, England, and the Low Countries engaged in nearly constant strife. Then in the late eighteenth century there began to emerge liberal regimes. At first hesitant and confused, and later clear and confident as liberal regimes gained deeper domestic foundations and greater international experience, a zone of peace became established among the liberal states.

One key example of this peace was Anglo-American relations. During the nineteenth century, the USA and Great Britain engaged in nearly continual strife, including one war, the War of 1812. However, after the Reform Act of 1832 defined representation as the formal source of the sovereignty of the British parliament, Britain and the USA settled their disputes diplomatically despite, for example, British grievances against the North's blockade of the South, with which Britain had close economic ties. Nearly a century later, despite severe Anglo-French colonial rivalry, liberal France and liberal Britain formed an *entente* against illiberal Germany before the First World War. In 1914–1915, Italy, the liberal member of the Triple Alliance with Germany and Austria, chose not to fulfil its treaty obligations to support its allies. Instead, it joined in an alliance with Britain and France that prevented it from fighting other liberal states, and then subsequently declared war on Germany and Austria. And despite generations of Anglo-American tension and Britain's wartime restrictions on American trade with Germany, the USA leaned towards Britain and France from 1914 to 1917, before entering the war on their side. Nowhere was this special peace among liberal states more clearly proclaimed than in President Woodrow Wilson's War Message of 2 April 1917:

> Our object now, as then, is to vindicate the principles of peace and justice in the life of the world as against selfish and autocratic power and to set up amongst the really free and self-governed people of the world such a concert of purpose and of action as will henceforth ensure the observance of those principles. (Wilson 1924: 378)

Beginning in the eighteenth century, a zone of peace, which the liberal philosopher Immanuel Kant called the 'pacific federation' or 'pacific union', was slowly established among liberal societies. Today, more than 100 liberal states with at least three years of consolidation make up this zone of peace.[6] Most are in Europe and North America, but they can be found on every continent (see Map 3.1).

Of course, the outbreak of war in any given year, between any two given states, is a low-probability event. The occurrence of a war between any two adjacent states, considered over a long period of time, is more probable. Thus the near absence of war between liberal states, whether adjacent or not, for almost 200 years may have significance. More significant, perhaps, is that when states are forced to decide on which side of an impending world war they will fight, liberal states will tend to wind up on the same side, despite the complexity of the paths that take them there. These characteristics neither prove that the peace among liberals is statistically significant nor that liberalism is the peace's sole valid explanation.[7] But they do suggest that we consider the possibility that liberals have indeed established a separate peace—but only among themselves.

Foreign relations among any other group of states with similar social structures or with compatible values or pluralistic social structures are not similarly peaceful.[8] Feudal warfare

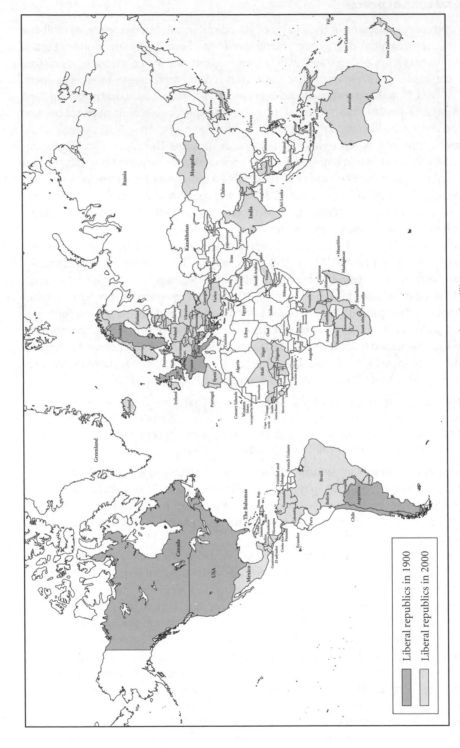

Map 3.1 Liberal republics in 1900 and 2000. *Note:* Only countries with populations greater than 1 million.

was frequent and very much a sport of the monarchs and nobility. Civilizations may clash, but there have been as many wars within Islam or Christianity as between them. There have not been enough truly totalitarian fascist powers (nor have they lasted long enough) to test fairly their pacific compatibility, but fascist powers in the wider sense of nationalist military dictatorships clearly fought each other in the 1930s in Eastern Europe. Communist powers have engaged in wars more recently in East Asia, when China invaded Vietnam and Vietnam invaded Cambodia. Equally, we have not had enough democratic socialist societies to consider the relevance of socialist pacification. The more abstract category of pluralism does not suffice. Certainly Germany was pluralist when it engaged in war with liberal states in 1914; Japan as well in 1941. But they were not liberal. Peace among liberals thus appears to be a special characteristic.

Here the predictions of liberal pacifists are borne out: liberal states do exercise peaceful restraint and a separate peace exists among them. This separate peace provides a solid foundation for the crucial alliances of the USA with the liberal powers (NATO, the US–Japanese alliance, the alliance with Australia and New Zealand), and it appears impervious to the quarrels with allies that have bedevilled many US administrations. It also offers the promise of a continuing peace among liberal states, and with increasing numbers of liberal states, it announces the possibility of a self-enforcing global peace without establishing a world state.

Imprudent aggressiveness

Aside from restraint in warring against other liberal states, liberalism carries with it a second effect—what David Hume called 'imprudent vehemence' or aggression against or enmity towards non-liberals (Hume 1963: 346–347).[9] Peaceful restraint seems to work only in liberals' relations with other liberals; liberal states have fought numerous wars with non-liberal states.

Many of these wars have been defensive, and thus prudent by necessity. Liberal states have been attacked and threatened by non-liberal states that do not exercise restraint in their dealings with liberal states. Authoritarian rulers both stimulate and respond to an international political environment in which conflicts of prestige, of interest, and of pure fear all lead states towards war. Thus war and conquest have characterized the careers of many authoritarian rulers and ruling parties—from Louis XIV and Napoleon to Mussolini's fascists, Hitler's Nazis, and Stalin's communists.

But imprudent aggression by the liberal states—**liberal imprudence**—has also characterized many of these wars. Both liberal France and liberal Britain fought costly expansionist colonial wars throughout the nineteenth century. The USA fought a similar war with Mexico in 1846–1848, waged a war of annihilation against the Native Americans, and intervened militarily against sovereign states many times before and after the Second World War. Liberal states invade weak non-liberal states and display exceptional degrees of distrust in their foreign policy relations with powerful non-liberal states.[10]

Nonetheless, establishing the statistical significance of Hume's assertion appears remarkably difficult. The best statistical evidence indicates that 'libertarian' or 'democratic' states appear to be more war-prone.[11] War-proneness is not, however, a measure of imprudent aggression since many wars are defensive. But that does not mean that we can simply blame warfare on the authoritarians or totalitarians, as many of our more enthusiastic politicians would have us do.[12] Liberal states acted as initiators in twenty-four out of the fifty-six interstate wars in which they participated between 1816 and 1980, while non-liberals were on the initiating side in ninety-one out of the 187 times in which they participated in interstate wars (Chan 1984: 636). Liberal **metropoles** (imperial centres) were the overwhelming participators in **extrasystemic wars**, colonial wars, which we can assume to have been by and large initiated by the metropole (see below). Furthermore, the USA intervened in the Third World more than twice as often in the period 1946–1976 as the Soviet Union did in 1946–1979 (Clemens 1982: 117–118). Further, the USA devoted one-quarter and the Soviet Union one-tenth of their respective defence budgets to forces designed for Third World interventions, where responding to perceived threats would presumably have a less than purely defensive character (Posen and Van Evera 1980).

We should recall as well that authoritarian states have a record of imprudent aggression. It was not semi-liberal Britain that collapsed in 1815, but Napoleonic France. It was the Kaiser's Germany that dissolved in 1918, not republican France and liberal Britain and democratic America. It was imperial Japan and Nazi Germany that disappeared in 1945, not the USA or the UK.[13] It is the contrast with ideal rational strategy and even more the comparison with liberal accommodation with fellow liberals that highlight the aggressive imprudence of liberal relations with non-liberals. Moreover, most wars seem to arise out of calculations and miscalculations of interest, misunderstandings, and mutual suspicions, such as those that characterized the origins of the First World War. Yet we still find expressions of aggressive intent and apparently unnecessary vehemence by liberal states characterizing a large number of wars.[14]

In relations with powerful non-liberal states, liberal states have missed opportunities to pursue the negotiation of arms reduction and arms control when it has been in their mutual strategic interest, and they have failed to construct wider schemes of accommodation that are needed to supplement arms control. Prior to the outbreak of the First World War, this is the charge that Lord Sanderson levelled against Sir Eyre Crowe in his response to Crowe's classic memorandum on the state of British relations with Germany.[15] (see Box 3.2).

BOX 3.2 Relations with powerful non-liberal states

In developing relations with powerful non-liberal states, evidence of deeply held suspicion appears to characterize US diplomacy towards the Soviet Union. In a fascinating memorandum to President Wilson written in 1919, Herbert Hoover (then one of Wilson's advisers) recommended that the President speak out against the danger of 'world domination' which the 'Bolsheviki'—a 'tyranny that is the negation of democracy'—posed to free peoples. Rejecting military intervention as excessively costly and likely to 'make us a party in re-establishing the reactionary classes in their economic domination over the lower classes', Hoover proposed a 'relief programme' designed to undercut some of the popular appeal which the Bolsheviks were garnering in both the Soviet Union and abroad. Although acknowledging that the evidence was not yet clear, he concluded: 'If the militant features of Bolshevism were drawn in colours with their true parallel with Prussianism as an attempt at world domination that we do not stand for, it would check the fears that today haunt all men's minds.' (Herbert Hoover to President Wilson, 29 March 1919, Paterson 1978: 95).[i]

[i] The actual US intervention in the Soviet Union was limited to supporting anti-Bolshevik Czechoslovak soldiers in Siberia and to protecting military supplies in Murmansk from German seizure.

In the post-Second World War period, and particularly following the outbreak of the Korean War, US foreign policy equated the 'International Communist Movement' (all communist states and parties) with 'communist imperialism' and with a domestic tyranny in the Soviet Union that required a Cold War contest and international subversion as means of legitimizing its own police state. Secretary of State John Foster Dulles most clearly expressed this conviction, together with his own commitment to a strategy of 'liberation', when he declared: '[W]e shall never have a secure peace or a happy world so long as Soviet communism dominates one-third of all the peoples that there are, and is in the process of trying at least to extend its rule to many others' (US Senate 1953: 5–6)).[16]

Imprudent vehemence is also associated with liberal foreign policy towards weak non-liberal states, such as the many in the Third World. This problem affects both conservative liberals and welfare liberals, but the two can be distinguished by differing styles of interventions.

Protecting 'native rights' from 'native' oppressors, and protecting universal rights of property and settlement from local transgressions, introduced especially liberal motives for imperial aggression. Ending the slave trade and encouraging 'legitimate trade' (while protecting the property of European merchants) destabilized nineteenth-century West African oligarchies. Declaring the illegitimacy of *suttee* (self-immolation as practised by widowed women in India) and domestic slavery also attacked local cultural traditions that had sustained the stability of indigenous political authority. Europeans settling in sparsely populated areas destroyed the livelihood of tribes that relied on hunting. When the locals retaliated defensively in force, the settlers called for imperial protection (De Tocqueville 1945: 351). In practice, once the exigencies of ruling an empire came into play, liberal imperialism resulted in the oppression of 'native' liberals seeking self-determination in order to maintain imperial security, avoid local chaos, and preclude international interference by another imperial power attempting to take advantage of local disaffection.

Thus nineteenth-century liberals, such as British Prime Minister William Gladstone, pondered whether Egypt's proto-nationalist rebellion (1881–1882) was truly liberal-nationalist (they discovered that it was not) before intervening to protect strategic lifelines to India, commerce, and investment.[17] These dilemmas of liberal imperialism are also reflected in US imperialism in the Caribbean where, for example, following the Spanish–American War of 1898, Article III of the Platt Amendment gave the USA the 'right to intervene for the preservation of Cuban independence, the maintenance of a government adequate for the protection of life, property, and individual liberty . . . ' (Paterson 1978: Vol. I, 328). (See also Box 3.3.)

The record of liberalism in the non-liberal world is not solely a catalogue of oppression and imprudence. The North American West and the settlement colonies—Australia and New Zealand—represent a successful transplant of liberal institutions, albeit in a temperate, underpopulated, and then depopulated environment and at the cost of Native American and Aboriginal rights. Similarly, the twentieth-century expansion of liberalism into less powerful non-liberal areas has also had some striking successes. The forcible liberalization of Germany and Japan following the Second World War and the long covert financing of liberal parties in Italy are the more significant instances of successful transplant. The covert financing of liberalism in Chile and occasional diplomatic démarches to nudge aside military threats to non-communist democratic parties (as in Peru in 1962, South Korea in 1963, and the Dominican Republic in 1962[18] and again in 1978) illustrate policies that, though less successful, were

BOX 3.3 The 2003 invasion of Iraq: geostrategic and liberal factors at work

The invasion of Iraq in 2003 illustrated another intervention, one widely regarded as imprudent. US and UK hostility stemmed from factors that any great power and any state committed to the international rule of law would have found provoking. These included Saddam Hussein's record of aggression against his neighbours (particularly Kuwait), the implicit threat he posed to the security of oil supplies in the Persian Gulf, and his unwillingness to assure the international community that he had eliminated programmes to acquire weapons of mass destruction as he had been required to do as part of the settlement of the first Gulf War in 1991 (UN Security Council Resolution 687). Visibly liberal factors and goals were also at work. Saddam's genocidal campaigns against the Kurds and his record of flagrant abuses of the Iraqi population shaped his international reputation.

But the particular circumstances of the run-up to the 2003 invasion appeared more significant than either of the longer trends in hostility. The Bush administration, aware that the American public held it responsible for preventing another 9/11 attack and benefiting from a public that politically rewarded a 'war on terror presidency', read—and presented to the public—almost every piece of pre-invasion intelligence according to the most threatening interpretation.[i] The Bush administration attempted to justify the war by denouncing alleged Iraqi programmes to build weapons of mass destruction (WMDs) and alleged Iraqi ties to 9/11 and al-Qaeda (for which no support could be found afterwards), and it promised to induce a transformative spread of democracy in the region, beginning with Iraq.[ii]

Reacting to the insurgency that greeted the invasion, the poor planning that characterized the occupation, and the mounting US and Iraqi casualties, by 2005 a majority of the US public, and publics of other democracies earlier, had turned against the war. The long-term results of the invasion and effort to democratize Iraq were far from clear. Iraq had experienced a referendum on a constitution and national elections, but splits among its three major communities (Shia, Sunni, and Kurd) threatened an escalating civil war. Even aggressive liberals who might have welcomed a democratic transformation of the region questioned the method in light of the disputed legality of the invasion and the long-run costs expected by some to amount to two trillion dollars.[iii]

[i] One instance was the neglect of information widely available in the Bush administration that Niger was very unlikely to have sold uranium ore to Iraq. The charge that it did nonetheless wound up as the notorious sixteen words in the President's 2003 State of the Union Address justifying the march to war (Lichtblau 2006).

[ii] For an informative collection of speeches by President Bush and Secretary Powell justifying the war and by Senator Byrd and others criticizing those rationales see 'Why Attack Iraq?' (Gutmann and Thompson 2005: 45–60, 88–95). Goldsmith (2002) and Franck (2003) offer thoughtful pro and con legal analyses, while Pollack (2002: Chapters 5 and 11) and Kaufmann (2004) provide pro and con policy analyses.

[iii] Bilmes and Stiglitz (2006) estimate one trillion dollars as the low figure and two trillion the high, taking into account the long-term medical and other indirect costs associated with the war.

directed towards liberal goals. These particular post-war liberal successes are also the product of special circumstances: the existence of a potential liberal majority, temporarily suppressed, which could readily be re-established by outside aid, or unusually weak oligarchic, military, or communist opponents.[19] (See Box 3.4.)

Elsewhere in the post-war period, when the USA sought to protect liberals in the Third World from the 'communist threat', the consequences of liberal foreign policy on the non-liberal society often became far removed from the promotion of individual rights or national security. In Vietnam and elsewhere, intervening against 'armed minorities' and 'enemies of free enterprise' meant intervening for other 'armed minorities', some sustained by oligarchies and others resting on little more than US foreign aid and troops. Indigenous liberals simply

---

BOX 3.4 President Obama's grand strategy? 'A just and lasting peace'

In his Nobel Peace Prize lecture in December 2009, less than a year after taking office, President Obama modestly acknowledged that his prize seemed designed more to reward aspiration than accomplishment. He then outlined his aspirations for a just and lasting peace in words that resonated with liberal theories of foreign policy. Separating himself from Gandhian pacifism, Obama acknowledged that war was sometimes necessary. Separating himself from George Bush's militarism, he also saw international law and just war doctrines of self-defence as applicable to all states. Obama then joined Clinton and Blair in insisting that just wars must be broadened to include humanitarian wars that protect a people from massacre, and concluded by outlining what it takes to make a just and lasting peace practicable: first is adequate deterrence and sanctions against aggression and massacres; second is not merely an absence of conflict, but a positive commitment to the 'inherent rights and dignity of every individual.' For, argued Obama, 'I believe that peace is unstable where citizens are denied the right to speak freely or worship as they please; choose their own leaders or assemble without fear'. As examples, Obama added: 'Only when Europe became free did it find peace. America has never fought a war against a democracy'. Third, this lasting peace must be bolstered with 'economic security and opportunity'.

Inspiring as the speech was, a speech is not the same as policy. After all, in it Obama promised to close Guantanamo (still open two years later). But a speech by a head of government is more than a single individual's private thoughts. It tends to be widely vetted within the bureaucracy as an expression of a government's policy intentions. And it serves to coordinate government action and generates reputational costs if it is flouted.

---

had too narrow a base of domestic support. These interventions did not advance liberal rights, and to the extent that they were driven by ideological motives, they were not necessary for national security.

To the conservative liberals, the alternatives were starkly cast: Third World authoritarians with allegiance to the liberal capitalist West, or 'communists' subject to the totalitarian East (or leftist nationalists who, even if elected, are but a slippery stepping stone to totalitarianism) (Kirkpatrick 1979)).[20] Conservative liberals are prepared to support the allied authoritarians. The communists attack property in addition to liberty, thereby provoking conservative liberals to covert or overt intervention, or 'dollar-diplomacy' imperialism. The interventions against Mossadegh in Iran, Arbenz in Guatemala, Allende in Chile, and the Sandinistas in Nicaragua appear to fall into this pattern (Barnet 1968: Chapter 10). President Reagan's simultaneous support for the military in El Salvador and guerrilla 'freedom-fighters' in Nicaragua also tracks this pattern, whose common thread is rhetorical commitment to freedom and operational support for conservative free enterprise.

To the social welfare liberals, the choice was never so clear. Aware of the need for state action to democratize the distribution of social power and resources, they tend to have more sympathy for social reform. This can produce, on the part of 'radical' welfare liberals, a more tolerant policy towards the attempts by reforming autocracies to redress inegalitarian distributions of property in the Third World. This more complicated welfare-liberal assessment can itself be a recipe for more extensive intervention. The conservative oligarchs or military bureaucrats with whom the conservative liberal is well at home are not so congenial to the social welfare liberal, yet the communists are still seen as enemies of liberty. In their foreign policy, left liberals justify extensive intervention first to encourage, and then to sustain, Third

World social democracy in a political environment that is either barely participatory or highly polarized. Thus Arthur Schlesinger recalls President Kennedy musing shortly after the assassination of President Trujillo (former dictator of the Dominican Republic): 'There are three possibilities in descending order of preference, a decent democratic regime, a continuation of the Trujillo regime [by his followers] or a Castro regime. We ought to aim at the first, but we can't really renounce the second until we are sure we can avoid the third' (Schlesinger 1965: 769; also quoted in Barnet 1968: 158). Another instance of this approach was President Carter's support for the land reforms in El Salvador, which one US official explained in the following analogy: 'There is no one more conservative than a small farmer. We're going to be breeding capitalists like rabbits' (Simon and Stephen 1981: 38). President Clinton's administration seems to have succumbed to a similar dose of optimistic interventionism in its conviction that friendly nations could be rebuilt democratically in both Somalia and Haiti, although democracy had never existed in the first and was led in the second by Jean Bertrand Aristide, a charismatic socialist and an eloquent critic of American imperialism.

Complaisance and isolationism

The third effect apparent in the international relations of liberal states is David Hume's second assertion, that of 'supine complaisance'. This takes two forms: one is the failure to support allies; the other is a failure to oppose enemies.

Liberal states have often been shortsighted in preserving their basic preconditions under changing international circumstances, particularly in supporting the liberal character of the constituent states. Self-indulgent isolationism or appeasement by democratic majorities, reluctant to bear the fiscal cost, has failed on occasion—as it did with regard to Germany in the 1920s—to provide the timely international economic support for liberal regimes whose market foundations were in crisis. Liberal democratic majorities failed in the 1930s to provide military aid or political mediation to Spain, which was challenged by an armed minority, or to Czechoslovakia, which was caught in a dilemma of preserving national security or acknowledging the claims (fostered by Hitler's Germany) of the Sudeten minority to self-determination. Farsighted and constitutive measures seem to have only been provided by the liberal international order when one liberal state stood pre-eminent among the rest, prepared and able to take measures, as did Britain before the First World War and the USA following The Second World War, to sustain economically and politically the foundations of liberal society beyond its borders. Then measures such as British antislavery and free trade, the US loan to Britain in 1947, the Marshall Plan, NATO, GATT, the IMF, and the liberalization of Germany and Japan helped construct buttresses for the international liberal order (Kindleberger 1973; Gilpin 1975; Krasner 1976; Hirsch and Doyle 1977; Ikenberry 2001).

Of course, ideologically based policies can also be self-indulgent. Oligarchic or authoritarian allies in the Third World do not find consistent support in a liberal policy that stresses human rights. Conservative and realist critics claim that the security needs of these states are neglected, and that they fail to obtain military aid or more direct support when they need it (the Shah's Iran, Humberto Romero's El Salvador, Somoza's Nicaragua, and apartheid South Africa). Equally disturbing from those points of view, communist regimes are shunned even when a détente with them could further the strategic interests of the USA (China before 1976, Cuba). Welfare liberals particularly shun the first group, while laissez-faire liberals baulk at close dealings with the second. In both cases economic interests or strategic interests are allegedly slighted.[21]

A second manifestation of complaisance lies in a reaction to the excesses of interventionism. A mood of frustrated withdrawal affects policy towards strategically and economically important countries. Just as interventionism seems to be the typical failing of the liberal great power, so complaisance characterises declined or 'not quite risen' liberal states.[22] Following the exhaustion of wars, representative legislature may become especially reluctant to undertake international commitments or to fund the military establishment needed to play a geopolitical role. Purely domestic concerns seem to take priority, as they did in the USA in the 1920s. Rational incentives for **free riding** on the extended defence commitments of the leader of the liberal alliance also induce this form of complaisance. During much of the nineteenth century the USA informally relied upon the British fleet for many of its security needs. During the Cold War, the Europeans and the Japanese, according to some American strategic analysts, failed to bear their 'fair' share of defence burdens.

Liberalism, if we take into account both Kant and Hume, thus carries with it three legacies: peace among liberals, imprudent vehemence towards non-liberals, and complaisance towards threats. The first legacy appears to be a special feature associated with liberalism and it can be demonstrated both statistically and through historical case studies (Owen 1996; O'Neal and Russett 1997; Rousseau 2005). The latter two legacies cannot be shown to be special to liberalism, though their effects can be illustrated historically in liberal foreign policy and reflect laissez-faire, and social democratic, welfare variants. But the survival and growth in the number of liberal states suggests that imprudent vehemence and complaisance have not overwhelmed liberalism's efficacy as a form of governance.

Liberal foreign policy analysis

Liberalism has complicated implications for theories of foreign policy (Nincic 1992; Zacher and Matthew 1995; Doyle 1997; Moravcsik 1997). Defined by the centrality of individual rights, private property, and representative government, liberalism is a domestic theory. Transposed to the international plane, liberals share a common framework or zone of peace with fellow liberals, where they vary according to whether property or welfare should guide international preferences and whether the risks of isolation are greater or less than those of internationalism. Foreign policy analyses strive to account for these patterns by focusing on whether individual rights, domestic commercial interests, or a more complicated combination of both, together with republican institutions and international perceptions, shape policy.

Liberal theorists agree with the realists that states exist under anarchy, but they disagree as to the nature of anarchy. Unlike the realists, liberals do not assume that international anarchy is a 'state of war'—a time 'wherein', in Hobbes's phrase, 'the will to contend by battle is sufficiently known' (Hobbes, *Leviathan*: 100). The realist 'state of war' is a time in which all states fear the possibility of war such that they are driven into contests of relative 'positional' (Grieco 1988) zero-sum games that produce balance of power alignments. Thus temporary cooperation is only possible within an alliance. Instead, the contest among liberal states can be a positive- or negative-sum game within a separate zone of peace among fellow liberals. A failure to inform others may undermine coordination when liberals are seeking compatible goals. In more competitive situations, a failure to trust others may undermine cooperation when each would prefer at least one alternative to a failure to cooperate. But their inter-liberal security dilemma is generally solved by stable accommodation, rather than balancing. They can come to appreciate that the existence of other liberal states constitutes no threat, but instead constitutes an opportunity for mutually beneficial trade and (when needed) alliance against non-liberal states.

Thus liberals differ significantly from the realists. But liberal theorists also differ from each other, and they do so in systematic ways. Like realists, each of the liberal theorists must make assumptions about human nature, domestic society, and international structure as found in Kenneth Waltz's three images (Waltz 1959). Liberals pay more attention to domestic structures and individual differences than do realists, and believe that the international system (or Third Image) has a less than overriding influence and so distinguish themselves not only from structural realists but also from almost all realists. For the present analysis, we can identify three types of liberals: **First Image Lockean** (human nature), **Second Image Commercial** (societal), and **Third Image Kantian** (republican internationalist). Each of these images can explain the three features of liberal foreign relations, and each highlights special aspects and reveals difficult choices within liberal foreign policy.

Locke's international system, like that of realists such as his fellow seventeenth-century philosopher Thomas Hobbes, is anarchic. But the Lockean state is based on representation and ultimately on consent, while the Hobbesian state is indifferent to these matters as long as the state is sovereign. Locke's citizens, like Hobbes's, are rational independent individuals. The difference then lies in the importance that Locke attributed to the duties to protect life, liberty, and property that Locke thought accompanied citizens' rights to the same. It is these duties that lead just commonwealths to maintain peace with each other provided, i.e. that their natural partiality and the poorly institutionalized character of world politics do not overcome their duties to try to resolve disputes peacefully.

But partiality and weak international institutions are difficult to overcome, and so imprudent aggression and complaisance often occur. Thus Locke portrayed an international condition of troubled peace, only one step removed from the realist state of war and one fraught with 'Inconveniences' that could deteriorate into war through the combined effects of bias, partiality, and the absence of a regular and objective system of adjudication and enforcement. There is, for example, much of Hobbesian rational unitary egoism in the Lockean 'Federative Power', with its pursuit of 'national advantage'. Locke is prepared, unlike most liberals, to delegate foreign policy to the executive, trusting that no better institution can pursue the public interest. In troubled times, Lockean international 'Inconveniences' might well approach a nearly general state of war. But we also see one crucial difference. Locke's statespersons, like his citizens, are governed by the duties of natural law—life, liberty, and property. Lockean states are then distinguished by a commitment to mutual trust under the law. In the literature explaining the logic of negotiation, trust is crucial for stable agreements, and all rational egoistic bargainers will want to cultivate a reputation for it (Heymann 1973; Dunn 1984).

The commercial liberals—a second tradition of liberal scholarship focusing on Second Image domestic social forces—highlight the pacifying international effects of markets and commercial capitalism. The tradition that Albert Hirschman has called *doux commerce* (soothing commerce) originates in the eighteenth-century attack on the realist doctrine of relative economic power then advocated by the Mercantilists (Hirschman 1982). Although the commercial liberals such as Smith and Schumpeter argued that representative government contributed to peace—when the citizens who bear the burdens of war elect their governments, wars become unattractive—for them, the deeper cause of the zone of liberal peace was commerce. After all, democracies had been more than war-prone in history. Thucydides' story of democratic Athens was familiar to all with a classical education. Passions could wreak havoc among democrats as well. What was new was manufacturing and commerce—capitalism. Thomas Paine, the eighteenth-century radical American democrat, announced: 'If commerce were permitted to act to the universal extent it is capable, it would extirpate the system of war' (Paine 1995: Chapter 5). Paine contributed to a growing recognition of a powerful insight systematically developed by Enlightenment philosophers: war does not benefit commercial manufacturing societies. This view was articulated most comprehensively by the great Scottish philosopher–economist Adam Smith, and was then extended into a general theory of capitalist pacification by the Austrian economist Joseph Schumpeter.

Like the realists, Schumpeter regarded the international system as anarchic. Like many realists (including Hobbes), he regards citizens as individualistic, rational, and egoistic, and usually materialistic. But Schumpeter sees the combination of democracy and capitalism as opening up a revolutionary transformation of domestic state and social structure. These societies are as self-interestedly deterministically pacific as the Hobbesian Leviathan is bellicose. Hobbesian Leviathans, after all, were merely Hobbesian individuals writ large, with all their individual competitiveness and egoism. Schumpeter's state is a structured whole, distinct from its parts, transformed as it were by an 'invisible hand' (to borrow the classic commercial metaphor from Adam Smith). According to Schumpeter (1955: 68), when the people's energies are daily absorbed in production, 'economic rationalism', or the instability of market competition, necessitates calculation. It also 'individualizes' as 'subjective opportunities' replace the 'immutable factors' of traditional hierarchical society. Rational individuals then demand democratic governance. Market capitalism and **democratic majoritarianism** make individual material egoism and competitiveness into pacifism. Democratic capitalism means free trade and a peaceful foreign policy simply because they are, Schumpeter claimed, the first best solutions for rational majorities in capitalist societies. This is the heart of the contemporary enthusiasm, expressed by many liberal politicians, for global democratization and capitalism as the inevitable and pacific routes to peace at the 'end of history.'[23] It does well in accounting for the sometimes complaisant liberal attitude towards threats and provides another account of the liberal peace, but doesn't quite offer a convincing account of liberal aggression.

Thus First and Second Image liberals differ from each other. Schumpeter makes the peace, which is a duty of the Lockean liberal statesman, into the structured outcome of capitalist democracy. Both highlight for us powerful elements of liberal world politics. But if there is a long state of peace between liberal republics, Locke offers us a weak explanation for it. (How do they avoid partiality and bias so regularly in their relations?) He also misses the persistent state of war between liberals and non-liberals. (Why are the liberals so regularly more partial here?) Schumpeter misses the liberal sources of war with non-liberals, unless we should blame all these wars on the non-liberals.

Kant and the republican internationalists try to fill these gaps as they illustrate the larger potential of the liberal tradition. Immanuel Kant's 1795 essay 'Perpetual Peace' offers a coherent explanation of two important regularities in world politics—the tendencies of liberal states simultaneously to be peace-prone in their relations with each other and unusually war-prone in their relations with non-liberal states. Republican representation, liberal respect, and transnational interdependence (to rephrase Kant's three 'definitive articles' of the hypothetical peace treaty he asked states to sign) are three necessary and, together, sufficient causes of the two regularities taken in tandem.

Kant's theory held that a stable expectation of systemic peace among states would be achieved once three conditions were met. He calls them the 'definitive articles' of the hypothetical peace treaty he wants states to sign. Together they constitute a liberal republic and explain the foundations of the **three features of liberal foreign relations**. We can rephrase them as follows.

- **Representative republican government** which includes an elected legislative, separation of powers, and the rule of law. Kant argued that together those institutional features lead to caution because the government is responsible to its citizens. This does not guarantee peace. It should select for popular wars.

- **A commitment to peace based upon a principled respect for the non-discriminatory rights** that all human beings can rightfully claim. This should produce a commitment to respect the rights of fellow liberal republics (because they represent free citizens, who as individuals have rights that deserve our respect) and a suspicion of non-republics (because if those governments cannot trust their own citizens, what should lead us to trust them).[24]

- **The possibility of social and economic interdependence** Trade and social interaction generally engender a mix of conflict and cooperation. A foreign economic policy of free trade tends to produce material benefits superior to optimum tariffs if other states will retaliate against tariffs, as they usually do. Liberalism produces special material incentives for cooperation because, among fellow liberals, economic interdependence should not be subject to security-motivated restrictions and, consequently, tends to be more varied, less dependent on single issues, and less subject to single conflicts.[25] (See Box 3.5.)

Kant suggested that each was necessary and together they were sufficient to establish a secure expectation of peace. The first principle specifies representative government responsible to the majority; the second and third specify the majority's ends and interests. Together the three generate an expectation of peaceful interaction among fellow liberals—the liberal zone of peace—and suspicion towards non-liberals. Liberal aggressive imprudence and complaisant indifference are the choices that elected legislatures and executives make, reflecting the preferences (ideas, ideals, and interests) of the governing coalitions elections

---

BOX 3.5 The liberal foreign policy process

Liberalism could shape foreign policy in democracies either because public opinion is liberal and demands it, or because the political elite has liberal values and implements them. But a more likely process is that neither the public nor the elite is united in a single set of values, and that the elite typically manages policy but non-liberal members of the elite are deterred from choosing anti-liberal policies because they have good reason to doubt that anti-liberal policies would be sustained by a majority of the public at the next election.

produce. When galvanized by international threats or pushed by commercial interests, elected governments become aggressive towards non-liberals. When exhausted by war, they become complaisant. Governing coalitions also choose conservative, laissez-faire, or reformist social welfare variants of liberalism which, as discussed, lead to differing foreign policies.

Mitigating trade-offs

If a concern for protecting and expanding the range of international freedom is to shape liberal strategic aims, then foreign policy towards both liberal and non-liberal worlds should be guided by general liberal principles. At a minimum, this should mean rejecting the realist balance of power as a general strategy by refusing to balance against the capabilities of fellow democratic liberals, and trusting the **liberal community**. At its fullest, this also means going beyond the standard obligations of general international law. Membership in the liberal community should imply accepting a **positive duty** to defend other members of the liberal community, to discriminate in certain instances in their favour, and to override in some circumstances the domestic sovereignty of states in order to rescue fellow human beings from intolerable oppressions such as genocide and ethnic cleansing. Authentically liberal policies should in some circumstances call for attempts to secure personal and civil rights, to foster democratic government, and to expand the scope and effectiveness of the world market economy as well as to meet those basic human needs that make the exercise of human rights possible. (See Table 3.1.)

In order to avoid the extremist possibilities of its abstract universalism, liberal policy should be constrained both by a respect for consequences measured in terms of liberal values and by a geopolitical budget. Strategy involves matching what we are prepared to spend with what we want to achieve; it identifies aims, resources, threats, and allies. Balancing the first two, minimizing the third, and fostering the fourth are the core elements of a **liberal foreign policy** that seeks to preserve and expand the community of liberal democracies without violating liberal principles or bankrupting liberal states (Muravchik 1991; Deudney and Ikenberry 1991/92; Smith 1994).[26]

Liberals should not embark upon **crusades for democracy** because in a world armed with nuclear weapons, crusading is suicidal. And in a world where changes in regional balances of power could be extremely destabilizing for ourselves and our allies, indiscriminate provocations of hostility (such as against the People's Republic of China) could create increased insecurity (for Japan and ourselves). Liberals—even liberal hyperpowers such as the US—simply do not have the excess strength that frees them from the need to economize on dangers (as the USA painfully rediscovered in Iraq and Afghanistan).

Instead, **liberal strategy** for expanding the international community of liberal states should lean towards the defensive. It should strive to protect the liberal community, foster the conditions that might allow the liberal community to grow, and save the use of force for clear emergencies that severely threaten the survival of the community or core liberal values. The strategy should first *preserve*—protecting the community and managing and mitigating the normal tensions among liberal market economies—and then *expand*. Ruling out an offensive state strategy, one should rely primarily on transnational civil society for expansion by three methods; it should begin with 'inspiration', and call upon 'intervention' only when necessary.

Table 3.1 The liberal community by date[i]

Historical period	Country	Total number
18th century	Swiss Cantons,[ii] French Republic 1790–1795, USA 1776–	3
1800–1850	Swiss Confederation, USA, France (1830–1849), Belgium (1830–), Great Britain (1832–), Netherlands (1848–), Piedmont (1848–), Denmark (1849–)	8
1850–1900	Switzerland, USA, Belgium, Great Britain, Netherlands, Piedmont (1861), Italy (1861–), Denmark (1866), Sweden (1864–) Greece (1864–), Canada[iii] (1867–), France (1871–), Argentina (1880–), Chile (1891–)	13
1900–1945	Switzerland, USA, Great Britain, Sweden, Canada, Greece (1911, 1928–1936), Italy (1922), Belgium (1940), Netherlands (1940), Argentina (1943), France (1940), Chile (1924, 1932), Australia (190l), Norway (1905–1940), New Zealand (1907), Colombia (1910–1949), Denmark (1914–1940), Poland (1917–1935), Latvia (1922–1934), Germany (1918–1932), Austria (1918–1934), Estonia (1919–1934), Finland (1919–), Uruguay (1919–), Costa Rica (1919–), Czechoslovakia (1920–1939), Ireland (1920–), Mexico (1928–), Lebanon (1944–)	29
1945	Switzerland, USA, Great Britain, Sweden, Canada, Australia, New Zealand, Finland, Ireland, Mexico, Uruguay (1973, 1985), Chile (1973, 1990–), Lebanon (1975), Costa Rica (1948, 1953–), Iceland (1944–), France (1945–), Denmark (1945–), Norway (1945–), Austria (1945–), Brazil (1945–1954, 1955–1964, 1985–), Belgium (1946–), Netherlands (1946–), Italy (1946–), Philippines (1946–1972, 1987–), India (1947–1975, 1977–), Sri Lanka (1948–196l, 1963–1971, 1978–1983, 1988–), Ecuador (1948–1963, 1979–), Israel (1949–), West Germany (1949–), Greece (1950–1967, 1975–), Peru (1950–1962, 1963–1968, 1980–), Turkey (1950–1960, 1966–1971, 1984–), Japan (1951–), Bolivia (1956–1969, 1982–), Colombia (1958–), Venezuela (1959–), Nigeria (1961–1964, 1979–1984), Jamaica (1962–), Trinidad and Tobago (1962–), Senegal (1963–), Malaysia (1963–), Botswana (1966–), Singapore (1965–), Portugal (1976–, Spain (1978–), Dominican Republic (1978–), Ecuador (1978–), Peru (1980–1990), Honduras (1981–), Papua New Guinea (1982–), El Salvador (1984–), Argentina (1983–), Uruguay (1985–), Mauritius (1987–), South Korea (1988–), Taiwan (1988–), Thailand (1988–), Pakistan (1988–), Panama (1989–), Paraguay (1989–), Madagascar (1990–), Mongolia (1990–), Namibia (1990–), Nepal (1990–), Nicaragua (1990–), Poland (1990–), Hungary (1990–), Czechoslovakia (1990–)	68

(*continued*)

Table 3.1 (*continued*)

Historical period	Country	Total number
1990–	Switzerland, USA, Great Britain, Sweden, Canada, Australia, New Zealand, Finland, Ireland, Mexico, Uruguay, Costa Rica, Iceland, France, Denmark, Norway, Austria, Brazil, Belgium, Netherlands, Italy, Philippines, India, Sri Lanka, Ecuador, Israel, West Germany, Greece, Turkey, Japan, Bolivia, Colombia, Venezuela, Jamaica, Trinidad and Tobago, Senegal, Malaysia, Botswana, Portugal, Spain, Dominican Republic, Ecuador, Honduras, Papua New Guinea, El Salvador, Argentina, Mauritius, South Korea, Taiwan, Thailand, Panama, Paraguay, Madagascar, Mongolia, Namibia, Nicaragua, Poland, Hungary, Czechoslovakia (1990), Singapore (1993), Pakistan (1998), Russia (1991–1999), Jordan (1991–2001), Nepal (2003), Bulgaria (1990–), Chile (1990–), Mongolia (1990–), Albania (1991–), Bangladesh (1991–), Benin (1991–), Cape Verde (1991–), Croatia (1991–), Estonia (1991–) Latvia (1991–), Lithuania (1991–), Ukraine (1991–), Slovenia (1991–), Zambia (1991–), Armenia (1992–), Indonesia (1992–), Macedonia (1992–), Mali (1992–), Romania (1992–), Burkina Faso (1993–), Guatemala (1993–), Lesotho (1993–), Yemen (1993–), Guinea-Bissau (1994–), Malawi (1994–), Mozambique (1994–), South Africa (1994–), Georgia (1995–), Ghana (1995–), Sierra Leone (1998–), Kuwait (1999–), Nigeria (1999–), Tanzania (1999–), Bosnia-Herzegovina (2000–), Djibouti (2000–), Niger (2000–), East Timor (2002–), Gambia (2002–), Kenya (2002–)	103

This is an *approximate* list of 'liberal regimes' (through 1994, thus including regimes that were liberal democratic as of 1990) drawn up according to the four 'Kantian' institutions described as essential: (1) market and private property economies; (2) polities that are externally sovereign; (3) citizens who possess juridical rights; (4) 'republican' (whether republican or parliamentary monarchy) representative government. The last of these includes the requirement that the legislative branch have an effective role in public policy and be formally and competitively (either inter- or intra-party) elected. Furthermore, I have taken into account whether male suffrage is wide (i.e. 30%) or, as Kant would have had it, open to 'achievement' by inhabitants (for example, to poll-tax payers or householders) of the national or metropolitan territory (Kant's *Metaphysics of Morals*, in *Kant's Political Writings*, p. 139). This list of liberal regimes is thus more inclusive than a list of democratic regimes or polyarchies (Powell 1982: 5). Female suffrage is granted within a generation of its being demanded by an extensive female suffrage movement; and representative government is internally sovereign (including especially over military and foreign affairs) as well as stable (in existence for at least three years). (Banks and Overstreet 1983; *The Europa Yearbook* 1985; Gastil 1985; McColm and Freedom House Survey Team 1991; Finn *et al.*, 1995). The contemporary list, excluding liberal regimes with populations less than one million, includes all states categorized as 'Free' by Freedom House and those 'Partly Free' (four political and five civil liberties or more free).

[ii] There are domestic variations within these liberal regimes. For example, Switzerland was liberal only in certain cantons; the USA was liberal only north of the Mason–Dixon line until 1865, when it became liberal throughout. These lists also exclude ancient 'republics', since none appear to fit Kant's criteria (Holmes 1979).

[iii] Canada, as a commonwealth within the British empire, did not have formal control of its foreign policy during this period.

Preservation

Above all, liberal foreign policy should strive to preserve the pacific union of similarly liberal societies, which is not only currently of immense strategic value (being the political foundation of both NATO and the US–Japanese alliance), but is also the single best hope for the evolution of a peaceful world. Therefore liberals should be prepared to defend and formally ally with authentically liberal democratic states that are subject to threats or actual instances of external attack or internal subversion. Liberals have taken for granted and underestimated the importance of the democratic alliance. Their alliances in NATO, with Japan, and in ANZUS, and alignments with other democratic states, are not only crucial to their present security, but the best hopes for long-term peace and the realization of their ideals. Liberals should not treat them as once useful but now purposeless Cold War strategic alignments against the power of the USSR.

Global problem-solving, ranging from climate change to nuclear proliferation to economic growth, will require diplomacy that involves all states, including China and Russia and many other non-democracies. For these purposes liberal states will need to work across ideological divides and strengthen **multilateral institutions** such as the UN, IMF, World Bank, and WTO. But the liberal world also needs to strengthen its own collective security multilaterally, not replacing the UN with an 'alliance of democracies,' but supplementing it with democratic collective security.[27] The current need to redefine NATO and the increasing importance of the US relationship with Japan offer us an opportunity to broaden the organization of liberal security. Joining all the democratic states together in a single democratic security organization would secure an important forum for the definition and coordination of common interests that stretch beyond the regional concerns of Europe and the Far East. With the end of the Cold War, pressures towards regionalism are likely to become increasingly strong. In order to avoid the desperate reactions that might follow regional crises such as those of the 1920s and 1930s, a collective security organization for liberal democracies seems necessary. It could reduce pressures on Japan and Germany to arm themselves with nuclear weapons, mitigate the strategic vulnerabilities of isolated liberal states such as Israel, and allow for the complementary pooling of strategic resources (combining, for example, Japanese and German financial clout with American nuclear deterrence, and with American, British, and French expeditionary thrust). The expansion of NATO on the European continent is one part of this security umbrella. It should include all established democratic members and then establish a transitional category for all democratizing states that have yet to experience two democratic elections.

However, much of the success of multilateral management will rest on shoring up its economic supports. 'Above $6000 GDP per capita', Adam Przeworski and colleagues have noted, 'democracies are impregnable and can be expected to live forever' (297). Below that per capita income level, steady low-inflation economic growth is one key to protecting democratic government (Przeworski *et al.* 1995: 298). Unilateral solutions to national economic growth (exchange rate depreciation, increased taxation) may be necessary, but they are not sufficient and some (long-term protectionism) are neither. Avoidance of a costly global economic recession calls for continued trade liberalization and expansion of international investment to match whatever contractions of governmental spending and private consumption are needed to contain national inflationary pressures.

Discovering ways to manage global interdependence will call for difficult economic adjustments at home and institutional innovations in the world economy. Under these circumstances, liberals will need to ensure that those suffering losses, such as from market disruption or restriction, do not suffer either a permanent loss of income or exclusion from world markets. Although intense economic interdependence generates conflicts, it also helps to sustain the material well-being underpinning liberal societies and to promise avenues of development to Third World states with markets that are currently limited by low income. To this should be added mutually beneficial measures designed to improve Third World economic performance. Export earnings insurance, international debt management assistance, export diversification assistance, and technical aid are among these. In the case of the truly desperate poor, such as is the condition of some of the populations of Africa, more direct measures of international aid and relief from famine are required, as a matter of both political prudence and moral duty.

Furthermore, if measures of temporary economic protection are needed, liberal states should undertake these measures only by international negotiation and only when the resulting agreements are subject to a regular review by all the parties. Otherwise, emergency measures could reverberate into a spiral of isolationism. Thus the liberal community needs to create a diplomatic/international atmosphere conducive to multilateral problem-solving. Foreign policies conveying a commitment to collective responsibility in US diplomacy will go far in this direction (Bergsten *et al.* 1978; Cooper *et al.* 1978; Stiglitz 2002: Chapters 10 and 16).

Expansion

Preserving the community is important in part because there are few direct measures that the liberal world can take to foster the stability, development, and spread of liberal democratic regimes. Many direct efforts, including military intervention and overt or covert funding for democratic movements in other countries, discredit those movements as the foreign interference backfires through the force of local nationalism.

Therefore much of the potential success of a policy designed to foster democracy rests on an ability to shape an economic and political environment that indirectly supports or instigates democratic governance and creates pressures for the democratic reform of authoritarian rule.

Politically, there are few measures more valuable than an active human rights diplomacy, which enjoys global legitimacy and (if successful) can assure a political environment that tolerates the sort of dissent that can nourish an indigenous democratic movement. There is reason to pay special attention to those countries entering what Huntington (1981b) has called the **socio-economic transition zone**—countries having the economic development typically associated with democracy (see also Przeworski 1995). For them, more direct support in the form of electoral infrastructure (from voting machines to battalions of international observers) can provide the essential margin persuading contentious domestic groups to accept the fairness of the crucial first election.

Following the Second World War, the allied occupation and re-making of Germany and Japan, and the Marshall Plan's successful coordination and funding of the revival of Europe's pre-war industrial economies and democratic regimes offers a model of how much can be achieved with an extraordinary commitment of resources and the most favourable possible environment (Schwartz 1991). In practice today, short of those very special circumstances, there are few direct means to stimulate democratic development from abroad apart from *inspiration*.

Inspiration

The simplest programme for liberal expansion is to be the 'City on a Hill'. The success of liberalism at home stands as an example for emulation and a refuge for beleaguered liberals in oppressive countries everywhere. Liberalism, moreover, taps into deep chords of common humanity that lend confidence that all may some day follow a similar path towards liberation, allowing for the appropriate national and cultural differences. Peoples will *liberate themselves* by *modernizing themselves*. One liberal 'strategy' is simply to live up to their own principles at home, and wait for others to modernize themselves.

Francis Fukuyama's striking argument about the 'End of History' presents a radical restatement of the liberal modernization theme, bringing together both its materialist and idealist strains. His study envisions the failure of all forms of autocracy, whether in Eastern Europe or elsewhere, and the triumph of consumer capitalism and democracy under the irresistible onslaught of modernization. Today, however, we have mounting evidence that free-market capitalism may not even be the quintessential capitalist answer to growth under the conditions of late-late capitalism. The most striking rates of growth of the post-war period appear to have been achieved by the semi-planned capitalist economies of East Asia—Taiwan, South Korea, Singapore, Japan, and now China and India. Indicative planning, capital rationing by para-statal development banks and ministries of finance, managed trade, and incorporated unions—capitalist syndicalism, not capitalist libertarianism—seemed to describe the wave of the capitalist future.[28]

While China's current success (10% growth annually) with 'market–Leninism' or 'national corporatism' seems to confirm the non-liberal path, the potential for liberalism need not be completely discounted. Economists have raised concerns about whether Asian capitalism can evolve from capital accumulation to 'total factor productivity', which may require a loosening of indicative planning. Thus in China market forces have stimulated the formation of thousands of business and professional groups and greater village-level (democratic) self-management. Another route to democratization lies in the institutional routinization of authority, what Minxin Pei has called 'creeping democratization' in the Chinese context (Pei 1995). Even when leaders are opposed to democratization and even when the forces of civil society lack the power or the interest to promote a democratization of the state, democratization may 'creep' in. When leaders seek to defend their authority by recruiting allies, ceding to them competency embodied in institutional routines and government structures, the beginnings of constitutional checks and balances are set in motion. Representing diverse and sometimes extensive interests, the new institutions limit arbitrary power and begin to delegate power in their turn, further institutionalizing a regime. Step by step, the foundations of the rule of law are laid, as they are now (albeit slowly) in China, where new clusters of authority in the National People's Congress—such as the court system and the legal profession, and village councils—are emerging.

Here the roles of global civil society and international civil politics are particularly important. Tourism, educational exchanges, and scientific meetings spread tastes across borders; indeed, such **transnational** contacts with the liberal world seem to have had a liberalizing effect on the many Soviet and East European elites who visited the West during the Cold War, demonstrating both Western material successes (where they existed) and regimes that tolerated and even encouraged dissent and popular participation (when they did) (Deudney and Ikenberry 1991/92). The international commitment to human rights, including the Helsinki Watch process, found a reflection in Gorbachev's 'universal human values'. The 'Goddess of Liberty' erected in Tian'anmen Square represented another transnational expression of ideas shared on a global basis (see Chapter Seventeen).

Intervention

Liberal principles can also help us think about whether liberal states should attempt to rescue individuals oppressed by their own governments. Historically, liberals have divided on these issues.[29] Traditionally, and in accord with current international law, states have the right to defend themselves, come to the aid of other states aggressed against, and take forcible measures to protect, where necessary, their citizens from wrongful injury and release them from wrongful imprisonment (Cutler 1985). However, modern international law condemns sanctions and force designed to redress the domestic oppression of states. The UN Charter is ambiguous on this issue, since it finds human rights to be international concerns and permits the Security Council to intervene to prevent what it determines to be 'threats' to 'international peace and security'.[30]

Choosing a foreign policy of non-intervention has important moral foundations. Non-intervention helps to encourage order—stable expectations--in a confusing world without international government. It rests on a respect for the rights of individuals to establish their own way of life free from foreign interference. The basic moral presumption of liberal thought is that states should not be subject to foreign intervention, by military or other means. Therefore states should be taken as representing the moral rights of individuals unless there is clear evidence to the contrary. Although liberals and democrats have often succumbed to the temptation to intervene to bring 'civilization', metropolitan standards of law and order, and democratic government to foreign peoples who have expressed no demand for them, these interventions find no justification in a conception of equal respect for individuals. This is simply because it is to their sense of their own self-respect and not our sense of what they should respect that we must accord equal consideration.

What it means to respect another's sense of self-determination is not always self-evident. Ascertaining what it might mean can best be considered as an attempt at both subjective and objective interpretation. One criterion is **subjective**. We should credit the voice of their majority. Obviously, this means not intervening against states with apparent majority support. In authoritarian states, however, determining what the wishes of the majority are is particularly difficult. Some states will have divided political communities with a considerable share, but less than a majority, of the population supporting the government, a large minority opposing, and many indifferent. Some will be able to suppress dissent completely. Others will not. Therefore widespread armed resistance sustained by local resources and massive street demonstrations against the state (and not just against specific policies) can provide evidence of a people standing against their own government. Still, one will want to find clear evidence that the dissenters actually want a foreign intervention to solve their oppression. The other criterion is **objective**. No group of individuals, even if apparently silent, can be expected to consent to having their basic rights to life, food, shelter, and freedom from torture systematically violated. These sorts of rights clearly cross-cut wide cultural differences.

Whenever either or both of these violations take place, one has a *prima facie* consideration favouring foreign intervention.[31] But even rescuing majorities suffering severe oppression or individuals suffering massive and systematic violations of human rights is not sufficient grounds to justify military intervention. We must also have some reasonable expectation that the intervention will actually end the oppression. We need to expect that it will end the massacre or address starvation (as did India's intervention in East Pakistan and Tanzania's in Uganda). Or, if pro-democratic, that it has a reasonable chance of establishing authentic self-determination, rather than (as J. S. Mill warned) merely introducing puppet rulers who, dependent on outside support, soon begin to replicate the oppressive behaviour of the previous rulers. Moreover, the intervention must be a proportional response to the suffering now endured and likely to be endured without an intervention. Countries, any more than villages, cannot be destroyed in order to be saved. We must consider whether means other than military intervention could achieve the liberation from oppression. And we must ensure that the intervention, if necessary, is conducted in a way that minimizes casualties, most particularly non-combatant casualties. In short, we must be able to account morally for the expected casualties of an invasion, both to our own soldiers and the non-combatant victims. Lastly, interventions should incorporate a normal sense of fallibility, together with a decent respect for the opinions of the entire community of nations. Meeting these standards requires, wherever feasible, a resort to multilateral organizations to guide and legally legitimate a decision to violate the sovereignty of another state.

Conclusion

Liberal foreign policy presents both a promise and a warning. Alliances founded on mutual strategic interest among liberal and non-liberal states have been broken, economic ties between liberal and non-liberal states have proved fragile, but the political bonds of liberal rights and interests have proved a remarkably firm foundation for mutual non-aggression. A separate peace exists among liberal states. But in their relations with non-liberal states, liberal states have not escaped from the insecurity caused by anarchy in the world political system considered as a whole. Moreover, the very constitutional restraint, international respect for individual rights, and shared commercial interests that establish grounds for peace among liberal states establish grounds for additional conflict irrespective of actual threats to national security in the relations between liberal and non-liberal societies. And in their relations with all states, liberal states have not solved the problems of international cooperation and competition. Liberal publics can become absorbed in domestic issues, and international liberal respect does not preclude trade rivalries or guarantee farsighted collective solutions to international security and welfare.

 Key points

- For more than two centuries, liberal countries have tended to maintain peaceful relations with each other. Liberal democracies are each other's natural allies.

- Therefore a fundamental postulate of liberal foreign policy is preserving and expanding the liberal zone of peace.

- Liberalism contributes to the understanding of foreign policy by highlighting how individuals and the ideas and ideals they espouse (such as human rights, liberty, and democracy), social forces (capitalism, markets), and political institutions (democracy, representation) can have direct effects on foreign relations.

- But liberalism has also proved to be a dangerous guide to foreign policy, often exacerbating tensions with non-liberal states.

- The foreign policy question essential for all democracies is thus: Can the liberal peace be effectively preserved and expanded without provoking unnecessary danger and inflicting unnecessary harm?

- Scholars have analysed liberalism's effects by distinguishing three key interpretations of liberal foreign policy: individualist, commercial, and republican.

 ## Questions

1. What characteristics identify a typical liberal state? How well does an actual liberal state that you know—the US, UK, France, Germany, Japan, South Africa—match those characteristics?

2. What differences are said to distinguish individualist, commercial, and republican liberalisms? How and why do their foreign policies differ?

3. What might the citizens and leaders of liberal states do to improve the prospects that the good features of liberal foreign policy (the liberal peace) are enhanced and the bad ones (imprudence, intervention-ism) constrained?

4. Under what circumstances should a liberal theorist of foreign policy support or reject international military intervention?

5. What should a liberal theorist expect to happen in US–European relations and US–Chinese relations if Europe unites in a powerful democratic federation or China both continues to grow and democratizes? Would these expectations differ from those that a realist balance of power theorist would expect?

 ## Further reading

Brown, M., Lynn-Jones, S., and Miller, S. (eds) (1996), *Debating the Democratic Peace* **(Cambridge, MA: MIT Press).**
A valuable collection of essays by proponents and critics of the democratic peace proposition.

Doyle, M.W. (1997), *Ways of War and Peace* **(New York: W. W. Norton).**
A wide-ranging survey of international relations theory, including liberalism, realism, and socialism, and their policy implications.

Kant, I. (1795), 'Perpetual Peace', in H. Reiss (ed.), *Kant's Political Writings* **(trans. H. B. Nisbet). (Cambridge: Cambridge University Press, 1970).**
Written in 1795 by the great German philosopher Immanuel Kant, when there were few if any liberal republics; nonetheless, the classic source for the liberal peace.

Mill, J. S. (1859), 'A Few Words on Nonintervention', in G. Himmelfarb (ed.), *Essays on Politics and Culture* **(Gloucester, MA: Peter Smith, 1973).**
The classic nineteenth-century liberal defence of both non-intervention and liberal imperialism.

Rousseau, D. (2005), *Democracy and War* **(Stanford, CA: Stanford University Press).**
A quantitative assessment of the democratic peace, with insightful case studies.

 Visit the Online Resource Centre that accompanies this book for more information:
www.oxfordtextbooks.co.uk/orc/smith_foreign/

4

Constructivism and foreign policy

TRINE FLOCKHART

Chapter contents

 Reader's guide

This chapter is about one of the newer theories in international relations—constructivism. As a 'newcomer' constructivism has been viewed with scepticism from within the discipline and from foreign policy making circles alike, where many have questioned its utility and its ability to say anything about 'the real world of policy'. This chapter aims to show that although some of its concepts and propositions may seem unsettling at first, constructivism is a useful tool not only for understanding foreign policy, but also as a guide for prescribing foreign policy. The chapter starts out by discussing what constructivism is, outlining the constructivist view that anarchy exists in different forms with major implications for how agents act. The chapter then outlines some of the main propositions and conceptual tools of constructivism, especially its views on identity, social construction, rules, and practice. Although many of the propositions and concepts may appear a little abstract, the chapter uses examples from 'the real world' of European security, to show constructivism's alternative understandings of NATO's role after the end of the Cold War and in present-day European security. The chapter points out that theory matters in foreign policy making—including constructivism—because different theories imply different policies and may make alternative policy options visible which would otherwise easily have been overlooked.

Introduction

On 1 July 1991 the Warsaw Pact ceased to exist after its European members withdrew their support and military contributions to the organization, bringing an end to a 36-year-long foreign policy based on a military stand-off between the Soviet-led Warsaw Pact and the US-led NATO Alliance. The event immediately sparked off speculation about NATO's future and which policy options would be available in the new security environment. The general wisdom in realist circles was that without a clear threat NATO had outlived its purpose, famously expressed by Kenneth Waltz, who proclaimed that although 'NATO's days were not numbered—its years were'.[1]

This example raises the question of why students and practitioners of foreign policy should care about abstract theories that proclaim to be able to say something about foreign policy and even to prescribe the 'right' foreign policy option (Walt 1998:29). The answer might (partly) be that we need theories as a form of organizing principle to make sense of a complex world. Without theories, we would simply be overwhelmed by the masses of information that have to be processed in the making and understanding of foreign policy. Yet, as indicated by the example above, theories do more than organize data, they also imply different policy options and they contain different assumptions about how the world works.

Neither realists nor liberals were able to correctly predict the consequences of the demise of the Warsaw Pact for NATO, yet they have retained their dominant position in international relations, albeit now challenged by the constructivist perspective. At the time neither of the two dominant theories, nor most foreign policy practitioners, were able to imagine a more, rather than a less, influential role for NATO, where the Alliance would be teaching the 'new Europeans' democratic norms and the appropriate behaviour for gaining membership in the 'Western club'—and in the process changing identities and interests and deeply ingrained foreign policy practices. Curiously, although constructivism has arguably been able to best capture the finer nuances of NATO's post-Cold War role, and has offered the most persuasive alternative interpretations of the momentous changes in international relations and their foreign policy implications, realist and liberal perspectives are still the 'theories of choice' among foreign policy makers and scholars of International Relations (IR). This suggests that scholars and foreign policy practitioners not only hold firm belief systems about substantial policy matters, but also that the assumptions of realism and liberalism might resonate more easily with a generation of academics and foreign policy makers, who are themselves schooled in realist and liberal theories, and to whom the constructivist perspective is an unknown entity and perhaps a bit too abstract.

If decision makers do hold on to their belief systems (as suggested in the original Foreign Policy Analysis (FPA) research) the long-held preference for realist and liberal perspectives is not surprising as constructivism challenges both theories on a number of important points—especially deeply ingrained assumptions about how the world works. The constructivist conviction that 'the world is of our making' (Onuf 1989) challenges the realist view that we can do little to change things, as unpleasant as they might seem, and the liberal perspective of a particular route to human progress. This chapter aims to unpack the basic assumptions and policy relevance of constructivism so that it might increasingly be included in the conceptual toolbox used by students and (future) policy makers in their attempt to understand and do foreign policy. The chapter explores the nature of constructivism and its added value for explaining and understanding foreign policy using European security as an illustrative example.

What is constructivism?

The failure of the two mainstream theories to predict, and initially even to explain, the end of the Cold War is usually seen as having facilitated constructivism's arrival in the IR discipline. It is true that the failure of realism in predicting the momentous events, its overall static nature, and its initial insistence after the Cold War that essentially nothing had changed,[2] contributed to the rapid spread of constructivism into IR from the early 1990s onwards. However, the origins of constructivism in IR can actually be traced back to the early- to mid 1980s,[3] where critical and post-modern theories suggested alternative readings of the very notions of reality, truth, and structure (Smith 1995: 25) and questioned widely accepted understandings of concepts of IR and subfields such as the study of foreign policy (see Chapter Five).

Although constructivism is presented in this book as one of the mainstream theories, many would actually say that constructivism is an approach rather than a theory. This view is grounded in the understanding that constructivism has nothing substantial to say about who or what are the main actors, problems, or issues in international relations. Constructivism offers no solutions to specific problems in international relations, nor does it prescribe any particular policy directions. Indeed, constructivism can be seen as an empty vessel that merely specifies a social ontology without, however, specifying which social relationships it is concerned with. Moreover constructivism is 'empty' in the sense that it does not challenge the ideological convictions of either realism or liberalism, and it is neither optimistic nor pessimistic by design (Adler 1997: 323). Even so, constructivism does offer alternative understandings of some of the most central themes in international relations such as the meaning of anarchy and balance of power, the relationship between state identity and interest, and the prospects for change (Hopf 1998: 172). Moreover, with its roots in critical theory and post-modernism, constructivism has remained committed to problematizing that which is taken for granted and to 'making strange' what is commonly regarded to exist (Pouliot 2004: 323).

Applied constructivism

Strictly speaking, it is true to say that constructivism is not a theory in the sense that realism and liberalism provide visions of particular world orders. However, constructivism is perhaps closer to being a substantial theory than its critics suggest, and it certainly holds considerable potential as an applied framework for understanding foreign policy. This is especially clear in relation to European security, where arguably constructivism is closest to becoming a substantive theory, as constructivists are concerned with the specific question of how old practices of rivalry and war-making can be changed through institutionalization, which might over time change identities, interests, and practices. This form of constructivism could be called 'applied constructivism' and builds on the work of, amongst others, Karl Deutsch and his associates (Deutsch 1957) who theorized that changed interactions across borders might lead to new social relationships and eventually lead to the establishment of a 'security community'.[4] Since the publication of *Security Communities* (Adler and Barnett 1998), the concept of a 'security community' has experienced a revival in IR thinking. The security community literature has since produced convincing empirical evidence that the processes taking place in, for example, the enlargement of NATO and the European Union, or through some forms of democracy promotion, are aimed precisely at forging new relationships based on friendship and cooperation rather than rivalry or enmity, and that identities and interests have been fundamentally changed in the process.

The clearest constructivist statement on these processes is found in the influential article 'Anarchy is What States Make of It' by Alexander Wendt (1992). Wendt asked if it is really the case that the absence of political authority in the international system forces states into the patterns of behaviour based on self-help, as suggested by realists. His answer was a clear 'no'. Self-help and power politics do not follow logically from anarchy, because self-help is not a structural feature, as suggested by Waltz, but an institution based on particular inter-subjective understandings about self and other that are reinforced through agents' practice. The argument builds on one of the most central features of constructivism, which holds that people act towards objects (including other people) on the basis of the meanings the object (or person) has for them. This means that states act differently towards enemies than they do towards friends because enemies are threatening and friends are not (Wendt 1992: 396). Moreover, Wendt suggested the existence of three different 'cultures of anarchy' character-ized by different institutions. The three cultures of anarchy could be conflictual and based on self-help as suggested by realists, competitive and based on rivalry as suggested by many liberals, or friendly and based on cooperation as suggested by, for example, Deutsch. The implication was that not only is anarchy what states make of it, but that cultures of anarchy can be changed.

The argument that anarchy is not necessarily based on conflict and self-help was a dev-astating blow to neorealism, but it was also a completely new conceptual tool for thinking about options for foreign policy making, as it opened up entirely new possibilities where the overarching question became how to change from one culture to another. If, as main-tained by Wendt, the only reason why we might be in a self-help system is because prac-tice made it that way (Wendt 1992: 407), then practice could also 'un-make' a conflictual culture. In the aftermath of the Cold War, constructivists argued that it was precisely in such 'un-makings' of past conflictual patterns that NATO and the EU could play important roles.

The big question here, of course, is how we move from one culture to another, because once a culture has become institutionalized, it is difficult to change. To answer this question, it is necessary to take a closer look at some of the essential parts of constructivism which provide a conceptual toolbox for understanding how agents' shared knowledge, identities, and interests are interlinked and may contribute to changing deeply embedded practices and structural conditions. Doing so, however, requires a fundamental break with some of the real-ist and liberal assumptions about how the world works. (See Box 4.1)

The essence of constructivism

Constructivism differs from realism and liberalism on a number of crucial points, some of which may appear a little unsettling to those who have been schooled in the so-called ration-alist thought which underpins realism and liberalism. Moreover, all essential elements of con-structivism are interconnected in ways that can also make it difficult to divide constructivism into 'bite-sized' pieces. In this section I will first present some of the essentials of constructiv-ism divided into four core propositions, and in the next section I will illustrate how these core propositions of constructivism can be utilized to answer the question identified above—how foreign policy might be able to effect change from one form of anarchy to another.

The four key constructivist propositions and some of the key constructivist concepts can be summarized as follows:

BOX 4.1 Ego and Alter on a desert island

Relations, whether conflictual, competitive, or friendly, are always a product of social interactions rather than just material capabilities. To illustrate this point, Wendt uses an example of two space avatars, Alter and Ego, who meet on a desert island for the first time. From their first encounter on the beach, their relationship will develop from their initial understanding of the situation and from the development of shared understandings through their interactions, which might lead to enmity, competition, or friendship, depending on their actions and reactions. The 'material structure' is the same in each situation where both have themselves and a knife and are on the same desert island. Think about which 'culture of anarchy' is likely to result from the three desert island situations outlined below.

SITUATION 1 Ego notices Alter on the island. Ego judges the situation as potentially threatening and approaches Alter brandishing his knife.

SITUATION 2 Ego notices Alter on the island. Ego considers that Alter will be a competitor for the known scarce resources on the island, but wonders if Alter knows of other resources. Ego approaches Alter with his knife in his belt, but his hand resting on it.

SITUATION 3 Ego notices Alter on the island. Ego wonders if Alter might want to cooperate on digging a well (and whether he might like to play chess). Ego approaches Alter with his hand outstretched and the knife simply dangling from his belt.

How will Alter respond and what will be Ego's interpretation of Alter's response—which shared understandings and practices might develop?

---

1. A belief in the social construction of reality and the importance of social facts.

2. A focus on ideational as well as material structures and the importance of norms and rules.

3. A focus on the role of identity in shaping political action and the importance of 'logics of action'.

4. A belief in the mutual constitutiveness of agents and structure, and a focus on practice and action.

Social construction and social facts

As the name 'constructivism' indicates, the major common proposition by constructivists is that reality, which we mostly take as given, is in fact a project under constant construction. Constructivists understand the world as coming into being rather than existing as a pre-given entity. Moreover, as argued in the seminal work *The Social Construction of Reality* (Berger and Luckmann 1966), our understanding of reality is derived from inter-subjective knowledge and the interpreted nature of social reality. The fact that constructivism is often called *social* constructivism is indicative of the considerable role attached to the social processes of inter-action for the production of shared knowledge about the world. From this perspective, constructivists agree that although some aspects of reality clearly exist as 'brute facts' whose concrete existence is not contested, their meaning is. Ayer's Rock, or Uluru, in Australia clearly exists, but its significance and meaning varies greatly depending on whether it is regarded from a European or an Aboriginal perspective. Similarly, a North Korean nuclear warhead may look similar to a French nuclear warhead, and both have the same devastating consequences, but despite their similar material attributes, we attach different meanings to each. This is of relevance to the 'cultures of anarchy' because different meanings will also imply different practices and different foreign policy choices, as witnessed in the different American foreign policies *vis-à-vis* a nuclear-armed France and a nuclear-armed North Korea.

Apart from brute facts with different shared meanings, constructivists agree that there are portions of reality that are regarded as facts only through human agreement and which are made observable only through human practice. As suggested by Vincent Pouliot (2004: 320), all constructivists share a focus on those portions of the world that are treated *as if* they were real. Many of the most important concepts and understandings in international relations—even the state—are social facts rather than brute facts. Social facts exist only through human agreement and shared knowledge reinforced through practice. A common example of a social fact is money, which is clearly more than its material existence—what matters is the shared meanings we attach to money and the practices surrounding it. Without shared agreement that pieces of paper can be swapped for goods and services, money would no longer exist because it exists *only* through practice. International relations also consist of social facts that have no existence outside the meanings and practices associated with them. Over time social facts become reified through social relationships, rules, and routine practices so that they appear as an objective reality with an independent existence from those who constructed the social fact in the first place. Therefore key questions for constructivists are necessarily: How are social facts socially constructed and how do they affect global politics (Pouliot 2004: 320)? How can they be changed and even 'un-constructed'? (See Box 4.2.)

BOX 4.2 NATO—a social fact?

NATO clearly exists, and as seen in Libya, Afghanistan, the Balkans, and elsewhere is an important foreign policy actor. Yet who or what exactly is NATO? What do we mean when we say that NATO has bombed targets in Libya? In material terms NATO is an ageing headquarter building on the outskirts of Brussels, a home-page, and an international staff, and apart from a few AWACS reconnaissance planes, a command structure, and a few other very limited assets, NATO has no military forces of its own. Yet, despite the limited material manifestations of NATO, the organization clearly has a presence in international politics and security, and is commonly considered to be an objective reality with the ability to act (to have agency). Yet NATO only exists as a social fact constituted by social relationships, shared practice, and shared understandings.

NATO was established in 1949 through the signing of the North Atlantic Treaty which committed its signatories to come to the help of any fellow NATO member in case of attack. Therefore NATO's presence and existence as a foreign policy actor is based on the promise contained in a document that is more than sixty years old, and the shared meaning attached to that document, the shared identity and shared values of its members, and the many shared practices which have since been established. Moreover, NATO exists through its actions in concrete foreign and security policy, where during the Cold War it acted as the most important forum for foreign policy *vis-à-vis* the Soviet Union, and where since the end of the Cold War it has been engaged in forging new social relationships with former enemies.

Ideational and material structures

The insistence that the world is socially constructed is linked to the second essential proposition of constructivism—that structure cannot be understood through reference only to material forces such as natural resources and military power, but that it consists of both material and ideational factors. Constructivists emphasize the importance of shared knowledge about material factors, rules, symbols, and language, which all shape how we interpret the world and the actions of others. Neither actions nor material forces have meaning outside shared forms of knowledge, and it is collective meanings along with material forces that constitute the structure, and which organize our actions. For constructivists it is simply impossible to get a grasp on reality by only looking at the material world. In this sense constructivism directly challenges the materialism of neorealism and neoliberalism, which see the most fundamental feature of society as the distribution of material forces. Constructivists argue that although structure consists partly of material facts, as the example above of the Korean and French nuclear warheads shows, material facts alone have no meaning without understanding the social context, the shared knowledge, and the practices surrounding it. In the case of nuclear weapons, one North Korean nuclear warhead matters more to the USA than many French or British nuclear warheads because the meaning of the latter is interpreted within a social context of friendship, where cooperation is the dominant practice, rather than being interpreted within a social context of enmity.

Structures are often codified in formal rules and norms, which agents are socialized into following (Wendt 1992: 399). The rules that are followed may be formal rules that exist in a written or spoken form, but they may also be a less formal form of rule conceptualized as norms, which are usually taken for granted, are unquestioned, and are associated with specific identities and belonging to a specific community or social group. Norms are collective understandings that make behavioural claims on those actors who (because of their identity) see the norm as salient. A norm will specify the appropriate behaviour for an agent with a given identity. In that sense norms are at once cognitive 'maps' for actors to determine what is appropriate and inappropriate behaviour, and are also a major constitutive influence on actor identities and interests. Constructivists agree that norms have a structural function, which is both constraining and constitutive, but only in so far as the norm is seen by the agents themselves as of relevance—norms in this sense can be thought of as 'structures of relevance'.

Moreover, norms are important for constituting social relations because to become a member of a certain social group, such as NATO or the EU, applicant states have to follow the norms of the group to which membership is desired. The implied logic here is that structural change can be brought about by changing the norms of certain actors, especially if those actors seek membership of a new social group. The idea that norms could be changed in order to change identities and interests had already been used in the immediate aftermath of the Second World War in (West) Germany and Japan, but has since been adopted as a major foreign policy project in the aftermath of the Cold War as policy makers realized the eagerness of the Central and East European states to gain membership of the 'Western club'. Within a short space of time, both the EU and NATO, together with other international actors, had engaged in a gigantic project to socialize the norms of the West based on liberal and democratic ideas to those Central and Eastern European states who wished to become members of

---

BOX 4.3 Rules matter

Constructivists believe that rules are a necessary element for all but the most elementary forms of interaction, and they contend that rules are often followed blindly—even in situations where we might think that no rules exist. For example, tourists in London very quickly find out about the unspoken rule on the Underground not to stare at fellow passengers seated opposite you. Instead, travellers on the Underground learn the practice of directing their gaze above their fellow passenger, a practice that is expertly exploited by advertisers with very detailed advertising boards.

Rules matter because they provide order and predictability and they provide guidance for how to behave. Rules are general imperative principles, which require or authorize certain behaviour (Bull 1977/1995: 52). Rules may have the status of formalized law, but they may also be morality, norms, custom or etiquette, or simply operating procedures or 'rules of the game'.

The importance of diplomatic rules was clearly visible at the Copenhagen Climate Summit in 2009. In a desperate bid to get a result from the complicated negotiations and a far too crowded agenda, the Danish hosts used unorthodox procedures and went against diplomatic etiquette and the UN principle of equality. The result was not only confusion among delegates, but also consternation and a slowdown in the proceedings as much energy was consumed in 'finding out what was going on'. The disappointing outcome can now be blamed on 'failure to follow diplomatic etiquette' rather than the political unwillingness of some states to agree to the terms of the proposed agreement.

NATO and the EU (Flockhart 2006). In the process, new identities and new social relationships were constructed, which changed the logic of anarchy in Europe (between East and West) from one characterized by enmity and self-help to one characterized by friendship and a practice of cooperation. (See Box 4.3.)

Identity, interests, and 'logics of action'

The third core feature of constructivism is its focus on identity. Identity is the agent's understanding of self, its place in the social world, and its relationships with others. An understanding of self is always dependent on an 'other' for its constitution and, although relatively stable, is a condition that is always in a process of reconstitution and is always supported by a narrative to ensure biographical continuity that makes any changes seem natural. Constructivists place a key importance on identity because it is believed that identities strongly imply a particular set of interests or preferences in respect of choice of action (Hopf 1998: 175). This view of identity as constitutive of interests and action stands in stark contrast to the realist and liberal assumption that actors in international politics have only one pre-existing identity—that of a self-interested state engaged in producing and reproducing a predictably stable world.

By conceptualizing agents in international politics as influenced by their identity, constructivists also acknowledge the importance of the historical, cultural, political, and social context of the agents in question, as these are (some of) the factors that would have contributed to the construction of identity in the first place. Constructivists maintain that a sole focus on material factors provides an incomplete basis for analysis. For example, in a materialist interest-based analysis Denmark and Sweden would be assumed to be 'like units' as small states and therefore would be assumed to display similar patterns of action. Yet Sweden's self-identity as a middle power rather than as a small state has had profound effects for Swedish policy choices, such as a long tradition of a policy of armed neutrality and an expectation of 'being heard' in international negotiations—a policy that stands in contrast to the seemingly similar state Denmark, whose self-understanding as a small state has produced a foreign policy based on protection through alliances and close military cooperation with trusted partners.

Constructivists attach such importance to identity because to have a particular identity also implies that actors will be following the norms that are associated with the identity, which suggests that some forms of action are more appropriate than others. As norms specify behaviour, it is clear that a normative structure will define certain forms of behaviour as appropriate and others as not. Therefore constructivism stands in contrast to realism and liberalism by assuming that people are not simply led by assumed interests based on rational cost–benefit calculations, but that they will consider options for action reflexively and consider whether the action is appropriate for their identity.

March and Olsen (1989) include both logics of action in their analysis of political institutions. They agree with realists and liberals who think that action is driven, in their words, by a 'logic of consequences'. In this logic the assumption is that agents calculate the consequences of a particular course of action and will choose the action that offers them the most utility. However, they contend that actors may also act from a 'logic of appropriateness', where the assumption is that as agents are rule followers, they will try to follow rules that associate particular identities to particular situations (Risse 2003: 163), and they will consider which action is the most appropriate behaviour for them. The two logics are useful for understanding the kind of reflections that precede foreign policy action, but they should not be seen as exclusive to each other. Constructivists assume that agents will try to do the right thing in accordance with their identity, but they acknowledge that much will depend on the context of the situation, or indeed that some actions may simply be the result of habit. The point is that it cannot *always* be assumed that *all agents only* utilize the 'logic of consequence'. (See Box 4.4.)

Agents, structure, and practice

The fourth key feature of constructivism is the claim that structures and agents are mutually constituted. This is a view that is based on the work known as **structuration** by Anthony Giddens, which holds that structures influence agents, but that agents are also able to influence structure through their practice. As has been shown in relation to all four core propositions of constructivism, constructivists place a great deal of importance on the role of routinized practice. It is through practice that social facts are externalized and habitualized, and thereby ensured an independent existence from the agents who first constructed the social fact, and it is through practice that institutions such as self-help or cooperation become embedded. However, once it is embedded as taken for granted day-to-day routines, practice will not only underpin the existence of social facts and institutions, but may also be constitutive of structure and identity (Adler 2008: 196). Moreover, it is through practice that a stable cognitive environment is ensured, which is itself what reinforces the individual's identity and provides agents with confidence that their cognitive world will be reproduced. This is of relevance for the prospects for effecting change from one culture of anarchy to another.

BOX 4.4 Logics of action

Since the elections in Burma and the subsequent release of Aung San Suu Kyi from house arrest in 2011, the prospects for political change seem to have improved significantly. Regardless of the (as yet uncertain) outcome, the new situation has called for reconsiderations of foreign policy and diplomatic relations with Burma. It seems clear that states' foreign policy considerations are influenced by 'logics of consequence' as well as 'logics of appropriateness'.

Imagine that a liberal state and a strong supporter of human rights and a supporter of the economic sanctions imposed on Burma since 1997 is now reconsidering its foreign policy options *vis-à-vis* a Burma which shows strong, though not irreversible, signs of political change. The liberal state might have the following considerations.

New investments in Burma have been prohibited since 1997, with detrimental economic consequences for Burma and for foreign investors. However, in the context of the global financial crisis (GFC), and with the prospects of political change in Burma, the negative consequences of economic sanctions have become less tolerable, whilst the reasons for maintaining economic sanctions are less convincing. Therefore our liberal state might conclude that the costs of maintaining economic sanctions are greater than any further political benefits to be achieved through political sanctions. The logic would suggest lifting, or at least easing, the economic sanctions.

Burma has a huge potential as a tourist destination, yet during the years of political isolation and economic sanctions, tourism in Burma has been regarded as inappropriate because travel there was seen as an implicit support of the military regime. However, with the signs of political change, 'responsible' tourism is viewed as a means of supporting local communities economically and of increasing social and cultural exchanges between Burma and the outside world. Therefore tourism in Burma would no longer constitute inappropriate action.

What other considerations from a 'logic of consequence' and from a 'logic of appropriateness' might be part of a process of reformulating the foreign policy of a liberal state *vis-à-vis* Burma. What would be the position on human rights?

The logic of structuration assumes a *mutually* constitutive relationship between agent and structure. Yet, as argued by Ted Hopf, constructivism effectively places a premium on structure, because although structuration logically implies the possibility of change through agents' practice, constructivists also assume that agents reproduce their own constraints through daily practice (Hopf 1998: 180). Therefore, from this perspective, constructivists conclude that although change is possible, it is difficult to bring about. This view is reiterated by Jeffrey Checkel, who contends that the causal arrows in constructivism mainly go one way—from structure to agent—because constructivists, despite their arguments about mutually constituting agents and structure, have focused on structure-centred approaches in their empirical work (Checkel 1998: 342). Indeed, constructivism has difficulty in explaining where the powerful structures (norms) come from and why and how they change over time (Checkel 1998: 339).[5] Moreover, the mutual constitution, which clearly implies a causal flow from agents to structures, is precisely where foreign policy to effect change is located. This suggests that, for constructivism to be really useful as an analytical framework for foreign policy, more sustained attention to agency is needed. This is precisely why there is a need for 'actor-specific' complements to constructivism (as suggested by Valerie Hudson in Chapter One) such as psychological and cognitive influences on decision makers.

Foreign policy is by definition an agent-level activity, performed by various policy makers (agents) within both domestic and international environments and therefore responsive to the structures of both. The fact that foreign policy makers are subject to at least two sets of structural influences complicates the task of FPA significantly. Moreover, it is clear that the actions which foreign policy makers are engaged in, and which are the very focus of analysis in FPA, are often *not* routinized social practices for externalizing particular normative structures, but on the contrary non-routine actions designed to effect change. Yet, as we have seen, the power of social practices rests in their capacity to reproduce and thus to reify the inter-subjective meanings that constitute social structures and actors alike (Hofp, 1998: 178), and not in their power to effect change. In fact, some cognitive constructivists would point to the fact that actors will have a profound reluctance to change what is a reassuringly stable situation (Giddens 1991). It stands to reason that if humans aim to minimize uncertainty and anxiety and prefer always to confirm their existing beliefs about the social world, they also prefer stability to change. This is a finding that echoes the findings from FPA research on belief systems, which seemed to suggest highly unyielding beliefs among foreign policy makers.

As can be seen from the above, constructivists place a great deal of importance on the role of routinized practice. It is through practice that social facts are externalized and habitualized, and thereby ensured an independent existence from the agents who first constructed the social fact. However, once practice is embedded as taken-for-granted day-to-day routines, it will not only underpin the existence of social facts, but may also be constitutive of structure and identity (Adler 2008: 196). Furthermore, it is through practice that a stable cognitive environment is ensured, which may also reinforce the individual's identity and provide agents with confidence that their cognitive world will be reproduced. This is of relevance for the prospects of effecting change from one culture of anarchy to another—a point that was acknowledged by Wendt as he pointed to the self-perpetuating quality and path dependency of institutions such as self-help, rivalry, or cooperation. Therefore although it is through practice that the mutually constitutive relationship between agency and structure is operationalized, and it is through practice that change is made possible, it is also because of the very same practices that change is difficult to achieve. Clearly these are dilemmas which have important implications for foreign policy and for the prospects of changing a culture of anarchy.

Two questions arise out of the above: how to understand foreign policy, and how to undertake intentional transformation. The first question is important because if foreign policy is a practice, then logically change through foreign policy will be an almost impossible undertaking for the reasons outlined above. On the other hand, foreign policy can also be understood as 'action', which is agent behaviour that is linked to intention and directed at a specific goal (Taylor 1964). Foreign policy clearly contains both pre-intentional practice based on taken-for-granted routines (Swidler 2001), but it also contains intentional action based on conscious decision making and reflexive processes designed to achieve a specific goal which may well be a change from the status quo. Therefore in order to be fully able to utilize constructivism for the analysis of foreign policy, it is necessary to distinguish between 'foreign policy as practice' and 'foreign policy as action'.

The second question is important because if both structures and agent-level practice imply a tendency for stability rather than change, it is necessary to ask under what conditions change through intentional foreign policy might take place. This is a complicated question, which all IR theories grapple with, and which can only be briefly touched on here. However,

BOX 4.5 Practice and action in foreign policy

It is useful to distinguish between practice-based foreign policy and action-based foreign policy. Practice-based foreign policy draws on practice seen as 'unconscious or automatic activities embedded in taken-for-granted routines' (Swidler 2001: 84) contributing towards stability rather than as a factor contributing towards change. Change will take place mainly as a result of disruptive events, but can also take place gradually through changes in agent practice or through persuasion and argument (Risse 2000; Crawford 2002). Practice-based foreign policy is performed mainly through diplomatic embedded practices and conventions where, for example, the rule of sovereign recognition is reproduced in every diplomatic dispatch and ambassadorial handshake (Dunne and Koivisto 2010). Action-based foreign policy, on the other hand, is behaviour that is intentional, reflexive, and related to a specific goal (Taylor 1964). Action-based foreign policy is performed mainly through foreign policy decisions intended to solve a problem or to introduce new thinking, such as the adoption by the UN Security Council of the Responsibility to Protect, a principle which is intended as a policy to change the established sovereignty-related practice of non-intervention. Therefore action-based foreign policy is sometimes an initial step towards changing practice. Both are crucial for understanding foreign policy, but they are not always easily separated.

the implication of the above analysis is that transformative change is most likely to follow a disruptive event, which has made existing structures and existing shared meanings seem inadequate for the new situation. Constructivists speak of a situation of cognitive inconsistency following a so-called 'critical juncture', meaning that agents' cognitive environment no longer makes sense to them and that existing rules and norms can no longer be used as a cognitive map for identifying appropriate behaviour. Even agents' sense of self and other may have become unclear. In such a situation new structures of knowledge and identity can be adopted, which in turn can open up a window of opportunity for intentional policy change through the adoption of new rules followed by changes in practice, identity formations, and the reconstitution of shared knowledge. In such cases the possibility exists for changing embedded institutions in one culture of anarchy to a different logic of anarchy. (See Box 4.5.)

Constructivism meets foreign policy

The chapter started out by pointing to realism's and liberalism's limited expectations for NATO in the post Cold War security environment. The limited role envisaged for NATO is puzzling because NATO has always been more than just a defence alliance, with its role defined by NATO's first Secretary General, Lord Ismay, as 'keeping the Russians out, the Americans in, and the Germans down'. Formulated a little more diplomatically and using constructivist terminology we might say that NATO's post Cold War roles could be defined as (1) still keeping member states safe from threats to their security, (2) still maintaining a common identity, shared knowledge, and shared understandings among all its members, and (3) still engaging in transforming relationships and practices between NATO members and former adversaries through the socialization of appropriate behaviour for NATO membership. In other words, NATO's roles after the end of the Cold War remained pretty much the same, but with different conceptions of self and other and with more states becoming acquainted with the rules and norms of the Alliance and learning appropriate behaviour.[6]

Keeping NATO members safe

NATO came out of the Cold War with a major identity crisis and a deep sense of cognitive inconsistency as it was clear that its established practices and shared knowledge about the world no longer provided the necessary cognitive map as a guide for appropriate behaviour. From a constructivist perspective, NATO was faced with an existential crisis (a critical juncture) which, although experienced as unpleasant, could facilitate transformative change to be undertaken. The depth of the crisis must have concentrated the mind because within a relatively short timespan NATO had redefined itself as a more political alliance and the threat was reformulated as political instability and uncertainty. Not only was this an example of reconstitution of NATO's own identity and its understanding of 'the other', but it also turned out to be a very precise prediction, vindicated by the Yugoslavian tragedy that unfolded on the European continent throughout the 1990s. As suggested by Shea (2010), amidst the tragedy of the situation 'the Balkans were good for NATO' because the conflicts allowed NATO to undertake foreign policy action, which reinforced its new identity as a European security and foreign policy actor, and which allowed it to establish new security practices based on the new structural environment such as the ability to 'go out of area'.

Although NATO's foreign policy actions since the Balkans have been less successful, especially in its operation in Afghanistan, it has now fundamentally altered its identity from an old-fashioned static defence alliance to a modern expeditionary security organization and has altered its policy making from a practice-based to an action-based foreign policy *vis-à-vis* a growing number of external security challenges. This has necessitated internal processes to establish new shared knowledge and interpretations of NATO's founding document, the North Atlantic Treaty, where NATO's role is now defined as protecting members' *security* rather than members' *territory*. Therefore if NATO members' security is challenged through events in, for example, Afghanistan, Libya, or the Gulf of Aden, the new shared understanding of the founding treaty and of NATO's identity and role suggests a foreign and security policy role for the Alliances in such places.

Maintaining shared understandings

NATO has always been overtly concerned with maintaining Alliance cohesion—especially between the European and North American components. Without such cohesion the nuclear guarantee would not be credible and NATO's major commitment that 'a threat against one member is a threat against all' would simply not be credible. Therefore, to be able to show unity, NATO has engaged in a practice of intensive negotiation prior to all decisions, which all had to be agreed in unity. The extensive practical cooperation has reinforced a 'culture of anarchy' among the member states based on friendship and shared values and shared understandings of what constitutes appropriate action.

This is a process that can best be conceptualized as an internal process of socialization of Western norms and shared values and appropriate behaviour for member states. The process has been ongoing throughout NATO's history, starting with the enlargements to include Greece and Turkey in 1952, West Germany in 1955, Spain in 1982, and twelve further enlargements after the Cold War. All new members have entered the Alliance with considerable 'baggage', without a fully constituted democratic norm set, and with issues relating to being able or willing to follow a 'logic of appropriateness' for a NATO member. These internal processes of socialization have been highly successful as new members have acquired the new norm set reasonably fast, and (generally speaking) have behaved appropriately within the context of NATO membership and engaged in extensive cooperation resulting in fundamentally altered security and foreign policy practices—not just within NATO, but individually as well. It seems fair to say that these internal processes of socialization are perhaps NATO's most important foreign policy achievements, albeit that they are often overlooked as examples of foreign policy.

Reconstitution of new social relationships

Just as NATO has always been engaged in the construction of shared knowledge and maintaining a unified identity, early in its history it became involved in the task of establishing new relationships and new practices for interaction and appropriate behaviour. Therefore NATO was as much a forum for establishing and cementing peaceful relations and new social relationships with new practices among the European member states, as it was a defence alliance designed 'to keep the Soviets out'.

From a constructivist perspective, the end of the Cold War was a critical juncture which presented NATO with new opportunities as a socializing agent for establishing new social relationships and changed practices. Much like the situation with Ego and Alter on the beach (Box 4.1), NATO was in a situation where different 'futures' were possible depending on its actions and the response of the Soviet Union and former Warsaw Pact members. The action chosen by NATO in June 1990 was to 'stretch out the hand of friendship'[7] to the countries in Central and Eastern Europe. This chosen role was subsequently followed up with practice and action with the establishment in December 1991 of the North Atlantic Cooperation Council (NACC) in which all former adversaries participated, followed in 1994 with the Partnership for Peace (PfP) programme, and culminating in 1999 with membership for the Czech Republic, Poland, and Hungary, as well as the establishment of the Membership Action Plan (MAP) which was a consultation programme for prospective members. The point here is that all these initiatives can be seen as examples of a NATO foreign policy designed to effect change through the socialization of states that were not members of NATO, and which might never become members of NATO (Gheciu 2005). The process has been one of mutual constitution as NATO has presented a number of options and expectations, and the prospective members have then defined their relationship with NATO through their actions and engagement. Although a dozen countries have already joined NATO, the process is by no means finished.

NATO recently also opened up for enhanced cooperation with Russia on missile defence and other defence-related issues, whilst at the same time announcing that it will develop a missile defence system. The situation bears a close resemblance to the example in Box 4.1 with Ego and Alter on the beach. An announcement that NATO was adopting a missile defence within a social context of enmity would almost certainly have been detrimental to NATO–Russia relations. However, within a social context of planned cooperation and shared understandings about the missile defence, a situation of (limited) cooperation may be facilitated. It is hoped that this important foreign policy initiative will result in a radically changed relationship with Russia, by changing the relationship from one based on rivalry to one based on cooperation in policy areas where both are believed to have shared interests and shared security concerns. Should the initiative turn out to be successful (which is far from certain), it may have the potential not only for fundamentally changing security practices between NATO and Russia, but also for effecting important structural change.

Conclusion

From a constructivist perspective, it is clear that over the past two decades NATO has followed a constructivist foreign policy by continuing its efforts to establish a culture of anarchy based on friendship and cooperation among its members and a growing number of partners, whilst at the same time maintaining its role identity as a defence alliance. In focusing only on this latter role, realism saw NATO's years as numbered, because it is precisely within this role that NATO was most challenged by the end of the Cold War, and where it has had to undertake significant change in its conceptions of self and other and work hardest on establishing new shared knowledge and redefining appropriate behaviour. The statist nature of realism lacked the conceptual tools for seeing such change as possible. The two traditionally dominant theories also lacked a conceptual toolbox enabling NATO's foreign policy to be understood as being not only about material capabilities and interest-based cooperation, but also about the continuous reconstitution of identities and shared knowledge, reinforced through security practices that facilitate a culture of anarchy based on friendship and cooperation rather than on rivalry or enmity.

Constructivism has come a long way in the last couple of decades, and even foreign policy practitioners have since acknowledged the role of NATO, and similar international organizations, as agents for effecting change—not through force but through normative power and the ability to change long-held identities and embedded practices. Therefore the answer to the question posed by Stephen Walt—about why students and practitioners of foreign policy should care about abstract theories such as constructivism—is that they have considerable explanatory power in relation to the durability of institutions. At the same time, to ignore constructivism as a guide to foreign policy practice is to overlook policy alternatives to the standard claim that there is no alternative to the rational pursuit of the national interest.

 Key points

- Constructivism offers different understandings of some of the most central themes in foreign policy making, and implies different policy options from the two mainstream theories.

- Constructivists ask how old practices of rivalry and war making can be changed through institutionalization, which might over time change identities, interests, and practices.

- Constructivism asks where interests come from and assumes that different identities will have different interests, which will lead to different foreign policies.

- One of the central features of constructivism holds that people act towards objects (including other people) on the basis of the meanings that the object (or person) has for them.

- Constructivists see structure as material *and* ideational, where ideational structures are codified in formal rules and norms which agents are socialized into following.

- Constructivism assumes a mutually constitutive relationship between agent and structure, although the influence of structures on agents has been in the forefront of constructivist theorizing.

- Constructivists reject the assumption that agents always calculate the consequences of their actions, but argue that they will also consider which action is the most appropriate for their identity, even if such action may have costly consequences.

 ## Questions

1. Why should students and practitioners take note of constructivism?

2. Why is constructivism sometimes called an approach rather than a theory?

3. Why does self-help not necessarily follow logically from anarchy?

4. What are social facts?

5. Why is shared knowledge so important to constructivists?

6. Why is identity such an important concept in constructivism?

7. Why are rules and norms so important to constructivists?

8. What is meant by the phrase 'The social construction of reality'?

9. What is the role of 'practice' in constructivist theorizing and how should it be distinguished from 'action'?

10. What is the relationship between structures (ideas, norms, material facts) and agents (people, states, international organizations) in constructivist thinking?

 ## Further reading

Adler, E. (2002), 'Constructivism and International Relations', in W. Calsnaes, T. Risse, and B. Simmons (eds), *Handbook of International Relations*: 95–118 (London, Sage Publications).
In this essay Adler provides a very detailed and in-depth overview and introduction to constructivism. It is quite a difficult text, but well worth reading.

Adler, E. (2008), 'The Spread of Security Communities: Communities of Practice, Self-Restraint and NATO's Post Cold War Transformation', *European Journal of International Relations*, 14: 195–230.
This article applies a constructivist and practice theory approach to NATO in the post Cold War period.

Checkel, J. (1998), 'The Constructivist Turn in International Relations Theory', *World Politics*, 50: 324–8.
Although a review article of three constructivist books, the article gives an excellent outline of constructivism and draws attention to constructivism's lack of focus on agents.

Hopf, T. (1998), 'The Promise of Constructivism in International Relations Theory', *International Security*, 23, 171–200.
An excellent article which clearly outlines the difference between conventional and post-modern constructivisms.

Wendt, A. (1992), 'Anarchy Is What States Make of It: The Social Construction of Power Politics', *International Organization*, 46: 391–421.
This is the article that most clearly sets out anarchy as practice, and which gives a full account of the three cultures of anarchy.

 Visit the Online Resource Centre that accompanies this book for more information:
www.oxfordtextbooks.co.uk/orc/smith_foreign/

Discourse analysis, post-structuralism, and foreign policy

LENE HANSEN

Chapter contents

 ## Reader's guide

This chapter provides an introduction to how discourse analysis can be used to study foreign policy. Within International Relations, discourse analysis is associated with post-structuralism, a theoretical approach which shares realism's concern with states and power, but differs from realism's assumption that states are driven by self-interest. It also takes a wider view of power than realists normally do. Post-structuralists hold that states, and other political entities, strive to uphold particular visions of themselves and that they do so through policy discourses. Foreign policy discourse plays a crucial role in the construction of these visions as it draws a line between the state and what makes up its identity on the one hand, and that which is different from and outside the scope of the state on the other. Taking post-structuralist assumptions to the study of foreign policy, this perspective implies a focus on the way that foreign policy decisions are legitimated or undermined within the wider public sphere. Epistemologically and methodologically, to understand foreign policy as discourse implies analysis of texts, and this chapter lays out the most important insights and challenges that come with this form of analysis.

Introduction

Discourse analysis has been brought into the discipline of International Relations (IR) and its subfield of Foreign Policy Analysis (FPA) by scholars from the IR approach known as post-structuralism. The first post-structuralist works appeared in the 1980s when scholars like Ashley (1987), Der Derian (1987), Walker (1987), and Shapiro (1988) used the theories developed by post-structuralist philosophers, most prominently Michel Foucault and Jacques Derrida, to draw attention to the power of language. The concept that post-structuralists used to emphasize this power was discourse—that is, in short, linguistic systems through which meaning is generated (Foucault 1974: 38). Or, as Doty (1996: 6) puts it, 'A discourse delineates the terms of intelligibility whereby a particular "reality" can be known and acted upon'.

Using the concept of discourse, post-structuralists show that the distinction between international relations and domestic politics is neither given nor based on objective features within these two realms, but that it is maintained through academic and policy discourses and practices. More directly, foreign policies are dependent upon particular representations of the countries, places, and people that such policies are assisting or deterring, as well as on representations of the national or institutional Self that undertakes these policies. Post-structuralists are keen to point out that language is not a transparent medium that simply conveys the empirical world, but rather, as Shapiro (1988: 11) states it, is 'a kind of practice'. As a consequence, one should ask not whether statements are true or not, but which values, norms, and identities are being created in language. Language has 'political power', not because it is always clear what is being said, but because it is 'a medium of both communication and mystification' (Walker 1986: 495).

These assumptions about the power of language underpinned the introduction of discourse analysis into IR. There was a need for an IR perspective, post-structuralists argued, that theorizes foreign policy as a discursive practice and which uses those theories to produce critical analysis of the way in which states and international institutions construct their foreign policies and, through them, their own and others' identities. Post-structuralism first came to the field of IR in the mid-1980s, a time when the Cold War had reached a heightened intensity following the Soviet Union's invasion of Afghanistan. Many scholars, particularly in Security Studies, were deeply concerned not just with the analytics but with the politics of nuclear deterrence, and post-structuralists shared that concern. They argued, for example, that US President Ronald Reagan's famous description of the Soviet Union as an 'evil empire' was a striking indication of the power that discursive representations asserted. But post-structuralists were not confining themselves to the study of global security. Underdevelopment, colonialism, and North–South economic relations were also on the research agenda.

The arrival of post-structuralism and discourse analysis did not go unnoticed. In a landmark article taking stock of Security Studies in 1991, Walt warned against the field being 'seduced' by post-structuralism, holding that it is 'a prolix and self-indulgent discourse that is divorced from the real world' and that it is 'mostly criticism and not much theory' (Walt 1991: 223). At the time of Walt's writing, what was at stake was not so much that post-structuralists abstained from analysis of 'the real world' or building 'theory', but rather that there were fundamental disagreements as to what 'the real' and 'theory' were. Such debates have continued and may not be resolved as they concern deeper ontological and epistemological differences.

During the 1990s and 2000s, post-structuralism expanded theoretically and empirically through an engagement with issues on the contemporary political agenda, including the ethics and politics of humanitarian interventions (Campbell 1998), European integration and identity formation (Neumann 1999; Hansen and Wæver 2002), and the War on Terror (Walker 2006). Post-structuralism has been and is, in short, driven by current events, arguably more so in the field of security than constructivism (Buzan and Hansen 2009: 219). This attention to foreign policy decisions and processes in 'the real world' provides an empirical meeting ground between discourse analysis and other forms of FPA.

To say that there is a strong nexus between post-structuralism and discourse analysis in IR is to underscore that discourse analysis is not simply a technique or methodology, but part of a larger substantial approach to foreign policy and international relations. One should note, though, that not all post-structuralists work exclusively with discourse analysis—there are, for example, those who take a more psychoanalytical approach drawing on Jacques Lacan (Epstein 2011)—and that discourse analysis comes in other forms than the post-structuralist one associated with Foucault which is dominant in IR and therefore the focus of this chapter (Titscher *et al.* 2000). Many constructivists (see Chapter Four) are also analysing linguistic processes, and the boundary between them and post-structuralism is sometimes blurred (see, for example, Weldes 1999), but the institutional and sociological trajectories that have anchored these two perspectives in IR vary, and their theorization of language and identity are also not identical (Buzan and Hansen 2009: 199). This is particularly true for those constructivists who draw on the work of the German philosopher Jürgen Habermas.

Because of the nexus between discourse analysis and post-structuralism, we need to have a good sense of the kind of an IR approach that post-structuralism is before moving to how discourse analysis is applied in empirical studies of foreign policy. This is also important because post-structuralism is often presented as the most radical or non-mainstream perspective on the terrain of IR (Adler 1997). The first part of this chapter shows that one should take this description with a pinch of salt because post-structuralism was developed in part through a critical engagement with the realist tradition and it shares this tradition's concern with power and state sovereignty. The next part of the chapter turns to the more concrete theoretical principles that inform post-structuralist discourse analysis. It also looks at the research designs and methodological techniques that discourse analysts use, and it offers a series of examples and four learning boxes featuring mini-case studies. The conclusion sums up, locates post-structuralist discourse analysis in relation to the field of FPA, and discusses the strengths and weaknesses of post-structuralist discourse analysis.

Post-structuralism

Chapter Two began by pointing out that 'Realism is the foundational school of thought about international politics around which all others are oriented'. This statement is perhaps nowhere as apt as in the case of post-structuralism. Going back to the 1980s, authors like Ashley (1981), Der Derian (1987), and Walker (1987) were deeply engaged with the realist tradition and they expressed great sympathy for what they saw as the historically sensitive and philosophically rich tradition of classical realism. In contrast, they were critical of the universalizing, structuralist, and positivist stance of neorealism. Thus a good way to introduce post-structuralism is to point out how it draws upon, but also challenges, realism's three core assumptions laid out in Chapter Two: groupism, egoism, and power-centrism.

Groupism—from universality to historicity

Realism assumes that humans gather in groups to survive and that such groups need to be glued together by 'we-feelings'. Post-structuralism agrees that the state stands at the core of modern political life, and it adds that state sovereignty implies, in Walker's words, a separation between the 'inside' of the state and the international on the 'outside' (Walker 1993). The inside–outside distinction has a territorial component, beginning with the Peace of Westphalia in 1648, and it implies that states have the sovereign authority to make, implement, and enforce decisions within their own borders. No similar authority exists above the state. But state sovereignty is not only a description of the alignment of states and territories, it installs two fundamentally different ways of thinking about politics. Domestically, we have an ordered public sphere, a social contract that makes governments and parliaments legitimate and responsible, and individuals who accept that they cannot take the law into their own hands. Between states there is no similar social contract, realists maintain, and 'politics' is replaced by the reign of power.

The domestic social contract may be an idealized rather than accurate description, and states have repeatedly sought to enforce 'order' upon other states through either institutional collaboration or physical violence. Yet, hold post-structuralists, the *idea* of politics as fundamentally different inside and outside is effective in that it is the benchmark which is consistently invoked and against which transgressions are compared. As Weber (1995) argues, military and political interventions may at first seem to undermine sovereignty, at least for the state being subject to intervention. Yet interventions do uphold sovereignty as a political principle. Most interventions are legitimated as defending the sovereignty of a 'people' threatened by 'its' government, or as supporting the sovereignty of leaders who are under illegitimate 'attack' by domestic rebels or foreign forces; additionally, military interventions help to strengthen the sovereign status of the intervening powers. At the general level, post-structuralists hold that the power of the inside–outside distinction resides in its ability to provide a compelling answer to the question of 'who we are'—i.e. 'citizens of particular states who have the potential to work toward universal standards of conduct by participating in statist political communities' (Walker 1990: 12).

There is considerable resonance between realism's groupism assumption and post-structuralism's account of the inside–outside distinction, but there are also three important ways in which post-structuralism breaks with realism. First, realists see no need to problematize the groupism assumption, whereas post-structuralists hold that the assumption is only 'there' because it is sustained through practices. Such practices include academic practices ranging from the way that classical philosophical treatises are being used to support claims about human nature, order, and conflict to contemporary theories about international relations and foreign policy practices that reproduce the inside–outside distinction's self-evident status (Campbell 1992).

Second, post-structuralists hold that realism's groupism assumption must be historicized, because to describe Neolithic tribes, medieval empires, and modern nation-states as all being 'groups' hides the true diversity of political life. In the words of Ashley (1987: 419), we are prevented from seeing our current world of state sovereignty as 'a historically effected mode of political community vying with other modes and owing its precarious existence to historical practices and the strategic play of power'. Offering a historically sensitive analysis, Walker (1990: 10) points out that the principle of hierarchical subordination, which preceded state sovereignty, permitted 'an understanding of the world as a continuum from low to high, from the many to the few, from God's creatures to God, from the temporal to the eternal'. Rather than distinct national spaces where citizens (or some of them) are equal, medieval Europe was organized as one large political space with individuals arranged in hierarchies. Comparing the medieval principle of hierarchical subordination with that of modern state sovereignty one also finds two different forms of foreign policy: the sovereign state conducting its foreign policy towards other states, and a more messy medieval set of political and religious authorities conducting 'foreign' policy within and between empires. To point to the historical specificity of state sovereignty is also to hold that it might change. Looking to the future, post-structuralists use medieval hierarchical subordination to argue that one universal world order is problematic because it is unlikely that we could have a political community without some form of hierarchy. State sovereignty locates 'difference' on the outside, whereas hierarchical subordination situates it on the inside by arguing that there are natural hierarchies between categories of people within an empire or imperial system.

Third, post-structuralists challenge realism's grounding of its groupism assumption in philosophical principles, human nature, or historical recurrence. The inside–outside distinction 'works', holds post-structuralism, not because it identifies 'how the world is', but because the domestic and international are defined as the radical opposite of each other—by referring to each other, they stabilize their existence (Ashley 1987). This argument draws upon the work of the French philosopher Derrida who held that language should be viewed as a semiotic structure where words only obtain their meaning as they are juxtaposed to what they are not. Yet, in contrast with structural linguistics, which assumed such sign systems to be relatively stable, Derrida emphasized that these systems were inherently unstable and thus in need of support. In terms of the inside–outside distinction, this implies that the outside is known as the radical opposite of the inside and, vice versa, the inside is only meaningful because it is the antitheses of the outside. Foreign policies, and theories about them, are required to keep this distinction in place.

Egoism—from human nature to performativity

The second assumption that realism makes is that self-interest motivates political behaviour and that egoism is rooted in human nature. Post-structuralists agree in so far as they see politics, including foreign policy, as driven by interests, but they hold that such interests are discursive, that is they are articulated in language by foreign policy actors who hold that, say, going to war against al-Qaeda or protecting the domestic automobile industry is in the American interest. As summed up by Weldes (1999: 15) 'National interests . . . are social constructions that emerge out of a ubiquitous and unavoidable process of representation'. Post-structuralists hold in a similar way that 'intentions' are constituted in discourse, rather than something that actors have prior to foreign policy practices. Post-structuralists are also critical of the assumption that human nature is egoistic and the intertwined assumption that humans are rational.

It is important to stress that post-structuralism's critique is not empirical-psychological, i.e. post-structuralists are not claiming that humans are really altruistic or irrational. Post-structuralism 'does not try to get to the thoughts or motives of the actors, their hidden intentions or secret plans' (Wæver 2002: 26), but focuses on public texts. The post-structuralist point is rather that the egoism–altruism and rationality–irrationality dichotomies are being deployed in ways that come to structure our ability to think about foreign policy in much the same way as the inside–outside distinction does. Such dichotomies have a long tradition as being the taken-for-granted foundation for philosophical arguments as well as more con-crete statements about international relations. Post-structuralists seek through deconstruc-tion to bring out the 'cultural contingency' of such dichotomies and thereby challenge their unquestioned power (Gregory 1989: xvi). Deconstruction involves two moves. It shows, first, how paired concepts depend upon each other and how one is valued as superior to the other. It then shows how the seemingly inferior concept is 'superior' in the sense of being required for the superior concept to 'work'. This leads, for example, to the conclusion that rational man and the irrationality of the international depend upon each other (Ashley 1989).

Taking post-structuralism's deconstruction of realism's assumptions about human nature from the level of the individual to that of the state and its foreign policy, the state is seen as a subject constituted in discourse. This implies a break with the assumption, which underpins most of FPA—that the state is a rational actor or subject given prior to foreign policy decisions (for an exception see Chapter Fourteen). Campbell (1992: 8) advocates instead that 'foreign policy be understood as a political practice central to the constitution, production, and main-tenance of [American] political identity'. In other words, foreign policy plays a central role in producing not just the boundary between inside and outside, but the 'we' who enact foreign policy. Because post-structuralism came into IR during the 1980s when relations between East and West were tense, it was at first much concerned with those identity dynamics where the national or alliance Self was constituted in relation to a radically different Other. The cen-tral example was that of the USA and NATO on the one hand, and the Soviet Union and the Warsaw Pact on the other. Taking the history of the USA as a case in point, Campbell argued that while identity need not in principle require something that was radically Other, only something that was different, in the case of the state there was a 'temptation to treat differ-ence as otherness' (Campbell 1992: 56). This led to a larger debate within post-structuralism on whether states needed enemies in order to be. For example, Neumann (1996) and Milliken (1999b) held that to see the state as requiring enemies or radical Others would lead to too monolithic a conception of the Other. It might also cause discourse analysts to overlook for-eign policies—or elements within them—which were more nuanced and less Othering (Buzan and Hansen 2009: 218–19). It also raised the question of what forms 'the Other' could take. For instance, Wæver (1996: 122) argued that 'Europe's Other is Europe's own past which should not be allowed to become its future'. This in turn generated the possibility that foreign policy could be constructed around overcoming violence within rather than on 'the outside'.

As the example of Europe shows, there might be historically powerful accounts that as-cribe a particular identity to a given state—or other foreign policy subjects such as NATO—but identity is never given independently of discourse. In other words, identities are invoked as the precondition for foreign policy decisions and implementations, for example by the claim that 'we are going to war against the Taleban to protect the liberal values that define who we are'. Yet such identities are also only established as they are invoked as the precondition for action. Theoretically, identity is in short, following post-structuralist theorist Judith Butler (1990: 25), performative—it is 'constituted by the very "expressions" that are said to be its re-sults'. This understanding of identity sets post-structuralism aside from those constructivists like Wendt (1999: 224–8) who theorize identity as comprising elements that are pre-social or intrinsic. For post-structuralists, identity is always social and discursively constituted. Thus where constructivists explain phenomena such as NATO's post Cold War survival by the institution's liberal values and identity (Risse-Kappen 1996), post-structuralists ask which threats, values, and identities were being invoked by central foreign policy actors as the reason why NATO is and should be surviving (Constantinou 1995; see also Chapter Four). Because identity is theorized as performative in post-structuralist discourse analysis, it cannot operate as an explanation, nor can it be tested against other 'variables' explaining foreign policy decisions or behaviour.

Post-structuralism's concern with how identity is being constituted also leads to a broad view of what foreign policy is. For example, Campbell analyses not only Foreign Policy—the traditional domain of FPA—but foreign policy, that is the practices through which 'otherness' is constituted in relation to 'our' identity. Such 'little foreign policies' might be restricted to the domestic arena, but they might also link up with Foreign Policy as when communism and homosexuality were linked in Cold War US discourse (Campbell 1992: 176). Post-structuralism's view of foreign policy as reliant upon discourses that produce and maintain identity also implies a critical concern with who becomes marginalized in foreign policy making, i.e. with those who are formally bared from the venues where decisions are taken or who might lack the resources to engage in public debates. But post-structuralism is also asking which subject positions are being made available and who is marginalized as a result. For example, women who are sex trafficked are frequently referred to as helpless, powerless, and innocent 'victims' or as illegal immigrants. These two subject positions lock women into problematic choices between accommodating to the 'victim' position or running the risk of being criminalized (Aradau 2008).

Power—from capability to discourse

The third realist assumption is that 'Power is the fundamental feature of politics' (Chapter Two), and as the discussion above has already made clear, power is also fundamental to post-structuralists. Post-structuralists understand 'language as power' because it is through discourse that subjects, objects, actors, and identities are being constituted. As Barnett and Duvall (2005) have pointed out, this is a different way of conceptualizing power than the one we find in realism. In realism, power is understood as 'compulsory power', as control over others, and this implies a focus on 'how one state is able to use material resources to advance its interests in direct opposition to the interests of another' (Barnett and Duvall 2005: 50). Empirically, this leads to a privileging of great power analysis. Post-structuralism, by contrast, theorizes power as 'productive power', i.e. 'the constitution of all social subjects with various social powers through systems of knowledge and discursive practices of broad and general social scope' (Barnett and Duvall 2005: 55). Empirically, as noted above, this is coupled to a wider concern, not only with great powers, but also with those marginalized by the discourses of the powerful. One group of such marginalized people are those who are stateless or struggling as asylum seekers and migrants to 'get a (new) state'. Post-structuralism also takes power to be always present in that discourses inevitably constitute subjects who are variably equipped to speak with authority about a given issue. This assumption sets post-structuralists apart from those constructivists who, in the tradition of Habermas, hold that there are certain situations where 'relationships of power and social hierarchies recede in the background' (Risse 2000: 7).

Post-structuralism's conception of power as discursive, or discourses as power, has on occasion lead to two misunderstandings: that post-structuralism disregards materiality, and that it takes language to be transparent or truthful. On the question of materiality, post-structuralists agree that materiality—and expressions of materiality such as the realist 'balance of power' axiom—are important, but they hold that materiality is ascribed significance through discourse. Thus someone holding nuclear weapons—a material capability—is constructed radically differently if that 'someone' is an allied state or a terrorist group. Therefore decisions about potential acquisition of material capabilities are based on discursive constructions of who are trustworthy allies and who are enemies to be deterred. Post-structuralist discourse analysis always assumes that 'foreign policy meaning' must be ascribed to material issues, or, put differently, that materiality cannot simply generate 'its' foreign policy effects. There is no way of observing political power in ways that are not mediated by language and symbols; for example, the Soviet Union during the Cold War could not be grasped by a simplistic aggregation of its economic and military assets.

On the question of the transparency or truthfulness of language, those focusing on foreign policy behaviour often hold that 'talk is cheap': states might say one thing and do another. This, the argument goes, should caution against assigning much explanatory power to language. Post-structuralists reply in response that one should indeed be careful not to assume that language is a transparent medium that simply mirrors what goes on in the world. That said, foreign policy actors cannot dispense with providing reasons why they undertake a particular policy. For example, Western countries with troops in Afghanistan have stated that they are there in part because they want to help Afghan women. Regardless of whether this is 'just talk' or 'real', the status of Afghan women has become a topic of debate in national and international forums. In other words, language is the medium through which foreign policy actors seek to make their policies appear legitimate, necessary, and 'realistic' to their relevant audiences. Thus to what extent such audiences accept a given foreign policy or refuse to do so on the grounds that it is 'cheap' or 'incoherent' is in itself an important question.

Studying foreign policy discourses

Post-structuralism provides the theoretical foundation from which scholars move to the more concrete study of foreign policy discourses. We will now turn to how post-structuralist discourse analysis has tackled a series of more specific theoretical and analytical issues that arise when foreign policy is understood as discursive practice.

The politics of representation

In short, post-structuralists see language as the central social medium through which meaning is generated. This implies that foreign policies have to be connected, through discourse, to justification for why these policies are necessary, plausible, and possible. Foreign policy discourses must, more specifically, provide representations of the 'problem' that policies are aimed at solving (Shapiro 1988). Such representations can be of a particular head of state as laid out in Box 5.1, but they might also be of countries (think of the Soviet Union during the Cold War), wars (as ethnic hatred or genocide), or populations (of 'natives' as primitives whom 'we' help civilize through colonial rule (Doty 1996)). In other words, discourse analysis seeks to provide a 'road map' which shows as accurately as possible the main foreign policy positions and the representations that sustain them. The discursive power of representations comes out most strikingly when competing representations are mobilized, as in the case of the representation of Saddam Hussein in the lead-up to the war against Iraq in 2003 (see Box 5.1).

One should recall that discourse is an analytical concept, not something that exists 'out there' in the real world. Therefore to study the representations that legitimize foreign policies is to make analytical decisions. We need, more specifically, to identify those 'key representations' (Hansen 2006), or 'nodal points' (Laclau and Mouffe 1985), that structure debates on a foreign policy issue. Finding such representations can sometimes be rather straightforward, as in the case of Saddam Hussein, but may also require more analytical work to identify exactly which representations do most of the 'structuring'. Key representations need not be those terms that are most frequently articulated, but rather those that allow us to identify the main combinations of representations and policies, and which have the status of being 'building blocks' around which variations can be placed (Hansen 2006: 52). To take the example of the Western debate on the Bosnian War in 1992–1995, there were two key representations: of the war as a 'Balkan' war, and of the war as 'genocide' (Hansen 2006). These two

---

BOX 5.1 The productive power of representations—the case of Saddam Hussein

Representations of heads of states often play crucial roles in foreign policy debates. In the lead-up to the war against Iraq in 2003, the question was not only whether Iraq possessed weapons of mass destruction, but whether, in the apt formulation by Mearsheimer and Walt (2003: 52), 'the combination of Saddam plus nuclear weapons is too dangerous to accept'. Policy thus hinged on the materiality of weapons of mass destruction as well as the identity of Saddam Hussein. Two texts illustrate how competing representations of Hussein led to different policy recommendations. The first text, 'President George Bush Discusses Iraq in National Press Conference', found at http://georgewbush-whitehouse.archives. gov/news/releases/2003/03/20030306-8.html, constitutes Hussein as a 'direct threat' to America and to 'all free people'. His threatening status is linked to the fact that Hussein is a 'dangerous dictator' and a 'master at deception', and his regime is 'a cancer'. The likelihood that weapons of mass destruction will be used is strengthened by Hussein's 'long history of reckless aggression and terrible crimes' and his and his country's links to terrorism. The invocation of a link between 'Hussein' and 'terrorism' establishes an ambiguous affinity between the two: on the one hand, 'Hussein' is not explicitly claimed to be 'a terrorist'; on the other, his support thereof brings him close to the fundamentalism, anti-Western hatred, and irrationality of the terrorist subject. In terms of the policy options available, Bush draws the conclusion that one cannot contain Hussein, and if he fails to prove that Iraq is disarmed, then the USA must go to war. The second text, 'An Unnecessary War' by prominent realists Mearsheimer and Walt, published in the January/February issue of *Foreign Policy*, takes issue with the view that Hussein cannot be contained just like the Soviet Union was (Mearsheimer and Walt 2003: 56). The precondition for containment being a viable policy is that the subject contained is rational, i.e. it understands that an aggressive act would lead to its own destruction. Going through the political and military history of Saddam Hussein, Mearsheimer and Walt (2003: 52) argue that Hussein's 'behaviour was far from reckless' and that his willingness to stay alive and in power as well as his rationality is demonstrated by his being deterred on previous occasions (Mearsheimer and Walt 2003: 55).

representations called for two different kinds of foreign policies: preventing the West from being 'dragged into the Balkans' or making it responsible for stopping atrocities. Based on these two 'basic discourses' one can move on to analyse how variations develop, for instance how the representation of the war as a humanitarian crisis modified the Balkan discourse. One might also study the range of specific policies that a representation 'allows' in particular settings—for instance, how 'robust' should a response be to 'properly' counter 'genocide'?

The aim of foreign policy discourse analysis is, in short, to identify and analyse the main discursive structures as well as the more subtle differences and variations. We should remember that because post-structuralism sees materiality as constituted through discourse, there is not an extra-discursive realm that the truth of representations can be measured against. To continue with the example of the Bosnian War, the representation of the war as 'Balkan' was not based on how many people were killed, but on a particular reading of history. Therefore discourse analysis asks not whether a representation is true or false, but what the political implications of adopting a particular representation are.

The scope and stability of foreign policy

Discourse analysts study official foreign policies, but may also broaden the scope to include political parties not in government, the media, NGOs, and others who engage in foreign policy debates. Some even examine the way in which popular culture supports or undermines official representations. But even if one takes a narrow view of foreign policy, it is possible that texts that one would not normally think of as foreign policy texts are singled out as significant—for an example see Box 5.2.

BOX 5.2 A wide conception of foreign policy texts—the case of *Entropa*

Discourse analysts study 'normal' foreign policy texts, such as declarations and parliamentary debates, but also popular culture and images that are brought into the realm of foreign policy. One example of an 'unusual' foreign policy text is that of the artwork *Entropa*, which was commissioned by the Czech Republic to commemorate their incoming EU Presidency in January 2009. *Entropa*, which was made by the Czech artist David Cerny and hung on the Council of the European Union's building, consisted of 27 models, each referring to a member of the EU . Bulgaria was enraged over being depicted as a Turkish squat toilet, and its ambassador sent formal letters of protest to the Czech EU presidency and to Javier Solana, the Secretary General of the Council of the EU. Betina Joteva, first secretary for the Bulgarian office to the EU, said that, 'I cannot accept to see a toilet on the map of my country. This is not the face of Bulgaria' (quoted in Hines and Charter 2009). The Czech government mobilized two discourses in its response. Speaking through a discourse of diplomatic accommodation, the Deputy Prime Minister Alexandr Vondra stated, 'I apologise to Bulgaria and its government if it feels offended', and he expressed his government's willingness to remove the Bulgarian part of the sculpture, a promise which was fulfilled on 20 January, when 'Bulgaria' was covered by a black blanket (BBC News 2009). Yet, at the same time, Vondra, a former dissident, also invoked a freedom of speech discourse: 'We wanted to prove that 20 years after the fall of the Iron Curtain, there is no censorship' (BBC News 2009). The discourses of diplomatic accommodation and anti-communist freedom of speech are in tension with one another, thus showing how foreign policy makers may seek to juggle the demands of multiple audiences.

The advantage of taking a broader view that incorporates more than official foreign policy discourse is that one gains an understanding of the positions that official foreign policy has to fight off or accommodate. A broader view also provides an understanding of what competing discourses agree upon. For example, in Danish debates over the EU, one finds competing constructions of 'Europe', but an agreement that 'Denmark' is and should remain a sovereign nation-state (Hansen 2002).

The question of how stable a foreign policy discourse is might also be approached by looking more critically, or deconstructively, at the stability of official texts. As noted above, foreign policy discourses seek to present themselves as stable, i.e. the representation of 'what happens' should be consistent, and there should be a 'fit' between the foreign policy advocated and its representation. Discourse analysts look critically at how such 'stability attempts' may hide more ambiguous positions. A concrete example of how textual instability can be brought out is provided in Box 5.3.

As noted above, post-structuralist discourse analysis is bracketing intentions, and therefore we cannot say whether textual instability is intentional. What we can do is situate a given text within the context of previous texts and ask what kind of genre it belongs to. To take the example of NATO's statement on Libya analysed in Box 5.3, this is a diplomatic text and the drafting and wording of such texts is carefully attended to by foreign policy bureaucracies. Thus the instability that the statement charts is one that allows NATO members flexibility in terms of how 'Libya' is represented and thus how NATO policies might be adjusted in the future.

BOX 5.3 Textual instability—the case of NATO and Operation Unified Protector

Following in the wake of two UN Security Council Resolutions in early 2011, NATO undertook 'military action' in Libya. This operation was explained by a wealth of official texts published on NATO's homepage (www.nato.int). One of them was 'Statement on Libya following the working lunch of NATO Ministers of Foreign Affairs with non-NATO contributors to Operation Unified Protector', issued on 14 April 2011. This text is only one page, but nevertheless it provides a good illustration of how foreign policy texts might seek to incorporate instability. First, NATO is affirming 'our support' to the sovereignty, independence, territorial integrity and national unity of Libya', i.e. dividing Libya between a part run by Gaddafi and one run by those opposing Gaddafi is ruled out. As to the question of who is 'the opposition', the Statement refers in places to 'the Libyan people', but also to 'the Contact Group'. However, the relationship between these two subjects is unstable. Is 'the Contact Group' the (only) legitimate representative of 'the Libyan people' or is there a split between this political institution and 'the people'? The statement abstains from a further discussion, which seems sensible given that the ability of the Contact Group 'to represent' 'the people' is difficult to assess empirically. However, as a textual instability it leaves the part of 'the people' who might be in support of Gaddafi or in opposition to Gaddafi as well as the Contact Group in a political limbo. Second, the statement is also ambiguous on what conditions in Libya NATO is trying to remedy. It begins by referring to 'the continuing violence and atrocities in Libya perpetrated by the regime against its own people', and this constitution of 'what happens' accomplishes two things: it defines the situation as one of extreme transgressions ('atrocities'), and it attributes political responsibility to Gaddafi's regime. Moving to the closing sentence of the statement, 'atrocities' have been replaced by the less dramatic 'crisis', and there is no longer a political agent that has brought this situation about. As a consequence the demand for action is lessened.

Change and genealogy

Our account of representations and foreign policy has so far proceeded as if this was set on a rather static terrain, but foreign policy is, like all policy making, dynamic. What falls within the gambit of foreign policy changes over time, and the policy on a given issue often shifts in the time that passes from when the issue appears on the agenda of decision makers and until it is—or can be claimed to having been—solved. A dynamic discourse analysis traces the way in which discourses wax and wane, i.e. how policy makers change their representations of 'the problem' and 'the policy' as events unfold. There are two main routes through which shifts in foreign policy are produced. The first route goes through pressure at the level of the discourse itself. Such pressure might come from actors in the domestic setting who claim that the policy undertaken is unable to handle the foreign policy problem in question adequately, for instance to bring democracy and security to Afghanistan, that it is at odds with the national interest, or that it proves too costly to bring about. Pressure might also come from other states who argue that they have 'done enough' and now it should be country X, Y, or Z's turn to provide, say, famine relief or peacekeepers.

The second route through which shifts are produced is through changes in the foreign policy 'issue' itself. For example, a massive change in Western discourse followed the dismantling of the Soviet Union. Yet, looking back upon Western discourses during the latter half of the 1980s, we find much scepticism that Gorbachev was willing to create, or accept, real changes to East–West relations. In other words, it took a fair amount of time before the linguistic and material changes in the former Eastern block led to a thorough revision of Western discourses. One might also examine the ability of established discourses to accommodate specific 'material challenges', such as the way in which the George W. Bush administration responded to the photos from Abu Ghraib, which challenged the administration's discourse on how American security personnel conduct themselves abroad. The response, which was not entirely stable or universally accepted, was to construct 'Abu Ghraib' as the product of 'a few bad apples', who showed 'un-American behaviour' (see also Chapter Nine). Thus the question is what capacity discourses have for accommodating 'material shifts', and if discourses change, what those changes imply.

Another way to ensure that discourse analysis includes a dynamic element is to ask how history is mobilized within foreign policy debates and discourses. As several of the examples mentioned above have illustrated, history—'our' history as well as the history of other places and peoples—often plays an important and explicit role in foreign policy discourses. To take one of those examples, 'Europe's past' is prominent in discourses on the purpose and identity of the EU. Representations that have been used in the past are likely to echo part of their prior use as they are 're-used' in the present. But history does not simply assert itself and determine the choice or specific content of a representation, it is always told in a particular manner and with particular political effects. Therefore history should be studied through what Foucault called a genealogical perspective (Foucault 1984). A genealogy starts from the present and asks how what we 'know' now has become the understanding of history, and what has been excluded or marginalized by current representations. To the extent that genealogies or conceptual histories of current representations have already been carried out, one can rely upon them when conducting discourse analysis. If they do not exist, one might have to produce them using primary sources. For an example of the power of past representations, and a genealogical approach to representations of the past, see Box 5.4.

> ### BOX 5.4 Genealogy—the case of the Bosnian War as 'Balkan'
>
> One of the key representations in the Western debates on the Bosnian war (1992–1995) was that of the war as 'Balkan'. This representation made the Bosnian War the sequel to the First and Second Balkan Wars of 1912 and 1913, and it was argued that 'the Balkans' was a place saturated with 'ancient hatred', where people had fought each other for 500 years. A genealogical reading allows us to see the power of this reading of history, and it also allows us to question it. As Todorova's *Imagining the Balkans* (Todorova 1997) and Goldsworthy's *Inventing Ruritania* (Goldsworthy 1998) point out, 'the Balkans' was first coined in the early nineteenth century, but only became prominent by the turn of the twentieth century; thus its history is much shorter than the 500 years claimed by the 1990s' catch phrase of 'ancient hatreds'. Moreover, the Western concept of 'the Balkans' has a much more complex history than one would assume if one sticks to the texts of the 1990s. The most prominent discourse of the nineteenth century was one that admired, and romanticized, the Balkans for their heroic, proud, brave, and wild peoples. Another discourse appears in the first decades of the twentieth century, and it constructs 'the Balkans' as 'young clients of civilization' (d'Estournelles de Constant 1914: 8) who have been abandoned by Europe, but who have the capacity to become part of 'civilization'. It is not until in the 1920s, after the First World War and with the concept of 'Balkanization', that the conception of 'the Balkans' as a threatening radical Other arises. In short, genealogy undermines the use of 'the Balkans' as a trans-historical entity and switches the attention from 'what the Balkans is' to 'what role does "the Balkans" play in legitimizing our foreign policies?'

Conclusion—the scope, strengths, and weaknesses of discourse analysis

Discourse analysis makes an assumption that foreign policies rely upon representations and that such representations are articulated in language, and this leads to a concern with public texts. As in the case of constructivism (see Chapter Four), there has been little attempt to link explicitly to the subfield of FPA (Wæver 2002: 27), although when we look at the kind of analysis that post-structuralists carry out using discourse analysis, they are indeed concerned with foreign policy. Comparing discourse analysis with other approaches to foreign policy, we see that this is an approach that is less concerned with group decision making, organizational processes, and bureaucratic politics than with the public defence of the decisions that arise from these (see Chapter One). This may in part be a pragmatic decision for some discourse analysts in that conducting a detailed discourse analysis that incorporates genealogy and traces texts constituted as significant for foreign policy *and* studying the bureaucratic environment and 'behind the scenes' decision-making processes is just too much.

Post-structuralist discourse analysis requires detailed knowledge of the discursive and political setting which is studied, including knowledge of how current texts are connected to past ones and which representations and terms have become so institutionalized that they no longer need to be explicitly invoked. In terms of research design and methodology, this disposes discourse analysis towards a small number of case studies and this in turn provides a contrast with large-*N* research projects such those of comparative foreign policy (Wæver 2002; see also Chapter One). It also sets post-structuralist discourse analysis apart from content or framing analysis that draws conclusions from data that document the frequency of explicitly articulated words.

The scope, theoretical assumptions, and methodological techniques of discourse analysis provide it with strengths and weaknesses. Its strengths reside in its ability to provide rich analysis of the discursive structures that underpin foreign policies. In terms of its weaknesses, those depend on who one asks. Those who think that FPA should identify the causes that explain foreign policy are not convinced by discourse analysis's constitutive post-positivist epistemology. Those who deem psychological processes of such significance that these must be taken into account will find that discourse analysis offers them limited theoretical and methodological assistance. And those who argue that groups and individuals who are marginalized, or even silenced, by foreign policy decisions should be at the centre of critical analysis are sceptical of the focus of discourse analysis on public texts and discourse and its (alleged) downplaying of global–local structures of exploitation.

One challenge to discourse analysis is worthy of particular attention because it engages the boundaries of discourse analysis from within. Working with discourse analysis, Neumann (2002: 628) has expressed 'an impatience with what could, perhaps unkindly, be called "armchair analysis"; by which I mean text-based analyses of global politics that are not complemented by different kinds of contextual data from the field, data that may illuminate how foreign policy and global politics are experienced as lived practices'. Supporting Neumann's call for a turn to practice, Pouliot (2008: 265) has further argued that discourse analysis 'evacuates the practical logics' that make foreign policy discourse possible.

For discourse analysts, this is a useful opportunity to think critically about the scope and limitations of one's analysis, particularly how one might combine discourse analysis with other forms of FPA, including those of 'lived practice'. First, as Neumann shows, one might expand the scope of study from that of official foreign policy to how diplomats and others 'practice' foreign policy, thereby potentially transforming it. Methodologically, this expansion of scope would be paralleled by including interviews, fieldwork, or participant observations. The crucial question here is whether the data one gathers is subjected to a discourse analysis where one's own potential textual contribution (for instance, interview questions) is made part of the analysis, or whether interviews are used to uncover decision-makers' 'hidden intentions', 'real reasons', or 'actual experiences', that is 'the truth' that lies behind discourse.

Second, discourse analysis could be linked to the study of small-group decision makers and bureaucratic politics. One cannot assume that the discourse found here is identical to the discourse which is publicly articulated, but one can assume that the discussions, the eventual output, and the policy's implementation must relate to public discourses. If it does not, decision makers and bureaucrats stand the risk of missing the boat on what makes a foreign policy 'sellable' to those outside the narrow foreign policy making corridors. Studying the way that Danish and British diplomats handle the opt-outs of their countries from EU treaties, Adler-Nissen (2008) shows, for instance, how diplomats negotiate the institutional and discursive constraints imposed upon them. Memoirs by peace negotiators such as David Owen (Owen 1995) and Richard Holbrooke (Holbrooke 1998) provide another indication of how foreign policy makers navigate between the discursive positions laid out by politicians and the media.

Third, the methodology of discourse analysis is per definition tied to texts, and it is often hard to get 'public textual data' that documents the life of the inner circles of decision makers and bureaucrats. When such text appears, it is usually in the form of a memoir published at a distance from the events one seeks to study or from anonymous sources. While both forms of textual material are valuable in terms of gaining an understanding of how decision making and institutional processes unfold, they are in fact 'public texts' and can be studied as such using discourse analytical theory and method. In other words, such accounts do not provide an unmediated pre-public-textual window into the 'inner workings' of decision makers and bureaucrats. Discourse theorists ask instead how the discourses invoked in those texts are situated on the broader political and discursive terrain, and how the authors constitute themselves as having a privileged insider authority that allows them to claim that they 'really know' an issue.

 ## Key points

- Discourse analysis has come into International Relations and the study of foreign policy through post-structuralism.
- Post-structuralism argues that foreign policies should be understood as discursive practices through which identities are being constructed.
- Post-structuralism emphasizes power and conceptualizes it as productive; i.e. power is asserted as subjects are constituted in discourse.
- Discourse analysis examines the way in which representations are mobilized and linked to foreign policies.
- Discourse analysis builds on an understanding of language as simultaneously structured and unstable.
- Discourse analysis assumes that history is important, but that its meaning is always constituted in discourse.
- Discourse analysis is predominantly focused on public texts, but can be expanded to include interviews and fieldwork.

 ## Questions

1. What is a discourse?
2. How does post-structuralism differ from realism?
3. Why is identity important to foreign policy?
4. How does discourse analysis conceptualize power?
5. What is a representation and how do representations impact foreign policies?
6. How can one assess the stability of a foreign policy?
7. What kinds of text should one choose when conducting discourse analysis?
8. What are the strengths and weaknesses of discourse analysis?

 ## Further reading

Campbell, D. (1992), *Writing Security: United States Foreign Policy and the Politics of Identity* (Manchester: Manchester University Press) (2nd edn 1998).
The first book to theorize the constitutive relationship between state identity and foreign policy discourse and to apply that in a historical account of the USA from its discovery to the present. Much of the debate over post-structuralism in the 1990s and beyond evolves around this classic.

Doty, R. L. (1996), *Imperial Encounters* **(Minneapolis, MN: University of Minnesota Press).**
Doty provides a pedagogical, yet sophisticated, account of how post-structuralist theory can illuminate the discursive power asserted within colonial foreign policy.

Hansen, L. (2006), *Security as Practice: Discourse Analysis and the Bosnian War* **(London: Routledge).**
This book situates post-structuralist discourse analysis on the terrain of International Relations and provides detailed methodological guidelines for how texts should be read and selected and how research design can be built.

Milliken, J. (1999), 'The Study of Discourse in International Relations: A Critique of Research and Methods', *European Journal of International Relations,* **5: 225–54.**
Milliken's article gives a valuable introduction to discourse analysis and its key concepts. It was also one of the first texts to explicitly discuss discourse analytical methods.

Neumann, I. B. (1999), *Uses of the Other: 'The East' in European Identity Formation* **(Minneapolis, MN: University of Minnesota Press).**
Neumann offers a critical analysis of how identity has been theorized by post-structuralism and constructivism as well as a series of rich and illustrative studies of how Europe has constructed its Others.

Shapiro, M. J. (1988), *The Politics of Representation: Writing Practices in Biography, Photography, and Policy Analysis* **(Madison, WI: University of Wisconsin Press).**
Shapiro's classic is one of the first post-structuralist works showing the significance of representations for foreign policy across a range of genres.

Wæver, O. (2002), 'Identity, Communities and Foreign Policy: Discourse Analysis as Foreign Policy Theory', in L. Hansen and O. Wæver (eds), *European Integration and National Identity: The Challenge of the Nordic States* **(London: Routledge), 20–49.**
Wæver presents his widely used theory of European integration policies as layered discourses and discusses how discourse analysis relates to the field of FPA.

 Visit the Online Resource Centre that accompanies this book for more information:
www.oxfordtextbooks.co.uk/orc/smith_foreign/

Section 2

Analysing Foreign Policy: Actors, Context, and Goals

6

Actors, structures, and foreign policy analysis

WALTER CARLSNAES

Chapter contents

 Reader's guide

The starting point of this chapter is that the foreign policy of a given state is the product of a number of actors and structures, both domestic and international, and that it is the combination of these that makes this an uncommonly complicated field of study. The chapter then discusses how, in view of this complexity, these actors and structures have been treated in the literature on foreign policy analysis. The first step in this overview is to determine *what* is to be explained, i.e. the object of analysis (or explanandum). The second question is *how* foreign policy is explained, referring to the type of explanatory factors (or explanans) invoked in its analysis. The nature and role of actors and structures are then discussed in relation to these explanatory dimensions and the approaches they have generated within the field. Finally, two further issues are briefly raised—the agency–structure problem, and the question of whether an integrated framework is feasible—before concluding with a recommendation of how to resolve the former in terms of a constructive answer to the latter.

Introduction

Foreign policy is neither fish nor fowl in the study of politics, but an empirical subject matter straddling the boundary between the internal and the external spheres of a state. Such policy is conducted in complex internal and international environments; it results from coalitions of active actors and groups situated both inside and outside state boundaries; its substance emanates from issues of both domestic and international politics; and it involves processes of bargaining and compromise involving trade-off affecting the interests of both domestic and international groupings (Neack 2003: 8–11). This double-sided nature of foreign policy—of being 'at the hinge of domestic politics and international relations,' as one eminent scholar writes (Hill 2003: 23)—has complicated the analysis of foreign policy immensely since the very beginning of this field of study . It has also added significantly to the difficulties of conceptualizing, explaining, and assessing the role of actors and structures in foreign policy analysis.

In view of this complexity, is it worthwhile analysing this role? Yes, for the simple reason that **actors** and **structures** are always present in, and indeed crucial to, the making of foreign policy. Christopher Hill has expressed the intimate relationship between these two factors very well: 'Foreign policy making is a complex process of interaction between many actors, differentially embedded in a wide range of different structures. Their interaction is a dynamic process, leading to the constant evolution of both actors and structures' (Hill, 2003: 28). In other words, in the real world we find a number of actors, both domestic and international, who are closely involved in foreign policy decision making in one manner or another; and equally there are a number of structures on both sides of the domestic–international divide which decisively affect these actors in many different ways. A few elementary examples will suffice to illustrate the complex nature of this abundance of both actors and structures in the conduct of foreign policy.

First of all, who are the most important actors making foreign policy decisions? The obvious candidates are heads of state, heads of government, foreign ministers or secretaries of state, politburos, parliaments, parliamentary committees, political parties, and so forth. These are the politically responsible decision makers—democratically elected or not—acting internationally on behalf of the polities they represent. They should be distinguished from the wider array of civil servants and experts also involved in this process, in the first place within ministries of foreign affairs, but also within rival entities such as military establishments, economic ministries, and intelligence services, as well as lobbying firms, various think tanks, research institutes, and the media. In addition, while these actors are usually domestically based, they are often in contact—even acting in consort—with their counterparts in other countries, as well as with various governmental and non-governmental organizations, both domestic and international. Although by no means complete, this list suffices to illustrate the empirical complexity facing us here.

The same applies to structural factors affecting the making of foreign policy. In the realist tradition of International Relations (IR), such structural entities have usually been seen as belonging primarily to the international system, but this is clearly an exceedingly narrow conception of this phenomenon. Indeed, structures—political, cultural, psychological, economic, national, regional, global, technological, ideational, cognitive, and normative, to name some of the most important—are omnipresent in societies everywhere, existing in various degrees on all levels from the most isolated tribal groupings to the global system as a whole. Not all are equally important to foreign policy making, but many are vital and central to understanding and explaining its manifestations.

In summary, it is not only the inclusion of both domestic and international politics that complicates matters for the foreign policy analyst, but also the omnipresence of both actors and structures, and the intimate and reciprocal link between these two sets of factors. As a consequence, it is impossible to incorporate them fruitfully into explanations of foreign policy without analytically imposing some form of second-order intellectual 'structure' onto this exceedingly messy first-order domain of foreign policy making as an empirical object of study. In view of this, it is essential for the scholar to have some form of analytical framework or approach as a starting point. This is also, in various ways, what scholars of foreign policy have tried to establish over the years, at the same time as there remain fundamental disagreements about the most fruitful and feasible ways of achieving this goal. This chapter will present and briefly discuss some of the most prominent of these contending approaches to this field of study before concluding on a somewhat more positive and constructive note.

However, before proceeding with this overview, a brief terminological clarification needs to be made. In this chapter, the acronym 'FP' will be used instead of 'FPA' for the field of study usually called 'Foreign Policy Analysis' (upper case), even though the latter abbreviation is the normal one in the current literature. The primary reason is that this acronym situates the study of foreign policy within the broad field of international relations; FPA, by contrast, denotes a commitment to a separate sub-field with its own research questions and techniques.

Historical background

A fruitful starting point for understanding any field of study is to know something about its history. Thus it is important, on the one hand, to bear in mind that foreign policy as an academic subject matter has had strong roots in the broader domain of the policy sciences, focusing on the whole spectrum of the domestic public policy arena. This was particularly the case in the USA, where FP was first established as an academic subject matter shortly after the Second World War. However, almost concurrently a second major tradition emerged, which has left a stronger imprint on the subsequent evolution of the field. This is the induction into American thinking of **realism**, a doctrine which, mainly through the immense influence of Hans Morgenthau, a European émigré, came to dominate both the study and practice of foreign policy during the Cold War era. His main ambition, as that of most realists at the time, was to translate 'the maxims of nineteenth century's European diplomatic practice into more general laws of an American social science' (Guzzini 1998: 1). More specifically, by linking the concept of power to that of the national interest, Morgenthau believed that he could provide universal explanations for the external behaviour of all sovereign states.

During this period a more general scholarly development, known as **behaviouralism**, also gained dominance in the USA, proclaiming that the social sciences should aspire to be more 'scientific' by emulating the methodology of the natural sciences. This new scientific approach had a decisive effect on both the public policy and realist-oriented perspectives on the study of foreign policy. Its impact on the former was perhaps the more deep-going in the sense that it changed its character altogether from being an essentially idiographic and normative enterprise—i.e. analysing specific forms of policy or prescribing better means for its formulation and implementation—to one that aspired to generate and test hypotheses in order to develop a cumulative body of empirical generalizations. This inaugurated a period, which turned out to be relatively brief but intensive, during which the *comparative* study of foreign policy (CFP) came to dominate the field. The impact on realism was less fundamental, in so far as the behaviouralists never really challenged the underlying assumptions of realism, only its methodology. Realism nevertheless bifurcated into essentially two strands, with **neorealism** giving the structures of the international system an exclusive explanatory role, while **neoclassical realism** (a more recent and eclectic approach) retained the centrality of the concept of power while rejecting the exclusion of domestic factors in the explanation of foreign policy. Most neorealists have also claimed that, given their exclusive focus on how international structures decisively determine the behaviour of states in a systemic fashion, they are not interested—nor indeed competent—in explaining the specific foreign policies of any given state.

A third and more conceptual issue has deep historical roots as well, and is also central to the subject matter of this chapter. This is the crucial question of understanding what exactly constitutes the object to be analysed and explained in foreign policy, known as the explanandum (that which is to be explained or, to use neopositivist parlance, the dependent variable). While this definitional issue may seem trivial at first sight, it goes to the conceptual core of what distinguishes foreign policy from both domestic and international politics, the two major sub-disciplinary foci of political science. The stipulation and understanding of a given explanandum is also crucial to the appropriate choice of explanatory factors or explanans (that which does the explaining, or the independent variable) to be used in a given investigation. To be theoretically feasible and empirically fruitful, these must be analytically compatible with the object of analysis in such research.

The roles of both explanandum (object of analysis) and explanans (explanatory factors) in analysing foreign policy are discussed below. To simplify matters somewhat, this will be done in terms of two fundamentally different explananda currently in use in foreign policy analysis. The first is characterized by a focus on decision-making *processes* in a broad sense, while the second makes a clear distinction between such processes and *policy*, defined more narrowly as a choice of action in the pursuit of a goal, or a set of goals, often characterized as an undertaking. These, and the selection of explanatory approaches—explanans—in each case, will be discussed and analysed in turn, with a specific focus on the role of actors and structures in each.

The role of actors and structures in 'process' approaches to FP

Valerie Hudson has become the prime spokesperson for the first approach in a series of influential contributions to the field over the past decade or so. 'The explanandum of foreign policy analysis', she stipulates in the keynote article of the journal *Foreign Policy Analysis* when it was first launched in 2005, 'includes the process and resultants of human decision making with reference to or having known consequences for foreign entities' Hudson 2005: 2). She then elaborates further on this conceptualization:

> One may be examining not a single decision, but a constellation of decisions taken with reference to a particular situation. Furthermore, decisions may be modified over time, requiring an examination of sequences of decisions. Also, the stages of decision-making may be the focus of inquiry, from problem recognition, framing, and perception to more advanced stages of goal prioritization, contingency planning, and option assessment (Hudson 2007: 4).

The notion here is essentially that the object of analysis—foreign policy—is a question of what foreign policy decision makers are thinking and doing, i.e. their purposive behaviour. What they are up to is taking part in the dynamic and complex process of making foreign policy decisions on behalf of the state; hence this process as a whole is what needs to be examined and explained. Or, as she notes: 'The explanans of FPA [*sic*] are those factors that influence foreign policy decision-making and foreign policy decision-makers' (Hudson 2007: 5). Thus the focus is explicitly on 'human decisional behaviour', as Douglas Stuart has recently noted, adding that this 'makes this the most ambitious and multifaceted subfield of international relations' (Stuart 2008: 576). Because they aim to explore the process of foreign policy decision making as a whole rather than policy *per se*, scholars of this ilk sometimes use the acronym FPDM to describe the focus of their field of study (Mintz and Derouen 2010). As summarized by Hudson, foreign policy is 'centered on foreign policy decisionmaking (FPDM) as it is performed by human beings' (Hudson 2007:165).

This process specification of the object of analysis has some obvious consequences for the role assigned to actors and structures. A central question here is what function the state plays in approaches that focus on decision-making processes (rather than specific policies). Viewed in the context of the two major historical strands briefly discussed above, the choice here is between viewing the state in realist terms as the sole and independent *actor* in foreign policy, or viewing foreign policy actors in terms of the domestic functioning of a state, in which decisions are made by a number of elite decision makers acting on behalf of the state. The answer here is relatively clear-cut: states are not conceived as unitary actors but rather as an institutional *structure* within which, and on behalf of which, individual decision makers act. As Hudson emphasizes: 'States are not agents because states are abstractions and thus have no agency' (Hudson 2007: 6). As such, this type of approach is explicitly 'actor-specific', meaning that the actors are not generic entities but always specific individuals.

What roles do actors and structures play in the explanation of foreign policy decision making? A clear trend is discernible here: this type of approach tends to favour a **levels of analysis** framework, defined in its simplest form in terms of an individual level, a state level, and an international level of explanation (Neack 2003), with additional variants including a group decision-making level as well as one incorporating culture and national identity (Hudson 2007). Furthermore, the causal effects on the decision-making process of actors and structures are examined one level at a time, with actors dominating on the lower levels of analysis (individual and group decision levels), while structures take over the stage as the levels become more general and abstract (state, cultural, and international levels). As readily acknowledged by Hudson, this poses a problem for this type of FP, since although it is 'fairly straightforward to examine each separate level of analysis', theoretical integration across levels 'must be possible, but . . . remains a promise unfulfilled for the time being' (Hudson 2007: 165, 184). (See Box 6.1.)

BOX 6.1 Levels of analysis in foreign policy

Although in the 1950s Kenneth Waltz had already enquired into how war and peace can be explained by distinguishing between three 'images', it is David Singer, in a landmark piece published in 1961, who can lay claim to having introduced the 'level-of-analysis' problem to IR (Waltz 1959; Singer 1961). But whereas Waltz's question had been concerned with what sociopolitical level in which to locate the causes of war and peace—whether in man, the state, or the state system—Singer's discussion is in terms of only two levels: the state system and the international system. Although there has been confusion on this issue (in both Singer's analysis and the subsequent literature), his question is essentially whether the behaviour of states (the explanandum) is to be explained in terms of causal factors (explanans) on the level of the international system, or on the level of the state itself. His answer is clear: it all depends on the type of question(s) asked. Here he differs from Waltz, who ended up opting for the explanatory level of the international system, calling explanations of state behaviour in terms of the state and/or the individual as 'reductionist' (Waltz 1979). However, both agree that explanations of *foreign policy*—as distinct from international politics more broadly defined—cannot be couched in terms of the systemic level. Singer's formulation of the problem also has another implication, which has remained largely unchallenged as well as problematic: that levels of this kind cannot be integrated or combined.

The role of actors and structures in 'policy' approaches to FP

Studies focusing on explaining the choice of specific *policies* rather than decision-making processes do so because they view policies as *resulting* from such processes rather being part of them. Charles Hermann, discussing many years ago 'that which is to be explained' (the explanandum), wrote of foreign policy that 'it is the discrete purposeful action that results from the political level decision of an individual or group of individuals', and as such it is 'not the decision, but a *product* of the decision' (C.F. Hermann 1978: 34; my emphasis). Amongst scholars writing in this tradition there is considerable consensus today around a view of the explanandum which emphasizes the *purposive* nature of foreign policy actions, the centrality of *policy*, and the crucial role of *state boundaries* (Carlsnaes 2002). Graham Allison and Philip Zelikow have explained the rationale for conceptualizing foreign policy in this sense as follows.

> When we are puzzled by a happening in foreign affairs, the source of our puzzlement is typically a particular government action or set of actions . . . These occurrences raise obvious question: *Why* did the Soviet Union place missiles in Cuba? *Why* were 500,000 soldiers in the Persian Gulf? *Why* did Germany give up the Deutsche-Mark? *Why* did the United Nations do so little to defend Srebrenica in July 1995? In pursuing the answers to these questions, the serious analyst seeks to discover why one specific state of the world came about—rather than some other (Allison and Zelikow 1999: 2–3).

The important point to notice here is that by so clearly distinguishing a foreign policy *action* from the decision-making *process* preceding it, the authors are not foreclosing any particular approach to answering the 'why' question. Indeed, the whole point of Allison's original study—and the reason why it had such an impact on the field in general—was his success in showing that the same questions could be answered in different ways, depending on what kind of explanatory model, or conceptual 'lens', was being used. (See Box 6.2.)

What are the implications for the role of actors and structures of such a specification of the object of analysis (or explanandum)? Contrary to process-oriented approaches, this perspective does not a priori view either actors or structures in any particular way, since the focus here is on 'policy undertakings', not the behaviour of any particular entity within a specific structural environment (such as 'decision making'). This is also why this perspective—à la Allison's 'lenses'—is able to harbour a number of different and not necessarily compatible analytical approaches.

One way of classifying the various options to be found in the literature, which is both convenient and appropriate in the present context, is to ask once again what role structures and actors play in the explanation of foreign policy actions. The fact is that these two concepts point to a deep-rooted and long-standing tension which exists within this field of study, as indeed in the social sciences in general, between approaches tending to privilege either structure- or actor-based forms of explanation. This is in marked contrast to the decision-making tradition, which is able to accommodate both actor- and structure-based explanations essentially by assigning them to analytically distinct levels of analysis. What complicates matters further is that we also find different approaches within each of these two perspectives, which will therefore have to be discussed separately.

BOX 6.2 Graham Allison's explanations of the Cuba Missile Crisis in 1962

One of the most influential twentieth-century studies of foreign policy is Graham Allison's *Essence of Decision: Explaining the Cuban Missile Crisis*, first published in 1971, with a second and substantially updated edition appearing in 1999 (with Philip Zelikow as co-author). This study focuses on thirteen days in October 1962, during which a crisis erupted when John F. Kennedy learned that the Soviet Union was in the process of installing intermediate-range ballistic missiles in Fidel Castro's Cuba. This action was viewed as an unacceptable provocation by the President and his key advisors, who consequently felt impelled to insist that the Soviets withdraw these missiles. The US government considered three options in this context: to invade Cuba, to conduct air strikes against the missile sites, or to impose a naval blockade of Cuba. The President finally chose the third option, a tactic that turned out to be successful. Allison's purpose is to explain why and how this choice was made, and he does this in the form of first constructing three different conceptual models or lenses (*rational actor, organizational behaviour, and governmental politics*), and then using each in three separate empirical chapters to explain and assess the actions taken by Kennedy and his advisors during these thirteen days. He does not claim that these three models are the only feasible options in explaining the puzzles generated by this crisis, but he does show how our view of events such as these are strongly influenced by the 'basic assumptions that we make, categories we use, our angle of vision', and that by 'comparing and contrasting the three frameworks, we see what each magnifies, highlights, and reveals as well as what each blurs or neglects' (Allison and Zelikow 1999: x). What has made this study so influential is that although it purports to explain the same events, it comes to the conclusion that different explanations are reached depending on the conceptual model employed. As against most schools of thought at the time, it thus called into question the assumption that social science can achieve, and therefore should aim for, clear-cut and 'objective' explanations of social actions. Today this notion that all explanations, predictions, and evaluations are inescapably theory-laden is more or less taken for granted and, at least within IR, Allison's study must be given much credit for this. The importance of conceptual models applies equally to policy makers, which explains why this is one of the most widely read and influential foreign policy studies amongst foreign policy decision makers as well.

Approaches based on a structural perspective

Realism

Although, as we have noted above, the realism espoused by Morgenthau suffered a decline with the ascendancy of neorealism, both approaches to foreign policy analysis nevertheless remain strong today, albeit in different forms. Hence, while Kenneth Waltz (the originator and still the most eminent proponent of neorealism) continues to insist on the inapplicability of neorealism to the analysis of foreign policy (Waltz 1996; for a contrary view, see Elman 1996), one finds variants of it which focus on precisely such policies. In contrast, latter-day neoclassical scholars following in Morgenthau's footsteps have no such qualms, and hence continue to focus squarely on explaining foreign policy and nothing else.

With regard to the former, a distinction should be made between **aggressive** and **defensive** forms of **neorealism** (Rose 1998). During the past two decades, aggressive realism has been pre-eminently represented by John Mearsheimer, who has argued that whereas the Cold War, based on bipolarity, military balance, and nuclear weapons produced peace in Europe for 45 years, its demise will, contrary to conventional wisdom, necessarily have negative effects in the long run. This pessimistic scenario follows from a strict application of neorealist tenets, especially the view that in so far as the structure of the international system invariably fosters conflict and aggression, rational states continue to be compelled to pursue offensive strategies in their search for security (Mearsheimer 1995: 79–129).

Defensive neorealists, on the other hand, do not share this pessimistic and essentially Hobbesian view of the international system, arguing instead that although systemic factors do have causal effects on state behaviour, they cannot account for all state actions. Furthermore, instead of emphasizing the role played by the distribution of power in the international system, scholars belonging to this school have pointed to the importance of the source, level, and direction of threats, defined primarily in terms of technological factors, geographic proximity, and offensive capabilities but also perceived intentions (Rose 1998: 146).

Finally, **neoclassical realists** share with neorealists the view that a country's foreign policy is primarily formed by its place in the international system and in particular by its relative material power capabilities. However, these theorists also argue that the impact of systemic factors on a given country's foreign policy will be indirect and more complex than neorealists have assumed, since such features can effect policy only through factors on the domestic level (Rose, 1998: 146). Or, as noted by Walt, the causal logic of this approach 'places domestic politics as an intervening variable between the distribution of power and foreign policy behavior' (Walt 2002: 211). As a consequence of the stress on the role of both systemic and domestic variables, research within neoclassical realism is generally conducted in the form of theoretically informed narratives that trace how different factors from both levels combine to forge the particular foreign policies of states (Rose 1998: 153); for a recent overview of this field, see Taliaferro *et al.* (2009).

In summary, realism in its various strands is essentially a structural orientation for the simple reason that at its central core lies the notion of state power, which is defined either in terms of the structure of the international system, as in neorealism, or as a combination of domestic power resources and international structures. The state is the core actor in both instances, and its capacity to act is determined by material factors, and especially by shifts in these, be they external or internal to the state.

Neoliberal institutionalism

Although not generally touted as an approach to the analysis of foreign policy, it is obvious that the type of focus that usually goes under the name of **neoliberal institutionalism** (or simply neoliberalism) is as relevant to the study of foreign policy as are realism and neorealism in their various configurations. Indeed, in so far as this school of thought is posited as an alternative to realism, it also represents an alternative approach to foreign policy analysis (Baldwin 1993).

Neoliberal institutionalism is a structural, systemic, and 'top-down' view for some of the same reasons that neorealism constitutes such an approach. It assumes that states are the primary actors in the international system, that they behave like egoistic value maximizers, and that the international system is essentially anarchic, i.e. non-hierarchical in distinction from domestic polities (Baldwin 1993: 8-14).

What then is distinctive about the neoliberal institutionalist approach to foreign policy analysis? Very briefly, the following: whereas both neorealists and neoliberals view foreign policy making as a process of constrained choice on the part of states acting rationally and strategically, the latter understand this constraint not primarily in terms of the international configurations of power capabilities facing states, but in terms of an anarchic system which, while it fosters uncertainty and hence security concerns, can nevertheless be positively affected by the creation of **regimes** providing information and common rules, thereby fostering international cooperation to at least some degree (Keohane 1993). Thus, instead of viewing international institutions as epiphenomenal and hence constituting a 'false promise' (Mearsheimer 1994–95), neoliberal institutionalists emphasize that such institutions do matter—that they 'make a difference in the behaviour of states and in the nature of international politics' (Stein 2008: 212). Or as noted by K.J. Holsti, how states 'defend and pursue their purposes is tempered by international institutions that encompass ideas, norms, rules, and etiquette . . . [which] have a moderating influence on the plans and actions of their sovereigns' (K.J. Holsti 2004: 306–7). Furthermore, by adding a focus on the role of international institutions to neorealism, neoliberals claim that they have added to the explanatory power of neorealism without undermining its main structuralist assumptions.

Social constructivism

Although **social constructivism** (or simply constructivism) is essentially a meta-theoretical standpoint in the study of social phenomena, and hence is foundational to political analysis rather than being a specific analytical or theoretical approach within IR, here—following a common practice within the literature—it is used to designate a more or less coherent body of thought in IR, including FP. Its core assumptions are that reality is socially constructed in the form of social rules and inter-subjective meanings, and that this affects our knowledge of it: how we see the world as well as ourselves, and how we define our interests and proper ways of behaviour (see Adler 2002; revised in Carlsnaes *et al.* 2012).

Although constructivism consists of an increasingly broad spectrum of views, we will focus here only on the so-called 'modernist' or 'thin' type, which predominates in foreign policy analysis. This approach can be said to consist, first of all, of a *normative–ideational* strand, which conceives of norms qua ideas as aspects of social structure emerging from the purposive behaviour of actors in specific communities and that these, in turn, shape such behaviour by constituting the identities and actions of such actors (Hoffmann 2010: 2). Challenging mainstream assumptions of the international system as essentially consisting of power calculations and material forces, early normative constructivists thus 'worked to demonstrate that shared ideas about appropriate state behaviour had a profound impact on the nature and functioning of world politics' (Hoffmann 2010: 2). With particular reference to foreign policy behaviour, the goal was to show how such behaviour is enabled or constrained by normative and ideational factors, i.e. how these influence states' understanding of the external material world. A second research focus, often intertwined with the first, centres on the notion of *identity* to highlight the socially constructed nature of the state and its interests. As noted by Bruce Cronin, 'identities provide a frame of reference from which political leaders can initiate, maintain, and structure their relationships with other states' (Cronin 1999: 18), and as such it 'is a constructivist concept if there ever was one' (Berenskoetter 2010: 2). Indeed, as Paul Kowert has recently claimed, most of 'constructivist scholarship in foreign policy . . . dictate[s] a concern with state identity' (Kowert 2010: 2). Although human interaction is essential for establishing and upholding these norms, ideas, and identities, constructivism is nevertheless a structural approach, since the explanation of the policy choices made by decision makers is in terms of the effect of social structures (broadly defined) on the individual actor rather than with reference to any innate characteristics of such actors.

To sum up, although these three different structural approaches to FP do not exclude actors in their analyses, what primarily unites them is that in each instance structural factors rather than actors are invoked as the dynamic factor 'causing' a particular state to behave in a particular way in the conduct of its foreign policy. In the approaches to be discussed below, the tables are turned in favour of the explanatory power of actors and their characteristics in one form or another.

Approaches from an actor-based perspective

Cognitive and psychological approaches

Although research on the **cognitive** and **psychological** characteristics of individual decision makers has been viewed with considerable scepticism by scholars pursuing structural explanations of foreign policy, this has in fact been one of the growth areas within FP over the past quarter of a century (Hudson 2007). As against the **rational choice** assumption—common to both realism and neoliberal institutionalism—that individuals are in principle open-minded and adaptable to the dictates of structural constraints, it is based on the contrary assumption that they are to a considerable degree impervious to such effects because of the 'stickiness' of their underlying beliefs and the way they process information, as well as a number of other personality and cognitive traits.

From having focused on the study of attitudes and attitudinal change in its earliest years, psychological analysis underwent a 'cognitive revolution' in the 1970s. Instead of the conception of the 'passive' actor underlying previous work, a new viewed emerged, stressing the individual as 'problem-solver' rather than malleable agent (Rosati 1995: 52–54). This was also a period when studies of how the characteristics of leadership—beliefs, motivations, decisional and interpersonal styles—affected the pursuit of foreign policies first received serious attention, a focus which has continued to this day (M.G. Hermann and Preston 1998). Under this rubric one can also include small-group approaches, including a focus on the effects of 'groupthink' (Garrison 2010), as well as prospect theory, which reputedly 'has evoked the most interest among students of foreign policymaking' (Kahler 1998: 927). James Taliaferro has provided us with the most recent and up-to-date review of this approach and its current applications in FP (Taliaferro 2010). Role theory, first introduced into FP by Kal Holsti (K.J. Holsti 1970) and most recently discussed by Cameron Thies (Thies 2010), should also be mentioned in this context.

Although there is much overlap between studies of this kind and those discussed above under the rubric of foreign policy decision making, they should nevertheless be clearly distinguished from each other for at least two reasons. The first is the fundamental difference in the explanandum focused on, which in the case of the FPDM approach is the decisional process itself, whereas here it is intentional policy behaviour—the question why a particular policy undertaking was chosen. The second is that while the scholars discussed here are exclusively engaged in finding psychological and cognitive causes (or 'theories') for explaining given policy choices, the FPDM framework goes well beyond the individual actor level to account for the particular nature of a given decisional process.

Bureaucratic politics approach

The main rationale of the so-called **bureaucratic politics** (or governmental) approach to the analysis of foreign policy, popularized by Allison, is to explain why decisions often take the form of 'resultants' as distinct from what any person or group intended, and it does this not in terms of given preferences and strategic moves (as in rational choice thinking) but 'according to the power and performance of proponents and opponents of the action in question' (Allison and Zelikow 1999: 256). At the same time, the power involved in such interaction is primarily bureaucratic rather than personal, in so far as the actors taking part in these bargaining games represent sectional or factional rather than individual interests. In other words, what we find here is the view that foreign policy can best be explained in terms of bureaucratic infighting, and that this necessitates an examination of the interaction of individuals in their organizational environments rather than, as in cognitive–psychological approaches, in terms of their predispositions as decision makers. Although earlier claimed as, and criticized for, being excessively US-centred in its empirical applicability, it is slowly finding its way to Europe and elsewhere (see Jones 2010).

New liberalism

Although liberalism itself has roots going back to the early history of FP, Andrew Moravcsik must be given primary credit for having put **new liberalism** on the contemporary IR and FP agendas (Moravcsik 1997). In his view, three core assumptions underlie this challenge to neo-realism and neoliberalism. The first is the primacy of societal actors over political institutions, the implication of which is that being based on a 'bottom-up' view of the political system, individual and social groups are treated as prior to politics, because they define their interests independently of politics and then pursue these interests through political exchange and collective action. Second, state preferences represent the interests of a particular subset of society, in the sense that state officials define state preferences and act purposively in world politics in terms of these interests. Third, state behaviour in the international system is determined by the configuration within it of interdependent state preferences, i.e. by the constraints imposed on a given state by the preferences of other states (Moravcsik 1997: 520).

This framework differs from the actor-based approaches discussed above primarily because of its emphasis on the role of societal actors rather than politically appointed individuals or small-group actors in the formation of the foreign policies of states. In this sense it broadens the scope of explanation beyond the purely political or governmental, and as such places the analysis of foreign policy in a broader sociopolitical context than any of the other approaches discussed here.

Interpretative actor perspective

The final approach to be discussed here shares with social constructivism an interpretative epistemology, i.e. understanding actors as reflexive entities in an inter-subjective world of meaning. However, whereas the logic of the former is to interpret individual actions in terms of social rules and collective meanings, this perspective approaches the explanation of foreign policy by focusing on the thinking and actions of individual decision makers. 'Here the concern is to understand decisions from the standpoint of the decision-makers by recon-structing their reasons,' Hollis and Smith thus write. 'The foreign policy behaviour of states depends on how individuals with power perceive and analyse situations. Collective action is a sum or combination of individual actions' (Hollis and Smith 1990: 74).

An illustrative example of this type of essentially atheoretical form of analysis is Philip Zelikow and Condoleezza Rice's detailed study of German reunification (Zelikow and Rice 1995). It offers an insider's view of the innermost workings of the top political elites of the United States, the Soviet Union, West Germany, East Germany, Britain, and France in the crea-tion, following a series of top-level negotiations, of a reunited Germany. Their analysis examines the reasoning behind their choices and proffers an explanation of the immense changes that occurred during the year following the collapse of the Berlin Wall in terms of this reasoning and its effects. The assumption underlying this type of analysis is the counterfactual argument that if the main actors in this historical process had not reasoned and made choices in the way they did, the history of this period would have been different.

Conclusion

The purpose of the above discussion has been to give an overview of how FP scholars have tried to deal with the many actors and structures which exist in the real world in which foreign policy is made, and which therefore, in one way or another, are involved in the formation and pursuit of such policies. As we have seen, some scholars give pre-eminence to the role of actors in such explanations, while others, while similarly intent on explaining specific policies, place their bets on the prime importance of structural factors in explain-ing such actions. A third group, focusing on decision-making processes rather than on policies, casts its net much wider, incorporating both actors and structures in the form of a levels of analysis framework. Thus, whereas scholars aiming to explain policies can be said to practise a logic of inclusion and exclusion, of privileging either actors or structures, those focusing on decision-making processes take the opposite tack of including all pos-sible factors which may play a role in the general activity of foreign policy decision making. The first two groups also differ in terms of applying either a top-down or bottom-up ana-lytical procedure, in the sense that structural explanations generally take the first form, while actor-based explanations take the second. This is not the case with scholars explain-ing decision-making processes, for which this problem does not seem to exist in so far as each level of analysis is treated separately and on its own merits in a 'fairly straightforward' manner (Hudson 2007: 165).

These differences within FP point to at least two important issues. The first is commonly referred to as the **agency–structure problem**, the implications of which are neatly illustrated in the discussion above: scholars focusing on explaining policies either view actors as the prime cause of policy actions, or give structures this role, and when both are present (as in decision-making analyses), they are essentially treated as separate factors not interacting with each other. The problem is that it is generally recognized that in real life actors and structures do not exist in such a zero-sum relationship but, rather, that human agents and social structures are in a fundamental sense dynamically interrelated entities, and that hence we cannot account fully for the one without invoking the other. None of the approaches discussed above has resolved this problem, since each tends to privilege either actors or structures in their explanations, or treats them separately on different levels of analysis. (See Box 6.3.)

This raises a second problem: the feasibility and/or need for an integrated or synthetic framework in FP, incorporating both structures and actors and the dynamic interaction over time between the two. Hudson is quite frank about such a need: 'the true promise of Foreign Policy Analysis . . . must be theoretical *integration*: the integration of theory across several levels to develop a more complete perspective on foreign policy decisionmaking' (Hudson 2007: 165). As to the feasibility issue, she openly acknowledges that this remains 'a promise unfulfilled for the time being' (Hudson 2007: 184).

My own view is that a synthetic framework for analysing foreign policy is indeed feasible, but only if the explanandum is defined as purposive policy behaviour rather than in process terms. The second step is a recognition and acceptance of the empirical fact that all foreign policy actions, small or large, are linked together in the form of *intentions*, *cognitive–psychological* factors, and the various *structural* phenomena characterizing societies and their environments, and hence that explanations of actual foreign policy actions must be able to give accounts that do not by definition exclude or privilege any of these types of explanans.

My own favourite method of conceptualizing such a synthetic analytical framework consists of a simple tripartite approach to explaining foreign policy actions (the explanandum) consisting, respectively, of an *intentional*, a *dispositional*, and a *structural* dimension of explanation (the explanans), as follows (Carlsnaes 1992). (See Figure 6.1.)

BOX 6.3 The agency–structure problem in FP

The agency–structure problem focuses on the empirical claim that human agents and social structures are fundamentally interrelated, and hence that explanations of social actions must incorporate both. Or, as noted by Colin Wight: 'In the social world both agents and structures are necessary for any social act to be possible' (Wight 2007: 111). The 'problem' is that although such views of reciprocal implication are generally taken for granted, we nevertheless 'lack a self-evident way to conceptualise these entities and their relationships', as Alexander Wendt has noted. Although he did this in 1987, in the first discussion of this issue in IR, it is fair to say that the problem is yet to be resolved to the satisfaction of most IR theorists. One persistent stumbling block is the continued influence of two types of explanations in IR, which deny either the need or the possibility of such a resolution: methodological individualism, claiming that social outcomes can be explained solely in terms of the characteristics of individuals (a 'bottom-up' notion), and methodological structuralism, which accords such powers to structures (a 'top-down' notion). A second issue that has caused considerable controversy is the claim that agents and structures 'constitute' each other, and that this is essentially the nature of the link between them. This means that although agents and structures mutually affect each other, this relationship is not of a causal nature. Here, Wendt has argued in terms of this link providing explanations of what an entity *is*, as for example in the master–slave relationship—the one actor constitutes the other (see Wendt 1998). As against this, Wight has argued that the 'relationships that constitute them as certain types of social actors *are* what causes them to behave in certain ways' (Wight 2007: 117). A third body of controversy (and confusion) concerns the relationship between agency-structure, micro–macro, and level-of-analysis issues, all of which are closely related, sometimes conflated with one another, but, which it is argued by some scholars, should nevertheless be kept analytically apart. The most recent discussion of these issues—as of the agency-structure *problematique* in general—is provided by Wight in his penetrating and exhaustive book on this topic (Wight 2007: 102–20).

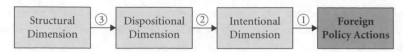

Figure 6.1 Three dimensions for explaining foreign policy actions.

Although conceptualized as analytically autonomous, these three dimensions should be viewed as closely linked in the sense that they can be conjoined in a *logical step-by-step* manner to produce *increasingly exhaustive* (or 'deeper') explanations of foreign policy actions.

The starting point in such an explanation would be to focus on the first link, i.e. the relation between a given foreign policy action and the intention or goal that it expresses (arrow 1 in Figure 6.1). This is a *teleological* relationship, giving us the specific reason(s) for, or goal(s) of, a certain policy undertaking. This is also a *necessary* first step, given the inherently intentional nature of the explanandum. The study of German unification by Zelikow and Rice (1995) is an excellent example of such an approach, giving us a 'thick' description of top-level negotiations and statecraft at its best. However, scholars who are also interested in giving *causal* in addition to intentional explanations will want to go further than this. This distinction can also be described in terms of an 'in order to' and a 'because of' dimension in explanations, in which the former refers to actions pursued intentionally (i.e. 'in order to' achieve a certain aim), while the latter aims to indicate those prior or underlying mechanisms which 'caused' a given actor to have this but not that intention. Thus scholars not satisfied with merely tracing descriptively the reasoning behind a certain action will want to ask why one rather than another intention in the form of a policy undertaking was being pursued in the first place.

In such an analysis the next step would be to trace the link between the intentional and the dispositional dimensions, with a view to finding the particular and underlying psychological–cognitive factors which have *disposed* a particular actor to have this and not that preference or intention (arrow 2 in Figure 6.1). In the analysis of such dispositions the primary focus would be on the underlying *values* (or 'belief systems') which motivate actors to pursue certain goals, as well as on the *perceptions* which make actors see the world in particular ways ('world views'). This is where cognitive and psychological approaches to the explanation of foreign policy enter into the analytical picture. In the case of German unification, for example, in-depth leadership analyses of the various individual statesmen, not pursued by Zelikow and Rice, would be relevant in determining the actor dispositions of the main protagonists.

This leaves us with the question of how structural factors are to be incorporated into this framework, since they are present in neither of the first two dimensions. In my view, they do so in terms of a third, 'deeper' and very powerful structural dimension, always underlying and thus affecting the cognitive and psychological dispositions of individuals (arrow 3 in Figure 6.1). These structural factors—domestic and international, social, cultural, economic, material, or ideational—do so in many ways, but essentially as a consequence of being perceived, reacted to, and taken into account by actors, and it is in this sense that structural factors can be said to influence, condition, or otherwise affect—either by constraint or by enabling—human values, preferences, moods, and attitudes, i.e. actor dispositions as here conceptualized. It is also by causally affecting the dispositional characteristics of the agents of policy in this manner that one can say that structural factors—via their effects on the dispositions of actors (and only in this manner)—also determine the particular types of intentions motivating policies (thus combining all three arrows). In the case of German unification, such structural factors would be the end of the Cold War, the economic decline of the Soviet Union, the group dynamics of the persons involved in the negotiations, the continued consolidation of a peaceful European Community, and the central importance of democracy—to name but a few.

If this approach to foreign policy analysis provides an *integrative* framework, linking both individual decision makers and social structures across state boundaries, does it resolve the *agency–structure* problem? No, not as it stands, for although it combines actor and structural features (which is a step forward), it privileges structures over actors in so far as the former are viewed as having causal effects on the latter, but not the latter on the former. In short, it is a logically *static* framework, which can be used to explain *single* foreign policy actions but not a series of such actions over time. However, once we view policy undertakings with reference also to their actual *outcomes*—which may be intended or unintended, extensive or marginal— a *dynamic* component enters into the picture. In other words, in so far as these outcomes have subsequent effects over time on both the structures and actors determining the foreign policy undertakings of a particular state, we have a case of mutual interaction between the two (see Carlsnaes 1992). To quote Hill once again, this conceptualization of the reciprocal relationship neatly encapsulates the notion that 'Their interaction is a dynamic process, leading to the constant evolution of both actors and structures' (Hill 2003: 28).

In conclusion, this is but one possible way, outlined in the barest detail, in which to conceptualize an integrative framework for the analysis of the roles of actors and structures in foreign policy actions, as well as a dynamic model of the agency–structure relationship. Nevertheless, much remains to be done to consolidate further a field of study which, despite some lean years in the shadow of the vibrant theoretical developments and debates within the larger discipline of IR, is now ready once again to make more space for itself.

 Key points

- In the real world we find a number of actors, both domestic and international, who are closely involved in the formulation of foreign policy. Equally, there are a number of structures on both sides of the domestic–international divide that decisively affect these foreign policy actors and their behaviour in many different ways.

- The combination of these factors complicates the conceptualization, explanation, and assessment of the role of actors and structures in foreign policy analysis well beyond what is the case, for example, in the study of either domestic or international politics, since it involves both of these as well as the interplay between them.

- As a consequence, it is not feasible to incorporate actors and structures fruitfully into explanations of foreign policy without analytically imposing some form of *second-order* theoretical or intellectual 'structure' onto this exceedingly messy first-order domain of foreign policy making as an empirical object of study. In other words, it is essential for the scholar to have some form of *analytical framework* or *approach* as a starting point.

- This is also, in various ways, what scholars of Foreign Policy (FP) have tried to do over the years, and hence it is only in terms of these attempts to structure this field of study analytically that a reasonable and fruitful examination and discussion of the role of actors and structures within it can proceed.

- The first such second-order conceptualization is that of the explanandum—the phenomenon that is to be explained, often also referred to as the dependent variable. Two different types of such explananda can be found in the current literature: scholars focusing on foreign policy as a decision-making *process*, and scholars (a much larger group) focusing on *policy* conceived as a product of such processes. In the first, actors are viewed as those individuals partaking in decision making, whereas structures are primarily those of the state, on behalf of which decisions are made. In the second, the role of actors and structures is left undefined, since the focus is on policies defined as undertakings or commitments, which are neither actor-like nor structural in nature.

● The second and more important analytical category of relevance here is that of the explanans—those factors scholars point to in order to explain a certain phenomenon, often also referred to as independent variables. Scholars focusing on explaining foreign policy qua *processes* tend to invoke the explanatory role of actors and structures in terms of the notion of analytically separate 'levels of analysis', some of which are actor-based and others structural. On the other hand, scholars who view their object of analysis in *policy* terms tend to do so from either of two perspectives: those highlighting structures as explanatory factors (a top-down view), or those who privilege actors in this role (a bottom-up view).

● In view of this array of contending approaches to the study of the role of actors and structures in FP, it is generally agreed that there is a strong need at present for scholars to facilitate integrative frameworks of analysis, as well as to break the habit of viewing actors and structures as two mutually exclusive rather than constitutive and interactive entities. One such suggestion in the form of an analytical framework is offered at the end of the chapter.

Questions

1. Why is the study of the role of actors and structures in foreign policy important?

2. Why is it necessary to employ approaches or frameworks of analysis when studying actors and structures in foreign policy?

3. Give a brief sketch of the historical development of foreign policy analysis.

4. What characterizes 'behaviouralism', and what effects did it have on the subsequent development of the field of foreign policy analysis?

5. Give a brief characterization of 'process' approaches to foreign policy analysis, and how they treat actors and structures.

6. What, in your view, is the essential difference between 'process' and 'policy' approaches to foreign policy analysis?

7. Give a brief outline and comparison of the various approaches to foreign policy analysis based on a structural perspective, and the role which actors and structures play in these.

8. How do the cognitive and psychological approaches discussed in the chapter differ from process-oriented approaches?

9. Give a brief analysis of the agency–structure problem and its relevance to foreign policy analysis.

10. Evaluate the 'synthetic' framework suggested in the conclusion.

Further reading

Allison, G.T. and Zelikow, P. (1999), *Essence of Decision: Explaining the Cuban Missile Crisis* **(2nd edn) (New York: Longman).**
The second and much revised and updated edition of one of the twentieth-century classics in foreign policy analysis, much read by students, scholars, and decision makers alike.

Carlsnaes, W. and Guzzini, S. (eds) (2011), *Foreign Policy Analysis,* **Vols 1–5 (London: Sage).**
A five-volume collection of some of the most seminal contributions to FP since the Second World War. Although obviously a subjective choice, this collection is intended to present a broad picture of the analytical diversity of the field.

Hill, C. (2003), *The Changing Politics of Foreign Policy* (Basingstoke: Palgrave Macmillan).
One of the few recent substantive books in the field, by one of Britain's foremost foreign policy scholars.

Houghton, D.P. (2007), 'Reinvigorating the Study of Foreign Policy Decision-Making: Toward a Constructivist Approach', *Foreign Policy Analysis* 3: 24–45.
A recent and constructive example—still too rare—combining American and European traditions within the field.

Hudson, V.M. (2007), *Foreign Policy Analysis: Classic and Contemporary Theory* (Lanham, MD: Rowman & Littlefield).
The most recent theoretically oriented American textbook, by a leading member of the younger generation of foreign policy scholars with roots in the comparative foreign policy tradition.

Snyder, R.C., Bruck, H.W., Sapin, B., Hudson, V.M., Chollet, D.M., and Goldgeier, J.M. (2002), *Foreign Policy Decision-Making (Revisited)* (Basingstoke: Palgrave Macmillan).
A latter-day resuscitation of one of the real classics of early foreign policy analysis, much cited but rarely emulated.

Wight, C. (2007), *Agents, Structures and International Relations* (Cambridge: Cambridge University Press).
Currently the definitive study of the agency–structure debate, and worth penetrating if one wants to get a real grip on the meta-theoretical and theoretical issues involved in studying actors and structures in the making of foreign policy. However, not for the theoretically faint-hearted.

 ## Web links

http://www.cfr.org/ Web site of the *Council of Foreign Relations,* perhaps the best single source for users searching for up to date information and insights about international politics.

http://www.foreignaffairs.org/ Website of *Foreign Affairs*, published by the Council of Foreign Affairs in New York; probably America's most influential mainstream publication on international affairs and foreign policy.

http://www.foreignpolicy.com/ Website of *Foreign Policy,* a major policy journal published by the Carnegie Endowment for International Peace, Washington, DC; oriented towards the analysis of global politics, economics, and ideas.

http://www.chathamhouse.org.uk/ Founded in 1920 and based in London, Chatham House is one of the world's leading organizations for the analysis of international issues.

http://www.brook.edu/fp/fp_hp.htm Website of the Foreign Policy Studies Program at the Brookings Institution, one of the most respected American think tanks in international affairs.

 Visit the Online Resource Centre that accompanies this book for more information:
www.oxfordtextbooks.co.uk/orc/smith_foreign/

Foreign policy decision making: rational, psychological, and neurological models

JANICE GROSS STEIN

Chapter contents

 Reader's guide

This chapter looks at the contribution that rational models of choice can make to foreign policy analysis. It then examines cognitive models which identify the boundaries to rationality in decision making. The chapter then looks at new research in neuroscience which recasts the role of rational models and highlights the importance of emotions. It concludes with suggestions for system design that can improve foreign policy decision making.

Introduction

In early 2007, the Munk School of Global Affairs at the University of Toronto assembled a group of scholars to think broadly about the meaning of rationality in foreign policy and conflict resolution. Among them were two recent Nobel Prize laureates and a distinguished philosopher. We asked our colleagues to wrestle with a practical problem, that of 'applied' rationality. They followed in the footsteps of scholars and policy makers, who for thirty years have debated the elements of a solution to the Israel–Palestine conflict. The outlines of a 'rational' solution are broadly known on both sides of the divide: two independent states and a shared Jerusalem. Yet the conflict is still raging and people are still being killed. What stands in the way of a rational solution to this enduring conflict? Why can the governments on both sides not move towards a rational compromise that is known to the participants as well as outsiders? If analysts and political leaders on both sides know the broad outlines of a rational solution, why can't they get there?

This deceptively simple question masks a host of complex issues. What does it mean to 'know' a rational solution? What is a 'rational' solution in a real-world setting? Rational by what criteria? From whose perspective? If one or more of the parties to the conflict rejects the solution, are they necessarily 'irrational'? Are there good reasons why solutions that scholars might consider 'rational' are not chosen by government leaders? All these questions point to even bigger questions. How rational are political leaders when they make big and important foreign policy decisions? How well do concepts of rationality, as developed by philosophers or economists, travel into the world of politics and foreign policy making? The short answer: not very well at all.

Commonsensical understandings of rationality

This chapter could get badly off track by investigating the many meanings of rationality. The focus of this chapter is much narrower—how we understand foreign policy decision making. I put forward two commonsensical models of rationality in decision making. In the first, **rational decision making** refers to the process that people *should* use to choose. In a rational decision-making process, people should be logical and orderly. Their preferences should be ranked, at least intuitively, in such a way that if I prefer A to B, and B to C, then I prefer A to C. If I prefer peace to all-out war, and I prefer all-out war to low-level insurgency, then I should prefer peace to insurgency. If I violate this requirement of 'transitive' preferences—if I prefer C to A, or insurgency to peace—then I am ruled out as a rational decision maker. We need to look elsewhere—and we will in this chapter—to explain choices that violate the axioms of rationality.

As part of the process of making informed choices, rational decision makers should be good at attending to new information that comes along as they are making their choices; they need to 'update' their estimates in response to new reliable information that contains significant evidence. The attentive reader may notice all sorts of caveats here: 'reliable' information that comes from a 'trustworthy' source, 'new' information or information that the decision maker did not previously have, and 'significant' or diagnostic evidence that speaks to the likelihood of some of the consequences the policy maker is considering. When President Bush was considering whether or not to go to war against Iraq, he was told that Saddam Hussein had sought to buy yellow cake uranium from Niger. This information was new to the President—he had not heard it before—and it was diagnostic: it signalled that Saddam was probably seeking to develop unconventional weapons. What the information was *not*, however, was reliable or trustworthy, and at least one official quickly identified it as unreliable; therefore it should have been discounted or excluded from any kind of consideration. The reliability of information is a threshold barrier that any piece of evidence should cross on its way into the decision-making process. However, determining the trustworthiness of any piece of information is often very difficult to do. Indeed, 'rational' processes of information management are often swamped by the quick intuitive processes and deep cognitive biases that political leaders use to interpret evidence.

So far, this picture of a rational decision maker approximates common sense. People who make important choices about foreign policy need to be logical, discriminating while open to new evidence, and 'coherent' and 'consistent' in responding to logical arguments.[1] Rational decision makers are those who are open to arguments and evidence, free of serious blinkers as they weigh the evidence and think about the likely consequences of options. The minimal commonsensical requirements of rationality in foreign policy decision making expect that policy makers can learn from history, and that they can draw some propositions from the past and apply these propositions in an appropriate way to the future as they weigh the likely consequences of the options they face (Jervis 1976; Vertzberger 1990; Tetlock and Breslauer 1991; Levy 1994; Tetlock 1998a).

The second, more demanding, models of rational choice expect far more from decision makers. Borrowing heavily from micro-economics, they expect decision makers to generate **subjective probability estimates** of the consequences of the options that they consider, to update these estimates as they consider new evidence, and to maximize their subjective expected utility. Rational decision makers choose the option that promises to give them what is likely of greatest value to them. In other words rational choosers are reasonably good estimators of probability and efficient in the choices that they make.[2]

To put these requirements more formally, theories of rational choice in foreign policy treat both initial preferences and expectations as given and exogenous. Models of rational choice are powerful because they can identify the strategy that leaders should choose, given their preferences and expectations. They take original preferences as given and specify the optimal choice. In so far as formal models of rational choice discuss the process of choosing, they assume that people are 'instrumentally rational'. Given their existing preferences, people are expected to engage in an appropriate end–means calculation. Formal models of rational choice do not claim to explain the beliefs and expectations which *lead* to choice, and therefore, in a fundamental sense, leave out most of what is important in explaining foreign policy. Rational decision makers resolve the conflicts they face in multi-attribute problems by measuring along a single attribute—that of subjective utility—and simply trading off to find the best outcome. Rational choice appears to do away with the conflict of choice by measuring along a single dimension. They assume a common yardstick which makes complex measurements simple.

How well do these models mirror processes of choice in foreign policy? Not well at all. There is by now abundant evidence that foreign policy decision makers, and people more generally, rarely meet these standards. This evidence will surprise some readers because, as a species, we are intuitive causal thinkers and like to think of ourselves as rational; in many ways, a discussion of the deep limits to human rationality goes against the grain. The most important evidence of the limits to rationality comes from well-established work in psychology, specifically from the new, still tentative, research results in neuroscience which are challenging the most fundamental tenets of the rational model. The work of neuroscientists is important for the analysis of foreign policy because it is re-introducing conflict as a key feature in the choices made by decision makers. What makes the work of psychology and neuroscience even more important is that the two tend to converge, a factor of real importance in analyses of foreign policy.

Psychological models: the 'cognitive revolution'

Forty years ago, psychologists began a 'cognitive revolution' as they rejected simple behaviourist models and looked again at how people's thought processes shaped the choices they made. They brought the 'mind' back into psychology. Although this was not its main purpose, the cognitive revolution can be understood largely as a commentary on the limits of rationality. Much of the work accepts rational choice as the default position and then demonstrates its boundaries. Research has now accumulated to show that people rarely conform to the expectations of the rational model (Kahneman *et al.* 1982; Hogarth and Goldstein 1996; Dawes 1998). The grounds for pessimism are twofold: the difficulty of making inferences (as models of rational choice anticipate), and the limitations of the human mind.

Cognitive psychology has demonstrated important differences between the expectations of rational decision models and the processes of attribution, estimation, and judgement people frequently use. It explains these differences by the need for simple rules of information processing and judgement that are necessary to make sense of uncertain and complex environments. Human beings have a preference for *simplicity*. They are also averse to ambiguity and want *consistency* instead. Further, they misunderstand fundamentally the essence of probability (Dawes 1998; Tetlock 2006), making them intuitively *poor estimators*. Lastly, humans have risk profiles that depart from models of rational choice; as a result, we are far more *averse to loss* than we are gain-seeking. Together, these four attributes compromise the capacity for rational choice and affect the decision-making abilities of leaders and officials who are responsible for foreign policy.

Simplicity

Political leaders making decisions about the world need to order that world, making its complexities somewhat simpler. To do so, they unconsciously strip the nuances, context, and subtleties out of the problems they face in order to build simple frames. When they look to the past to learn about the future, political leaders tend to draw simple one-to-one analogies without qualifying conditions. In 1991, President George Bush called Saddam Hussein 'another Hitler', with little attention to what was different either about the two men or about Iraq in 1990 and Germany in 1938. Yet fitting Saddam into an existing frame through use of **analogical reasoning**—reasoning based on analogy—gave the President a readily accessible script about how to respond to Iraq's invasion of Kuwait (Khong 1992).

Drawing arguments from a complex historical past is even more challenging. When NATO leaders decided to take over responsibility for military operations in Afghanistan from the USA in 2005, there was a relatively straightforward discussion about the importance of preventing 'terrorists' from regaining control of southern Afghanistan. Policy makers were partly correct. al-Qaeda, now in its third generation, was certainly one element, but what made Afghanistan so challenging to outside forces was its own indigenous insurgency and strong warlords who coexisted with al-Qaeda. Global terror, local insurgency, local warlords, and a local economy fuelled by narcotics interacted together to create an environment of far greater complexity than the simple one-dimensional construction of the challenge that policy makers used. Their simplified definition of the problem limited the options that policy makers then considered—it both pushed other options off the table and blinded decision makers to some of the likely consequences of the option they chose to 'fight terror'. We all need to simplify a noisy, distracting, and complex environment in order to see patterns, but typically we oversimplify badly. Political leaders are no exception.

Consistency

Cognitive psychologists have produced robust evidence that people strongly prefer consistency, that they are made uncomfortable by dissonant information, and that they consequently deny or discount inconsistent information to preserve their beliefs. This drive for consistency impairs the processes of estimation and judgement. The well-established tendency to discount inconsistent information contributes significantly to the persistence of beliefs. Indeed, exposure to contradictory information frequently results in the strengthening of beliefs (Anderson *et al.* 1980; Anderson 1983; Hirt and Sherman 1985). People, it seems, are hard-wired to be conservative.

The lengths to which policy makers will go to defend policy forecasts gone wrong are quite remarkable (Tetlock 1998b). For example, some of the strongest proponents of regime change in Iraq during 2003, when confronted with the steep violence four years later, insisted that they had been right but that Iraq's leaders simply had not risen to the challenge. Others insisted that they had been right to support the invasion, but that they had underestimated the gross incompetence of the Bush administration. Politicians on both sides of the argument did not revise their fundamental arguments when confronted with strongly discrepant evidence, but shifted responsibility to the incompetence of others which, they insisted, they could not have been expected to foresee. Why they should not have been expected to see the sectarian divisions among a brutalized population or the hubris which infected planning for the war remains unexplained.

Much of the work of cognitive psychology has been done in the laboratory with students; experts have questioned how well such results travel into the political world. That question has been largely put to rest by a remarkable study of political forecasts in different cultures, where experts on foreign policy generally continued to defend their forecasts even though what they expected did not happen (Tetlock 2006). Tetlock identifies seven categories of belief-system defences: challenging whether the local conditions required by the forecast were satisfied; invoking the unexpected occurrence of a shock; invoking a close-call counterfactual—'I almost got it right'; using an 'off-on timing' argument—'I'm ahead of my time, history will prove me right'; declaring that international politics is hopelessly indeterminate and consequently unpredictable; defiantly asserting that they made the 'right mistake' and would do it again; and insisting that unlikely things sometimes happen (Tetlock 2006: 129).

Conservative foreign policy makers in the Bush administration implicitly argued that local conditions were not satisfied when they blamed Iraq's leaders for failing to seize the opportunity that they had been given. The problem was not with their forecast (i.e. that the removal of a regime by force would open the door to democracy) but with the would-be democrats. A defence that 'all things were not equal', that an unexpected shock changed the direction, is also a comforting defence against error. NATO officials acknowledge that they did not expect the ferocity of the Taliban insurgency in 2005, but insisted that their fundamental forecast of accelerating reconstruction and stability in Afghanistan would be proved correct over the longer term. This defence combines the unexpected shock with an argument about timing to rescue the forecast.

Some of the most intriguing defences by experts claimed that they were almost right. Who could have expected Saddam to have got rid of his weapons programmes, experts insisted, when they failed to uncover unconventional weapons programmes in post-invasion Iraq. But, they insisted, had the USA not invaded, he undoubtedly would have forged ahead with nuclear weapons as the international sanctions weakened. They would have been vindicated with the passage of time, they insisted, had the USA not removed Saddam from power. Here too, experts draw on 'close-call counterfactuals' and arguments about timing to preserve their belief systems. Closely related was the argument by those who got it wrong that it was better to have overestimated than underestimated his weapons programme. Better safe than sorry, they said.

Tetlock confirms the same kind of self-serving bias in argumentation among political experts that cognitive psychologists have documented in the laboratory. He also finds a relationship between the size of the mistakes and the activation of defences. The more confident experts were in their original forecast, the more threatened they were when they were faced with disconfirming evidence, and the more motivated they were to use one or more of the seven defences to preserve their beliefs. '**Defensive cognitions**', Tetlock argues, 'are activated when forecasters most need them' (Tetlock 2006: 137). When political experts most needed to revise their judgements, they were least open to revision. This same pattern was also very much present among American decision makers during the Vietnam War.

The evidence we have reviewed thus far suggests that belief change is very difficult. Yet at times belief systems or schemas do change, at times dramatically. Theories of **cognitive consistency** expect that the least central parts of a belief system, i.e. those with the fewest interdependent cognitions, will change first. People will also make the smallest possible change; they will change their beliefs incrementally, generate a large number of exceptions and special cases, and make superficial alterations rather than rethink their fundamental assumptions. Political leaders in the USA were generally resistant to changing their beliefs about the Soviet Union after Mikhail Gorbachev came to power. In the face of counter-evidence, three years after he became General Secretary, senior policy makers in Washington were arguing that Gorbachev's strategy was to lull the West while the Soviet Union recovered, and therefore the USA should continue to be both sceptical and cautious.

Cognitive psychologists suggest some conditions that facilitate change (Jervis 1976: 288–318; Tetlock 2006). There is evidence that greater change will occur when information arrives in large batches rather than bit by bit. Cognitive models suggest that when people are confronted with overwhelmingly discrepant information, when there is no other way to account for large amounts of contradictory data, beliefs can change dramatically (Jervis 1976: 288–318). When central beliefs do finally change, they generally trigger far-reaching changes in related peripheral beliefs.

Change in belief is also related to content. Not all beliefs or expectancies are equivalent; they vary in strength and in the person's commitment to them. The most common distinction is between long- and short-term beliefs. Beliefs that have relatively short-run consequences are less resistant to change, while beliefs with longer-term consequences tend to persist. In foreign policy, the 'inherent bad faith model' is an example of a long-term belief that is impervious to new information (Jervis 1976; Stuart and Starr 1982). Long-term belief in another's hostility is easy to confirm and difficult to disprove almost regardless of the objective circumstances. That kind of dynamic is obvious in the enduring conflict between Israel and Palestine. It is difficult to persuade Israelis, short of a dramatic gesture that is irrevocable and self-binding in the way that President Sadat's visit to Israel in 1979 was, that Palestinian intentions have changed. It is impossible to persuade Palestinians, confronted daily by occupation, that Israel's intentions could change. Any disconfirming evidence is discounted to preserve the consistency of long-term inherent bad-faith images on both sides. In foreign policy, conflict persists because images are so difficult to change. Deeply rooted cognitive processes systematically work against rational expectations of appropriate, diagnostic updating. When beliefs and arguments do change, they generally change in uneven ways that reflect the somewhat arbitrary patterns in the information and basic processes of attribution. Neither of these has very much to do with rational expectations. However, there is some evidence that is more encouraging. It comes from the close analysis of differences among foreign policy experts in their willingness to entertain the possibility that they were wrong. Not all experts are resistant to change all the time.

Drawing on a well-known distinction made by Isaiah Berlin, Tetlock classified foreign policy experts as 'foxes' or 'hedgehogs'. Hedgehogs know 'one big thing' extremely well and extend what they know into other domains of foreign policy analysis. Foxes, on the other hand, know many small things, are generally sceptical of grand overarching schemes, stitch together explanations with different threads of knowledge, and are sceptical of prediction in world politics (Berlin 1997; Kruglanski and Webster 1996: 263–8; Tetlock 2006: 73–5). Applying this to the realm of foreign policy analysis, one could suggest that hedgehogs tend to be deductive generalists in confronting evidence, while foxes are more likely to be inductive pragmatists, more likely to search for new information, and more open to new information.

The evidence shows that the foxes do much better at short-term forecasting within their broad domain of expertise than do hedgehogs. The worst performers were hedgehogs who made long-term predictions, usually with considerable confidence. Hedgehogs are generally people with strong needs for structure and closure, who are most likely to discount and dismiss inconsistent evidence when it contradicts their preconceptions. The more knowledge hedgehogs have, the better equipped they are to defend against inconsistency. Foxes, however, are sceptical of deductive approaches, more likely to qualify analogies by looking for disconfirming information, more open to competing arguments, more prone to synthesize arguments, more detached, and, not surprisingly, more likely to admit they were in error and move on. The hallmark of the foxes is their more balanced style of thinking about the world. Foxes have 'a style of thought that elevates no thought above criticism' (Tetlock, 2006: 88, 118). It is this capacity for critical sceptical thinking that enhances their capacity to learn. When foxes are in positions of political responsibility, foreign policy is likely to be more adaptive over time. Hedgehogs are far more likely to drive policy in a consistent direction.

Poor estimators

People are not intuitive probability thinkers. They depart systematically from what objective probability calculations would dictate in the estimates they make. 'Human performance suffers,' argues Tetlock, 'because we are, deep down, deterministic thinkers with an aversion to probabilistic strategies that accept the inevitability of error' (Tetlock 2006: 40). Foreign policy experts are no exception. Where we can compare their estimates with those that would be generated by objective calculations of probability, experts do surprisingly poorly. Highly educated specialists in foreign affairs approached only 20% of the ideal across all exercises (Tetlock 2006: 77). This is so because they think causally rather than pay attention to the frequencies with which events occur. Experts tend to overestimate the likelihood of war, for example, because they can easily imagine the causal pathways to war, a highly salient occurrence that they have likely studied. They pay less attention to the frequency of wars over an extended period of time (Tversky and Kahneman 1983; Koehler 1996: 1–53: 293–315).[3]

To make matters worse, probable states of the world are very difficult to estimate because we do not have repeated trials with large numbers in world politics. Foreign policy analysts generally do not live in a world of risk, where the probability distributions are known and they only have to estimate the likelihoods. Perhaps in international economics and finance and in global health, analysts know the probability distributions of recessions, deflation, and epidemics. Analysts, even the best informed, do not know the probability of another attack by militants against civilian infrastructure in the USA or the UK. There have been too few such attacks to generate any reasonable estimate of likelihood. Here foreign policy analysts work in a much tougher environment, one of uncertainty where they have no access to probability distributions. This world of uncertainty is one they particularly dislike, and it is under these conditions that experts, just like other people, seek the certainty, the false certainty, of order and control.

In this world of uncertainty, experts search for the relevant categories in which to anchor their judgements. Cognitive psychology has identified a number of **heuristics** and biases that people use in environments of risk and uncertainty that can impair processes of judgement (Nisbett and Ross 1980; Kahneman *et al.* 1982; von Winterfeldt and Edwards 1986). Heuristics refer to the rules or indicators which leaders use in order to test the propositions embedded in their own schemas. Heuristics help describe how decision makers actually process information, using convenient short cuts or rules of thumb. Three of the best-documented heuristics are availability, representativeness, and anchoring. The *availability heuristic* refers to people's tendency to interpret present information in terms of what is most easily available in their cognitive repertoire (Tversky and Kahneman 1973). *Representativeness* refers to people's proclivity to exaggerate similarities between one event and a prior class of events (Jervis 1986: 483–505). *Anchoring* refers to the estimation of a magnitude by picking an 'available' initial value as a reference point and then making a comparison (Fiske and Taylor 1984: 250–6, 268–75). (See Box 7.1)

In all three cases, what is available in a cognitive repertoire has an undue influence on how an individual influences the likelihood of a future event. What we know, and what we can access, has a disproportionate impact on our forecasts. Anchoring, availability, and representativeness were all at play for years in Britain, where policy makers were likely to forecast negative consequences from 'appeasement' because of the salience of Munich in British history. British decision makers paid correspondingly less attention to the unwanted escalation that could come from the threat of force. 'Hedgehogs' who are expert on what happens 'when we knuckle under to dictators' are especially likely to discount any negative consequences from the threat of force.

Cognitive biases also lead to serious errors in attribution which can confound policy making. People exaggerate the likelihood that other's actions are the result of their own prior behaviour and overestimate the extent to which they are the target of those actions; cognitive psychologists call this pattern of attribution the 'egocentric bias'. One of the most pervasive biases is the **fundamental attribution error**, where people exaggerate the importance of dispositional over situational factors—in other words, explaining the disliked behaviour of others as a result of their disposition, while explaining their own behaviour based on the situational constraints that they face (Fiske and Taylor 1984: 72–99). When explaining behaviour that they like, people simply reverse the pattern of inference. When the government of North Korea makes a concession in the talks about its nuclear programme, analysts in Washington see that concession as a function of the constraints Pyongyang faces, but explain their own willingness to participate in the talks as evidence of their search for a peaceful compromise.

BOX 7.1 Heuristic processing

Heuristics, those rules or indicators that serve as cognitive 'short cuts' or 'rules of thumb', often play into decision making without us being aware of it. The following study by Kahneman and Tversky (1983) revealed the common use of heuristic processing. How would *you* answer this questionnaire?

The Linda problem

Linda is 31 years old, single, outspoken, and very bright. She majored in philosophy. As a student, she was deeply concerned with issues of discrimination and social justice, and also participated in antinuclear demonstrations.

Please rank the following statements by their probability, using 1 for the most probable and 8 for the least probable.

(a) Linda is a teacher in a primary school.

(b) Linda works in a bookstore and takes yoga classes.

(c) Linda is an active feminist.

(d) Linda is a psychiatric social worker.

(e) Linda is a member of Women Against Rape.

(f) Linda is a bank teller.

(g) Linda is an insurance salesperson.

(h) Linda is a bank teller and is an active feminist.

The results of the study revealed that 85% of respondents indicated that Linda was less likely to be a bank teller than both a bank teller and a feminist. According to the representativeness heuristic, subjects make their judgements according to the perceived similarity between the statement and the description of Linda.

Kahneman, D. and Tversky, A. (1983), 'Extensional versus Intuition Reasoning: Conjunction Fallacy in Probability Judgment', *Psychological Review*, 90: 293–31. Reprinted with permission.

When North Korea cuts off the talks, it is doing so, analysts argue, because of its determination to acquire nuclear weapons in violation of the rules. A tough response to North Korea is dictated by the constraints that Western powers face. The double standard in reasoning is glaringly obvious.

To make matters worse, foreign policy experts suffered from the classic **hindsight bias**, in which they systematically misremembered what they had predicted. They claimed that they had assigned a higher probability to outcomes that did happen, and gave less credit to their opponents for getting it right than they deserved. The strength of the 'hindsight bias' was striking because these experts knew that their original judgements had been recorded and that these records were accessible. How can we explain this kind of bias in the face of evidence that these experts knew existed? Tetlock argues as follows:

> A fuller explanation must trace hindsight bias to a deeper cause capable of producing genuine self-deception: the largely unconscious cognitive processing that is automatically activated . . . that allows us to rapidly assimilate the observed outcome into our network of beliefs about what makes things happen. People manage to convince themselves, sometimes within milliseconds, that they 'knew it all along' (Tetlock 2006: 139–40).

Loss aversion

Foreign policy decision makers, like people generally, are not neutral about risk. Cognitive psychology has generated robust evidence that loss is more painful than comparable gain is pleasant, and that people prefer an immediate smaller gain rather than taking a chance on a larger longer-term reward (Kahneman and Tversky 1979, 2000; Tversky and Kahneman 1992). People systematically overvalue losses relative to comparable gains. These propositions about risk have held up across a wide variety of cultures and situations.

The impact of loss aversion on foreign policy decision making is considerable. Leaders tend to be risk averse when things are going well and relatively risk acceptant when things are going badly—when they face a crisis in which they are likely to lose or have lost something that matters to them. Leaders are also likely to take greater risk to protect what they already have—the 'endowment effect'—than to increase their gains. They are also likely to take greater risk to reverse losses, to recapture what they once held, than they would to make new gains. And when decision makers suffer a significant loss, they are far slower to accommodate to these losses than they would be to incorporate gains. Finally, leaders reverse their preferences and make different choices when problems are reframed as losses rather than gains.

These general findings apply directly to foreign policy choices. President Sadat of Egypt, for example, never 'normalized' for the loss of the Sinai to Israel in 1967. Even though Israel had an obvious advantage in military capabilities, Sadat was undeterred and, highly motivated to recapture the Sinai, he designed around Israel's military strengths and launched a war in 1973 (Stein 1985, 1996). Under these kinds of conditions, theories of rational deterrence which do not systematically build in aversion to loss are likely to mislead foreign policy decision makers by generating undue confidence.

This review of the need for simplicity and consistency, the impediments to probabilistic thinking, and the predisposition to loss aversion are often treated, as we saw earlier in this chapter, as *deviations* from rational models of information processing, estimation, and choice. Rational choice remains the default and these 'deviations' are treated as limiting conditions. I disagree. These 'deviations' are so pervasive and so systematic that it is a mistake to consider rational models of choice as empirically valid in foreign policy analysis.

Neuroscience, emotion, and computation

We are at the edge of an exciting revolution in our understanding of the human brain and how it works. New imaging technology is allowing scientists for the first time to 'watch' the brain as it thinks, feels, remembers, and chooses; the pictures they are seeing are revolutionizing understandings of thought and decision. Even though the experimental results are still far from definitive, two results stand out. First, many decisions seem not to be the result of a deliberative thought process, but preconscious neurological processes. The brain can absorb about eleven million pieces of information a second, but can only process forty consciously. The unconscious brain manages the rest. Second, many decisions seem to be the product of strong emotional responses. (See Figure 7.1.)

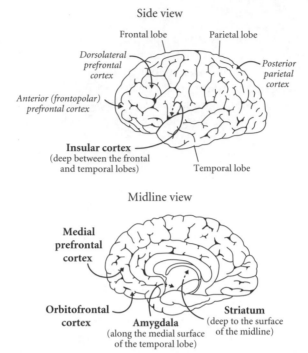

Notes: Lateral (side) and medial (midline) views of the human cerebrum, identifying areas critically associated with decision making. Areas in bold have consistently been associated with emotional processing, while areas in italics have consistently been associated with higher-level cognitive processes

Figure 7.1 The human cerebrum

Source: Cohen, J. (2005), 'The Vulcanization of the Human Brain: A Neural Perspective on Interactions Between Cognition and Emotion', *Journal of Economic Perspectives*, 19: 9. Reproduced by permission of Jonathan D. Cohen, Department of Psychology and Princeton Neuroscience Institute, Princeton University.

Scientists now make a very strong, and startling, claim. There is growing consensus that emotion is 'first', because it is automatic and fast, and that it plays a dominant role in shaping behaviour. We know now that emotion operates in part below the threshold of conscious awareness (LeDoux 1996; Winkielman and Berridge 2004). Contrary to conventional wisdom, we generally feel *before* we think and, what is even more surprising, we often act *before* we think. There is widespread consensus that the brain implements 'automatic processes' which are faster than conscious deliberations with little or no awareness or feeling of effort (Bargh *et al*.1996; Bargh and Chartrand 1999). Not surprisingly, the conscious brain then interprets behaviour that emerges from automatic, affective, processes as the outcome of cognitive deliberations (Camerer *et al.* 2005: 26).

A useful way of thinking about emotion and cognition is to see affective processes as those that address the go–no-go questions, the questions that motivate approach–avoidance, while cognitive processes are those that answer true–false questions (Camerer *et al.* 2005: 18 Zajonc 1980, 1984, 1998). Choice clearly invokes both kinds of processes. Establishing truth claims about states of the world is usually not enough for people to make a choice. What matters to me, what I value, is an emotional as well as a cognitive process, and is important in what I decide to do, whether I go, or I don't go, whether I approach or I avoid. Whether or not I am treated fairly is an emotional as well as a cognitive judgement and, in this sense, emotion carries utility.

How do neuroscientists analyse emotion and cognition? Some conceive of two separate operating systems in the brain: emotion and reason.[4] 'Emotions influence our decisions,' argues Jonathan Cohen. 'They do so in just about every walk of our lives, whether we are aware or unaware of it, and whether we acknowledge it or not' (Cohen 2005: 1). Emotions are automatic processes associated with strong positive or negative response. The brain, Cohen explains, has different kinds of mechanisms: one, which includes emotional responses, can respond automatically, quickly, and definitively but is relatively inflexible; cognition is less rapid and has limited capacity but is more flexible. There is a trade-off between the speed and specialization of emotions and the generality of reflection. In the circumstances of modern life, these systems may prescribe different responses and the outcome of this competition determines choice (Camerer *et al.* 2005). This branch of neuroeconomics has explicitly brought conflict back into decision making. Choice is a conflict between emotion and computation. (See Box 7.2.)

Kahneman calls the first, emotion-based, system of decision making 'intuitive' and 'associative', and the second system of cognitive decision making 'reasoned' and 'rule-governed'.[5] The first system is preconscious, automatic, fast, effortless, associative, unreflective, and slow to change. The second system is conscious, slow, effortful, reflective, rule-governed, and flexible. The vast majority of decisions are made through the first system, which draws heavily on emotions and in a competition between the two always trumps the rule-governed reasoned system. It is extraordinarily difficult, Kahneman concludes, for the second system to educate the first.

The well-known 'ultimatum game' highlights the computational, cognitive, and emotional elements at play in decision making (Figure 7.2). The game comes out of economics but has relevance to international politics as well. One partner has access to a given resource—wealth,

---

BOX 7.2 Scientists create 'trust potion'

Scientists create 'trust potion'

A key hormone helps determine whether we will trust lovers, friends, or business contacts, scientists claim. Exposure to an oxytocin 'potion' led people to be more trusting, tests by University of Zurich researchers found. They report in the journal *Nature* that the finding could help people with conditions such as autism, where relating to others can be a problem. But one expert warned it could be misused by politicians who want to persuade more people to back them.

'Some may worry about the prospect that political operators will generously spray the crowd with oxytocin at rallies of their candidates' (Dr Antonio Damasio, University of Iowa College of Medicine).

Oxytocin is a molecule produced naturally in the hypothalamus area of the brain which regulates a variety of physiological processes, including emotion.

Story from BBC NEWS:

http://news.bbc.co.uk/go/pr/fr/-/1/hi/health/4599299.stm

Published: 2005/06/02 Ó BBC MMV

vast natural resources, highly sophisticated military technology—and can propose how the resource should be split. If the other party accepts the proposal, then the resource is divided as they have agreed. If the split is rejected, neither receives anything and the game is over, and conflict probably follows.

Rationally, the second party should accept anything that is offered, because anything is clearly better than nothing. And again, the first party, knowing that for the other anything is better than nothing, should rationally offer as little as possible. The game has been played across a wide range of situations and cultures, with a remarkably consistent outcome. Contrary to what rational models would expect, offers of less than 20% of the total are generally rejected out of hand. Why? Perhaps those who rejected the offer were worried about their bargaining reputation for the next round, as rational deterrence theory says they should. But players responded the same way even when reputational effects were removed from consideration, when they were told that they would play the game only once. When asked why they rejected an offer that would give them something, players responded that the offer was humiliating, insulting, patently unfair. They responded quickly and intuitively to an offer which gave them something, but humiliated them in the process.[6] Their rejection was driven by a strong negative emotional response.

According to this experimental economics game, first studied by Güth et al. (1982), two players interact anonymously and only once, so reciprocation is not an issue. The first player proposes how to divide a sum of money with the second player. The second player can either accept or reject the proposed division: if the second player accepts the division, the first gets his demand and the second player gets the rest; on the other hand, if the second player rejects the division, neither player receives anything.

Illustratively this game can be demonstrated by the example below:

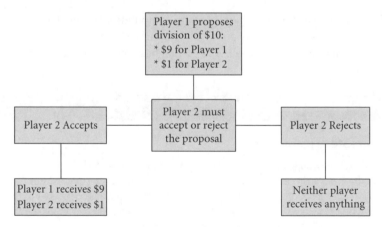

Rationality would suggest that the second player accept whatever division is proposed, because anything is better than nothing. However, consistently, the second player rejects the proposed division when offers are less than twenty per cent of the total. Why? Emotional reasons: the second player tends to find such low offers 'humiliating', 'insulting', and 'unfair', thereby denying both players anything (Cohen 2005: 13–15).

Figure 7.2 The 'ultimatum game': how would you choose?

Source: The negotiation style known as the 'ultimatum game' was introduced by experimental economists Güth, W., Schmittberger, R., and Schwarze, B. (1982), 'An Experimental Analysis of Ultimatum Bargaining', *Journal of Economic Behavior of Organization*, 3: 367–88, © Elsevier 1982.

Emotion is an individual embodied experience. How can the study of emotion be extended to the analysis of foreign policy and to decision making which, even when decisions are made by individual leaders, takes place in a collective context on behalf of others? Emotions are meaningful in a social context (Saurette 2006: 507–8)? It is only with a shared sense of what constitutes appropriate social behaviour, for example, that a person, a people, or a government feels humiliated at all. When the flag of one nation is burned by another, the humiliation and anger that follows flow from a shared understanding that the burning of a flag is a deliberately insulting and hostile act. Physiological processes are layered by social knowledge which shapes the appropriateness of anger, fear, and happiness. It is in this sense that emotions need to be conceived as not only an individual but also a social process (Ross 2006).

Scholars in international relations are now beginning to look carefully at the neuroscience of emotion. Research on emotion is having a significant impact on the analysis of a wide range of global issues: the logic of deterrence (Mercer 2005, 2010), cooperation and the solution of collective action problems (Rilling *et al.* 2002; Mercer 2005), nuclear proliferation (Hymans 2006); the War on Terror (Bennett 2002; Saurette 2006; Bleiker and Hutchison 2008; Crawford 2009), revenge, anger, and humiliation as motives for war (Gries 2004; Saurette 2006; Löwenheim and Heimann 2008), and patterns of ethnic and civil conflict (Kaufman 2001), conflict resolution, and post-conflict reconciliation (Edkins 2003; Hutchison and Bleiker 2008)—all issues that are central to foreign policy decision makers in the twenty-first century.

Psychological models have long informed the study of deterrence (Jervis *et al.* 1985; Lebow and Stein 1994), but building emotions into the explanation is shedding new light on old problems. The credibility of signals, an essential component in theories of deterrence, compellence, and bargaining, is not only a property of the sender, as some formal models of signalling suggest, but also a function of the beliefs of the receiver (Mercer 2010). These beliefs are not only cognitive but are emotional as well. The emotional cues that signals evoke—fear, anger—matter in so far as these emotions then prompt beliefs and action in turn. Research demonstrates that fear prompts uncertainty and risk-averse action, while anger prompts certainty and risk acceptance. Threats that evoke fear, unless they evoke loss avoidance, are likely to prompt hesitancy and a risk-averse response; indeed, that is the purpose of most deterrent threats. However, frightening threats are less likely to be successful when they are designed to compel adversarial leaders to act.

Conclusion

We are at a hinge moment in the development of theory and evidence on decision making. Much that has been taken for granted is now being questioned as new avenues of research and theory open. The work that this chapter has reviewed looks largely at individual decision making, and it is a big step from individual to collective decision making. We need to be very careful in generalizing from the individual to the collective; indeed many believe that it is inappropriate to do so.

It is a well-established fallacy to give the properties of an individual to a collective entity. Bureaucracies and states do not think or feel—the individuals within them do. A government, as a collective entity, does not calculate and make rational choices—policy makers do. It is impossible to aggregate individual preferences without significant distortion. As other chapters in this volume look explicitly at models of collective decision making (see Chapters Six and Fourteen), it remains to ask here: How important are *individual* models of choice in foreign policy analysis?

Presidential systems often give great scope to the choice of the president who seeks advice and delegates authority, but reserves to him/herself the central decisions in foreign policy. Here, individual models of choice are very relevant. Even in parliamentary systems, prime ministers increasingly make decisions after consulting a handful of advisers, and only after they have decided do they bring the issue to cabinet (Stein and Lang 2007). Here too, individual models of decision making are relevant. It is in the framing of decisions and in the implementation phase that more complex models are necessary. In other words, what comes before and after choice often constricts the space for decisions.

A second question grows out of the research this chapter has examined. There is strong robust evidence that most human choice is preconscious and strongly and quickly influenced by emotion. How relevant is this evidence to public choice in foreign policy? We cannot yet answer this question with confidence, but the survey of foreign policy analysts suggests that the more general patterns we have identified are present in foreign policy decision making as well (Tetlock 2006). Despite their expertise, foreign policy makers are no less biased than other people.

If we assume that foreign policy makers do not deviate significantly from these general patterns, then we face a third question. Does this new evidence about choice constrain what we can do to improve the quality of decision making in foreign policy? That is the power of models of rational choice—they set norms and standards. The new research should not discourage foreign policy analysts from efforts at improving decision making, but these efforts might need a different focus.

The pioneering work of Damasio (1994), LeDoux (1996), and Panksepp (1998) joined together emotion and reason. The revolutionary impact of Damasio's research was to make it clear that people with impaired emotional capacity cannot make rational choices. Reason presupposes emotion. At the same time, the conscious brain can condition preconscious choices after the fact. In other words, there is an opportunity to prime neural responses, to educate our brains for the next time. Cohen argues that the brain has been 'vulcanized'; just as rubber is treated with a substance to improve its strength, resiliency, and usefulness, so neurological systems leave room for reason over time (Cohen 2005: 19). The capacity to reason and reflect protects people against impulsivity over time. When these protections are not adequate, social and technological innovations can help to protect people against themselves. For example, people discount the future badly and consequently do not save enough for their retirement. When the default was changed so that people needed to opt out of enforced savings which were deducted from their monthly pay, savings for retirement grew dramatically. Neuroeconomists call this 'libertarian' or 'asymmetric' paternalism; libertarian because people still have choice, but paternalistic because default options are set to produce individual and collective benefit (Camerer et al. 2003). It is not hard to imagine extending these kinds of options to foreign policies which deal with the environment, health, and arms control.

The new research emerging from neuroscience does not eliminate the possibility of learning and change. Reflection may come after choice, but it prepares decision makers for the next decision. The challenge is to understand far better how and when emotions are engaged, when they improve decisions, and how emotions engage with reflection and reasoning (Ochsner and Gross 2005). Neuroscience research on choice certainly does not preclude priming the unconscious mind through both repetitive patterning and systems design, what some of have called the 'free won't' (as distinct from 'free will'). In this context, research on learning and change, largely neglected, becomes especially important in foreign policy analysis (Tetlock and Breslauer 1991; Levy 1994; Stein 1994).

Rational models of decision making can be used in three important ways. First, they are useful as an aspiration, or a norm, but only with the full realization that foreign policy decision makers are unlikely ever to meet that norm. They are not descriptive theories of choice (Elster 1986: 1). Second, the creative use of rational choice models has uncovered many counter-intuitive and non-obvious paradoxes and traps that can be very instructive to those who make decisions. Knowing the traps of games of Prisoner's Dilemma and the risks of Chicken can serve as salutary warnings for those who, for example, must make life-and-death decisions about when and how to use military force. Finally, rational choice models can be designed into the small cracks that neuroscience opens up and highlights as spaces that can be used to correct some of the worst biases in decision making.

Leaders who are aware of the dynamics of choice can build in compulsory delays and waiting periods which leave time for reflection and analysis. They can design the equivalent of automatic check-offs in foreign policy by putting in place systems of checklists before decisions are finalized. They can seek out their critics and expose themselves, quite deliberately, to counter-arguments. They can demand worst-case scenarios and anticipate how they would respond were the worst to happen. They can insist on verification of the information that they think is most important to their decision. Leaders can design the open spaces that they need for deliberation, reflection, and analysis once they acknowledge their impulsive emotion-driven choice. It is precisely in these open spaces that foreign policy analysis, working with the dynamics of choice, can make its most significant contribution.

 Key points

- Rational models have poor empirical validity. People rarely conform to the expectations of a rational model, which suggests there is something beyond rationality that explains human choices.

- Cognitive psychology reveals that people prefer simplicity and consistency, making them poor estimators; people are also more averse to loss than they are gain-seeking.

- Political leaders unconsciously make use of analogical reasoning to simplify a complex environment, at the risk of oversimplifying the situation.

- Foreign policy experts have been classified as 'foxes' or 'hedgehogs'. Hedgehogs know 'one big thing' and are poor at making long-term predictions; they are more likely to drive policy in a consistent direction even when they are wrong. Foxes, on the other hand, know 'many small things' and are particularly strong at providing short-term forecasts; they are more likely to drive policy in a more dynamic, adaptive direction.

- Many decisions seem to be the result of strong emotional responses. Neuroscience enables us to 'see' how the brain reaches certain forms of behaviour, therefore making the work of neuroscientists an important resource for the analysis of foreign policy.

 Questions

1. When are rational choice models inadequate?

2. What does cognitive psychology tell us about human behaviour that is relevant to foreign policy analysis?

3. Do you knowingly engage in heuristic processing? Give examples of how heuristics affects your decision making.

4. Do you consider yourself to be a 'hedgehog' or a 'fox'? What are the advantages of being one or the other if you are in a position of political leadership? Can you identity 'hedgehogs' and 'foxes' among today's leaders?

5. Why are analysts of foreign policy looking to the work of neuroscientists? What does the physiology of the brain reveal about decision making?

6. How does human emotion affect foreign policy decision making? Give examples of how emotion can positively and negatively determine response in decision making.

7. How can we proceed in foreign policy analysis knowing that decision making is often done at a pre-conscious level?

8. What can we do to improve the quality of decision making in foreign policy?

 ## Further reading

Goldstein, E.B. (2007), *Cognitive Psychology: Connecting Mind, Research and Everyday Experience* (2nd edn) (Belmont, CA: Wadsworth).
This book introduces cognitive psychology and the theories of cognition, with a final chapter on 'reasoning and decision-making'.

Hudson, V. and Singer, E. (1992) *Political Psychology and Foreign Policy* (Boulder, CO: Westview Press).
This book discusses the impact of psychological processes on foreign policy decision making.

McDermott, R. (2004), 'The Feeling of Rationality: The Meaning of Neuroscientific Advances for Political Science', *Perspectives on Politics*, 2: 691–706.
This article discusses the uses of neuroscience in understanding decision making in politics.

Mintz, A. (ed.) (2003), *Integrating Cognitive and Rational Theories of Foreign Policy Decision-Making* (Basingstoke: Palgrave Macmillan).
This edited volume draws from both cognitive and rationalist ideas to examine how foreign policy decisions are made, using case studies and experimental analysis.

Yetiv, S.A. (2004), *Explaining Foreign Policy: U.S. Decision-Making and the Persian Gulf War* (Baltimore, MD: Johns Hopkins University Press).
In this book a theoretical framework on foreign policy decision-making is presented and tested using the Persian Gulf War of 1991 as a case study.

Zak, P.J. (2004), 'Neuroeconomics', *Philosophical Transactions of the Royal Society of London (Biological Sciences)*, 359: 1737–48.
This paper introduces the emerging transdisciplinary field known as 'neuroeconomics', which uses neuroscientific measurement to examine decision making. The role of emotions is examined in social and strategic decision-making settings.

 Visit the Online Resource Centre that accompanies this book for more information:
www.oxfordtextbooks.co.uk/orc/smith_foreign/

Implementation and behaviour

ELISABETTA BRIGHI AND CHRISTOPHER HILL

Chapter contents

 Reader's guide

This chapter looks at what is known as the 'implementation phase' of foreign policy making, i.e. the period in which decisions are translated into action. Implementation can lead to very big problems—and surprises—for decision makers, whose intentions often get left behind in the complexities of practice.

In order to throw light on why this should be so we first of all look at the theoretical problems involved in deciding where a foreign policy action ends and its environment begins, for the difference between the 'inside' of state decision making, and the 'outside' world of international relations is by no means as clear as has been traditionally supposed. We then go on to illustrate the variety of problems which states encounter when trying to implement their foreign policies, and the range of instruments—diplomatic, military, economic, and cultural—which are available to them. The chapter finishes by outlining the endless loops which connect—and blur together—ends and means in foreign policy, and by identifying the key lessons which practitioners need to keep in mind.[1]

Introduction

The phase of implementation is that in which actors confront their environment and in which, in turn, the environment confronts them. In essence, this phase implies an interactive strategic process which is very often important when it comes to translating foreign policy objectives into practice, and decisive when it comes to turning practice into desired outcomes. This first half of this chapter will be dedicated to examining some of the most typical features and dilemmas of the phase of implementation. This phase requires crossing the boundary between actors and the outside world, if outcomes are to be shaped on the basis of stated objectives. The second half of the chapter will look at the practical choices over means and modes through which states conduct foreign policy. The exercise of channelling intentions into outcomes, via the use of instruments, is complex and rarely a mere technicality; indeed, it has the power to change foreign policy in the process.

By way of introduction to this set of issues, the chapter will firstly look at theory and present some general remarks on the issue of how to conceptualize foreign policy implementation as a form of **strategic and dialectic** interplay between a foreign policy actor and its environment. As we shall see, the essential insight of what will be presented here is that a successful implementation of any foreign policy depends not only on a clear definition of objectives and a sound choice of **instruments** (issues which will be dealt with in the second half of the chapter), but also, and rather crucially, on the interplay between the actor's strategy and the context surrounding it. Accordingly, it also depends on the actor's ability to adjust to unforeseen circumstances. The second section will move on to examine in more detail what we mean by **context** when dealing with foreign policy; in doing so, we will present a picture of the 'international' seen from the perspective of the actor. This will involve two steps: on the one hand, we will draw different pictures of the 'perimeter' of the 'international' (from the regional to the global); on the other, we will look at the many dimensions of which the 'international' is made and explore their interconnectedness. Thirdly and finally, we will shift the perspective to consider implementation from the point of view of both the actor and the context, and will focus on some of the dilemmas and synergies inherent in the process of connecting the 'domestic' and the 'international' while pursuing one's foreign policy objectives. **Implementation** thus emerges as a complex and fully political activity; a 'boundary' process which connects actors to their environments via the pursuit of foreign policy.

When actors meet their environment—theoretical issues

The issue of how social and political actors pursue courses of action and, through actions, succeed in attaining their objectives is a conundrum of interest not just to foreign policy analysts, but to all social scientists. How is it that sometimes even the best laid plans do not succeed in achieving one's goals? And conversely, what does it take to turn situations to one's own advantage? These puzzles confront foreign policy makers daily in their efforts to project their country's interests and goals abroad, and go to the heart of the 'problem' of implementation in foreign policy. Hardly a technicality, implementation is in fact a fully political activity, not least in the sense of reflecting a clash of wills between different actors, or between actors and their often intractable environment.

Despite the rather inchoate literature which has developed around it, the best place to start for considering the question of foreign policy behaviour and implementation from a theoretical point of view remains the so-called 'agency–structure debate' (*inter alia* Wendt 1987; Hollis and Smith 1991; Carlsnaes 1992; Wight 2006). At its most basic level, the debate concerns the vexing question of whether action can be explained from the 'inside' of actors, or from the 'outside'. Is it possible to find the roots of actions in the actor's preferences, interests, and meanings, or is it rather the external context, constraints, and patterns which steer actors in certain directions and not in others?

As some of the most compelling literature in foreign policy analysis has now made clear, foreign policy can be fully considered as a form of action (Carlsnaes 1989); indeed, foreign policy is an important site of political agency in contemporary world politics (Hill 2003). In this sense, the agency–structure debate does have something to say about foreign policy, and in fact it has interesting things to say primarily about the phase of behaviour and implementation.

Consider the following counterfactual. If an actor (for instance a state) existed in perfect isolation (or, alternatively, if it were all-powerful), it would have surely no problem in translating intentions, motivations, and desires into objectives. Indeed, objectives and outcomes would be practically the same; the process of implementation would be quite smooth, either because it would be accomplished in a vacuum, or because the actor would be fully in control of the context, able to manipulate it at will.

World politics, however, hardly resembles this picture. The international scene is made up of actors, states, and non-states, each with their own set of interests, objectives, and priorities— not necessarily in conflict, but very often distinct from one another. Therefore, for all but the most powerful actors, a degree of resistance is bound to be encountered in the process of 'having one's own way' in the system with the intent to produce desired outcomes. Further, even the most powerful actors might not be in the position to manipulate the environment around them fully, because of either failures of judgement or disadvantageous asymmetries in other important dimensions besides that of power (e.g. information or legitimacy).

How can one come to an elegant formalization of the set of issues and processes with which actors on the international scene are confronted when trying to implement their objectives, thus producing foreign policy behaviour? The argument advanced here is that in order to conceptualize behaviour and implementation, foreign policy analysis needs to adopt a **strategic–relational approach** (for the original statement of the model, see Hay (1995, 2002); for a full application to foreign policy, see Brighi (2005)). The intuition at the heart of the strategic–relational model—a type of **systems approach**—is that foreign policy behaviour is produced via a dialectic interplay between the actor's own *strategy* on the one hand and *context* on the other hand. The approach is called **strategic** in that actors are conceptualized as oriented towards the attainment of stated goals. Furthermore, in the process of elaborating appropriate courses of action, actors inevitably have to take into account the strategies of all other players. It is also **relational** because it assumes that actors and their behaviour only become intelligible when analysed in relation to their proper context. In turn, the context only becomes truly 'real' when looked at from the perspective of the individual actor in question; therefore it always exists in relation to something , or some other actor.

The strategic–relational model was first introduced in political science in order to reject the view that (political) action could be reduced to either external constraints or internal preferences. If it is reasonable to assume that both elements are in play most of the time, what becomes interesting is to investigate how constraints and preferences interact, sometimes clashing and sometimes producing virtuous synergies.

If one applies this approach to foreign policy, certain aspects of implementation become intelligible. Firstly, the strategic–relational approach tells us that neither strategy nor context taken in isolation can explain the success or failure of a certain foreign policy to deliver an intended outcome. An exclusive focus on the domestic political process cannot explain those instances in which outcomes deviate from intentions (which is the rule rather than

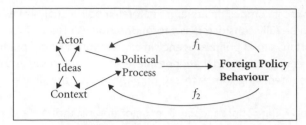

Figure 8.1 The strategic–relational approach to foreign policy (Brighi 2005).

the exception). Conversely, an exclusive focus on context places too much emphasis on the constraints and opportunities shaping action, and cannot convey any real sense of intentionality.

A schematic illustration of the model is provided in Figure 8.1.

In thinking about this model as applied to foreign policy implementation and behaviour, three considerations seem particularly relevant. Firstly, with regard to context we should avoid the fatalism usually associated with the term 'structure' in much International Relations (IR) literature. Context is not a monolithic, impenetrable, entity which pre-exists actors, and against which actors stand virtually powerless. Rather, **context** is here mainly intended as *other actors*, no more and no less than the set of relations which they entertain and the patterns they have generated. Even the material environment, which is an important and arguably 'objective' part of the context, becomes fully meaningful only through the relations that actors establish with one another. The coexistence of different actors, their interaction and complex aggregation of interests, is what makes 'the international' an uneven terrain for foreign policy. The likelihood of achieving an objective is dependent on how strategically placed the actor is on this terrain; in other words, given its position in relation to the context, some actions will be more successful than others. Moreover, and even more fundamentally, because of its inherently *relational* nature, context means different things to different actors, depending not only on where they are placed, but also on how they interpret the features of the terrain surrounding them. The cycles of isolationism and interventionism in US foreign policy, for instance, are to be understood not so much as resulting from an objective change in the country's position in the world but, perhaps more importantly, as a result of different interpretations of the same position, with its balance of constraints and opportunities.

Secondly and relatedly, there is a constant **interplay** between actors and context, and it is through this interplay that behaviour is produced. This in turn does not play itself out at the material level only, but is mediated by the role of ideas and discourses. Thus it is important not just to take into account the way the context responds to the actors' behaviour, but also the way such responses are filtered through perceptions, paradigms, and narratives, eventually to be internalized in the political process.

Thirdly and finally, just as there is a constant interplay, so is there a constant **feedback** from the actor to the context and vice versa. Once produced through an interactive process, foreign policy behaviour feeds back into the context (Figure 8.1f_2), restructuring the environment or leaving it unchanged, and into the actor itself (Figure 8.1f_1), by making adaptation possible. Think for instance of the various repercussions of US foreign policy actions in the

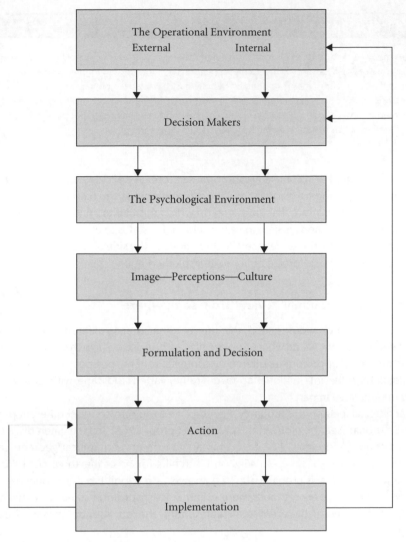

Figure 8.2 The place of implementation in the foreign-policy-making process. The arrows represent the flow of decision making and the main lines of feedback.

Source: Adapted from Brecher (1974: 7).

Middle East. These have not only changed the context at the regional, if not international, level, but have impacted on the US itself, sometimes causing a domestic reaction against involvement and at other times an upsurge of nationalism.

Figure 8.2, building on the work of Michael Brecher among other **systems theorists** who have worked on the subject, outlines the processes of action, reaction, and feedback which characterize the foreign policy making process, creating endless loops of policy and implementation rather than the clear progression of stages, formulation–choice–decision–action, which a rationalist approach might be thought to presuppose. (See Box 8.1.)

> **BOX 8.1 Systems theory**
>
> **Systems theory** is the approach, deriving from natural science but associated in political science mostly with the work of David Easton, which sees most phenomena as interrelated through processes of input, output, and feedback from the environment. The system is characterized primarily by a process of **homeostasis**, or dynamic equilibrium through interaction of the various forces involved. This can be as true of international politics, for example via the balance of power, and foreign policy, via the instinct for political survival, as it is of natural features such as body temperature or climate.

Since both strategy and context are important in foreign policy, we now take a closer look at each in turn, starting from the latter. 'The international' is the natural context of foreign policy, and yet there is more than one sense in which this habitat, natural as it may be, provides a rather complex and challenging environment for states to operate in. The section that follows will look at why this is the case. We then move to the side of strategy, so as to examine how the 'domestic' affects foreign policy in its implementation.

Ideas of the 'international': a view 'from somewhere'

As illustrated in the previous section, the 'international' means different things to different actors, depending not only on where they are placed, but also on how they (actively) interpret the constraints and opportunities offered by context. From the perspective of a single foreign policy actor, then, the 'international' appears a rather varied landscape, with features that can be only manipulated in part.

The ecological metaphor is probably a good place to start to consider different pictures of the 'international' (see the pioneering Sprout and Sprout 1965). In fact, when discussing the reach of a country's foreign policy, it is customary to turn to geographical/geometrical metaphors such as 'circles' or 'spheres'. Winston Churchill's image of the 'three circles' of British post-war foreign policy is probably the best known case in point, but one only has to think about how diffuse the expression 'sphere of influence' is to understand how this mode of language is ingrained in the exercise of representing the 'outside', or 'abroad' (Dodds and Atkinson 2000).

From the perspective of a single foreign policy actor, the 'international' has at least two dimensions: **horizontal and vertical**. Horizontally, the international unfolds on the *continuum* from proximity to distance, from 'near' to 'far', from regional to global. Vertically, the international is stratified into a number of functional layers: political, social, economic, military, normative, and so on. Without any doubt, when called to formulate interests and implement objectives, the greatest challenge for foreign policy makers is to harmonize the two dimensions and keep a certain degree of internal consistency within each.

In horizontal terms, the implementation of foreign policy objectives starts from the environment closest to the actor, which means the neighbouring states usually grouped in a region. Regional environments are specific to where actors are placed, and depend on how concentrated or widely spread their interests are. For most continental European countries, for instance, the regional environment coincides with the borders of Europe. However, as the case of Europe well testifies, the regional borders of an actor's foreign policy are far from fixed.

They are constantly susceptible to being renegotiated following historical, political, or simply ideological developments. Witness the fate of Eastern Europe, hardly a foreign policy priority for most European states before 1989 (with a few notable exceptions such as Germany, France, or Italy) and now considered to be part of a single European region (Wallace 1990). Consider also how geographical proximity does not by definition ensure inclusion in the region of interest to foreign policy–geography must always be read in conjunction with politics. Thus, for instance, despite erupting at the heart of the continent geographically, the Balkan wars were at first dealt with as if at the periphery of Europe (Simms 2001). Conversely, it was the political and ideological bond of communism which connected geographically distant states (as with Cuba's or North Korea's relations with the former Soviet Union) in a relatively homogeneous environment.

If all states have a region of priority for their foreign policy, only a few can really aspire to a have a genuinely global frame of reference. That the 'international' is more and more frequently equated with the 'global' testifies to the success of the globalization paradigm, but does not *de facto* imply the possibility for all actors to exercise a wide-ranging foreign policy. Yet, given the technological revolution and the power of ideas, foreign policy as a *political activity* has the potential to be global in both its causes and its effects—and has not, contrary to expectations, become obsolete. In fact, there is a sense in which, in conditions of globalization, *all politics has become foreign policy* in one way or the other.

And yet, not many actors can elaborate, let alone afford, a truly global foreign policy. The USA has most notably laid claim to this status, particularly since the end of the Cold War, reinforced in the wake of the 2001 attacks. However, despite its overwhelming military and economic power, America's vision of an effective global reach has been only partly fulfilled, suffering a number of important setbacks.

Interestingly enough, it is precisely in the phase of *implementation* that the USA's foreign policy designs have most frequently failed. If we look back at the strategic–relational model presented earlier in the chapter, this is not at all surprising. A failure to take into account the strategic and interactive nature of foreign policy means a high likelihood of problems at the implementation phase. As analysts have noted, many of the difficulties encountered by the USA in its foreign policy (let alone military) projection are due to a poor appreciation of the crucial relation between ends and means on the one hand, and between foreign policy actions and context, on the other. This alone would explain much of the frustration encountered, without considering the additional failure to take into account the mediation of ideas and their impact on such an interplay. At another level, it simply means that even the USA cannot dominate everything in a complex world, a fact that it does not always acknowledge.

For middle and small states, the 'global' remains but an aspiration, or a rhetorical commitment. The case of Britain is instructive here: despite the New Labour pledge of a foreign policy informed by global normative commitments, the difficulties of implementing such a grand design have been countless over the last decade, in economic, military, and political terms (Dunne and Wheeler 1999). More generally, as some of the literature has made clear, one of the paradoxical effects of globalization has been that of reinforcing the regional dimension, pushing middle to small states especially to strengthen the regional scope of their foreign policy (on the rise of regionalism, see Hurrell (1995)).

Thus, the perimeter of the 'international' varies greatly depending on the actor considered, and especially on its position in the context, on the resources at its disposal, and on the strategic value of these resources. But there is also a second dimension along which actors measure the 'international', and that is the vertical axis of functional differentiation. Thus, the 'international' results not just from its horizontal extension but from its stratification in different layers, the most important being political, economic, military, normative, and cultural. Two qualifications must accompany such a characterization, however. Firstly, the hierarchy among layers is by no means fixed; indeed, the traditional distinction between 'high politics' and 'low politics', which claimed a primacy for political and military issues (Hoffmann 1966), is increasingly problematic in a world in which issues such as culture have become (or rather, have returned to be) the terrain of greatest contestation. At the very least, what counts as 'high' or 'low' politics changes from actor to actor, and is inevitably subject to political, let alone idiosyncratic, considerations. Secondly, while analytically separable, these layers are at least marginally interlinked, partly because any given foreign policy has effects at many different levels, and partly because layers overlap in important ways, empirically as well as conceptually.

The political layer of the 'international' is formed by the complex web of interrelations which bind actors together. Diplomacy is one, the traditional but critical expression of the existence of such a web, which consists of far more than just international institutions or 'regimes'. Moreover, in conditions of globalization, the political dimension of the 'international' acquires, at least potentially, further depth in three directions (Held and Archibugi 1995). Firstly, the domestic politics of states, especially large ones, becomes a factor in this interdependence, affecting other actors through their foreign policies and sometimes also their own domestic politics. Secondly, the progressive formation of a 'global public sphere' means that political interdependence gradually comes to feature processes of normative adjudication and contestation, until recently exclusive to life inside states. Thirdly, a variety of actors, state and non-state, participate in the interdependence which makes up the political layer of the 'international'. However, this does not happen on a condition of parity, as states still express their agency through channels which are far more institutionalized, accountable, and varied than those at the disposal of non-state actors.

The political dimension of the 'international' has important areas of overlap with the social and normative layer. Diplomacy is in fact one of the key institutions of what the English School of International Relations calls the 'society' of states, or 'international society' (Bull and Watson 1982). Norms are another important component, in both their more codified version (international law) and their informal variety (customs). More generally, this is the level at which ethical concerns play themselves out. The extent to which these have come to affect foreign policy is nowhere more apparent than in the wave of 'humanitarian interventions' which was initiated in the early 1990s (Wheeler 1997). This practice provides evidence that foreign policy must now confront an environment which has elements of society—and a society composed of individuals and social movements, as well as states (Linklater 1998).

The economic layer is, if possible, even more pluralistic in its inclusion of a variety of actors of different nature. Not surprisingly, here the superiority states enjoy is far less marked than at the political level, partly because of the less hierarchical nature of economic transactions and partly because economic interdependence has often thrived irrespective of the international political systems in place (Strange 1988). However, economic issues are constantly susceptible to being highly politicized: witness the case of natural resources, and how this issue has become a matter of greatest concern for the foreign policy of states, especially emerging powers such as China (Alden 2007).

At yet another level, foreign policy must take into account the existence of patterns of military alignments, both cooperative and adversarial. According to some theories of international relations, most notably neorealism, this is the layer which is ultimately the most significant in foreign policy terms. While this may be true in the sense that military affairs carry with them the greatest threat, that of physical annihilation (Aron 1966), security problems are usually multifaceted and often derivative of political, economic, or cultural conflicts (Omand 2010). Still, the asymmetrical distribution of military power, and in particular of nuclear weapons, is a major fact for foreign policy makers in all states.

Finally, there is an important cultural dimension to the 'international' which decision makers cannot afford to leave out in their effort to implement foreign policy objectives. It is not just that cultural factors such as religion have come back, supposedly to ignite fundamentalism and terrorism, but that these factors today play an increasingly important role in all international relations (Petito and Hatzopoulous 2004). This is due on the one hand to the forced **contiguity** among different cultures brought about by globalization, and on the other to the decline of that modern paradigm which marginalized all forms of culture (religion *in primis*), confining them to the realm of the private. Foreign policy now finds itself dealing with these issues as priorities, and with the complications produced by their entanglement with all the remaining dimensions.

To sum up, the context of foreign policy means different things to different actors, according to who and where they are. The 'international' is a kaleidoscopic formation which develops both horizontally, extending from local to regional to global, and vertically, layering political, economic, military, normative, and cultural dimensions. Despite its varied complexion, context is often perceived as a whole, as a 'system', by foreign policy makers (Hill 2003: 164). And yet, interestingly enough, the greatest challenge for them is precisely how to ensure that all these dimensions do not contradict each other. There is, in fact, a natural **centrifugal** tendency that threatens consistency and coherence in foreign policy. Complexity breeds specialization, if not fragmentation. Thus, it is very frequent for economic foreign policy to deviate from that officially played out at the political level; this in turn is often in tension with the principles governing the normative dimension of the 'international', and so on. The exercise of making these different logics work in synergy in the pursuit of coordinated objectives is certainly one of the most daunting challenges for all foreign policy makers.

Balancing 'inside' and 'outside': implementing foreign policy

If implementation is about reaching out into the environment to transform one's objectives into outcomes, one should not think of this process as exclusively directed *to*, let alone *from*, the outside. On the contrary, the implementation of goals in foreign policy involves an important domestic or 'internal' component. More specifically, it involves an act of balancing, and indeed a process of interplay between what goes on inside the actor and its projection towards the outside. As the strategic–relational model presented above illustrates, all of these dialectical processes take place in the political process and are mediated by the impact of ideas and discourses.

There are at least two general ways in which the 'domestic' is implicated in foreign policy implementation, aside from the very fundamental role of deciding which objectives to pursue in the first place. To start with, implementation presupposes not only the capacity to pursue

goals with effective **means**, but more generally the ability of governments to extract and mobilize resources from their audiences, both material and immaterial, and channel them into
the pursuit of given objectives (Mastanduno *et al*. 1989). The most classic example of mobilization happens, of course, when states go to war. In the kinds of 'total wars' experienced in the
twentieth century, entire societies were involved in sustaining the war effort (*nations* go to
war, as the expression has it), with their economy and culture transformed by the will to attain
war *aims*. But more prosaically, either simply through the collection of taxes or through more
specific actions, societies take a direct or indirect part in realizing foreign policy aims. Secondly, but relatedly, at least in democratic societies, the 'domestic' enters the picture of implementation in the form of the *consensus* needed to sustain the foreign policy projection
necessary to attain objectives (Lamborn 1991). When a modicum of consensus is missing,
foreign policy is undermined from below; as a result, implementation is potentially much
weaker, or can be even at risk. In fact, if consensus breaks down entirely, a crisis can erupt to
threaten not only the foreign policy in action, but the survival of the government itself.

In general, therefore, implementation always develops on two levels, 'domestic' and 'international', which are in constant interaction. This is what the political scientist Robert Putnam
had in mind when he imagined foreign policy as a 'two-level game' (Putnam 1988; Evans *et
al*. 1993). Using this metaphor, Putnam focused on the issue of how democratic foreign policy tends to be internationally and domestically constrained in the specific context of multilateral economic bargaining. As the literature in Foreign Policy Analysis (FPA) has made clear,
this intuition can be applied to foreign policy *lato sensu*, and indeed encapsulates an essential feature of the process of implementation. In the words of Wolfram Hanrieder, the first
foreign policy analyst to examine this issue in detail, implementation hinges on a 'compatibility–consensus' balance and unfolds within a 'double constraint' (Hanrieder 1971). In order
to be successful in achieving their objectives, actors need to pursue a foreign policy that is
compatible with the context and, at the same time, supported by a reasonable degree of
agreement inside the state. Thus implementation calls for an attention to both fronts, domestic and international, and foreign policy makers need to make them work in tandem as
much as possible.

But the exercise of balancing the domestic and the international does not exhaust the ways
in which these ambits can be connected in the phase of foreign policy implementation. In
fact, sometimes it is the dynamic interplay, or synergy, between them which is of most interest. This happens, for instance, whenever the attainment of a foreign policy goal has domestic
implications, or vice versa. In fact, sometimes *domestic* objectives are achieved via particular
foreign policies, whereas *foreign* policy objectives are pursued via *domestic* policies. When this
happens, the synergistic (or dialectic) nature of foreign policy manifests itself most clearly,
and the process of interplay between actor, context, and foreign policy at the heart of the
strategic–relational model seen above comes full circle.

As for the first possibility, the choice of many countries to join the EU provides a good case
in point. Naturally, entry into the EU is portrayed primarily as a foreign policy issue; negotiations, after all, take place at the level of the foreign policy apparatus. And yet, there is a sense
in which historically the entry into the EU (or the European Community before Maastricht)
was pursued by policy makers primarily for domestic purposes. Think of the pursuit of enlargement by Spain or Greece during the 1970s and 1980s, and how this was functional to the
overriding domestic objective of democratic consolidation. The same logic applies today to

some of the applicants from former Eastern Europe (Tovias and Ugur 2004). Further, there is no doubt that part of the controversy surrounding the accession of Turkey to the EU—in both parties—originates from concern over the set of domestic objectives which accession is supposed to facilitate, most notably political reform.

Examples of the opposite case are also frequent, and indeed very relevant to the current predicaments of some democratic states. Today's conditions of globalization, and especially multiculturalism, mean that minorities become the focus of concern as the result of foreign policy entanglements which then blow back into one's own society (Hill 2007). For instance, the high degree of suspicion, and accompanying restrictive policies, attaching to Muslim citizens in the USA and Britain after the terrorist attacks of 2001 and 2005, respectively, are the indirect consequence of foreign policy engagements in the Middle East, and reverberate in turn on relations with major Muslim states such as Saudi Arabia and Pakistan. Therefore, as argued in this section, a degree of interplay between the domestic and the international in the process of foreign policy implementation is inevitable, and indeed necessary for its success. This is true in at least two ways: firstly, domestic participation features in the implementation phase in terms of either the need for consensus or the specific resources to be mobilized; secondly, it is through foreign policy that the 'domestic' can become the channel by which the 'international' is pursued, and vice versa.

Exerting influence

All foreign policy, by definition, is about the outside world. While the issues of the definition of 'outside' and the boundaries between 'us' and 'them' are highly contested, they are discussed elsewhere in this book. The purpose of this section is to examine the practical problems which occur when foreign-policy-making processes collide with the world for which they are intended. Intention, however, is itself a variable phenomenon in this context. Some foreign policy is initiated at home, whether by a new government, a strong-minded leader, or pressures from below, such as those represented by nationalism. But many other foreign policy positions are reactions to events beyond borders, and thus either to the initiatives of others or to chains of events which have spiralled beyond any single actor's control. Either way, a policy can be rational or not, and compatible or not, with other aspects of the government's programme. Yet whatever its internal logic it still has to face up to the problem of implementation, i.e. the putting of a policy into practice through engagement with other independent actors, which are often physically beyond reach.

Implementation has several meanings in FPA, two of which are focused on here: on the one hand is the issue of the channels through which foreign policy aims are translated into practice, involving the often complex relationship between ends and means; on the other are the difficulties which states have in *operating* in what is literally a 'foreign' and quite often a highly intractable world, and how they *adapt* their behaviour on the basis of the interaction with, and feedback from, that outside world. Those who work more on the policy-related side of FPA have always written about the challenges represented by a particular instrument, particularly diplomacy and military force. Detailed research has also been conducted on propaganda and the use of economic sanctions, while key figures like Alexander George have underscored the links which exist between instruments, as in his influential work on 'coercive diplomacy', which has now spawned the subfield of 'defence diplomacy' (George 1994). More directly, however, theoretical work is also vital to an understanding of implementation, whether relating to the bureaucratic dimension, or to the underlying problems of planning and rationality. Graham Allison has been the most influential figure on both counts, providing a bridge, as he does, into the work of economists and administrative theorists like Herbert Simon and Charles Lindblom (Allison and Zelikow 1999; see also Chapters Six and Seven).

The above two meanings of implementation will be explored by looking at the following in turn.

- The **variety of relationships** that exist with the outside world because of the many different kinds of states conducting foreign policy and the varying challenges that their external activities involve. For instance, the implementation of British policy towards New Zealand is a rather more straightforward matter than its conduct towards Belarus. Despite the much greater geographical distances between the parties to the first relationship, the degree of 'foreignness' (i.e. political and cultural distance) is far less than in the second.

- The **foreign policy instruments** available to decision makers as they contemplate the best way to translate their intentions into actions which have a chance of success in the international environment. The main instruments fall into four categories: political, military, economic, and cultural/ideological. Yet any analysis of them soon encounters complex problems, in the first instance of the choices over the use of which instrument for what purpose, and in the second instance over the relationship between the instruments themselves and the underlying capabilities which make them possible.

- The **theoretical issues** raised by any discussion of the ends–means relationship in foreign policy. In the context of implementation, this means the issues of rationality, slippage, and complexity. It also means some particular reflections on one of the central concepts in all IR, namely power. The key issue here is the distinction between power as a *means*, and as a *context*.

The practical importance of context

FPA is a comparative field of study which generates observations of varying degrees of generality. Sometimes its insights will need to be heavily qualified through the particularity of period and circumstances, while others will amount to propositions of wide applicability. In terms of implementation, it is unarguable that the follow-through phase of decision making (which in this case is more properly termed action, or **agency**) always has the capacity to raise new problems and to derail the original intentions. If this now seems an unremarkable statement, it was not always the case. Even today, rationalists often do not make allowances for the fact that choices and trade-offs are not the only determinant of outcomes—choices are not self-executing. For their part, in their enthusiasm, politicians very often neglect to factor in either the 'foul-up' factor or the inconvenient unwillingness of outsiders to conform to the roles expected of them. It is enough to mention the gap between intentions and outcomes on the part of the proponents of the Iraq war to make the point.

Great powers, small powers

However, this kind of high-level generalization is only a start. To understand implementation more fully we also need fine-grained work on the basis of distinctions between the kinds of actors producing foreign policies, and between the kinds of relationship in which they are engaged. On the first count, for example, it might be thought that great powers (to say nothing of the world's only superpower) would have far fewer problems in implementing their external policies than small and/or weak states. But this is not necessarily the case. It depends, crucially, on what aims are being sought. Despite its status as a middle power, and the considerable array of means at its disposal, Britain is torn between aspiration and (in)capacity. It has, for instance, failed to fulfil many of the foreign policy aims dictated by its 'new' global agenda. This is only in part due to the fact that 'the global' has been used primarily as a rhetorical strategy, as mentioned above. More interestingly, it was the very nature of some foreign policy aims, most notably those of a normative kind, which was difficult to match with the means used to pursue them.

A small country which overreaches itself, in terms of seeking to change the whole character of the international system (as Fidel Castro's Cuba has occasionally tried to do, and as Hugo Chavez became fixated on in Venezuela) risks even greater complications, if not outright failure. On the other hand, this is not to say that they will achieve nothing. If they have already discounted the risks and the unlikelihood of achieving the stated goals, they may still fulfil lesser, and probably unstated, goals of a satisfying kind. Thus for four decades Muammar Gaddafi in Libya managed to defy predictions of his demise and, despite his undoubtedly erratic behaviour and the hostility of the USA, exerted a disproportionate degree of influence in the Maghreb and sub-Saharan Africa. By extension, a small country which remains modest in its goals may have relatively few problems of implementation because it will be too cautious to attempt anything which antagonizes the more powerful, or exposes it to other kinds of potentially destructive blow-back.

Conversely, the USA often encounters serious problems of implementation with its foreign policies, precisely because it has global interests and is active on almost every front. As the 'hegemon'/'leader of the free world', it has a forward stance on so many issues that almost inevitably it runs into difficulties in some of them. **Overstretch** is a term which refers to a structural condition over a historical period (Kennedy 1988). It refers to the tendency of great powers to take on imperial commitments which they cannot sustain, financially or militarily. In particular circumstances, it may take the form of a foreign policy which is undertaken without the available resources to follow it through, even if in principle the state in question should have no problem in doing so. The USA discovered this truth in Somalia in 1993, from where it withdrew after only a few casualties, concluding (possibly with undue haste) that there was not the domestic support for a long engagement. The Soviet Union suffered the same fate in Afghanistan, after much longer and much greater losses, during the years following their invasion in December 1979.

Thus, the foreign policy designs of great powers have most frequently failed in relation to implementation. This result, though puzzling, can be illuminated through the strategic-relation model presented in the first part of the chapter. Two of its insights must be kept particularly in mind. Firstly, given the constant interplay between strategy and context, successful implementation requires a certain degree of flexibility to accommodate on-going feedback processes. A foreign policy which is projected to the outside without much understanding of such interplay is likely to backfire, as recent American foreign policy has vividly demonstrated. Secondly, a successful implementation depends also on the crucial relation between ends and means. No matter how powerful or big a state is, the pursuit of foreign policy aims is contingent on the ever-important choice of the appropriate means.

Multilateralism and the complexity of action

The military dimension is not the only one in which problems of implementation arise. Tony Blair apparently succeeded in getting the G8 to commit to a policy of debt cancellation in Africa during the Gleneagles Summit of July 2005, only to find that many of his partners simply failed to live up to their promises. This is one example among many which demonstrates that, almost by definition, any foreign policy action depends on others for its full implementation. If being pursued bilaterally or multilaterally, it will require the cooperation of partners. But even then, and certainly in all unilateral actions, it depends on how the majority of actors affected, whether hostile, supportive, or just indifferent, respond to the action. If they choose to take an interest in the subject, for whatever reason (and the indifferent may decide to take a stance just to give themselves leverage on something else), these actors are likely to create friction, add costs, or at least complicate the implementation of the policy. Even if they are neutral on the substance, their technical assistance may still be needed, as with the controversial (and therefore secret) rendition flights of US aircraft in ferrying presumed terrorists to and from their detention centres.

Despite the controversy of recent years between the USA and its allies as to whether unilateralism, multilateralism, or 'effective multilateralism' (the compromise position) is the preferred approach to international relations, the reality is that most implementation entails some or other form of **multilateralism**. Occasionally states indulge themselves in pure myopic solipsism, as with the wild calls of Iranian President Ahmadinejad for Israel to be wiped off the map. Even then, their real aim is usually to rally support in a particular quarter or to provoke reactions in another. But for the most part, states take for granted the fact that success in foreign policy will require mobilizing support, neutralizing hostility, shaping the balance of influence, and (increasingly) winning the rhetorical wars which characterize the modern multilayered international system. Often this work takes place within formal international organizations, whether universal through the UN system, or partial, in the form of networks of allies, regional partners, or the 'like-minded'. But just as much is ad hoc, cutting across institutional boundaries and not restricted by formal rules or agreements. Even in its moment of maximum self-assertion, when it disregarded the Article 5 offer of help from its NATO allies immediately after 9/11, the USA was collaborating pragmatically with a wide range of countries involved in the hunt for al-Qaeda members. The 'War on Terror' could not be other than a collective affair, even if it also divided the world crudely into 'those who are for us, and those against us'. In other words, the deployment of the immense national power which the USA has at its disposal is in itself no guarantee of effective implementation. The very use of the famous 'axis of evil' image was an attempt to mobilize the international community on one side by 'othering', or scapegoating, a small number of seemingly irresponsible states.

Therefore implementing foreign policy usually requires the simultaneous use of various levels and techniques of international cooperation: bilateral, multilateral, and transgovernmental— that is, links between parts of one state's machinery and parts of another, as with the privileged links between the French and German ministries of Defence which produced the joint brigade in the late 1980s. Not all of these will be visible to the public; indeed many, perhaps most, will operate at the level of what used to be called 'secret diplomacy'. Secrecy is an overrated quality these days, as relatively few activities require the absolute darkness associated with the preparation of, say, a surprise attack. Even in those cases, it is impossible to maintain absolute surprise. There were plenty of indications of Hitler's impending attack on the USSR in June 1941, of Israel's on Egypt in 1967, or of Argentina's on the Falkland Islands in 1982 for those who wanted to listen, or were capable of reading the signs correctly. In the contemporary media-driven environment, it is especially difficult to keep something secret for long, as the Reagan administration discovered in 1986-1987, when its attempts to use money from arms deals with Iran to fund illegal military campaigns in Central America (the Iran–Contra affair) were exposed with serious consequences for its policies on both fronts.

All this is to say that most foreign policy implementation involves a tangled web of connections with other states, or at least parts of other states, which is both necessary and a serious complication of agency, as it may compromise the aspiration towards a single rational strategy as well as the control of outcomes. If foreign policy inevitably means subcontracting out various parts of the endeavour to different parts of the state bureaucracy and to outside entities, then those subcontractors have the capacity to refract, distort, and even subvert the policy's original intentions. This is the strategic–relational approach in practice—looking inside as well as outside the state. One might adapt Truman's famous remark about General Eisenhower, as the latter prepared to take over the Presidency: 'He'll sit here, and he'll say, "Do this! Do that!" *And nothing will happen.* Poor Ike—it won't be a bit like the Army' (cited in Neustadt 1960: 9).

Inside any political machinery, and even more so in the complex world of international relations, 'orders' may easily be issued, but that is only the beginning of the process of attempting to achieve one's goals. Moreover, this is true for all kinds of states, whatever their size or level of sophistication.

The instruments of foreign policy

When it comes to choosing the instruments with which to act, the differences between states do come into play. The wide variation in state capacities is a key determinant of what can even be attempted in the outside world. The larger states will possess the full portfolio of potential instruments, from the hardest of hard power to the most subtle and indirect cultural influences. They will also have the capacity to act well beyond their own locality, perhaps globally. They simply have more people, more contacts, and more money than the others. It is, indeed, a plausible definition of a **superpower** that it can expect to determine outcomes in any geographical arena and via any available instrument. At the other end of the spectrum, it will be a major challenge for a micro-state just to preserve its autonomy. Its foreign policy will have no further ambition than to assist in the achievement of basic domestic policy goals through diplomacy alone. Between these two extremes, most states survive on the basis of a limited and patchy range of instruments, possessing armed services of highly variable size, quality, and scope, embassies in some parts of the world but not all, the ability to exert economic influence according to levels of development and/or the lottery of geographical position, and probably very limited cultural outreach.

Any understanding of how states approach the problem of deciding on the best means of implementing their foreign policy must remember two dicta: firstly, instruments are themselves dependent on underlying capabilities, which are in turn a function of the resources at the disposal of the society in question; secondly, decision makers do not choose instruments as the surgeon selects the scalpel—rather, the nature of the available instruments tends to shape their policy choices in the first place. These points are expanded in what follows.

Resources refers to what the French school referred to as the 'basic forces' of foreign policy (Renouvin and Duroselle 1968; Merle 1987), i.e. a country's sum total of (dis)advantages derived from climate, position, geography, population size, education, tradition, and level of development. These things are not unchangeable—the Law of the Sea Treaty expanded territorial waters from 12 to 200 miles in the 1970s, and the Channel Tunnel was finally built in 1994—but for the most part they change slowly. This is on the assumption that territorial expansion is not generally acceptable. Where it does occur, as with Israel's conquests of 1967, the parameters of both security and access to raw materials (in this case water) can change dramatically. Resources are a critical factor in determining a state's choices in foreign policy, although there is no simple correspondence between the possession of an asset and the ability to exert influence, as with Nigeria's wasting of its oil revenues or Indonesia's failure to translate its status as the world's fourth most populous country (c. 238 million) into an equivalent political ranking. Conversely, states with no apparent resource advantages, such as Singapore and Switzerland, have managed to achieve both security and prosperity. Thus resources have to be managed effectively. What really makes possible the pursuit of an effective foreign policy are capabilities, which in turn determine the range of possible instruments at the disposal of decision makers.

Capabilities are resources made operational but not yet translated into the specific instruments (like propaganda or the use of force) which may be applied in practical politics (See Figure 8.3.). Accordingly, they are the elements which an intelligent government will always seek to improve, to give itself a better chance of implementing an effective foreign policy, but which will be seen more as a long-term investment than as providing an immediate pay-off. Into this category fall such factors as the strength of the national currency, the size and proficiency of its armed forces, and the skills of its people—this last was the reason why Prime Minister Blair continually stressed the importance of education to the UK's position in the world, both economic and political.

On the other hand, such capabilities are of importance in themselves and to the well-being of any society; their role in underpinning foreign policy is incidental except in cases where leaders see the latter as providing their primary goals. This was evidently true for Hitler and Mussolini, who provided full employment as a means to pursuing their country's international greatness, rather than the reverse. This means that foreign policy and its implementation is to a large extent at the mercy of factors beyond its control and of long-term developments. It is for this and other reasons that the second dictum referred to above applies: that decision makers cannot choose on an abstract rational basis the instrument which would best serve their immediate purpose. They are limited not only by the size and wealth of their country (i.e. by basic resources), but also by the decisions of their predecessors in office to develop (or not) a particular capability which would have made possible the preferred instrument. And that in turn will have depended on the priority given to external policy. France in the 1880s was determined to reverse the humiliation it had suffered at the hands of

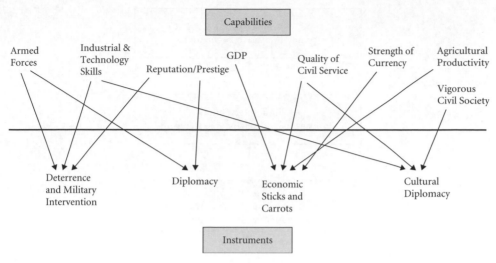

Figure 8.3 Links between the principal capabilities and instruments of foreign policy.

Germany in 1870–1871, and focused on educational reform and population growth (but not with great success) as the means of doing so. Israel has made foreign and defence policy the overriding priority throughout its existence, although it has only been able to do so through unwavering US support. But for many states foreign policy is rather like an expensive insurance policy whose dues seem disproportionate to the risks they face. They often neglect the relevant capabilities or divert them in other directions, especially if they are able to free-ride on more activist allies. They may also misunderstand the link between capabilities and instruments, assuming more choice when it comes to implementing a foreign policy than they in fact possess. To put it at its simplest, if they have allowed weapons procurement to run down or have closed embassies for financial reasons, they will have much less leverage available to them when the need arises. In such circumstances misperceptions are common, and may be fatal.

The actual **instruments** of foreign policy, that is to say the forms of pressure and influence available to decision makers, represent an ascending scale of seriousness in terms of the commitment of resources, the impact on third parties, and the according degree of risk in use (see Figure 8.4). This scale is akin to the spectrum from soft to hard power now familiar in the discussion of international politics (Nye 2004; Parmar and Cox 2010). If a problem occurs which requires a foreign policy response, it would take a particularly irrational leader (it can happen) to go straight for the high-risk option (interestingly now referred to as the 'nuclear option' in everyday speech). The pragmatic initial response is to discuss the issue with other relevant states, i.e. to employ diplomacy. If that is unproductive, there may be some attempt to incentivize compliance by various forms of positive or negative sanctions, not all of them economic. Appeals to an adversary's own domestic opinion, through public diplomacy or employing civil society in direct cultural linkages, may have some chance of weakening his/her political base.

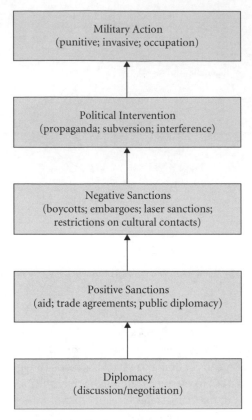

Figure 8.4 The ascending scale of foreign policy instruments.

Failure at this level then leaves the initiating state with a serious choice. Does it go on to escalate the dispute by exerting punitive measures (assuming it has that opportunity), which will almost certainly raise the level of tension between the two parties to the point where it might as easily spiral out of control as produce compliance, or does it decide to cut losses and back off, with the possible consequences of international humiliation and domestic criticism? The same choice, but of an even more serious kind, awaits further down the road if and when sanctions turn out to have been ineffective. This was the dilemma faced by the USA and Britain in 1998 as they attempted to enforce the no-fly zones in southern Iraq on Saddam Hussein, and to press him to renounce the suspected programmes of biological and chemical weapons production. The economic sanctions which had been in place since 1991 seemed not to be working, and indeed were attracting ever more criticism on the grounds of their damaging impact on Iraqi civilians. Yet to abandon them without any alternative course of action would have been to hand a diplomatic victory to Saddam, and perhaps to encourage him to develop further 'weapons of mass destruction' (WMDs). This reasoning produced Operation Desert Fox, namely the major air attacks on southern Iraq launched by the USA and UK in December 1998. In time, catalysed by 9/11, it led to the aim of regime change and the full-scale invasion of Iraq (Kampfner 2004).

The ladder of escalation in the use of foreign policy instruments is a tendency rather than an absolute rule. It conforms to a rational ideal type which may only be honoured in the breach. Powerful states are able to use different instruments simultaneously or in rotation. They are certainly able to benefit from the law of anticipated reactions by keeping the mere possibility of escalation in the minds of their weaker adversaries, who may decide that prudence is preferable to any kind of risk. Lesser powers have fewer options, and not just in relation to hard power. Their embassies may be restricted to a few major capitals plus the UN network, their economic weakness will rule out any use of sanctions, and their ability to project themselves abroad culturally will be very limited. This does not mean that they are totally hamstrung; if prepared to take risks, like Castro or Kim Jong il, they may have surprising degrees of success, even over long periods, by being prepared to defy all their opponents' instruments, short of regime change itself. If, conversely, they do not wish to attract hostility, they may still have some capacity to implement effective policies so long as they show creativity and do not become over-ambitious. Julius Nyerere of Tanzania fitfully displayed these characteristics in the 1960s and 1970s, giving his country an influence on African politics that it has not had since his departure (Nzomo 1999: 184–6). More recently, President Morales of Bolivia has raised his similarly weak country's profile with a shrewd mixture of diplomatic activism and dignified restraint.

Power, and the ends–means relationship in foreign policy

The concept of **power** is a common thread not only in the story of implementation but in the analysis of foreign policy more broadly. All action implies the exercise of power to a greater or lesser extent, both as a means and as a context. In the former sense power, and thus foreign policy, is an inherently relational activity in that it only exists in relation to some object or some other party (Baldwin 1985). In the latter sense, as context, power impinges on foreign policy through its unavoidability; if decision makers behave as if the power of others, or their own lack of it, is not relevant, they will soon suffer some unpleasant shocks. Conversely, if they become overconfident about their power position, or interpret it too narrowly, they risk the usual result of hubris—a hostile coalition and probable failure (Nye 2008). Complacency is also a routine danger. The European states engaged in the Barcelona Process after 1995 assumed that while they might not be able to solve the Israel–Palestine dispute, their diplomatic and economic engagements with the countries of the southern shore of the Mediterranean were sufficient to promote stability. This proved, in 2011, to be a fundamental miscalculation.

In a theoretical sense, power is often defined as getting A to do what they might not otherwise do, or even consider doing. Yet in order to understand the way in which power both works in the implementation process and can be drained away during this crucial phase, it needs to be disaggregated and contextualized. In the inevitable shorthand talk in IR of 'great powers', 'power politics', and the like, FPA provides a useful corrective by employing middle-range theory to explore the different levels and processes beneath the surface of events. As we saw in Part I, the FPA perspective allows us to unpack the interplay of structures with agency, and in a much more concrete way than the usual discussion of that relationship. It tends to be sceptical of single-factor explanations, whether at the level of the motivations, actions or effects of foreign policy. Equally, it shows—and most clearly in the particular context of implementation—how ends and means exist in a perpetual loop of interconnectedness, with the latter often determining the former.

The **rational model**, which stresses setting one's goals in line with available power and then choosing the most appropriate instrument to achieve them, rarely conforms to actual foreign policy practice. In confronting an unexpected problem, decision makers often turn to the first potential solution to hand, bearing in mind the need to build a coalition of support within the government and (at times) to carry domestic public opinion with them. They may then be sucked into an unforeseeable tunnel of events which throw up yet further choices over ends and means. This was evident in the Balkans during the 1990s, as the Western states grappled with the complex consequences of the disintegration of Yugoslavia, finally taking on commitments to *de facto* protectorates in three countries (Bosnia, Macedonia, Kosovo), and (in the case of the EU) accepting a major enlargement of membership across the whole region. The many complex instruments thus deployed were ostensibly as a *means* towards the *ends* of stabilization and pacification, but the longer they stay in place the more difficult it is to distinguish the two. Indeed, most foreign policy implementation is best judged not via a snapshot in the moment, but over the long term in relation to changing goals and the flexible use of a range of means.

Certainly, leaders need to be clear and reflective about their goals and about the ends–means relationship, but in foreign policy they should not be under any illusion that the latter can be held steady, or that any given means can be relied upon to deliver results. The implementation phase of policy making always involves some loss of momentum through transaction costs, political friction, and disillusion. Because decisions are never self-executing (except in the case of Saddam Hussein, who is said to have literally executed one death sentence on a ministerial colleague), leaders rely on subcontracting to bureaucratic agents, some of whom may take the opportunity to slow down or undermine the policy, or even to run their own policies in competition, under the cover of agreement. More likely, they will just be guilty of inefficiency, but this can still endanger the original policy. As John Kennedy famously said during the Cuban Missile Crisis of 1962 (after one of his spy planes had strayed over Soviet territory, strictly against his orders), 'There's always some son-of-a-bitch who doesn't get the word' (Allison and Zelikow 1999: 241).[2]

Conclusion

The key points which emerge from the analysis of the confrontation between foreign policy and the world in which it has to operate all qualify rationalist notions of power and the ends–means relationship. They stress the importance of understanding the interplay between context and policy, between structures and actors. And they highlight the huge potential for slippage between intentions and outcomes, between actions and consequences. Indeed, foreign policy decisions should be seen primarily as heightened moments of commitment in a perpetual process of action, reaction, and further action at many different levels and involving a range of different actors, inside and outside the state, all of which need to be taken into account. In short, they are best understood through the strategic–relational model. The most important thing for practitioners to remember is that the point of decision in foreign policy is usually only the start of a long process of immersion in a fluid and unpredictable external environment. The onset of implementation denotes not the end of politics, but simply a new phase of it.

Key points

- Foreign policy is not self-executing; the implementation phase is critical to success.

- The means of foreign policy can distort and even transform its original ends.

- The implementation of foreign policy needs to be highly flexible—it is self-defeating to rely on one instrument alone, or one strategy for too long.

- The international environment is fluid and difficult to manage. Foreign policy makers should be alert to the constant feedback it provides and adapt to its changing circumstances, however clear their initial objectives.

- Implementation takes place in several different arenas simultaneously—the local, the states system, the global/transnational, and even the domestic (of both the acting and the receiving state).

- Implementation can be a purely technical executive matter. For the most part, however, it is as political—and therefore as ethical—a dimension as any other aspect of foreign policy.

 Further reading

Cohen, R. (1991), *Negotiating Across Cultures: Communication Obstacles in International Diplomacy* (Washington, DC: US Institute of Peace).
A richly informed analysis of culturally derived misperceptions in foreign policy.

George, A. and Simons, W.E. (eds), with contributions by D.K. Hall (1994, 2nd edn), *The Limits of Coercive Diplomacy* (Boulder, CO: Westview).
The best discussion of how force and diplomacy are often combined, if not always to good effect.

Hill, C. (2003), *The Changing Politics of Foreign Policy* (Basingstoke: Palgrave Macmillan).
A wide-ranging discussion of the conduct of foreign policy, with much attention given to the problems of acting in an intractable environment.

Jervis, R. (2010), *Why Intelligence Fails: Lessons from the Iranian Revolution and the Iraq War* (Ithaca, NY: Cornell University Press).
A sophisticated discussion of one of the key issues in foreign policy implementation from one of the world's leading analysts.

Nye, J.S. (2004), *Soft Power: the Means to Success in World Politics* (New York: Public Affairs Books).
The fullest statement of the argument that even major powers need the full range of foreign policy instruments.

Wolfers, A. (1962), *Discord and Collaboration: Essays on International Politics* (Baltimore, MD: Johns Hopkins University Press).
A classic, containing several essential essays, on the nature of goals and the ends–means problem.

 Visit the Online Resource Centre that accompanies this book for more information:
www.oxfordtextbooks.co.uk/orc/smith_foreign/

The role of media and public opinion

PIERS ROBINSON

Chapter contents

 Reader's guide

This chapter introduces students to debates on the relationship between public opinion, media, foreign policy, and international politics. The first three sections discuss the interconnected influences between public opinion, media, and the making of foreign policy. Here, the extent to which both public opinion and media can influence foreign policy formulation in a bottom-up fashion and, conversely, the way in which governments can influence media and public opinion are reviewed. The fourth section integrates these debates with theoretical frames used in the study of international relations, namely realism, liberalism, and critical approaches. The chapter concludes by discussing contemporary debates concerning new media and the 'War on Terror'.

Introduction

Do public opinion and media matter for our understanding of foreign policy and international politics? To most observers the answer appears obvious. We live in a world of instantaneous communication facilitated by technologies such as the internet, mobile phones, social networking technology, and satellite-based communication, as well as the arrival of 'global' 24-hour news channels such as CNN and Al Jazeera. Indeed, it sometimes seems that little of any importance happens in the world that is not subject to the gaze of both media and the public. Politicians continually claim to have to manage the pressures created by media criticism and public disapproval. At the same time, political actors from the President of the USA to groups such as al-Qaeda attempt to utilize media to project power. For example, in May 2003, US President George Bush alighted upon a US aircraft carrier to declare 'mission accomplished' in Iraq. The aim, at least in part, was to create a visible symbol of success for both the American public and a global audience. At the same time, it is likely that those who planned the attacks on the World Trade Center and the Pentagon in 2001 were aware of how the ensuing destruction would be relayed around the world, and how the stunning pictorial quality of the attacks would be a factor in their foreign policy impact.

If the role of media and public opinion matter, how have academics approached them? Perhaps surprisingly, the discipline of International Relations (IR) tends to pay little attention to public opinion and media. The dominance of realism (see Chapters Two, Ten, and Sixteen), with its focus upon inter-state relations and tendency to discount the domestic-level workings of states, is in part to blame. More importantly, IR academics have often lacked the theoretical and conceptual tools available to Communications scholars. This has left many scholars of IR with a loose sense that both the media and public opinion are key variables in analysing foreign policy, but without the tools with which to understand how and why. Providing a start toward rectifying this particular shortcoming is one aim of this chapter.

In contrast, the subfield of Foreign Policy Analysis (FPA), with its focus upon explaining decision making, accords media and public opinion far greater analytical significance. Here, consideration of media and public opinion has been one part of a growing literature analysing the impact of *societal groups* upon foreign policy making (Hudson 2005: 19). Also, individual-level explanations focusing on the psychology of decision makers have shown how *some* decision makers value public opinion and therefore come to be influenced by it when formulating foreign policy (e.g. Foyle 1999). More generally, analysis of the interaction between public opinion, media, and foreign policy contributes to the ability of FPA to provide the complex 'ground' (Hudson 2005: 1) upon which the often abstract study of IR rests. In other words, understanding foreign policy *processes* at the international level requires a detailed examination of the influences on foreign policy *decisions* made at the state level.

Two perspectives dominate academic debate, the **pluralist model** and the **elite model**. The pluralist model assumes that power is dispersed throughout society (including across the media and the public) so that no one group or set of interests dominate. As such, pluralist accounts maintain that media and publics are independent from political influence and therefore can (and should) act as powerful *constraints* upon governments. As will be examined, recent debate revolves around the **CNN effect**, whereby independent news media coverage pressures policy makers to pursue a particular course of action during a crisis. Conversely, the elite model assumes that power is concentrated within elite groups who are able to dominate politics and society. As such, elite accounts maintain that both media and public opinion are subservient to political elites. From this perspective, media have a rather less independent form of influence—acting as mouthpieces for government officials, operating to mobilize publics in support of their policies.

This chapter has two aims. The first is to introduce concepts, arguments, and theories relating to public opinion, media, and foreign policy. The second is to integrate these with existing theoretical frameworks in IR. I begin by discussing the two distinct areas of enquiry that traditionally structure academic analysis. The first section examines whether public opinion influences foreign policy formulation, as argued by the pluralist model, or whether the public are politically impotent, as argued by the elite model. The second section looks at whether the media can influence foreign policy formulation, as argued by the pluralist model, or whether the media are fundamentally subservient to the foreign policy process, as argued by the elite model. In the third section, consideration is given to possible methods of reconciling elite and pluralist perspectives. Analysing these debates provides the foundation for understanding how media and public opinion matter for IR. The chapter concludes by examining the role of news media and public opinion as important components in three leading theoretical frameworks; as illustrated, realist, liberal, and critical approaches all have differing assumptions and claims regarding the media and public opinion. Lastly, attention is given to contemporary developments, including new communications technology and recent ideological imperatives including the current 'War on Terror', and the potential impact of these upon public opinion, media, and foreign policy.

Public opinion and foreign policy

In a democracy, a government is supposed to be responsive to the public. That is to say, the opinions of people living within a democratic state are expected to be reflected in government policy, including its foreign policy. The processes by which these opinions come to influence government policy include direct elections, opinion polls, and the representation of public concerns via media. As such, the expectation in a democracy is that the pluralist model *should* hold true. It is also useful to note that, with respect to the foreign affairs of democratic states, 'the public' can be divided into distinct categories, each with different perspectives on international affairs. For example, research on US public opinion has traditionally categorized US citizens as either *isolationist* or *internationalist*. Isolationists oppose their government taking an active role in world affairs; conversely, internationalists prefer a more active role for the US in global affairs and support the idea of the USA being involved in organizations such as the United Nations. Other scholars, as we shall see, have differentiated between those citizens who are interested in international affairs and those (arguably the majority) who pay little attention to matters beyond their own country.

In fact, early academic opinion questioned the wisdom of the pluralist model, arguing that most of the public were too ill-informed to hold coherent, and therefore influential, views on foreign affairs. The most dismissive analysis claiming public ignorance of international affairs came from the pioneering work of Gabriel Almond, who sought to understand the opinions of the American public in the context of post Second World War debates over isolationism and internationalism. Almond (1950) distinguished between a numerically small *attentive public* and a much larger *mass public*: the former possessed sufficient knowledge to hold coherent views on foreign affairs; the latter was ill-informed and unstable, prone to irrational changes in opinion. At worst, the mass public possessed *non-attitudes* with respect to international politics. Further research during the 1950s and 1960s, mainly conducted in the USA, supported a further claim, namely that the public, however ill-informed, ultimately had little impact upon foreign policy (Holsti 1992). Overall, this academic consensus challenged both the *empirical reality* of the pluralist model and its *desirability* as an analytical framework and, by implication, advocated the *existence* and *desirability* of the elite model. At the same time, it is also worth noting the context of this early research which revolved around concerns within the US foreign policy and political establishment that US citizens were *too* isolationist. The concern was that US policy makers would be unable to take on the global role necessary to counter the 'communist threat' because of an 'irrational' public which failed to 'realize', and indeed support, the need for an internationalist foreign policy. As such, an *internationalist* perspective shared between academics and policy makers perhaps shaped the claims being made in favour of the elite model and at the expense of the pluralist model.

Whatever the accuracy of the early consensus around the elite model, the Vietnam War (spanning the 1960s and 1970s) provided a new context by which to view the relationship between public opinion and foreign policy. US military failure, combined with widespread public opposition to the war, raised questions of whether or not public opinion had undermined US war efforts. Indeed, by the early 1970s, many researchers argued that public opinion was more *rational, stable, and influential* than previously suggested. Consequently, whether because people had become more informed and influential over time, or simply because earlier research had simply been wrong, there existed stronger grounds to support the existence of the pluralist model. The most prominent of such studies was John Mueller's *War, Presidents and Public Opinion* (Mueller 1973). Mueller's thesis was simple, but powerfully demonstrated. Analysing the relationship between US public support for the Korean War and the Vietnam War and the number of US casualties during each of these conflicts, he found that as the number of casualties increased, support for each war declined. As such, US citizens responded in a relatively informed and rational manner; as more soldiers were killed, support for the two wars was withdrawn as revealed through opinion polls, public protests, and ultimately political damage to US Presidents Harry Truman and Lyndon Johnson, respectively. The implication of Mueller's analysis is that public opinion can matter during wars that become protracted and costly in terms of casualty counts.

Since then, despite intensive research, there remains minimal academic consensus between the contrasting elite and pluralist perspectives. For some who argue the existence of the elite model, public opinion continues to have minimal impact on policy, if only because of the multitude of other factors that influence policy makers. This perspective emphasizes the ability of governments alone to lead, and indeed mobilize, public opinion by actively *promoting* particular foreign policy decisions. For example, in the run-up to the 2003 Iraq War, the British and US governments devoted significant time and resources (including the publication of *intelligence dossiers*) to ensuring that the British and American public believed that Saddam Hussein possessed weapons of mass destruction and constituted a threat (Jones 2010). For others (e.g. Margolis and Mauser 1989), public opinion acts at most as a *broad constraint* on foreign policy formulation, whereby policy makers consciously devise policy with an awareness of what the public will and will not accept. So, for example, during the 1999 air war against Serbia, the Clinton administration's options were limited by the knowledge that political support from sections of the US public, in particular those with isolationist sentiments, could be lost if troops were killed in a war that appeared irrelevant to US interests. As a consequence, the Clinton administration adhered to a policy of air strikes and avoided the riskier option of deploying ground troops (Robinson 2002: 94–110).

Others, in support of the pluralist model, find evidence that public concerns can and do play a major role in foreign policy formulation (Risse-Kappen 1991), primarily through citizens punishing and/or rewarding politicians via elections. Perhaps more usefully, other pluralist accounts have sought to provide a more differentiated understanding whereby, under certain circumstances, public opinion plays a greater or lesser role in policy formulation. For example, Foyle (1999) argues that public influence on foreign policy in the USA depends on the normative position of the president regarding the desirability of public influence on his policy, and his need for public support in order to carry through a policy. Some US presidents, whom Foyle labels as 'delegates', believe that public opinion is desirable and necessary and thus are indeed influenced by public opinion. Other US presidents, labelled as 'guardians', believe that the public should never be considered when formulating foreign policy and therefore are not influenced by public opinion.

Overall, the range of positions on questions of public opinion and its influence upon foreign policy seems daunting and contradictory. In part, this is due to the difficulty of actually identifying and measuring influence; academics *cannot* peer inside the minds of policy makers and see influence at work. Moreover, the task of disentangling a single factor, like public opinion, from the wide range of other factors influencing decision makers is a technically difficult task for researchers. Given this uncertainty, it is perhaps best for foreign policy students to first recognize the diversity of academic opinion, and second concede that there is some truth in all the positions. For those who advocate the elite model, there exist prominent examples whereby governments ignore public opinion on matters of foreign policy. For example, in the run-up to the 2003 Iraq invasion, opinion polls repeatedly showed a majority opposition to the war amongst the UK public, and yet the government still proceeded with the war. For those who claim that public opinion influences politics, as indicated by the pluralist model, the subsequent rise in both military and civilian casualties caused large numbers of both the UK and the US publics to perceive the war in Iraq as ill-conceived and wrong, punishing the respective governments of both countries in subsequent elections.

Finally, the greatest limitation of much research into public opinion and foreign policy is its tendency to ignore a crucial intervening variable—the media. And yet the media are clearly central to the public opinion–foreign policy nexus. For example, the pluralist model of public opinion–foreign policy *assumes* that public opinion is *independent* of both government and media. For this to occur, two conditions must be met. First, media must present *objective* information to the public and not simply views that are defined by foreign policy officials. Second, the public must be capable of consuming and processing the information they read and hear in the media in order to form their own *independent* opinion. Conversely, the elite model *assumes* either that the media are, along with public opinion, irrelevant to the concerns of politicians and foreign policy makers, or that the media function only to communicate the viewpoints of policy makers to a public who then passively absorb what they read and hear. As we shall see, these assumptions about the media and their relationship to both foreign policy officials and the public are open to debate. And it is to the question of the media that we now turn.

Media and foreign policy

Within democratic states, the media are supposed to facilitate full and open debate on important issues. The term used to refer to this role is the **public sphere**. Within this sphere, **news media**, including television news, newspapers, and other news formats such as current affairs programming, should help to educate, inform, and facilitate debate. In doing so, a societal consensus can be reached which can then influence government policy. News media are also expected to perform a *watchdog* function, scrutinizing and holding to account the government and also *representing* the opinions of the public. In order to do this, the media strive to be *objective*. That is to say, the aim of the news media is to provide neutral and truthful information untainted by political bias. Amongst news media, an important distinction is to be made between *television* media and *print* media. Television news, for example the British Broadcasting Corporation's (BBC's) *Six O'Clock News*, focuses upon the reporting of unbiased daily political and social events. Conversely, the print news media often practise partisan journalism, catering to differing political agendas and perspectives. In Germany, for example, the *Frankfurter Allgemeine Zeitung* newspaper reflects the interests and values of the right, while in France *Le Monde* articulates left-of-centre views. Overall, however, the expectation in democratic states is that power is sufficiently devolved across television and newspapers to enable a free and independent media. In other words, media systems are expected to conform to the pluralist model. Conversely, in authoritarian or totalitarian states, news media are subject to state control. For example, within the now defunct Soviet Union, the *Pravda* newspaper acted as the mouthpiece for the Kremlin and was committed to helping mobilize the Soviet public to achieve the goals of socialism. Such media systems are understood to conform to the elite model.

In fact, similar to the early elite model of consensus on public opinion and foreign policy, initial analysis of the role of media questioned whether media actually did perform its democratic pluralist role with regard to foreign policy. For example, in *The Press and Foreign Policy*, Bernard Cohen (1963) found that at best media perform an **agenda-setting** role, whereby the media caused policy makers to pay attention to issues that they had raised, but ultimately had little impact on how policy makers then chose to respond to those issues. However, the Vietnam War marked the start of new arguments regarding the impact of media on policy formulation. This war, sometimes described as America's first television war, appeared to some to have been lost because of the relentless flow of violent images and critical reporting by US journalists. Indeed, in his memoirs, President Nixon (1978: 350) famously wrote:

> More than ever before, television showed the terrible human suffering and sacrifice of war . . . the result was a serious demoralization of the home front, raising the question whether America would ever again be able to fight an enemy abroad with unity and strength of purpose at home. (See the photographs on p. 174.)

Whatever the validity of these claims (see Box 9.1), the quantity of studies based on the pluralist model increased throughout the 1980s and 1990s. Two arguments underpinned claims of a more powerful media, in what came to be known as the CNN effect. The first concerned the rise of 24-hour news channels, such as the US-based Cable News Network (CNN), which appeared to have widened the exposure of international events, thereby increasing the pressure on policy makers to respond to issues raised by journalists. At the same time, the end of the Cold War had brought to an end an ideological prism of anti-communism that had bonded policy makers and journalists. Released from the Cold War prism, journalists were, it was presumed, freer to criticize foreign policy (see Box 9.3). As we shall see in our discussion of IR theory, one important component of this debate focused upon the power of media to facilitate humanitarian intervention during post Cold War crises in war-torn countries such as Iraq and Somalia (see also Box 9.3).

Challenging the CNN effect thesis, however, has been the elite model literature that highlights the close relationship between news media and official sources (Hallin 1986; Herman

Influential images from Vietnam: children fleeing napalm.

Source: Photograph taken by Bettman (8 June 1972). Distributed by Corbis.

Influential images from Vietnam: execution of an alleged Vietcong prisoner.

Source: Photograph taken by Eddie Adams. Distributed by PA.

BOX 9.1 Hallin and US media coverage of the Vietnam War: Cold War ideology and spheres of consensus, controversy, and deviance

Daniel Hallin's seminal study, *The Uncensored War* (Hallin 1986), directly challenges the claim that US media coverage adopted an *adversarial*, or *oppositional*, stance toward the US war in Vietnam. Following a detailed content analysis of US newspaper and televison news, Hallin found that US media coverage of the war was broadly supportive up until 1968, with coverage serving to highlight the bravery of US soldiers and ignoring the impact of the war on the Vietnamese population. However, in 1968 communist forces launched the Tet offensive which involved an uprising throughout pro-US South Vietnam. As fighting spilled onto the streets of South Vietnamese cities, US journalists were able to witness the extent of communist support throughout South Vietnam which, in turn, raised doubts about US military claims to be winning the hearts and minds of the South Vietnamese.

At this point, according to Hallin's research, critical reporting did start to emerge in mainstream US media. However, this was not so much because journalists were starting to oppose the war, but because the Johnson administration itself had started to argue publicly over the course of the war. Specifically, the US political establishment had become divided between *hawks*, who believed victory needed to be achieved whatever the cost, and *doves* who argued that the price of victory in Vietnam was not worth paying. Hence, rather than critical reporting being the result of journalists adopting an oppositional stance, it was actually generated by journalists mirroring the debate within the US foreign policy elite. Moreover, US mainstream media rarely reported the views of the anti-war movement in America who argued not that the war was unwinnable, but that it was an immoral and ill-conceived act of aggression. Hallin explains media performance through reference to both the *ideology of objective journalism*, whereby US journalists depend heavily upon official sources in Washington when defining the news agenda, and Cold War ideology which united policy makers and journalists along an anti-communist agenda.

The result of the ideology of anti-communism was that journalists were unable to perceive the Vietnam War as anything but a necessary and just struggle against communism. From this study, Hallin developed his concept of spheres to characterize how US media covered international affairs (Figure 9.1). The sphere of consensus relates to areas where elite agreement over policy exists (e.g. Vietnam policy prior to 1968). Here, media coverage remains relatively passive and reflects the consensus in existence. The sphere of legitimate controversy comes into play when elites are in disagreement over policy (e.g. during and after the Tet offensive in Vietnam); here journalists reflect elite disagreement and criticism of policy emerges in media reports. The sphere of deviance relates to arguments and debates that fall outside the boundaries of elite-legitimated debate (e.g. the arguments of the anti-Vietnam War movement). According to Hallin, US mainstream media, because of their reliance upon US official sources, rarely produce reports that fall into this sphere.

and Chomsky 1988). For example, Lance Bennett's **indexing hypothesis** (Bennett 1990) describes how US journalists follow foreign policy elites in terms of both the news agenda and the framing of foreign affairs issues, rather than striking out independently. As Bennett describes, US journalists tend simply to *index* news coverage to debates occurring within Washington. This arises from the need to avoid upsetting major political and economic interests, the deference of journalists towards official sources, and the vast quantity of information supplied by government to journalists. It is important to note that a variety of formulations of the elite model of media–state relations exist (Hallin 1986; Herman and Chomsky 1988; Bennett 1990), each with a different degree of emphasis regarding the proximity of media to state elites. However, all indicate that, far from presenting some kind of objective reality, media coverage of international affairs is largely subservient to elite groups.

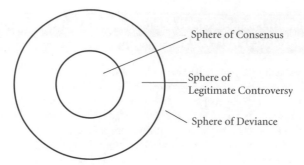

Figure 9.1 Spheres of consensus, controversy, and defiance.

Source: By permission of Oxford University Press Inc. Originally published in D.C. Hallin (1986), *The Uncensored War: The Media and Vietnam* (New York, Oxford University Press), p 117.

In addition to the issue of *indexing*, advocates of the elite model argue that the extent to which audiences are able to consume news and, in turn, form their own independent opinion is more limited than assumed by the pluralist model. Here, the concepts of **agenda setting** (Cohen 1963; McCombs and Shaw 1972), **priming** (Iyengar and Kinder, 1987), and **framing** (Entman 1991) indicate ways in which public opinion can be shaped. Agenda setting refers to the media's ability, by focusing on some issues rather than others, to direct people to think to about those issues. Priming refers to the ability of the media to prepare and direct publics to the issues by which they should judge their leaders. Framing refers solely to the way in which the actual presentation of news information influences how people perceive specific issues. For example, analysing US public opinion, media, and the 1991 Gulf War, Iyengar and Simon (1994) drew on opinion polls and news coverage in order to demonstrate how media focus on the Gulf crisis led to the public defining the crisis as the most important political issue at the time. The media had both set the agenda and directed the public as to what was the most important issue to think about. Their analysis also demonstrated that US citizens were, accordingly, primed to judge how well President George Bush Snr handled the war. Finally, Iyengar and Simon (1994) argue that media coverage of the war was framed in terms of event-orientated (**episodic**) coverage that focused upon military matters, such as military technology and the progress of the war, and tended to downplay **thematic** coverage that dealt with broader diplomatic issues and matters related to the rationale and justification for war. According to their analysis, this framing of the news tended to increase viewers' support for military action. (See Box 9.2.)

Procedural versus substantive criticism and influence

The CNN effect thesis appears incompatible with the elite model. If media are beholden to foreign policy elites, how can it be that coverage shapes and influences what those elites do? Part of the problem for researchers has been the difficulty of accurately measuring media influence. As with the question of public influence, researchers cannot directly observe influence occurring within the minds of policy makers, and the multitude of factors influencing any given decision complicate efforts to measure the precise impact of the media.

BOX 9.2 Framing the news: the Korean Airline and Iran Air shootdowns

The concept of *framing* has emerged as a central tool of analysis in identifying and unpacking political bias within news media reports. In essence, the concept of framing refers to the way in which the use of language, the selection of facts and images, and the degree of attention devoted to a particular issue can lead seemingly objective news reports to convey a highly politicized and biased representation of that issue. In his seminal study 'Framing US Coverage of International News: Contrasts in Narratives of the KAL and Iran Air Incidents', Robert Entman (1991) shows how US media framed two similar events in dramatically contrasting ways. In this article, Entman analyses US media coverage of two events involving the shooting down of a civilian airliner. The first was the shooting down of a Korean airliner in 1983 by a Soviet fighter aircraft after it had strayed into Soviet airspace. The second involved the shooting down of an Iranian airliner in 1988 by a US warship in the Persian Gulf after the airliner flew toward a US navy battle group.

Entman argues that both events were broadly similar in that they involved mistakes by military personnel that led to the destruction of civilian airliners and large loss of life. As such, if news media were objective, coverage of both events should have been broadly similar. However, US media representation of the two events was strikingly different. In the case of the Soviet shootdown, US media coverage accorded far greater attention than that of the US shooting down of the Iranian airliner in terms of column inches and space. For example, the *New York Times* devoted 286 stories to the KAL shootdown and only 102 stories to the Iran Air shootdown. In terms of selection of facts, coverage of the KAL shootdown focused upon the responsibility of the Soviet authorities and the claim that they knowingly ordered the destruction of the airliner. Conversely, coverage of the Iran Air shootdown focused upon the limited information available to US naval personnel regarding the movements of Iranian airliners. Furthermore, the victims of the KAL shootdown were *humanized*, whilst those of the Iran Air shootdown were described more often in *neutral* terms. Overall, according to Entman, the variation across both cases in terms of space, selection of facts, language, and visual imagery led to a *moral outrage* framing of the KAL shootdown and a *technical fault* framing of the Iran Air shootdown. Following from this, Entman argued that US media did not cover the two events objectively, but rather represented both events in ways which were conducive to the political interests of the US government. The *moral outrage* frame supported the Reagan administration's 'evil empire' rhetoric levelled at the Soviet Union at that time, whilst the *technical fault* frame served to reduce public criticism of US government policy in the Persian Gulf.[i]

i For further information on framing and news media coverage see Entman's *Projections of Power* (Entman 2004).

Moreover, when both policy makers and journalists are interviewed about the influence of the media, differing perspectives and interests cloud their opinions. Policy makers are sometimes prone to blame media influence for unsuccessful foreign policy decisions. For example, the ill-fated intervention in Somalia in 1992 was widely attributed to US media forcing policy makers to respond to the humanitarian crisis in the country. Other policy makers, committed to notions of rational decision making, are inclined to deny that they are ever influenced by media reports that by their nature are often incomplete and incorrect. At the same time, journalists might be inclined to oversell their power and importance. These problems introduce a significant degree of uncertainty to elite and pluralist debates over media influence.

BOX 9.3 Media power and the CNN effect debate

We can identify two routes by which media coverage may influence policy (Livingston and Riley 1999). The *indirect route* refers to the process by which media reports influence public opinion, which in turn can then influence policy makers who are sensitive, via the democratic process, to public opinion. The *direct route* refers to the process by which policy makers are directly affected by what they see and read in the media. So, for example, when images of civilian deaths during the Bosnian conflict were broadcast by CNN, some senior policy makers would react to such images on a personal level and be moved to 'do something' to prevent further loss of life.

With respect to of types of effect, four distinct categories of effect can be identified; a *CNN effect*, an *accelerant effect*, an *enabling effect*, and an *impediment effect* (Livingston 1997; Robinson 2002). The *CNN effect* occurs when media coverage plays a direct role in *causing* policy makers to adopt a particular policy. This *does not* mean that media was the only reason that policy makers chose a particular policy option, but it *does* mean that without media pressure, the policy would not have been adopted. Generally, when academics talk of media influence, it is the *CNN effect* they have in mind. For example, George Kennan (1993) argued that it was emotive images of starvation that caused US policy makers to intervene in Somalia. In the absence of those images, no intervention would have occurred. In fact, evidence for the CNN effect has been hard to find. For example, a decade of research into this phenomenon has failed to provide consistent evidence of strategic foreign policy initiatives (e.g. humanitarian intervention) being caused by media pressure. More commonly, research has found evidence of an *accelerant effect*, whereby the decision making process is speeded up by media attention. However, whilst often cited by both policy makers and academics, the *accelerant effect* does not entail media causing a particular policy outcome; rather, this type of effect suggests that policy makers respond *quicker* to a particular issue, but do so in precisely the *same ways* that they would have done without media attention. For example, in relation to the crisis in Northern Iraq 1991, media attention to the Kurdish Crisis might have speeded up the US decision to intervene but, in any case, that decision would have been made at some later point.

Another effect is that the media can *enable* policy makers to pursue a policy by building public support for that policy (Wheeler 2000: 165). For example, it could be argued that the 9/11 attacks on the USA, and the fact they were communicated to the US public in horrific real-time reporting, was crucial in helping to mobilize public support in favour the Bush administration's 'War on Terror' and military action in Afghanistan and Iraq. Therefore the attacks, and their mass-mediated nature, helped to build a constituency amongst US citizens for a more interventionist foreign policy. Finally, the *impediment effect* is linked to the *Vietnam syndrome*. Here, it is a fear over negative media coverage of US casualties and its impact on public opinion that constrains policy makers and prevents them pursuing a policy. For example, during the air war against Serbia in 1999, the Clinton administration limited military options to air strikes in order to avoid US casualties. A factor in this decision was the desire to avoid negative publicity of US casualties during an already politically controversial operation. (For recent debate on the CNN effect and media power, see Special Issue 'The CNN Effect Revisited', *Media, War and Conflict*, 4:3–95, 2011.)

For students, however, it is useful to also understand that these apparently divergent positions on the role and influence of media are not necessarily mutually exclusive, but rather can be understood in greater depth when taking into account their **procedural** and **substantive** influence. The term 'procedural' is used to describe media criticism and influence that relates to debates over the actual *implementation* of policy decisions. The term 'substantive' has been used to describe criticism and influence that relates to the underlying *justifications* and *rationale* for particular foreign policies. For example, analysing US media during the Vietnam War, Hallin (1986) found that, whilst media coverage became critical of the implementation of policy in Vietnam (principally that the war policy was failing), it rarely questioned whether the USA was in fact justified in attempting to exert control over the destiny of the Vietnamese population (see Box 9.1). Therefore media influence and criticism remained at a *procedural level* and was never intensified to the *substantive level*.

Once this distinction is introduced, it becomes easier to understand what have at times been somewhat dogmatic debates between academics subscribing to elite models of media–state relations and those who adhere to the CNN effect thesis and the pluralist model. There is evidence to indicate that the media are both critical and influential at a procedural level. For example, Nik Gowing (1994) argues that during the 1992–1995 war in Bosnia, the British government responded to media criticism through the implementation of *cosmetic policy* responses, such as short-term humanitarian issues that included the airlifting of limited numbers of injured civilians out of the war zone. Influence on *tactical policy* could be seen in limited military responses to human rights abuses that included limited air strikes on various combatants in the conflict. However, substantive-level influence—of the kind that might have changed the overall strategy aimed at containment of the conflict but not forcing an end to the war—was more limited. In short, media criticism and influence tend to be bounded within certain limits which, in turn, are often set by foreign policy elites.

To sum up, two competing visions of media–state relations dominate the current debate. One, the CNN effect thesis, places significant emphasis on the ability of the media to shape and influence foreign policy decisions. The other, the elite model of media–state relations, paints a picture of media subservience to the foreign policy establishment. In fact, both viewpoints possess some truth, and the important distinction lies in the *level* of criticism and influence (procedural versus substantive) being considered. (See Box 9.4.)

Media, public opinion, and theoretical frames

Having set out the diverse array of arguments concerning the relationship between public opinion, media, and foreign policy, we can now turn to the task of integrating these competing arguments with major IR schools of thought. As we shall see, each of the major IR schools of thought can be linked to the different arguments and models discussed earlier.

Realism

Broadly speaking, media and public opinion are presented by realist theory as irrelevant to understanding international politics. Why is this the case? For realists, international politics can be *described* and *explained* as the outcome of inter-state power struggles. For realist theory, the most important actor to consider is the state, and the domestic structure of a state has minimal bearing upon how that state behaves. Whether a state is democratic, totalitarian, or authoritarian, the anarchic nature of the international system forces it to pursue its self-interest in order to survive. Consequently, foreign policy is formulated not under the influence of domestic media and publics, but by foreign policy elites who, under the influence of an anarchic international system, define and pursue the national interest. As such, realism argues that

---

BOX 9.4 Beyond the elite–pluralist dichotomy: new approaches to theorizing the media–foreign policy nexus

Whilst elite and pluralist perspectives continue to influence academic debate, recent research has attempted to develop models that capture both these theoretical perspectives and therefore provide a more nuanced and differentiated understanding of media–state relations. For example, many academics now argue that both elite dissensus (Hallin 1986), when there is disagreement within the political and foreign policy establishment, and unexpected events (Lawrence 2000) that occur beyond the control of governments can considerably open up the boundaries of media criticism and influence. So, for example, during the build-up to and the invasion of Iraq in 2003, debate occurred amongst politicians and within the foreign policy community in the UK over the justification for the war. As a consequence, media coverage was much more critical and perhaps influential in terms of shaping public and elite perceptions of the war (e.g. Robinson *et al.* 2010). At the same time, unexpected or uncontrolled events (such as the abuse of Iraqis by coalition forces) which spread through the world's media meant that the UK and US governments were subjected to varying levels of criticism and dissent from their respective domestic media.

Other recent accounts that attempt to bridge the elite–pluralist divide include the *political contest model* (Wolfsfeld 1997) and *policy–media interaction model* (Robinson 2002). These models emphasize variables such as levels of policy certainty (Robinson 2002) and control over the political environment (Wolfsfeld 1997). For example, when a government is uncertain over policy, media and public opinion can exert greater influence on policy formulation. Alternatively, when policy is set in place, the potential for media influence wanes. Wolfsfeld argues that sometimes a government can lose control of the political environment, which in turn leads to a more critical media and space for non-elite challenges. He demonstrates how the Israeli government lost control over the political environment during the 1987 Palestinian uprising, the *intifada*; as a consequence media mobilized support for the Palestinians and criticized Israeli policy.

Finally, Baum and Groeling (2010) present a novel theoretical work in their book *War Stories*, in which the elites are understood to dominate the media and public environment during the early stages of a war, but that over time elite discord and the reality on the ground (casualties and costs of war) endow media and publics with greater autonomy from, and power over, a US government and its war policy. Also, in *Pockets of Resistance*, Robinson *et al.* (2010) explore evidence for the diversity and variability of the British media during the 2003 invasion of Iraq. In short, the applicability of the elite and pluralist models can be argued to vary across time and circumstance.

---

foreign policy is generated by forces *external* to the state, rather than forces *internal* to the state such as media and public opinion.

However, there is more to the realist analysis. Implicit in realist theory are various **normative** components. The first such component is that foreign policy *should* be immune from public and media influence, otherwise a state might be prevented from pursuing its national interest. For example, a public might remain opposed to a war necessary for their national interest. Here, the assumption underpinning realism is that foreign policy elites are more likely to do what is in the nation's interest and that, just as Almond (1950) argued, publics are largely ignorant and ill-informed about international affairs. The second normative component is that mobilization of the public and the media in support of the national interest is morally correct. Here, the realist assumption is that moral communities are defined by state boundaries and that both media and public opinion should reflect this reality. So, when a state goes to war, for example, it is *right* that the media help to mobilize the public in support of war.

Regarding debates about public opinion and media discussed earlier, the *elite model* is compatible with realist theory, by claiming that public opinion and media *are* led by government and that domestic factors are irrelevant to foreign policy. Conversely, the realist claim concerning the irrelevance of domestic factors is weakened if one accepts the pluralist model's argument that public opinion and media *do* influence foreign policy formulation. Further, the argument that the media are limited to *procedural-level criticism* is consistent with realist theory. For example, the media might come to criticize the means by which a war is being fought—as was the case regarding the use of cluster bombs during the 1991 Gulf War—but leave uninterrogated the justification for the war. Indeed, much research into media coverage of war highlights a broad tendency to uncritically mobilize support for both military and government war objectives. Of course, this is not the place to suggest which line of argument is 'correct'; the central point here is that realism rests upon the assumption that the elite model is correct and that pluralist models are in error. As such, the validity of realist assumptions can be usefully analysed and debated through reference to both elite and pluralist models.

Liberalism

Unlike realism, liberalism places far greater analytical importance on the role of public opinion and media. As a theory of international relations, liberalism focuses on the rules and norms that have evolved between states (see Chapter Three). Central to liberalism is the belief in, and commitment to, developing rule-governed behaviour between states that, in turn, can lead to greater levels of cooperation and reduced levels of conflict. A key component of liberal theory is the **democratic peace thesis**, and it is here that particular claims regarding public opinion become crucial to liberalism. The democratic peace thesis maintains that liberal democracies are war averse because, at least in part, the consent of the public is required. Because, as liberalism assumes, people generally prefer peace to war, public opinion acts as a powerful constraint on elected leaders and therefore on the external behaviour of a state. In order for this to occur, it must be the case both that public opinion constrains foreign policy formulation and that media are independent of government when covering international affairs. In short, the democratic peace theory assumes that pluralist models of media and public opinion are correct and that elite models are in error. The level of academic disagreement on these issues, as discussed earlier, suggests that such assumptions are open to contestation.

At the international level, liberal claims regarding free speech and the global free flow of information (in part facilitated by media communications technology) have been associated with the progressive spread of liberal values. For example, Joseph Nye (1996) argues that:

> [o]rganizations such as the U.S. Information Agency are vital to the task of aiding democratic transitions. . . . USIA'S international broadcasting arm, the Voice of America, has in the last few years become the primary news source for 60% of the educated Chinese. America's increasing technical ability to communicate with the public in foreign countries, literally over the heads of their rulers via satellite, provides a great opportunity to foster democracy.

Here, communications technology becomes a key mechanism by which **soft power,** the 'ability to get what you want by attracting and persuading others to adopt your goals' (Nye 2004), can be projected. With respect to **complex interdependence** and regimes, the pluralization of transnational information flows facilitated by the internet and global media have 'opened the field to loosely structured network organisations ... who are particularly effective in penetrating states without regard to borders and using domestic constituencies to force political leaders to focus on their preferred agendas' (Keohane and Nye 1998: 83). For example, NGOs successfully coordinated political pressure through media *vis-à-vis* environmental talks leading to the Kyoto Agreement and the anti-landmine campaign that led to the Ottawa Agreement (Keohane and Nye 1998: 92). As such, the kind of networking and media promotion available by virtue of the contemporary information environment facilitate the emergence of new regimes.

Other, liberal, arguments persist regarding the internet and its tendency to undermine the control of authoritarian states over what their populations see and hear. The assumption here is that the free flow of information through global media and the internet are part of **globalization** processes and have a progressively liberalizing effect around the world. Significant debate during the 1990s revolved around the emergence of a new norm of humanitarian intervention, whereby the international community intervened in the internal affairs of a state to uphold human rights (see Chapter Twelve). For some, a key factor in developing this norm is the media. For example, in *Civil Society and Media in Global Crises*, Martin Shaw (1996) argues that during the 1991 Kurdish crisis in Northern Iraq, Western media highlighted the suffering of Kurds fleeing attacks from Saddam Hussein's forces. As a consequence of relentless and emotive coverage, Western leaders were forced into conducting what was widely seen to be the first case of humanitarian intervention (see Box 9.3). As such, the media is understood to be a central component in ensuring that states respond to human rights concerns.

Again, as with the democratic peace, these arguments rest upon a series of assumptions regarding the role and function of media and public opinion. To the extent that media and publics are capable of both influencing and driving foreign policy, liberal theories are strengthened. Whatever the empirical validity of such claims, which are open to debate as discussed earlier in this chapter, the key point is that important liberal claims rest upon the validity of the pluralist model.

Critical approaches

Critical approaches to the study of IR (Marxism and critical theory) call into question existing political and economic orders through a process of explaining and understanding their origins.[1] In fact, it is noteworthy that the empirical description of the public opinion–media–foreign policy nexus made by realists is similar to critical approaches. Both assert the subservience of public opinion and media to the state, and work with an elite understanding of the foreign policy–media–public opinion relationship. For realists, this is part due to the need for foreign policy elites to be free to pursue the national interest unfettered by an 'irrational' media and public, and in part because the state is assumed to represent the interests of those people contained within its borders. For critical approaches, however, the state is a function of political and economic structures that enable domination by a socio-economic elite. Central to the maintenance of this inequality is the role of the mass media which serves to reflect and propagate the interests of elites, whose particular world view is then transmitted to the population whose opinions are manipulated or 'manufactured'.

One notable account in this vein is *Manufacturing Consent: The Political Economy of the Mass Media* by Herman and Chomsky (1988). These authors emphasize the commercial imperatives acting upon news organizations. According to Herman and Chomsky, there are significant ovelapping interests between the US state and major US business conglomerates of which the mass media is but one part. Consequently, news stories that run contrary to these interests are unlikely to surface. It is important to note that such radical critiques are not just arguing that the media within liberal democratic states functions to promote liberal and capitalist values to both domestic audiences and wider global publics. If this were the case, the only disagreement between the liberal and the critical positions would be a normative one; that is to say, liberals support the promotion of liberalism and free market economics, whilst critical approaches would challenge the promotion of these and, instead, seek to change the existing order. Rather, the core of the radical critique is that Western mainstream media perpetuate an image of Western democracies (and in particular the USA) as inherently benign, peaceful, and committed to high moral standards when, in fact, the foreign policies of those states are riddled with self-interested economic and political objectives that often lead those states to support violent and illiberal policies. As such, the media are not free and autonomous, but rather mobilize—through deception—citizens in support of the actions of their governments. For instance, in support of their case, Herman and Chomsky document how US media functioned to promote anti-communism by highlighting human rights abuses committed by communist states and downplaying similar abuses committed by allies of the USA during the 'struggle against communism'.

In addition, critical approaches highlight ways in which global information flows are dominated by powerful states and vested economic interests. For example, whilst CNN might indeed be described as global media, some argue that its news agenda and framing of events reflect the interests of First World elites. Again, whilst liberals point to the ability of the media to provoke humanitarian concern for suffering people in poorer parts of the globe, as was the case during the 1984 Ethiopian famine (Philo 1993), critical approaches argue that such responses are superficial and allow affluent audiences in the West to avoid confronting global inequalities that enable famine and crisis to occur in the first place (De Waal 1997).

Central to these critical analyses, of course, is the position that the media are subservient to the state and that public opinion is moulded by—but does not itself mould—foreign policy elites who form part of a broader societal elite. As such, critical accounts emphasize the extent to which both media and public opinion are shaped by broader political-economic power structures and, therefore, rest upon the validity of the elite model.

Conclusion: new technology and the 'War on Terror'

Whilst academics continue to debate the relative merits of the various theories, models, and arguments outlined in this chapter, a broader set of concerns have come to dominate debate in recent years. Essentially, these new issues examine the extent to which media and public opinion have grown in influence because of the proliferatio of new forms of communications technology, such as the internet, and the emergence of global media such as CNN and

Al-Jazeera (see Box 9.5); conversely, they also examine the extent to which the rise of new political issues, such as the 'War on Terror', have decreased the influence of media and public opinion. I shall deal with each in turn.

New technology

The emergence of truly global forms of communication such as satellite broadcasting, which facilitate real-time reporting of global events, along with the internet, which provides a forum for anyone to promote their own political agenda free from the constraints of state-based media systems, have radically pluralized the relationship between publics, media, and the state, at least according to some. In a globalized world of instant communication, governments—as the traditional architects of foreign policy—appear less able to manage and manipulate information and ideas, and hitherto weak and marginalized groups have sometimes been able to exploit communications technology. For example, analysing the David and Goliath struggle between the indigenous Chiapas guerrilla army and the Mexican state during the early 1990s, Dougas Kellner claims that '[f]rom the beginning, the peasants and guerrilla armies struggling in Chiapas, Mexico used computer data bases, guerrilla radio, and other forms of media to circulate news of their struggles and ideas' (Kellner 1998: 182). Other examples of the inability of states to suppress 'bad news' are the images of torture and abuse by American soldiers at Abu Ghraib in Iraq where, ultimately, the US government could do little to prevent the global circulation of such images through the internet. Most recently, many commentators have asserted the importance of social media such as Facebook, and other Web 2 technologies, in facilitating uprisings throughout the Arab world.

BOX 9.5 The Al-Jazeera effect?

Since its launch in the mid 1990s, the Qatar-based 24-hour satellite news channel Al-Jazeera has emerged as a significant, and at times controversial, news channel. Principally committed to providing *independent* and *objective* news reporting throughout the Middle East, the first effect of Al-Jazeera was to enable the creation of an Arabic public sphere where genuine criticism and debate could be aired. This contrasted with existing Arab news media that were widely seen as beholden to Middle Eastern governments. As such, Al-Jazeera is seen by many as a democratizing force in the Middle East. However, since 9/11 Al-Jazeera has increasingly been criticized by the US and British governments on the grounds that its reporting is *biased* and, unhelpful, in the 'War on Terror'. For example, for broadcasting tapes of Osama bin Laden delivering statements, Al-Jazeera was accused of providing a public platform for the al-Qaeda terrorist network. Also, during the 2003 Iraq War, Al-Jazeera incurred criticism from both the US and British governments for transmitting images of dead coalition soldiers. In its defence, Al-Jazeera has maintained that it has attempted to report controversial events objectively without privileging any one perspective. But what is the overall effect, if any, of an independent 24-hour Arab-based news channel on global affairs? On the one hand, its influence on Western publics is probably minimal; most people in the West continue to watch 'Western' news channels. On the other hand, the popularity and credibility of Al-Jazeera throughout the Arab world means that attempts by the West, and in particular the USA, to influence perceptions during its 'War on Terror' through *soft power projection* is far more limited than if, for example, CNN was the information source of choice in the Arab world. For more read *Al Jazeera Effect: How the New Global Media Are Reshaping World Politics* (Seib 2008).

Broadly speaking, such claims challenge both the realist and the critical approaches discussed earlier and support liberal arguments regarding the influential and transformative potential of both media and public opinion. Despite the quantity of such claims in recent years, some have come to question quite how empowering new communications technology has actually been (e.g. Robinson *et al.* 2010: 167–70). With respect to the aforementioned examples, instances like the Chiapas can be argued to be relatively rare and exceptions to the rule, and there is no firm evidence that the Arab uprisings were causally dependent upon web-based communications technology. Certainly, and overall, there is little evidence to support the thesis that marginalized groups have become much more powerful as a consequence of developments in communications technology. With respect to the issue of Abu Ghraib, recent research has suggested that, whilst a problem issue for US authorities, most mainstream US media represented the issue in a manner relatively congenial to the US government by representing the events as *abuses* by a *few soldiers* rather than as the consequence of an 'administration policy of torture' (Bennett *et al.* 2006: 467). More generally, realists can still point to the fact that, for all the talk of the emergence of a global media sphere and global public, most audiences maintain a 'stubborn preference' for national, regional, and even local news (Carruthers 2000: 202). Also, critical approaches point to the concentration of ownership and competition across the global media industry to highlight the political–economic imperatives that, in their view, encourage media outlets such as CNN and Sky News to eschew in-depth reportage for a focus on **infotainment**. Overall, realists and critical approaches still present a serious challenge to both the theoretical and empirical cogency of liberal pluralist claims.

The 'War on Terror'

As noted earlier, much debate during the 1990s revolved around the impact of the end of the Cold War stand-off between the USA and the Soviet Union. Freed from an ideological bond that united policy makers and journalists, media, it was argued, became more influential and adversarial. The current question influencing research and theorizing concerns how new issues, such as the 'War on Terror', have limited the extent to which both media and publics are autonomous from state-directed foreign policy. Specifically, since the events of 11 September 2001, the geopolitical landscape has been dominated by the Bush Administration's 'War on Terror'. For some academics (Domke 2004; Jackson 2005), the 'War on Terror' functions as a new ideological imperative, effectively replacing that of Cold War era anti-communism (see Box 9.1), which is now limiting media independence and the perception by Western publics of global affairs. From this perspective, the 'War on Terror' frame provides journalists with a template with which to understand global events and a powerful rhetorical tool with which to justify a more aggressive and interventionist foreign policy agenda. This has already been seen during the build-up to and war against Iraq when the US government justified the invasion of Iraq as part of the 'War on Terror'. For liberals, the appearance of new issues, such as the 'War on Terror', challenge their claims for the existence of a more adversarial and independent post Cold War media. For realist and critical approaches the 'War on Terror', and its impact upon both media autonomy and public perceptions of global affairs, confirms the subservience of both media and publics to broader political and economic forces.

Quite where the truth lies between these various positions must be for the reader to decide and for academics to continue to debate. But as we have shown throughout this chapter, media and public opinion remain important for IR theory, whether as a powerful constraint upon state action (the liberal position), a source of mobilization for the state (the realist position), or the mechanism by which structures of inequality and domination are maintained (the critical position). Perhaps the most significant question facing researchers is the extent to which political and economic forces constrain and manipulate media and publics and the extent to which technological developments have strengthened the independence of media and publics from those forces. At the heart of this debate remains the central question of whether peoples of the world have become any more, or any less, informed about global affairs.

 Key points

- Research on public opinion, media, and foreign policy falls into two principal categories examining (a) the public opinion–foreign policy relationship and (b) the media–foreign policy relationship.
- Pluralist accounts maintain that both public opinion and media have a significant impact on foreign policy.
- Elite accounts maintain that both public opinion and media are subservient to the state and therefore do not influence foreign policy.
- For realists, public opinion and media should be mobilized in support of the state.
- For liberals, public opinion and media *should* provide an important input to foreign policy decision making and can transform international politics.
- Critical approaches maintain that media are mobilized in support of the state and elite interests, but that this situation is to be criticized as fundamentally undemocratic.
- Recent debate has revolved round the impact of new communications technology and the 'War on Terror' upon the power and influence of media and public opinion.

 Questions

1. What influence, if any, can public opinion have on foreign policy formulation?
2. In what ways, and to what extent, can media influence public opinion?
3. Assess the relative cogency of elite and pluralist models of media–state relations.
4. To what extent do you agree with the realist perspective on media and public opinion?
5. To what extent do you agree with the liberal perspective on media and public opinion?
6. Critical accounts argue that media and public opinion are manipulated by elite interests. To what extent do you agree?
7. What impact has new technology had on the public opinion–media–foreign policy nexus?
8. To what extent *should* public opinion and media shape foreign policy?

 Further reading

Entman, R. (2004), *Projections of Power: Framing News, Public Opinion and US Foreign Policy* (Chicago, IL: University of Chicago Press).
Comprehensive introduction to the concept of frames, detailing their impact upon both public and foreign policy.

Foyle, D. (1999), *Counting the Public In: Presidents, Public Opinion and Foreign Policy* **(New York: Columbia University Press).**

A good example of a contemporary account arguing that that public opinion can influence policy.

Herman, E., and Chomsky, N. (1988), *Manufacturing Consent: The Political Economy of the Mass Media* **(New York: Pantheon).**

Provocative and widely read example of the elite perspective, arguing that US media function to mobilize support for elite interests.

Robinson, P. (2002) *The CNN Effect: The Myth of News, Foreign Policy and Intervention* **(London: Routledge).**

Provides a contemporary theoretical and empirical analysis of the CNN effect debate highlighting the contrasting roles that the media can play in policy formulation.

Shaw, M. (1996), *Civil Society and Media in Global Crises* **(London: St Martin's Press).**

A good example of the pluralist position, detailing the case of the 1991 Kurdish Crisis and arguing that the media had a powerful impact upon public opinion and foreign policy.

Visit the Online Resource Centre that accompanies this book for more information:
www.oxfordtextbooks.co.uk/orc/smith_foreign/

10

The primacy of national security

BRIAN C. SCHMIDT

Chapter contents

 Reader's guide

The aim of this chapter is to explore the concept of national security. Although national security is a familiar concept in foreign policy, it is, at the same time, an essentially contested concept. This chapter introduces students to some of the competing conceptions of national security, beginning with the traditional realist understanding of national security that has had a significant influence on both the academic field of International Relations and foreign policy makers. The chapter then provides a brief overview of the field of security studies. The chapter concludes by linking the theoretical controversy about the meaning of national security to the American foreign policy debate on grand strategy.

Introduction

National security is a key concept for those who engage in the analysis of foreign policy. This is equally true for practitioners who are engaged in the process of formulating their respective state's foreign policy. One of the core objectives of foreign policy is to achieve national security. Yet while national security is a paramount goal, there is a great deal of ambiguity about the actual meaning of the concept. As Arnold Wolfers (1962) noted over fifty years ago, national security is an ambiguous symbol. National security means different things to different people, and there is no universally agreed understanding of what the term signifies (see Box 10.1). Although the traditional meaning of national security is most often associated with the notion of protecting, and ultimately securing, the physical survival of the nation-state from external threats in the form of a military attack, this certainly does not exhaust all of the possible meanings. Wolfers was concerned that while the term 'national security' was beginning to be widely used by scholars and policy makers after the Second World War, the concept actually lacked a precise meaning. Moreover, he was worried that the pursuit of national security was being limited to military means when there were many non-military policies such as diplomacy that could be employed.

The ambiguity surrounding the concept of national security stems from a number of factors. First, the term 'security,' like that of other concepts such as power, is extremely broad and can be viewed from a variety of competing perspectives. Writing in 1983, Barry Buzan, in his highly acclaimed book *People, States, and Fear*, re-confirmed Wolfers' point by arguing that security remained an underdeveloped concept (Buzan 1983). A key question, therefore, is what do we really mean by security? Is security limited to military concerns or should other issues such as health, the economy, and the environment be included as 'security issues'? Unfortunately, the answer to this question depends on how one answers the related question of what or who is the proper referent object of security. Who, or what, are we attempting to secure? Depending on your perspective, there are a number of possible referent objects: individuals, families, nation-states, regions, the society of states, and even the globe. Although the traditional perspective holds that the referent object of security is the nation-state, there are those who endorse the concept of **human security**, pointing instead to the possibility of individuals being the referent object of security. If we take seriously the idea that the aim of national security is to secure individuals, a diverse range of issues and concerns enters the framework of analysis. This includes the point that the state itself, as in the most recent cases of Libya and Syria, can represent a threat to the security of an individual in the form of arbitrary arrests, unlawful detention, torture, and lack of respect for basic human rights. As Buzan reminds us, 'for perhaps a majority of the world's people threats from the state are among the major sources of insecurity in their lives' (Buzan 1991: 45).

Yet even if we remain wedded to the state as the traditional referent object of national security, this does not resolve the ambiguity of the concept. There is another complicating factor that must be considered when pondering the meaning of national security—threats. The

---

BOX 10.1 Competing conceptions of national security

'A nation has security when it does not have to sacrifice its legitimate interests to avoid war and is able, if challenged, to maintain them by war.' (Lippmann 1943: 51)

'Any feminist definition of security must therefore include the elimination of all types of violence, including violence prod uced by gender relations of domination and subordination.' (Tickner 1992: 58)

'National security is the preservation of a way of life. . . . It includes freedom from military attack or coercion, freedom from internal subversion and freedom from the erosion of the political, economic and social values which are essential to the quality of life.' (Canadian National Defence College, quoted in Buzan 1991: 17)

'National security is about the protection of core values, that is, the identification of threats and the adoption of policies to protect core values.' (Leffler 2004a: 131)

'National security is the ability of a nation to protect its internal values from external threats.' (Bock and Berkowitz 1966: 134)

'National security refers to the preservation of the country's highest values as these are purposefully threatened from abroad, primarily by other states, but by other external actors as well.' (Nordlinger 1995: 10)

concept of security only makes sense against the backdrop of threats; yet if there is little agreement on the meaning of security, the same is also true of threats. The assessment and definition of a threat is always subjective, and this is true for both individuals and states. In both cases, fear, which is deeply subjective, is the motivating factor behind the quest for security. In making the distinction between individual and state security, Buzan draws attention to the radical implications this has for how one defines threats. It is often the case that the military means a state uses to defend itself against a threat from a rival state can prove to be the source of an individual's threat. Feminist scholars, for example, have shown that women suffer disproportionately from large defence expenditures which frequently result in a reduction of social expenditures that place women and children in a vulnerable and fearful situation.[1] One of the debates among those who study national security today is what constitutes the most significant security threat. The traditional realist view that threats are defined solely in terms of the ability of a state to use military force against another state seems, for many, to be increasingly antiquated. In the context of globalization, threats are increasingly being conceptualized in terms of transnational terrorism, economic deprivation, environmental degradation, global pandemics such as HIV/AIDS, and cyber-warfare.

Not only is there a debate about what constitutes a threat to national security, there is also a debate about the sources of threats. This is one of the reasons why the study of foreign policy is beholden to theories of international relations. Theories are simplifying devices that help analysts decide what to focus on and what to ignore. As explained in the next section, realist theories focus on the external sources of national security threats. Threats are seen as emanating outside the boundaries of the sovereign state and arising from the anarchical international system. Others, including those informed by critical theory, emphasize both the internal *and* external sources of threats (Booth 2005). Critical theories aim to broaden what they perceive to be a narrow realist agenda focused on state security and military threats. The threat of poverty, environmental degradation, and domestic repression of essential human rights arguably all reside inside the state and pose a direct security threat to the lives of individual human beings. Focusing on how political discourse and ideas contribute to the prevailing meanings of these terms (McSweeney 1999), constructivists argue that both security and threats are social constructions. Constructivists are not only interested in examining the existing identities of actors and meanings of key concepts, but also in the social processes that can lead to changes in the way we understand concepts such as security. Ideally, constructivists look to the possibility of establishing 'security communities' (Adler and Barnett 1998) whereby states share a collective sense of identity and security. Finally, there are approaches that attempt to combine the insights of the aforementioned theories. The best example of this is Melvyn Leffler's national security approach which simultaneously attempts to integrate external and internal factors into a comprehensive approach to studying **national security policy** (see Box 10.2).

Realism and national security

The primacy of national security owes much to the realist school of International Relations theory. Realists paint a grim picture of world politics that resembles Thomas Hobbes' pessimistic account of life in a state of nature, which he viewed as synonymous to a state of war of

US Air Force.

Source: US Air Force photo.

BOX 10 .2 Leffler's national security approach

The genius of Leffler's (2004a) national security approach is that it combines multiple levels of analysis, and bridges the divide between internal and external variables. Leffler's approach, which draws on the insights of Wolfers and Buzan, provides a comprehensive framework for studying national security. He defines security as the protection of domestic core values from external threats. This obligates students of foreign policy 'to look at the structure of the international system as well as the domestic ideas and interests shaping policy' (Leffler 2004a: 123). To determine core values, the analyst must look inside the state and examine the actors, ideas, interests, and processes that lead to the determination of core values. External threats, Leffler argues, only emerge in relation to how a state defines its internal core values. While external threats are defined in terms of the risks they pose to core values, they are also influenced by changes in the international system. Finally, Leffler also acknowledges the crucial role that individuals play in national security policy. Policy makers' perceptions matter with respect to both how core values and national identity are defined as well as how external dangers are perceived and constructed. Thus Leffler is able to offer an approach to understanding national security that incorporates individuals, domestic politics, and the international system.

all against all. In a world where threats loom large, realists argue that states are compelled to seek power in order to ensure their own security. The core objective of foreign policy is to ensure the survival of the state. For realists, the fundamental national interest of all states *is* national security. While significant differences exist among realists, Dunne and Schmidt (2011) argue that realists of all stripes subscribe to 'three S's'—statism, survival, and self-help— that together help to account for the primacy of national security.

Statism

According to realists, the state is the main actor and sovereignty is its distinguishing trait. By identifying the state as the central actor in international politics, realists consider the overriding objective of national security to be the security of the state. Buzan agrees that the state is central to the concept of security and argues that national security—acting as a compass for the state's foreign policy—is devoted to protecting the four component elements of a state: its physical base (population and territory), the idea of the state (nationality and organizing ideologies), its institutions (the machinery of government), and finally its sovereignty (Buzan 1991: 65–96). Realists argue that it is the attribute of sovereignty that provides both security and order to the political community living inside the territorial boundaries of the state. Within this territorial space, sovereignty denotes the supreme authority of the state to make and enforce laws. Internally, realists operate under the assumption that the problem of security is solved; most of the time individuals do not have to worry about their own personal security. Externally, however—in the relations among independent sovereign states—insecurities, dangers, and threats to the very existence of the state are enduring features of international politics. Realists largely explain this on the basis that the very condition for order and security—namely, the existence of a sovereign—is missing from the international realm.

Anarchy is the term that realists use to indicate that international politics takes place in an environment that has no overarching central authority. Structural realists (neorealism), in particular, attribute security, competition, and war to the absence of world government and to the relative distribution of power in the international system. For structural realists, the condition of anarchy—that is, the fact that there is no 'higher power' to ensure peace among sovereign states—is often viewed as synonymous with a state of war. This does not mean that every state is constantly at war, but rather that war is always a distinct possibility. Waltz explains that 'competition and conflict among states stem directly from the twin facts of life under conditions of anarchy: States in an anarchic order must provide for their own security, and threats or seeming threats to their security abound' (Waltz 1989: 43). This illustrates the realist argument that national security is a pervasive concern of states and explains why survival is ultimately the central goal of foreign policy.

Survival

It is largely on the basis of how realists depict the international environment that they conclude that the first priority of state leaders is to ensure the survival of their state. Under anarchy, the survival of the state cannot be guaranteed because the use of force culminating in war is a legitimate instrument of **statecraft**. Force can be used both to wage war and to threaten war as an element of **coercive diplomacy**. Realists argue that the ever-present possibility of force being used in the anarchical international system causes states to fear one another. Along with anarchy, there are two additional factors that generate insecurity among states. The first is that most states possess some offensive military capability that can potentially be used against a rival state. Second, states are most often uncertain about the intentions of other states. On the basis of these factors, Mearsheimer (2001: 3) concludes that states, especially great powers, have a strong incentive to seek a maximum amount of power in the belief that this is the best path to security.

While realists do view the accumulation of power, especially military power, as the best route to achieving national security, this traditional realist formula is not immune from controversy. First, while realists largely base their foreign policy analysis on the role of power, there is a good deal of variation in how individual realists conceptualize power (Schmidt 2005). **Structural realists**, for example, define power in terms of capabilities, and calculate this on the basis of the sum total of national attributes, including size of population and territory, wealth, and military strength. Yet because realists determine force to be the ***ultima ratio*** or last resort of international politics, military power emerges as the most important factor in assessing the relative power of a state and its relative position in the international system. However, this can prove to be problematic because there are many instances in which a state with superior military power is unable to achieve its foreign policy goals—the USA's misadventure in Iraq is a dramatic example. Classical realists such as Hans Morgenthau (1954) had a more expansive and nuanced notion of power that included both tangible elements, such as geography, natural resources, industrial capacity, and military preparedness, and non-tangible elements, such as national character, national morale, and the quality of a nation's diplomacy. As a perceptive scholar of international politics, Morgenthau recognized that one of the most complicated tasks of foreign policy analysis was to evaluate how the individual elements of power contributed to the overall power of one's own state compared with that of others.

A second controversy, which is rooted in the debate between defensive and offensive realists, is whether states are primarily security or power maximizers. This debate has direct implications for the analysis of foreign policy (see Chapter Two). According to **defensive realism**, states are fundamentally security maximizers. The international system, according to defensive realists, only provides incentives for moderate behaviour, and expansionistic policies to achieve security are generally not required because the international system is basically benign. In order for a state to ensure its own survival, defensive realists recommend a foreign policy that only seeks an appropriate, rather than a preponderant, amount of power. Defensive realists argue that expansionistic foreign policies most often prove to be counterproductive because they cause other states to form a counterbalancing coalition. In addition to balancing, defensive realists highlight a number of intervening variables, such as geography, technology, and military doctrine, which result in conquest rarely paying.

Rather than security maximizers, **offensive realism** argues that states are power maximizers continually searching for opportunities to gain more power relative to other states. Unlike defensive realists, offensive realists do not believe that security in the international system is plentiful. Nor do they believe that balancing behaviour is as frequent and efficient as defensive realists contend. According to Mearsheimer, the anarchical structure of the international system, coupled with the deep uncertainty that states have about the current and future intentions of other states, compels foreign policy makers to maximize their state's relative power position. For offensive realists, it is obvious that the best way to achieve national security is to be the most powerful state in the international system. National security is a function of power; as such, more powerful states are less vulnerable to being attacked than weaker states. Therefore offensive realists conclude that all states are continuously searching for opportunities to increase their power relative to other states.

Self-help

National security, realists argue, is ultimately an individual effort. Realists maintain that states act on the basis of **self-help**, meaning that they must each take the appropriate steps to ensure their own survival in the anarchical international system. Realists do not believe it is prudent for a state to entrust its survival to another actor or international institution such as the United Nations. Rather, security can only be realized through self-help. While each state must undertake its own measures to achieve national security, there is no guarantee that this goal will be achieved. There are many reasons why the goal of achieving national security can be thwarted. First, a state may have an expansive notion of security that is simply unachievable. Second, a state may lack the capabilities to achieve its vision of national security. Third, even if a state has a reasonable conception of national security and possesses the necessary means to implement it, realists highlight the anarchical system as an obstacle to achieving security. The ability of a state to achieve national security is often contingent on the behaviour of other states, and yet the international system lacks a mechanism to coordinate all of the individual foreign policies. Tragically, the rational pursuit of national security can sometimes lead to irrational collective outcomes. The best example of this is known as the **security dilemma**, where the goal of pursuing one's own security often fuels the insecurity of other states. According to Wheeler and Booth (1992: 30), 'security dilemmas exist when the military preparations of one state create an unresolvable uncertainty in the mind of another as to whether those preparations are for "defensive" purposes only (to enhance its security in an uncertain world) or whether they are for offensive purposes (to change the status quo to its advantage)'. This type of security dynamic can be seen taking place in a number of volatile regions in the world. States find it very difficult to trust one another and often view the intentions of others in a negative light. Thus the military preparations of one state, even if they are purely for defensive national security purposes, are likely to be perceived as threatening and matched by neighbouring states. The irony is that, at the end of the day, states often feel no more secure than before they undertook measures to enhance their own security.

Realists recommend that the best route to national security is to accumulate power for yourself, and ensure that no other state acquires a preponderance of power. For realists, the **balance of power** is a key component of national security and a central dynamic in foreign policy making. The balance of power dictates that if the survival of a state or a number of weak states is threatened by a hegemonic state or coalition of stronger states, they should each seek to increase their own military capabilities (internal balancing) or join forces by establishing a formal alliance (external balancing), seeking to preserve their own independence by checking the power of the opposing side. The mechanism of the balance of power seeks to ensure an equilibrium of power, in which case no single state or coalition of states is in a position to dominate all the others. The latest controversy concerning the balance of power is whether the USA is so powerful that balancing is no longer an operating principle of international politics (Brooks and Wohlforth 2008). While many American foreign policy officials have advocated a grand strategy of primacy, which is discussed below, others have pointed out that such a strategy is doomed to fail as other states will inevitably seek to counterbalance the USA (Walt 2005).

Security studies and national security

The outset of the Cold War rivalry between the USA and the Soviet Union immediately after the conclusion of the Second World War helped to establish the primacy of national security concerns. In 1947, the US Congress passed the National Security Act which established a number of new foreign policy institutions including the Department of Defense, the Central Intelligence Agency, and the National Security Council. These institutions were aimed at providing the president and senior foreign policy officials with better information for pursuing national security. The advent of nuclear weaponry dramatically elevated the prominence of national security and heightened the existential threat to the physical survival of the nation-state. Although realists as far back as Machiavelli (1469–1527) had made the survival of the state the essence of statecraft, the existence of thousands of thermonuclear weapons in the arsenals of the USA and the Soviet Union profoundly raised the stakes of national security. As national security concerns came to dominate the foreign policy agenda of the USA and its allies, the new academic field of security studies was born. Tracing the evolution of this subfield is a helpful exercise in coming to terms with the primacy of national security.[2]

David Baldwin (1995: 119) was correct to point out that if security studies is 'defined as the study of the nature, causes, effects, and prevention of war', then it is wrong to assume that this subfield only emerged after the Second World War. Baldwin reminds us that between the creation of the field of International Relations—which in the UK is commonly taken to be the establishment of the Woodrow Wilson Chair of International Politics in 1919 at the University College of Wales, Aberystwyth—and the beginning of the Cold War, a fair amount of attention was devoted to the issue of how to achieve security. Much of this attention was focused on how to avoid another cataclysmic world war. Rather than achieving security through military force, inter-war scholars tended to focus on international institutions such as the League of Nations, disarmament, collective security, arbitration, and various other diplomatic instruments. The focus on non-military instruments of statecraft began to shift in the late 1930s and early 1940s as war engulfed the world for a second time in twenty years. A new body of literature began to appear that accentuated the conflictual nature of international politics, and emphasized the role of military force in achieving national security. The Cold War rivalry between the USA and the Soviet Union, symbolized by the nuclear arms race, served to underline the primacy of national security.

It was in this context that the subfield of security studies gained prominence. Those working in this new field unequivocally identified the state as the referent object of security and conceptualized threats in military terms emanating from outside the borders of the state. Most embraced realist theory, arguing that the best route to achieving national security was through the acquisition of military capabilities and the formation of alliances. Writing in 1966, Bock and Berkowitz claimed that the field of national security 'concerns itself with studying how nations plan, make, and evaluate the decisions and policies designed to protect their internal values from external threats' (Bock and Berkowitz 1966: 134). Twenty-five years later, Walt confirmed the field's realist underpinnings by claiming that security studies 'may be defined as the study of the threat, use, and control of military force' which 'explores the conditions that make the use of force more likely . . . and the specific policies that states adopt in order to prepare for, prevent, or engage in war' (Walt 1991: 212). For foreign policy analysts who regarded the use of armed force as a legitimate means of attaining security, the Cold War posed a particular conundrum: Did military force continue to have utility in the nuclear age?

The issues surrounding nuclear weapons animated much of what Walt refers to as the 'Golden Age' of security studies. Beginning with Bernard Brodie's The Absolute Weapon (Brodie 1946), discussion was focused on the impact of atomic weaponry on national security. According to Walt, the central question in the field was straightforward: 'How could states use weapons of mass destruction (WMDs) as instruments of policy, given the risk of any nuclear exchange?' (Walt 1991: 214). For Brodie, nuclear weapons negated the Clausewitzian principle that war was a continuation of politics by other means, arguing that the nuclear revolution rendered obsolete traditional notions of winning or losing a war. Any use of nuclear weapons by either the USA or the Soviet Union would result in what Robert McNamara, who was US Secretary of Defense from 1961 to 1968, termed mutually assured destruction. According to Brodie, the role of nuclear weapons was to prevent a Third World War through the policy of **deterrence.** The theory of deterrence rests on the credible threat to punish another state if it undertakes certain unacceptable actions such as attacking one's own state. When applied to nuclear weapons, deterrence formed the basis of the doctrine of mutually assured destruction (MAD), whereby both the USA and the Soviet Union were vulnerable to a massive retaliatory nuclear attack should either decide to undertake a first-strike blow against their opponent.

Under such a 'balance of terror' scenario, the argument was that no rational actor would risk using nuclear weapons because it would be suicidal. From this perspective, apart from a minimal defensive role in deterring an attack, nuclear weapons actually lacked military utility. Yet a complete consensus on this point never existed during the Cold War as other national security experts sought to retain the military utility of nuclear weapons and assimilate them as usable instruments of war and foreign policy tools of a last resort (Wohlstetter 1959; Gray 1982). For these scholars, the scenario of nuclear Armageddon envisioned by proponents of MAD did not preclude the possibility of using nuclear weapons in a limited manner (Kissinger 1957). Moreover, this 'maximalist' school of nuclear strategists found it preposterous for American national security policy to rest on a position of being vulnerable to a Soviet nuclear attack—the cornerstone of MAD. Despite the immense technological difficulties, the maximalist school argued that achieving a position of invulnerability to a long-range nuclear missile attack would be a superior national security strategy. As evidenced by the USA's continuing attempt to implement some sort of missile defence, it is apparent that the quest for invulnerability has not been abandoned.

While the study of national security during the Cold War was dominated by realists working in the subfield of security studies, this is no longer the case today. Several factors explain this development. First, a number of critical thinkers challenged the assumptions of realism that underpinned the conventional thinking about nuclear weapons and national security. These included Mikhail Gorbachev, the last President of the Soviet Union, who concluded that nuclear weapons could never be used as military instruments of power or built into foreign policy strategies. Second, a new generation of scholars, who were opposed to the realists' conception of state security and their notion of military threats, entered the field of security studies (Buzan et al. 1998). And third, issues concerning human rights, the environment, and economic development were increasingly construed in terms of national security. Together, these developments contributed to a new view of security that was conceptualized in terms of human security. The alternative human security paradigm replaced states with individuals as the dominant referent of security, and focused on non-military sources of threats to the welfare of human beings. (See Box 10.3.)

National security and American grand strategy

Even if we continue to rely on the mainstream understanding of national security as the protection of territory and core values from foreign threats, this does not answer the question of the best strategy for achieving national security. This crucial component of a state's foreign policy is termed **grand strategy,** which is defined as the overall vision of a state's national security goals and a determination of the most appropriate means by which to achieve these goals. Grand strategy can be viewed as a three-step process. First, foreign policy officials must determine their state's vital security goals. Second, they must identify the main source of threats to these goals. And finally, they must ascertain the key political, economic, and military resources that can be employed as foreign policy options to realize their national security goals. All foreign policy officials go through a similar process, even though the resulting grand strategies tend to be quite different from one another. This stems from the point mentioned earlier concerning the differing ways in which both security and threats are conceptualized. It is also a function of the different capabilities that states possess as well as a host of other factors determining their national power, including their geographical size and location. Great powers, for instance, typically have a more expansive notion of security and proportionately face more (and larger) threats than smaller powers. And insular states face a different set of security threats than land-locked states.

Since the end of the Cold War there has been a debate over the best grand strategy for the USA to follow, and here we will consider three different grand strategies: neo-isolationism,

---

BOX 10.3 Human security

The concept of human security arose in the early 1990s and was the collective result of efforts to place individuals at the centre of strategies to achieve security. The 1993 UN Development Programme (UNDP) *Human Development Report* announced, 'The concept of security must change—from an exclusive stress on national security to a much greater stress on people's security, from security through armaments to security through human development, from territorial security to food, employment, and environmental security' (UNDP 1993: 2). In the following year, the 1994 UNDP *Human Development Report* was devoted to the concept of human security, which it defined as 'safety from the constant threats of hunger, disease, crime and repression' and 'protection from sudden and hurtful disruptions to the patterns of our daily lives—whether in the home, in our jobs, in our communities or in our environment' (UNDP 1994: 23).

Human security has been promoted by the governments of Canada and Norway, and embraced by numerous agencies in the United Nations as well as by many NGOs. All share the belief that a broader conception of security is needed that goes beyond a narrow focus on protecting states from external threats. In 2003, the Canadian Department of Foreign Affairs and International Trade published a report entitled 'Freedom from Fear: Canada's Foreign Policy for Human Security'. The report identified five foreign policy priorities for achieving human security: public safety, protection of civilians, conflict prevention, governance and accountability, and peace and support operations (www.humansecurity.gc.ca).

liberal internationalism, and primacy. Although the Goldwater–Nichols Act of 1986 obligates American foreign policy officials to submit a National Security Strategy (NSS) to Congress, most of these reports have not proved to be controversial. However, this was not the case with the 2002 NSS submitted by the George W. Bush administration shortly after the 9/11 terrorist attacks. Some analysts concluded that Bush's grand strategy represented a radical break with the past, while others argued that the continuities were more striking than the innovations. (See Box 10.4.)

On a close reading of the 2002 NSS, one can identify a variety of different grand strategies, thus raising the question of the overall coherence of America's national security. The same can be said of President Obama's 2010 NSS which focuses on renewing American leadership for achieving national security (www.whitehouse.gov/issues/foreign-policy).

Neo-isolationism

Neo-isolationism, also known as an 'interest-based' foreign policy or a 'strategy of restraint', harks back to an earlier period of American foreign policy when the USA was not as deeply involved in managing the affairs of other states, and had not assumed the role of global hegemon. Like earlier advocates of this view, neo-isolationists are not arguing that the USA should cut itself off from the rest of the world, but rather that the best method of preserving national security is for America to focus first and foremost on its own national interests. While the Cold War may have necessitated a more activist role to achieve American national security, neo-isolationists argue that this is no longer the case; what is required instead is a restricted conception of the American national interest in terms of the physical protection of the territory and people of the USA as well as its continued economic prosperity. The core argument of neo-isolationism is that the USA is extraordinarily secure from external threats,

---

BOX 10.4 The Bush Doctrine: continuity or change?

The 2002 National Security Strategy along with a number of speeches, such as President Bush's 2002 West Point commencement address, formed the basis of the Bush Doctrine. The core elements of the Bush Doctrine include a commitment to preserving the pre-eminent position of the US, aggressive democracy promotion, unilateralism, and a willingness to use force preventively. The Bush Doctrine proved to be controversial, especially as it provided a key rationale for the 2003 invasion of Iraq. But does it represent a radical departure in American foreign policy?

Leffler argues no. 'Bush's goals of sustaining a democratic peace and disseminating America's core values resonate with the most traditional themes in U.S. history. . . . The U.S. quest for an international order based on freedom, self-determination, and open markets has changed astonishingly little' (Leffler 2004b: 22–3).

Daalder and Lindsay argue yes. George W. Bush has launched a revolution in American foreign policy. . . . he discarded or redefined many of the key principles governing the way the USA should act overseas. He relied on the unilateral exercise of American power rather than on international law and institutions to get his way. He championed a proactive doctrine of pre-emption and de-emphasized the reactive strategies of deterrence and containment. He promoted forceful interdiction, preemptive strikes, and missile defenses as a means to counter the proliferation of weapons of mass destruction' (Daalder and Lindsay 2003: 2).

which they argue is a function of its favourable insular position, weak neighbours to the North and South, immense military capabilities, and strong relative standing in the global distribution of power, all of which allows for a drastic reduction in America's security commitments to Europe, Asia, and much of the rest of the world.

According to neo-isolationists, America has more than enough power to guarantee its security, and its overriding national security objective should be to safeguard its position by greatly limiting its involvement in the affairs of other states. Indeed, as evidenced by its enormous budget deficits, America is eroding its own power position by continuing to underwrite the security of other states in Europe and Asia. Moreover, because it is spreading its military presence around the world and enlarging the alliance that it created in 1949 (NATO) other states are actually attempting to counterbalance the USA in a more systematic fashion than if it simply focused on its own backyard. Neo-isolationists make the following recommendations: dismantle NATO, remove American troops from states such as Japan and Germany, reduce defence spending, and, most importantly, focus on America's own needs and interests in order to preserve its security.

Perhaps the strongest criticism of a neo-isolationist grand strategy was 9/11, which demonstrated that the USA is not nearly as secure as many had assumed. Yet neo-isolationists have a response, namely that there is a direct correlation between America's overseas military presence, particularly in the Middle East, and terrorism directed at the USA. The threat of terrorism can be greatly diminished if the USA exercises restraint, reduces its overseas military presence, and refrains from meddling in the affairs of other states. In this manner, isolationism is a national security strategy which can be pursued through a restrained foreign policy. The Pentagon may have no choice, as drastic cuts to the defence budget are necessary to rein in the federal deficit.

Liberal internationalism

Proponents of a liberal internationalist foreign policy argue that neo-isolationists fail to understand that America is secure and prosperous precisely because the USA has exercised global leadership since the end of the Second World War. As a liberal hegemon, America has played a vital role in maintaining international peace which has direct benefits to both the USA and the rest of the world. President Obama's NSS largely equates national security with renewed American leadership. Compared with neo-isolationists, advocates of a liberal grand strategy have an expansive notion of the American national interest. This includes an interest in world peace, as liberals argue that threats in the form of small wars, civil unrest, and human rights violations in one part of the world can quickly spread to other parts. In a globalized interdependent world, the USA is not immune from traditional military threats or from newer security threats including terrorism, WMDs, and global climate change. American national security, according to liberal internationalists, thus hinges on global security, requiring it to actively pursue world peace, free trade, democracy, and human rights. From the perspective of liberal internationalism, a peaceful world would be one populated by democratic states which respect human rights and pursue free trade.

In order to achieve America's national security goals, liberal internationalists argue that the USA must act multilaterally with other states in the pursuit of common goals. Given the manner in which liberal internationalists define both the goals of, and threats to, American national security, it would be impossible to address these in a unilateral manner. A single state acting alone is not going to curb global warming, stem ethnic conflict, or thwart acts of terrorism. The 2010 NSS proclaims that international cooperation is needed to meet common security challenges, and recommends that the USA work through international institutions and traditional alliance partners, and forms new partnerships with other key centres of influence (www.whitehouse.gov/issues/foreign-policy). A liberal internationalist grand strategy is predicated on the construction of multilateral institutions that are believed to provide cooperative solutions to pressing security and economic issues. Liberal internationalists remind us that the USA has played a key role in the creation of important multilateral institutions such as the United Nations and the World Bank, arguing that such institutions continue to serve American interests by providing legitimacy and a rule-based setting for its foreign policy behaviour. Moreover, these multilateral institutions are instrumental in achieving the core liberal national security goals of democracy, free trade, and human rights.

It should be self-evident that a liberal internationalist grand strategy is firmly anchored to the theory of liberalism (see Chapter Three). This strategy calls on the USA to promote the spread of democracy and liberty around the world. The USA is better able to pursue its interests and reduce security threats when other states are also democracies. Closely related to the argument about the pacifying effect of democracy is the liberal idea that the promotion of free trade increases the prosperity of more and more people, which in turn creates the conditions for democratic governance. Free trade is believed to foster greater interdependence among states, which diminishes the economic gains that any state could expect to incur by going to war. Finally, the creation of international institutions and norms is viewed as the best mechanism for managing the array of political, economic, and environmental problems that arise in a globalized world. In this manner the three key ideas of liberal theory—democracy, interdependence, and institutions—are vital elements of a liberal internationalist grand strategy.

Primacy

A foreign policy of primacy seeks to preserve America's position as the undisputed pre-eminent power in the international system. Peace among the great powers and American national security are held to rest on a preponderance of US power. Since the end of the Cold War, the USA has been the sole super-power in the international system. Proponents of primacy view this as an extremely advantageous position for achieving national security and argue that America's grand strategy should be one of preventing any future great powers from challenging the power of the USA. This is to be achieved by outspending all other states to preserve full-spectrum military dominance, stationing troops around the globe, underwriting the security of allies such as Germany and Japan, and actively working to prevent the rise of powers such as China and Iran which could pose a challenge to American primacy. A multipolar world is viewed as inherently threatening and inimical to US interests. To prevent the emergence of a multipolar international system, advocates of primacy recommend that the US continue to commit its military power and act as the pacifier in Europe, Asia, the Persian Gulf, and other strategic regions.

While liberal internationalists and proponents of primacy both have a broad conception of American national security, there are some important differences. Most importantly, those endorsing primacy argue that liberals often put transnational interests ahead of American interests. According to advocates of primacy, interventions to spread democracy or defend human rights are not vital to American national security. America's interest in peace is instrumental in the sense that a world order underwritten by US power is a strategy for maintaining primacy. Advocates of primacy concur with liberal internationalists about the benefits of American leadership, but they disagree that it is always necessary to exercise leadership in a cooperative manner with other states. Although multilateralism has certain advantages, unipolar powers have the benefit of being able to act unilaterally to advance their own interests regardless of what other states think. Thus, when the situation warrants—such as when dealing with rogue states armed with WMDs—advocates of primacy do not hesitate recommending that the USA acts alone. The role of institutions in achieving American national security is viewed as restraining rather than enabling American power. The cornerstone of a grand strategy of primacy is to keep America in its pre-eminent position and the rest of the world off balance.

There is a good deal of evidence to suggest that the USA has based its foreign policy on a grand strategy of primacy. Yet it is worthwhile asking whether this strategy is sustainable. First, realists remind us that states are fearful of any state holding a preponderance of power, and there is evidence to suggest that attempts to counterbalance the USA are underway. Second, it is evident that the USA's attempt to achieve absolute security through primacy has made some states feel insecure which, in turn, has led them to increase their military capabilities. Third, states with preponderant power often succumb to the imperial temptation of overextending themselves in unnecessary and costly wars. Thus rather than trying to preserve the impossible, namely unipolarity, many realists advocate a policy of offshore balancing that attempts to maintain America's relative power and national security in an emerging multipolar world.

Conclusion

There is no disputing that national security is a serious matter. The chapter began with Wolfers' observation that national security is an ambiguous concept, and subsequent sections have substantiated his important insight. This insight leads to the conclusion that, notwithstanding the importance of the concept, one should not overlook the fact that there is no objective universal understanding of national security. Before assuming the primacy of national security in the analysis of foreign policy, it would be wise to begin by critically evaluating how the concept is being employed. And as we have seen, it is impossible to analyse the concept of security without simultaneously considering the types of threat that one is facing. Realists are united in arguing that the goal of national security is the physical protection of the state, and that states face numerous threats that arise from the anarchic international system. In the face of such threats, realists encourage states to pursue power in order to achieve a measure of national security. Yet a core paradox of the realist's prescription is that while states are encouraged to pursue their own policies to achieve national security, there is no mechanism to coordinate these individual efforts, which sometimes results in a good deal of international insecurity, including armed conflict.

While realists are able to provide an explanation for the primacy of national security, there are numerous critics who disagree with the manner in which realists conceptualize security. Those advocating some form of human or common security seek to replace the state as the referent object of security with either individuals or larger collectivities such as world society. They also seek to expand the range of threats beyond narrowly defined external military threats. These challenges to the realist model are to be welcomed for they force us to think critically about the meaning of national security without necessarily refuting the primacy of national security. The study of grand strategy reveals that there are a number of different foreign policies that a state can adopt in the pursuit of national security. These diverse strategies reflect different ways of conceptualizing security and threats. The study of foreign policy illustrates that security and threats, no matter how they are conceptualized, are enduring issues that account for the primacy of national security.

Key points

- National security is an essentially contested concept—it means different things to different people.
- The three S's of realism, statism, survival, and self-help contribute to the primacy of national security.
- The prominence of realism and the onset of the Cold War helped to establish the primacy of national security concerns to both academics and policy makers.
- Debates about grand strategy are explicitly related to competing conceptions of national security.

Questions

1. What does Wolfers mean when he writes that national security is an ambiguous symbol?
2. How does realist theory contribute to the primacy of national security?
3. How do the three S's of realism account for the primacy of national security?
4. What is the relationship between the theory of realism and the field of security studies?
5. During the Cold War, how did scholars conceive of the relationship between nuclear weapons and national security?
6. What is the meaning of national security?
7. How does a focus on the concept of human security change your understanding of national security?
8. What is the best grand strategy for the USA to achieve national security?

Further reading

Brown, M., Cote, O., Lynn-Jones, S.E., and Miller, S. (2000) (eds), *America's Strategic Choices* (revised edition) (Cambridge, MA: MIT Press).
An informative survey of the competing American grand strategies for the post Cold War period.

Gray, C. (1999), 'Clausewitz Rules, OK? The Future is the Past—with GPS', *Review of International Studies*, 25: 161–82.
One of the UK's leading strategists arguing for the continuing relevance of realism.

UNDP (1994), *Human Development Report 1994: New Dimensions of Human Security* (New York: Oxford University Press).
The landmark publication that helped to launch the debate on the issue of human security.

Katzenstein, P. (ed.) (1996), *The Culture of National Security* (New York: Columbia University Press).
A distinctive constructivist approach to the topic of national security.

Wolfers, A. (1962), *Discord and Collaboration: Essays on International Politics* (Baltimore, MD: Johns Hopkins University Press).
A timeless collection of essays which includes 'National Security as an Ambiguous Symbol'.

Visit the Online Resource Centre that accompanies this book for more information:
www.oxfordtextbooks.co.uk/orc/smith_foreign/

Economic statecraft

MICHAEL MASTANDUNO

Chapter contents

 Reader's guide

This chapter focuses on the relation between economic instruments of statecraft and broader foreign policy goals and strategies of states. In general, it is difficult for economic sanctions to achieve major foreign policy objectives, despite their popularity as a foreign policy strategy. The end of the Cold War has led to an increase in the use of sanctions, but not necessarily in their relative effectiveness. However, even if sanctions do not always succeed, governments still find them useful as part of a broader foreign policy strategy to signal their intentions, send important messages, and complement military action or diplomacy.

The chapter also argues that the positive use of economic incentives has considerable promise as an instrument of statecraft, and deserves more systematic attention in the study of foreign policy. It concludes with the enduring question of whether economic interdependence leads to harmony, as liberals expect, or conflict among states, as realists expect, and finds that it depends on the future expectations of policy makers, the nature of the military balance, and the form that economic interdependence takes.

Introduction

Statecraft can be defined as the use of instruments at the disposal of central political authorities to serve foreign policy purposes. The instruments of statecraft fall commonly into three main categories: diplomatic, military, and economic. This chapter focuses on **economic statecraft**—the use of economic tools and relationships to achieve foreign policy objectives. Economic statecraft may be negative, involving the threat or use of sanctions or other forms of economic coercion or punishment, or it may be positive, involving the use of economic relationships as incentives or rewards. In addition, the use of economic statecraft may be unilateral, involving efforts by one government, or multilateral, involving attempts by multiple governments to coordinate their economic resources or policies to influence the behaviour of a target country or government.

Economic statecraft has a long history, dating back at least to the Peloponnesian Wars of ancient Greece. Foreign policy students should note that economic statecraft has been used with increasing frequency during the twentieth century, as countries in the international system became more interdependent and a global economy formed. By drawing countries and their citizens into tighter economic networks across borders, the liberal world economy has provided an accommodating structural environment, opening more opportunities for governments to employ economic statecraft, both positively and negatively.

The best-known empirical study of economic sanctions analysed 174 instances of their use between 1914 and 2000 (Hufbauer *et al.* 2007). It is not surprising that powerful states—those with strong economies and many economic instruments at their disposal—are more likely than weaker states to initiate economic statecraft as a key foreign policy measure. The USA has been the most prolific practitioner of economic sanctions since the Second World War, and Russia (formerly the Soviet Union) and the countries of Western Europe have frequently resorted to sanctions as well. Having only twice organized multilateral economic sanctions, against South Africa and Rhodesia, during the Cold War, the UN Security Council has since become more active, authorizing sanctions in at least ten instances and against a variety of targets including Iraq, Somalia, Libya, Serbia, Haiti, Rwanda, and Iran (Cortwright and Lopez 2000).

Because economic instruments are used so prominently in foreign policy, it is important to understand how and why governments use them, and the extent to which they are effective. Indeed, economic sanctions often fail to achieve the most ambitious political objectives (e.g. forcing a government to end a military occupation or driving a dictator from power) that governments seek through their use. This has led some scholars to conclude that economic measures are not effective instruments of statecraft (Pape 1997). Others highlight that economic statecraft can serve multiple and varied objectives (Baldwin 1985). The key point is that even if sanctions do not solve major foreign policy problems, a variety of economic instruments may still be useful to governments for signalling intentions, complementing diplomacy, building a political consensus, or even paving the way for the use of military force. Economic statecraft is part of the wider array of foreign policy instruments that states have at their disposal; more often than not, economic measures are used in conjunction with diplomatic and military ones as part of any government's overall approach to addressing foreign policy problems and opportunities.

The next section of this chapter provides an analytical framework by discussing the wide variety of economic instruments which states employ in the interest of foreign policy, and the range of objectives they seek to accomplish with their use. The third section then examines international economic sanctions, focusing on the reasons behind their use and the circumstances under which they are likely to be effective. It provides a broad review of the twentieth-century experience, including the renewed interest and frequency of sanctions use after the Cold War. The interplay of economic sanctions, diplomacy, and military force, so crucial to understanding the broad schema of foreign policy, is then explored, and the section ends with a discussion of how globalization, democratization, and the end of the Cold War are likely to affect the incidence and effectiveness of sanctions.

The fourth section discusses the issue of positive economic statecraft. Under what conditions can the promotion of trade, aid, or investment induce other states to change their foreign policy behaviour? Positive economic statecraft has received relatively little attention in the political science literature. The logic of positive economic statecraft is explained, several recent cases are explored, and the potential effectiveness of negative and positive economic measures is assessed comparatively. The discussion also moves from the level of the state to the systemic level in examining the link between economic interdependence, peace, and war. Will the deepening economic integration among countries of the world lead to international stability, as liberal logic suggests, or be a source of conflict? A brief concluding section summarizes the main arguments of the chapter.

Economic statecraft: instruments and objectives

Governments seeking to employ economic statecraft as part of their foreign policy have a variety of possible instruments at their disposal. Among the most common are **trade restrictions**. Countries that rely heavily on exports or imports—either generally or upon particular commodities—are potentially vulnerable to economic **influence attempts** against them. In 1973, OPEC countries used the 'oil weapon' against the USA and other Western countries by restricting their access to this vital natural resource in an effort to influence Western policies in the Arab-Israeli war. The UN sanctions directed against Iraq following the 1990–1991 Persian Gulf War were intended to prevent Iraq from earning hard currency by selling its oil on world markets. For over forty years the USA has maintained—initially with the support of other governments but for the most part unilaterally—a comprehensive trade embargo against Cuba designed to undermine the authority of Fidel Castro's communist regime.

Financial sanctions have become increasingly popular and are often used alongside trade restrictions to enhance the pressure on a target government. Specific measures include cutting off economic or military aid, or—as in the attempt by the USA to pressure Chile between 1970 and 1973—blocking a country's access to multilateral lending institutions such as the World Bank or the Inter-American Development Bank. The freezing of assets belonging to a target government or its leaders which are held in banks under the legal jurisdiction of the sanctioning government is another tactic. The USA froze Iranian assets held in US banks in 1979–1980 in an effort to compel Iran to release American hostages. Similarly, after 11 September 2001, the USA and its partners froze the assets of suspected terrorist groups, and governments that assisted them, as part of the larger effort to combat the spread of international terrorism.

Many countries, especially developing ones, rely heavily on direct foreign investments—such as the building of factories, the construction of oil and gas pipelines, or the creation of communications infrastructures—to further their economic growth and development. Thus **investment restrictions** are a potentially formidable economic sanction. Restrictions on energy exploration and production investments have been used frequently by Western countries against oil-rich, but technologically dependent, target states in the Middle East and North Africa such as Iran, Iraq, and Libya. During the 1980s, Western governments and private lobbying groups pressured multinational corporations to forego a variety of investments in South Africa as a means of pressuring the white minority government to initiate reforms and share power with the black majority population.

Finally, **monetary sanctions**, most commonly the buying and selling of large quantities of a target state's currency in order to manipulate its exchange rate, can be used to force a government to change its political behaviour by threatening it with the prospect of a financial crisis. In 1956, the US Treasury sold large quantities of British pounds to force down the value of that currency and prod the British government to rethink its policy in the Suez crisis. France employed a similar tactic against the USA in the 1960s by selling dollars in exchange for gold in order to pressure the USA to accept reforms of the international monetary system. During the 1930s, the government of imperial Japan proliferated 'puppet' or alternative currencies in different parts of China, with the intent of discrediting China's existing currency and thereby weakening China's hold on its own territory (Kirshner 1995). During the 2000s, analysts debated the possibility that China, holding more than a trillion dollars in US debt instruments, might one day try to coerce the USA politically by threatening to dispose of its holdings and thereby drive down the value of the dollar (Drezner 2009).

As the above discussion suggests, governments use economic sanctions to satisfy a range of foreign policy objectives. One category involves attempts to alter the *domestic politics* of a target country. The USA, through legislation such as the Jackson–Vanik Amendment of 1974 (see Box 11.1), has long used the threat of economic sanctions against governments that it has judged to maintain inadequate human rights practices with regard to their own populations. During the early 1990s, Russia imposed sanctions against Latvia, Estonia, and Turkmenistan to gain greater protection for ethnic Russian minorities living within those countries. Russia continues today to use its control over natural resources, especially oil and gas, to coerce its neighbours such as Georgia, Moldova, and Ukraine to adopt policies more accommodating to Russia (see Chapter Twenty-Three.) Similarly, West European governments employed sanctions against Algeria, Malawi, and Togo to promote or protect democratization, while UN

BOX 11.1 The Jackson–Vanik Amendment

The Jackson–Vanik Amendment was part of the US Trade Act of 1974, named for its co-sponsors, Senator Henry Jackson and Congressman Charles Vanik. The Amendment stipulates that the USA may grant most favoured nation trading status to certain (mainly communist) countries, only if the US resident certifies that those countries allow the right of free emigration to their citizens. The Jackson–Vanik Amendment is an example of economic statecraft. It promises an economic reward—a normal trading relationship with the powerful USA—if countries improve their emigration practices, and threatens an economic penalty—the denial or removal of most favoured nation status—if countries do not.

The original intent of this legislation was to convince the Soviet Union, during the part of the Cold War known as détente, to allow more of its Jewish citizens to emigrate to the West. The Jackson–Vanik Amendment was controversial, viewed by the Soviet Union as an infringement on their sovereignty, and by its American supporters as a necessary measure to justify normal trade with a repressive communist regime. Even though the Cold War has ended and the Soviet Union has collapsed, the Jackson–Vanik Amendment remains in force and still applies to US trade relations with Russia. The People's Republic of China was subject to the provisions of Jackson–Vanik until 2001. When it joined the World Trade Organization in that year, the USA removed it from coverage under the Amendment.

sanctions against Rwanda in 1994 were intended to prompt governing authorities to end genocide and civil war.

Second, countries often use sanctions to influence the *foreign policy behaviour* of a target government. Italy invaded Ethiopia in 1935, the Soviet Union invaded Afghanistan in 1979, and Iraq invaded Kuwait in 1990. In each case, a collection of countries reacted by devising economic sanctions against the aggressor in the hope of forcing an end to the conflict and ideally the withdrawal of troops. UN and US sanctions against Libya and Iran during the 1990s were intended to discourage those countries from supporting international terrorism. The USA sanctioned India and Pakistan in 1993 and again in 1998 to protest against their respective nuclear weapons programmes and to deter them from undertaking nuclear proliferation. The USA recently relaxed its restrictions with regard to India, as part of a broader foreign policy effort to improve relations between the two countries.

Some sanctions are intended to influence the domestic or international behaviour of a target state; others are employed specifically to affect its economic or military *capabilities*. NATO's trade embargo against the Soviet Union and Warsaw Pact countries throughout the Cold War was primarily intended to slow the growth of their military capabilities by denying them access to the latest civilian and military technologies of the West. The UN sanctions against Saddam Hussein's Iraq during the 1990s were similarly a means of economic containment. By restricting the regime's access to oil revenues, the UN coalition hoped to limit Saddam Hussein's capacity to rebuild Iraq's military at home and threaten force against its neighbours abroad.

In some cases, sanctions are intended less to affect the behaviour or capabilities of a regime, and more to bring about *regime change*—the undermining of the very existence of the regime itself. The UN sanctions against Rhodesia and South Africa were intended primarily to isolate and force the political capitulation of the white minority regimes ruling those countries. The US sanctions against Cuba, beginning in 1960, were a central part of the effort to oust Fidel Castro and his communist regime from power. The long-standing Arab boycott of Israel was intended to hasten the demise of the Jewish state (Losman 1979). US sanctions against North Korea during the 2000s were intended in part to hasten the collapse of that country's communist government.

The discussion thus far has focused on the negative or coercive uses of economic sanctions. It is important to bear in mind that economic statecraft can also be positive. Sanctioning governments have 'carrots' as well as 'sticks' at their disposal. Just as trade denial can be used to change behaviour, weaken capabilities, or induce regime change, so trade promotion—the promise or actuality of expanded trade—can be a means to influence a government's domestic or foreign policies or to strengthen its capabilities. Governments can promise to increase aid, encourage foreign investment, or support a country's currency in exchange for desirable changes in that country's behaviour. One of the most celebrated cases of positive, and successful, economic statecraft was the Marshall Plan of 1948–1953. By transferring significant resources from the USA to Western Europe, the US government managed to strengthen the economic capacity and political stability of its Cold War allies, and drew them more closely into the alliance against the Soviet Union. More recently, the EU has mastered the art of positive statecraft, using the promise of economic rewards in the broader context of EU enlargement to lock in desirable changes in the domestic and foreign policies of its central European neighbours.

Economic sanctions: not always successful, but still useful

The brutality of modern warfare, experienced by the great powers of Europe during the First World War, led international diplomats to search for alternatives to war as a means to settle international disputes and contain aggression. It is not surprising that, in light of the emergence of a liberal world economy, the framers of the League of Nations turned to an economic instrument, specifically economic sanctions, as a possible substitute for war (Doxey 1996). The League Covenant called on member states to use economic sanctions as their primary response to aggression by one League member against another, and to use military force only as a last resort. When Italy invaded Ethiopia in 1935, League members did come together to impose sanctions against Italy. But the sanctions failed to halt or reverse Italy's aggression, and League members were not prepared to take the next step and go to war. This sanctions episode ended with the humiliation of the League, which subsequently collapsed at the beginning of the Second World War.

The UN Charter, crafted near the end of the Second World War, similarly held out an important role for economic sanctions as a collective response to international aggression and conflict. Once again, the hope of governments that sanctions might resolve fundamental international conflicts was not rewarded. The post-war record of well-publicized sanctions attempts mirrored the unhappy experience of the League sanctions against Italy. The following are among the most celebrated cases of sanction failures, a cumulative record that may lead scholars reflecting on the post-war experience to conclude that economic sanctions were for the most part an ineffective instrument of statecraft.

During the 1950s, the USA and its NATO allies hoped that comprehensive economic sanctions would retard the economic growth and undermine the political authority of the communist regimes of the Soviet Union and Eastern Europe. However, communist economic growth progressed and political legitimacy endured despite the sanctions, and by the early 1960s American attempts to maintain the sanctions created considerable political friction within the Western alliance. A Western economic embargo against the People's Republic of China—launched with the hope of undermining the nascent communist regime—had similarly failed by the end of the 1950s and, worse, created political controversy within NATO (Mastanduno 1992). The Soviet Union's own sanction attempts met a similar fate. In 1948, for example, Stalin used economic denial in an effort to force the renegade communist leader Tito of Yugoslavia into compliance with Soviet preferences for its other client states. Yet Tito defied Stalin, increased his domestic popularity, and took Yugoslavia on a more independent path.

The attempt by Arab states to use an economic boycott to strangle the state of Israel in its infancy clearly failed, although it had some success in altering the foreign policy behaviour of the West. The United Nations imposed comprehensive economic sanctions against Rhodesia after its Unilateral Declaration of Independence in 1965. Initially, the Rhodesian regime and economy withstood the sanctions; the minority government did not collapse until 1979, when it capitulated to military force brought to bear by the black resistance movement. The UN arms embargo against South Africa, beginning in 1963, did not prevent that country from becoming the most formidable military power in southern Africa. US sanctions against the Soviet Union following its invasion of Afghanistan neither forced Soviet leaders to reconsider nor prevented them from undertaking a decade-long, ultimately unsuccessful, attempt to pacify that country. Finally, in perhaps the greatest case of sanctions failure, Fidel Castro managed to defy US sanctions for over four decades, and his regime outlasted that of the Kennedy, Johnson, Nixon, Ford, Carter, Reagan, Bush, Clinton, and Bush administrations. In 2009, President Barack Obama tried a modified approach by maintaining the broad trade embargo while lifting some restrictions on the ability of Americans to travel to the island. He also allowed US telecommunications firms to begin operating in Cuba, hoping that the infusion of money and information might provide support to opponents of the regime led as of 2006 by Fidel's brother, Raul Castro.

Why is it difficult for sanctions to succeed?

The logic of economic sanctions as a foreign policy tool is relatively straightforward. The imposition of economic pain on the target country is intended to compel political change. Economic pain may force the target government directly to reconsider its behaviour. Alternatively, it may create political divisions within the government which lead to policy change, or it may prompt the suffering target population to apply pressure for policy change or even change in the government itself. The greater the economic pressure, the more likely it is that these political effects will be felt.

The first challenge that sanctioners must confront is the difficulty of maximizing economic pain. States facing economic sanctions can sometimes turn, even at considerable political and economic cost, to alternative economic partners. Cuba was traditionally highly dependent on the large neighbouring US economy; the Cold War context gave the Castro regime the opportunity to switch its political allegiance, selling its sugar to the Soviet Union instead and buying (technologically inferior) plant and equipment from Eastern Bloc countries. Facing Western sanctions during the 1950s, China tied its economy more closely to that of the Soviet Union. By the 1960s, the Soviet Union was able to sidestep American sanctions by trading instead with America's own allies in Western Europe and Japan who were no longer prepared to follow the American lead. Yugoslavia defied the Soviet sanctions by turning its trade to and accepting economic aid from the non-communist West. The Arab boycott forced Israel to look outside its immediate neighbourhood, primarily to the USA and Western Europe, for goods and markets. Sanctions imposed by the USA and the EU on Sudan in the 2000s, in response to the Sudanese government's role in the mass killings in Darfur, were frustrated by the participation of Chinese, Indian, and Malaysian companies in the Sudenese oil industry.

Target states have options even if virtually all other states are cooperating in sanctions. During the 1990s, Iraq managed, at a high cost, to smuggle goods through Jordan and to find an array of illicit middlemen to move its oil onto world markets. South Africa found private buyers in various states willing to violate the UN arms embargo. Throughout the Cold War the Soviet Union ran a systematic programme of stealing Western technology or purchasing it from Western companies willing to risk the penalties that their own governments would impose on them if their activities were exposed.

Some states respond to sanctions as an externally imposed protectionist barrier that forces the domestic economy to produce, at higher cost, what had previously been imported. At the time UN sanctions were imposed, the Rhodesian economy produced about 600 different manufactured goods. By 1971, it produced about 3800 goods (Losman 1979). In effect, the sanctions forced the diversification of the domestic economy.

The second challenge for sanctioners is that even the imposition of considerable economic pain does not necessarily translate into the desired political changes. Sanctions, in fact, often have the opposite effect of that intended. Instead of leading to political disarray at home and the disintegration of the target government, the imposition of sanctions can result in political *integration* within the target country. This is sometimes referred to as the **rally round the flag effect**—sanctions create a sense of solidarity within the target country as citizens and their leaders draw closer together in response to what is perceived—or depicted by opportunistic leaders—as an external threat or attack on the country. Throughout his long tenure Fidel Castro was masterful at blaming the mostly self-imposed problems of the centralized Cuban economy on 'Yankee imperialism'. He depicted food shortages as the result of US sanctions rather than as an inevitable drawback of the inefficient and overregulated state of the Cuban agriculture sector. In Rhodesia, the white minority government and its supporters drew closer together in defiance of international sanctions and in the interest of protecting their privileged status.

This integrative effect of sanctions is similar to what has been documented as a common psychological response to military attack. Instead of breaking the morale of publics under siege, strategic bombing during the Second World War seemed to strengthen the resolve and defiance of the various European populations in the face of enemy attack. The USA found the North Vietnamese to be similarly defiant in the face of the systemic and destructive bombing campaign that the US air force carried out in the Vietnam War.

Third, the imposition of sanctions can be costly to the sanctioner as well as the target, making it difficult to sustain political support over time within a coalition of sanctioning states. Despite taking a confrontational stance towards the Soviet Union, in 1981 President Reagan lifted the US grain embargo in response to political pressure from US farmers closed out of the lucrative Soviet market. The 'front-line' states of Zambia, Botswana, and Zaire, despite their political support of international sanctions and their intense political opposition to apartheid, found themselves reluctantly trading with Rhodesia because cutting off that source of trade would have been prohibitively costly economically. International sanctions imposed against Iraq in 1991 began to fall apart around 2000 because France, Russia, and other coalition states were no longer willing to forego the economic benefits of participation in the Iraqi energy sector. Many analysts believe that China would prove reluctant to use its monetary power against the USA because by hurting the US economy it would simultaneously hurts its own, owing to the deep interdependence between the two large economies.

Fourth, sanctions can create political and public relations problems for the senders when their effects fall disproportionately on innocent victims. The very effectiveness of economic sanctions in imposing economic pain on the populations of Iraq and Haiti during the 1990s helped to create humanitarian crises in those two countries and to turn world public opinion against the sanctioning states. The sight of children without food or the elderly without access to needed medical supplies or care deflected international attention away from the evils of Saddam Hussein's regime and focused it instead on the immorality of sanctions as 'weapons of human destruction' (Mueller and Mueller 1999).

In recent years this last problem has led governments to rely more heavily on **smart sanctions**, i.e. sanctions that limit damage to the general population in favour of more precise targeting on the assets of the ruling elite. The idea is to move away from comprehensive trade sanctions that depress the overall economy, and focus upon measures that directly affect a dictatorial regime and its wealthy supporters. Financial sanctions, such as the freezing of bank assets, and travel sanctions, such as refusing to allow the targeted elite access to international destinations, are among the types of smart sanctions employed since the end of the Cold War against elites in Libya, Iraq, and North Korea. Targeted sanctions against the assets of Colonel Gaddafi's close supporters appear to have mattered in Libya's 2003 decision to abandon its weapons of mass destruction programme and to bring suspected terrorists to trial (Cortright and Lopez 2002). In 2007, the UN Security Council sanctioned Iran for its refusal to suspend uranium enrichment. A key element of the sanctions was the freezing of bank assets of members of, and firms owned by, Iran's Revolutionary Guards. Smart sanctions, like smart weapons, are designed to create the desired political outcome while minimizing collateral damage against innocent victims within the target country. (See Box 11.2.)

Why governments still find sanctions useful

The discussion thus far raises a puzzle. If sanctions are apt to fail and may even have costly and negative unintended consequences, why do governments continue to rely on them? The simple answer is that governments find sanctions to be a useful instrument of statecraft—even if sanctions by themselves cannot accomplish the most ambitious foreign policy objectives. Sanctions often accomplish *some* objectives, even if not the most ambitious. They may also complement the other instruments of statecraft that states draw upon in their foreign policies, helping diplomacy or military force to work more effectively. Indeed, in some circumstances, sanctions are the best, or least undesirable, choice for a government facing an unattractive set of foreign policy options.

Three points need to be considered regarding the usefulness of sanctions. First, critics of sanctions often draw their negative conclusions about the questionable effectiveness of sanctions by focusing only on the most public and difficult objectives that a sanctions attempt

---

BOX 11.2 The tools of economic statecraft—illustrative techniques

Comprehensive trade embargo

Selective trade embargo

Freezing of financial assets

Restrictions on foreign direct investment

Dumping of another currency to depress its exchange rate

Restrictions on foreign aid

Increases in economic aid

Preferential trade arrangements

Support for the value of another currency

Encouragement of foreign direct or portfolio investment

might hope to accomplish. If the Soviets were not driven out of Afghanistan, or the Rhodesian government was not toppled, then sanctions are presumed to have failed. However, foreign policy is more complex, and influence attempts by governments often have multiple objectives (Baldwin 1985). Sanctions may satisfy some, if not all, of a state's goals. In the Rhodesian case, sanctions failed to achieve the ideal outcome—the rapid capitulation of the Smith regime. But the principal sanctioning state, Britain, had additional objectives (Rowe 1999–2000). Some members of the British Commonwealth were clamouring for a military response to Rhodesia's independence declaration. Britain wished to avoid that outcome and to hold the Commonwealth together. As a tangible sign that Britain took Rhodesia's defiance seriously, the sanctions were a sufficiently forceful response to satisfy other Commonwealth states and simultaneously deflect pressure for a costly war.

Similarly, one could argue that Western sanctions against the Soviet Union failed to undermine the Soviet economy or topple the communist regime. Yet by focusing on the denial of advanced technology, the sanctions almost certainly made it more costly and difficult for the Soviet Union to keep up in a technologically intensive arms race with the West. The sanctions also served the important political objective of isolating the Soviet Union and signalling that it was a 'second-class citizen' in the international community—a message that clearly irritated Soviet leaders from Khrushchev to Gorbachev. Sanctions against white minority regimes in South Africa and Rhodesia, particularly when initiated by 'friendly' Western states, played a similar role in exacerbating the international isolation of these states. The UN sanctions maintained against Iraq during the 1990s neither undermined Saddam Hussein's regime nor brought desirable changes in his behaviour. But they did help to degrade Iraq's economic and especially military capabilities, rendering Iraq a far less formidable military adversary when the USA attacked again in 2003. Even the US sanctions against Cuba, generally acknowledged to be a failure, may have had some value in signalling to other states in the region that defiance of the USA would be very costly economically, even if one could survive it politically.

Second, governments frequently use sanctions as part of a broader foreign policy strategy, involving other instruments of statecraft, to achieve their objectives. Economic sanctions, for example, might pave the way for the eventual use of military force. The US experience with Iraq during 1990–1991 demonstrates this point well. When Iraq invaded Kuwait in 1990, many states in the international community found Saddam Hussein's behaviour objectionable, yet were not prepared to go to war with Iraq over it. War could only be a last resort after other options had been exhausted. By painstakingly assembling an international coalition for sanctions, the USA demonstrated that it was willing to explore options short of military force. Even though the sanctions did not 'work' by themselves, they played a vital role in enabling US officials to build a credible coalition for the eventual use of military force.

The interplay of sanctions, force, and diplomacy is evident in other cases as well. In South Africa and Rhodesia, unpopular governments were eventually brought down not by sanctions but by domestic resistance movements. But those domestic forces were themselves aided by economic sanctions. Sanctions were a credible indicator that the international community was on the side of the resistance movements and against the perpetuation of the white minority regimes. A critical turning point in the South African case came in 1986, when two long-standing geopolitical allies of the apartheid regime, Britain and the USA, turned from opposing to supporting an international sanctions effort.

Third, the utility of sanctions is best judged in the context of *alternative* courses of action available to decision makers. Decision makers often ask not 'Will sanctions work?' but 'What better options do we have?' In some situations, decision makers find sanctions to be the relatively most attractive option, even if the chances of success are small. The Soviet invasion of Afghanistan in 1979 left the USA without any obviously attractive options in response. Doing nothing might actually have been a risky choice. It might have signalled to the Soviet Union that the USA, recently defeated in Vietnam and simultaneously facing the collapse of its ally and a humiliating hostage crisis in Afghanistan's neighbour, Iran, might be paralysed politically and unprepared to defend its regional interests. This could tempt the Soviets to try to take advantage of US weakness in Iran, a miscalculation that could in turn lead the two superpowers to stumble into a regional war. On the other hand, the USA did not want to risk war itself by responding too aggressively to the Soviet invasion. An intervention by US forces against the Soviet occupiers in Afghanistan could similarly lead to the Third World War. US officials needed a response which indicated that they took the Soviet action seriously and disapproved of it, were not prepared to go to war over it, but were prepared to defend their vital interests in the region in the event that the Soviets moved militarily from Afghanistan into Iran. Economic sanctions—even if they could not actually oust the Soviets from Afghanistan—helped to serve these purposes. They conveyed to the Soviet leaders that the USA would no longer conduct business as usual. The grain embargo (which ultimately hurt the USA more than the Soviet Union economically because the Soviets could eventually find other suppliers) sent this message, as did the US refusal to participate in the 1980 Moscow Olympics. The sanctions were complemented by public diplomacy; in what became known as the Carter Doctrine, the US President stated publicly that the USA would be prepared to use whatever means were necessary to protect its allies and defend its vital interests in the Persian Gulf. (See Box 11.3.)

The most authoritative quantitative study of economic sanctions concludes that, with a broad definition of success, sanctions attempts during the 1990s were successful about 33% of the time (Hufbauer *et al.* 2007). Sanctions tend to be most successful when the objectives are relatively modest, when the target is relatively small and weak, and when the sender avoids high costs to itself.

How does the end of the Cold War matter?

I noted earlier that economic sanctions have been used with increasing frequency since the end of the Cold War. Sanctions have become a weapon of choice for Western governments

---

BOX 11.3 The objectives of economic statecraft—general categories

Influence another country's domestic policies

Influence another country's foreign policies

Weaken or strengthen another country's economic or military capabilities

Undermine the government or political system of another country

and the UN Security Council. But are there reasons to believe that economic sanctions will be any more effective than they were during the Cold War? The international structural changes at the end of the Cold War, along with developments in the world economy (globalization) and in world politics (democratization), have created a new international environment for sanctions attempts (Jentleson 2000). Each of these developments is consequential for sanctions but, taken together, there is no reason to expect that sanctions will be systematically any more effective in the future than they have been in the past.

The end of the Cold War predictably brought forth a surge of sanctions optimism. The Cold War had created a stalemate in the international community. Western allies might agree to sanction their Eastern adversaries, or vice versa, but there were very few issues on which *all* the great powers might agree to place their collective political influence. The collapse of the East–West divide reopened the possibility of great power collaboration that had been envisioned at the founding of the United Nations. Optimism escalated after Iraq's 1990 invasion of Kuwait; all the great powers, including Iraq's traditional benefactor Russia, lined up together in support of multilateral economic sanctions.

The subsequent post Cold War experience has been more sobering. The major powers have agreed to impose sanctions collectively for a variety of reasons against a variety of targets including Serbia, Rwanda, Somalia, Libya, and Cambodia. However, there is no concert of major powers policing the world by lining up *consistently* on the same side of salient international conflicts. The collective sanctions against Iraq, maintained for almost a decade, began to unravel during the late 1990s. The USA and Britain proved eager to maintain a comprehensive embargo, but Russia and France were anxious to resume a more normal trading relationship. The case of Iran provoked similarly uncoordinated attitudes. The USA has pushed consistently for a confrontational policy of economic and diplomatic containment. The EU has traditionally favoured a more accommodating strategy of economic engagement, although in recent years it has moved closer to the US position. Russia has proved most concerned to reap the economic benefits of bilateral trade with Iran; it has been willing to agree at best to limited and targeted sanctions related to Iran's nuclear activities.

Similarly, for much of the post Cold War period the USA has consistently favoured stricter economic sanctions against North Korea. Japan, China, and South Korea initially opted for forms of engagement, although by 2009 provocative behaviour by North Korea had swung Japan and South Korea closer the the US position. However, China has remained reluctant to impose serious economic restrictions on North Korea. America and Europe have taken the lead in sanctioning Syria for its support for international terrorism and, more recently, its brutal crackdown on its own population supporting democratic reform in the context of the Arab Spring. However, as of 2011 Russia argued that sanctions would constitute inappropriate interference in Syria's domestic affairs. In short, the end of the Cold War means that there is greater potential for great power cooperation on sanctions, but no guarantee that agreement will be forthcoming either on overall foreign policy strategy (containment versus engagement) or on the willingness to bear the economic costs that sanctions entail.

Globalization—the process by which more and more countries are integrating more meaningfully into the liberal world economy—has important cross-cutting implications for economic sanctions. On the one hand, globalization makes the 'Rhodesian solution' of diversifying far more difficult to carry out. Domestic economic insulation and domestic substitution for imports and exports are a less viable response to sanctions in a globalized economy. As countries become increasingly dependent on the world economy, they become potentially more vulnerable to international sanctions attempts by other actors in the system. Very few countries choose to 'hide' from the contemporary world economy, and those that do (e.g. North Korea) pay an extraordinary price in terms of economic prosperity and development. On the other hand, globalization also increases the possibility that a target country can seek out alternative markets and suppliers, undermining the effectiveness of sanctions. Globalization has increased the volume and complexity of international economic transactions, and makes it harder for any coalition of countries, unless it is a universal coalition, to control all the possible external partners that might benefit from evading or ignoring multilateral sanctions against a particular target.

These cross-cutting effects of globalization help us to understand the seemingly paradoxical impact of sanctions against Iraq and Haiti during the 1990s. In these two cases, the domestic economy was severely damaged by sanctions and the general population suffered significantly. However, elites managed to emerge relatively unscathed and in some cases were economically even better off as a result of sanctions. The reason may be that in these sanctions targets, as in most countries, elites were better positioned than members of the general population to take advantage of the international networks and connections offered by globalization. The overall economy suffered the vulnerability impact of globalization, but elites took advantage of the opportunity offered by alternative markets and suppliers. In other words, globalization increases the likelihood that comprehensive sanctions can transform into foreign policy weapons of human destruction that do not necessarily lead to meaningful political change. This makes the development and implementation of precisely targeted smart sanctions all the more imperative.

During the 1990s democratization spread from Eastern Europe to Latin America to East Asia and even parts of Africa. The logic of economic sanctions suggests that democratization should, in general, increase the likelihood that the pain of economic sanctions will translate into meaningful political change. Governments in democratic settings are more sensitive to the pressures and demands of their constituents. All things being equal, democratic targets will be more vulnerable to sanctions attempts than autocratic ones. But there is one important caveat—the 'rally round the flag effect' mentioned earlier. A common response to externally imposed sanctions is the assertion of nationalism, and there is no reason to expect that nationalist responses will be weaker in democratic than in autocratic settings. Democratic governments may be just as capable as their autocratic counterparts in framing sanctions attempts as pitting 'us against them' in order to maintain their own political position and their ability to withstand external pressure to change their behaviour.

Conversely, the lack of democratization means that autocratic governments are better positioned to shift the burden of sanctions to a more repressed population that has limited political resources. Autocratic governments in the Soviet Union during the Cold War, in Iraq after the Cold War, and in Cuba across both periods proved effective in shifting the burden and minimizing the overall impact of sanctions on their political autonomy at home. Alternatively, in Guatemala in 1993 and Paraguay in 1996, business and professional classes newly empowered by democratization processes and with much to lose in the event of sanctions pressured their respective governments to accommodate the demands of the international

community and turn back anti-democratic coup attempts by government and military officials (Jentleson 2000: 157).

Economic incentives: an under-appreciated instrument of statecraft?

Positive economic statecraft can be defined as the provision or promise of economic benefits
to induce changes in the behaviour of a target state.[1] It is important to distinguish between
two types. The first involves the promise of a well-specified economic concession in an effort
to alter specific foreign or domestic policies of the target government. I call this version **tactical linkage**; others refer to 'carrots' or 'specific positive linkage'. A second version, which I term
structural linkage and others refer to as 'general positive linkage' or 'long-term engagement',
involves an effort to use a steady stream of economic benefits to reconfigure the balance of
political interests within a target country. Structural linkage tends to be unconditional; the
benefits are not turned on and off according to changes in target behaviour. The sanctioning
state expects instead that sustained economic engagement will eventually produce a political
transformation and desirable changes in target behaviour.

Tactical linkage and long-term engagement are each informed by a different logic. Tactical
linkage operates at a more immediate level; the sanctioning state calculates that the provision
of a particular type of economic reward will be sufficient to convince policy makers in the
target to reconsider their existing policies. For example, immediately after the Second World
War, the USA offered sizeable reconstruction loans to Britain, France, and the Soviet Union—
in exchange for political concessions. The British and French were generally willing to accommodate US demands that they liberalize their domestic and foreign economic policies; the
Soviets were not. In 1973, European states and Japan offered economic inducements in the
form of aid and trade concessions to Arab states during the OPEC crisis in a largely successful
attempt to ensure that they would receive access to oil supplies at predictable prices. In 1982,
the USA offered to increase sales of coal to its West European allies to discourage them from
a gas pipeline deal with the Soviet Union. This influence attempt failed.

Long-term engagement, however, works at a deeper level, and its logic was most clearly
articulated in the classic work of Albert Hirschman (Hirschman 1980 [1945]). The sanctioning
government provides an ongoing stream of economic benefits which gradually transform
domestic political interests in the target state. Over time, 'internationalist' coalitions that
favour interdependence with the sanctioning state will form and strengthen, and will exert
influence over the policy of the weaker state in a direction preferred by the sanctioning state.
Hirschman demonstrated how Nazi Germany used an array of economic inducements to
inculcate economic dependence, and eventually political acquiescence, on the part of its
weaker central European neighbours during the inter-war period.

Political scientists have traditionally devoted relatively little attention to positive economic
statecraft. There are, for example, no databases of instances of economic inducement, with
assessments of success and failure, along the lines of those that Hufbauer *et al.* (2007) and
Jentleson (2000) have compiled for negative economic sanctions. Economic sticks have com-
manded more attention than economic carrots. This was especially true during the Cold War,

when the two dominant powers and their respective alliances were largely self-sufficient and economically independent of each other. Since there was so little economic cooperation, the study of superpower and inter-bloc economic interaction emphasized economic warfare, or negative sanctions.

The end of the Cold War has brought a changed global situation and a revival of scholarly interest in positive economic statecraft. The major powers of the world are now economically interdependent, as they were during the late nineteenth century. An understanding of great power politics once again requires an understanding of economic relationships and of the links between economics and foreign policy. During the Cold War, US–Soviet relations focused on arms control and the management of political and ideological competition. Today, and particularly in the context of the great financial crisis that began in 2008, the focus in foreign relations among the USA, the EU, China, Japan, and Russia is as much on issues of economic reform, trade policy, and currency competition as on the traditional 'high politics' of military competition and alliance cooperation. As economic relations take centre stage in foreign policy, the traditional lines between high politics and low politics become blurred. It is not surprising that scholars have begun to rediscover the agenda of positive economic statecraft. For example, a recent book argues that US foreign policy objectives would be better served by employing carrots rather than sticks, even in relations with seemingly intractable states such as Iran and North Korea (Nincic 2011).

The Cold War endgame, and in particular Germany's reunification, highlighted the key role of economic inducements. Beginning in 1969, West Germany used economic statecraft to build the political foundation for reconciliation with one of its most distrustful neighbours, Poland. When West Germany finally seized the opportunity to reunify in 1989, a reassured Poland did not stand in the way (Davis 2000). Similarly, West German leaders used a steady stream of economic inducements over two decades to inculcate Soviet dependence on German commerce and credits and to signal Germany's benign foreign policy intentions. Soviet leader Gorbachev counted on Germany, more so than any other Western state, to provide much-needed economic support. The German government responded in 1989–1990 with food aid and sizeable economic credits. The clinchers, which paved the way for Russian acquiescence to unification on Germany's terms, included a five billion Deutschmark credit, a willingness to allow Russia to buy goods from the eastern zone of Germany with roubles rather than hard currency, and a commitment to provide financial support for the post-unification resettlement of the Red Army in Russia (Newnham 2002).

Since the end of the Cold War, economic engagement has proved to be a key foreign policy strategy in relations both among major powers and between stronger and weaker states. The USA and the EU have used economic incentives, with mixed success, in an effort to integrate Russia and Central and Eastern Europe into a Western-centred world political economy. European states view economic engagement as the appropriate strategy to adopt with regard to a potentially revisionist Iran; the USA prefers economic containment. China has sought to deepen economic interdependence with Taiwan as a means to reduce incentives for Taiwanese independence. Most prominently, the USA has adopted economic engagement as the focal point of its strategy towards a rising potential challenger, China. US officials recognize that China's integration into the world economy will increase its economic and potential military power. But they also expect—or hope—that the very process of integration will soften

Chinese intentions and encourage China to be a more accommodating, rather than a more revisionist, rising power. In light of the rapid growth of Chinese economic and even military capabilities, a good part of the future of international politics hinges on the outcome of this high-stakes experiment in economic statecraft.

Positive and negative economic statecraft

The revival of interest in economic inducements naturally raises the issue of the relationship between positive and negative means of economic statecraft. We can conceive of positive and negative measures as substitutes or complements. As substitutes, we can identify both strengths and drawbacks of relying on positive economic statecraft.

There are good reasons to expect positive measures to be more effective than negative ones. Threats tend to inspire resistance and resentment in the target government; a typical response to the promise of rewards is hope and expectation. Negative sanctions often produce the 'rally round the flag' effect. Positive sanctions do not, and have the potential to undermine the target government by creating transnational coalitions between groups in the sanctioning and target countries at the societal level. Positive sanctions have a tendency to encourage the target government to cooperate with the sanctioning government on other issues; negative sanctions create a general reluctance to cooperate. With negative sanctions, multilateral cooperation is a necessity and there are strong incentives for third parties to break the embargo in order to gain above-normal profits. Positive sanctions do not require multilateral support, and alternative economic partners typically cannot gain by undercutting the sanctions. Business interests in the sanctioning state tend to mobilize against negative sanctions, but they are likely to support positive ones that coincide with their natural interest in expanding economic interaction.

However, positive economic measures have potential drawbacks as well. Governments that indicate a willingness to 'pay' for good foreign policy behaviour may find themselves subject to continual demands for payment. After North Korea precipitated a potential nuclear crisis, the USA offered it economic concessions in 1994 to forego its nuclear ambitions. About ten years later, the North Korean government precipitated another nuclear crisis, and made clear its expectation that once again economic concessions should be forthcoming. A second and related problem concerns the political repercussions of 'trading with an enemy'. Even if positive economic measures stand a relative chance of success, governments might be reluctant to reward a government that they otherwise find to be politically or morally repugnant. The USA faces this dilemma in relations with Iran. The normalization of bilateral economic relations has the potential to bring Iranian political concessions, but at the cost of diluting the overall US effort to isolate politically this charter member of the 'axis of evil'.

Positive and negative measures can also be used as complementary instruments of statecraft. Positive economic sanctions can set up the threat or use of negative sanctions by developing the economic dependence of the target on the sanctioning country. Similarly, negative sanctions can structure opportunities for the use of positive measures. Once negative sanctions have been in place, lifting them is a change from the status quo for which sanctioning states can derive some concession in return. The USA used this tactic in 1980 to facilitate the return of hostages from Iran, and Western states employed it against Serbia to persuade it to accept the Dayton Accords of 1995. The long-standing US embargo of Cuba holds open this possibility as well.

The relationship between positive and negative economic statecraft is relatively unexplored territory for foreign policy analysis. Now that positive measures have been rediscovered, the next step will be to study their effectiveness more systematically, both on their own and in relation to the more familiar forms of economic sanctions.

Economic interdependence: source of political harmony or conflict?

The previous section discussed the renewal of positive economic sanctions at the level of foreign policy analysis. It is important to consider the systemic implications as well. If economic interdependence can be used to strengthen alliances and improve relations with adversaries, does its presence lead more generally to peaceful relations among states?

Liberals argue that economic interdependence decreases incentives for conflict by tying peoples more closely together and increasing the costs of economic disruption to high or prohibitive levels. States eventually come to recognize that they can no longer afford war because it jeopardizes the economic benefits of interdependence. Realists, in contrast, generally argue that economic interdependence is more likely to lead to state conflict. It heightens the potential for political friction and exposes the vulnerabilities of insecure states in an anarchic setting.

It is not surprising that one can find empirical support for either position. One study reinforces the liberal view by finding that since 1850 the level of international trade has been inversely related to the occurrence of major power wars (Mansfield 1994). Others find a significant correlation between increased interdependence and democracy, and a reduction in the likelihood of military conflict. Realists counter with evidence that during the inter-war years dependence on strategic mineral imports created incentives for states to use aggressive foreign policies, even if that meant disrupting economic interdependence. In her survey of twenty studies of interdependence and conflict, Susan McMillan (1997) reports that ten studies support the liberal position, four support the realist, and six come up with mixed results.

Rather than seek a paradigmatic winner, it may be more useful to search for intervening variables that help to explain the circumstances under which economic interdependence leads to war or peace. For example, high levels of interdependence can lead to either peace or war depending on policy makers' future expectations. If policy makers are pessimistic that they will gain future trade benefits, they may be willing to resort to war even if, as before the First World War, levels of economic interdependence are high (Copeland 1996). Alternatively, Peter Liberman argues that whether interdependence leads to peace depends on the perception of the military balance between offence and defence (Liberman 1999–2000). Interdependence leads to conflict when major powers are both trade-dependent and facing a security situation in which defence is generally stronger than offence. The need to prepare for the possibility of a protracted conventional war raises the stakes and exposes the vulnerabilities of trade-dependent states. Stephen Brooks suggests that the modern form of interdependence is more likely than the nineteenth-century version to lead to peaceful state relations because contemporary globalization is characterized not only by deep trade links but also by transnational production networks (Brooks 2005). These studies raise the debate over interdependence and war to a more sophisticated level, beyond the set-piece battles between liberal and realist positions.

Conclusion

This chapter has focused on economic instruments of statecraft and advances four main arguments. First, despite their popularity as a foreign policy tool, it is difficult for economic sanctions to achieve major foreign policy objectives. The end of the Cold War has led to an increase in the use of sanctions, but not necessarily in their relative effectiveness. Second, even if they do not always succeed, governments find sanctions useful as a device to signal their intentions, send important messages, and complement military action or diplomacy. Third, the positive use of economic incentives has considerable promise as an instrument of statecraft and deserves more systematic attention from students of the subject. Finally, the enduring question of whether economic interdependence leads to harmony or conflict among states is best answered conditionally. It depends on the future expectations of policy makers, on the nature of the military balance, and on the form that economic interdependence takes.

 Key points

- Economic statecraft is part of the wider array of foreign policy instruments that governments have at their disposal, and is frequently used in conjunction with diplomatic and military measures in response to foreign policy problems and opportunities.

- Economic statecraft may be positive, involving the use of rewards or incentives, or negative, involving threats or punishment.

- Economic sanctions usually fail to achieve ambitious foreign policy objectives. But they are still useful to governments in signalling intentions, complementing diplomacy, building a political consensus for the eventual use of military force, or withstanding pressure to resort to military force.

- Recent structural changes such as the end of the Cold War, the rise of globalization, and the spread of democracy worldwide each have important implications for the practice of economic statecraft.

- Positive economic statecraft has become more important since the end of the Cold War. Scholars should pay as much attention to positive economic statecraft as they do to economic sanctions.

- Whether economic interdependence leads to peace, as liberals believe, or to political conflict, as realists believe, depends on a number of intervening variables, including the future expectations of policy makers, the nature of the military balance, and the form that economic interdependence takes.

 Questions

1. Under what circumstances are economic sanctions likely to be effective?
2. How do realists and liberals differ in their understanding of the relationship between economic interdependence and peace?

3. If economic sanctions do not seem to work very well, why do governments resort to them so frequently?

4. What are 'smart sanctions', and why have they become so popular?

5. Why do some scholars believe that economic incentives are more likely to succeed than economic threats?

6. Is economic statecraft best understood as a complement to the use of military force, or a substitute for the use of military force?

7. Identify and explain the significance of the 'rally round the flag' effect.

8. What impact does globalization have on the effectiveness of economic statecraft?

 ## Further reading

Baldwin, D. (1985), *Economic Statecraft* **(Princeton, NJ: Princeton University Press).**
An authoritative study of economic statecraft from the perspective of decision-making theory, systematically comparing economic with other instruments of statecraft.

Cortright, D. and Lopez, G. (2002), *Smart Sanctions: Targeting Economic Statecraft* **(New York: Rowman & Littlefield).**
A systematic examination of negative economic sanctions that are precisely targeted.

Doxey, M. (1996), *International Sanctions in Contemporary Perspective* **(Basingstoke: Palgrave MacMillan).**
An excellent introduction to the history and logic of economic sanctions undertaken by multilateral institutions.

Drezner, D. (2009), 'Bad Debts: Assessing China's Financial Influence in Great Power Politics', *International Security*, **34: 7–45.**
An analysis of China's potential to use monetary pressure against the USA.

Hirschman, A. (1945) [1980], *National Power and the Structure of Foreign Trade* **(Berkeley, CA: University of California Press).**
The classic work on the theory and logic of positive economic statecraft.

Hufbauer, G.C., Schott, J., Elliot, K.A., and Oegg, B. (2007), *Economic Sanctions Reconsidered* **(Washington, DC: Peterson Institute for International Economics).**
A comprehensive study of cases of economic sanctions during the twentieth century.

Kirshner, J. (1995), *Currency and Coercion: The Political Economy of International Monetary Power* **(Princeton, NJ: Princeton University Press).**
A study of economic statecraft with special emphasis on the use of monetary and financial instruments.

Losman, D. (1979), *International Economic Sanctions: The Cases of Cuba, Israel, and Rhodesia* **(Albuquerque, NM: University of New Mexico Press).**
In-depth analysis of three celebrated cases of sanctions failure.

Nincic, M. (2011), *The Logic of Positive Engagement* **(Ithaca, NY: Cornell University Press).**
Theory and case studies on the use of economic inducements in US foreign policy.

 Visit the Online Resource Centre that accompanies this book for more information:
www.oxfordtextbooks.co.uk/orc/smith_foreign/

Duties beyond borders

MICHAEL BARNETT

Chapter contents

 Reader's guide

This chapter explores why states proclaim duties to those beyond their borders, the apparent expansion of those duties over the last two decades, and the implication of this development for understanding the purpose and practice of foreign policy. The chapter begins by discussing what is meant by duties beyond borders and considers its relationship to the concepts of sovereignty and cosmopolitanism. It then proceeds to examine how realist, liberal, constructivist, and decision-making theories (the latter particularly central to Foreign Policy Analysis (FPA)) explain the existence and expansion of these duties. The chapter then examines why states failed to halt the genocide in Rwanda in 1994 but did intervene in Libya in 2011, with a particular focus on the decision-making process in the USA. The chapter closes by examining the growing tension between a foreign policy defined by realpolitik and a foreign policy that is increasingly affected and defined by intensifying interdependence in a range of issues and transnational connections between peoples.

Introduction

Much of foreign policy analysis concerns how states make and implement policies that are designed to further the interests of states, typically defined by power or wealth. This analytical focus presumably captures an important empirical reality and normative claim. The empirical reality is that most states most of the time construct their foreign policies in order to maximize their security. The normative claim is that governments *should* behave this way because as the representative of the nation they should protect *its* interests. In other words, the duties of states should extend no further than their territorial boundaries. Yet occasionally states do seem to care about more than themselves and their interests, acting on behalf of distant strangers and in defence of global ethics. In fact, states appear to be increasingly expressing a commitment to aiding those who reside outside their borders; many are advocating debt relief for the world's poorest countries, spreading human rights in order to protect societies from authoritarian leaders, working to increase access to medicines for the poor, and carrying out humanitarian interventions. When juxtaposed against the standard claim that states pursue only their self-interest, their willingness to sacrifice for and expend energy to improve the welfare of those living in other lands is an impressive anomaly, to say the least. If states are accepting more duties beyond borders, or at least act as if they do, one reason is because of deepening interdependence and intensifying transnational connections. States are expected by international society and their domestic society to pursue not only power but also a sense of purpose—a purpose that has an ethical and normative content. Yet do states actually back up their expressions of sympathy with concrete action? If they do, why, and how can such expressions be encouraged and acted upon? If not, why not, and what should and can be done to align talk and action?

Duties beyond borders

The language of duties suggests that individuals have obligations and moral responsibilities to others. International relations scholars traditionally assume that duties stop at the border's edge. States have obligations, first, foremost, and last, to their citizens. Citizens have duties, but to their compatriots and to the state. Scholars will highlight two reasons why duties do not cross borders. One is the existence of social contracts among citizens and between citizens and the state. A state's constitution is such a contract, defining the responsibilities and duties which states and their citizens have to each other. The other reason is the presumption that the territorial state defines the boundaries of the community in every sense. The state also contains a community or nation in which individuals exhibit solidarity and have a shared identity, history, and sense of fate. This is why International Relations (IR) theorists frequently contrast the 'community' that exists on the inside with the 'anarchy' that exists on the outside. As yet, there is no global contract or constitution and the concept of the international community is nothing more than an empty slogan, limiting the duties of states to their citizens and their territorial boundaries.

An alternative perspective suggests that state sovereignty does not limit our obligations to distant strangers. States frequently pursue more than simply their interests defined as power and wealth; they also follow their ethics and principles, promoting human rights, providing development assistance, and delivering relief to the victims of natural and man-made disasters. If the concept of sovereignty appears to put a brake on the concern for others, the concept of **humanity** pushes us forward. Drawing from the idea that individuals possess basic inalienable rights, the claim is that all individuals have a common humanity. The principle of humanity leads to a general commitment to 'prevent and alleviate human suffering wherever it may be found', 'to protect life and health and to ensure respect for the human being', and to 'promote mutual understanding, friendship, co-operation and lasting peace amongst all peoples.'(Pictet 1979).

Humanity, in this fundamental way, is connected to **cosmopolitanism**—the claim that each person is of equal moral worth and a subject of moral (Brock and Brighouse 2005). But the case for the existence of duties across borders does not rest on philosophical principles alone. The fact is that people do not act as if their obligations are limited by borders—they frequently express concern for and provide assistance to those in distant lands. There is ample evidence that both peoples and states give to others whom they do not know and do so without expecting much in return, as evidenced in the reflections by Bill Gates in Box 12.1. We do not close our hearts or our wallets to distant strangers in need.

An impressive range of foreign policy practices now reflect a duty to strangers, including foreign aid, human rights promotion, development assistance, global health initiatives, and on and on, but perhaps the surest expression of the idea of duties across borders is **humanitarianism**, the provision of life-saving relief to those whose lives are in danger. Although the concern for and sense of obligation to distant strangers are as old as antiquity, over the last 200 years we have seen an impressive expansion of a humanitarian system—and particularly so over the last two decades. Today, a vast institutional network, comprised of states, international organizations, and transnational non-governmental organizations (NGOs), aims to save lives and eliminate the root causes of suffering and violence. There are many reasons behind this remarkable development, but a critical factor is the dynamic relationship between the development of activist organizations that insist that their governments do what they can to relieve the suffering of others, governments who believe that it is in their political and strategic interests to respond positively to these pleas, growing forms of interdependence, transnational connections, and information flows that increase the awareness of the desperate circumstances of millions of people. The growing awareness that others are at risk and the sense that states and others can do something about it (because of new communication and transportation technologies) can create new ways of judging the ethical character of a state's foreign policy and sentiments by citizens that if states can act to save lives, then they should. In general, the startling growth of a network of states, international

---

BOX 12.1 Valuing human life

For Bill Gates, the founder of Microsoft, the ideal of valuing human life equally began to jar against reality some years ago when he read an article about diseases in the developing world and came across a statistic that half a million children die every year from rotavirus, the most common cause of severe diarrhoea in children. He had never heard of rotavirus. 'How could I never have heard of something that kills half a million children every year?' he asked himself. He then learned that in developing countries, millions of children die from diseases that have been eliminated, or virtually eliminated, in the USA. That shocked him because he assumed that, if there are vaccines and treatments that could save lives, governments would be doing everything possible to get them to the people who need them. As Gates told a meeting of the World Health Assembly in Geneva last year, he and his wife, Melinda, 'couldn't escape the brutal conclusion that—in our world today—some lives are seen as worth saving and others are not.' . . . The belief in the equal value of all human life . . . is prominent on the website of the Bill and Melinda Gates Foundation, where under Our Values we read: 'All lives—no matter where they are being led—have equal value.'

Peter Singer on Bill Gates, 'What Should A Billionaire Give—and What Should You?' New York Times Sunday Magazine, 17 December 2006, p. 60.

organizations, and transnational NGOs that are dedicated to relieving the suffering of others suggests that individuals and states are feeling a greater sense of obligation to those in distant lands.

Theories of foreign policy and duties beyond borders

Our standard theories of foreign policy tend to discount the existence of duties beyond borders. Most famously and critically, **realist** theories observe that states do not exhibit much of a duty to others and commend them for this neglect; the state's national interest is to protect the nation and distractions can lead to self-destructive foreign policy behaviour. These observations of the past and recommendations for the future flow from realism's foundational principles. According to realism, the state's national interest is defined by the quest for survival and power. Although realists offer various reasons why states are so self-absorbed, most credit anarchy: in the absence of a supranational authority that can preserve the security of the state, it is a self-help world in which states must learn to help themselves because no other state will. The state, then, has a duty to protect the national interest defined as power, security, and wealth. Importantly, realists do not deny the existence of a community. A community exists, but it is limited to those who live within the confines of the state. There is a community on the inside and an anarchy on the outside—and the state's job is to protect the community from anarchy.

This starting point leads realists to make two important claims regarding any duty to others. To begin, beware whenever states claim that they are doing something for someone else. Such claims are mere smokescreens, ideological props that are intended to legitimate their more primeval foreign policy goals. To be sure, sometimes states will help others, but rarely will they do so when it actually costs them something. In fact, states are most likely to help others when it furthers their other interests. When Vietnam intervened in Cambodia in 1978 and put an end to the genocide, when India intervened in Eastern Pakistan in 1971 to protect the Bengalis, and when Tanzania toppled Idi Amin in Uganda in 1978 and put an end to the killing, their actions had humanitarian consequences but these states were largely motivated by geostrategic interests. Japan is providing more foreign assistance than ever before, but a major reason is because it expects to gain status and influence in return. The realist perspective nicely reminds us that states rarely sacrifice for others and will frequently deploy high-minded ideals to camouflage their true motives.

Second, realists also have a normative argument. The function of the state is to protect the national interest and it has no business squandering its resources and manpower to try and help others. In 1993, Samuel Huntington is purported to have observed that American soldiers have no business dying to stop the right of Somalis to kill each other. Although Huntington might appear to be gratuitously callous, arguably he is only saying what most Americans believe—and Americans are hardly unique. Few states volunteered to send their troops into Somalia, and few societies asked their governments to reconsider. Although states might be willing to provide food aid and financial assistance to those in need (but hardly ever in adequate amounts), rarely are they willing to sacrifice their citizens' lives. States do not and should not have duties across borders. If states did begin to act on behalf of others, they would quickly find themselves overwhelmed with the demands of millions of suffering souls, deplete their own national resources, and undermine their primary foreign policy interests.

Liberalism contains a mixture of claims suggesting that states do and should have duties beyond borders. One prominent strand focuses on the prominence of domestic politics and interest groups in shaping the foreign policy of a state (Moravcsik 1997). Perhaps the first and most famous example of domestic mobilization that changed a state's foreign policy was the anti-slavery movement in Britain in the early nineteenth century. Drawing from stories of suffering by slaves and ideas of Christian charity, many religiously inspired individuals and organizations worked tirelessly to change the attitudes of the British people towards slavery, and influenced the British's government ultimate decision to abolish slavery and to combat the slave trade. In the USA ethnic, religious, and national associations lobby the US government to provide assistance to their compatriots. One of the first instances of US aid took place in the late nineteenth century when Irish immigrants in the USA lobbied the government to provide relief to a famine-stricken Ireland. Today evangelical and human rights organizations are working together on a range of issues, including action to end the violence in the Sudan and to combat sex trafficking. This 'left–right' partnership has proved to pack a very powerful 'one-two' punch with members of Congress. One of the most important foreign aid programmes in the USA is PL 480, which sends export surplus agricultural products to developing countries. A major reason why this programme receives Congressional support is that it is championed by the American farmers, who financially benefit from the arrangement.

Another strand of liberalism focuses on interdependence (Keohane and Nye 2000). One dimension of interdependence is our awareness of the plight of others. Visual images have proved to be one of the most important developments in the growth of humanitarianism and a powerful weapon in the arsenal of activist organizations.

The development of photojournalism and war reporting in the mid-nineteenth century proved instrumental in creating a citizens' movement to bring relief to wounded soldiers, leading directly to the creation of the International Committee of the Red Cross and the development of international humanitarian law. The coverage of the devastation caused by the Second World War helped to spur the development of relief organizations such as CARE and international humanitarian organizations such as the UN High Commissioner for Refugees. Today, satellite technology, 24-hour cable news programmes, and the worldwide web put before us a constant barrage of searing images, transforming what might have been anonymous events into global spectacles. Floods in Pakistan, earthquakes in Haiti, and government crackdowns on protestors in the Arab world now get global attention and, frequently, action.

These growing connections are not only visual, they also are causal. Sometimes individuals are compelled to act because they believe that it is the moral thing to do. At other times it is because they believe that their actions are partially responsible for the suffering of others. When labour organizations in the West campaign to stop inhumane conditions in the factories in Southeast Asia that are exporting basketball shoes to the West, part of their argument is that consumers in the West enjoy low prices because of the exploitation of foreign workers. Arguments in favour of more economic assistance and debt relief for Africa frequently include arguments that imperialism contributed to Africa's current plight and inequitable post-colonial trading practices have perpetuated it.

A third strand of liberalism considers how a liberal identity leads to a sense of obligation to others (Tesón 2003). Here, liberalism refers not to a leftist position in politics but rather to a belief in human reason, liberty, autonomy, and freedom. During the nineteenth century, many Western liberal states began to express an obligation to help the 'uncivilized' peoples—those who were viewed as not having been exposed to or adopted Western standards—and to share with them the scientific and medical advances that helped to bring progress and prosperity at home. Although these sentiments were first and most forcefully voiced by many religious and missionary organizations which drew on Christian notions of charity, in the nineteenth century great secular liberal thinkers, such as John Stuart Mill, similarly argued that the civilized peoples must help the uncivilized develop the mental and physical tools necessary to enjoy the fruits of their freedom. These notions of humanitarianism quickly fed into the belief that colonialism was justified because the West could and should help civilize the rest of the world; concepts like 'mission civilatrice' and the 'white man's burden' had a positive association and reflected a sense of duty from the haves to the have-nots. However, not everyone believed that liberal states had a right to interfere in the lives of others; some protested that Westerners do not always know what is best, that other cultures should be respected, and that colonialism was leading to exploitation and not emancipation. There are twentieth and twenty-first century versions of these debates. Coalitions have formed in favour of humanitarian intervention, peace-building, democracy promotion, and human rights, united by the belief that the international community must act to help the world's poor, weak, and vulnerable. Yet various critics of these seemingly high-minded self-sacrificing people are claiming that they are knowingly or unknowingly part of broader imperial projects. Are today's liberals vulnerable to the charges levelled at well-intentioned missionaries and colonial administrators?

As discussed by Flockhart in Chapter Four, **constructivist** theories explore how the state's identity shapes its interests and how its identity and interests are together influenced by international society. This perspective suggests various reasons why states might express a duty to others. To begin with, a state's interests are not defined by security and wealth alone but also include various principles such as a commitment to human rights and the spread of democracy. As E.H. Carr noted in his magisterial *The Twenty Year's Crisis* (Carr 1964), a foreign policy motivated by the pursuit of power alone is unsustainable; the populace wants to believe that their country's foreign policy is also driven ethical principles of right and wrong. The USA has long demonstrated a commitment to democracy promotion, which many suggest comes from an American identity which believes that it is a 'city on the hill' and has an obligation to promote freedom abroad.

Moreover, like individuals in society, states care about what other states in international society think about them—they want their foreign policies to appear legitimate. In this view, states are respected not for their ability to aggressively pursue their national interests but rather for their willingness to defend universal principles. Furthermore, in contrast with realism's claim that community is limited solely to the nation-state, constructivists posit the existence of a transnational community which encourages states and their societies to be concerned about the welfare of others. This community need not be global—it can also be regional. Arabs and Muslims see the community as defined by Arab-speaking and Islamic peoples, respectively, and exhibit a commitment to those Islamic and Arab populations who are experiencing hardship or violence (especially when the assaults originate from outside the community)—hence the tremendous obligation felt by many Arabs to the Palestinians.

Decision-making theories (as found within FPA itself) add another layer of possibility for whether states decide to aid or not. As noted by Stein in Chapter Seven, while our theories of IR have implicit understandings of why states make the decisions they do, decision-making theories examine the actual processes by which those decisions are made and critically examine whether the reasons given by decision makers conform to the theory's expectations. Realism, liberalism, and constructivism invite us to think through the foreign policy decision processes that might lead to the decision to aid or not to aid. As realism might expect, if humanitarian intervention is rare, it is because most militaries object to putting their troops at risk and have the bureaucratic power to get their way. As liberalism might predict, NGOs can identify pressure points within the government that enable it to assemble a policy in favour of positive action, which is much easier if that action is not viewed as compromising the national interest. The major proponents of PL 480—religious and relief organizations—persuaded members of Congress and the Department of Agriculture that exporting surplus agricultural production would help American farmers, the poor abroad, and America's image. Constructivist theories would be more attentive to how the state's identity is likely to shape its willingness to provide aid because those foreign policy practices are deeply related to its national culture. For instance, Canada's national identity is reputed to be inclined towards positive international action, and that inclination is housed in foreign policy bureaucracies.

Are foreign policies becoming kinder and gentler?

There is growing evidence that states feel motivated and compelled to help distant strangers: the creation of the UN's Millennium Development Goals, the humanitarian interventions in Somalia, Kosovo, and East Timor, the outpouring of assistance to the victims of the Tsunami in December 2004, and the mobilization of citizens' movements around debt relief, human rights, landmines, and environmental protection. States and peoples appear increasingly prepared to take action and commit resources for the world's most vulnerable populations. How do we explain this?

Realists would encourage us to dig a little deeper and not stop until we find the bedrock of the state's true motives—security, power, and wealth. States will not sacrifice their interests for high-minded principles. They might contribute to good causes on occasion, but certainly not when it will cost them much. Consequently, states will 'talk a good game' (in terms of their international commitments and interests) but will ultimately only disappoint those who are gullible enough to believe that they will deliver on their promises. If states talk a good game, it is because they believe that the language of ethical action (and the vehicle of ethical projects) can be appropriated to advance their national interests. Also, sometimes they will make a half-hearted effort to help others in order to avoid more costly action. In 1993 many European states were willing to provide relief to the Bosnians as a way of trying to avoid any kind of forceful military intervention; thus humanitarianism became a 'fig leaf' for political inaction. Finally, being seen as a 'do gooder' can be beneficial for the international prestige of states. In response to the tsunami that occurred at Christmas 2004, many states entered into a 'bidding war' to demonstrate who cared the most—all the while expecting that they would get good publicity and gain influence by being seen as the most benevolent. States do not help others unless there is something in it for them.

Liberal theories point to various developments. One is globalization. The communications revolution, the simple fact that images from one part of the globe can be instantaneously transmitted to another, makes us keenly aware of what is happening elsewhere; in this respect, the 'CNN effect' (see Chapter Nine) is illustrative, albeit hyped. Human rights organizations are able to take advantage of this revolution to mobilize domestic opinion and to try and pressure their governments to act on behalf of others. In the USA a very active grassroots movement to 'save Darfur' was partly responsible for keeping the Bush administration focused on atrocity crimes. People also travel more than ever before and have a growing connection to faraway places. Not only are individuals more aware of the fates of others, but because of a revolution in transportation technologies they can more easily do something about it. Therefore one reason why Europeans were so affected by the tsunami in 2004 was because many had visited the very beach communities that had been swept away (and indeed were killed on holiday there). Not only are individuals more aware of the fates of others, but because of a revolution in transportation technologies they can more easily do something about it.

Constructivist theories point to how growing interconnections and a deepening international society are having an impact on the state's identity and interests. Several factors come into play. States are transforming their conceptualization of what constitutes a stable international order. Where once this order was believed to derive purely from sovereignty and deterrence, prevalent understandings suggest that states which are organized around democracy, an unfettered private sector, and the rule of law are more likely to be stable and respectful of their citizens and their neighbours. This belief is most evident in the claim that democratic states do not wage war on one another. Consequently, states increasingly promote democracy and human rights because these principles are viewed as inextricably tied to their own security interests. Moreover, a deepening international society, the fundamental interdependence of the security of states, and the perceived centrality of human rights in the creation and maintenance of a just and stable international order has shaped how many national leaders think about the purpose of the state's foreign policy. In the context of the NATO intervention in Kosovo, British Prime Minister Tony Blair offered a doctrine for the international community which argued that a more interconnected world requires a more interconnected set of foreign policies that consider not just interests but also values (see Box 12.2) Another reflection of this new thinking is the concept of a 'good international citizenship' championed by former Australian Foreign Minister Gareth Evans. He argued that the best way to secure international order is by strengthening international institutions and rules, the need for self-restraint and pragmatism, and the recognition that an ethical foreign policy is not about earning merit badges but rather about acknowledging that a principled international order is a stable international order.

Liberal and constructivist approaches help to explain why foreign policies are increasingly expressing a duty to others. Yet it is hard to shake the realist retort that this is little more than cheap talk—especially when action is most needed.

> **BOX 12.2 Tony Blair's doctrine of the international community, given at the Economic Club, Chicago, 24 April 1999**
>
> The most pressing foreign policy problem we face is to identify the circumstances in which we should get actively involved in other people's conflicts. Non-interference has long been considered an important principle of international order. And it is not one we would want to jettison too readily. One state should not feel it has the right to change the political system of another or foment subversion or seize pieces of territory to which it feels it should have some claim. But the principle of non-interference must be qualified in important respects. Acts of genocide can never be a purely internal matter. When oppression produces massive flows of refugees which unsettle neighbouring countries, then they can properly be described as 'threats to international peace and security'. When regimes are based on minority rule they lose legitimacy—look at South Africa.
>
> Looking around the world there are many regimes that are undemocratic and engaged in barbarous acts. If we wanted to right every wrong that we see in the modern world then we would do little else than intervene in the affairs of other countries. We would not be able to cope. So how do we decide when and whether to intervene? I think we need to bear in mind five major considerations.
>
> First, are we sure of our case? War is an imperfect instrument for righting humanitarian distress, but armed force is sometimes the only means of dealing with dictators. Second, have we exhausted all diplomatic options? We should always give peace every chance, as we have in the case of Kosovo. Third, on the basis of a practical assessment of the situation, are there military operations we can sensibly and prudently undertake? Fourth, are we prepared for the long term? In the past we talked too much of exit strategies. But having made a commitment we cannot simply walk away once the fight is over; better to stay with moderate numbers of troops than return for repeat performances with large numbers. And finally, do we have national interests involved? The mass expulsion of ethnic Albanians from Kosovo demanded the notice of the rest of the world. But it does make a difference that this is taking place in such a combustible part of Europe. I am not suggesting that these are absolute tests. But they are the kind of issues we need to think about in deciding in the future when and whether we will intervene.
>
> http://www.number10.gov.uk/output/Page1297.asp

The tragedy of Rwanda

Rwanda should give pause to any claim that there has been an ethical revolution in global affairs. Beginning on 6 April 1994 in only 100 days roughly 800,000 people lost their lives in a genocide. What did the UN do? It had 2500 UN peacekeepers on the ground in Rwanda, but instead of adding more troops and giving them a mandate to protect civilians, it reduced the operation to a skeletal force of 250 and ordered them not to protect civilians. What might have caused this inhumane response?

Although the causes of the genocide are complex, some aspects are essential background information (see Map 12.1). Rwanda has two ethnic groups, Hutu and Tutsi. In pre-colonial times these were largely economic groups—the Tutsi owned cattle and were in the minority but were the ruling class, and the Hutu who were peasants and were the vast majority but on the lower economic and political rung. When Belgium took over the colonial mandate from Germany after the First World War, they saw Hutu and Tutsi not as interconnected economic groups, in which it was possible to move from one category to another, but rather as mutually exclusive racial groups in which individuals were destined by birth to be a member of one group or the other. Belgium decided that Tutsis were destined to rule because of their racial superiority, which hardened the divisions and increased the conflict between Tutsi and Hutu. When Rwanda gained independence in 1961 there was a reversal of fortunes, and the majority Hutu now kept down the Tutsi. Many Tutsis fled the country. In 1989, Tutsis in exile in Uganda formed the Rwandan Patriotic Front (RPF) and attacked Rwanda from the north the following year. In response, the Hutu-led Rwandan government clamped down on the Tutsi population and Hutu extremism flowered. Ethnic hatred and conflict filled the land. In 1993 the Rwandan government and the RPF signed a peace treaty, known as the Arusha Accords, and the UN sent a peacekeeping mission to try and keep the peace and implement the agreement. However, beneath the peace treaty there existed tremendous mistrust between the two parties and growing fear among Hutu extremist groups that the Tutsis, their mortal enemy, were about to re-take political power.

The political instability and growing ethnic violence exploded on 6 April 1994 when President Habaryimana was killed. The UN Security Council now had to decide the fate of the Rwandans. Although there were many reasons why the Security Council decided to reduce the peacekeeping force, a central factor was that states would not provide reinforcements. Simply put, if the UN operation was going to be effective it would need more troops, but if no troops were forthcoming then the beleaguered and vulnerable operation could protect neither the Rwandans nor themselves. Because no state volunteered to send their forces into the violent maelstrom, the Security Council felt that it had little choice but to stand aside. Why

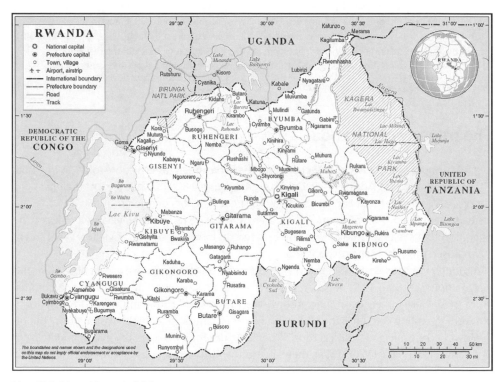

Map 12.1 Map of Rwanda (UN).

Source: Map ref no. 3717, Rev. 9 January 2004, Department of Peacekeeping Operations, UN Cartographic Sections.

were states unwilling to send troops? They concluded that it was not worth sacrificing their own citizens to save Rwandans, a quintessentially realist conclusion.

The USA's decision to oppose an intervention highlights many of the issues previously discussed. There was no overlap between American strategic and economic interests and Rwanda. Indeed, one recent event dramatized the dangers of allowing the heart to guide American foreign policy—Somalia. In response to a civil-war-induced famine in Somalia and the inability of the UN to protect the aid agencies that were delivering food, in November 1992 President Bush dispatched American military forces to keep the preying warlords at bay. What began as a humanitarian mission became a nation-building exercise. The warlord Mohammed Aideed, who believed that this development would frustrate his ambitions to seize political power, began to battle UN and then American forces. A particularly violent episode occurred on 3 October 1993, leaving eighteen American soldiers dead. Congress's reaction was fast and furious, accusing President Clinton of neglecting American interests and doing 'social work'. In response, Clinton decided to withdraw American troops and learned that there was a heavy political price to pay when America became too involved in humanitarian affairs.

The Clinton administration's decision-making process on Rwanda reflected the conclusion that there was no tangible reason why the USA should get involved in a country that was so disconnected from American interests and so soon after Somalia (see Box 12.3). A tell-tale indicator of the administration's lack of concern was the absence of any high-level meetings during the first weeks of the genocide. The Pentagon dominated the decision-making process. Not only did it oppose putting American troops on the ground, but it opposed any intervention whatsoever because of the fear that if the UN intervened and failed then the USA would have to pick up the pieces. So, rather than worry about a slippery slope, the Pentagon decided it was better to keep the UN off the slopes altogether. A handful of State Department officials contemplated a more proactive response, but Somalia was the great conversation stopper.

The lack of action did not appear to bother Congress or the American public. The only speeches in Congress on the subject cautioned against intervention and reminded the Clinton administration of the lessons of Somalia. The Congressional Black Caucus, which typically advances African issues, was focused on Haiti and had little to say about Rwanda. Unlike the initial American response to Somalia, except for a handful of human rights organizations there was no constituency in the USA demanding that something be done. Nor was there any CNN effect—in part because there was no CNN. In the USA the single most covered international event during the month of April 1994 was the election in South Africa, and the single most widely covered national event was the O.J. Simpson saga. Even if journalists had wanted to cover the story, it was nearly impossible to get into Rwanda. This story of neglect and indifference was repeated in countries around the world.

The world did not completely ignore Rwanda. As the RPF routed the Rwandan army, in June and July nearly two million Hutu, the greatest single refugee movement since the Second World War, fled to the neighbouring countries of Tanzania, Burundi, and, mostly, Zaire (now the Democratic Republic of Congo), where they established refugee camps the size of cities that quickly became incubators of disease and death. The media now rushed to cover the emergency. Partly in response to the shame of having done nothing to stop the genocide, in July the international community jumped into action and began providing life-saving relief.

> **BOX 12.3 Anthony Lake on why the Clinton administration's decision to not intervene**
>
> I wish I could say [Rwanda] had even become an abstraction. I think the problem here for me, for the President, for most of us at senior levels, was that it never became a serious issue. We were focusing on the edges of the problem. . . .
>
> But we never came to grips with what in retrospect should have been a central issue—do we do much more to insist that the international community intervene and go out and find the troops that are necessary, or even contemplate an American intervention itself? That issue just never arose.
>
> Given the broader context, it was seen as impossible to contemplate American intervention, because nobody was for it. My great regret is, again, that we and I did not say, 'Let's test the limits of this possibility. Too many people are dying. We cannot accept that this is inconceivable. I want to see a more rigorous analysis of the answers to the questions in PDD 25'. I was in more of a position to do it, but I didn't do it, any more than editorial writers and NGOs, other governments, the UN Secretariat, anybody.
>
> [Those outside of government who wanted an intervention] should be trying to create more noise about this situation, which would help us, inside, who had any concern about this issue. Noise means television interviews. Noise means newspaper articles. Noise can even mean peaceful demonstrations, etc. . . .
>
> An issue like this, where you are swimming uphill, upstream, and where, if you're thinking about an intervention in a Rwanda, you were really going against the conventional wisdom in the context and you had no allies on the outside—it would take a president or a national security adviser to push it through. [I]t would have taken quite a push. There's no question in my mind that, in the end, the President would have had to push it.
>
> From PBS Documentary, *Ghosts of Rwanda*: http://www.pbs.org/wgbh/pages/frontline/shows/ghosts/interviews/lake.html

Although many innocents were saved, so too were the perpetrators of the genocide. The remnants of the Hutu militias and military commandeered the camps and took control of the distribution of aid in order to further their political power and to exchange that aid for weapons that they could use in their next round against the Tutsis.

The international community's indifference to Rwanda brought tremendous shame to the UN Security Council and the UN itself. In response to the failure in Rwanda and the humanitarian interventions in Kosovo and East Timor, UN Secretary-General Kofi Annan urged the UN General Assembly in 1999 to consider adopting a doctrine for humanitarian intervention. Although most states were lukewarm to a doctrine that might impose obligations on them and circumscribe their state sovereignty, Canada, a booster of UN peacekeeping and humanitarian action, sponsored an international commission—the International Commission on Intervention and State Sovereignty (ICISS). After extensive worldwide consultations, the ICISS proposed a 'responsibility to protect'—when states fail in their obligations to protect their citizens, the international community inherits that responsibility (see Box 12.4). The UN General Assembly adopted core features of this document at the 2005 World Summit. The very adoption of this document and its language of international responsibility to victims of mass violence suggest a growing sense of mutual obligations. The challenge, of course, is to back up such grand talk with action. If this is to take place, domestic publics must pressure their state officials to act in an organized fashion, and be willing to hold them electorally accountable if they do not. As the Clinton National Security Advisor, Anthony Lake, told various human rights organizations who wanted the USA to intervene to stop the genocide, it will only happen if people 'make some noise.'

BOX 12.4 The International Commission on State Sovereignty on the 'Responsibility to Protect'

The Charter of the UN is itself an example of an international obligation voluntarily accepted by member states. On the one hand, in granting membership of the UN, the international community welcomes the signatory state as a responsible member of the community of nations. On the other hand, the state itself, in signing the Charter, accepts the responsibilities of membership flowing from that signature. There is no transfer or dilution of state sovereignty. But there is a necessary re-characterization involved: from *sovereignty as control* to *sovereignty as responsibility* in both internal functions and external duties.

Thinking of sovereignty as responsibility, in a way that is being increasingly recognized in state practice, has a threefold significance. First, it implies that the state authorities are responsible for the functions of protecting the safety and lives of citizens and promotion of their welfare. Secondly, it suggests that the national political authorities are responsible to the citizens internally and to the international community through the UN. And thirdly, it means that the agents of state are responsible for their actions; that is to say, they are accountable for their acts of commission and omission. The case for thinking of sovereignty in these terms is strengthened by the ever-increasing impact of international human rights norms, and the increasing impact in international discourse of the concept of human security.

[R]esponsibility to protect resides first and foremost with the state whose people are directly affected. This fact reflects not only international law and the modern state system, also the practical realities of who is best placed to make a positive difference. The domestic authority is best placed to take action to prevent problems from turning into potential conflicts. When problems arise the domestic authority is also best placed to understand them and to deal with them. When solutions are needed, it is the citizens of a particular state who have the greatest interest and the largest stake in the success of those solutions, in ensuring that the domestic authorities are fully accountable for their actions or inactions in addressing these problems, and in helping to ensure that past problems are not allowed to recur.

While the state whose people are directly affected has the default responsibility to protect, a residual responsibility also lies with the broader community of states. This fallback responsibility is activated when a particular state is clearly either unwilling or unable to fulfill its responsibility to protect or is itself the actual perpetrator of crimes or atrocities; or where people living outside a particular state are directly threatened by actions taking place there. This responsibility also requires that in some circumstances action must be taken by the broader community of states to support populations that are in jeopardy or under serious threat.

International Commission on Intervention and State Sovereignty http://www.iciss.ca/menu-en.asp

Libya: case of interests or responsibilities?

The international community's intervention in Libya in March 2011 suggests how a combination of interests and values can push even lukewarm powerful states into a supporting role. The uprising in Libya can only be understood in the context of an 'Arab Spring', a stunning moment when Arab civil society organizations, citizens, and protest movements joined forces to call for an end to authoritarianism. Beginning in Tunisia, the long-awaited revolt of the Arab people against their dictatorial governments was occurring across the region, from the Persian Gulf to

North Africa. This development not only caught Arab leaders by surprise, but it also caught Western governments unprepared, unsure how to encourage peaceful change, and even wondering whether the Middle East was better with the devil it knew rather than the uncertainty and instability that might accompany the toppling of these long-existing regimes.

The USA was particularly challenged by this turn of events. It had strong alliances with many of the governments that were the target of pro-democracy movements, including Bahrain and Egypt. Yet it also sympathized with the broad call for political change, human rights, and democracy. This seemed to be a situation in which American interests and its values pulled in different directions, and it chose to avoid specific principles in favour of examining each situation case by case. However, its one consistent position was that the regimes had to respect the right of the people to protest peacefully, and both publicly and privately cautioned the regimes against using deadly force.

The USA's attempt to maintain a cautious foreign policy became impossible to sustain when the Libyan people chose to join the cause for political change. Strongman Muammar Gaddafi had been in power since 1969. Although Libya and the West had moved towards a détente, he was still reviled because of his inflammatory rhetoric, his radical policies, his link to terrorism, and his penchant for intervening in the region. Consequently, when a major rebellion was launched in eastern Libya, there was a groundswell of sympathy for the rebels in the West. The USA also backed the rebels, but it had little interest in providing military support, wary of becoming bogged down in another part of the Islamic world and potentially hurting the legitimacy of the rebels. But then the military campaign turned against the rebels, and Gadaffi's son called the rebels 'cockroaches' and threatened to turn the streets of Benghazi red with blood. This set off alarm bells around the world and in Washington. 'Cockroaches' was the language used by the Hutu elite to describe the Tutsi, and thus was immediately associated with genocide. The Libyan government was threatening to level the city, treating civilians as legitimate targets. And Gadaffi, widely called crazy and a madman, seemed to be the sort of leader whose threats of atrocity should be believed. Genocide appeared to be imminent.

Although the USA remained guarded, the rest of the world was increasingly agitating for a military intervention. The reasons were many and complicated. There was widespread support for the Arab Spring, and worry that if Gadaffi got away with using force then other Arab leaders might see this as a precedent. Gadaffi had no friends and many enemies, and so there was no one who was prepared to come to his defence. The African Union appeared to give its support for protecting civilians. Perhaps the greatest surprise of all, though, was when the Arab League, whose members had long defended sovereignty against any form of intervention and whose leaders would probably have liked to use force against their population as a last resort to stay in power, voted to authorize international action to defend civilian populations.

With these developments there was a ferocious debate in the Obama administration regarding how to respond. Although aware that it looked increasingly feckless, many Obama officials, especially in the military, argued that the USA could not involve itself in another conflict. Yet those who argued against met their match when several Obama officials, namely Secretary of State Hilary Clinton, US Representative to the United Nations Susan Rice, and National Security Adviser Samantha Power, argued in favour of military intervention. Although they argued that intervention was in American national interests, they did so with the memory of Rwanda and other cases of American indifference to genocide. Hilary Clinton had long advocated that America should do what it could to save civilians.

Susan Rice, who had been an adviser to President Clinton on Africa in the National Security Council during Rwanda, used her first speech as American representative to the United Nations to passionately defend the responsibility to protect. Samantha Power, a strong voice for human rights who had written a Pulitzer Prize winning book, *A Problem from Hell*, which documented the failure of the USA to stop genocide in the twentieth century, used her position in the National Security Council to argue that Libya should not become Obama's Rwanda. Tony Lake was right that if the USA was going to act against possible crimes against humanity then Americans needed to make noise (see Box 12.3), but he probably had not imagined that the noise would be made by his foreign policy advisers in the Oval Office.

Conclusion

This discussion of the idea of a duty to aid highlights how states are seemingly torn in two different directions. There is the primacy of realpolitik and the expectation that the fundamental purpose of the state's foreign policy is to protect its national interest. Not only does anarchy drive states towards this conclusion, so too do most of the powerful bureaucracies in the foreign policy process and most publics. Governments and societies are not inherently heartless. Rather, when forced to choose between interests and ethics, they generally choose interests if the ethical choice imposes a real cost or sacrifice.

Yet a distinguishing features of modern global politics is a thickening of international society. Although it might be far-fetched to posit the existence of an international community, there now exist rules, norms, and principles that bind states and societies together producing an 'internationalization' of ethics. Consequently, there are genuine expectations that states pursue not only their self-interest but also the interests of the international community, and those imply the interests of states *and* people. While there is no expectation that states become committed cosmopolitans, there is the expectation that they will not use sovereignty as an excuse for not engaging in principled action. Although sometimes states do pursue a righteous path, they are also motivated to gain the status, legitimacy, and influence that come from those who comply with the international community's expectations and universal aspirations.

The pull of realpolitik and the push of internationalization mean that foreign policy officials recognize the extent to which they are expected to broaden the ethical purpose of their foreign policy while also safeguarding the national interest. This can have various effects. It can lead to a growing sense of hypocrisy—where states seem to deliver nothing but disappointment and empty promises. Yet the very existence of hypocrisy suggests that there are new international standards that states are expected to respect, especially if they want legitimacy, status, and standing. Another possible consequence is that social movements, activist groups, religious organizations, and advocacy networks will draw from these ethical expectations to push their governments to measure up. While states are unlikely to deliver on their ideals when it potentially undermines the national interest, increasingly the foreign policies of states are expected to pursue a broader purpose, and various domestic organizations provide a continual reminder of what is to be expected. Sometimes the world surprises us by trying to live up to its ideals.

Key points

- A widely held view is that governments have duties to their citizens but not to those outside their lands.

- While sovereignty suggests that the community is bounded by the territorial state, the concepts of humanity and cosmopolitanism suggest transnational connections and affiliations.

- While realist theories acknowledge that there is growing pressure on states to care about the welfare of others, they will find ways to avoid any such commitments, use those expectations to further their primary motives, or follow through only when it is not costly.

- Liberal theories argue that globalization is having various effects that increase the demand for states to become more ethically minded.

- Constructivist theories identify how a growing sense of community and tighter global connections are causing government leaders to rethink the purpose of their foreign policy and imagine themselves as global citizens.

- Instead of intervening to stop the genocide in Rwanda, the UN reduced its presence. The UN Security Council's decision not to intervene was shaped by the fact that states were not willing to contribute troops to any operation.

- The US decision-making process reflected the primacy of national interest and the absence of countervailing factors that might have pressured government officials to reconsider their policies.

- The backlash against the UN's perceived moral bankruptcy shaped Kofi Annan's challenge to the General Assembly to consider a new stance on humanitarian intervention. The Responsibility to Protect Doctrine provided the ethical foundation for a duty to aid but did not address the fact that states still have very little incentive to engage in costly action.

 Questions

1. Is there a growing sense of community?

2. What kinds of duties should we have to distant strangers?

3. Has the purpose of foreign policy changed? If so, how and why?

4. What price do governments pay if they fail to live up to high-minded ideals? What price do they pay if they try to do so but fail? What credit do they get if they help others?

5. Do voters reward politicians when they carry out their ethical obligations to others?

6. Do you think that ethics should play a role in foreign policy?

7. Which domestic actors and government bodies are most likely to argue for an ethical foreign policy?

8. What is the best way to influence the state's foreign policy so that it helps those in need?

 Further reading

Barnett, M. and Weiss, T. (2008), 'Humanitarianism: A History of the Present', in M. Barnett and T. Weiss (eds), *Humanitarianism in Question: Politics, Power, and Ethics* (Ithaca, NY: Cornell University Press).
Provides an introduction to the idea of humanitarian action since its birth in the early nineteenth century.

Hochschild, A. (2006), *Bury the Chains: Prophets and Rebels in the Fight to Free an Empire's Slaves* (New York: Mariner Books).
A highly readable account of the history of British abolitionism.

International Commission on Intervention and State Sovereignty (2001), *A Responsibility to Protect* (Ottawa: International Development Research Centre).

Keck, M. and Sikkink, K. (1998), *Activists Beyond Borders* (Ithaca, NY: Cornell University Press).
A compelling examination of the growing role of international activists in global politics and how they operate internationally and domestically to alter the state's foreign policy purpose.

Power, S. (2002), *A Problem from Hell: America in an Age of Genocide* (New York: Times Books).
A Pulitzer Prize winning examination of the failure of the USA to stop the genocides of the twentieth century, including a very powerful and exhaustive examination of the Clinton administration's indifference to Rwanda.

Wheeler, N. (2000), *Saving Strangers: Humanitarian Intervention in International Society* (New York: Oxford University Press).
A sophisticated exploration of how changes in international society have affected the willingness of states to engage in humanitarian intervention.

Wheeler, N. and Dunne, T. (1998), 'Good International Citizenship: A Third Way for British Foreign Policy', *International Affairs*, 74: 847–70.
A good overview of how foreign policy leaders are attempting to find a new purpose for their foreign policies given changes in international society.

Web links

http://eeas.europa.eu/human_rights/index_en.htm *EU and Human Rights*

http://geo.international.gc.ca/cip-pic/ips/ips-overview2-en.asp *Statement on Canada's Foreign Policy*

 Visit the Online Resource Centre that accompanies this book for more information: **www.oxfordtextbooks.co.uk/orc/smith_foreign/**

Section 3

Foreign Policy Case Studies

Teaching foreign policy cases

STEVEN L. LAMY

Chapter contents

 ## Reader's guide

Case studies have been used in law schools and medical schools across the world for a number of years. Additionally, some of the better public policy schools around the world use case studies in many of their degree programmes. For about twenty years, programmes in international relations in the USA, Canada, Australia, and Russia have been integrating case studies into their Foreign Policy and International Relations courses. This chapter introduces the case method of teaching. This is an active teaching and learning strategy which requires that students and instructors *inhabit* or go inside a decision-making situation and explore complex issues through a rigorous process of questioning that encourages critical analysis, evaluation, and assessment of existing policy and policy processes and creative problem-solving.

Introduction

> Forget about PowerPoint and statistics. To involve people at the deepest level, you need stories. Essentially a story expresses how and why life changes. Stories are how we remember; we tend to forget lists and bullet points. (McKee 2003)

It may seem strange to have a chapter on case teaching and learning in a book with theoretical and analytical chapters and a series of research case studies. This is not surprising if you consider that many universities across the world are moving away from traditional *passive learning* lectures and examinations to more student-centred *active learning* strategies including, but not limited to, problem-based learning and case studies. **Active learning** is primarily about critical thinking and learning by doing. Students engage in higher-order thinking tasks of analysis, synthesis, and the evaluation of competing arguments and policy ideas. One element of the globalization process is the increasing competition for students and faculty from anywhere in the world and the dissemination of successful teaching strategies which might be used to attract these students. In addition, students interested in careers in foreign policy should be looking for academic programmes that offer an opportunity to explore the complexity of real decision-making situations and analyse, evaluate, and then suggest alternatives in critical foreign policy issue areas. Short of internships or other forms of on-the-job training, case studies provide the best teaching method to prepare students for leadership and decision making in foreign policy. As someone who has taught foreign policy for over twenty-five years, I was convinced to try case teaching and other active learning strategies when I read an anonymous author's argument for active learning:

> The concept of learners as receivers of information should be replaced with a view of learners as self-motivated, self-directed problem-solvers and decision makers who are developing the skills necessary for learning, who develop a sense of self-worth and confidence in their ability to participate in a changing global society.

Many of us who teach foreign policy have our students read and discuss the classic text *Thinking in Time* (Neustadt and May 1986). This book includes a number of domestic and foreign policy case studies and the authors address it to 'those who govern or hope to do so'. The goal of their text is to encourage decision makers to use history to frame better questions and to 'provide useful stories for analysis, evaluation and advocacy' of certain policies. Like their cases, the cases in this book focus on significant foreign policy situations and each chapter provides sufficient information for discussions that may provide useful lessons for policy makers and analysts. Students reading these cases have a chance to learn about critical issues in global politics and learn about the importance of critical variables in shaping foreign policy, for example the role of the media and popular opinion (Chapter Nine) and the importance of psychological factors in shaping the choices leaders make (Chapter Seven).

We are more likely to find successful seminars and engaging lecture classes where students are partners in the learning process—engaged in a simultaneous process of learning and teaching. This process is led or facilitated by the instructor, but in a case class the learning experience depends on students teaching each other as they *inhabit the story* as presented in the case study. Students might be asked to apply analytical theories to explain foreign policy behaviour, consider how theoretical traditions (see Section 1) that might define a nation-state's operational code or dominant belief system shape foreign policy choices, learn about the various stages of the foreign policy process, and evaluate foreign policy strategies and suggest alternatives. Case teaching requires a commitment from both instructors and students to be well prepared and to be willing to participate in an open exchange of ideas. Case teaching is active learning at its best. No one is protected from a 'cold call' question in a good case discussion, and 'opting out of the class' for the day is never an option. Similarly, case discussions encourage cooperative preparation, research, and problem-solving, and student-centred learning.

So how is a case class in foreign policy analysis different from a traditional lecture course or a discussion-oriented seminar? In a case class, students inhabit a foreign policy making situation or are placed inside a complex and difficult foreign policy crisis and are asked to practice essential skills for all social scientists—learning to *describe, explain, predict, and prescribe*. A case discussion is interactive, exploratory, and student-centred. Students are engaged with the text by asking questions, suggesting explanations, challenging decision makers, and learning with their colleagues in the course. Faculty members are in the middle of this process—facilitating and structuring the students' contributions rather than lecturing, providing all the answers, and playing the role as the wise sage on the stage.

A professor must be willing to let the discussion move into unanticipated areas, guided more by student interests than by a set of predetermined questions. One student described her experience in a case seminar as a 'voyage into unexplored intellectual territory' with the professor and his/her questions as the travel guide: 'The questions force students to explore every part of the landscape. Soon we [the students] start seeing sections of the territory that our instructor has overlooked. We are not just tourists in a case class. We become the explorers and at times the guide'. Golich (2000: 12–13) states that case studies provide four different opportunities for students. First, they provide detailed descriptions of issues and factors that help shape foreign policy decision making. Second, students are provided with examples of how theory can be used to explain and understand complex international issues. Third, students are put in decision-making situations and are asked to make difficult decisions. Fourth, students receive an opportunity to evaluate decision making and to suggest ways of improving the decision-making process and policy outcomes.

Another advantage of case teaching is that it provides an opportunity for professors and students to receive immediate feedback on how well they are doing as either teacher or learner. After each case discussion, it is common practice for the professor and students both to debrief the active learning experience and to assess the quality of the written case. *How well does the case represent the foreign policy process? How important are the decision-maker's core beliefs in shaping foreign policy priorities? Are foreign policy priorities shaped more by external factors or domestic politics?* Rather than waiting for a midterm or final exams, students can apply concepts and theoretical ideas during the case discussion. Also, the instructor has a chance to assess how effective previous lectures or readings have been in helping students understand foreign policy. Any errors or misunderstandings are easily corrected in the case discussion or the debriefing. The interactive nature of case discussions provides numerous opportunities for student assessment and a chance for professors and students to make adjustments aimed at improving student learning.

What are the differences between a research case and a teaching case?

Students and scholars read and write **research cases** for most of their social science courses. Although useful for discussion in our seminars, these do not work as well in a case teaching environment. What precisely are the differences between a research and **teaching case** study? Laurence Lynn (1999: 15–16) states that the basic difference is that a research case provides the answers and a teaching case requires that students discuss the case and discover the answers in the discussion process. He makes the following distinction.

Research cases may be used to illustrate appropriate, typical, or exemplary decision making: Here is what good work or good management looks like. But research cases are not useful in teaching critical thinking skills because the thinking has already been done, the findings already reached, the conclusions already included in the case. (Lynn 1999: 15–16)

Lynn suggests that a research case is like a lecture with the problem and the answers all neatly presented to the students instead of giving them a chance to explore alternative explanations and make a choice about what action to take in response to a policy problem or controversial issue.

All the cases in this book are written by scholars with expertise in foreign policy. Several of the authors are actually experienced practitioners of foreign policy. Although written primarily for teaching purposes, some of these cases have included what Lynn might call the 'answers'. The authors have provided some explanations, evaluations, and analysis of the behaviour of different actors in their cases. However, each case or narrative still provides some space for student discussion and analysis.

When the analysis is already included, the instructor's range of questioning is limited and the focus is usually on asking students to evaluate the 'answers' and provide alternative views. To illustrate, the instructor might ask if there are other ways of seeing the problems and issues in this case?

Good research cases include the most useful and appropriate tools of analysis, provide evaluations of the policy process and actual policy strategy, and often prescribe alternative approaches. Good teaching cases have **PDQ**: *personalities* fully developed, some *drama* related to a decision situation or international event, and direct *quotes* from these same actors that describe their role in the story. Students and faculty can explore these dramatic stories through a process of focused discussions that encourage interaction among students and result in the analysis, evaluation, and critical review of decision processes and policy outcomes. A good teaching case contains no right answers to questions raised by the issues discussed in the case. The instructor must ask the right kinds of questions that enable the students to *discover* the answers.

Lynn (1999: 117–119) identifies several qualities of an excellent or 'star quality' teaching case.

- There are *no obvious solutions to the problems* faced by the policy makers in the story. In foreign policy teaching cases, this might mean having the students identify the key players and review the positions they advocated and simply ask if there are any options that were not explored.
  - *What were the options suggested by Kennedy's Excomm in the Cuban missile case? Do you think they may have overlooked some options?*
  - *What would you have done?*
- The case includes an in-depth description of each of the *key players*. These could be individuals, organizations or key ministries, departments, or political parties. You need enough information so you might ask the students how their current position is influenced by the belief system of their key leaders or their past practices.
  - *Is there anything in the Canadian Liberal Party's past that would lead to an explanation for their leadership in the landmine campaign?*
  - *If not, is this all about Axworthy's personality and belief system?*
- The case must contain enough information to allow full exploration of the *contending positions* on a critical foreign policy event, decision-making situation, or policy problem.

The history must be correct and the famous journalist's questions must be answered: *who, what, where, and how?*

- *What was the official Chinese position on the Tian'anmen crisis?*
- *Who were the critics inside and outside China and how did they see the crisis? How did they react?*

• There should be enough puzzle in the case for students to practice their critical thinking skills of analysis and evaluation.

- *Why did the major EU powers go for the 'big bang' strategy?*

• The case should provide the necessary background information so the reader understands how the actual policy process works. What are the rules and procedures that determine how policies are made?

- *How did the foreign policy making process in the USA allow the neoconservatives to gain so much influence in the George W. Bush administration?*

Both research and teaching cases may provide the types of knowledge that both scholars and practitioners need to continue their work. **Substantive theory** provides knowledge of major foreign policy issues and standard foreign policy instruments and strategies. **Process theories** suggest ways to structure and manage the policy process and achieve policy goals (George 1993: 20–22). These two types of theory, together with a general understanding of the context or situation, are essential for good decision making in foreign policy. These are easily practised in a focused case discussion that is carefully managed by a prepared instructor. One effective way of combining theory and practice is to link cases with important articles or key texts. A case might be used to test a theory or provide illustrations that confirm the importance of decision-making variables, domestic politics, and the nature of the international system. Other uses of cases are discussed in the next section. (See Box 13.1.)

BOX 13.1 What makes a good teaching case?

Five criteria are needed for a good teaching case.

1. *Pedagogic utility* or what will the case teach? Will it illustrate a theory, show how beliefs shape decision making, or explore a contentious policy debate?

2. Does the case story *provoke conflict?* Case experts contend that controversy is the *essence of a good case discussion*. When there is controversy students must weigh contending positions and make assessments about who may be right or wrong or whether all sides seem to be wrong.

3. A third element is the value of decision-making situations or **decision-forcing** cases.
   A case that forces students to make a decision proves more effective at getting them to take the first-person perspective rather than looking on from the outside.

4. Can the case be *generalized* to other policy situations? Can lessons be learned from this case that applies to other cases?

5. Many experts maintain that good cases are brief. This allows for thorough discussion and helps students keep track of players, their interests, and their influence in the case.

Source: Dorothy Robyn, *What Makes A Good Case*, distributed by The Kennedy School of Government at Harvard.

Retrospective and decision-forcing cases

We generally use two types of case studies in our international relations classes—retrospective cases and decision-forcing cases. **Retrospective cases** present the history of an important issue or event. These cases may tell the story of a crisis, a conflict, policy debates, or policy problems from the perspective of all relevant actors. The story is told in great detail, focusing on the competing interests and tough choices faced by the critical decision makers. These cases usually provide excellent reviews of historical events. The inclusion of interviews and speeches by key players in the story lends itself to thoughtful analysis and evaluation of the decision-making process. In the Allison case (Chapter Fourteen), comments made by key players can help one reach a decision on which hypothesis best explains the Soviet decision to place missiles in Cuba. The speeches and comments made by key neoconservatives help us to understand their eventual impact on the Bush Iraq policy.

An experienced case instructor will develop a teaching plan which includes a variety of questions that 'take the story apart and put it back together again' with the course's teaching goals in mind. As shown in Box 13.2, learning in a case course is all about the questions and resulting conversations among all the class participants.

Decision-forcing cases encourage students to find answers to complex problems. These cases pose a problem with no obvious right answers. For example, a decision-forcing case in

---

BOX 13.2 It is all about the questions

In preparing case discussions, instructors and students should consider asking and anticipating different types of questions to explore the case. These include the following.

1. *Open-ended questions* (a good way to start a case)
   What do you know about the Indian economy? What do you know about the Arab–Israeli conflicts in the past?

2. *Analytical/diagnostic questions*
   What factors/variables might have shaped the Russian decision to support Iran in the dispute with the USA and the EU?

3. *Data-gathering questions*
   Who? What? Where? How?

4. *Comprehension questions*
   Why were the neoconservatives able to gain so much power in the George W. Bush regime?

5. *Evaluation/action questions*
   Do you think the Kennedy administration made the best choice? What would you have done in this situation?

6. *Hypothetical/prediction questions*
   With its access to energy resources, do you think Russia is likely to take a more active role in global politics? Will it seek to regain its superpower status?

7. *Generalizations/lessons questions*
   What could our current leaders learn from this case?

a business course might present a marketing or public relations problem with foreign policy dimensions. Both Hadfield's case on energy and foreign policy (Chapter Twenty-three) and Narlikar's case on India and the WTO (Chapter Eighteen) will work well in a political economy or global business course.

- Consider the challenges faced by the countries in Europe when they watched Russia cut off natural gas to Ukraine?

- What can the EU do to maintain energy supplies and protect their economic security? What are the alternatives to Russian energy supplies?

- Why has India become such an important player in the WTO? What does it mean to be a veto player?

- If you were appointed to a commission to reform the WTO's rules to accommodate new economic powers like India and Brazil, what changes would you make?

Two frequently discussed topics in many foreign policy courses are the issue of humanitarian intervention and the role of NGOs and transnational social movements in shaping foreign policy. Consider how Axworthy's chapter on landmines and human security (Chapter Fifteen) could be linked with a discussion about the humanitarian crisis in Somalia to create a great decision-forcing case. The first part of this case might present the crisis from the perspective of refugees and various UN and NGO relief agencies attempting to feed the people of Somalia who have fled regions controlled by al-Shabab, a militant group linked to al-Qaeda. Leaders of the weak Somali government have argued that as many as 3.5 million people may starve in this country because of the worst drought in sixty years. The second part might present the various proposals to end the suffering and violence in the region and the responses by governments, international and regional organizations, and various global civil society organizations. Here the students would look at the landmine campaign as a model for future humanitarian interventions and 'responsibility to protect' situations. The final section would not provide a solution but would be presented so as to force the students to make a choice.

- Given the facts in the Somalia situation and the past global actions of the landmine, responsibility to protect, and human security movements, what plan of action makes most sense to you? Why do you think this would work?

- How would you sell your programme to the government of Somalia and to various militant groups in the region? How will the UN or the global community implement this programme?

Most retrospective cases can become decision-forcing cases by just stopping the discussion at an appropriate point and asking students what they would have done differently in the same situation. Historical cases, like Dunne's Blair and Iraq case (Chapter Twenty-two), work very nicely as decision-forcing cases.

- After 9/11, what would you have advised Blair to do to become a legitimate pivotal power?

- What normative context could the UK promote to shape its identity and the global agenda?

The case chapters in this book work very well if linked with foreign policy cases available from the Kennedy School of Government at Harvard and the Institute for the Study of Diplomacy at

Georgetown. The instructor can easily design his/her questions so as to focus on key decision points and simply ask the students to evaluate the decision made and to suggest alternatives. Counterfactuals work well here as well.

- What if the USA had sent troops to Rwanda to contain the spread of genocide?
- Even if it had succeeded in this goal, would it have been viewed as an imperial action driven by strategic interests?

The best decision-forcing cases provide the reader with a thorough review of the problem or problems, the contending positions in the policy debate, and possible solutions. Those reading the case should have a clear idea of the costs and benefits of each proposed solution that have been presented by various participants in the policy process.

An important area of foreign policy focuses on *foreign policy and morality*. There are a number of decision-forcing cases that present very interesting and thought-provoking *ethical dilemmas*. These cases recreate the entire policy situation and present the options open to the key players, and then present the *tough choices* or ethical dilemmas faced by the players in the situation. As Dunne's case study (Chapter Twenty-two) on the UK government's response to the Iraq crisis illustrates, there was no straightforward choice facing Prime Minister Blair. The previous policy of containment had failed for complex reasons; moreover, 9/11 had put the West on a heightened sense of alert as to the threats to its security posed by its ideological enemies. In light of the assertive policy response to this situation advocated by the George W. Bush administration, was it feasible for the UK to risk the USA 'going it alone' and therefore jeopardizing the UK's wider security interests as well as encouraging the USA to act unilaterally? At the same time, by standing 'shoulder to shoulder' with the USA, the UK government risked being an accessory to a crime of aggression, thus doing untold damage to its claim to have an ethical dimension to its foreign policy. The UK case illustrates the complex moral ambiguities that exist in the real world of decision making. Leaving Saddam Hussein in power was morally wrong. An aggressive war of regime change was morally wrong. Considering the Blair government's focus on an ethical foreign policy, how do you explain his support for the Bush invasion of Iraq? As Hedley Bull once remarked, in international relations there is seldom one right outcome—often there are only 'terrible choices to be made'.

Case studies are being used in ethics programmes throughout the USA. Students at the US Naval Academy are using cases to explore issues related to just war and ethical decision making in times of war. Several of the war colleges and officer training programmes in the USA are also using case studies to prepare military officers for decision making in difficult cross-cultural situations and where ethical issues must be considered.

Learning about the foreign policy process with cases

Both retrospective and decision-forcing cases can be used to learn about the actual **policy-making process**, to help define key foreign policy problems, to explore critical concepts and strategies, and to illustrate the importance of key historical events which might serve as analogues for future decision makers.

In foreign policy courses, a well-written case will explore all **four phases** of the foreign policy process or a particular part of the process. The first phase is the **articulation or initiation** phase. Here, cases focus on those players who bring the issue to the attention of the policy makers, for example the role of NGOs and other global civil society actors in the landmine case or how the media and national-interest groups in the three major European powers framed and then promoted the 'big bang' strategy for EU enlargement. In a case discussion, this is where the students find out who the *key players* are in policy debates and, in particular, which groups or individuals are pushing a particular foreign policy agenda and why.

In the second phase of the foreign policy process, policy is actually made or formulated. In this **formulation** phase, students learn about which bureaucratic agencies are actually involved in crafting legislation like trade and aid policies and energy policy. In many Western states, such as the USA, Canada, and the UK, the executive branch or government make most foreign policy decisions. Parliaments rarely legislate independently in foreign affairs. Thus, cases show how the various ministers or advisers work out the policy and how they interact with members of the legislative branches. Graham Allison's organizational and bureaucratic models work well in explaining foreign policy decisions in this phase of the policy process.

An under-studied but important area of the policy process is the **implementation** phase or what happens once a foreign policy decision is made. This phase describes the agencies and individuals charged with carrying out the policy. Often, the final outcome is very different from the intent of the legislation. Think of Blair's idea of an ethical foreign policy for the UK. How does support for the Bush invasion of Iraq and the other military actions in Africa and the Middle East square with the emphasis on an ethical foreign policy?

The final policy phase is the **evaluation** phase. Here is where parliamentary committees, special commissions, government ombudsmen, or watchdog groups review the policy process and the policy outcomes and make recommendations to stay the course or change. The Iraq Study Group report (2006) is an example of a comprehensive evaluation of US policy. It includes an assessment of the current situation in Iraq, reviews some alternative courses of action in Iraq, and then proposes a new strategy for the future. Obviously, the media and many NGOs play a significant role in the assessment and evaluation of major foreign policy actions.

Cases may be written about all or one of these phases of policy making. Each phase will reveal the significance of various actors, decision rules, procedures, practices, and habits. There are cases that emphasize the importance of budget processes in shaping strategy and others that demonstrate how voting procedures might be used to either stop or support policy actions. It is hoped that, while participating in case discussions, students will learn who or what matters most in the various phases of the policy process.

Students might read textbooks to learn about the constitutional or formal rules that define how the policy process is intended to work. With case studies, the students are able to go inside the policy process and understand how decision makers think and act and how they interpret, adapt, and apply the policy-making rules and procedures. To illustrate, a case written about US foreign policy during the Iraq War would focus less on the US State Department, which is theoretically the centre of foreign policy activity, and more on the Pentagon and the Office of the Vice-President. Khong's case study (Chapter Sixteen) on the role of the neoconservative advisers who helped to shape the aggressive foreign policy of the George W. Bush administration clearly supports this point and suggests that ideas play an important role in constructing a foreign policy and individuals do matter. Cases consider changing contexts and the importance of individuals in any given situation. Students can read about how powerful personalities might manipulate others and interpret the rules and define the policy problem to serve their interests or to convince others to follow their lead—for example, the role Lloyd Axworthy played in designing and promoting the Ottawa Process or the leadership of Tony Blair in his attempt to give UK legitimacy as a pivotal power and to secure its goals of multilateralism, economic modernization, a special relationship with the USA, and an ethical state. Again, both retrospective and decision-forcing cases can be used to practise skills that are essential for policy making. **Problem definition** and **framing** are two of those critical skills. Many business schools and public administration programmes use short problem cases to help students learn to identify the various parts of public policy problems. In foreign policy, students might be presented with a complex situation, such as toxic waste dumping by global corporations in developing countries, and be asked to identify the problem from the perspective of different players in the case. The immediate goal here is for students to identify the obvious and less than obvious problems that define most of these situations and to understand how *world view*, or the *image of the problem*, and political and economic interests influence how the problem is defined and eventually how it is framed or presented to the public and key decision makers. The case discussion could end there but usually the next part would include a careful assessment of the policy responses being advocated by different players and a frank discussion of attempts to prevent future toxic waste dumping.

Another purpose of case teaching in foreign policy analysis is to use cases to explore critical foreign policy and international relations concepts. Lynn (1999: 109) calls these *concept application* cases, including analytical, theoretical, or process concepts. To illustrate, when talking about negotiations and trying to understand the constraints facing those involved in the bargaining process, an important concept is *two-level games*. Trade cases like the contributions on India and the WTO by Narlikar (Chapter Eighteen) and on energy and foreign policy by Hadfield (Chapter Twenty-three) show how domestic interests influence foreign policy choices and how leaders involved in international negotiations cannot make promises at the domestic level that will not be accepted at the international level, and vice versa. A case discussion provides illustrations or applications of core concepts and theoretical issues in foreign policy.

Finally, cases are often used to present a slice of history from the perspective of key actors or players in the process. Good cases provide enough substantive information about an event for students to be able to ask the right questions about foreign policy behaviour. Neustadt and May (1986) use historical cases as analogues in an effort to improve decision making and to consider the lessons of history in future decision making. Hagan (2000: 39) uses historical cases to outline the logic of how decision makers viewed the issues and to explore how they tried to make certain their views and preferences shaped the final policy outcome. Good foreign policy cases provide an opportunity not only to explore and evaluate competing theories like realism and liberalism, but also to test and compare the value of contending middle-range theories. It is to this analytical use of cases that we now turn.

Testing middle-range theories

Cases provide the opportunity to test theories, to apply middle-range theories to explain foreign policy behaviour. Cases can be used to set up theoretical puzzles such as: How might Vice-President Dick Cheney's belief system influence his choices? Do pro-Israeli interest groups influence US foreign policy toward the Middle East? What impact does the EU have on the foreign policies of its member states? However, cases are not limited to exploring middle-range theories based on *levels of analysis*. Because cases present complex stories, they are particularly useful in exploring some of the issues related to what Christopher Hill (2003) calls the changing context of foreign policy. Cases provide stories in which students can explore the critical **agency** question of who makes foreign policy and the **structure** question of how do the 'multiple environments in which agents operate shape the nature of the choices' available to states (Hill 2003: 26). Case stories provide excellent meeting places for exploring critical analytical questions: Is the state the primary foreign policy actor? Is the distinction between domestic and foreign policy no longer meaningful? Can foreign policy address ethical and normative issues without compromising national interests?

Cases provide students with a chance to see how variables at all four levels of analysis (i.e. individual, domestic, system, and global) interact with each other to shape the decision situation. Students usually dismiss the *layer-cake* image of the levels of analysis and, instead, decide that in real-world situations the interaction of these different factors creates a mixture of variables that offers less precise, but more comprehensive and appropriate, explanations for the behaviour of states. Parsimony is not always the goal when looking to explain the behaviour of states. The cases in this text all present very rich stories in which a variety of factors help to shape the decision processes in both state and non-state actors.

Good case study chapters—such as those which appear in this text—suggest to students that if one wants to explain foreign policy, it is important to understand that individuals matter, and that the domestic politics and economic, social, and cultural structures and attributes of each state contribute to what leaders decide to do. Students learn that states do not all respond to anarchy or bipolarity in the same way. Such an understanding challenges many of the **neorealist** assumptions about foreign policy behaviour. A few case examples might provide some insights here.

In *Keeping the Cold War Cold: Dick Cheney at the Department of Defense*, Mary Schumacher (1990) uses the case to explore the relationship between Congress and the Executive Branch. It presents a detailed account of Cheney's attempt to sell Congress a Defense Department budget without a post Cold War strategy. The politics of the budget process are described in some detail as Cheney confronts members of Congress more concerned with jobs in their districts than US national security interests. The case ends with a debate between Cheney and Senator Nunn about whether the budget shapes strategy or strategy shapes the budget. This case would fit well with Khong's contribution on the neoconservatives and domestic sources of foreign policy that focuses on the role of key ideas and personalities (Chapter Sixteen). Cheney appears again in this case, but so do Kagan, Kristol, and Richard Perle. In addition, both these cases lend themselves to a constructivist analysis that focuses on identity and ideas.

One of the more interesting ways to teach this case is to focus on the importance of **belief systems** in shaping policy debates and eventually policy decisions. Cheney's traditional realist **operational code** and his decision to single-handedly direct the budget process meant that, even with the end of the Soviet Union, the US defence budget was not going to change dramatically. Students often comment that this case illustrates how deeply embedded the Cold War–realist belief system is in US foreign policy circles. This is the belief system and operational code challenged by Axworthy's case about human security and landmines (Chapter Fifteen). His liberal internationalism is a direct challenge to realism and the neoconservative brand of what has been called democratic realism or militarized Wilsonianism.

In *The Dutch in Srebrenica: A Noble Mission Fails* (Lamy 2001), I present a case that focuses on the importance of domestic politics and political culture in shaping foreign policy. The case also explores the foreign policy of a 'like-minded' social democratic state and its attempt to establish its 'niche' in international diplomacy. As a traditional 'middle power', the leaders of The Netherlands were pushed by a powerful grass-roots campaign to end genocide in the former Yugoslavia. As firm believers in the UN, NATO, and other forms of multilateralism, the Dutch were deeply disappointed with the failure of these institutions to effectively coordinate a response to the tragic civil war in Yugoslavia. The 'safe areas' were difficult to protect, but they provided an answer to other political problems such as unwanted refugees and the need to fight wars with few, if any, casualties. This case provides a useful illustration of one of the critical dichotomies in international relations—national interests versus human interests. This case can be used to introduce students to the moral dimensions of foreign policy or to the human security agenda in international relations. Dunne's chapter (Chapter Twenty-two) would work well if taught with this case. He explores Blair's desire to create a niche for Britain as an ethical pivotal power.

All the cases in this text present very rich stories—*thick descriptions* of policy situations which present opportunities to explore a variety of analytical and policy lessons. A brief list of possible teaching themes and analytical lessons for each chapter is available on the Online Resource Centre which accompanies this book: www.oxfordtextbooks. co.uk/orc/smith_foreign/. Each of these lessons is revealed through the process of questioning and discussion that defines a useful active learning case discussion.

Conclusion: why cases work so well

In a case class, the responsibility of learning shifts from the faculty expert to a partnership between students and faculty. Students learn from well-crafted questions asked by the faculty member and from responses by their peers. An experienced faculty 'discussion leader' adjusts the case direction and revises questions based on the substance of the students' comments and questions. Rarely does a good case discussion closely follow a single teaching plan. However, a case class is not just an open-ended discussion. An instructor must devote significant time to mapping the case to focus and structure the discussion so as to encourage students to explore both theoretical and policy issues.

Students appreciate the pace of these classes, the interaction, pressure, and the relevance of the case stories, and the skills practised in good case discussions. A case class is a clear break from the passive lecture, and students seem to like sharing responsibility for the learning process. Students accept the fact that these classes are more demanding and they seem to appreciate that professors also have to devote more time and energy to case preparation. One student described a case course as one with a final exam every week. The student found the class demanding, but stated that the frequency of cases provided an opportunity to improve each week and get almost immediate feedback from the professor. There is little opportunity to relax in a case course that focuses on *preparation, presence, and performance* every session.

Not all faculty and students are comfortable with this approach to teaching and learning. Some critics claim that it is too time-consuming, taking away from valuable lecture time. Another frequently heard objection is that it can result in a shallow discussion of important issues. In an effort to cover the case and maintain a certain discussion pace some issues may be covered inadequately. Also, some colleagues claim that that to encourage participation and promote the process of interactive discussion, case instructors tread too lightly on students who are misinformed or might try to promote a certain point of view. Many of these points have merit and should be considered by all case instructors. But these are concerns that apply to any course and method of instruction. Cases work best when they are sandwiched between lectures and readings so that students see the connections. Again, they work well as part of an illustrated or experiential lecture. Consider how a lecture about economic globalization would be enriched by a case study on outsourcing corporations moving jobs from the USA to Ireland or the story of the unravelling of the recent Doha trade rounds.

As universities look towards technology to provide student-centred learning environments, they may be ignoring a more engaging teaching and learning strategy that requires no hardware or software. With case studies, students are asked only to think critically about why states behave the way that they do.

 ## Key points

- Research cases, like those in this text, provide answers by offering plausible explanations for policy choices. Teaching cases are written so that the instructor can ask questions that help students discover the answers.

- Useful teaching cases have PDQ: *personalities* thoroughly described, *drama* or *conflict* that is described in detail, and *quotations* from key players that tell the story from their perspective.

- Case teaching is a form of *active learning* that requires preparation and participation from students and their instructors. The responsibility for learning is shifted from the instructor to all members of the class.

- Case discussions provide an opportunity for both professors and students to assess how much they know and how well they are teaching and learning every time they discuss a case study.

- Well-written case studies provide students with the opportunity to learn about the policy process from the perspectives of key players in that process.

- Cases provide students with an excellent opportunity both to evaluate policy decisions and to test middle-range theories that might provide explanations for these decisions.

- Participation in a case discussion may be one of the best ways to help students practise a wide range of critical-thinking and problem-solving skills.

 ## Further reading

Lynn, L. (1999), *Teaching and Learning with Cases* (Chappaqua, NY: Seven Bridges Press–Chatham House).
A very thoughtful discussion of teaching and writing cases presented by a master case teacher. It also includes a broad discussion of the purposes of active learning and case- and problem-based learning.

Neustadt, R. and May, E.R. (1986), *Thinking in Time: The Uses of History for Decision-Makers* (New York: Free Press).

 Visit the Online Resource Centre that accompanies this book for more information:
www.oxfordtextbooks.co.uk/orc/smith_foreign

The Cuban Missile Crisis

GRAHAM ALLISON

Chapter contents

 Reader's guide

Lessons drawn from the Cuban Missile Crisis, or interpretations of it, continue to shape the thinking of American leaders, and others, about the risks of nuclear war, crisis confrontation, and foreign policy. The opening of extensive records, including tape recordings of most White House meetings and notes from previously secret files of many of the Soviet deliberations, makes it possible to reconstruct the calculations of both nations in addressing the three central questions: Why did the Soviet Union attempt to place offensive missiles in Cuba? Why did the USA choose to respond to the Soviet missile emplacement with a blockade of Cuba? Why did the Soviet Union decide to withdraw the missiles? These questions are tackled in the first part of the chapter. In the conceptual epilogue, the chapter provides readers with a précis of the three decision-making models first used in 1971 to examine the Cuban Missile Crisis in greater detail. Foreign policy students are urged to think critically about the predictability of foreign policy behaviour from rational, organizational, and governmental perspectives, and to apply their ideas to both the Cuban Missile Crisis and a host of other foreign policy dilemmas.[1]

Introduction

The Cuban Missile Crisis stands as a seminal event.[2] History offers no parallel to those thirteen days of October 1962, when the USA and the Soviet Union paused at the nuclear precipice. Never before had there been such a high probability that so many lives would end suddenly. Had war come, it could have meant the death of 100 million Americans and more than 100 million Russians, and millions of Europeans as well. Other catastrophes and inhumanities of history would have faded into insignificance. Given the odds of disaster—which President Kennedy estimated as 'between one out of three and even'—our escape is staggering (Steel 1969: 22).

In retrospect, this crisis proved a major watershed in the Cold War. For thirteen days, the USA and the Soviet Union stood 'eyeball to eyeball', each with the power of mutual destruction in hand. Having peered over the edge of the nuclear precipice, both nations edged backwards towards détente. Never again was the risk of war between them as great as it was during the last two weeks of October 1962. Thus an understanding of this crisis is essential for every serious student of foreign affairs.

Operation Anadyr

American sources and newly available material from the Soviet Union now permit us to reconstruct the Soviet arms build-up that culminated in the conversion of Cuba into a major strategic missile base.[3]

The Soviet government first gave arms to Cuba in the autumn of 1959. The Soviets and Cubans negotiated the next phase of military assistance in early 1962. The Soviet Presidium approved Cuban requests for additional weapons in April 1962, and the Soviets resumed arms shipments at a markedly increased pace in late July. By 1 September, Soviet arms in Cuba included surface-to-air missiles, coastal defence Sopka cruise missiles, patrol boats armed with anti-ship missiles, and more than 5000 Soviet technicians and military personnel.

The first Soviet nuclear ballistic missiles reached Cuban soil on 8 September. The **medium range ballistic missiles** (MRBMs) were secretly transported to Cuba beneath the decks of Soviet ships.[4] Additional MRBMs, missile trailers, fuelling trucks, special radar vans, missile erectors, and nuclear warhead storage bunkers arrived and were rushed to construction sites. Similar equipment to set up longer-range **intermediate range ballistic missiles** (IRBMs) soon followed. Unknown to the USA, Cuba received nuclear warheads for the MRBMs on 4 October, along with dozens of nuclear warheads for the Sopka coastal defence cruise missiles, six nuclear bombs for IL-28 medium jet bombers, and twelve nuclear warheads for short-range tactical nuclear rockets. (See Figure 14.1.)

The final decision to put missiles in Cuba was made in the Soviet Presidium, but the details of the operation—that is, the path from the general decision to the actual appearance of operational missiles in Cuba—were delegated to appropriate Soviet organizations. Standard Soviet operations, particularly where nuclear weapons were involved, imposed secrecy beyond anything approached in the American government. Secrecy deprived each organization of information about other organizations and made it impossible to keep the whole operation in view. Forced to take a narrower perspective, each organization tended to 'do what it knows how to'.

The clandestine shipping, unloading, and delivery of the missiles to the construction sites was a major organizational success, eluding all methods of detection until missiles were deployed in the field. This part of **Operation Anadyr** was planned by a specially created subunit of the operations branch of the Soviet General Staff, working closely with Soviet intelligence agencies. But once the weapons and equipment arrived in Cuba, the Group of Soviet Forces in Cuba took over.

At the sites, each team did what it knew how to—emplace missiles—literally according to the book. They had never installed MRBMs or IRBMs outside the Soviet Union before Cuba. A serious effort to camouflage the operation was possible. However, the units constructing the missiles had no routine for camouflage, never having camouflaged construction activity

Figure 14.1 Missile range map

Source: Reprinted by permission of the John F. Kennedy Presidential Library, Boston, MA.

in the Soviet Union. Moreover, the command had two competing goals: to be ready for action and to conceal its activity. The field organization had to choose which had priority. Camouflage would have created extreme discomfort for people working under the netting or plastic covers in the tropical heat. Working stealthily at night would have slowed the pace of construction and put the work even further behind schedule. An intelligence agency would probably have made a different choice, but a field organization in the business of deploying missiles could be expected to focus first on completion of preparation for possible combat, particularly when that directive came with a deadline.

When Gribkov, one of the Soviet staff planners, arrived in Cuba on 18 October to inspect the work, General Issa Pliyev, the Group of Forces commander, had some bad news: the missiles had very probably been discovered by the Americans. A U-2 had flown over the areas where the missiles were deployed on 14 October. Soviet air defences had observed the overflights but had taken no action. There had been more overflights on 15 and 17 October, which presumably were observed too.

Why were the U-2 flights not fired upon? Surface-to-air missiles (SAMs) were operational. But, Gribkov recalled, 'Moscow had sent them to Cuba to defend against air attack, not actual espionage. With no invasion thought imminent, the SAM commanders were not even allowed to use their radars to track your spy planes overhead' (Gribkov and Smith 1994: 58). Gribkov apparently had no inkling of Khrushchev's reported desire to use the SAMs against prying U-2s, despite the fact that Khrushchev himself had made sure that SAMs would go to Cuba before the missiles, to be ready to protect Cuban skies against overflying U-2s (Fursenko and Naftali 1997: 192–4). Pliyev was presumably equally ignorant. Standing orders to air defence units told them to fire only if attacked, perhaps to avoid provoking any incident or unwanted attention before everything was ready. The standing orders were undoubtedly written by someone who was not present when Khrushchev expressed his concerns, so the Soviet leader's intentions never entered the operational directives to the relevant implementing organizations.

There is evidence that, on 14 October, Pliyev suspected that the missiles had been discovered. On 18 October, Gribkov was told about this suspicion. But there is no evidence that the 'Soviet government' learned of these suspicions. Soviet Foreign Minister Andrei Gromyko met with Kennedy on 18 October and saw no sign that the Americans knew what was going on, confidently predicting that 'a USA military adventure against Cuba is almost impossible to imagine' (Gromyko 1995: 66–7). The Kremlin did not start seriously worrying about the American discovery of the missiles until 22 October, when they heard the news bulletins advertising Kennedy's forthcoming television address to the nation (Fursenko and Naftali 1997: 237–38, 242).

On 22 October, worried that Kennedy was about to announce an invasion of Cuba, the Presidium actually drafted an instruction authorizing Pliyev to use tactical nuclear weapons to repel it. Only after Soviet Defence Minister Malinovsky warned that the Americans might intercept the message and therefore use nuclear weapons first did the Kremlin step back to more conservative instructions directing Pliyev not to use the nuclear weapons without authorization from Moscow (Fursenko and Naftali 1997: 241–3; Kramer 1996–1997: 348–9).

Yet until the message from Moscow arrived, 'the tactical weapons were Pliyev's to deploy and, if he were cut off from contact with Moscow, to use as a last resort' (Gribkov and Smith 1994: 63). On 26 October, acting on his own authority, Pliyev ordered the movement of a number of nuclear warheads closer to the missiles that would carry them. Pliyev then reported his move to his superiors in Moscow. Unsettled, they sharply reminded him that he must wait for central authorization before using any weapons. But there were no technical safeguards to physically prevent nuclear use by field units. They relied instead on Pliyev's obedience.

The Americans did not even know that Soviet forces in Cuba had tactical nuclear weapons until late in the crisis. The American 'planners saw no sense in the island's defenders employing battlefield atomic weapons and thereby risking escalation' (Gribkov and Smith 1994: 141). Yet on 22 October, Khrushchev contemplated announcing not only that tactical nuclear weapons were lodged in Cuba, but that they were being turned over to Castro and the Cubans who would declare their readiness to use them against attack (Gribkov and Smith 1994: 28). Fortunately, Khrushchev reconsidered.

Why missiles in: four hypotheses

When, on 15–16 October, Kennedy and his advisers were informed that the USA had discovered Soviet **ballistic missiles** in Cuba, the President and most of his advisers were shocked. What Kennedy called 'this secret, swift, and extraordinary build-up of communist missiles' posed troubling questions indeed. Why did the Soviet Union undertake such a reckless move? What Soviet objective could justify a course of action with such a high probability of nuclear confrontation? Kennedy's senior advisers considered these questions when they convened at 11:50 a.m. on Tuesday, 16 October. Their discussion focused on four principal hypotheses.

Hypothesis one: Cuban defence

An analyst who knew nothing about the Soviet Union, except that it was a powerful country and that one of its important allies, Cuba, was at risk of attack by a large threatening neighbour, might infer that the powerful country would come to the aid of its weak friend. One of the first memos the CIA produced after the discovery of missiles in Cuba explained: 'The Soviet leaders' decision to deploy ballistic missiles to Cuba testifies to their determination to deter any active US intervention to weaken or overthrow the Castro regime, which they apparently regard as likely and imminent' (McAuliffe 1992: 141). Although the 1961 effort to invade Cuba with a force of CIA-trained Cuban exiles had failed disastrously, the Soviet Union had substantial reason to believe that the USA might return to do the job right.

Certainly Khrushchev and other Soviet officials defended the deployment of Soviet arms to Cuba in 1962 in just these terms, arguing that Soviet aid to Cuba was 'exclusively designed to improve Cuba's defensive capacity' (Larson 1986: 72). In support of the Cuban defence hypothesis, it is clear that Cuba was surely on Khrushchev's mind.[5] Indeed, for the Soviet General Staff, Khrushchev's plan 'was like a roll of thunder in a clear sky' (Gribkov and Smith 1994: 13). The only options they had examined relied on conventional arms alone.

Although persuasive, attempts to explain Soviet nuclear missiles in Cuba with the Cuban defence hypothesis will not withstand careful examination. If **deterrence**, meaning the prevention of a major attack, had been the objective, the presence of a sizeable contingent of Soviet troops would have been a better solution. If for some reason the Soviets believed that a nuclear deterrent was necessary, tactical nuclear weapons (i.e. weapons with a range of less than 100 miles) were available that could have been emplaced more quickly, at less cost, and with considerably less likelihood of being discovered before they were ready. In the end, Castro did accept longer-range missiles, but he worried that the deployment could provoke an intense crisis. So a final problem with the Cuban defence hypothesis is that the move actually made Cuba's position more, not less, perilous.

Hypothesis two: Cold War politics

The defining feature of the **Cold War** was the global competition between American and Soviet values and interests. Whenever one side lost, the other gained—and was seen to do so by others around the world. A rival might seize the opportunity to display the extent of its global power, especially so near its enemy's shores.

President Kennedy fell back on just this hypothesis of global politics when he responded to Defense Secretary Robert McNamara's initial assessment that the Soviet missiles in Cuba had little military significance. 'Last month,' Kennedy speculated, 'I said we weren't going to [allow it]. Last month I should have said that we don't care. But when we said we're *not* going to, and then they go ahead and do it, and then we do nothing, then I would think that our risks increase . . . After all, this is a political struggle as much as military' (May and Zelikow 1997: 92).

Intelligence experts around the government joined a few days later, estimating that '[a] major Soviet objective in their military buildup in Cuba is to demonstrate that the world balance of forces has shifted so far in their favor that the U.S. can no longer prevent the advance of Soviet **offensive power** even into its own hemisphere' (US Intelligence Board 1962: 214). If the USA accepted the build-up, it would lose the confidence of its allies in Latin America and around the world. Secretary of State Dean Rusk concluded that 'the hard line boys have moved into the ascendancy. So one of the things that we have to be concerned about is not just the missiles, but the entire development of Soviet policy as it affects our situation around the globe' (May and Zelikow 1997: 255).

Kennedy felt such global stakes keenly. On 21 October, Arthur Schlesinger Jr asked Kennedy why the Soviets had put missiles in Cuba. Kennedy gave three reasons. First, the Soviet Union would demonstrate that it was capable of bold action in support of a communist revolution, impressing China and healing a split between Moscow and Beijing that had widened since 1959. Second, the Soviets would radically redefine the context of the Berlin

The Cuban leader Fidel Castro giving a speech.

Source: © PA photos.

problem. Third, the Soviet Union would deal the USA a tremendous political blow (Schlesinger 1965: 742).

Despite the persuasiveness of Cold War arguments, this hypothesis ignores five key aspects of the situation. First, as Robert McNamara wondered publicly on several occasions, why did the Soviet Union need to probe the firmness of American intentions after the strong American stand on Berlin in 1961? Second, the size and character of the Soviet deployment went well beyond a mere political probe. To challenge American intentions and firmness, even a few MRBMs threatening the entire southeastern USA (including Washington) should suffice. What could the IRBMs or the planned deployment of submarine-launched ballistic missiles possibly add to the achievement of this objective? Third, the deployment of MRBMs and IRBMs, plus plans for a nuclear submarine base, jeopardized the essential requirement for a successful move on the Cold War chessboard, namely that it be a *fait accompli*. A small tailored nuclear deployment that became operational *before* it was discovered could have given the Soviet Union a Cuban enclave no less defensible than the Western enclave in Berlin. But the specific features of the deployment undermined this objective.

Fourth, the question of timing: Why launch such a provocative probe of American intentions at that moment, in the autumn of 1962? Was there some particular reason to try and humble the Americans at that particular time? What tangible gains could justify the risks? This remains unclear. Finally, why choose Cuba as the location of the probe? At no point on the globe outside the continental USA were the Soviets so militarily disadvantaged *vis-à-vis* the USA as in the Caribbean. If the Soviet probe provoked a forceful American riposte, a vivid Soviet defeat would make the whole venture counterproductive.

Hypothesis three: missile power

At the first meeting with his advisers, on the morning of 16 October, President Kennedy speculated that the **strategic balance of power** motivated the Soviet Union. 'Must be some major reason for the Russians to set this up,' he mused. 'Must be that they're not satisfied with their ICBMs.' Maxwell Taylor, chairman of the Joint Chiefs of Staff, thought that Kennedy's guess was on target (May and Zelikow 1997: 59).

Objectively, the Soviet Union faced a serious and widening 'window of vulnerability'.[6] In 1962 the Soviet government found itself with only twenty **intercontinental ballistic missiles** (ICBMs) capable of launching nuclear weapons that could reach American territory from bases inside the Soviet Union. The Soviets also had well-founded doubts about the technical reliability and accuracy of these missiles. In addition, Soviet strategic forces included 200 long-range bombers and only six submarines with **submarine-launched ballistic missiles** (SLBMs). The American strategic nuclear arsenal in 1962 was substantially more robust, consisting of at least 180 ICBMs, twelve Polaris submarines (each carrying twelve missiles), and 630 strategic bombers stationed in the USA, Europe, and Asia, from which they could attack Soviet targets from all angles. This arsenal was rapidly being expanded by the Kennedy administration.

A clear-eyed strategic analyst could quite reasonably conclude that in 1962 the Soviet Union had a problem. Moving their existing nuclear weapons to locations from which they could reach American targets was one option. As one of the staff planners, General Gribkov, later wrote, 'In one stroke he [Khrushchev] could readdress the imbalance in strategic nuclear forces' (Gribkov and Smith 1994: 13). Soviet missiles placed in Cuba would also outflank America's existing systems for early warning which were oriented towards the Arctic and other flight routes from the USSR.

There are two major objections to the missile power hypothesis. First, why did Khrushchev feel such extraordinary urgency to redress the strategic balance, rather than wait to develop his ICBM force into something more formidable? Second, why was Khrushchev willing to run such extraordinary risks to solve this problem? Director of Central Intelligence John McCone argued that Khrushchev had some great political prize in mind elsewhere in the world, and that he would use the missiles in Cuba in order to win it (McAuliffe 1992: 95).

Hypothesis four: Berlin—win, trade, or trap

President Kennedy was not satisfied with the missile power hypothesis, and wondered aloud to his advisers: 'If it doesn't increase very much their strategic strength, why is it—can any Russian expert tell us—why they . . . ?' (May and Zelikow 1997: 106). For Kennedy, a more plausible answer dawned on him shortly afterward. It must be Berlin. Khrushchev would use the missiles to solve the Berlin problem—on his terms. As a prelude to a confrontation over Berlin, Khrushchev's manoeuvre made sense. If the Americans did nothing, Khrushchev would force the West out of Berlin, confident that the missiles in Cuba would deter the Americans from starting a war. If the Americans tried to bargain, the terms would be a trade of Cuba and Berlin. Since Berlin was immeasurably more important than Cuba, that trade would also be a win for Khrushchev. If the Americans blockaded or attacked Cuba, Khrushchev could then use this as the excuse for an equivalent blockade or attack on Berlin. 'So that whatever we do in regard to Cuba,' Kennedy said, 'it gives him the chance to do the same with regard to Berlin' (May and Zelikow 1997: 256). Worse yet, Kennedy thought, America's European allies would then blame the loss of Berlin on the USA, since they would not understand why America felt the need to attack Cuba. The Alliance would be split and again Moscow would be the winner. In bargaining terms, Kennedy admired Khrushchev's move. 'The advantage is, from Khrushchev's point of view, he takes a great chance but there are quite some rewards to it' (May and Zelikow 1997: 256).[7]

The four hypotheses reviewed

Against this backdrop, the missile power and Berlin hypotheses offer the most satisfactory explanation of the thinking behind the Soviet move to send nuclear missiles to Cuba. Khrushchev would gain a quick and relatively cheap boost to Soviet missile power, and the Berlin crisis might be pressed to a successful conclusion. Foreign policy triumph in hand, Khrushchev could return to his hopes for Soviet domestic renewal, now better able to move resources from defence and heavy industry to the needs of his people. 'The Cuban missile venture,' Richter concludes, 'offered him the prospect, however slim, that he could emerge from this situation and salvage his already declining authority' (Richter 1994: 150).

But it must be acknowledged that the missile power and Berlin hypotheses, as well as the others considered above, fail to account for many other features of what the Soviets actually did. First, each of the four hypotheses assumes that the Soviet decision to emplace missiles necessarily led to a plan for *implementing* that decision, by installing air defences first to protect the bases and deter photographic reconnaissance, and then sending in nuclear weapons. But Soviet actions seemed inconsistent with this plan. It appeared to the Americans that the MRBMs were installed *before* the cover of SAMs was in place. Kennedy's adviser and speechwriter, Theodore Sorensen, expressed forcefully the bewilderment of the White House over this fact: 'Why the Soviets failed to coordinate this timing is still inexplicable' (Sorensen 1965: 673). We now know that in fact the Soviet Union did install the air defence cover on time, before the missiles were put in place, in order to shield the missiles from being discovered. Why, then, did the Soviet forces in Cuba permit the U-2 to fly over Cuba and spot the missiles?

Khrushchev's grand plan for unveiling his *fait accompli* presents a second difficulty. He planned to visit the USA and announce the true situation in the second half of November. Presumably by then the installation of the missiles would be complete. But even on the round-the-clock construction schedule adopted after the US announcement that the missiles had been discovered, only the MRBMs would be in place. The IRBM complexes would not have achieved operational readiness until December (McAuliffe 1992: 237). This further failure of coordination is difficult to understand.

A third puzzle arises over the Soviet omission of camouflage at the missile sites. At the White House meeting on the evening of 16 October, the intelligence briefer explained that they could spot the launchers, in part because 'they have a four-in-line deployment pattern . . . which is identical . . . representative of the deployments that we note in the Soviet Union for similar missiles' (Carter, in May and Zelikow 1997: 79). But a Soviet desire to be found out hardly squares with the extensive and effective camouflage and deception that shielded the transport of the missiles to Cuba and then from the docks to the sites.

Finally, why did the Soviet Union persist in the face of Kennedy's repeated warnings? Khrushchev did not ask his ambassador in Washington or any other known experts on the USA for a considered analysis of their judgement. Foreign Minister Gromyko later wrote that he had warned Khrushchev privately that 'putting our missiles in Cuba would cause a political explosion in the USA' (Gromyko 1989). According to Gromyko's account, Khrushchev was simply unmoved by this advice. Ambassador Dobrynin later complained that Khrushchev 'grossly misunderstood the psychology of his opponents. Had he asked the embassy beforehand, we could have predicted the violent American reaction to his adventure once it became known. It is worth noting that Castro understood this . . . But Khrushchev wanted to spring a surprise on Washington; it was he who got the surprise in the end when his secret plan was uncovered' (Dobrynin 1995: 79–80).

Why American blockade

According to Robert Kennedy, 'the fourteen people involved were very significant—bright, able, dedicated people, all of whom had the greatest affection for the US . . . If six of them had been President of the US, I think that the world might have been blown up' (Steel 1969: 22). The men advising President Kennedy differed sharply about what should be done. Given the difficulty of the challenges they confronted and the differences in their jobs and backgrounds, who should expect otherwise?

After discovering ballistic missiles in Cuba, the American government organized its crisis decision making around an informally selected inner circle of advisers who met either at the White House or at the State Department from 16 to 19 October. This process assumed a more regular formal quality in successive meetings of the National Security Council on 20, 21, and 22 October. The decision makers then narrowed again to an inner circle designed as the Executive Committee of the National Security Council, also known as the 'ExComm'. They met at the White House for the duration of the crisis. Because of the centrality of this crisis to the presidency of John F. Kennedy, evidence about what members of the US government were seeing, doing, and even thinking is much greater than for most events. With the publication of the secret tapes and most of the classified documents of the crisis, one can follow the perceptions and preferences of individual players with more confidence than usual. Unfortunately, even with the new evidence about the Soviet side of the equation, the Soviet decision-making process remains more opaque.

On Monday, 15 October, just as he finished delivering a speech to the National Press Club addressing the Soviet activity in Cuba and arguing that the build-up was 'basically defensive in character', Assistant Secretary of State Edwin Martin received a phone call. The caller informed Martin that offensive missiles had been discovered in Cuba. The U-2 photographs presented conclusive evidence of Soviet nuclear missiles in Cuba.

Kennedy was determined to stand fast. To fail to act forcibly could produce a number of undesirable outcomes. First, it would undermine the confidence of the members of his administration, especially those who in previous weeks had so firmly defended his policy towards Cuba. Second, it would convince the rest of the government that the administration had no leader, encouraging others to challenge his policies and destroying his reputation in Congress. Weakness in the face of the crisis would cut the ground from under fellow Democrats who were standing for re-election on Kennedy's Cuban policy. Failing to act forcibly would also drive the public to doubt Kennedy's word and his will, deepen dismay over the Bay of Pigs, and shake Kennedy's confidence in his own leadership. The entire circle of pressures to which Kennedy as a president had to be responsive pushed him in a single direction—vigorous action.

The Joint Chiefs of Staff (JCS) wanted an invasion to eliminate this threat. But their new chairman, Maxwell Taylor, wanted to gather more intelligence, pull it all together in the next few days while no one knew the missiles had been discovered, and then take the missiles, the bombers and MiG-21 aircraft, and the SAMs 'right out with one hard crack'. He estimated that it would take about five days to do the complete job from the air (May and Zelikow 1997: 342).

For Dean Rusk, the Secretary of State, the initial issues were diplomatic. His main suggestion was to try to get Castro himself to push the Soviets out. Rusk wanted to warn the Cuban leader that the Soviets were putting his regime in mortal danger and would in the end happily sell him out for a victory in Berlin. Kennedy thought that the proposal had no prospect, and no one outside the State Department spoke up for it.

For Secretary of Defense McNamara, the missiles were principally a political problem. In his view, the overall nuclear balance would not be significantly affected by the Soviet deployment. Therefore, at the start, McNamara was sceptical about the need for military action. He argued that no US air strike could be considered if the Soviet missiles in Cuba were operational and therefore could be launched in a retaliatory strike against the USA. McNamara raised the idea of *blockading* future weapons shipments to Cuba, but his suggestion did nothing about the missiles already deployed there except to warn the Soviets not to use them.

'Now, this alternative doesn't seem to be a very acceptable one,' he allowed. 'But wait until you work on the others' (May and Zelikow 1997: 113–14).

McGeorge Bundy, the National Security Adviser, was uncharacteristically reticent. Two days later, on 18 October, he advocated taking no action, fearing that the Soviets would retaliate in kind against Berlin. Then the next day, after agonizing further over the question, Bundy changed his mind again and supported an air strike against the missiles.

By 19 October, other positions had hardened. UN ambassador Adlai Stevenson joined McNamara in the ranks of the sceptics. McCone favoured Taylor's plan for an air strike. New overflights revealed for the first time that IRBMs had also been shipped to Cuba. This news tipped Taylor to join his JCS colleagues in support of an invasion to follow up the air strikes. Former Secretary of State Dean Acheson supported an air strike, but called for a narrow strike against the missile sites only, ignoring the Soviet bombers, fighter-bombers, and anti-aircraft units. Robert Kennedy and Rusk objected that any American surprise attack would be immoral, comparing it to Pearl Harbor.

But the most telling argument for President Kennedy, which he repeated in days to come, was the one he outlined for his subordinates on 18 October. An attack on Cuba would cause a retaliatory attack on Berlin which in return would instantly present Kennedy with no meaningful military option but nuclear retaliation. 'So' he said, musing aloud, 'the question really is what action we take which lessens the chances of a nuclear exchange, which obviously is the prime failure' (May and Zelikow 1997: 149, 145).

It is clear from Kennedy's taped recapitulation of a White House meeting on the night of 18 October and from the arguments he made to the unconvinced Joint Chiefs of Staff the next morning that the President was turning away from a surprise strike on the missiles (May and Zelikow 1997:171–2, 175–87). This left the intermediate option of the blockade originally broached by McNamara.

On the morning of 19 October President Kennedy met with the Joint Chiefs of Staff and found them adamant in support of an immediate air attack against Cuba that would retain the military advantages of surprise. Air Force chief of staff Curtis LeMay, confident of his own political base of support on Capitol Hill, was boldest in confronting the President. 'This blockade and political action, I see leading into war. I don't see any other solution. It will lead right into war. This is almost as bad as the appeasement at Munich' (May and Zelikow 1997: 178). Opinion was still generally divided between a blockade and an immediate air strike, with McNamara emerging as the chief advocate of a blockade–negotiate option. President Kennedy returned for a decisive White House meeting on 20 October, where McNamara presented the blockade–negotiate approach. Following the blockade, he said, the USA would negotiate for the removal of missiles from Turkey and Italy and talk about closing the US base at **Guantanamo** in Cuba. McNamara opposed an ultimatum demanding the removal of the missiles, saying it was too risky (US Department of State 1996: 126–36). Taylor, supported by Bundy, presented the case for an air strike to begin two days later on Monday, 22 October. Robert Kennedy agreed with Taylor that the present moment was the last chance to destroy Castro and the Soviet missiles in Cuba. Sorensen, who was sympathetic to the blockade–negotiation approach, disagreed.

Robert Kennedy then argued for a 'combination of the blockade route and the air strike route'. The blockade would be coupled with an ultimatum demanding removal of the missiles. If the Russians did not comply, the USA would proceed with an air strike. That, he explained, would get away from the Pearl Harbor surprise attack problem. Dillon and McCone then supported this option. Dillon suggested a 72-hour interval between the demand and action; McCone agreed (US Department of State 1996: 126–36). Rusk suggested a fourth option of a blockade. Instead of an ultimatum or an offer to trade US assets, the objective could simply be to freeze the situation. The Soviet missile installations in Cuba would be monitored by UN observation teams.

President Kennedy first sharply ruled out the blockade–negotiation variant, feeling that such action would convey to the world that the USA had been frightened into abandoning its positions. He then ruled in favour of the blockade–ultimatum option, urging that any air strike be limited only to the missile sites. The strike was to be ready by 23 October. The group also agreed that the blockade would be narrowly focused on Soviet arms deliveries, not on all shipments of vital supplies such as oil. Kennedy overruled suggestions that the blockade should be extended to the necessities of life in Cuba, reasoning that the Soviets might be less likely to reciprocate with an identical blockade of Berlin and the danger of an escalation to war would be reduced (May and Zelikow 1997: 237). The basic decision was made.

In the speech draft the next day, Kennedy sided further with the blockade–ultimatum faction. He removed an invitation to Khrushchev to come to a summit meeting to talk about the crisis. First they would see how Khrushchev dealt with the missiles in Cuba. We 'should be clear that we would accept nothing less than the ending of the missile capacity now in Cuba, no reinforcement of that capacity, and no further construction of missile sites' (US Department of State 1996: 126–36). The proposed blockade had several advantages. First, it was a middle course between inaction and attack—aggressive enough to communicate firmness of intention, but not as precipitous as a strike. Indeed, no possible military confrontation could be more acceptable to the USA than a naval engagement in the Caribbean. A naval blockade on the American doorstep appeared invincible. By flexing its conventional muscles, a blockade also permitted the USA to exploit the threat of subsequent non-nuclear steps in which the it would enjoy significant local superiority. Lastly, a blockade placed on Khrushchev the burden of choice for the next step. He could avoid a direct military clash simply by keeping his ships away.

At 7 p.m. on 22 October 1962, President Kennedy delivered the major foreign policy address of his career. Disclosing the American discovery of the presence of Soviet strategic missiles in Cuba, the President declared a 'strict quarantine on all offensive military equipment under shipment to Cuba' and demanded that 'Chairman Khrushchev halt and eliminate this clandestine, reckless, and provocative threat to world peace' (Larson 1962: 59–63). (See Box 14.1.)

The blockade began on the morning of 24 October, 500 miles off the coast of Cuba. The first Soviet ships carrying weapons would pass that line during the night of 23–24 October and, under this plan, they would be intercepted at dawn so that the American navy could conduct operations in daylight. The first Soviet ships approached the quarantine line on Wednesday 24 October, but halted and turned around just before challenging it.

Why Soviet withdrawal of missiles from Cuba

President Kennedy's announcement of the blockade emphasized that it was an *initial* step in a series of moves that threatened air strikes or invasion. No attempt was made to disguise the massive build-up of more than 200,000 invasion troops in Florida. Hundreds of US tactical fighters moved to airports within easy striking distance of targets in Cuba. On 27 October,

President Kennedy signs the Proclamation for the Interdiction of the Delivery of Offensive Weapons to Cuba.

Source: Photograph by Abbie Rowe in the John F. Kennedy Presidential Library and Museum, Boston, MA.

BOX 14.1 Excerpt from JFK's address to the American people, 22 October 1962

My fellow citizens, let no one doubt that this is a difficult and dangerous effort on which we have set out. No one can foresee precisely what course it will take or what costs or casualties will be incurred. Many months of sacrifice and self-discipline lie ahead—months in which both our patience and our will will be tested, months in which many threats and denunciations will keep us aware of our dangers. But the greatest danger of all would be to do nothing.

 The path we have chosen for the present is full of hazards, as all paths are; but it is the one most consistent with our character and courage as a nation and our commitments around the world. The cost of freedom is always high—but Americans have always paid it. And one path we shall never choose, and that is the path of surrender or submission.

Source: R.F. Kennedy (1969), *Thirteen Days: A Memoir of the Cuban Missile Crisis* (New York: W.W. Norton), paragraphs 29 and 30, p. 171.

McNamara called twenty-four troop-carrier squadrons of the Air Force Reserve to active duty—approximately 14,000 men.

 After hearing Kennedy's plans to address the American people, the Kremlin plunged into its own crisis deliberations. Unlike Kennedy, Khrushchev continued to rely upon his normal foreign policy process, consulting a small group of Presidium members aided by the defence and foreign ministers and the leading international expert from the Communist Party's Central Committee staff. When a formal decision was needed, Khrushchev convened the full Presidium.

Deliberations began with news of the impending Kennedy speech. Not yet knowing what Kennedy would say, Khrushchev feared the worst, namely that the Americans would simply attack Cuba. Therefore Kennedy's blockade announcement was greeted not with fear, but with relief by the Soviet leadership which considered it a weaker response that left room for political manoeuvre. The next day they issued a flat unyielding response to Kennedy's demands. Khrushchev's message to Kennedy on 24 October was defiant.

By the morning of 25 October, the Soviet leadership had received a tough terse reply to Khrushchev's defiant pronouncement of the previous day. Kennedy wrote, 'It was not I who issued the first challenge in this case'. Kennedy underscored his 'hope that your government will take the necessary action to permit a restoration of the earlier situation' (May and Zelikow 1997: 421). Khrushchev reconvened the Presidium. He switched to a tone of conciliation. He was ready, he said, to 'dismantle the missiles to make Cuba into a zone of peace'. He suggested the following: 'Give us a pledge not to invade Cuba, and we will remove the missiles'. He was also prepared to allow UN inspection of the missile sites. First, though, he wanted to be able to 'look around' and be sure that Kennedy really would not yield (Fursenko and Naftali 1997: 240–3). Khrushchev was stirred to action the next day by a series of intelligence reports, some false and based on little more than rumour, warning of imminent American military action against Cuba (Fursenko and Naftali 1997 257–8, 260–2). Khrushchev promptly sent instructions to accept UN Secretary-General U Thant's proposal for avoiding a confrontation at the quarantine line, promising to keep Soviet ships away from this line. He also dictated a long personal letter to Kennedy suggesting a peaceful resolution of the crisis. In the letter, he stated that if the USA promised not to invade Cuba, 'the necessity for the presence of our military specialists in Cuba would disappear' (Fursenko and Naftali 1997: 263). (See Box 14.2.)

For reasons that are still obscure, Khrushchev came to a judgement on 27 October that the Americans could be pushed harder. Perhaps he misjudged US resolve because of the way that the Americans were failing to enforce the quarantine. Khrushchev convened the Presidium and explained that he thought that the Americans would no longer dare attack Cuba. 'It is necessary to take into consideration that the United States did not attack Cuba.' Five days had passed since Kennedy's speech and nothing had happened. 'To my mind they are not ready to do it now.' Khrushchev would send another letter on Saturday, making a more concrete offer that acknowledged the presence of missiles in Cuba but which demanded that the USA withdraw its missiles in Turkey into the bargain. With that, 'we would win', he said (Fursenko and Naftali 1997: 274).

Khrushchev's manoeuvre created a significant problem. The lengthy discursive personal 'Friday letter' suggesting the withdrawal of Soviet missiles for a non-invasion pledge was sent secretly and was considered by the ExComm in secret. The 'Saturday letter' not only changed the terms of the deal, adding a new demand—the withdrawal of Turkish missiles as well—but it did so in a *public* message, making it politically impossible for Khrushchev's American counterparts to accept this compromise.

Kennedy had no difficulty accepting the terms proposed by Khrushchev's Friday letter: pledging not to invade Cuba if missiles were dismantled. But how to answer Saturday's

---

BOX 14.2 Excerpts from Khrushchev's letters to JFK (26 October 1962) during the crisis[i]

You are worried over Cuba. You say that it worries you because it lies at a distance of ninety miles across the sea from the shores of the USA. However, Turkey lies next to us. Our sentinels are pacing up and down and watching each other. Do you believe that you have the right to demand security for your country and the removal of such weapons that you qualify as offensive, while not recognizing this right for us?

You have stationed devastating rocket weapons, which you call offensive, in Turkey literally right next to us. How then does recognition of our equal military possibilities tally with such unequal relations between our great states? This does not tally at all.

Source: R.F. Kennedy (1969), *Thirteen Days: A Memoir of the Cuban Missile Crisis* (New York: W.W. Norton), paragraphs 6 and 7, p.198.

[i] On Friday 26 October, Khrushchev sent two letters to President Kennedy. The first, not made public, apparently took the 'soft' line that Russia would remove its missiles from Cuba in return for ending the US quarantine and assurances that the USA would not invade Cuba. The second took a harder line in seeking the removal of US missiles in Turkey in return for taking Russian missiles out of Cuba. [A notation from *Congressional Quarterly*]

---

proposal to trade NATO missiles in Turkey for Soviet missiles in Cuba—that was the problem. The USA could simply reject it, as many members of the ExComm urged. But Kennedy found that unacceptable. Kennedy judged that 'we're going to be in an insupportable position [if we reject Khrushchev's proposition] . . . It is going to—to any man at the UN or any other rational man—it will look like a very fair trade' (May and Zelikow 1997: 498).

If, on the other hand, the USA traded NATO missiles in Turkey for Soviet missiles in Cuba, what would be the consequences for the NATO Alliance and for American commitments elsewhere? As Bundy argued, a trade would make it 'clear that we were trying to sell out our allies for our interests. This would be the view of all NATO. Now, it's irrational and crazy, but it is a *terribly* powerful fact' (May and Zelikow 1997: 500). The struggle to avoid being impaled on one horn or the other of this dilemma made Saturday's deliberation the most intense and difficult of the crisis. As Sorensen recalled: 'our little group, seated around the Cabinet table in continuous session that Saturday felt nuclear war to be closer on that day than at any time in the nuclear age' (Sorensen 1965: 714).

Before the USA had to make the final decisions about military action, Khrushchev moved. Warning signs of imminent combat in Cuba arrived in Moscow during the day of 27 October, waking Khrushchev from his apparent complacency. A message arrived from Castro to Khrushchev. In it, Castro asserted that an American attack in the next twenty-four to seventy-two hours was 'almost inevitable'—probably a massive air strike but possibly an invasion. If the Americans did invade, Castro urged Khrushchev to consider the 'elimination of such a danger', plainly referring to the use of Soviet nuclear weapons against the Americans. 'However difficult and horrifying this decision may be,' Castro wrote, 'there is, I believe, no other recourse' (Castro, in *Cold War International History Project*: 1962). Air defences in Cuba then began shooting at American reconnaissance aircraft, and an American U-2 was shot down by Soviet SAMs in Cuba and its pilot was killed. Khrushchev was unnerved by Castro's message. A few days later, in another message to Castro, Khrushchev referred to this 'very alarming' message in which 'you proposed that we be the first to carry out a nuclear strike against the enemy's territory'. 'Naturally,' Khrushchev added, 'you understand where that would lead us. It would not be a simple strike, but the start of a thermonuclear world war' (Khrushchev, President's Office Files, 30 October 1962).

Kennedy asked Robert Kennedy and Theodore Sorensen to compose a response to Khrushchev. At 8 p.m., the public message to Khrushchev was simultaneously transmitted to Moscow and released to the press. According to this letter, 'The first thing that needs to be done is for *work to cease* on offensive missile bases in Cuba, and for all weapons systems in Cuba capable of offensive use to be rendered inoperable, under effective UN arrangements' (May and Zelikow 1997: 604). On the Turkish question, the letter said only that 'if the first proposition were accepted, the effects of such a settlement on easing world tensions would enable us to work towards a more general agreement regarding other armaments as proposed in your second letter which you made public' (May and Zelikow 1997: 604).

Kennedy then invited a small group to join him in the Oval Office to discuss the message that Robert Kennedy would convey personally to Ambassador Dobrynin. McGeorge Bundy summarized that meeting as follows:

> One part of the oral message we discussed was simple, stern, and quickly decided—that the time had come to agree on the basis set out in the President's new letter: no Soviet missiles in Cuba, and no US invasion. Otherwise, further American action was unavoidable . . . The other part of the oral message was . . . that we should tell Khrushchev that while there could be no deal over Turkish missiles, the President was determined to get them out and would do so once the Cuban crisis was resolved. (Bundy 1988: 432–3).

Bundy's next carefully chosen words reflect his unease: 'Concerned as we all were by the costs of a public bargain struck under pressure at the apparent expense of the Turks, and aware as we were from the day's discussion that for some, even in our closest councils, even this unilateral private assurance might appear to betray an ally, we agreed without hesitation that no one not in the room was to be informed of this additional message' (May and Zelikow 1997: 606). Reflecting the contract implicit in the proposal, he added: 'Robert Kennedy was instructed to make it plain to Dobrynin that the same secrecy must be observed on the other side, and that any Soviet reference to our assurance would simply make it null and void'. Robert Kennedy left immediately to meet Dobrynin at the Justice Department and deliver the private message. It was a masterful example of diplomatic doublespeak:

> I told him that this [the U-2 shootdown] was an extremely serious turn in events. We would have to make certain decisions *within the next 12 or possibly 24 hours* . . . I said those missile bases had to go and they had to go right away. We had to have a commitment by at least tomorrow that those bases would be moved. This was not an ultimatum, I said, but just a statement of fact. He should understand that if they did not remove those bases, then we would remove them. His country might take retaliatory action, but he should understand that before this was over, while there might be dead Americans, there would also be dead Russians. He then asked me about Khrushchev's other proposal dealing with removal of the missiles from Turkey. I replied that there could be no quid pro quo—no deal of this kind could be made . . . If some time elapsed—and . . . I mentioned four or five months—I said I was sure that these matters could be resolved satisfactorily. (Kennedy, President's Office Files, 30 October 1962)

Dobrynin heard the offer clearly and conveyed it to Moscow. A public message from Kennedy to Khrushchev arrived late on Saturday evening, 27 October, in Moscow. It laid out the deal that would entail the verified withdrawal of Soviet 'offensive weapons' in exchange for the non-invasion pledge.

Khrushchev opened the Presidium session on the morning of Sunday, 28 October, with yet another about-face in his assessment of the American danger. This time he told his Presidium colleagues that they were 'face to face with the danger of war and of nuclear catastrophe, with the possible result of destroying the human race'. He went on: 'In order to save the world, we must retreat' (Fursenko and Naftali 1997: 284). On the morning of Sunday, 28 October, Soviet leaders broadcast an urgent message over the radio, announcing that they would withdraw their missiles from Cuba.

In sum, the blockade did not change Khrushchev's mind. Only when coupled with the threat of further action in the form of alternatives did it succeed in forcing Soviet withdrawal of the missiles. Without the threat of air strike or invasion, the blockade alone would not have forced the removal of the missiles. The middle road, i.e. the blockade, may have provided time for Soviets to adjust to American determination to withdraw the missiles. But it also left room for the Soviet Union to bring the missiles to operational readiness. What narrowed that room was Khrushchev's belief that he faced a clear, urgent threat that America was about to move up the ladder of escalation.

President Kennedy and Nikita Khrushchev confer at the Soviet Embassy, Vienna, Austria.

Source: Photograph in the John F. Kennedy Presidential Library and Museum, Boston, MA.

Epilogue: three conceptual frameworks for analysing foreign policy

> The essence of ultimate decision remains impenetrable to the observer—often, indeed, to the decider himself . . . There will always be the dark and tangled stretches in the decision-making process—mysterious even to those who may be most intimately involved. (President J. F. Kennedy, in Sorensen 1963)

In thinking about problems of foreign affairs, professional analysts as well as ordinary citizens proceed in a straightforward non-theoretical fashion. However, careful examination of explanations of events like the Soviet installation of missiles in Cuba, reveals a more complex conceptual substructure. The concluding section of this chapter revolves around three central propositions.

1. **Professional analysts and ordinary citizens think about problems of foreign policy in terms of largely implicit conceptual models that have significant consequences for the content of their thought.**

Explanations show regular and predictable characteristics that reflect unrecognized assumptions about the character of puzzles, the categories in which problems should be considered, the types of evidence that are relevant, and the determinants of occurrences. Bundles of such related assumptions constitute basic frames of reference or conceptual models in terms of which analysts and citizens ask and answer the following questions: What happened? Why did it happen? What will happen? Assumptions like these are central to the activities of explanation and prediction. In attempting to explain a particular event, the analyst cannot simply describe the full state of the world leading up to that event. The logic of explanation requires **conceptual models** to single out the relevant critical determinants of the occurrence—the junctures at which particular factors produced one state of the world rather than another. Moreover, as the logic of prediction underscores, the analyst must summarize the various factors as they bear on the occurrence. Conceptual models not only fix the mesh of the nets that the analyst drags through the material in order to explain a particular action, but they also direct the analyst to cast nets in selected ponds, at certain depths, in order to catch the fish he/she is after.

2. **Most analysts explain and predict behaviour of national governments in terms of one basic conceptual model, the Rational Actor Model (RAM or Model I).**

In what is, in effect, the default posture, events in foreign affairs are understood as purposive acts of unified national governments. For example, in confronting the problem posed by the Soviet installation of strategic missiles in Cuba, the Model I analyst frames the puzzle: why did the Soviet Union decide to install missiles in Cuba? He/she focuses attention on the goals and objectives of the government. The analyst infers: if the government performed an action of this sort, it must have had a goal of this type. The analyst has explained this event when he/she can show how placing missiles in Cuba was a reasonable action, given Soviet strategic objectives. Predictions about what a nation will do are produced by calculating what a rational action in this certain situation would do, given specified objectives.

Although **Model I** has proved useful for many purposes, it is clear that it must be supplemented by frames of reference that disaggregate the government, focusing on the organizations and political actors involved in the policy process. Model I's grasp of national purposes and of the pressures created by problems in *inter*national relations must confront the *intra*national mechanisms from which governmental actions emerge. In its simplest form, the RAM links purpose and action. If I know an actor's objective, I have a major clue to his likely action. By observing behaviour and considering what the actor's objective might be, when I identify an objective that is advanced effectively by the action, I have a strong hypothesis about why he/she did whatever he/she did. The full RAM includes not only objectives but also calculations about the situation in which the actor finds him/herself. This context presents threats and opportunities that the agent packages as options with pros and cons. The actor chooses the alternative that best advances his/her interests. Thus in explaining what an agent did, or in making bets about what he/she is likely to do, an analyst must consider not only the actor's objectives but also the options identified, the costs and the benefits estimated to follow from each option, and the actor's readiness or reluctance to take risks. The core questions a Model I analyst seeks to answer in explaining a government action or estimating the likelihood of an action can be summarized succinctly. To explain (or predict) a phenomenon X (e.g. Soviet nuclear missiles in Cuba, October 1962):

Assume:
- X is the action of a state.
- The state is a unified actor.
- The state has a coherent utility function.
- The state acts in relation to external threats and opportunities.
- The state's action is value-maximizing (or expected value-maximizing).

Ask:
- What threats and opportunities arise for the actor (e.g. the balance of strategic nuclear forces in 1962)?
- Who is the actor (e.g. the Soviet Union, or its leader in 1962, Nikita Khrushchev)?
- What is its utility function (e.g. survival, maximization of power, minimization of coercion, etc?)
- To maximize the actor's objectives in the specified conditions, what is the best choice (e.g. Soviet installation of nuclear-armed missiles in Cuba)?

3. **Two alternative conceptual models, the Organizational Behaviour Model (Model II) and the Governmental Politics Model (Model III), provide a base for improved explanation and predictions.**

According to the Organizational Behaviour Model, what Model I analysts characterize as 'acts' and 'choices' are thought of instead as *outputs* of existing organizations functioning according to regular patterns of behaviour. Faced with the fact of Soviet missiles in Cuba, a **Model II** analyst focuses on the existing organizations and their standard operating procedures for (1) acquiring information, (2) defining feasible options, and (3) implementing a programme. The analyst infers: if organizations produced an output of a certain kind at a certain time, that behaviour resulted from existing organizational structures, procedures, and repertories. A Model II analyst has explained the event when he has identified the relevant Soviet organizations and displayed the patterns of organizational behaviour from which the action emerged. Predictions identify trends that reflect existing organizations and their fixed procedures and programmes.

It is clear that, for some purposes, governmental behaviour can usefully be summarized as action chosen by a unitary rational decision maker: centrally controlled, completely informed, and value maximizing. But we also know that, in fact, a government is not an individual. It is not just the president. It is a vast conglomerate of loosely allied organizations, each with a substantial life of its own. Government leaders sit formally on top of this conglomerate. But governments perceive problems through organizational sensors. Governments define alternatives and estimate consequences as their component organizations process information; governments act as these organizations enact routines. Therefore governmental behaviour can be understood, according to the second conceptual model, less as deliberate choices and more as *outputs* of large organizations functioning according to standard patterns of behaviour.

At any given time, a government consists of existing organizations, each with a fixed set of standard operating procedures and programmes. The behaviour of these organizations—and consequently of the government—in any particular instance is determined primarily by routines established prior to that instance. Explanation of a government action starts from this baseline. Clearly, organizations do change. Learning occurs gradually, over time. Dramatic organizational change can occur in response to major disasters. Both learning and change are influenced by existing organizational capabilities and procedures.

The characterization of government action as organizational behaviour differs sharply from Model I. Attempts to understand problems of foreign affairs in this frame of reference produce quite different explanations. About the Missile Crisis, the Model I analyst asks why 'Khrushchev' deployed missiles to Cuba, or why the 'USA' responded with a blockade and ultimatum. Governments are anthropomorphized as if they were an individual person, animated by particular purposes. In Model II explanations, the subjects are never named individuals or entire governments. Instead, the subjects in Model II explanations are organizations; their behaviour accounted for in terms of organizational purposes and practices common to the members of the organization, not those peculiar to one or another individual.

Model III focuses on the politics inside a government. According to this model, events in foreign affairs are characterized neither as unitary choice nor as organizational outputs. What happens is understood instead as a *resultant* of bargaining games among players in the national government. In confronting the puzzle posed by Soviet missiles in Cuba, a Model III analyst frames the puzzle: what bargaining among which players yielded the critical decisions and actions? The analyst focuses on the players whose interests and actions impact the issue in question, the factors that shape each player's perceptions and stands, the established 'action channel' for aggregating competing preferences, and the performance of the players. The analyst infers: if a government performed an action, that action was the resultant of bargaining among players in this game. A Model III analyst has explained this event when he/she has discovered who did what to whom that yielded the action in question. Predictions are generated by identifying the game in which an issue will arise, the relevant players, and their relative power and bargaining skill.

Model II's grasp of government action as organizational output, partially coordinated by leaders, enlarges Model I's efforts to understand government behaviour as the choices of a unitary decision maker. But beyond the Model II analysis lies a further, more refined, level of investigation. The leaders who sit atop organizations are no monolith. Rather, each individual in this group is, in his/her own right, a player in a central competitive game. The game is politics: bargaining along regular circuits among players positioned hierarchically within the government. Thus government behaviour can be understood according to a third conceptual model, not as organizational outputs but as the results of bargaining games. Outcomes are formed by the interaction of competing preferences. In contrast with Model I, the Governmental Politics Model sees no unitary actor but rather many actors as players—players who make government decisions not by a single rational choice but by the pushing and pulling that is politics.

Model III focuses on the players who are engaged in this interaction. Most players represent a department or agency along with the interests and constituencies that their organization serves. Because players' preferences and beliefs are related to the different organizations they represent, their analyses yield conflicting recommendations. Separate responsibilities laid on the shoulders of distinct individuals encourage differences in what each sees and judges to be important.

Model III analysis begins with the proposition that knowledge of the leader's initial preferences is, by itself, rarely a sufficient guide for explanation or prediction. The proposition reflects the fact that authoritative power is most often shared. The primary inspiration for Model III is the work of Richard Neustadt, though his concentration on presidential decision has been generalized to resultants of political bargaining among substantially independent players (Neustadt 1990).

None of the three analysts—Model I: The Rational Actor, Model II: Organizational Behaviour, and Model III: Governmental Politics—simply describes events. In attempting to explain what happened, each distinguishes certain features as the relevant determinants. Each combs out the numerous details in a limited number of causal strands that are woven into the most important reasons for what happened. Moreover, each emphasizes quite different factors in explaining the central puzzles of the crisis.

The outline of a partial synthesis of analysis using these three models begins to emerge as one considers the core questions each model leads one to ask in pursuing explanations or prediction.

Model I questions include:

- What are the objective (or perceived) circumstances that the state conceives as threats and opportunities?
- What are the state's goals?
- What are the objective (or perceived) options for addressing this issue?
- What are the objective (or perceived) strategic costs and benefits of each option?
- What is the state's best choice given these conditions?

Model II questions include:

- Of what organizations (and organizational components) does the government consist?
- What capabilities and constraints do these organizations' existing standard operating procedures (SOPs) create in producing *information* about international conditions, threats, and opportunities?

- What capabilities and constraints do these organizations' existing SOPs create in generating the menu of *options* for action?
- What capabilities and constraints do these organizations' existing SOPs establish for *implementing* whatever is chosen?
- Which organizations have the greatest stake in the outcome of what is chosen?

Model III questions include:

- Who plays? Whose views and values count in shaping the choice and action?
- What factors shape each player's (a) perceptions, (b) preferred course of action, and thus (c) the player's stand on the issue?
- What factors account for each player's impact on the choice and action?
- What is the 'action channel', i.e. the established process for aggregating competing perceptions, preferences, and stands of players in making decisions and taking action?
- Which players have the greatest stake in the outcome of the decisions that are made and the actions that are taken?

The central features of each model are summarized in Figure 14.2.

Thus the models can be seen as complements to each other. Model I fixes the broader context, the larger national patterns, and the shared images. Within this context, Model II illuminates the organizational routines that produce the information, options, and actions. Model III focuses in greater detail on the individuals who constitute a government and the politics and procedures by which their competing perceptions and preferences are combined. Each, in effect, serves as a search engine in the larger effort to identify all the significant causal factors without which the decision or action would not have occurred. The best analysts of foreign policy manage to weave strands from each of the three conceptual models into their explanations. By integrating factors identified under each model, explanations can be significantly strengthened.

The story of the missile crisis provides many opportunities for one to use the alternative lenses in re-analysing questions that members of the US government, and the Soviet government, answered at that time. For example, in preparing for President Kennedy's meeting with Foreign Minister Gromyko on Thursday, 18 October, the question arose whether Gromyko and his colleagues in the Soviet central circle expected the USA to discover missiles being installed in Cuba before they became operational. Would Gromyko reveal the missiles to Kennedy? Should Kennedy say something to him? Evidence of what the Soviets had actually done in constructing missiles in Cuba, including the standardized features of ballistic missiles at each of the sites, the absence of camouflage at the sites, and the near certainty that U-2s flying over these areas would take photographs of the missiles (as in fact they did), led some in the US government to conclude that the Soviet government *must* have expected the USA to discover the missiles. Indeed, the extraordinary and effective disguise of the missiles during shipment from the Soviet Union to sites in Cuba, on the one hand, and the absence of any equivalent camouflage at the sites, on the other, suggested to some that the Soviet government expected the USA to discover the missiles at about this time. If the administration had accepted that judgement, it might have developed a different script for the conversation with Gromyko.

The Paradigm	Model I	Model II	Model III
	National government Black box labelled. . . . Notional state Generic state Identified state Personified state	National government Leaders A B C D E F G What actually occurs Range of choice Structure of situation Innovation	National government (diagram of players A B D E F in positions) Players in positions (A–F) Goals, interests, stakes, and stands (n–z) Power Action-channels
Basic unit of analysis	Governmental action as choice	Governmental action as organizational output	Governmental action as political resultant
Organizing concepts	Unified National Actor The Problem Action as Rational Choice Goals and Objectives Options Consequences Choice	Organizational actors Factored problems and fractionated power Organizational missions Operational objectives, special capacities, and culture Action as organizational output Objectives–compliance Sequential attention to objectives Standard operating procedures Programmes and repertoires Uncertainly avoidance Problem-directed search Organizational learning and change Central coordination and control Decisions of government leaders	Players in positions Factors shape players' perceptions, priorities, preferences, stands Parochial priorities and perceptions Goals and interests Stakes and stands Deadlines and faces of issues Power What is the game? Action-channels Rules of the game Action as political resultant
Dominant inference pattern	Action = value maximizing means toward state's ends	Action (in short run) = output close to existing output Action (in longer run) = output conditioned by organization view of tasks, capacities, programmes, repertoires, and routines	Governmental action = resultant of bargaining
General propositions	Increased perceived costs = action less likely Decreased perceived costs = action more likely	Existing organized capabilities influence government choice Organizational priorities shape organizational implementation Special capacities and cultural beliefs Conflicting goals addressed sequentially Implementation reflects previously established routines SOPs, programmes, and repertoires Leaders neglect administrative feasibility at their peril Limited flexibility and incremental change Long-range planning Imperialism Directed change	Political resultants Action and intention Problems and solutions Where you stand depends on where you sit Chiefs and Indians The 51-49 principle International and intranational relations Misexpectation, miscommunication, reticence, and styles of play

Figure 14.2 Summary outline of models and concepts.

Source: Figure 'Summary outline of models and concepts', p 391 of *Essence of Decision* (2nd edn), by Graham Allison and Philip Zelikow. © 1999 by Addison-Wesley Educational Publishers Inc. Reprinted by permission of Pearson Education Inc.

Today, each of us can address this question ourselves. With the evidence available on 18 October, should one conclude that the Soviet government expected, or alternatively that it did *not* expect, the USA to discover the missiles at about this time? Here, Model II competes directly with Model I and yields precisely contrary conclusions.

The Missile Crisis maintains its special claim on policy makers and citizens alike because no other event so clearly demonstrates the awesome crack between the *unlikelihood* and the *impossibility* of nuclear war. The further one gets from the event, the harder it becomes to believe—existentially—that nuclear war could really have happened.

How could this crisis have gone nuclear?[8] To stimulate the reader's imagination, we will summarize what happened in the form of a scenario, and then spell out one path to Armageddon. Actual events are represented by eight steps.

1. The Soviet Union puts missiles in Cuba clandestinely (September 1962).

2. American U-2 flight photographs Soviet missiles (14 October 1962).

3. President Kennedy initiates a public confrontation by announcing the Soviet action to the world, demanding Soviet removal of their missiles, ordering a US quarantine of Soviet weapon shipments to Cuba, putting US strategic forces on alert, and warning the Soviet Union that any missile launched from Cuba would be regarded as a Soviet missile and met with a full retaliatory response (22 October).

4. Khrushchev orders Soviet strategic forces to alert and threatens to sink US ships if they interfere with Soviet ships en route to Cuba (23 October).

5. Soviet ships stop short of the US quarantine line (24 October).

6. Khrushchev private letter says the necessity for the Soviet deployment would disappear if the USA will pledge not to invade Cuba (26 October), followed by a second public Khrushchev letter demanding USA withdrawal of Turkish missiles for Soviet withdrawal of Cuban missiles (27 October).

7. USA responds affirmatively to first Khrushchev letter but says that, first, missiles now in Cuba must be rendered inoperable and urges quick agreement. Robert Kennedy adds privately that missiles in Turkey will eventually be withdrawn, but that the missiles in Cuba must be removed immediately and a commitment to that effect must be received the next day, otherwise military action will follow (27 October).

8. Khrushchev publicly announces that the USSR will withdraw its missiles in Cuba (28 October).

Consider, however, one obvious scenario for nuclear war beginning with steps 1–7 above but then proceeding hypothetically as follows.

1. Khrushchev reiterates that any attack on Soviet missiles and personnel in Cuba would be met with a full Soviet retaliatory response (28 October).

2. Soviet and/or Cuban forces fire upon US surveillance aircraft over Cuba on 28 October. A series of air strikes begins against Soviet missiles (destroying all operational ballistic missiles and killing a limited number of Soviet personnel) (29 or 30 October).

3. Soviet aircraft and/or medium-range ballistic missiles attack Jupiter missiles in Turkey (destroying ballistic missiles and killing a small number of Americans); Soviet and East

German forces interfere with traffic moving into Berlin; nuclear weapons in Cuba are dispersed to remaining operational forces on the island (31 October and 1 November).

4. In accord with obligations under the NATO treaty, US aircraft in Europe attack bases in the Soviet Union from which attacks against the Turkish bases had been launched; Berlin confrontation intensifies; US preparations to invade Cuba advance (4 November).

At this point, if not a step or two earlier, the Soviet government would be intensively considering possible pre-emptive nuclear strikes against the USA, especially command and control centres like Washington, in order to limit the damage inflicted by the overwhelming first strike they fear could come at any moment. If the Soviets preferred to place the burden of first use of nuclear weapons on the Americans, Moscow could use its conventional military forces to seize all of Berlin, thus forcing the Americans to decide whether they would indeed keep their promise to use nuclear weapons first to defend their allies. This scenario moves from frame to frame by a Model I analysis. Use of Model II and Model III would greatly enlarge the menu of nightmarish possibilities, adding misinformation, false warnings, accidents, and inadvertent clashes to the mix.

Other paths from what occurred to nuclear weapons exploding in the USA and Soviet Union start with unauthorized actions by individuals or units of both governments making choices that they clearly had the technical capability to make. For example:

- On 22 October, General John Gerhart, commander of North American Defense Command, ordered air defense commanders to load nuclear weapons onto F-106 fighter-interceptor jets—meant to destroy incoming Soviet bombers—and disperse them to dozens of remote airfields. This order violated the Air Force's 'buddy system' doctrine, which required at least two officers to be in physical control of a nuclear weapon at all times. One nuclear safety officer observed that 'by an inadvertent act', a single pilot carrying out this order 'would have been able to achieve the full nuclear detonation of the weapon'.[9]

- The US Navy had been using electronic eavesdroppers to monitor four Foxtrot class submarines that had slipped out of the Soviet submarine base at Gadzhievo on Kola Peninsula on the night of 1 October. The submarine commanders had only been given a vague instruction on how to respond to a US attack: 'If they slap you on the left cheek, do not let them slap you on the right one'. On the morning of 24 October, Nikolai Shumkov, commander of one of the four Soviet submarines, realized that a US destroyer was closing in on his vessel—not to sink the submarine, as it turns out, but simply to force it to the surface. Unknown to the destroyer's commander, there was a 10-kiloton nuclear torpedo stacked in the B-130's bow. With the push of a button, Shumkov could have unleashed the weapon, which had over half the destructive force of a Hiroshima-style nuclear bomb.[10]

The most frequently cited lessons of the Cuban Missile Crisis have emerged from Model I analysis. These include: (1) since nuclear war between the USA and Soviet Union would have been mutual national suicide, neither nation would choose nuclear war, and therefore nuclear war was not a serious possibility; (2) given its strategic nuclear advantage at the time, the USA could choose lower-level military actions without fearing escalation to nuclear war; (3) nuclear crises are manageable, as the Cuban Missile Crisis shows, since in situations where vital interests are at stake, leaders of both nations will think soberly about the challenge and their options and find limited actions to resolve disputes short of war.

Model II and Model III analysts caution against confidence in the impossibility of nations stumbling, irrationally in Model I terms, into the use of nuclear weapons, in the manageability of nuclear crises, or in understanding the recipe for successful crisis management. Through Model II lenses, the USA' success included crucial organizational rigidities and even mistakes. Except for the organizational and political factors that delayed an immediate military attack on Cuba, the probability of war would have been much higher. Except for the organizational and political dynamics that produced sufficiently persistent displays of American resolve to tilt Khrushchev's wildly oscillating estimates of American determination, Khrushchev might have proceeded with his plan to stage a nuclear confrontation in Berlin that could have proved even more dangerous. Only barely did the leaders of both governments manage to control organizational programmes that threatened to drag both countries over the cliff. In several instances, both Americans and Soviets were just plain lucky.

The lesson from Model II: nuclear crises between large machines, such as the US and Soviet governments of 1962, are inherently chancy. The information and estimates available to leaders about the situation reflect organizational capacities and routines as well as facts. The options presented to the leaders are much narrower than the menu that analysts might consider desirable. The execution of choices exhibits unavoidable rigidities of SOPs. Coordination among organizations is much less finely tuned than leaders demand or expect. The prescription: considerable thought must be given to the routines established in the principal organizations before a crisis, so that during the crisis the organizations will be capable of adequately performing the needed functions. In a crisis, the overwhelming problem will be that of control and coordination of large organizations. Given insurmountable limits to control and added dangers that can be created or compounded by the interacting plethora of the safety routines themselves, such crises must be *avoided*.

Lessons that emerge from Model III provide even less reason to be sanguine about our understanding of nuclear crises or about the impossibility of nuclear war. Actions advocated by leaders of the US government covered a spectrum—from doing nothing, to seeking a diplomatic bargain with Khrushchev at a summit meeting, to an invasion of Cuba. The process by which the blockade emerged included many uncertain factors. Had the Cuban Missile Crisis been Kennedy's first crisis, the participants in the decision-making group would have been different. Had McNamara been less forceful, the air strike could well have been chosen in the first day or two. Had Kennedy proved his mettle domestically in a previous confrontation, perhaps the diplomatic track would have prevailed and a major Berlin crisis could have erupted in November and December of 1962.

Thus the lessons of Model III terms are: (1) leaders of the US government can choose actions that they believe entail real possibilities of escalation to war; (2) the process of crisis management is obscure and exceedingly risky; (3) the interaction of internal games, each as ill-understood as those in the White House and the Kremlin, could indeed yield war, even nuclear war, as an outcome. If a president and his/her associates have to manage a nuclear crisis, the informal machinery, free-wheeling discussions, and devil's advocacy exemplified by ExCom have many advantages. But the mix of personality, expertise, influence, and temperament that allows such a group to clarify alternatives, even while it bargains over separate preferences, must be better understood.

Key points

- The Cuban Missile Crisis refers to the period of heightened nuclear tension between the Soviet Union and the USA during the thirteen days of 16–28 October 1962.

- The Soviet government decided to give arms to Cuba in 1959, steadily increasing the shipments. Soviet nuclear warheads reached Cuba in early October 1962 under the covert mission 'Operation Anadyr'.

- After American U-2 planes discovered the ballistic missiles in Cuba, the US government assembled a select inner circle of advisors known as the 'ExComm', who met at the White House for the duration of the crisis.

- In his address to the public on 22 October 1962, President John F. Kennedy declared a strict quarantine on all offensive military equipment under shipment to Cuba and called for Soviet Premier Nikita Khrushchev to eliminate the provocative threat to world peace.

- On 28 October, Soviet leaders announced that they would withdraw their missiles from Cuba.

- The Cuban Missile Crisis remains a formidable case study in world history for students of foreign policy analysis.

 Questions

1. What lay behind Soviet Premier Khrushchev's decision to deploy offensive missiles in Cuba?

2. Why did Fidel Castro permit the Soviet missiles to be deployed in Cuba?

3. At the height of the Cuban Missile Crisis, what options were considered by President Kennedy and the members of the Executive Committee?

4. Put yourself in the position of the American President. How would you have acted to resolve the Cuban Missile Crisis differently? What would be the consequences of your actions?

5. Why did the Soviet Union ultimately decide to remove the missiles from Cuba? Was this a 'victory' for the USA?

6. How close did the world come to nuclear annihilation in October 1962? As an ordinary citizen living in the USA, what would you have done during the bleakest times of the crisis?

7. If events had occurred differently and nuclear missiles had been launched, which areas do you think would have been most critically affected?

8. What steps have we taken since 1962 to ensure that such a potentially devastating nuclear crisis does not happen again?

 Further reading

Allison, G. (2004), *Nuclear Terrorism: The Ultimate Preventable Catastrophe* (New York: Times Books–Henry Holt).
This book addresses modern-day nuclear threats from a variety of sources. Selected by the *New York Times* as one of the '100 most notable books of the year'.

Glantz, D. M. (2001), *The Military Strategy of the Soviet Union: A History* (London: Routledge).
This book sheds light on the military strategy of the Soviet Union during an epoch when it was the most threatening enemy of the USA.

Kennedy, R.F. (1969), *Thirteen Days: A Memoir of the Cuban Missile Crisis* (New York: W.W. Norton).
This classic book offers an engaging narration of the Cuban Missile Crisis, and includes official documents of correspondence and speeches during the crisis.

Nathan, J.A. (ed.) (1992), *The Cuban Missile Crisis Revisited* (New York: St. Martin's Press).
This volume brings to light either significant re-evaluations of the crisis, or in some cases, truly startling challenges to the conventional wisdom surrounding much of the crisis.

Neustadt, R.E. (1990), *Presidential Power and the Modern Presidents: The Politics of Leadership from Roosevelt to Reagan* (5th edn) (New York: Free Press).
This book offers an insightful look into the executive power of American presidents, therefore accounting for the 'agency' around foreign policy decisions.

Visit the Online Resource Centre that accompanies this book for more information:
www.oxfordtextbooks.co.uk/orc/smith_foreign

Canada and antipersonnel landmines: the case for human security as a foreign policy priority

LLOYD AXWORTHY

Chapter contents

 Reader's guide

This chapter examines a defining moment in global diplomacy—the impact of the Ottawa Process on the use of landmines. Through this process, an international treaty to ban the use and trading of landmines was signed by 122 countries in 1997, with a number of other countries joining the treaty later. The dynamic between governments and NGOs leading up to the launch of the Ottawa Process is discussed. The method by which the Ottawa Process moved beyond established decision-making channels through the leadership and soft-power diplomacy of middle power countries such as Canada and various NGOs is then explored. Throughout the chapter, the parentage of the concepts of human security and the responsibility to protect is traced through the Ottawa Process, which in turn allows the reader to consider the process in terms of its utility as a model for recent international efforts, including the Commission on Intervention and State Sovereignty and the establishment of the International Criminal Court. Thus it provides a model for how the foreign policy role of middle powers can be directed towards normative/ethical standards and the establishment of an alternative global paradigm.

Introduction

In my university office, sitting on a side cabinet, is a landmine. It has been defused, fortunately, and mounted on a display board, a presentation given to me by a military group of de-miners in Bosnia a decade ago.

Visitors, especially students who gather weekly for a class in Canadian foreign policy, look at the crude weapon with its pineapple-shaped steel outer shell mounted on a sharp wooden stake with a mixture of curiosity and revulsion, often wondering aloud what kind of perverse mind can conceive and concoct such an evil device.

It is a truism that, since the cave dwellers, one of the major preoccupations of humankind has been how to deliberately kill other human beings, and of all the many destructive weapons of war that have been devised over the millennia, the landmine has been one of the deadliest. It not only wreaks havoc on combatants who are in conflict zones, but remains in the ground after the conflict is over, continuing to killing innocent civilians who traverse the ground that has been seeded by these hidden weapons.

I recall meeting a young Lebanese girl in a rehabilitation hospital outside Acre who had lost her arm by picking up a brightly coloured device thinking it was a toy, only to have it explode in her hand. Visiting a rehabilitation centre in Managua, Nicaragua, I met a group of young child soldiers involved in the Contra war who were painfully carving out of wood their own makeshift prosthetics. And there was a group of young women in Gulu, Uganda, who lost their legs or arms when they left the displaced persons camps set up by the government to forage for wood or water only to be overcome by strategically placed landmines, a tactic of the rebel Lord's Resistance Army.

The landmine in my office stands as a singular remembrance of the many landmine victims living and dead around the world and how this one weapon alone has been a source of so much suffering. It also serves another and more positive purpose. It is a reminder that

Halo Trust mine clearance in Angola.

Source: © CICR/ESKELAND, Lena.

humankind can do something to control, manage, and possibly eliminate weapons of 'mass destruction'. Each time I look at it sitting harmless and de-fanged, no longer capable of exploding in someone's face or gut, it brings to mind the enormous effort by many governments, hundreds of NGOs, and thousands of ordinary people a decade ago to rid the world of landmines. Because of that combined effort and through an extraordinary collaboration, a treaty banning the use and trading in landmines was forged which, as of 2007, has 156 signatories. Since the signing of the treaty there has been a concerted global campaign to eliminate landmine use by the world's military, to de-mine, destroy stockpiles, and support the rehabilitation of landmine victims. Such efforts are a testament to how **soft-power** political action (i.e. the cultivation of personal relationship building, the use of public diplomatic techniques of persuasion and communication, and cultural and ideological advocacy) by networks of committed **middle powers** and civil society groups can be taken on a global scale to provide for the basic protection and security of people.

It has also come to be seen as a different way of approaching international politics. The **Ottawa Process**, as the treaty-making effort came to be known, has acted as a model for several other campaigns designed to limit the use of force, establish new norms of international law, and provide protection for innocent people against the violation of their basic rights. It is seen by many as an alternative way of conducting global affairs in contrast with the realpolitik of national interest and foreign policies based upon the doctrine that might makes right. It demonstrated that world politics do not necessarily have to be the exclusive preserve of great powers or always determined by military force. Instead soft **middle power** contributions and

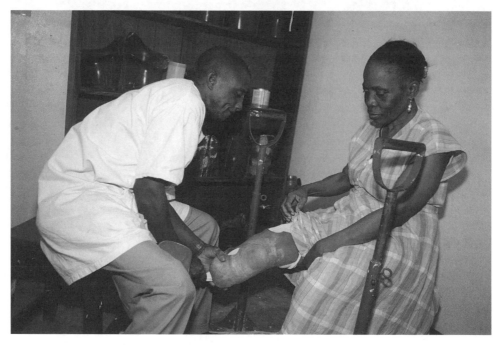

Orthopaedics.

Source: © CICR/DI SILVESTRO, Jean-Patrick.

Sign warning of mine danger in Sri Lanka.
Source: © CICR/BJÖRGVINSSON, Jon.

ethical foreign policies have demonstrated their viability within the dynamics of the international system, stimulating new ways of thinking about international cooperation.

The landmine treaty process was the spawning ground for the development of new ideas and practices centred on the notion of **human security** which emphasizes the security of individuals, presenting a counterpoint to the traditional concepts of national security. The parentage of the emerging global principle of **responsibility to protect** can also be traced back to the **Ottawa Process**. Adopted by the UN summit of world leaders in 2005 as part of the reform package, **responsibility to protect** sets a global standard to determine when the international community has the right to intervene in other nation-states to protect people. It stipulates that if a state is unwilling or unable to fight genocide, massive killings, and other massive human rights violations within its own borders, the responsibility must be transferred to the international community.

As the *Convention on the Prohibition on the Prohibition of the Use of Stockpiling, Production and Transfer of Antipersonnel Landmines and on their Destruction* (hereafter referred to as the treaty) has passed its ten-year milestone, there is good reason to review and reflect upon its construction, accomplishments, and what lessons it imparts about the role of soft and middle power for the present and the future.

To truly understand the treaty's impact, it will be necessary to start at the beginning, to describe the conference that took place in Ottawa, to explain how and why Canada made the transition from traditional international politics by initiating an out-of-the-box process designed to achieve an international treaty that heretofore had been blocked by big power machinations, and to discuss the means by which the treaty was actually written, signed, and implemented.

The context

The **Ottawa Process** began with the emergence of a strong group of NGOs who in the mid-1990's addressed the humanitarian devastation caused by landmines and the inability of traditional international disarmament institutions to respond adequately to the demand for change. While NGOs managed to generate a strong public will capable of addressing the problem of landmines, they needed nation-state partners to actually secure a treaty. The elements defining the uniqueness of the **Ottawa Process** are centred on the fact that certain states and NGOs used human relationships and strong negotiating skills to form a coalition of common interest based on the principles of **human security** (explored below) and transform the accepted norms of warfare.

States: stalemated

By the early 1990s, the landmine problem was given a fair amount of attention by a significant number of countries, thanks to the work of the NGO community. In 1992, the USA took an early lead by declaring a moratorium on the export of landmines. Senator Patrick Leahy of Vermont introduced several measures designed to limit the use of landmines. A number of governments followed suit with similar export bans. The French government called for a review of landmines in the UN **Convention on Certain Conventional Weapons** (CCW) (see Box 15.1). The Swedish government issued a call for a total ban while the Italian Senate

---

BOX 15.1 The Convention on Certain Conventional Weapons

Generally referred to as the Convention on Certain Conventional Weapons (CCW), the *Convention on Prohibitions or Restrictions on the Use of Certain Conventional Weapons Which May Be Deemed to Be Excessively Injurious or to Have Indiscriminate Effects* was initially concluded on 10 October 1980 and entered into force on 2 December 1983. It consists of an umbrella convention followed by a set of protocols that ban or restrict the use of weapons considered to cause unnecessary suffering to soldiers or civilians. Individual states have to ratify or accede to the Convention and to each Protocol. When the Convention came into force on 2 December 2 1983, there were 50 state signatories. Today there are 102, although not all have signed on to each Protocol.

Initially, the convention had three protocols: Protocol I on Non-Detectable Fragments, Protocol II on Prohibitions or Restrictions on the Use of Mines, Booby Traps and Other Devices, and Protocol III on Prohibitions or Restrictions on the Use of Incendiary Weapons. In October 1995, Protocol IV on Blinding Laser Weapons was adopted. In May 1996, amendments to Protocol II, which deals with landmines, were negotiated and both the amendments to Protocol II and the establishment of Protocol IV came into effect in 1998. In November 2003, Protocol V on Explosive Remnants of War was adopted. The convention can be accessed at: http://disarmament.un.org/ccw/.

ordered the Italian government to pursue an end to the production of landmines, a significant move for a country that was one of the largest suppliers.

In keeping with his country's early leadership on the issue, President Clinton's first speech to the UN General Assembly called for an eventual elimination of antipersonnel landmines. The president's groundbreaking statement was followed by a US-sponsored resolution in the General Assembly that urged states to exercise a ban on exports and to undertake 'further efforts to seek solutions to the problems caused by antipersonnel landmines, with a view towards [their] eventual elimination' (Clinton 1994)—a significant change in policy for the world's largest producer and user of landmines. Soon after, Belgium and Norway announced total bans on the production, export, and use of the weapon. This was a classic example of a big power country calling for action on an issue through the usual UN avenues. Meanwhile, in Canada my predecessor in foreign affairs, André Ouellet, had begun to advocate the non-use of landmines. This initiative was taken up by Canadian Prime Minister Chrétien at the G8 summit held in Halifax in June 1995. Within the Department of Foreign Affairs, a skilled group of Canadian Foreign Service officers had been formed to focus on the landmine issue. They became active on the diplomatic circuit, raising the issue with their international counterparts as the opportunity presented itself.

Also in June 1995, the first meeting of any significance on the use of landmines was held in mine-infested Cambodia. At the meeting, mine victims were directly involved. Their presence brought a counterbalance to the position of countries such as China and India that opposed any limitation on mine use. Moreover, the meeting's success in attracting widespread participation from developing countries helped turn the landmine problem into a truly global issue and generated optimism that the current structure of the international community had the ability to deal with it. Most countries wanted to begin with amendments to the CCW, which mentioned the need to protect civilians against the destruction of landmines, but limited its purview to international cross-border armed conflicts. The CCW also possessed no compliance mechanism. In this sense, while the treaty had begun to address landmines as a humanitarian issue, its restriction to international conflicts and lack of enforcement continued to uphold the principle of national sovereignty and, by extension, national security as a fundamental tenet of international politics.

A French initiative to convene a review conference of the CCW was agreed to, but after a series of prolonged meetings among the nation-state members of the UN Disarmament Conference (where NGOs were kept outside the room), the CCW review produced only a watered-down Protocol, agreed to on 3 May 1996. Based on achieving full consensus, the UN system of disarmament negotiation was, as is so often the case, held hostage to the position of the most recalcitrant members. There was clear blockage by a number of states including India, China, Cuba, and the five permanent members of the Security Council who wanted discussions confined to a forum that they controlled.

NGOs: an innovative strategy

Early leadership on the part of civil society and NGOs on the landmine issue began in the USA. The organization Veterans for Vietnam, led by Bobby Mueller, represented the many young Americans who returned from Vietnam with lost limbs due to landmines. They began a strong lobby in the USA.

The Veterans' group recognized the need to raise the issue at the international level and funded the start-up of a coalition of international NGOs headed by Jody Williams. By 1992, a powerful amalgam of humanitarian groups which included the International Red Cross, several NGOs interested in arms control and human rights, and a number of committed individuals, many of them victims of landmines explosions or the relatives of victims, formed the International Campaign to Ban Landmines (ICBL).

The coalition's strategy was to focus on the risk of landmines to individuals. The importance of this approach cannot be overemphasized. The tactic immediately moved the discourse out of the obscure realm of diplomatic and military arms control language and turned the focus instead on the destructive impact upon innocent civilians. The coalition's shift away from thinking about national security and towards thinking in terms of **human security** was an important development in those turbulent days of the 1990s, when old Cold War precepts were being discarded and replaced by new navigational coordinates.

This focus on **human security** gained strength with the help of the Landmine Survivors Network, which brought together survivors, their family members, and aid workers. The Network began appearing before international bodies, describing landmine experiences first hand and making a direct pitch to governments for assistance to victims. Their stories were greatly enhanced for the media by words of support from Pope John Paul II and the involvement of high-profile celebrities such as the late Princess Diana. Altogether, this demonstrated how civil society could raise the profile of issues, mobilize public support at a global level, and begin to shift the norms of people and government.

The International Red Cross played an essential role in documenting these cases and demonstrating the widespread damage caused by landmines around the world. They pointed out that landmines hidden in the ground prevented any form of development and cultivation, and were a serious impediment to economic renewal in war-torn countries. The Red Cross was also able to amass strong testimony from various military experts, including General Norman Schwarzkopf, the US commander in the first Gulf War, about the limited military utility of mines. He argued that they did not offer much in the way in protection and were frequently a great danger to troops.

Through the early and mid 1990s, armed with such compelling documentation and public support, civil advocates mounted skilful campaigns to change the perspective and position of governments. Their approach was to concentrate on a number of targeted countries, mobilizing public support and direct lobbying. The coalition tried to enlist government involvement through educational conferences and by building up close working relationships with sympathetic officials. At international meetings the group did not necessarily employ confrontational methods, but instead focused on the personal impact of strong individual pressure in the corridors.

One example of this approach occurred shortly after I became Foreign Minister. I was asked by the NGO Mines Action Canada to participate in an event on Parliament Hill at which the empty shoes of landmine victims would be piled in a heap. Pictures of the pile appeared in newspapers across the country; it was a graphic way of getting the message across, illustrating the tough but non-confrontational style of the NGOs.

While there was growing interaction between governments and NGOs, along with increasing media coverage, there was a serious divergence of approaches. Even before the meeting in France, the NGO activists increasingly took the position that only an outright ban or prohibition

Landmines kill kids.

Source: Photograph taken by John Rodsted of the International Campaign to Ban Landmines.

would end the suffering of so many victims. It was this argument, and the effectiveness with which NGOs dealt with landmines in human security terms, that would form the basis for the Ottawa Process, launched in Ottawa in 1996. It set the stage for Canada, along with other middle powers and in partnership with civil society groups, to seize upon the discourse of human security as a new dynamic of international security structures and to inject more soft power diplomacy into foreign relations.

States and NGOs come together in Ottawa 1996

Two important features of the conference in Ottawa need to be kept in mind. First, it was attended not only by representatives from more than seventy countries, but also by a large delegation of NGOs and several officials from the UN and the International Red Cross. The session was unusual, as international meetings go, as each of the participants had equal standing at the table. Secondly, the Ottawa session shifted the focus of the landmine movement away from Geneva, creating more space in which to carve out a new political path on the international political landscape.

The 1996 meeting was intended to organize a follow-up strategy after the disappointment of the CCW review. The event had been organized under Canadian auspices to map out a way to overcome the stalemate. It had been conceived as a fairly small gathering to promote an action plan, but as the conference approached, its momentum grew and it attracted widespread interest from a range of states and NGOs.

Of course, most governments still favoured working through the UN disarmament structures, where the consensus rule applied. However, those on the civil side of the movement saw this as a guaranteed recipe for stalemate. With NGOs present to make their case for a total ban (unlike in France), the encounter between NGOs and government proved combustible. Jody Williams, the head of the International Campaign, supported strongly by other civil groups, challenged the view of the UK, French, US, and Russian delegations that any negotiation must be confined to the established channels. When these governments refused to budge, suspicion grew that this was a 'big power' tactic to deflect serious efforts to cooperatively achieve a ban. Assessments that I received from the chair of the meeting were pessimistic. Two competing moods were at play in the corridors of the Conference Centre: an overwhelming sense of urgency and a growing feeling of frustration—feelings that I shared. As the conference began to wind down, I assembled a group of senior officials and staff in my tenth-floor office of the Pearson Building. The next afternoon was to be the wrap-up to the meeting and I was scheduled to give the benediction. What should I say?

It was then that a senior official—Paul Heinbecker, then the new Canadian Assistant Deputy Minister for Global Affairs—mentioned that the landmines team at the arms control division in the Department of Foreign Affairs and International Trade had been bandying about the possibility of short-circuiting the conventional process and setting up a separate track leading to a treaty banning landmines.

Setting up a negotiation track outside the UN framework was certainly not the traditional diplomatic approach, especially given the emphatic position of the big powers that only negotiation through established channels was acceptable. There had been no time to prepare the groundwork and there would be opposition from some very powerful players.

It would be seen as an audacious, even impudent, step for Canada to take, since we would be breaking the rules of accepted international behaviour and running the risk of falling flat on our face. Yet, in the absence of anything better, it was worth a try. I asked officials and staff to gauge potential support and to draft remarks for an announcement, and went home to sleep on the idea.

The next morning we reconvened in an anteroom of the main conference hall. Sitting around a small table was a crowd of officials from the Department of Foreign Affairs and International Trade who had been taking soundings and were confident that we could gain support from the NGOs and, importantly, from the President of the International Committee of the Red Cross, Cornelio Sommaruga. There would also be a core group of middle power states that had been working together on the landmines issue, even though some of them might resent our taking the lead. Could it succeed, given tough opposition from the large powers? No one knew. What was impressive, however, was that these officials, usually the voice of caution and prudent counsel, were ready to give it a go.

US President Harry Truman is famous for his saying that 'The buck stops here'. That morning in the crowded backroom of the Conference Centre, I understood what he meant. There was no one else to pass the decision to. I said, 'It's the right thing. Let's do it'. As the Saturday session drew to a close, with delegates voting on a declaration and an action plan, I waited in the wings to deliver the closing remarks with more than a twinge of nervousness. I knew I would be committing Canada to a course of action that defied traditional diplomatic niceties and procedures and challenged the positions of the permanent members of the Security Council. It would require an enormous expenditure of time, resources, and diplomatic capital. Yet, without it, the landmine campaign was headed towards a standstill.

Some necessary calls and contacts had been made. Peter Donolo of the Canadian Prime Minister's Office gave the green light. I spoke to UN Secretary-General Boutros Boutros-Ghali, who gave his blessing. A handful of key delegates were also given advance notice. But the circle of communication was limited to forestall any attempts to waylay the plan.

Finally, Ralph Lysyshyn, the Conference Chairman, asked me to the podium. I went through the normal list of thank-yous and words of appreciation, and then concluded: 'The challenge is to see a treaty signed no later than the end of 1997. The challenge is to the governments assembled here to put our rhetoric into action… The challenge is also to the International Campaign to ensure that governments around the world are prepared to work with us to ensure that a treaty is developed and signed next year' (Axworthy 1996). I then issued an invitation for all the delegates (and their friends) to come to Ottawa a year hence to sign the treaty.

The reaction in the hall was a mixture of surprise, applause, and incredulity. The NGO contingents rose to their feet. The representatives of many governments sat in their seats, too stunned to react, several barely suppressing their anger and opposition.

The crucial question was how many countries would follow our lead and return to Ottawa to sign a treaty banning landmines: we had just stepped out of the accustomed protocol of diplomatic deference to the powerful, and launched forth on an uncharted course of action. The only thing we could do was to forge a new path based on the principle of human security in partnership with the NGOs that had been so successful at turning the attention of the public and of politicians to the humanitarian impact of landmines.

The process

There was much about which to be nervous in launching the Ottawa Process. However, at the end of it the reward was not only an international landmine treaty, but also an alternative model that has many advantages over the top-down hierarchical 'coalition of the willing' model fashioned by the USA to support its invasion of Iraq (and other American-sponsored enterprises), and indeed over the present fashion for large-scale world conferences with casts of thousands engaged in a wild melee of activity, usually accompanied by massive protests at the perimeters of high fences. What emerged instead was a precedent that gave practice of international politics through what the political scientist Andrew Cooper describes as 'a bottom up, voluntary, mixed actor diplomatic approach' (Cooper 2005: iii). In Canada we worked out a three-track strategy: the achievement of full approval by our own government, the development of close working partnerships with the NGOs, and the development of a credible negotiating process among governments.

Gaining domestic support

The domestic track in our strategy—gaining the full approval and commitment of our own government—is one that is too easily overlooked. Clearly, Canada had to lead by example by getting rid of its own stockpile of mines, recruiting its own ministers and parliamentarians to the diplomatic cause, and providing funds for an effective global mine-action programme.

The key to achieving these outcomes was the Prime Minister. In Canadian foreign affairs, prime-ministerial approval, or at least acquiescence, is essential. It is particularly so when cooperation among various elements of the government is required. Fortunately, Prime Minister Chrétien supported the initiative, having first raised the landmines issue at the G7 meetings in Halifax in 1995. He pitched the treaty to his counterparts at various international meetings, and later made a special effort to enlist President Clinton during the crucial Oslo discussions. Chrétien was also instrumental in securing approval from Cabinet for a $100 million special fund to be used as a powerful signal of Canada's commitment. The most serious domestic obstacle was gaining agreement on eliminating our own stockpile of landmines, which had to be worked out with the Defence Department. Art Eggleton, the new Minister of Defence, proved very helpful in bringing Defence Department officials to an agreement. One of the carrots offered was that part of the $100 million landmines fund could be allocated to research at the Sheffield Testing Range in Alberta to look at alternatives to landmines. Another compelling factor was the experience of Canadian troops in the Balkans with landmines. There had been serious accidents; in one case a Canadian soldier, Mark Isfeld, lost his life removing landmines in Croatia. His family attended the October 1996 meeting in Ottawa and made a very moving presentation that struck a sympathetic chord among our own soldiers. On 7 November 1997, at a Defence Department testing range outside Ottawa, the Prime Minister, Art Eggleton, and I, along with Jody Williams (ICBL) and representatives of Mines Action Canada, presided over the explosion of the last remaining landmines held by Canada. We watched the weapons disappear in a whoosh of smoke. It was a major milestone in advancing our case.

Partnering with NGOs

Developing a close working partnership between states, NGOs, and international organizations such as the Red Cross was perhaps the most novel element of the Ottawa Process. As
already mentioned here, and as Richard Price discusses in his paper on the role of civil society
in the treaty process (Price 1998), these groups displayed an impressive ability to mobilize
public opinion and put pressure on governments: two thousand or so organizations in a coordinated network had successfully brought increasing attention to the problem and had
forced governments to account for their use of landmines. Now this network had to be en-
listed to focus upon a treaty process and on effectively shifting international norms. There
had to be synergy between the efforts of civil-based groups and sympathetic governmental
officials, as only governments could ultimately make legally binding decisions and tap into tax
revenues to pay for such decisions. Therefore, to be effective, governments and NGOs had to
be full partners.

Keeping this relationship healthy was not always easy. Often, citizen-based groups with
singular goals become frustrated with what they see as the delaying tactics of government.
They fail to accept the need to compromise or to balance competing interests. Equally, governments display unease and sometimes downright hostility towards people whom they see
as self-appointed public spokespersons, possibly usurping their role as elected representatives. There is frequently a reluctance to accept the advice and position of NGOs, simply because the officials feel they know more and dislike sharing their decision-making power. The
need to fast-track the treaty was a compelling reason to develop a close collaboration, with
the NGOs organizing public meetings and mobilizing direct pressure on parliaments and cabinets, while the core group of governments worked the diplomatic circle and funded the NGOs.

There were no mass meetings or barricade confrontations. The public pressure was highly
targeted, aimed at securing agreement by individual governments to a well-defined objective. One day I received a call from a European Foreign Minister asking if I could help turn off
the deluge of faxes from all over the globe that was flooding the offices of legislators in his
country. I told him that it was not in my purview to do so. Clearly, the message was being
delivered not through the traditional diplomatic state-to-state channels but through mobilization of the worldwide net of communication by NGOs.

Drafting the treaty itself was also a fully shared exercise—again a novel approach which led
to moments of tension between the partners, particularly when it involved a trade-off between the purity of the treaty and the need to sell it to the largest possible number of governments, especially the USA. However, in broad strokes there was a common front.

Diplomatic soft power

The aim of the diplomatic track was to use the art of persuasion and negotiation, capitalizing
on Canada's worldwide network of diplomatic missions as a basis for the treaty process.
Strained though they were by budget cuts, the offices housing Canadian Foreign Affairs and
Canadian International Development Agency officials became essential links in mobilizing a
global effort in a short period.

We in Canada started by enlisting a core group of middle power countries (states that
were not big powers but that still had some influence internationally and who had shown

interest in the landmine file), beginning with Austria, Norway, South Africa, New Zealand, Switzerland, Belgium, and Mexico, to act with us as a coordinating team. It is important to note that in each of these cases the governments of these countries had taken pro-disarmament positions not just on landmines but on other key issues such as nuclear weapons, reflecting a general interest in pursuing international cooperation towards limiting the risks of military action.

Together, we would host a series of diplomatic sessions that would both shape the elements of a treaty and emphasize the humanitarian, human security message about the damage to people. An appeal to conscience and common sense would put the opponents of the treaty, especially those arguing military utility, on the defensive. There were continuing consultations between officials of these respective countries along with representatives of the NGO groups in order to constantly plan and coordinate the necessary actions.

After meetings in Vienna to consider the wording of a treaty, in Brussels to enlist commitment to a total ban, and in Germany to look at the issue of verification, the various elements of a treaty were in place. Norway agreed to host the all-important negotiating session in Oslo in September 1997. In all these meetings, a core group of medium-sized and smaller countries with no 'big power' pretensions worked together with increasing unity of purpose, backed by Germany as a big-nation supporter and the eventual support of Britain and France which, thanks to their respective electorates, had brought into office sympathetic and supportive governments. The addition of these P-5 members added substantial credibility to the process and brought into play allies like Robin Cook, the UK Foreign Secretary, who used his eloquence and intelligence to great effect. The circle of involvement was continuously widening, generating a sense that this was a process that was building towards a successful outcome.

The same momentum was seen in other regions. In February, the South African government unilaterally announced a total ban on landmines just before convening an NGO conference on landmines in Maputo. Nelson Mandela, who undoubtedly had the benefit of advice from his partner, and child advocate, Graça Machel, went to work on persuading other African states. This was followed by a similar declaration from the Mozambique government during the conference, and by the pledge of support from forty-three members of the Organization of African Unity.

These were pivotal decisions, coming from countries that were the sites of extensive landmine pollution. It signalled that this was not to be another Western enterprise foisted on the developing world but the beginning of a regional, even global consensus. In the Americas, the experience of living and dying with landmines proved to be a powerful motivation for Central American and Caribbean countries. In the end, from the Western Hemisphere, only the USA and Cuba didn't sign. A tougher sell was required in Asia, where there was entrenched opposition from countries such as China, India, and South Korea, the last of these reflecting the strong commitment of both its own government and the USA to using mines in the Demilitarized Zone (DMZ) separating North Korea from South Korea.

Another important breakthrough was the conversion of Japan to support for the treaty, due primarily to the personal endeavour and political courage of the Foreign Minister (soon to be Prime Minister) Keizo Obuchi. His own bureaucracy was strongly opposed, but he pushed through a commitment for Japan to play an active role. We had several meetings together on the landmine issue where we talked about the human security idea, demonstrating the importance of strong personal relationships in helping to exercise soft power diplomacy.

America and the road to Oslo

The place where this soft power diplomacy would receive its major test was Oslo, where the draft treaty would be negotiated before moving to Ottawa for signature. The run-up to the Oslo meeting was given a major boost when ninety-seven countries declared at the Brussels conference in late June that they would sign the treaty. A media campaign was launched, using the status of such people as Princess Diana, Desmond Tutu, and the newly elected UN Secretary-General, Kofi Annan, to raise the public profile of the issue. Intense lobbying continued in capitals around the world.

The major sticking point was the position of the USA As we have seen, President Bill Clinton had delivered a stirring call at the UN to end the tyranny of landmines, but his administration was hamstrung by its own domestic political circumstances which had become increasingly hostile to any great leap forward towards a total ban on landmines. The 1994 election had given the Republicans control of the Congress, and there was a strong antipathy by many Republicans to any form of international agreement that appeared to constrain the use of any available options by the Pentagon. (See Box 15.2.)

Buttressing American political opposition was the hard-line position taken by Pentagon officials. They skilfully centred their opposition on three main conditions: the exclusion of the DMZ in Korea, an exemption for antipersonnel mines to be used as protective devices for anti-tank mines, and a delayed timetable for the treaty coming into effect. The Clinton Administration was reluctant to take on the senior military over specific items of military advice, especially given the deteriorating situation in the Balkans and in Haiti, situations that involved the deployment of US military forces against the will of Pentagon decision makers. While a general commitment to the idea existed in the administration, the landmines issue did not appear to merit a confrontation with an antagonistic congressional majority and the Joint Chiefs-of-Staff.

However, as Spring approached, the US administration recognized that an international consensus was building towards a total-ban treaty, and that the USA was now on the

---

BOX 15.2 US use of landmines

Despite a strong message in favour of the elimination of landmines at the outset of the treaty process, the USA has yet to join. At the end of his term, President Bill Clinton stated that the USA would sign by 2006. In a reversal of that statement, President George W. Bush implemented an alternative landmine legislation committing the USA to eliminating its stock of persistent landmines, while allowing for the continued development of non-persistent landmines after 2010. This, despite the fact that the USA is not known to have used antipersonnel landmines since the Gulf War in 1991, has not exported any landmines since 1992, and has already eliminated 1.2 million landmines (nearly half of its landmine stock) since 2004, thereby already complying with many of the articles of the Mine Ban Treaty.

The Obama administration has faced greater pressure from civil society groups to sign the treaty. On 18 May 2010, sixty-eight US senators, under the leadership of Senator Patrick Leahy, a long-time advocate against the use of landmines, signed and delivered a letter to President Obama urging his administration to sign the Mine Ban Treaty. In response to the pressure, Obama sent a delegation to the Second Review Conference in Cartagena and has since committed to a formal review of the US landmine policy.

outside of this initiative. That the treaty was moving ahead with or without the Americans demonstrates the extent to which it took place outside the more conventional international decision-making norms of the time. Efforts to bring the USA into the fold were marked by important questions and dilemmas. Undoubtedly their participation would have been a significant achievement as they were the largest producer and user of landmines. I believed, and continue to believe, that there was a chance to have the Americans sign on, and I was encouraged and aided in this effort by my close friend Senator Patrick Leahy, who had close connections to the administration. Still, one thing remained constant throughout: we could not compromise the integrity of the treaty. In March 1997, I raised the landmines issue with Madeleine Albright, the new Secretary of State, and expressed my hope for USA participation in the treaty-making process. At our first meeting, she expressed her own support, but reiterated the standard State Department response that they preferred the Geneva conference route. However, as the Americans became more aware of the progress of the Ottawa Process over the summer, she and I initiated talks at senior officials' level. In the meantime, however, the Brussels conference had set a high threshold for the treaty, calling for a total ban without exceptions or modifications. This made it very difficult at such a late stage to work out appropriate language that might allow the Americans to become part of the process. In a letter to other governments, Albright announced that Washington would participate in the Ottawa Process, which was a big step forward, but said that the USA would be seeking changes to the draft treaty based on their three main conditions. As a result, we headed into the Oslo meeting with the US decision to sign onto the treaty still up in the air.

Meeting in Oslo

The Oslo meeting began on 1 September 1996, with eighty-seven full participants and thirty-three observer nations. The dominant undercurrents were the issue of American demands for change and the question of whether having the USA as part of the global convention outweighed the consequences of accepting their modifications.

The president of the Oslo meeting was Jackob Selebi, a highly respected South African diplomat, but not someone who was prone to accommodating the Americans. He shared the view of many that this was simply a US tactic to delay or even scuttle an agreement. The civil groups bombarded the media in Oslo, arguing strenuously against any amendment to meet American demands. However, there were strong advocates responding to the American position: Japan, Australia, and Ecuador in particular argued for the necessary time to get the USA on board. This situation created a dilemma. We desired US participation, but not at the price of watering down the draft convention. In my speech to the Oslo meeting, I stated that there should be no major exceptions or amendments to the text that had been carefully developed over the preceding eleven months. Where there might be room for accommodation was in the entry-into-force terms, particularly as applied to the DMZ in Korea. While the negotiations continued in Oslo, the phone lines were busy between Ottawa and Washington. I was conversing with Madeleine Albright and Sandy Berger, head of the National Security Council, while the Canadian Prime Minister spoke to the US President. We requested US flexibility in return for an entry arrangement that would allow them time to make a change in the Korean DMZ.

Word of these discussions got back to the meeting in Oslo, and rumours circulated that we were giving in to the entire American demand. When the US delegation asked for extra time, I decided to instruct our delegation to agree, provoking charges that we were buckling. Despite the criticism from the NGOs that began to surface publicly in Oslo, I still thought it important to find a way to bring the Americans in without damaging the treaty, and felt that having them as signatories would be a big plus. The telephone diplomacy continued, with the Prime Minister and me on the phone to our respective counterparts late into the evening during the last twenty-four hours of the Oslo conference.

We came close to success, but ultimately the major stumbling block was not the Korean DMZ but the Pentagon's insistence on retaining an anti-tank mine system which used unconnected antipersonnel mines as guards (rather than the systems used by other armies, which wired them directly to the anti-tank device). Our argument was that the US Defence Department could use only the connected devices.

For a moment it looked as if this was going to work. Sandy Berger called me late in the evening to say that the USA would probably agree. I went home, told my wife that we had something to celebrate, and broke open a bottle of malt scotch. The feeling was short-lived. At about one o'clock in the morning, Berger called back to say that the president had ultimately decided that the opposition inside the Beltway would be too intense and that the USA wouldn't sign. The malt scotch came in equally handy after that call.

The good news was that we had a draft treaty that enjoyed widespread support. Now all we had to do was to hold together the coalition of pro-ban states with the NGO community until December, and continue to press reluctant governments to sign. This effort received a major boost on 1 October when Jody Williams and the International Campaign to Ban Landmines were awarded the Nobel Peace Prize for their work. The added attention helped to win over several governments.The treaty-signing ceremony that took place in Ottawa in December 1997 highlighted the magnitude of what had been accomplished. After strong speeches by the Canadian Prime Minister, the UN Secretary-General, Cornelio Sommaruga of the Red Cross, and Jody Williams of the ICBL, who gave a stirring reminder that the power of civil society is a form of superpower in the making, my role in the programme was to affix the first signature on the *Convention on the Prohibition of the Use of Stockpiling, Production and Transfer of Antipersonnel Landmines and on their Destruction*, which I did with great pride and satisfaction.

My signature, on behalf of Canada, was followed by 121 others. Beyond the signatures there was the endorsement of a major action plan and the pledging of more than $500 million for de-mining and victim assistance, a result of our officials having thought ahead to move implementation of the treaty forward before the ink was dry. Ratification was of course critical, and within fifteen months we had the requisite sixty ratifications; on 1 March 1999, the treaty came into force.

The path leading up to this signing was a new one for all involved, and as the treaty came into force we could begin to look back and seek to understand exactly how its success had been ensured. As the initiators of the process, it was crucial that Canada gained strong domestic support to gain credibility in its diplomatic efforts by modelling a new norm. It was this support, in conjunction with growing synergies between governments and civil society, that ensured that pressure came through both the soft power diplomacy of middle power countries and the targeted pressure of NGOs. What emerged was a new network of like-minded

---

BOX 15.3 The International Criminal Court

The International Criminal Court (ICC) was established by the Rome Statute of the International Criminal Court in July 1997 and is another example where civil society groups and individuals played a significant role in its creation. The ICC tries people for genocide, crimes against humanity, and war crimes. It is a court of last resort—if a case is investigated or prosecuted by a national judicial system, it will not act unless the national proceedings are not genuine.

The Rome Statute is an international treaty that entered into force on 1 July 2002, once sixty states had become parties. Currently, 114 countries are states parties, with Grenada and Tunisia scheduled to join by the end of 2011. Another 34 states have signed but have yet to ratify the treaty. The USA has not signed the treaty. Canada signed it in December 1998. To date, the Court has opened investigations into six situations: the Democratic Republic of the Congo, Uganda, the Central African Republic, Darfur, Sudan, the Republic of Kenya, and most recently the Libyan Arab Jamahiriya.

---

governments, NGOs, and key international organizations through which persuasion and diplomacy, as opposed to brute force, could be used effectively in the international arena. This network model was the beginning of the establishment of a more permanent human security architecture, which includes the **International Criminal Court**, and a model for future multilateral soft power negotiations on human security issues such as those currently underway with respect to cluster munitions. (See Box 15.3.)

Establishing a legacy

In a very real sense the impact of the landmines treaty ranges from the very direct result of saving lives in various killing fields around the world to being a catalyst for a new form of multi-actor diplomacy and a design for a new global political model. There are certainly some clear objective assessments that can be made by which to gauge the success of the treaty. A quick scan of the 2010 *Landmine Monitor Report* tells us that, since 1996, an estimated 45 million stockpiled landmines have been destroyed. In 2009–2010, over 225,000 antipersonnel landmines were destroyed and at least 198 square kilometres of mined areas were cleared. In June 2010 Nicaragua became the sixteenth state party to complete its clearance obligations, and even China, which is not a state party, has declared that its landmines have been cleared.

Support for the convention internationally continues to grow; there are currently 156 states parties to the treaty, representing 80% of states. The number of signatories tells us that there is increased support for the goal of eliminating antipersonnel mines. As a further testament to this fact, on an annual basis the UN General Assembly adopts a resolution calling for the universalization of the Mine Ban Treaty; the most recent vote in 2010 demonstrated the greatest response since 1997, with 165 in favour, none opposed, and 17 abstentions.

The degree of compliance and the sheer number of states parties to the treaty means that, even for those countries that have not formally joined, the treaty now acts as a global norm—a marker that measures their behaviour and stigmatizes non-compliance. Trade in landmines has been severely curtailed, and there is ongoing scrutiny by the NGO coalition monitoring process which reveals where there might be recidivism by signatory states and egregious use by those still outside the treaty. In the Afghanistan conflict zone it was reported that Pakistan was considering the use of landmines as a way of sealing its border against Taliban movements because of pressure from NATO coalition governments. The ensuing outcry forced those governments to reverse the pressure and demand a commitment to non-use of landmines by Pakistan.

This should not be taken to mean that landmines are not used anywhere nor that the risk to the safety and security of individuals from landmines has entirely disappeared. There are currently 66 states that are still affected by landmines, and in 2009 there were nearly 4000 reported casualties. The number of casualties, and the use of landmines by non-state actors (i.e. militias, rebel groups, terrorists), continues to be a serious problem. At the end of 2009 the Second Review Conference of the Mine Ban Treaty took place in Columbia and resulted in the adoption of the Cartagena Action Plan. The purpose of the summit was to review the achievements, but also to reiterate the continued threat of landmines and to garner a renewed commitment by states parties. (See Box 15.4.)

Still, the legacy and the meaning of the Ottawa Process go far beyond the banning of weapons and aid to victims. It set a new precedent in foreign policy by demonstrating the success with which soft power could be employed. Prior to the Ottawa Process, circumventing traditional diplomatic channels was not a viable option. From the nineteenth-century Concert of Europe (a series of meetings between the great powers of Europe initiated by Britain, Austria, Russia, and Prussia, and conducted between 1815 and 1822) to the present-day veto-wielding P5 Security Council members, the great powers have always occupied a place of privilege in international affairs. As such, the role of middle powers as a new collectivity, coupled with non-state actors like NGOs, represents an alternative foreign policy force through which the virtues and benefits of soft power diplomacy can be seen.

BOX 15.4 A treaty to ban cluster bombs?

On 23 February 2007 forty-six states signed a declaration in Oslo committing themselves to conclude, by 2008, a legally binding instrument that will prohibit the use, production, transfer, and stockpiling of cluster munitions and to establish a framework for cooperation and assistance that ensures adequate provision of care and rehabilitation for cluster munitions victims, clearance, risk education, and the destruction of stockpiles of prohibited cluster munitions. This process closely mirrors the campaign to ban landmines in terms of both the engagement of civil society and the role played by middle power countries. The Convention on Cluster Munitions was successfully negotiated by the 2008 deadline. It entered into force on 1 August 2010.

Cluster munitions are bombs that contain several smaller submunitions, often referred to as bomblets or grenades, which scatter over the area the size of two to four football fields when the larger explosive is detonated. Submunitions are designed to explode on impact; however, this does not always take place. Instead, a number of bomblets are left unexploded on the ground or burrowed into soft soil or sand, waiting to be detonated by a child, attracted by their bright colours, or by any other unassuming passer-by.

Cluster bombs have reportedly been used in Iraq, Afghanistan, Kosovo, and most famously in Lebanon, where estimates of the percentage of unexploded submunitions range from 25% to 40%. Explosions from these submunitions can kill anyone within a 50 metre radius and often result in multiple deaths because a group of people, often children, are gathered around the item, or the item is located in a populated area such as a town or village.

In the case of the landmine ban, the conventional path was strewn with roadblocks and infinite obstacles. The one instrument we had on hand to execute the ban—the Conference on Disarmament—also happened to be the campaign's most stubborn barrier. The only way to move beyond the 'lowest common denominator' approach was to walk a different path. But the path was not in existence . . . it was the type of path that Spanish poet Antonio Machado has written about—'the path that is made by walking'.

The path began not with governments and entrenched bureaucrats, but with citizen's groups. They were the ones who eventually forced state-level officials from their comfortable chairs and goaded them into motion. The techniques and tools used by pro-ban campaigners were not conventional by any means. Focusing on the humanitarian impact of what had hitherto been seen strictly as a disarmament issue helped give the landmine ban campaign the emotional force that it needed. Deciding to set a course leading directly to Ottawa broke new ground.

The Ottawa Treaty experience taught Canadians and other middle power countries about their inherent capacity to play a leadership role in a new kind of foreign politics by capitalizing on their diplomatic soft power strengths, working through a network of like-minded governments and NGOs. This capacity was held up through the implementation of the **human security** approach—putting the protection of individuals at the centre of foreign policy as opposed to relying only on traditional concepts of security which primarily emphasize the use of force and national security.

Canada now has a track record of drawing on the Ottawa Process experience to partner with civil groups and like-minded states on a variety of issues. Specifically, the process proved suitable to our national interest of working through collaborative, cooperative, multilateral, transnational institutions and to constrain the unilateral actions of the powerful. Other Canadian-inspired human security initiatives include the ICC, the protection of children, the Arctic Council, and the effort to organize a hemispheric drug network. The experiences of these various initiatives has led to the formation of the Human Security Network, an association of eleven states and nine NGO groups designed to tackle a variety of global issues through a networking of efforts (Box 15.5).

BOX 15.5 The Human Security Network

The Human Security Network (www.humansecuritynetwork.org) emerged out of the landmines campaign and was formally established in Norway in 1999. Members include Austria, Canada, Chile, Costa Rica, Greece, Ireland, Jordan, Mali, The Netherlands, Norway, Switzerland, Slovenia, and Thailand, and South Africa as an observer. The Network also maintains strong ties to academia and civil society. Its foreign ministers meet regularly to discussion questions pertaining to human security and to identify concrete areas for collective action. They have met in Bergen, Norway (1999), Lucerne, Switzerland (2000), Petra, Jordan (2001), Santiago de Chile (2002), Graz, Austria (2003), Bamako, Mali (2004), Ottawa, Canada (2005), and Bangkok, Thailand (2006).

Currently, the Network is involved in efforts to universalize the Ottawa Convention on Antipersonnel Landmines. It was also instrumental in the establishment of the International Criminal Court, and works on the protection of children in armed conflict, the control of small arms and light weapons, the fight against transnational organized crime, human development and human security, human rights education, the struggle against HIV/AIDS, addressing implementation gaps in international humanitarian and human rights law, and conflict prevention.

The pathway forged by the Ottawa Process led to a natural and logical outcome—a normative challenge to the precepts of state sovereignty. By working to advance the security and protection of individuals rather than state units, which is the gist of the human security approach, the coalition that grew out of the Ottawa Process defined an alternative foreign policy paradigm.

The crossroads in that paradigm shift took place as a result of the Kosovo intervention. While the human security discourse won an important victory with the landmine treaty, it was not until after the intervention by NATO forces in Kosovo in 1999 that the credibility of the human security concept was truly established. In the past, the notion of protecting individuals from new global threats had usually been seen by so-called hard-nosed critics as nothing more than posturing as an international do-gooder. Kosovo changed that. The ultimate test for a human security policy was a willingness to exercise military force to uphold the principles of protection.

Kosovo raised difficult questions about humanitarian interventions and the implications, and indeed obligations, of sovereignty. Old notions of national security predicated on the integrity and inviolability of borders made little sense when the threat posed by violence and conflict, international networks of predators and criminals, global pandemics, and massive natural disasters were at work. A new approach to the protection of people was necessary. The landmine campaign demonstrated that international politics could be conducted with a view to protecting people within a human security framework. Kosovo further demonstrated the need to solidify the principle into a more stable set of rules and tests for determining when and by what means international intervention could and should take place.

To help answer these questions, I undertook the establishment of the Commission on Intervention and State Sovereignty, charged with actually operationalizing the human security concept in internal conflicts. The Commission crafted a definition of sovereignty centred not on the prerogatives of the state but on its primary 'responsibility to protect' (R2P) its own citizens. If a state legitimately protects its citizens, it is fully entitled to its sovereign power. If it fails to do so, or becomes the perpetrator of a massive attack on the rights of its citizens, the international community must assume a function to protect.

R2P shifts the perspective from what sovereignty endows states *with* to what it obliges the state to *do*. If a state fails to protect its citizens or is itself the perpetrator of insecurity, there is a responsibility for the international community to take on the job. More specifically, in terms of today's definition it means that the act of intervention must be perceived from the perspective of the victim not the intervener. The report of the Commission on Intervention and State Sovereignty established that such a responsibility implies an evaluation of the issue from the perspective of the victim, not the intervener. If a state cannot provide the protection or is the author of the crime, then it forfeits its sovereign right and the international community steps in, not just to protect, but to prevent and rebuild (Commission on Intervention and State Sovereignty 2001). Built around this is a new, and arguably challenging, approach that seeks prevention, collaboration, and the establishment of a rule of law alongside the traditional facets of sovereignty. It establishes tests, and sets forth criteria for how to use power and for what purpose.

The R2P principle had a slow start. Its release took place just after 9/11 when the prime focus was counter-terrorism. However, by slow and patient diplomatic efforts using the Ottawa Process model the Canadian government, aided by its NGO allies and with the blessing of Secretary-General Kofi Annan, the idea began to take hold. It was picked up by the high-level commission on UN reform and became one of the key elements in the package of changes recommended by Secretary-General Annan to world leaders at the 2005 summit, where it was endorsed. When the Security Council decided to authorize a UN force for Darfur, it cited as its rationale the principle of the responsibility to protect.

That R2P represents one of the greatest challenges to traditional notions of state sovereignty that has emerged in recent history leaves it not without its critics. In 2009 some of these opponents tried to use a debate in the General Assembly on the Secretary-General's report on R2P to attack the principle itself. Civil society played an integral role in building support during the 2009 debate. The Global Centre for the Responsibility to Protect, among others, mounted very skilful campaigns with the media, which undoubtedly influenced opinion in various foreign ministries. The generally high degree of support for R2P was a pleasant surprise. Despite predictions that many members of the G-77 would vote to repeal or limit the 2005 adoption of R2P, the 2009 debate showed widespread support for R2P. Only four states (Venezuela, Cuba, Sudan, and Nicaragua) sought to roll back the 2005 resolution.

As a new global norm, R2P has had a staggering amount of success as a principle in such a relatively short amount of time. Operationally, it will take some time before the processes and procedures are fleshed out, but it is already being put into practice. While not being an explicit action under the R2P banner, in early 2008 Kofi Annan made the effort to intervene early in the political crisis in Kenya which had lead to an outbreak of violence and threatened to evolve into war. His efforts at early intervention led to a resolution of the crisis, preventing further violence, and has been lauded as an excellent example of R2P in action.

In 2011, a wave a popular uprisings desiring an overthrow of autocratic rule in favour of democracy spread across a significant portion of northern Africa and even into the Middle East. Early on, both Tunisia and Egypt saw the successful overthrow of the government in a relatively peaceful manner. Unfortunately, a similar popular movement in Libya against leader Muammar Gaddafi was met with the full brutal force of state and non-state forces loyal to the status quo. Reports of large-scale human rights abuses and a growing number of civilian casualties begged a response from the UN. Following a series of increasing international sanctions targeting Gaddafi and his entourage as well as diplomatic pressure to step down by the UN, and also by the US and France, which all went unheeded, the UN Security Council passed Resolution 1973, sanctioning the imposition of a no-fly zone in recognition of their responsibility to provide protection to civilians. The intervention is considered the first litmus test of the R2P principle.

There is still much work to be done regarding the appropriate application of the R2P principle as an example of human security in practice. We are facing constant and growing tension and confrontation between the classic principles of national interest and sovereignty and the need for global governance. The complexity of standards, rules, and institutions at an international level has become both intrusive and complex. This complexity is compounded by the efforts underway to erode broad multilateral jurisdictions in favour of bilateral and regional fixtures. As David Runciman said in *The Politics of Good Intentions*, 'A stable society of states seems to require both international oversight and national independence. No-one has worked out how to square the circle' (Runciman 2006: 20).

In fact, the responsibility to protect can become a way of squaring the circle and developing a template for reorganizing the global system around a principle that can apply to a wide variety of global issues and set in motion the re-invention of global governance. It becomes the guiding light for setting up a global public domain which holds individuals, corporations, international institutions, and nation states accountable to a set of standards of probity. It can also guide global stewardship in fields of security, poverty, aid, trade, and the environment.

This public space at the global level is emerging interlaced with new power centres and networks of decision making involving a much more varied set of civic actors, i.e. global citizens who believe that citizenship rights should trump market power and national sovereignty and that there must be a basic framework of international law holding all participants in the domain accountable.

This way of thinking emerged out of the Ottawa Process and it is a way of escaping from the messianic utopian claims of terrorists or those who seek a mission to save the world. It is a way of establishing a different sense of civic virtue which respects the rights of others and accepts the need to protect those rights. It is described by Sir Martin Gilbert, the noted British historian, as 'the most significant adjustment to national sovereignty in 360 years' (Gilbert 2007). As a foreign minister, I was basically a plumber fixing leaks. But I recognized that the leaks were more frequent because the architecture was frequently faulty. By the mid-1990s everyone was looking for improved solutions—better architecture. The human security idea proved to be the answer. As the Ottawa treaty conference came to an end, I sensed that for many participants this was a breakout from the dominance of great power politics towards an agenda that would put people's needs ahead of the raw power interests of the state. The Ottawa Process had flummoxed the experts who did not believe there could ever be anything more at stake than the exercise of naked self-interest. But the question was: Did it augur a change in perspective or was it an aberration? I would assert that the parentage of the human security concept and of responsibility to protect can be traced back to the Ottawa Process, and that these principles will shape global politics for years to come.

 ## Key points

- The 1996 Ottawa Process led to the establishment of an international treaty banning the use and trade of antipersonnel mines that is currently ratified by 156 countries.

- NGOs took an early lead in addressing the humanitarian devastation of landmines and attracted public support to the issue by reframing it as a humanitarian, or human security, issue, moving the focus away from arms control.

- The partnership that took place between NGOs and government in the build-up and execution of the Ottawa Process was novel, and it provided an alternative model for international politics.

- Middle power countries took the lead in the Ottawa Process, breaking away from established decision-making channels where more powerful nations had veto powers and where agreements were often watered down to suit the lowest common denominator. Instead, these countries worked with NGOs and used soft power diplomacy to achieve a ban on landmines.

- The parentage of the concept of human security and of the principle of the responsibility to protect can be traced back to the Ottawa Process.

 ## Questions

1. According to Dr Axworthy, the parentage of human security and 'responsibility to protect' can be traced back to the Ottawa process. What are the basis and logic of this statement?

2. Would a person examining the Ottawa Process from a realist perspective have a different assessment of it? If so, what might it be?

3. In his conclusion and his introduction, Axworthy presents his assessment of the impact and historical importance of the Ottawa Process. Is it possible to situate these arguments within a particular analytical framework? If so, which one and why?

4. This chapter emphasizes the way in which the Ottawa Process stepped away from the national security framework to focus instead on human security. Does it serve the interests of middle powers to sustain this framework across other international issues? What about big powers?

5. Dr Axworthy mentions that many politicians resent working with NGOs because they perceive them to be self-appointed spokespersons for the public who are usurping their role as elected representatives. Does this feeling reflect the existence of a real problem in terms of the democratic nature of initiatives in which NGOs are involved, or is it a red herring?

6. Axworthy discusses the success with which NGOs garnered public support for their cause by emphasizing the humanitarian impact of landmines. If they had emphasized the humanitarian impact of landmines, could governments have been as successful in affecting public opinion as NGOs were? Why or why not?

7. Thinking about international conventions and the rule of international law, are there any risks associated with conducting processes like the Ottawa Process outside traditional channels?

8. Does the stalemate that prompted the move outside traditional international decision-making channels indicate serious problems within existing frameworks? Does the Ottawa Process suggest strategies that can be used to address these problems?

 ## Further reading

Behringer, R.M. (2005), 'Middle Power Leadership on the Human Security Agenda', *Cooperation and Conflict: Journal of the Nordic International Studies Association*, 40: 305–42.
This article challenges the realist view of middle powers as followers of great power leadership by discussing a number of international initiatives led by middle power countries, including the Ottawa Process.

Lawson, R.J. (2002), *Ban Landmines! The Social Construction of the International Ban on Antipersonnel Landmines 1991–2001*, **Thesis for the Master of Political Science Carleton University (available online at: http://www.icbl.org/index/download/social_construction_of_ ban.pdf.**
This thesis provides a comprehensive overview of the Ottawa Process and of the roles played by relevant actors.

O'Dwyer, D. (2006), 'First Landmines, Now Small Arms? The International Campaign to Ban Landmines as a Model for Small-Arms Advocacy', *Irish Studies in International Affairs*, 17: 77–97.
This article challenges the argument that the Ottawa Process can serve as a model for future international efforts, arguing that it is best regarded as a one-off success.

Vines, A. (1998), 'The Crisis of Antipersonnel Mines', in M. Cameron, R. Lawson, and B. Tomlin (eds), *To Walk Without Fear* **(Toronto: Oxford University Press).**
An excellent discussion of the landmine issue and of the treaty.

Williams, J. and Roberts, S. (1995), *After the Guns Fall Silent: The Enduring Legacy of Landmines* **(Oxford: Oxfam).**
This book is an excellent overview of the impact of landmines, and provides an interesting perspective as it was written before the treaty process began.

Web links

www.stopclustermunitions.org The main source of information related to the campaign to ban cluster munitions.

www.icbl.org The International Campaign to Ban Landmines is the authoritative source for information on all aspects on the landmine ban and treaty and also provides many links to other sources of information, including a comprehensive index of landmine-related resources available both on and off line.

www.icrc.org/eng/mines The International Red Cross site dedicated to landmine issues.

http://www.hrw.org/advocacy/index.htm_Links to Human Rights Watch information and coverage of a range of arms and human security issues.

www.responsibilitytoprotect.org This website contains up-to-date information on the use of the R2P principle at the UN and in the media and discusses various initiatives underway to advance R2P.

http://globalr2p.org/ Global Centre for the Responsibility to Protect website.

 Visit the Online Resource Centre that accompanies this book for more information: **www.oxfordtextbooks.co.uk/orc/smith_foreign/**

Neoconservatism and the domestic sources of American foreign policy: the role of ideas in Operation Iraqi Freedom

YUEN FOONG KHONG

Chapter contents

 Reader's guide

Do ideas affect foreign policy, and if so, how? This chapter examines the claim that neoconservative ideas about foreign policy were decisive in persuading the George W. Bush administration to launch a preventive war against Iraq in March 2003. It identifies the key tenets of neoconservative foreign policy thought and shows that some of its major advocates won key positions in the Bush administration. However, the argument of the chapter is that, by itself, neoconservatism provides only a partial explanation of Operation Iraqi Freedom. A more satisfactory explanation would need to incorporate the following: the 9/11 attacks, the strategic placement of neoconservative ideas by its advocates in calmer times, the assumption that the USA would have no trouble waging a successful war, and the one percent doctrine. It is the combination of these events, ideas, and probability estimates that tipped the balance in favour of war.

Introduction

In the US elections of 2000, candidate George W. Bush sought to contrast his foreign policy approach with that of the Clinton administration, by using the idea of the USA as a 'humble nation'. 'If we're an arrogant nation', Bush argued, 'they'll resent us; if we're a humble nation,

but strong, they'll welcome us' (PBS Online News Hour 2000). Bush implied that his opponent, Vice-President Al Gore, was associated with the 'arrogant nation' approach of the Clinton Presidency, which saw America as the 'indispensable nation'.

Yet in the space of a few short years, the George W. Bush Presidency roused international
resentment against the USA on a scale inconceivable during the Clinton years. The strong
international 'rally behind America' sentiment in the aftermath of the 9/11 attacks was replaced by both dissent and resentment as the Bush administration launched a preventive war
against Iraq. The failure to find weapons of mass destruction (WMDs) in Iraq, the US mistreat-
ment of prisoners in Baghdad's Abu Ghraib prison, and the eruption of a vicious civil war in
Iraq made the international community dubious about the intentions, competence, and
moral stature of the USA. Domestically, mounting US casualties in the inconclusive Iraq war
led to plummeting approval ratings of the Bush administration. The American public's disenchantment and anger with the administration's handling of the war found expression in the
mid-term elections of 2006 when Democrats took control of the Senate and the House of
Representatives. A Democrat-controlled Congress in turn put pressure on the Bush administration to withdraw from Iraq. Images of the Vietnam quagmire became prevalent in domestic debates about the war. Domestically, and internationally, the George W. Bush administration
found itself besieged and demoralized.

From humble nation to a nation besieged. How did this happen? Many believe that the
answer lies in the influence of the neoconservatives and their foreign policy ideas upon
George W. Bush. As *Newsweek* put it, 'The neocon vision has become the hard core of American foreign policy.' *The New York Times* argued: 'They have penetrated the culture at nearly
every level from the halls of academia to the halls of the Pentagon.' And for Elizabeth Drew,
writing in *The New York Review of Books*, 'The neoconservatives . . . are largely responsible for
getting us into the war against Iraq' (cited in Muravchik 2004).

This chapter will examine the role of American neoconservatives and their ideas in the war
against Iraq. Neoconservative foreign policy thought emphasizes the moral necessity of distinguishing between the forces of good and evil in the international arena, the importance
of maintaining US military predominance, a greater willingness to use force, and deep distrust of international law and institutions. These ideas were not the only relevant factor in
bringing about Operation Iraqi Freedom; others included the 9/11 terrorist attacks, stopping
Saddam Hussein's WMD programme, spreading democracy in the Middle East, access to oil
resources, replacing Saudi Arabia with Iraq as America's security pillar in the region, and the
Israel lobby. Therefore the challenge for the foreign policy analyst is to select the most important of these factors, demonstrate when and how they came into play in the decision-
making process, and organize the analysis into a compelling narrative. I shall attempt to do
this by arguing that while neoconservative ideas were indeed important in the US decision
to launch a preventive war against Iraq, they were far from decisive. At least three other factors need to be taken into consideration. The most obvious of these are the 9/11 attacks on
the USA by al-Qaeda. In essence, no 9/11, no Operation Iraqi Freedom. Ideas, it would seem,
need to be activated by events. Second, the strategic placement of neoconservative ideas in
calmer times is also important. When 9/11 came, neoconservative ideas had developed
substantially and were ready to be put into action. Third, the two probability assumptions
made by the architects of the war are also critical. First, the assumption that militarily, the
operation would be a 'cakewalk', and second, the assumption that even if there was only a

low probability of Saddam's link to al-Qaeda over WMDs, the USA still had to treat it as a certainty. The assumption that it would be easy to defeat Saddam Hussein's army is consistent with the neoconservatives' faith in US military prowess. However, treating low-probability events as a certainty is not a neoconservative tenet. Rather, it is a post-9/11 mindset of vulnerability that permeated the Bush administration. As this chapter will demonstrate, it is precisely the coming together of these events (9/11), fears (perceptions of vulnerability), ideas (neoconservatism), and guesses (probability estimates) that set the USA on the path to war in Iraq.

Neoconservatism as a domestic source of American foreign policy

If the international environment compelled states to act predictably, the need for foreign policy analysis would not be so great. Both 9/11 and Pearl Harbor (1941) are examples of external attacks in which the USA had little choice but to retaliate by going to war against the state (Afghanistan) harboring the perpetrators, or the perpetrator state itself (Japan). The US reaction, in other words, seems reasonably obvious; no elaborate foreign policy analysis is needed to make sense of the decision. However, such externally dictated policies are rare. In most cases, even when there is a clear external dynamic, such as the threat posed by the Soviet Union during the Cold War or the rise of China today, the policy response of the USA is filtered through a domestic dynamic that may involve the president, his advisers, the relevant agencies, Congress, lobby groups, non-governmental organizations, and public opinion, many of whom may have different ideas or interests pertaining to the issue. The historian John Lewis Gaddis explained the two differing strategies of containment adopted by US administrations between the 1940s and 1980s in terms of the differing economic philosophies of the two main political parties. Republicans (prior to Ronald Reagan) favoured tight fiscal polices capable of reining in inflation, while Democrats (prior to Jimmy Carter) preferred expansive policies capable of generating employment. In his conclusion, Gaddis appeared pleasantly surprised by the decisiveness of the domestic sources of America's containment policy: 'To a remarkable degree, containment has been the product, not so much of what the Russians have done, or of what has happened elsewhere in the world, but of internal forces operating within the United States' (Gaddis 1982: 357).

The neoconservatives and their ideas can be understood as one of the more influential 'internal forces operating within the United States'. Irving Kristol, often regarded as the godfather of neoconservatism, locates its origins 'among the disillusioned liberal intellectuals of the 1970s' (Seltzer 2004: 33–7). What disillusioned these liberals was the Democratic Party's tilt to the left as a result of the domestic turmoil associated with the Civil Rights Movement and the Vietnam War. One manifestation of that tilt included the refusal or inability of liberals to defend themselves from attacks by radical students, professors, and civil rights activists on traditional values (implying moral self-doubt on the part of some segments of the American political elite); neoconservatives like Kristol found this moral self-flagellation excessive and even dangerous. Whatever America's errors, they felt, its political values and system were superior to the alternatives.

On social and economic issues, the 'first-generation' neoconservatives criticized the Democratic Party's approach to the welfare state which involved high taxes, welfarist programmes associated with the Great Society introduced under President Lyndon Johnson, and affirmative action policies. Although neoconservatives grudgingly accepted the need for the welfare state, they argued against a social engineering approach which rewarded undesirable social behaviour like single motherhood through the provision of welfare support; they also criticized policies in which schoolchildren were bused to schools beyond their neighbourhood in the name of racial integration. Neoconservatives argued for a moral regeneration of America, where there was clarity about the moral values that made the good life possible and where the right incentives would foster the desired kind of social behaviour (Stelzer 2004: 20–1).

On foreign policy, the neoconservatives were fervent anti-communists, emphasizing the ideological and moral superiority of democracy, while advocating the maintenance of a strong military (Kristol and Kagan 1996, 2004).[1] They rejected the moral angst prevalent among liberals that in Vietnam, the USA had fought an unjust war with unjust means. America may have lost the Vietnam War, but it was a 'noble war' which could have been won had the American public and media been less fickle. Neoconservatives, along with other political conservatives, or **hawks**, worked to counter the fallout from the Vietnam debacle by arguing for strong military budgets, even in times of economic strain, in the name of restoring the prestige and power of the US military. US military power had to be shored up because the neoconservatives of the 1970s saw the Soviet Union catching up with and even surpassing the military power of the USA The Team A versus Team B debates of the 1970s exemplify this concern about declining US power in the face of communism's perceived advance. Team B was set up in 1976 by CIA Director George H.W. Bush to address concerns that CIA analyses (Team A) of Soviet intentions and capabilities were too benign. Chaired by the conservative Harvard historian Richard Pipes, other members of Team B included Paul Nitze, Edward Teller, and Paul Wolfowitz. Team B's analysis of the classified intelligence data was more alarming: their report portrayed a Soviet Union bent on both military superiority and global Soviet hegemony (Mann 2004: 73–4).[2] Team B's assessments of the Soviet Union were given further credence by the Soviet invasion of Afghanistan in 1979.

In addition to Irving Kristol, other first-generation neoconservative figures included Jeane Kirkpatrick, Midge Decter, and Norman Podheretz. Their arguments for US domestic social and economic arrangements were featured in the pages of *The Public Interest*, edited by Kristol, while foreign policy issues were debated within the pages of *Commentary*, edited by Podheretz. By the 1980s, the 'second-generation neoconservatives', including intellectuals and policy makers such as William Kristol, Robert Kagan, Charles Krauthammer, Francis Fukuyama, Paul Wolfowitz, Elliott Abrams, Daniel Pipes, and Joshua Muravchik, were poised to carry the neoconservative torch forward (Ehrman 1995: 192). The main outlets for their writings were *The Weekly Standard*, edited by William Kristol, and *The National Interest*. A number of second-generation neoconservatives—Kristol, Abrams, Fukuyama, and Wolfowitz—also served in the Reagan and Bush Sr administrations. In power, they were inspired by Reagan's willingness to call a spade a spade, as in his 1983 'evil empire' speech about the Soviet Union. Wolfowitz and Abrams were also associated with regime change in the Third World. As Assistant Secretary of State for East Asian and Pacific Affairs, Wolfowitz was part of the decision-making team that used diplomacy to pressure President Ferdinand Marcos of the Philippines to leave office in 1986 when his clumsy attempts to prevent the democratically elected Mrs Cory Aquino from gaining power backfired. Abrams, as Assistant Secretary of State for Inter-American Affairs, was implicated in the Reagan administration's policy of providing funds, against the prohibitions of Congress, to the Contra rebels seeking to overthrow the Sandinista government of Nicaragua.

When the Cold War ended, neoconservatives found themselves without a clear **external Other**, or outside enemy upon which to focus. They also worried about the failure of the Bush Sr and Clinton administrations to maintain America's military strength and moral purpose. Many, including Richard Perle, Paul Wolfowitz, Jeane Kirkpatrick, and Joshua Muravchik, were disillusioned with US vacillation in the Balkans in the early 1990s (the late Bush Sr and early Clinton years) and agitated for the use of force against the Serbs in Bosnia. Others, like Charles Krauthammer, who adhered to a more restricted concept of US interests were opposed to US military involvement (Muravchik 2004: 243–57).

During the Clinton years, the neoconservatives found themselves on the ideological and political margins. The Clinton Presidency relied for its most important foreign policy decisions on non-disillusioned liberals like Warren Christopher and Anthony Lake, as well as moderate Republicans like Colin Powell and William Cohen. Although the neoconservatives carped from the foreign policy sidelines, some used this time very fruitfully. Most notable in this respect were William Kristol and Robert Kagan who, in the late 1990s, penned a series of neoconservative foreign policy tracts that would later exert great influence on the Bush administration. Kristol and Kagan's 1996 *Foreign Affairs* article, 'Toward a Reaganite Foreign Policy', is widely regarded as the seminal foreign policy statement of contemporary neoconservative thought.

Just as important as the contents of this essay was Kristol and Kagan's strategic approach to the battle of ideas. The authors sought to present a set of ideas with an apparent fit with the times which contrasted with existing approaches to foreign policy. They consciously rejected both the neo-isolationism advocated by Patrick Buchanan and the Wilsonian multilateralism of the Clintonites. The authors' main target—the approach it sought to displace—was conservative realism, the pragmatic realpolitik approach to foreign policy exemplified by Henry Kissinger and his protégé Brent Scowcroft. Kissingerian realpolitik was found wanting because it refused to advertise its moral purpose and was lax in doing what was necessary to maintain American military preponderance.

Kristol and Kagan also consciously and systematically embedded their neo-Reaganite foreign policy ideas into establishment circles during calmer times, when there appeared to be no serious threat to the USA. These were opportune moments to plant ideas, for the history of American foreign policy indicated that '[a]s troubles arise and the need to act becomes clear, those who had laid the foundation for a necessary shift in policy have a chance to lead Americans onto a new course' (Kristol and Kagan 1996: 29). For them, both the containment policy known as **NSC-68** and the Team A–Team B debates about Soviet intentions served as strategic thinking that laid the intellectual foundations for future policy shifts that would be triggered by external events. North Korea's invasion of the South in 1950 made it easy to choose the NSC-68 version of containment over George Kennan's more political/diplomatic approach, and the Soviet invasion of Afghanistan in 1979 also helped Team B win the debate about Soviet expansionism, facilitating the Reagan administration's massive military build-up in the 1980s. Guided by these historical lessons and

BOX 16.1 'Toward a Neo-Reaganite Foreign Policy'

'Toward a Neo-Reaganite Foreign Policy' (Kristol and Kagan 1996) is widely regarded as a seminal statement on neoconservative foreign policy thought. The authors argued that the international role of the USA is to exercise 'benevolent global hegemony', that is 'a leader with preponderant influence and authority over all others'. They believed that the USA was already in that position and they proposed to maintain that status via 'a neo-Reaganite foreign policy of military supremacy and moral confidence'. Such a policy would involve the following.

● A consistently strong defence budget that reinforces the power disparity between the US and would-be challengers.

● Educating Americans about the role they can play in understanding and supporting US armed forces as they carry out the 'responsibilities of global hegemony'.

● Having a clear moral purpose behind American foreign policy. The USA should be in the business of promoting democracy, free markets, and individual liberty abroad.

their underlying Hobbesian ideas about international relations, Kristol and Kagan were betting on even more drastic times when 'troubles arise and the need to act becomes clear'. Their conceptual and action blueprint would lie waiting until its trial by fire in Iraq. (See Box 16.1.)

The four tenets of neoconservative foreign policy thought

What then are the main tenets of the neoconservative approach to foreign policy? Drawing on the writings of Kristol and Kagan and others (Kristol and Kagan 1996, 2004; Halper and Clarke 2004; Fukuyama 2006), it is possible to organize neoconservatism's approach to foreign policy into four interrelated premises which together form a coherent philosophy.

The first premise of the neoconservative stance in foreign policy is **moral clarity** about the forces of good and evil in the international arena. This moral clarity or certainty is starkly articulated in terms of the internal characteristics of states—democratic leaders and liberal democracies are good; tyrants and tyrannical regimes are bad (Kristol and Kagan 1996; Fukuyama 2006: 48). Both democracies and totalitarian regimes cannot help but express their values when it comes to foreign policy, and the value-based policies of tyrannies such as Saddam Hussein's Iraq and Jiang Zemin's China are both geopolitical and moral affronts to the security and sensibilities of liberal democracies like the USA. For neoconservatives, therefore, morality and interest are, or should be, conjoined in US diplomacy: it is right and in the interests of the USA to act against regimes whose values and actions it considers morally abhorrent. Therefore the USA should not shy away from regime change and democracy promotion (Kristol 2004).

This premise contrasts with that of classical realists, who are dubious about injecting morality into their foreign policy, and who believe that morality and interests do not always go together. In the 1970s, for example, when the US Ambassador in Chile probed the Pinochet government about human rights abuses, Kissinger was reported to have asked his aides to tell '[US Ambassador] Popper to cut out the political science lectures!' (cited in Schoultz 1981:

111). For Kissinger, the geopolitical interest of having Chile on America's side during the Cold War trumped any moral unease that he or his Ambassador in Santiago harboured about Chile's human rights record. Kissinger and other conservative realists also refrained from using strong moral language in public to describe the other great but non-democratic powers with whom the USA had to coexist, and they went to great lengths to avoid branding these interlocutors as the evil empire or the butchers of Beijing. **Interest-based pragmatism** rather than value-based approaches is the *modus operandi* of classic realist foreign policy. However, as heirs to Reagan's 'evil empire' approach to tyrannies, neoconservatives pride themselves on undiplomatic straight talking, even in public. The policy implication of such strong moral discourse is *change* (e.g. regime change) or transformation, not *coexistence*.

The second premise of neoconservative foreign policy thought is that the USA should strive to preserve its **military pre-eminence** in the post-Cold War world. As the exemplar of liberal democracy, the USA should work towards what Kristol and Kagan call 'a benevolent US hegemony', meaning a situation where the USA 'enjoys [both] strategic and ideological predominance' in the world (Kristol and Kagan 1996: 20). From the neoconservative perspective, what most people in the world fear is US retrenchment and isolationism rather than US activism and hegemony. The neoconservatives' implicit theory of international relations is based on a preponderance of power, instead of a traditional balance of power, as the route to peace and stability. Classical realists do not mind being the pre-eminent power, but they do not believe that such a situation will last. As a result, they are more reticent about America's preponderant power post Cold War. This springs from their sensitivity to fact that—however virtuous the actions of the USA—others will find such preponderance unpleasant and even intolerable, and are likely to form counter-coalitions to balance against it. Neoconservatives worry less about such counter-coalitions for two reasons. First, they believe that fair-minded nations will appreciate the benevolent nature of US hegemony; second, nations that refuse to give the USA the benefit of the doubt will simply have to live with, or in fear of, America's overwhelming power. The latter points to the third tenet of neoconservative foreign policy thought.

The third tenet is that the USA should **leverage its military power**, i.e. be willing to use military force to pursue its foreign policy goals. This stems from a keen appreciation of America's technological edge and prowess. Paul Wolfowitz liked to express his awe for this prowess by marvelling at television images of the **Gulf War of 1990–1991** showing 'cruise missiles capable of making right angle turns.' But the neoconservative argument for the utility of force also stems from the first two premises: if one's ends are noble and good, one would be morally derelict if one did not use all the means at one's disposal—including military force—in pursuit of those ends (such as democratization). The desire to promote democracy by using force if necessary, coupled with a disregard for international law and international institutions, has earned the neoconservatives epithets of 'muscular Wilsonianism' and 'Wilsonianism on steroids' which do not necessarily displease them. Further, as the pre-eminent military power, few would have the resources or gumption to counter America on this terrain. Classical realists are far from reticent in using force when it comes to protecting US national/security interests, but in contrast with the neoconservatives, they recoil from using force to pursue primarily moral ends. For realists, one must unsentimentally assess the interests involved and not let morality intrude. Compared with the neoconservatives, the traditional realists are more cautious when it comes to leveraging American military power.

Fourth, there is also a deep scepticism on the part of the neoconservatives about the ability of international law and institutions to bring about peace and justice in this world (Halper and Clarke 2004: 11; Fukuyama 2006: 49). Institutions like the International Criminal Court and the United Nations are seen by neoconservatives as mechanisms used by weaker powers to tie down the USA. If the weaker nations had as much power as the USA, they would also be suspicious of these institutions. Here, the neoconservatives and the traditional conservative realists are not so far apart. Both appreciate the legitimating functions of international law and international institutions. However, the neoconservatives are much quicker at dismissing the latter when they obstruct US policy; they feel secure in doing so because of their faith in the moral rightness of their policies and because the USA has the power to pursue such policies.

The four tenets add up to a coherent philosophy of the purposes and methods of US foreign policy. For Kenneth Adelman, a self-identified neoconservative, neoconservatism is 'the idea of a tough foreign policy on behalf of morality, the idea of using our power for moral good in the world'(*Vanity Fair* 2007). The Kristol–Kagan formulation is even more ambitious. It amounts to a reversal of John Quincy Adams' warning that America should not go 'abroad in search of monsters to destroy'. Their retort: 'Why not?' In one of the most revealing passages in the Kristol and Kagan *Foreign Affairs* essay, they argue:

> The alternative is to leave monsters on the loose, ravaging and pillaging to their hearts' content . . . Because America has the capacity to contain or destroy many of the world's monsters, most of which can be found without much searching, and because the responsibility for the peace and security of the international order rests so heavily on America's shoulders, a policy of sitting atop a hill and leading by example becomes in practice a policy of cowardice and dishonor (Kristol and Kagan 1996: 31).

Kristol and Kagan were quite tentative about the identity of the main monsters. Ronald Reagan had slain the Soviet monster in the 1980s. In an elaboration of their thesis in 2000, they identified the missed opportunities of the 1990s in slaying monsters: Saddam Hussein, Slobodan Milosevic, and Kim Il Sung. Looking ahead, China was the other tyrannical regime 'with the power to do us or our allies harm' and where the USA 'should seek not coexistence but transformation [regime change]'. The slaying of these monsters would go a long way towards 'preserving and reinforcing America's benevolent global hegemony' (Kristol and Kagan 2004: 58, 70-71). (See Box 16.2.)

Neoconservatives and the slaying of the Iraqi monster

Kristol and Kagan felt sufficiently strongly about regime change in Iraq to send a letter to President Bill Clinton in January 1998 under the auspices of the Project on the New American Century (PNAC), co-signed by sixteen other grandees associated with Republican administrations. Among the signers were Elliott Abrams, John Bolton, Francis Fukuyama, Robert Kagan, Zalmay Khalizad, William Kristol, Richard Perle, Donald Rumsfeld, and Paul Wolfowitz (see Box 16.3). The letter argued that the existing policy of containing Iraq was not working and that the 'only acceptable strategy is one that eliminates the possibility that Iraq will be able to use or threaten to use weapons of mass destruction.' The signatories declared that '[i]n the

---

BOX 16.2 The four tenets of neoconservative foreign policy thought

- Moral clarity about forces of good and evil in the international arena: liberal democracies are good; tyrannies are bad.
- A benevolent US hegemony will be good for all.
- The USA should show a greater willingness to use military force to pursue its goals.
- International law and institutions are unreliable in obtaining peace/justice.

Applying the tenets of neoconservative foreign policy thought to Saddam Hussein's Iraq:

- Saddam is the No. 1 member of the 'axis of evil'; regime change leading to a democratic Iraq is the first step in democratizing the Middle East.
- Regime change in Iraq will remove a major adversary and reinforce US power in the Middle East.
- Saddam possesses WMDs, containment is not working, military force is the only way to achieve US goals.
- UN resolution is unnecessary; 'coalition of the willing' is sufficient.

BOX 16.3 PNAC 1998 signatories

Signatories of 1998 PNAC letter on Iraq who held a policy position in the Bush administration:

Elliott Abrams, Special Assistant to the President and Senior Director for Near East and North African Affairs, National Security Council
Richard Armitage, Deputy Secretary of State
Paula Dobriansky, Under Secretary of State, Democracy and Global Affair
John Bolton, US Permanent Representative to the United Nations
Richard Perle, Chairman, Defense Policy Board
Zalmay Khalizad, US Ambassador to Afghanistan (2003–05), and Iraq (2005–07)
Peter Rodman, Assistant Secretary of Defense for International Security Affairs
Donald Rumsfeld, Secretary of Defense
Paul Wolfowitz, Deputy Secretary of Defense
Robert Zoellick, US Trade Representative/Deputy Secretary of State

---

near term, this means a willingness to undertake military action as diplomacy is clearly failing' (Project for the New American Century 1998).

The case for a preventive war against Iraq was laid out in this letter. President Clinton neglected it. However, President George W. Bush appointed at least eight of the signatories—including Paul Wolfowitz, Elliott Abrams, John Bolton, Zalmay Khalizad, Richard Perle and Donald Rumsfeld—to important positions in his administration. To be sure, Rumsfeld is not usually thought of as a neoconservative. Neither is Vice-President Dick Cheney, unlike his two main aides, Lewis 'Scooter' Libby and Douglas Feith. The common thread that united these individuals was that they were sympathetic to regime change in Iraq. The ascension of these individuals to influential positions, especially within the Defense Department and the Vice-President's Office, meant that neoconservative foreign policy ideas moved definitively from the political fringe to the political centre. (See Figure 16.1.)

Figure 16.1 The ascent of the neocon.

Despite the seductiveness of the neoconservative foreign policy doctrine, it is doubtful that President Bush would have used military force to effect regime change in Iraq if not for 9/11. Having ideas and (some of) their advocates in high positions are important, but it was al-Qaeda's attack on the American homeland which tipped the balance in favour of neoconservative doctrine. The indiscriminate murder of innocents in the centres of American economic and military power was particularly galling to the neoconservatives. Here was a group of shadowy non-state actors, operating on a set of 'moral principles' that identified the USA as the chief obstacle to their dream of bringing back an eighth-century Islamic caliphate, and who viewed the killing of innocents as a legitimate policy in the pursuit of that end. Moral clarity, however perverse and distorted, was not something that al-Qaeda lacked. The terrorists were also strategic in their choice of landmarks; the World Trade Center and the Pentagon were symbols of American economic and military power, so the terrorists attacked the pre-eminent USA in the very sources of its pre-eminence. To the extent that there was no real return address for al-Qaeda (apart from for Afghanistan, harbouring Osama bin Laden), it would also seem difficult for the USA to respond directly with its military might, making it appear as a helpless giant. Had Bill Clinton or Al Gore been president, arguably they too would have targeted Afghanistan in the aftermath of 9/11. For the neoconservatives (and indeed for many around the world), the action of targeting Afghanistan was symbolic in its moral clarity; toppling the Taliban showed in no uncertain terms that those who harboured terrorists risked forcible regime change. It also demonstrated that the USA was not helpless; it could bring its military power to bear. In an important sense, however, the war in Afghanistan was a case of taking care of things too late—after one has been attacked. For National Security

Adviser Condoleezza Rice, 'The lesson of September 11' was 'Take care of threats early' (cited in Woodward 2002: 350).

Dealing with Saddam Hussein's Iraq would be the case where the USA would 'take care of threats early'. Despite receiving support from the USA during the Iran–Iraq war, Saddam Hussein made the mistake of threatening the interests of the West by invading Kuwait in 1990, thus shifting in Western eyes from a regional ally to a regional threat, particularly *vis-à-vis* Israel. After ejecting Iraq from Kuwait during Operation Desert Storm in 1991, the Bush Sr administration made a calculated decision not to move towards Baghdad to remove Saddam from power. However, leaving Saddam in power brought its own problems. He mercilessly suppressed the Shiite rebellion in southern Iraq in 1991; his military played cat and mouse games by firing at US war planes patrolling the 'no fly' zones; and he expelled the UN weapons inspectors in 1998, heightening suspicions that Iraq was intent on developing WMDs. Although these actions were persuasive enough for some (including the signatories of the 1998 PNAC letter) to argue for forceful regime change in Iraq, George W. Bush needed an extra push to set out on the path of war to Iraq. The 9/11 attacks provided that extra push.

Existing accounts of the deliberations leading to Operation Iraqi Freedom suggest that Secretary of Defense Donald Rumsfeld would have pursued Saddam Hussein regardless of his possession of WMDs or links to al-Qaeda. For Rumsfeld, the war in Iraq was about demonstrating American power to the rest of the world; he wanted to strike at something more substantial than Afghanistan in order to deter others from posing similar threats to the USA. Thus Rumsfeld's eagerness to attack Iraq was based on deterrence and demonstration of American power, rather than morality, which is why he is not normally seen as a neoconservative despite championing their cause of forceful regime change in Iraq. In two National Security Council meetings in the days after 9/11, Rumsfeld's position was to ask: 'Do we focus on Bin Laden and al Qaeda, or terrorism more broadly?' 'More broadly' was code for Iraq. In the 15 September meeting held at Camp David, Rumsfeld was more explicit: 'Is this the time to attack Iraq?' (Woodward 2002: 43, 84).

The answer was 'not yet' for most, especially the President. Bush and his advisers assumed that Saddam Hussein possessed WMDs. Successive National Intelligence Estimates had agreed, mistakenly as it turned out, that Baghdad possessed chemical and biological weapons (Woodward 2004: 194–9). But Bush wanted confirmation that Saddam Hussein was linked to the 9/11 terrorists before attacking Iraq. However, the National Intelligence Estimates were much more cautious about Saddam's links to al-Qaeda. There was much debate between the CIA and the administration about the existence and significance of a meeting in Prague between Mohammad Atta (one of the 9/11 hijackers) and the Iraqi Intelligence Chief. The debate was inconclusive. Instead, what clinched the argument in analysing the severity of the threat posed by Iraq for those who wanted war was the one percent doctrine.

The one percent doctrine

The one percent doctrine essentially argued that even with a one percent chance of a grave threat materializing, the USA should treat that threat as a certainty and act to eliminate it. To be clear, the one percent doctrine is not a neoconservative tenet; neither is it something derived from the four neoconservative premises discussed above. It is a probability estimate made by an administration that felt existentially vulnerable after 9/11; a vulnerability encapsulated by National Security Adviser Condolezza Rice's quip about the fear of 'smoking guns turning into mushroom clouds' (cited in Woodward 2004: 179).

Vice-President Dick Cheney was among to first to articulate the doctrine in a briefing by the CIA concerning a group of Pakistani scientists involved in disseminating nuclear knowledge to other Islamic actors. Although the evidence was inconclusive, Cheney argued that '[i]f there's a one percent chance that Pakistani scientists are helping al-Qaeda build or develop a nuclear weapon, then we have to treat it as a certainty in terms of our response'. For Cheney, it was not about the 'analysis or finding a preponderance of evidence', but rather about the appropriate US response (Suskind 2006: 65). Similarly, when the President was briefed by the FBI about a group of Americans in Lackawanna, Wisconsin, who had attended training camps in Pakistan, he enquired whether they might engage in terrorist acts. The FBI was '99 percent sure that we can make sure that these guys don't do something—if they are planning to do something'. But Bush's retort was: 'under the rules we were playing at the time, that's not acceptable' (Suskind 2006: 159).

The one percent doctrine provides an operational answer to a key element of the Bush doctrine of preventive war. As Bush's articulation of his doctrine in his 2002 State of the Union address put it: 'I will not wait on events, while dangers gather. I will not stand by, as peril draws closer and closer. The United States of America will not permit the world's most dangerous regimes to threaten us with the world's most destructive weapons' (White House, 2002). For such a doctrine to be operational, it needs to have an answer to the question of when the peril posed by the world's most dangerous regimes is close enough to warrant action. The one percent doctrine—even when interpreted figuratively instead of literally—suggests that even when the chances of such threats materializing are very low, the USA cannot afford to wait; it needs to act to remove the source of the threat.

It is unlikely that the one percent doctrine was a pretext cooked up by the Vice-President's office. Students of war maintain that a crucial element in war decision making involves the making of two estimates. One, estimating the probability of what you want to avoid materializing if you do not fight; two, estimating the probability of winning if you choose to fight. In examining the first probability, it is not difficult to understand why, post 9/11, US policy makers would take a radically different attitude towards such low-probability–high-impact events— especially when it comes to WMDs (thought to be) possessed by an arch enemy of the USA. According to some sources, Paul Wolfowitz believed from the beginning that there was a 10–50% chance that Saddam Hussein was involved in the 9/11 attacks (Woodward 2002: 83). Others were not so sure. However, if the 'insecurity threshold' is lowered to one percent, i.e. the USA would not even tolerate a one percent chance of insecurity, it would be virtually impossible for Saddam Hussein (or indeed any threat) not to be caught within that threshold. **Prospect theory**, a psychological theory of decision making under different frames of reference, would shed light on this line of thinking. Decision makers who see themselves as operating in the domain of gain tend to choose risk-averse policies; when they find themselves in the domain of loss—as Bush and his advisers must have found themselves—they are inclined to pick high-risk options (Quattrone and Tversky 1988). The one percent doctrine, inasmuch as it focuses on 'our response' (and springs from the domain of loss) implies a risk-acceptant strategy.

The second probability estimate that decision makers need to make involves ascertaining their chances of success. What precisely did success mean in the case of Operation Iraqi Freedom? Winning the war and deposing Saddam Hussein? Of that they had no doubt. On the broader aspects of success, which included establishing a democratic government in a peaceful and stable society, the Bush administration was also supremely confident, to the point of negligence. This is evidenced in the early decision by the Defense Department to shut out the State Department from the task of post-war planning, despite the State Department having already established a team devoted to post-war reconstruction. Faulty assumptions about the nature of Iraqi society, inadequate post-war planning, and above all incompetence in post-war reconstruction allowed the USA to snatch defeat from the jaws of victory (Galbraith 2006; Woodward 2006). As of May 2007, over 60,000 Iraqi civilian were reported dead, 3400 American and 250 coalition soldiers had been killed, and the civil war between the Shiites and Sunnis continued with no sign of abatement. Even if order and stability are eventually achieved by the Iraqi government with the help of the coalition forces, the human, financial, and moral costs of Operation Iraqi Freedom will be fiercely debated by future generations in America and elsewhere.

Douglas Feith, Undersecretary of Defense, whom General Tommy Franks called the '[expletive deleted] stupidest guy on the face of the earth' (cited in Woodward 2004) was the official in overall charge of post-war reconstruction. Widely seen as a neoconservative, Feith's faith about the ease with which post-war Iraq could be stabilized is consistent with neoconservative beliefs about the moral superiority of democracy and the military prowess of the USA. With Saddam Hussein deposed, Iraqis would be out in the streets to welcome the coalition forces as liberators. A democratic Iraq would serve as a beacon for other states in the Middle East. But these neoconservative hopes reveal a blind spot. Neoconservatives such as Feith may push for forceful regime change, but they seem less concerned with post-war reconstruction and the challenges of nation building. Francis Fukuyama has argued that first-generation neoconservatives were profoundly ambivalent about social engineering and nation building, a view which informed their critique of domestic welfare programmes in the USA (Fukuyama 2006: 49). Second-generation neoconservatives appear even less interested in nation building abroad. They chose not to pay it much attention and as such proved utterly incompetent in those same areas in which they were then required to act. If the moral situation is so clear and US power so benevolent, few would dare to challenge the USA; therefore in neoconservative eyes the post-war reconstruction of Iraq should be like a cakewalk. That the situation in Iraq since 2003 has been anything but a cakewalk has led some neoconservatives, like Kenneth Adelman, to admit that neoconservatism has been discredited for a generation; even William Kristol is willing to acknowledge that neoconservatism has been damaged although he remains insistent that it is still relevant.

Neoconservatism in the context of other factors

Major events in world politics tend to be overdetermined when we engage in post-fact analysis of their principal causes. This chapter has attempted to provide an analytical narrative of the events, ideas, and assumptions leading to Operation Iraqi Freedom. The narrative has been organized around the role of neoconservatism as a necessary but not sufficient condition of Operation Iraqi Freedom. Only when it operated in conjunction with US perceptions of vulnerability after the 9/11 attacks, estimates of probability of success if force was used, and the one percent doctrine, did neoconservatism become a powerful causal force behind the decisions of 2002–2003.

For some, this acknowledgement of neoconservatism as one of the major factors behind the preventive war of 2003 may be giving it too much credit. So it may be useful to entertain the following thought experiment: if neoconservative foreign policy ideas had not existed, would the Bush administration still have launched a preventive war against Iraq in the post-9/11 environment? Would not perceptions of sheer vulnerability and sureness about battle-field success, plus the one percent doctrine, have been enough to tilt the decision in favour of using force to topple Saddam? Perhaps, but neoconservatism did bring several key items to the table: its warning (in the mid-1990s) about troubles that beckon (giving it predictive cred-ibility and prescience when serious troubles came), its confidence in American power, and, perhaps most of all, its moral clarity about the evilness of Saddam Hussein's regime and po-tential for democratic change in the Middle East. In a recent analysis of agenda setting and the war in Iraq, Michael Mazarr focused on how the 'anti-Saddam' policy entrepreneurs had in-serted and kept the regime change agenda alive in Washington policy circles, and how 9/11 allowed them to push through that policy. He did this without once mentioning 'neocon-servatism' or 'the neoconservatives' (Mazarr 2007). Mazarr is perceptive both about the gen-eral role of agenda setting and the specific importance of events such as 9/11 in catapulting one's agenda to the top of the policy process, but his account begs the question of how the anti-Saddam policy first originated or what actually united the entrepreneurs pushing the policy. This is where neoconservatism comes in: with its recognition of America's military su-periority, its moral distaste for tyrants, and its willingness to use American power to get rid of them, Saddam Hussein's Iraq fell naturally within the crosshairs of the neoconservatives' stra-tegic sights long before 9/11. In other words, Saddam Hussein was the tyrant who emerged most fit for the neoconservative purpose. Neoconservatives may also have wished to aim at China or North Korea, but as these states possessed nuclear weapons, 'regime change' would probably require different and more challenging methods. Given the Iraq quagmire, the very question of regime change in US foreign policy is now likely to be up for grabs. In that sense neoconservatism does add value to our understanding of the path to war: it is more than an ideational backdrop but less than a decisive cause.

The other factors mentioned at the beginning of this chapter, including the need for oil resources, the Israel lobby, and the geopolitics of making Saudi Arabia the new security pillar in the Middle East, have not been given pride of place in this analysis because they have not featured prominently in published accounts of the Bush administration's decision making on Iraq. Moreover, these factors also fail the following counterfactual thought experiment: if X (e.g. the Israel lobby) did not exist, would the Bush administration have gone ahead with Operation Iraqi Freedom? The answer seems to be 'yes' whether we are thinking of oil or the Israel lobby. While secure and affordable oil supplies is a key factor in America's national se-curity strategy, the fear of Saddam spreading WMDs to terrorists was overwhelming. Iraq's oil, to the extent that it featured in the internal deliberations, was seen as a means of revenue for the Iraqis to rebuild their economy after the invasion. Similarly, the argument that the Israel lobby, through organizations like American–Israel Public Affairs Committee (AIPAC) and indi-viduals like Wolfowitz, was critical in persuading the Bush administration to attack Iraq, thereby enhancing Israel's security while undermining that of the USA, is problematic (Mear-sheimer and Walt 2006). While it is true that many in the Bush administration were staunch friends of Israel, the thrust of the analysis presented here suggests that their concerns focused primarily on safeguarding the security of the USA. Discussions of the risks posed by WMDs, including the one percent doctrine, focused on the danger to the USA, and not allies such as Israel. If regime change in Iraq also enhanced Israel's security, that would be a bonus. In other words, given the heightened vulnerability felt by the Bush administration, it did not need the Israel lobby to push for preventive war against Iraq.

Conclusion

This chapter has sought to provide an analysis of the conditions under which neoconservatism became an important causal factor in the Bush administration's decision to launch a preventive war against Iraq. Neoconservative foreign policy thought has been examined as a necessary but insufficient condition for the initiation of Operation Iraqi Freedom. The chapter highlighted the strategic way in which neoconservatives planted their ideas in the foreign policy discourse and anticipated emerging threats that might catapult their ideas into action. In that sense, neoconservatives were more prescient than those who envisaged the end of all ideological struggles in world politics and who expected issues of political economy to dominate with the demise of the Cold War. However, without 9/11 the neoconservative ideas would not have had the influence they did, especially when it comes to the Iraq war and forceful democratic change in the Middle East. If 9/11 helped coalesce President Bush and his advisers around the policy recommendations of the neoconservatives, probability estimates about the likelihood of victory in Iraq and Saddam's propensity to share WMD technology with al-Qaeda were equally critical in persuading the administration that war was worthwhile and necessary. Post-9/11, US policy makers were unwilling to countenance even a one percent chance of Saddam's proliferating WMD technology to those who may threaten the security of the USA.

Neoconservative ideas then were important, though not decisive, in the run up to Operation Iraqi Freedom. But to the extent that neoconservatism stood ready to be the guiding philosophy behind the invasion once the other relevant factors fell into place, it is interesting to end this analysis by speculating about the future of neoconservatism as a force in American foreign policy. Two questions present themselves. First, has neoconservatism been discredited by the war in Iraq? Neoconservatives argue 'no'; in fact, some have even suggested that the Obama administration's escalation of the war in Afghanistan in 2009 and creation of a 'no-fly zone' in Libya in Spring 2011 show that neoconservative principles remain very salient. Obama's actions—leveraging on American military strength in Afghanistan and using military force in the name of protecting human rights in Libya—seem consistent with neoconservatism's emphasis on moral rightness and using military force to pursue US goals. Which prompts the second question: their protestations notwithstanding, were Obama and his advisers also guided by neoconservative principles? I will answer the first question with a 'yes' and the second question with a 'no.'

'The difficulties and troubles in Iraq have damaged neoconservative advocates of the war,' William Kristol wrote in 2004. Moreover, according to Kristol, the 'failure in execution has been a big one. It has put the neoconservative "project" at risk'. Yet Kristol believed that 'in another sense, neoconservatism is today stronger than ever, for it continues to provide the most plausible basic guidance for America's role in today's world' (Kristol, in Stelzer 2004: 76). In focusing on the incompetence and errors of execution of the Bush administration, Kristol and his fellow neoconservatives imply that their basic ideas—namely a moralistic and values-based approach to foreign policy that leverages on US military power to depose tyrants and spread democracy—remain sound. The problem lay in the poor planning and implementation errors of an incompetent group of officials. More neutral observers would agree that colossal incompetence was present in huge doses during the planning of the war and the reconstruction of Iraq after the war. But they will also point to the moral and political hubris that are part and parcel of neoconservatism's foreign policy thought.

In arrogating to themselves the role of moral arbiter, and rejecting the 'decent opinions' of the rest of the world, the neoconservatives failed to see that what was morally clear to them was not so clear to others. Even within the USA, the moral clarity emphasized by the neoconservatives was contested by liberals. In wanting to use America's predominant military might to pursue their values-based policies, they also overestimated the ability of military force to produce the outcomes they wanted, such as a stable and democratic Iraq and Middle East. In assuming that theirs would be a 'benevolent hegemony', they blinded themselves and those who adopted their recommendations to the universal negative reaction to their 'project.' The price that the USA and its allies paid for this hubris was enacted on the streets of Baghdad and other Iraqi cities almost daily from 2003 to 2007 in the form of suicide bombings as well as attacks against coalition troops.

Perhaps even more devastating was the damage done to America's prestige and reputation: poll after poll since the invasion pointed to the alarming rise in negative perceptions of the USA by much of the rest of the world. In other words, the blind spots of neoconservatism contributed as much to the debacle of Iraq as the incompetence of the Bush administration. Paradoxically, the tenets so prized by neoconservatives and by which they are defined—the importance of moral clarity (in world politics), the idea of the USA as a benevolent hegemon, and the military reputation and might of America—have all been undermined by their 'project' in Iraq. It is doubtful that the neoconservative ideas behind the war can be resurrected as a plausible or philosophical guide to American foreign policy in the near future.

A second reason why neoconservatism is unlikely to be resurrected as the guiding philosophy of US foreign policy any time soon is because one of its key unspoken assumptions—a strong and vibrant US economy—imploded with the subprime and financial crisis of 2008. Three years on, the American economy has yet to recover, debt levels continue to be unsettlingly high, and her leaders are deadlocked on whether to raise taxes or cut spending, leading to the first ever downgrade of America's creditworthiness status by Standard & Poor's. In the absence of a strong economy, the cost of sustaining America's wars (and in the longer term its military prowess), not to mention its 'benevolent hegemony', will be increasingly hard to bear. Just before the Iraq War, Donald Rumsfeld and Paul Wolfowitz ridiculed the estimate by their White House colleague and Head of the National Economic Council, Larry Lindsey, that the war would cost $200 billion. They countered with figures in the region of $50–$60 billion (*Timesonline* 2008). We now know that even Lindsey's figures were far off; in the decade since 9/11, the wars in Iraq and Afghanistan have cost $800 and $443 billion, respectively (Belasco 2011: 1)

Barack Obama inherited his predecessor's two unfinished wars and a broken economy. He moved to a quick drawdown of the US role in Iraq, while seeking to augment the US effort to prevent a Taliban comeback in Afghanistan. Operation Iraqi Freedom formally ended in August 2010 with President Obama's declaration that America's combat mission was over. His administration oversaw the withdrawal of 90,000 troops from Iraq between 2009 and 2010; however,

50,000 US troops would remain in Iraq until the end of 2011 to train and support the Iraqi security forces. To be sure, the drawdown in Iraq was made possible by the 'surge' strategy enacted by the George W. Bush administration in 2007, which stabilized the security situation in Iraq.

As president, Barack Obama was confronted with an Afghanistan in peril. His predecessor's preoccupation with Iraq had allowed the Taliban to regroup, such that by 2008 it posed a serious threat to the government of Hamid Karzai. In November 2009 Obama decided to send an additional 30,000 troops to Afghanistan—the 'surge'—to arrest and reverse the Taliban's gains, and ultimately to shore up the Karzai regime. Obama's decision to execute the surge in Afghanistan and his responses to the Arab Spring uprisings of 2011—withdrawing support from the presidents of Egypt and Syria and using military force against Libyan President Muammar Gaddafi—have led some to suggest that the administration's foreign policy is hard to differentiate from that of George W. Bush or one informed by neoconservative tenets.

This is true only in a superficial sense. Obama was confronted with a deteriorating situation in Afghanistan and he chose to fight instead of throwing in the towel. Since no American president can countenance 'losing' Afghanistan on his watch, neoconservatism is neither necessary nor sufficient in elucidating Obama's surge decision. Many liberals who opposed the war in Iraq felt, like Obama, that the USA could not withdraw from Afghanistan; a time-limited 'surge' to stabilize the situation (informed perhaps by the perception that the 'surge' in Iraq had worked) was seen as the compromise outcome. Similarly, the process by which the Obama administration decided to use force in Libya and the way it limited its military role are telling. There was none of the looking for dragons to slay demeanour of the neoconservatives: Obama would have preferred Libya to follow the precedents of Tunisia and Egypt, where despots friendly to the USA abdicated power as the popular uprisings appeared unstoppable. Only when Gaddafi turned his military against the Libyan insurgents and people did the USA, at the instigation of France and Britain, opt for the military option. The clearest difference between Libya and Iraq was, of course, that in the former the USA and NATO obtained the backing of the UN Security Council (Resolution 1973) as well as that of the Arab League. This willingness to subscribe to international institutions and law directly contradicts one of the key tenets of the neoconservative approach which sees international law and institutions as unreliable and unnecessary.

Preliminary accounts of the Libyan intervention also suggest that if there is one guiding idea behind the Obama administration's decision to use force, it has to do with the lessons of Rwanda. Secretary of State Hilary Clinton, US Permanent Representative to the UN Susan Rice, and National Security Council senior staffer Samantha Powers—all of whom had vivid memories of the USA and the United Nations standing by while hundreds of thousands of Tutsis were massacred by the Hutus in 1994—played crucial roles in persuading the President to intervene in Libya. The reservations of Obama's Secretary of Defense Robert Gates and National Security Council Adviser Thomas Donilon notwithstanding, Obama was receptive to the argument that the most serious blight on the foreign policy of the Bill Clinton administration was its failure to stop the genocide in Rwanda. Like Hilary Clinton, Rice, and Powers, Obama was keen to avoid the spectre of 'another Rwanda' as Colonel Gaddafi turned his troops on the Libyan insurgents. Senator John Kerry, who was privy to the White House debate, characterized it as 'healthy', adding that 'the memory of Rwanda, alongside Iraq in '91, made it clear' that action was necessary, provided that international support was forthcoming (*New York Times* 2011). Whether this account of Obama's decision making tells the complete story will have to await the declassification of the deliberations, but it strikes this analyst as compelling (see Khong 1992).

A war that was initiated over the threat posed by Saddam's non-existent WMDs and that has exacted, as of June 2011, over 4450 American lives, with 32,000 Americans wounded (Brookings, 2011), can only be termed a success if one puts an extreme premium on the democratization of Iraq. The latter, moreover, was a secondary objective. If President George W. Bush and his neoconservative advisers had had a crystal ball that had told them what Operation Iraqi Freedom would cost—in lives, in money, and in US prestige, not to mention the 10,000 Iraqi military–security and 100,000 civilian fatalities (Brookings Institution 2011)—it is unlikely that they would have prosecuted the war. The American people are also clear on this: 59% of Americans see it as a mistake and 72% feel that the costs have exceeded the gains (*New York Times* 2010). Given this balance sheet, the neoconservative ideas that helped usher in the war will remain easy targets for those who prefer a less moralistic and militaristic approach to dealing with America's challenges.

 Key points

- Ideas can impact on foreign policy under certain conditions.
- Influential analysts have argued that neoconservatives and their ideas played a critical role in persuading the Bush administration to launch a preventive war against Iraq in March 2003.
- The tenets of neoconservative foreign policy thinking include: (a) moral clarity in foreign affairs; (b) preserving American pre-eminence; (c) willingness to use military force to achieve US goals; and (d) distrust of international law and institutions.
- While it is true that a number of Bush administration officials were neoconservatives, their ideas were only translated into action when other enabling factors fell into place.
- These factors are the strategic placement of neoconservative ideas into the foreign policy discourse, the 9/11 attacks by al-Qaeda, the one percent doctrine, and the belief that the US could achieve its war aims in Iraq.

 Questions

1. Do interests tend to trump ideas in the making of foreign policy?
2. In what sense is neoconservatism a 'domestic source' of American foreign policy?
3. What is the link between neoconservative foreign policy and domestic policy thinking?
4. 'No neoconservative ideas, no Operation Iraqi Freedom.' Do you agree?
5. If al-Qaeda had launched its attack when Bill Clinton was president, would Clinton have also gone after Iraq in due course?
6. Is counterfactual analysis a good way of assessing the importance of rival variables/explanations in foreign policy analysis? What might be some of the drawbacks?
7. What does it mean to say that a foreign policy event is 'overdetermined'?
8. Is the one percent doctrine meant to be taken literally?
9. What evidence would you look for to demonstrate that oil and/or the Israel lobby were crucial factors behind Operation Iraqi Freedom?
10. 'The idea of using force to effect regime change in Iraq remains valid and noble. What is criminal is the sheer incompetence of the Bush administration in tackling the post-invasion reconstruction of Iraq.' Do you agree?

11. Which of the three schools of international relations—realism, liberalism, and constructivism—will have least trouble recognizing the neoconservative approach to foreign policy?

12. Does the US 'surge' in Afghanistan (2009) and the use of military force against Libya during the 'Arab Spring' (2011) suggest that Obama and his advisers are closet neoconservatives?

 Further reading

Farnham, B. (ed.) (1994), *Avoiding Losses/Taking Risks: Prospect Theory and International Conflict* (Ann Arbor, MI: University of Michigan Press).
A thoughtful elaboration and application of prospect theory; case studies include decision-making during the Munich crisis, the Iran hostage rescue mission, and Russia's Syria policy.

Goldstein, J. and Keohane, R. (eds) (1993), *Ideas and Foreign Policy: Beliefs, Institutions, and Political Change* (Ithaca, NY: Cornell University Press).
Provides an analytical framework and well-chosen case studies for examining the role of ideas in foreign policy.

Gordon, M. and Trainor, B. (2006), *Cobra II: The Inside Story of the Invasion and Occupation of Iraq* (London: Atlantic Books).
A detailed and vivid account of the decisions and manoeuvring behind the invasion and occupation of Iraq, told from the military's point of view.

Kagan, R. and Kristol, W. (eds) (2000), *Present Dangers: Crisis and Opportunity in American Foreign and Defense Policy* (San Francisco, CA: Encounter Books).
A group of 'conservative internationalists' join forces to flesh out what a Reaganite foreign policy might look like in the twenty-first century. The pre-9/11 focus on states is interesting.

Kaplan, L. and Kristol, W. (2003), *The War over Iraq: Saddam's Tyranny and America's Mission* (San Francisco, CA: Encounter Books).
A book-length neoconservative argument for regime change in Iraq, accompanied by a critique of the Iraq policies of the first Bush and Clinton administrations.

Mann, J. (2004), *Rise of the Vulcans: The History of Bush's War Cabinet* (New York: Viking).
An excellent introduction to the personalities and ideas of the Bush national security team; the only drawback is the absence of a chapter on Bush's national security thinking.

Norton, A. (2004), *Leo Strauss and the Politics of American Empire* (New Haven, CT: Yale University Press).
An insightful essay on the teachings/mannerisms of the political philosopher Leo Strauss and how they have impacted on the neoconservatives.

Rothkopf, D. (2005), *Running the World: The Inside Story of the National Security Council and the Architects of American Power* (New York: Public Affairs).
An engaging history—enlivened by interviews—of the National Security Council, with an informative chapter on the Council under Condoleezza Rice.

Tetlock, P. and Belkin, A. (eds) (1996), *Counterfactual Thought Experiments in World Politics: Logical, Methodological, and Psychological Perspectives* (Princeton, NJ: Princeton University Press).
The primer of counterfactual analysis in world politics; the introduction by the editors provides useful criteria for assessing counterfactual arguments.

 Visit the Online Resource Centre that accompanies this book for more information:
www.oxfordtextbooks.co.uk/orc/smith_foreign/

17

China and the Tian'anmen bloodshed of June 1989

ROSEMARY FOOT

Chapter contents

 ## Reader's guide

This case study examines two main matters of importance to the study of foreign policy: first, the power of domestic groups and transnational non-state organizations to generate global interest in domestic conditions within particular societies, and the way that this increased attention can influence the foreign policies of states; secondly, how policies undertaken for domestic reasons can have foreseen, but often unforeseen, external consequences powerful enough to lead to revised foreign and domestic policies. The chapter demonstrates that it can be artificial to divide the domestic and external spheres of policy making, a feature of some foreign policy analysis models. The empirical focus of this chapter is on the foreign policy consequences of the Chinese leadership's decision in June 1989 to use the Chinese People's Liberation Army (PLA) to clear demonstrators from the streets of Beijing as well as from Tian'anmen Square. That 1989 decision led to hundreds, possibly thousands, of Chinese losing their lives, and many thousands suffering injury. China's decision in 1978 to adopt 'open-door' economic reform policies is a significant part of the build-up to the Tian'anmen crisis of 1989, as are the dramatic changes in the Soviet bloc in the second half of the 1980s. Important too is that global attention to human rights steadily increased over a similar period, leading to the emergence of human rights diplomacy as a significant feature of state practice. These developments necessitated China's diplomatic engagement with this issue area and subsequently resulted in some domestic legal reform, as well as a modest change in its behaviour towards humanitarian crises in global politics.

The external consequences of China's open door policy

In the immediate aftermath of Chairman Mao Zedong's death in 1976, the supreme leader of the People's Republic of China (PRC) since 1949, China's one-party state was in crisis. The ten years of turmoil associated with the 'Great Proletarian Cultural Revolution' (Box 17.1) in China had been economically and politically disastrous for the country. It was understood that a new basis for the Chinese Communist Party's (CCP's) right to rule had to be established. This right would now begin to rest on the improvement of living standards for ordinary Chinese and the introduction of rules and procedures that would provide some confidence that the Maoist era excesses would never occur again. In December 1978, Deng Xiaoping, having finally consolidated his hold on power, introduced a set of economic reform policies, labelled the 'Four Modernizations' (Box 17.2), which represented a revolutionary break from the past. He also placed in power other officials who would support these aims, such as Hu Yaobang, who became General Secretary of the CCP from 1980 but was removed from power in 1987, and Zhao Ziyang, the Premier from 1980 to 1989. With Hu's removal from power, Zhao took on his position as General Secretary, only to lose power himself and be put under house arrest at the height of the Tian'anmen crisis.

Economic consequences of reform

China's 'open door' reform policies opened up new opportunities for economic, cultural, and political contacts between Chinese and their counterparts overseas. Foreign trade increased, and foreign direct investment flowed into China at ever expanding rates. Average economic

---

BOX 17.1 The Great Proletarian Cultural Revolution 1966–1976

The Cultural Revolution officially started in China in May 1966. It lasted about ten years, but the most violent phase was brought to a close in 1969. The targets were those in the Party, government, and army whose alleged aims were to replace the 'dictatorship of the proletariat' with the 'dictatorship of the bourgeoisie'. Mao called on young people to 'rebel' and to root out 'bourgeois revisionists'. So-called 'Red Guard' organizations were formed. Factionalism among them led to serious violence. Schools and universities were shut and some students attacked their former teachers, accusing them of supporting feudalism and betraying the Chinese revolution. Neither were senior Party or state figures spared from this turmoil. As matters veered out of control, Mao called on the PLA to restore order and get the students back to their classes. This resulted in widespread disillusionment, especially among the young. (Saich 2004: 45–54)

BOX 17.2 The Four Modernizations policy

The Four Modernizations had first been introduced by China's Premier, Zhou Enlai, in 1974. But political conditions were not yet ripe for these policies to be implemented. Their time came in December 1978, when they were introduced again at the Third Plenum of the 11th Central Committee. The four areas for modernization were agriculture, industry, science and technology, and defence. Since 1989, and in part connected with the CCP's sense of obligation to the PLA for its role in putting down the demonstrations in June of that year, the defence budget has increased each year substantially more than the rate of inflation.

growth rates from that time onwards have been impressive, usually reaching double figures. China became a member of the World Bank and the International Monetary Fund in 1980, and a major recipient of the former's largesse shortly thereafter. In June 1984, the US government made it legal for the Chinese government to purchase its weaponry under the US Foreign Military Sales Act. By 1989, the USA had become China's major export market and other countries found the Chinese market of growing attraction.

Students and other intellectuals were also major beneficiaries of the reform effort. Their previously underutilized or denigrated skills now became crucial to the success of the reforms. Chinese students started to be trained overseas (for example, some 75,000 received visas to study in the USA between 1979 and 1989), they had greater access to foreign publications, and were able to take advantage of the explosion of publishing outlets inside China itself. As increasing numbers went abroad, they observed a dramatic gap in living standards between their own country and that experienced elsewhere. Particularly striking were the levels of development enjoyed by the Chinese communities of Hong Kong, Singapore, and Taiwan.

Political consequences and the ending of the Cold War

Economic disparities were not the only things on the minds of students and intellectuals. Reform-minded academics, such as the astrophysicist Fang Lizhi, exiled during the Cultural Revolution to one of China's remote provinces, toured university campuses in 1985. He exhorted students to press for democracy and a more open political system (Mitter 2004: 257). In early 1989, he began a campaign to free political prisoners. He was the first prominent intellectual to launch a public attack on Marxist–Leninist ideology and to declare that the success of democratic states was due to their recognition of the 'basic rights of the people, or human rights', especially freedom from fear of arbitrary arrest (Foot 2000: 68).

Fang had drawn inspiration from the writings of the humanist Albert Einstein and the dissident Soviet physicist Andrei Sakharov. Others, too, would be influenced by the actions and arguments of dissidents from eastern Europe. Dramatic political changes were taking place over the second half of the 1980s in the Soviet bloc, especially with the advent to power in March 1985 of Mikhail Gorbachev, the Secretary-General of the Communist Party of the Soviet Union. Gorbachev introduced the policies of *perestroika* (restructuring) and *glasnost* (opening), and became recognized in China as a major liberal reformer. Several of his decisions resonated with reformist Chinese. In 1987, the new Soviet leadership decided to release all its political prisoners. In 1989, it introduced the **Sinatra doctrine** which signalled Soviet approval of eastern European attempts to reform 'doing it their way'. In Poland, the government negotiated with and then re-legalized the independent trade union *Solidarity*, allowing it to participate in elections in June 1989. Hungary threw open its border with Austria and citizens flooded through from all parts of the bloc. At the end of the year, the Berlin Wall fell and the Warsaw Pact, the eastern European counterpart to the North Atlantic Treaty Organization, disbanded. In December 1991, the Soviet Union itself imploded. The Cold War in Europe was over.

These developments were of major concern to a one-party state for two main reasons. First, these new freedoms were an inspiration to reform-minded Chinese, especially the intellectual elites. As an editor of a youth magazine in China put it in May 1989: 'China needs a Gorbachev . . . we had a little one, Hu Yaobang, but he was purged by the conservative old men. We lead the Soviet Union in economic reform, they lead us in political and intellectual reform.' (Kent 1993: 178)

Secondly, China's strategic value to the West, and to the USA in particular, inevitably began to diminish over this period. The Beijing government had been in tacit alignment with the West against the Soviet Union, but now that the USSR under Gorbachev had taken a new political direction, some political figures, especially in the USA, no longer saw this degree of alignment with China as necessary. Instead, democratic reform in China was seen as an appropriate next step.

The human rights issue before Tian'anmen

Up to this point the fact that China, unlike eastern Europe, was not democratizing and offered only poor levels of human rights protections to its people had not garnered a great deal of international attention. For example, US President Jimmy Carter, whose administration between 1977 and 1980 had articulated an intention to place human rights matters at the heart of US foreign policy, had finally negotiated full diplomatic relations with the PRC at the end of 1978. However, whereas Carter offered succour to Soviet dissidents, he did not do the same to their equivalents in China. Beijing escaped attention because, at least until the late 1980s, Moscow was deemed the major enemy. But, more than that, there was sympathy for the task that the Chinese leadership had set itself. Beijing was understood to be embarking on fundamental reforms and many believed that it had to be given the chance to make progress with that agenda. China's leaders had admitted to the excesses of the past and claimed that they would introduce mechanisms to ensure that those abuses would never be witnessed again. Beijing's more cooperative stance in a number of major foreign policy arenas was of sufficient promise that praise rather than criticism seemed to be in order, at least to many Western governments.

However, China's greater openness, the growth in the number and resources of transnational human rights organizations, and the ability of such groups to transmit information to others about human rights abuse inside states came together in ways which ensured that China's behaviour would no longer escape such scrutiny. The Beijing government could not make progress with its open-door policies and at the same time prevent external probing into its domestic conditions. Groups such as Amnesty International, the most prestigious of the transnational human rights non-governmental organizations (NGOs), took up the challenge of studying China and produced its first report on conditions there in 1978, concentrating on major abuses such as arbitrary arrest, the use of torture, and detention without trial. The US-based Human Rights Watch began to take an interest in China in the 1980s, testifying before the US Congress and producing its own reports critical of Chinese practices.

Improved foreign access to Tibet provided information about Chinese governmental repression in that region. Growing publicity on the plight of those Tibetans who were struggling for autonomy or independence energized Tibetans abroad, internationalized the Tibetan struggle, and prompted Amnesty to take up the cases of those arrested for political or religious reasons. A Tibetan lobby became active in London, New York, and Washington. The US Congress, which had become far more assertive on human rights questions from the early 1970s, took note of the increasing levels of unrest. In 1987, it invited the Dalai Lama to Washington. The following year, the Tibetan spiritual leader spoke before the European Parliament. When China declared martial law in Tibet in March 1989, the Western media, human rights NGOs, and some political figures took up the Tibetan cause even more vigorously.

Thus there were a number of developments in China's foreign relations that were not fully anticipated when it introduced its reform policies after 1978. That opening led to greater exposure to foreign ideas and new thinking about how to organize China. Chinese citizens as well as the Chinese government had begun to explore the concept of rights, prompting the government to sign up to a number of the core human rights covenants such as, in 1986, the *Convention Against Torture and Other Cruel, Inhuman or Degrading Treatment or Punishment*, and to celebrate in 1988 the 40th anniversary of the Universal Declaration of Human Rights. At the same time, greater openness in China exposed those overseas to new information about conditions within Chinese society.

This increased openness was occurring at a time of other important changes in global society, making more complex the environment in which state policies had to be negotiated. Governmental protection of the human rights of its citizens had begun to be expected of the modern legitimate state. Over the course of the 1970s and 1980s Western states, together with Japan, had introduced a human rights element in their foreign policies, even if that element had not as yet affected relations with China. Human rights NGOs were growing in number and had increased resources at their command. At the same time, China's value as a tacit partner in an anti-Soviet containment policy was beginning to diminish as the Cold War started to unravel in Europe. When the Chinese leadership decided in June 1989 to use force to suppress the demonstrations that were rocking the Chinese capital, these important shifts in the political and normative climates ensured that its actions would be widely condemned.

The Tian'anmen crackdown

The death from a heart attack of the former reformist Party General-Secretary, Hu Yaobang, on 15 April sparked the 1989 demonstrations. The demonstrators soon came to be made up of a wide range of groups—workers, intellectuals, journalists, and entrepreneurs. However, the core members came from the universities, especially Peking University. Other cities joined in with their own protests, but attention was riveted on the capital, Beijing.

Soon after Hu's death had been announced, white flowers and other tributes began to pile up at the Martyrs' Monument in Tian'anmen Square, a huge public space located opposite the Forbidden City, at the heart of Beijing. Hu was praised as a leading reformer, a democrat, and liberal. A few days later, an estimated 30,000 students took their protests to the doors of Zhongnanhai, just west of the Square, a compound that houses most of China's leaders. Hu's funeral on 22 April was another opportunity to gather, and at least 100,000 people managed to circumvent the efforts of the security forces to stop them meeting in Tian'anmen. Protests and marches continued from then on, the numbers ebbing and flowing in late April and early May as some demonstrators returned to their campuses or workplaces, and others replaced them. Politically significant events such as the formation of the Beijing Autonomous Workers' Federation, and a similar autonomous grouping for students indicated the kinds of objectives that some of the participants had. Others were calling for freedom of the press and measures to root out corruption among the political elite. (See Map 17.1)

The Chinese leadership seemed at a loss as to how to respond and was split between those who wanted to negotiate (notably Zhao Ziyang) and those who wanted to take a tougher stand (particularly Li Peng). Those in support of a more conciliatory stance lost ground, the role of

BOX 17.3 Key political dates

The broader context

1978 Third Plenum of the 11th Central Committee introduces the 'open-door' economic reform policies, known as the Four Modernizations.

1979 Democracy Wall activist, Wei Jingsheng, is sentenced to 15 years in prison. He had called for a Fifth Modernization—democracy in China.
China and the USA establish full diplomatic relations on 1 January.

1980 China enters the IMF and World Bank.

1982 China becomes a member of the UN Commission on Human Rights.

1986 Student demonstrations lead to the purge of Hu Yaobang.

1988 China celebrates the fortieth anniversary of the Universal Declaration of Human Rights.

1989 March. Martial law is declared in Tibet.

The lead-up to the Tian'anmen bloodshed

1989 15 April, death of Hu Yaobang. Funeral held 22 April 1989. 13 May students begin a hunger strike in Tian'anmen Square. 15 May, the Soviet leader, Mikhael Gorbachev, arrives for his summit visit. There is an extensive media presence.

Martial law is declared on 20 May.

Zhao Ziyang, the Party General Secretary, is removed from power on 22 May and put under house arrest. He is eventually replaced by Jiang Zemin.

3–4 June, PLA troops clear the Square and fire on demonstrators elsewhere. The fear of civil war increases. Conservative estimates are that several hundred lose their lives and many thousands are injured.

5 June, international condemnation of Chinese action begins to build. The USA, other Western governments, and Japan impose sanctions over the course of that month. This also affects lending policies of the World Bank and Asian Development Bank.

President Bush sends secret envoys to Beijing at the end of June to find a basis for sustaining ties. These two envoys are sent again at the end of the year, this time openly. The US Congress and media react furiously when that first secret visit is discovered.

An August meeting of the UN Sub-Commission on human rights passes a resolution condemning China's action.

1990 10 January, the Chinese government lifts martial law in Beijing and starts to release some of those detained in the aftermath of the Tian'anmen bloodshed.

June 1990, China allows Fang Lizhi and his family to leave for the USA.

Preparations for the Gulf War involving a UN resolution authorizing the use of force result in a number of contacts between US and Chinese officials.

29 November, China abstains on UN Resolution 678 authorizing the use of force in Iraq. 1 December, China's foreign minister meets President Bush.

1991 In August, Japanese PM Kaifu becomes the first head of government to visit the leadership in Beijing.

1992 January, Deng Xiaoping tours southern China to signal that economic reforms must be allowed to continue.

China signs the nuclear Non-Proliferation Treaty, having promised as much to PM Kaifu in 1991.

external factors contributing strongly to that outcome, although the absence of detailed consideration of alternative strategies to coercion also played a part. Gorbachev was due in Beijing for a summit with Chinese leaders, a significant event in that it marked the formal ending of serious tension between China and the Soviet Union. The Sino-Soviet dispute dated from the late 1950s, and had culminated in border conflict in 1969 and the militarization of their long, shared, border. The May 1989 summit was designed to mark the formal end of that hostility. China wanted the world to witness the dramatic improvement in its national security; thus it invited the world's press to cover the events. Little did the government realize when it issued that invitation that the summit would coincide with major unrest in the capital.

Some among the students rightly saw the Gorbachev visit as an opportunity to internationalize their struggle. They called for a hunger strike and set up camp in Tian'anmen Square two days before the Soviet Secretary-General arrived. Deng Xiaoping was incensed. As he put it on 13 May, 'Tian'anmen is the symbol of the People's Republic of China. The Square has to be in order when Gorbachev comes. We have to maintain our international image. What do we look like if the Square's a mess?' (Nathan and Link 2001: 148). But China's paramount leader was not to have his way. The Soviet leader's visit became 'a sideshow'. With enormous crowds blocking the path, the Chinese government could not deliver Gorbachev to the designated media sites (Suettinger 2003: 44). Gorbachev's welcoming ceremony had to take place at the airport rather than in the symbolic Tian'anmen Square. For his meetings with China's senior leaders, Gorbachev had to enter by the back rather than the front door of the Great Hall of the People, located on the west side of the Square.

As far as the foreign media were concerned, the hunger strikers made for better coverage than the Soviet leader anyway. Indeed, even the domestic media gave the hunger strike detailed attention, until the leadership curbed its enthusiasm. Within a day or so, some of the strikers began to collapse and were rushed to hospital. The Chinese leader, Zhao Ziyang, and other senior leaders paid visits to hospitals in an attempt to stop this form of protest. Zhao claimed that the student calls for democracy and rule of law matched the aims of the Party and government and he would ensure fulfilment of their aims. But such conciliation disturbed other Party leaders. Martial law was declared on 20 May and PLA forces started to move into position. Zhao, unwilling to support the establishment of martial law, was removed from power on 22 May, to be replaced by Jiang Zemin, the erstwhile Shanghai Party Secretary.

It is from this time that Chinese officials began strongly to link the demonstrators with foreigners deemed antagonistic to the Chinese regime, whether in America, Hong Kong, or Taiwan. The USA and its Voice of America overseas radio reports were singled out for 'manufacturing rumors and inciting turmoil' (Nathan and Link 2001: 334). Adding fuel to this particular fire was the installation in the Square on 29 May of the 'Goddess of Democracy', a 27-foot plaster statue modelled on America's Statue of Liberty and made by students from Beijing's Central Academy of Fine Arts. For Beijing's officials, it was as if the students were 'trying to make American freedom and democracy their spiritual support' (Nathan and Link 2001: 332).

On 1 June, on orders from Li Peng, China's State Security Ministry produced a report on 'Western infiltration'. According to Nathan and Link, 'it was viewed as providing one of the best justifications for the military action that was about to occur' (Nathan and Link 2001: 338). It made several important points about why and how foreigners were manipulating the current unrest. First, it stated that the PRC had 'always been a major target for the peaceful evolution methods of the Western capitalist countries headed by the United States'. The USA was making use of

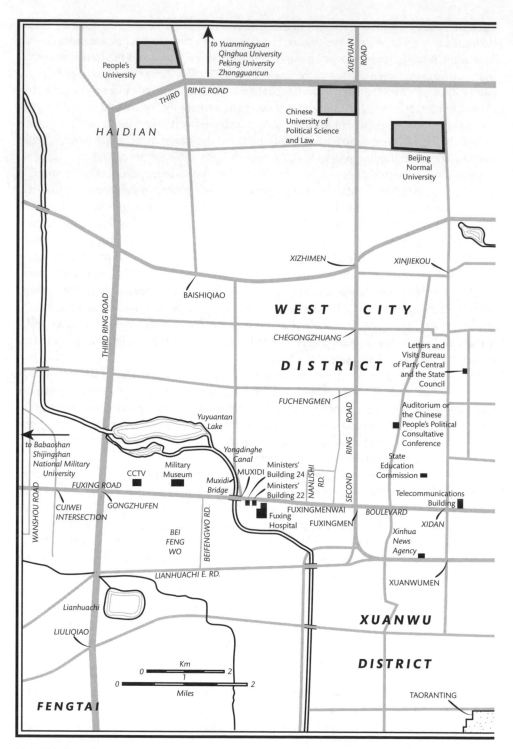

Map 17.1 Map of Beijing

Source: © A.Karl/J.Kemp, 2000.

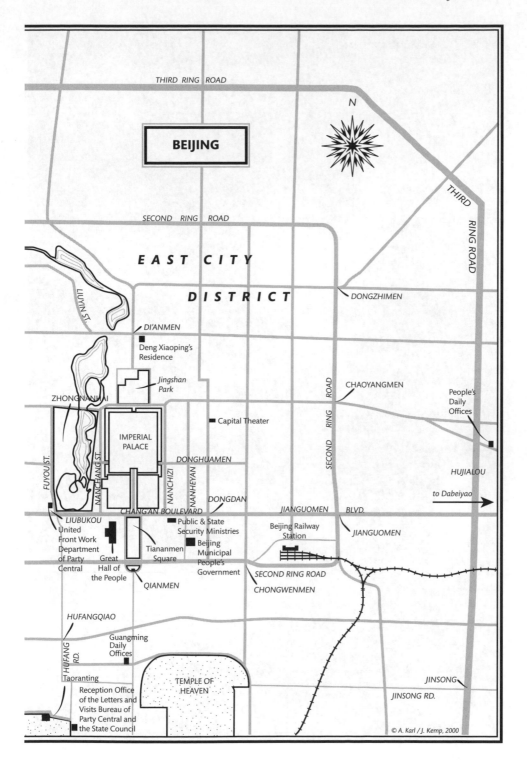

THIRD RING ROAD

N

BEIJING

THIRD RING ROAD

SECOND RING ROAD

E A S T   C I T Y

LIUYIN ST.

D I S T R I C T

DONGZHIMEN

DI'ANMEN

Deng Xiaoping's
Residence

ZHONGNANHAI

Jingshan
Park

CHAOYANGMEN

People's
Daily
Offices

Capital Theater

IMPERIAL
PALACE

SECOND RING ROAD

FUYOU ST.

NANCHANG ST.

DONGHUAMEN

NANCHIZI

NANHEYAN

HUJIALOU

to Dabeiyao

DONGDAN

CHANG'AN BOULEVARD

JIANGUOMEN   BLVD.

LIUBUKOU
United
Front Work
Department
of Party
Central

Public & State
Security Ministries

Great
Hall of
the People

Tiananmen
Square

Beijing
Municipal
People's
Government

QIANMEN

Beijing Railway
Station

JIANGUOMEN

SECOND RING ROAD

CHONGWENMEN

HUFANGQIAO

HUFANG
RD.

Guangming
Daily
Offices

Taoranting

Reception Office
of the Letters and
Visits Bureau of
Party Central and
the State Council

TEMPLE OF
HEAVEN

JINSONG

JINSONG RD.

© A. Karl / J. Kemp, 2000

'Goddess of Democracy' plaster statue.

Source: Photograph taken by P. Turnrey, Distributed by Corbis.

China's reform policies to infiltrate the minds of the populace, including intellectuals and Party officials, in order to 'cultivate so-called democratic forces' within the country. More seriously still, the report accused the USA of using the current 'turmoil' in the capital to support those who wanted to overthrow the communist government. US officials and its media, it alleged, were encouraging the demonstrators in their actions, and spreading the kinds of rumours that only served to make them more intransigent during the negotiations. The report ended on an emotional and somewhat hysterical note which in its phrasing marked a return to the pre-reform era: 'Many facts demonstrate that the international monopoly capitalists and hostile, reactionary foreign forces have not abandoned for a moment their intent to destroy us. It is now clear that murderous intent has always lurked behind their protestations of peace and friendship. When the opportunity arises they will remove the façade and reveal their true colors. They have only one goal: to annihilate socialism' (Nathan and Link 2001: 348). The next day, China's leaders took the decision to clear the Square by force if necessary. Numbers in the Square had already significantly diminished by that point, but this fact did not lead to a reconsideration of that fateful decision. Neither did it cool the official rhetoric. Now the demonstrators were described as 'terrorists' and 'hooligans' involved in a 'counter-revolutionary riot'. Allegedly, they drew their support from those who opposed China in the USA, Hong Kong, and Taiwan. (Suettinger 2003: 58). As the policy solidified behind the decision to use force, Deng Xiaoping adamantly stated that there was to be no bloodshed in the Square itself (Nathan and Link 2001: 370).

The army moves in

In fact, most of the deaths occurred about three miles west of the Square. PLA troops used live ammunition on a large crowd that had gathered in the district of Muxidi. Some in the crowd responded with rage and took their revenge on the soldiers. Others among the troops, out of control by this stage, chased after those civilians who were fleeing from the scene, shooting them in the back when they caught up with them. The PLA entered Tian'anmen Square just after midnight on the morning of 4 June, and cleared it by about 5.30 a.m. with no loss of life. Yet, elsewhere in Beijing, and sometimes in areas close to the Square, the killings and violence continued. For a time, civil war seemed a real possibility. The Chinese government's official figures on the casualties were 241 killed and about 7000 wounded (Nathan and Link 2001: 436). However, independent and other non-governmental observers put the figures much higher. The Chinese authorities hunted down as many of the leading demonstrators as they could, or failing that those they could accuse of 'disturbing the social order'. Many of those arrested were jailed; some were summarily tried and sentenced to death, a penalty swiftly enacted. Many others were sent to labour reform camps.

Immediate foreign policy consequences

Sanctions

Governments around the world expressed regret, concern, or utter condemnation, with China's Asian neighbours tending towards the gentler form of rebuke. The West, however, immediately backed up its words with a variety of sanctions.

For example, on 5 June the USA suspended weapons' sales and exchanges between military leaders. By 20 June, it had begun to use a wider variety of foreign policy tools: it had banned all exchanges with the Chinese government above the level of assistant secretary, halted a civilian nuclear cooperation agreement, and instructed its representatives at the World Bank and Asian Development Bank to postpone consideration of new loans to China. Some 45,000 Chinese in the USA had their visas extended. The US government allowed Fang Lizhi and his wife and son to seek protection in America's Beijing Embassy. This particularly angered the Chinese leadership since it had labelled Fang a 'counter-revolutionary'. Members of the US Congress, enraged by the events they had been witnessing on their televisions and lobbied hard by Chinese residing in the USA, demanded that the executive branch take more punitive actions. The bloc in Congress antagonistic to China had grown stronger. It now comprised a coalition not only among those concerned to protect human rights, but also among those who favoured independence for Taiwan, feared China's growing economic challenge to American workers, or abhorred China's 'one-child' family planning policies (Zweig 1991: 71). The US President, on the other hand, was reluctant to go much further, believing that contacts with the Chinese regime were important to maintain. He had a strong personal interest in China, deriving from his period in 1974 when he headed the first US liaison office in Beijing, the precursor to the Embassy established in 1979 once full diplomatic relations had been negotiated. For him, longer-term strategic questions were of more importance than the short-term, if regrettable, events involving the demonstrators.

The European Community (now European Union) as well as individual European states announced a set of sanctions similar to those enacted in the USA. These included a ban on sales of military equipment and on high-level ministerial visits, and the suspension of government-guaranteed loans. Japan followed suit, terminating a major loan negotiation and recalling a

Protestor in front of tanks near Tian'anmen Square.

Source: Photograph taken by Jeff Widener on 5 June 1989. Distributed by PA.

number of banking and other commercial staff. Australia cancelled a prime ministerial visit, and New Zealand a planned visit of its Minister of Police.

It has been estimated that Tian'anmen cost China about US$11billion in bilateral aid over four years. China also experienced a two-year decline in its credit rating, foreign investment, exports, and tourist visits. However, the damage went well beyond the economic, significantly tarnishing China's international image. Expressions of regret over the carnage came from many governments, even those, such as the Brazilian and Malaysian governments, usually unwilling to comment on internal upheavals in other countries. The French government gave publicity to the dissident cause when it offered political asylum to those leading activists who had escaped after 4 June, and awarded them an honoured place in the bicentenary Bastille Day parade. The French Communist Party also strongly criticized the Chinese government for firing on its own citizens. The UN Secretary-General called on the Chinese government to exercise the 'utmost restraint', and the UN's Special Rapporteur on Summary and Arbitrary Executions, whose 1989 report had already pointed to unlawful Chinese killings in Tibet, appealed to the government to curb its excesses. Some 1200 or more employees from the UN Secretariat sent an open letter to the UN Secretary-General asking for a special session of the UN Commission on Human Rights. This could not be arranged, but the Sub-Commission of this body met in August 1989 for its annual meeting. Li Lu, a student on China's wanted list, gave his dramatic version of the Tian'anmen events, leading a member of China's delegation to walk out. The Sub-Commission passed a condemnatory resolution which, despite the mildness of its wording, was the first ever resolution to criticize a permanent member of the UN Security Council for its human rights violations (Foot 2000: 115–19).

Perceived foreign involvement and China's decision to use force

Why did the Chinese government authorize the use of force knowing that its economy, foreign relations, and international image would be badly damaged? Why was it so intransigent about continuing the negotiations with the students? Deng Xiaoping has provided an important insight into the thinking of the Chinese leaders over this period. As he graphically put it on 2 June 1989: 'The causes of this incident have to do with the global context. The Western world, especially the USA, has thrown its entire propaganda machine into agitation work and has given a lot of encouragement and assistance to the so-called democrats or opposition in China—people who are in fact the scum of the Chinese nation . . . This turmoil has taught us a lesson the hard way, but at least we now understand better than before that the sovereignty and security of the state must always be the top priority'. He went on: 'Some Western countries use things like "human rights", or like saying the socialist system is irrational or illegal, to criticize us, but what they're really after is our sovereignty' (Nathan and Link 2001: 358). Deng could not believe that the protestors were acting alone, and feared that the main objective was the overthrow of the socialist regime. He also stressed the two longer-term considerations that were essential if the country was to reach its development goals: stability at home and a peaceful environment abroad. This has proved to be a constant refrain of China's leaders to this day.

Deng also made a strong bid for the country to continue with its open-door economic reform policies. But how was this to be achieved given that hard-line Beijing officials, who felt that the openness had gone too far, were now in a stronger position? And how could this be achieved in the face of a Western sanctions policy?

China's foreign policy response to sanctions

The unacceptability of China's behaviour had been made plain, but the message from China's international interlocutors was not without its ambiguities. The Beijing government set about exploiting those ambiguities, using its special attractions as a growing market, its regional strategic importance, and its position as a UN Security Council member able and willing to exercise a veto.

Bilateral diplomacy

According to China's then foreign minister, Qian Qichen, Beijing recognized that Japan was the weak link in the sanctions policy and the most appropriate government for it to target. Beyond Japan's economic interests in China, its abhorrent practices during its occupation of China from 1931 to 1945, its sense of belonging not only to the developed West but also to Asia, and its sympathy for China's concern to maintain stability made Japan reluctant to sustain sanctions. On 1 August 1989, Qian met the Japanese foreign minister, Mitsuzuka Hiroshi, in Paris where discussions on the Cambodian peace settlement were being held. Hiroshi told his Chinese counterpart that he had advised Western governments not to adopt harsh sanctions against China or unduly isolate it (Qian 2005: 150). In fact, the Japanese government moved swiftly to re-establish ties, offering a small gift of $1million for flood relief in August 1989, and lifting the freeze on current aid projects. Restrictions on travel to Beijing were formally removed in September and Japanese business activity in the Chinese capital began to revive. With the lifting of martial law in Beijing on 10 January 1990 and then Beijing's granting of permission in June that year for Fang Lizhi and his family to leave the country, Japan restarted the negotiations on the loans package. Prime Minister Kaifu capped these improvements in relations in August 1991 when he became the first head of government from the G7 countries to visit the new leadership in Beijing. However, he exacted some *quid pro quo* from China when he obtained its commitment in principle to sign the nuclear Non-Proliferation Treaty.

European governments followed a similar trajectory. They also viewed the lifting of martial law as an opportunity to remove sanctions, except in the areas of military sales and military contacts. France, Italy, and Germany, for example, offered new loans and sought out opportunities at the United Nations for meetings with China's high-level officials. Spain became the first European country to send a foreign minister to Beijing in November 1990, with Qian Qichen reciprocating in February 1991.

However, for Beijing, the actions of the US government were key. Here the Chinese leadership was in luck because US President George H.W. Bush had retained a conviction that China should not be isolated. At a press conference on 27 June 1989, a time when Congress was calling for harsher US measures to be adopted against China, Bush explained his position: 'If you look at the world and you understand the dynamics of the Pacific area, good relationships with China are in the national interest of the United States' (Suettinger 2003: 94). On a number of occasions after 4 June, the US President tried to talk to Deng Xiaoping on the telephone, but to no avail. He finally wrote the Chinese leader a letter, extraordinary in its content and telling in its emphasis. Calling on the Chinese to exercise 'clemency' towards the students, it began with affirmations of friendship and respect for Chinese history, culture, and tradition. It pleaded with Deng to understand that the US public and Congress had demanded that the US President authorize punitive sanctions against China. As the representative of these domestic actors, they expected the US President to tailor his foreign policy towards China in light of the Tian'anmen bloodshed, whether or not he wanted to react in ways Americans deemed appropriate (Suettinger 2003: 79; Qian 2005: 131). The Chinese only responded positively to the President's case when he asked if he could send secret envoys to Beijing, their task being to find concrete ways of improving the relationship.

That visit took place at the end of June 1989. The two American officials were required to impress on the Chinese that they had to take some action to take the sting out of the sentiment being expressed in America. If not, harsher sanctions were likely, including the possible denial to China of its **most-favoured nation (MFN) trading status**, which would be coming up for review in the US Congress in June 1990. Such status was valuable to Beijing economically because it reduced tariffs on Chinese goods sold in the USA. At this point, however, the Chinese were unwilling to offer any concessions.

Bush began a series of unilateral acts, including authorizing private discussions between the US Secretary of State James Baker and his Chinese opposite number during the Paris conference on Cambodia, as well as at the UN in September. US and Chinese officials also held talks on China's admission to the General Agreement on Tariffs and Trade (the forerunner to the World Trade Organization). Shortly after a second US mission to China—this one made public and organized for the end of 1989—the Chinese began to conciliate. The Beijing government lifted martial law on 10 January 1990 and on 18 January released 573 prisoners who had taken part in the Tian'anmen demonstrations. The US administration conciliated again, this time authorizing an Export–Import Bank loan and announcing that it would no longer disapprove of World Bank lending to China. It was now the turn of China. In moves timed to coincide with the MFN debate in the US Congress, Beijing released another 211 prisoners, and agreed to purchase US$4billion of Boeing aircraft, as well as quantities of US wheat. At the end of June, Fang Lizhi was allowed to leave the US Embassy and he and his family made their way to the USA.

The Gulf War 1990–1991 and UN Security Council action

Perhaps it is the late Saddam Hussein whom the Chinese have most to thank for the restoration of high-level contacts between Chinese and Western, especially American, officials. His decision to invade Kuwait, and the US decision to obtain a UN resolution approving its use of force to reverse this action, immediately placed China in an advantageous position. As a permanent member of the UN Security Council, China had veto power. US officials wanted China's support—either through a vote in favour or an abstention—for that resolution. American officials went into action. Those stationed in Beijing and Shanghai hinted that the Gulf War represented an opportunity for China to improve its relations with the USA. The US Secretary of State, James Baker, met Qian Qichen in Cairo in November, according to Qian offering to lift more of the US sanctions if China gave its support to the resolution (Qian 2005:145–6). Over the course of the Gulf crisis, China voted for all ten UN resolutions that imposed political, military, and economic sanctions on Iraq, but only abstained on Resolution 678 (29 November 1990), which provided for the use of force to compel Iraq to withdraw from Kuwait. It was that resolution that provided China with its bargaining leverage: Chinese officials implied, to the very last minute, that use of the Chinese veto was still a possibility. To rule that out, the US administration agreed that China's foreign minister would be received in Washington after China had voted in favour of the UN resolution. In fact, Beijing abstained, but a meeting with President Bush still went ahead on 1 December (Suettinger 2003: 113–15).

Thus, in the period immediately after Tian'anmen, the Chinese government noted that its possession of certain economic and strategic attributes posed foreign policy dilemmas for states that hoped to benefit from those attributes. Such states would be forced to rank their policy interests and, in general, China found that, while human rights concerns were featured, they did not appear at the top of many governments' lists.

The deepening of China's involvement with human rights

The realization of the contingent nature of other states' policies in this issue area gave the Beijing government some breathing space. Nevertheless, China also recognized that the matter of human rights could not be wished away even if other governments did not always want to give it priority in their relations with Beijing. America's President might have wanted a stable relationship with a strategically important state, but Congressional opinion was less favourably disposed to China. Debate over whether to impose human rights conditions on the renewal of China's MFN status became standard for the rest of the 1990s, until China applied to join the World Trade Organization (it became a full member in 2001). These types of debates, the establishment in the USA of a Commission on International Religious Freedom, and the annual US State Department human rights report ensured regular consideration of human rights conditions in China, and domesticated US foreign policy towards China in a way that has been difficult to overcome. Indeed, the Tian'anmen crackdown and its policy consequences still cast a shadow over Sino-American relations. Every meeting between senior US and Chinese officials includes some discussion of human rights issues and of specific cases of alleged abuse. These encounters act to accentuate the perceived ideological divide between the two states.

China's rapid escape from the sanctions imposed after Tian'anmen by the Western world and Japan in some respects increased the domestic pressure on these governments to try and sustain some influence over Beijing's human rights policies. Governments that identified themselves as democratic and protective of human rights provided opportunities for domestic groups to demand that they live up to that identity. Human rights 'dialogues', as they were called, between the Chinese and Western governments became the norm from this time, and are now held with about 20 countries. These governments also used what leverage they had to induce China to enter more fully into the international human rights regime.

From the late 1990s onwards China did make various adjustments, including signature of the two core human rights documents: in 1997 the International Covenant on Economic, Social and Cultural Rights (which it ratified, with a major reservation, in 2001), and in 1998 the International Covenant on Civil and Political Rights (which it has still not ratified). It also accepted other intrusions into its domestic space: for example, inviting in 2005 the UN Special Rapporteur on Torture and other Cruel, Inhuman or Degrading Treatment or Punishment to visit, and, in response to a UN call, issuing a National Human Rights Action Plan covering 2009–2010. Domestic legislation was also revised—including in the administration of capital punishment—and a 2004 Amendment to China's Constitution affirmed that 'the State respects and protects human rights'. Were these changes to be fully implemented and made legally enforceable, then undoubtedly the level of human rights protection in China would be much improved.

However, when various Chinese activists have tested the limits of these changes they have often found them wanting. The Chinese document, Charter 08, written in deliberate emulation of the founding of Czechoslovakia's Charter 77, explicitly linked China's domestic struggle for human rights with universalist principles and a global movement. As Charter 08 put it: '2008 . . .

marks the sixtieth anniversary of the promulgation of the Universal Declaration of Human Rights, the thirtieth anniversary of the appearance of the Democracy Wall in Beijing, and the tenth of China's signing of the International Covenant on Civil and Political Rights'. It went on to demand answers from the Beijing government to several key questions including whether it would 'continue with "modernization" under authoritarian rule', or instead would 'embrace universal human values, join the mainstream of civilized nations, and build a democratic system?' (quoted in *New York Review of Books* 2009: 54). Shortly after, several of the authors and signatories of this document were detained in policy custody. On International Human Rights Day, 8 December 2009, the 2010 Nobel Peace Laureate Liu Xiaobo—a leading figure in the promulgation of Charter 08 and former protagonist in the 1989 protest movement—was charged with inciting subversion. Liu, in fact, has spent much of the period since June 1989 in prison for his activities in support of democracy and human rights.

Thus the Chinese government has made it clear that any organized challenge to one-party rule will not be tolerated, and its willingness to participate in the international human rights regime or to promote rights domestically is circumscribed by this determination. To ensure that the internet and other similar technologies cannot be used to organize any form of serious dissent it has placed blocks on Facebook, Twitter, and what it regards as sensitive internet sites. Internet regulation from 2011 has been consolidated under a newly established State Internet Information Office.

China's emergence as a significant global actor

As China's significance as a global actor has increased, especially as a result of its profound economic rise relative to major economies such as that of the USA and Japan (see Figure 17.1), other governments have less leverage over its human rights policies and China itself

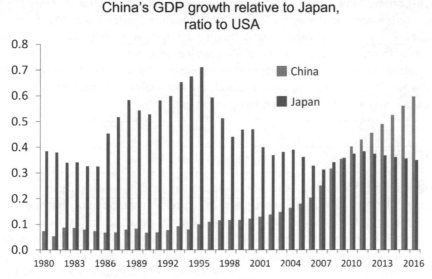

Figure 17.1 China's GDP growth relative to Japan, ratio to USA.

Source: IMF, *World Economic Outlook database*, April 2011.

approaches human rights diplomacy with greater confidence. Beijing is very willing to attack the human rights track records of its major critics in the USA and Europe. It has also become more dismissive of their criticisms, especially since it can counter that its policies have brought many millions of Chinese out of poverty and that its citizens now enjoy a greater amount of autonomy from state interference—provided that they do not overstep the limits outlined above—than had been the case in earlier decades.

However, while these arguments carry weight in world capitals, China's domestic conditions are still subject to some external scrutiny. Moreover, because China has emerged as a major global actor, this scrutiny is coupled with heightened attention to China's own behaviour towards rights-abusing governments and towards moves to deepen the international protection of human rights. For example, as a permanent member of the UN Security Council and given its strong rhetoric in support of the UN role in global politics, the Chinese government had little choice but to participate in debates leading to the adoption of 'The Responsibility to Protect' outlined in the World Summit Outcome document of September 2005 (United Nations 2005). That document affirmed that 'each individual state has the responsibility to protect its populations from genocide, war crimes, ethnic cleansing and crimes against humanity' and that where it was 'manifestly failing' to uphold its duties, the international community, through the UN Security Council, would be prepared to take collective action. China has also engaged in UN debates on the protection of civilians in armed conflict, and authorized UN Peacekeeping Operations that include humanitarian mandates (Foot 2011). Although it has worked hard to protect its interests in rights-abusing states such as Myanmar and Sudan, for example, even in such cases it acquiesced in the passage of a 2008 condemnatory resolution singling out Myanmar at the UN Human Rights Council, and in 2006 pressed the Sudanese government to accept a hybrid African Union–UN peacekeeping force (Kleine-Ahlbrandt and Small 2008).

Thus the Chinese government has moved from a position in August 1989 where it told the UN Sub-Commission on Human Rights that its condemnatory resolution that month represented interference in its domestic affairs, to a more nuanced statement in 2005 to the effect that 'when a massive humanitarian crisis occurs, it is the legitimate concern of the international community to ease and defuse the crisis' (People's Republic of China 2005). These represent modifications, if minor ones, in China's positions on questions related to sovereignty, but they probably would not have come about in the absence of a UN role in promoting responsible sovereignty as a part of the global human rights regime.

Conclusion

Human rights have become a feature of China's foreign and domestic policies for a variety of reasons, but much of this can be traced to China's reform and opening that began in late 1978. In the early 1970s, Beijing was not linked by air to any major city in Asia, most parts of the country were closed to foreigners, living standards had long stagnated, and foreign trade was an insignificant factor in the economy. China's level of technological advancement generally lagged ten to twenty years behind world levels, and some thirty to forty years in specialized areas. No longer willing to tolerate these outcomes of the Maoist years, domestic reforms coupled with new foreign policies began to be introduced. The Chinese leadership realized that it would need the help of its best brains and some of the technological know-how from the developed world. Young Chinese were sent abroad, foreigners were let in, and Deng Xiaoping authorized integration into a wide variety of international institutions.

With the loosening of political and economic constraints, debate in China over the country's needs took off. China's leaders veered between encouraging that debate, and then attempting to rein it in when it seemed to get beyond their control—1989 was one such year when it did get beyond their control. Rather than seeing the demonstrators' criticisms as a new source of ideas about the route to full modernization, the leadership explored few alternatives other than the use of force. It categorized the unrest as counter-revolutionary rebellion, instigated from abroad, and designed to overthrow the CCP.

The foreign policy consequences of China's decision to authorize the PLA to shoot at its own citizens in June 1989 were far-reaching. For a time, China was as isolated from the West as it had been in the 1960s. Its behaviour had drawn the criticism of the UN's human rights bodies, an unusual occurrence for a permanent member of the UN Security Council. Great damage occurred to its image as a reforming state committed to improving the lives of its citizenry. True, contacts with the West and Japan were soon renewed after the Tian'anmen bloodshed, and China used its bargaining power to good effect, but neither these governments nor China itself could entirely put aside the negative spillovers in their bilateral relationships from the human rights issue. The global environment in which Chinese policies have to be negotiated comprises a multiplicity of actors and a complex series of governance requirements. NGOs, the media, domestic political lobbies, and UN bodies continue to monitor violations as well as improvements, and Western governments still give human rights a place in their foreign policies towards China.

As China's power has grown, especially from the mid-2000s, there has been some recalibration in China's approach to human rights and in the approach of those engaged in human rights diplomacy with the Beijing government. China has undoubtedly become more dismissive of the criticisms of its human rights record and has sought to gain greater control over the issue in both the domestic and international environments. Global actors have shifted some of their attention away from China towards China's relations with rights-abusing governments, pressing Beijing to use what leverage it has to effect positive change inside other societies.

Beijing has shown some limited responsiveness to that latter demand, formulating a position that acknowledges a state's responsibility to prevent large-scale human rights abuses from occurring, but also accepting that in conditions of a state's 'manifest failure' to provide those protections, it is the duty of the international community to respond—though, in its view, this should rarely be a response that involves the use of force.

These subtle changes in position in its global diplomacy owe much to the open-door policies of late 1978 and Beijing's decision to foster economic growth and development based on integration with global institutions. That decision coincided with a period when human rights had become, as Michael Ignatieff once put it, the 'dominant moral vocabulary in foreign affairs' (Ignatieff 2002). The border between global and domestic has become ever more porous, it seems, with consequences that can affect the human rights policies of even the most wary of states.

Key points

- China's economic reform policies opened Chinese to ideas from overseas, and loosened the constraints on discussion of China's political trajectory. Political reform became a topic of debate inside China throughout the 1980s.

- The foreign policy consequences of the decision to use force against the demonstrators were initially severe. China's economy and international image were damaged.

- The Tian'anmen bloodshed transformed overnight the domestic context of America's China policy. It brought together a broad coalition of actors antagonistic to the authoritarian Chinese government. This places continuing constraints on Sino-American relations.

- Human rights groups, domestic and transnational, became more influential from the 1980s in the framing of democratic governments' foreign policies towards China.

- China's economic power and potential, and its growing influence as a regional and global strategic actor, served to weaken the West's sanctions policy.

- China, as a Permanent Member of the UN Security Council, threatened to use its veto at a crucial time, i.e. during the 1990 debate over Resolution 678 authorizing the use of force against Iraq. That threat also helped China to breach the sanctions.

- China has been forced to engage with the international human rights regime in a deeper way since 1989, both because of the criticisms that followed the Tian'anmen crackdown and because it has emerged as a significant global actor in world politics.

- As China's economic strength and political influence have grown, especially since the 2000s, it is now better able to control to its advantage the form of its participation in human rights diplomacy, but its actions towards rights-abusing governments now prompt critical global attention.

 Questions

1. Why did the Chinese government accuse the USA in particular of interference during its deliberations in May and June 1989?

2. Why did the Soviet leader's visit in May 1989 lead to a hardening of the Chinese leadership's resolve to end the demonstrations?

3. Was President George H.W. Bush wrong to be so conciliatory in the face of US domestic criticism and Chinese unwillingness to stop the crackdown?

5. Why did the sanctions policy start to weaken in 1990 and 1991?

6. Did the Chinese leadership appropriately assess the trade-off between the security of the one-party regime in China and its international status?

7. Which were the most significant of the foreign policy consequences of China's decision to use force.

8. Given that states quite quickly dropped most of the sanctions against China, why did Beijing engage in a global debate over human rights rather than ignore the topic?

9. Does the evolution of China's role in the global human rights regime illustrate the strengths or weaknesses of human rights diplomacy?

 Further reading

Goldman, M. (1995), *Sowing the Seeds of Democracy in China* (Cambridge, MA: Harvard University Press).
Analyses the reform debate among intellectuals inside China until the Tian'anmen crackdown of June 1989.

Kent, A. (1999), *China, the United Nations, and Human Rights: The Limits of Compliance* (Philadelphia, PA: University of Pennsylvania Press).
Examines China's levels of compliance with its international human rights treaty obligations.

Oksenberg, M., Sullivan, L.R., and Lambert, M. (eds) (1990), *Beijing Spring, 1989: Confrontation and Conflict. The Basic Documents* (Ithaca, NY: M.E. Sharpe).
An early compilation of documents and commentary that sets out to explain the decision to use force.

Risse, T., Ropp, S.C., and Sikkink, K. (eds) (1999), *The Power of Human Rights: International Norms and Domestic Change* (Cambridge: Cambridge University Press).
Develops a five-step 'spiral model' of human rights behaviour ranging from repression to rule-consistent behaviour.

Ross, R.S. (2001), 'The Diplomacy of Tiananmen: Two-Level Bargaining and Great-Power Cooperation', *Security Studies* 10: 139–78.
This article argues that domestic political conflict in China and then in the USA was a major determinant of the bilateral relationship, shaping their respective foreign policies between 1989 and 1992.

Teitt, S. (2011), 'The Responsibility to Protect and China's Peacekeeping Policy', *International Peacekeeping*, 18: 298–312.
Demonstrates the Chinese role in shaping the norm of the 'Responsibility to Protect' and that norm's potential impact on the protection of civilians caught up in armed conflict.

Wan, M. (2001), *Human Rights in Chinese Foreign Relations* (Philadelphia, PA: University of Pennsylvania Press).
Argues that China views its human rights diplomacy through the lens of realpolitik. Wan investigates this via chapters on the USA, Europe, Japan, and the United Nations.

Zhao, D. (2001), *The Power of Tiananmen: State–Society Relations and the 1989 Beijing Student Movement* (Chicago, IL: University of Chicago Press).
Examines the socio-cultural elements behind the students' decision to rebel in 1989.

 ## Web links

http://www.amnesty.org Amnesty International produces regular reports on human rights conditions in China and an annual survey of several countries, including China.

http://www.HRIChina.org Human Rights in China is an NGO, based in New York, of Chinese scholars and activists. It acts as a news, research, and discussion forum on human rights issues in China and publishes the journal *China Rights Forum*.

http://www.hrw.org Human Rights Watch produces regular reports on human rights conditions in China and an annual survey of countries, including China.

http://www.fmprc/gov/cn/eng/ Official website in English of China's Foreign Ministry and the first step to finding official statements, press briefings, and documents connected with the ministry's full range of activities.

http://www.humanrights.cn/index.asp Produced by the China Society for Human Rights Studies, which was established in March 1993. The Society describes itself as the largest national NGO in the field of human rights in China, but it often parrots a government line. However, it is a source of information on documents, laws and regulations, as well as on international exchanges.

 Visit the Online Resource Centre that accompanies this book for more information:
www.oxfordtextbooks.co.uk/orc/smith_foreign/

India and the World Trade Organization

AMRITA NARLIKAR

Chapter contents

 Reader's guide

This chapter analyses India's rise in the World Trade Organization (WTO), within the context of its foreign policy and its attempts to establish itself as an emerging power. The case study highlights two points. First, it demonstrates that the pathway to power that India has chosen within the WTO differs in interesting ways from the pathways that it has adopted in other international regimes. India's negotiation behaviour varies according to international institutions, and is often a function of careful adaptation within the specific structures and processes specific to the institution. The chapter provides a systematic analysis of the precise negotiation strategies, coalitions, and framing tactics that India has adopted to successfully establish itself as a major player in the WTO. Second, the chapter shows that several conventional explanations of foreign policy, including the role of domestic interest groups, bureaucratic politics, and ideational change, provide us with only partial and inadequate insights into India's successes in the WTO and ways it has achieved them. Critical to understanding the question of India's rise in the WTO is the role of the negotiation processes that it has adopted within a very specific institutional context. One of the conclusions of the chapter is that rising powers are seldom entirely revisionist or status quo; rather, their revolutionary, revisionist, or status quo aspirations vary according to the regimes they operate in.[1]

Introduction

India's rise from a struggling developing country to an acclaimed 'BRICs' economy has been meteoric.[2] This is reflected partly in India's soaring growth rate which makes it one of the fastest-growing economies in the world. Even in 2010, when most of the economies of the developed world were reeling from the global financial crisis, India maintained a growth rate of 8%. A Goldman Sachs study on the BRICs has predicted that in 30 years' time the Indian economy could be the largest in the world after the USA and China. India further demonstrated its military prowess via its nuclear tests in 1998. The economic and military indicators of India's rise have been accompanied by its emergence as a seasoned, proactive, and institutionally engaged player across international institutions. It has not only averted the risk of being branded a pariah state because of its acquisition of nuclear weapons, but, through successful diplomacy, it has actually managed to legitimize its status as a nuclear weapons state by signing a bilateral deal with the USA. It is a regular invitee to G8 summits through annex groupings such as the G5 or the outreach group, and is also a key player in the Leaders' Level G20. In the WTO, it has proved its ability to block the negotiation process until its demands are met; in meeting after meeting, negotiators from the developed world have reiterated that no deal would be possible without the Indians on board.

In this chapter, I investigate India's emergence as a core player in the WTO. This case study is important for two reasons. First, it illustrates that the foreign policy of India (or other emerging powers for that matter) cannot be fully understood without a close analysis of the international institutional context within which it plays out. As this chapter goes on to argue, India's rise in the WTO is a product of decades of learning to negotiate within the specific multilateral rules of the organization (as well as its predecessor, the General Agreement of Tariffs and Trade, GATT). Second, the case study illustrates that even after certain structural conditions are met, such as large market size and rapid economic growth, the rise of a country to the status of a recognized great power is not automatic. Rather, the process whereby a state's rise is negotiated matters in terms of both recognition by other parties and the outcomes that the state is able to generate.

The argument proceeds in seven parts. Following this introduction, I focus on some of the schizophrenic aspects of India's foreign policy when examined across issue areas. I highlight the contradictions in India's foreign policy in security areas versus economic areas to show the importance of understanding institutional contexts and processes in either case. In the third section, I focus specifically on the evidence of India's rise within the WTO. The fourth section explores plausible mainstream explanations for India's apparent rise to power, including growing market size, changing ideology, and the role of domestic interest groups in influencing foreign economic policy. All three have serious limitations. In the fifth section, I propose an alternative explanation. India's emergence as a key player in the WTO cannot be explained without an in-depth understanding of India's negotiation behaviour. This behaviour is in many ways specific to the regime, and has been learnt over decades through participation and adaptation within the institution. The sixth section discusses some of the problems that India's WTO diplomacy raises within the trade context as well as its broader foreign policy goals. The seventh and concluding section summarizes the findings of the chapter and its implications for Foreign Policy Analysis.

India's schizophrenic rise

India's rise is not institution-specific. In addition to its invitations to G20 summits and key small-group meetings in the WTO, India is seen as one of the most serious contenders for a permanent seat in the Security Council. Its diplomacy in establishing itself as a legitimate nuclear weapons' state has been unusually successful. But the processes whereby this rise is negotiated vary fundamentally across regimes. A brief examination of India's foreign policy on nuclear issues versus trade issues in recent times illustrates the differences—even contradictions—across issue areas.

In its role in the WTO, India has adhered to and further developed its long-established tactics of building coalitions with developing countries, standing up to the developed world, and saying no even when it incurs costs as a result. Recall that these tactics of engaging with and speaking up for the Third World are not qualitatively new; after all, India was a founder member of the Non-Aligned Movement, which had its first meeting in Bandung in 1955. It was an active and leading member of the G77—a group of developing countries that came together at the first meeting of the UN Conference on Trade and Development in 1964—and participated subsequently in the call for a fairer economic system via the demand for a New International Economic Order. In the first nearly 45 years of its independence, such demands fitted well with its domestic programmes for economic development based on import-substituting industrialization. But even after the launch of its programme of economic liberalization in 1991, India did not abandon these positions. As argued in the fifth section of this chapter, India has continued to be a tough negotiator in the WTO. It still acts as a leader of coalitions involving developing countries, makes concessions to smaller members, tolerates free-riding, and fights for causes of global justice and fairness. India, whilst rising in the WTO, retains at least some of its old ideals. But this is not the only face of Indian foreign policy.

India's Janus-faced foreign policy is evident when we compare elements of its traditional Third World-ist positions in the WTO against its pragmatic bilateralism on nuclear weapons. The USA–India deal on civilian nuclear cooperation, which was approved by the US Congress in December 2006, effectively welcomes India into the club of legitimate nuclear weapons states (despite the fact that India is not a signatory to the Non-Proliferation Treaty). Far from pursuing idealistic Third World-ist causes, the new nuclear India now seeks a freezing of the regime which prevents acquisition of nuclear weapons by other countries, and which is actively policed by 'responsible' nuclear powers including India. This strategy was borne out in 2005 in India's unprecedented support in favour of an IAEA resolution against Iran's nuclear activities; India ended up siding with the US camp, and several leaps away from its traditional adherence to positions of non-alignment. When asked about the implications of India's move closer to the USA on its Third World allies, a senior official in the Ministry of External Affairs responded, 'My heart bleeds for them!' (interview with author, New Delhi, January 2006).

The two sets of negotiating positions—one that represents India as 'the voice of the voiceless' (interview with Indian trade diplomat, October 2003), and the other that represents India as the forward-looking, pragmatic, and powerful strategist—do not easily add up. These contradictions are partly a function of bureaucratic politics within India: the drive for closer relations with the USA has come from the Ministry of External Affairs, whereas the Ministry of Commerce is in charge of India's negotiations in the WTO. But, as argued in the third section of this chapter, underlying both bureaucracies is India's common political culture which is rooted in an old anti-colonial view that resents Western powers. To understand the different faces of India's rising power, we must locate them within the specific international regime contexts. India's pathway to power in the WTO, given the rules of the institution and its experiences within it, differs fundamentally from the pathway to power into the club of legitimate nuclear powers. In the following pages, we will trace and analyse India's negotiation strategy within the WTO, and we will return to the question of its inconsistencies with other regimes in the Conclusion.

From the margins of the GATT to the core of the WTO

Three sets of indicators point to India's rising power in the WTO: participation in the negotiation processes, effective use of the dispute settlement mechanism (DSM), and proven ability to block the negotiations until certain demands are met.

First, it has become a regular invitee and active member of all the small-group decision-making meetings in the WTO where 'consensus' for the plenary meetings is shaped. This is true for meetings at all levels in the WTO: ministerial meetings, heads of delegations meetings, and expert level meetings. Such meetings usually bring together all those parties who must be on board for an agreement to be reached. One example is the Group of Five Interested Parties in 2004, which included Australia, Brazil, the EU, India, and the USA, and was instrumental in breaking a preceding stalemate in the negotiation process via the 'July Package'. In 2006, India was party to the G6 consultations (which included Australia, Brazil, the EU, India, Japan, and the USA), which attempted to break the deadlock on agriculture. In July 2008, India was part of a similar set of consultations involving seven countries. Participation in these meetings is no small sign of recognition (see Box 18.1 on decision-making processes in the WTO and the problems encountered by developing countries in the past; Box 18.2 provides a timeline of the major events in the multilateral trading system).

The second indicator of India's rising influence in the WTO is its active and growing participation in the DSM of the organization. In the entire history of the GATT, i.e. from 1947 to 1994, only one panel report was adopted involving India. Today, it has brought nineteen cases as complainant to the DSM, is respondent in twenty cases, and is third party in sixty-seven cases. Next only to Brazil's use of the DSM, these figures are not only the highest amongst developing countries, but are also comparable with developed countries (other than the EU and the USA). This rise in India's use of the DSM is partly a function of the greater stakes that it has in the multilateral trading system. But equally importantly, these figures reveal a qualitative jump in India's familiarity and skill in using the system.

The third, and perhaps even more convincing, indicator is India's emergence as a power in the WTO which has now successfully blocked the negotiation process. Theoretically, by virtue of the 'consensus' principle, all members of the organization can block a negotiation. In practice, however, few developing countries have exercised such a veto effectively. This is because developing countries have fewer alternatives available to them than developed countries, and their threats to block are unlikely to be believed. Narlikar and Odell (2006) cite an ambassador from a small developing country on why developing countries find it difficult to block: 'The US can block a consensus but not [my country]. If you block, the entire weight of the organization comes down on you. The problem is that on other issues I need others to be flexible. If I block on this issue, I am in trouble on the other issue'. Indeed, India had attempted in the past to hold up the negotiations—as leader of the G10 coalition in the run-up to the launch of the Uruguay Round, and as leader of the Like-Minded Group in the

BOX 18.1 The World Trade Organization: decision-making and developing countries

The World Trade Organization (WTO) was born in 1995. Before its creation, the multilateral trading system was managed by its predecessor—the General Agreement on Tariffs and Trade (GATT). The WTO, albeit a formal organization with a much wider scope and a stronger DSM, retains many features of the GATT, particularly its decision-making procedures.

India was one of the original contracting parties that signed the GATT. Even though eleven of the original twenty-three signatories were developing countries, participation in the GATT was not easy for them. Theoretically, the GATT was a one-country–one-vote institution, but most decisions were taken on the basis of 'consensus', i.e. decisions would be arrived at as long as no party present objected to the proposed decision. On paper, a consensus norm gives the power of a veto to any member, irrespective of size or any other criteria. In practice, however, the consensus norm deterred the participation of developing countries in two ways.

First, the consensus norm requires a presence in the meeting, and few developing countries had enough staff on their missions (if they had missions at all) to have an informed and active presence in meetings. It also requires an open show of hands, which made smaller and weaker players reluctant to stand up to the more powerful countries. Second, there were several informal processes underlying consensus-based decision making. These involved small-group consultations, many of which were by invitation only, and to which developing countries were often not invited. In fact, most important decisions were taken amongst the Quad group comprising Canada, the EU, Japan, and the USA. For these reasons, the GATT was often referred to as the 'Rich Man's Club'. Brazil and India were amongst the few developing countries which were invited to small-group meetings, but even they found it difficult to participate effectively in the almost 'English club atmosphere' of the GATT.

The WTO retains the same decision-making processes; in fact, Article IX:1 of the Agreement establishing the WTO explicitly states codifies the consensus norm. The WTO came under severe criticism, most visibly at the Seattle Ministerial of 1999, for its exclusive decision-making processes from which the majority of developing countries were excluded. India was a prime mover in raising these demands. As a result, the WTO has made some attempts to improve the transparency of decision-making processes. But many developing countries have continued to complain about inadequate resources to negotiate effectively, inability to use the DSM, and the dominance of the developed world—especially the EU and the USA—in setting the agenda via drafts of ministerial conferences and using the informal processes of decision making to unfair advantage. It is against these institutional odds that India's new-found status must be assessed to be fully appreciated. When facing deadlocks, a group of four to six members now gets together to build consensus; for the past few years, India has been an active participant in such meetings. This is no mean achievement, especially given the expanded membership of the organization which now includes over 150 countries.

run-up to the Doha Development Agenda. However, in both cases members of the coalitions were gradually bought off with carrots and sticks. As the coalition collapsed, India found itself isolated in the endgame and ended up having to give in with few returns (see Narlikar and Odell 2006; see also Box 18.3 on coalitions that India has been involved in). It is the ability of India now to successfully and effectively block the negotiations that has changed.

India, together with Brazil, was a leader of a coalition of developing countries—the G20—at the Cancun Ministerial Conference in 2003 which refused to succumb to pressures from the

BOX 18.2 Trade rounds in the GATT and WTO: a timeline

Year	Place and name of round	Subjects covered
1947	Geneva	Tariffs
1949	Annecy	Tariffs
1951	Torquay	Tariffs
1956	Geneva	Tariffs
1960–1961	Geneva—Dillon Round	Tariffs
1964–1967	Geneva—Kennedy Round	Tariffs and anti-dumping measures
1973–1979	Geneva—Tokyo Round	Tariffs, non-tariff measures, 'framework' agreements
1986–1994	Geneva—Uruguay Round	Tariffs, non-tariff measures, rules, services, intellectual property, dispute settlement, textiles, agriculture, creation of the WTO, etc.
2001-present day (was due for completion by January 2005)	Doha—Doha Development Agenda (DDA) Major events within DDA: Launch in Doha Ministerial 2001 Deadlock at Cancun Ministerial 2003 Deadlock broken in 'July Package' 2004 2004-2005—Recurrent stalemate Hong Kong Ministerial 2005—no major breakthroughs July 2006—Negotiations indefinitely suspended February 2007—Negotiations resumed June 2007—Stalemate continues July 2008—'July Package' discussed, deadlock continues Since 2008—Despite risk and rise of trade protectionism, and urgency of concluding Doha deal emphasized across organizations and countries, deadlock persists	Most wide-ranging in scope yet, covering critical areas such as agriculture, non-agricultural market access, reform of the dispute settlement system etc. Seeks to address development concerns

EU and the USA until the demands of its members were met. Unlike former coalitions, this coalition did not collapse on the last ministerial conference, and the proceedings ended in stalemate. The other coalitions involving India (as listed in Box 18.3) have displayed a similar pattern of resilience. Partly as a major economy in its own right, and partly because it enjoys the backing of coalitions involving large numbers of developing countries, India's presence is

BOX 18.3 Select coalitions involving India:[i] from the Uruguay Round to the Doha Development Agenda

Coalition	Timing	Membership	Agenda
G10	Lead-up to Uruguay Round launch, 1982–1986	Argentina, Brazil, Cuba, Egypt, India, Nigeria, Nicaragua, Peru, Tanzania, Yugoslavia	Opposition to the inclusion of the 'new issues' of services, TRIPs, and TRIMs
Like-Minded Group	Formed at Singapore Ministerial Conference 1996; continued until Cancun Ministerial Conference 2003	Cuba, Dominican Republic, Egypt, Honduras, India, Indonesia, Malaysia, Pakistan, Tanzania, Uganda, Zimbabwe + Jamaica and Kenya as observers	'Implementation issues', institutional reform, and opposition to the Singapore issues
G20	Formed at the Cancun Ministerial Conference 2003; continues to date	Original signatories: Argentina, Bolivia, Brazil, Chile, China, Colombia, Costa Rica, Cuba, Ecuador, El Salvador, Guatemala, India, Mexico, Pakistan, Paraguay, Peru, Philippines, South Africa, Thailand, Venezuela	Opening up of the agricultural markets of developed countries
G33	Proposal in July 2003; coalition crystallizes at Cancun Ministerial 2003; continues to date.	Antigua and Barbuda, Barbados, Belize, Benin, Botswana, China, Congo, Côte d'Ivoire, Cuba, Dominican Republic, Grenada, Guyana, Haiti, Honduras, India, Indonesia, Jamaica, Kenya, Korea, Mauritius, Madagascar, Mongolia, Mozambique, Nicaragua, Nigeria, Pakistan, Panama, Peru, Philippines, St Kitts and Nevis, St Lucia, St Vincent and the Grenadines, Senegal, Sri Lanka, Suriname, Tanzania, Trinidad and Tobago, Turkey, Uganda, Venezuela, Zambia, Zimbabwe (actually 42 members)	Strategic Product and Special Safeguard Mechanism for developing countries
NAMA-11	Formed just before the Hong Kong Ministerial 2005; continues to date	Argentina, Brazil, Egypt, India, Indonesia, Namibia, Philippines, South Africa, Tunisia, Venezuela	Seeks flexibilities to limit market opening for industrial goods

This table includes only those coalitions in which India has played a leading and proactive role.

seen as crucial to any agreement. This is evidenced in its presence in all critical consensus-building small-group consultations in the Doha negotiations. Not only does India see itself as having the ability to block negotiations and broker compromise, but it is also seen in this capacity by other countries; in speech after speech, the USA and the EU have acknowledged that a Doha deal will be impossible to achieve without India (with its ally Brazil, and more recently China) on board. India's dramatic move from the margins of the GATT and early WTO to its core processes today needs explanation.

The political economy of rising influence

International political economy offers us several useful insights into how India has managed to acquire influence in the WTO. I examine three mainstream explanations—market size, the role of ideas, and domestic interest groups—before offering an alternative explanation in the next section.

The lure of the market

The first explanation for India's rising power in the WTO is simply in terms of market power. Several studies suggest a 'global power shift in the making' which is driven by rapid economic growth (Hodge 2004; see also Wilson and Purushothaman 2003). And grown India has, at a rate of 7.5% between 2002 and 2006. In 1991, foreign direct investment (FDI) in India was less than US $2 billion; in 2004, FDI stock in India was near $39 billion (Chakraborty and Nunnenkamp 2006). Based on such figures, India is projected to be the third largest economy in thirty years, preceded only by the USA and China. Of course India could not escape the worldwide tremors caused by the global economic downturn of 2008. But even at its lowest, India's growth rate was a respectable 5.8% in 2009, and returned to an impressive 8% in 2010. India's increasing power in the WTO may well be seen as simply, or at least primarily, a function of this economic growth.

This is a plausible explanation, but an insufficient one. On closer inspection, we find that India's shares in world trade are still relatively small: it ranked as fifteenth largest exporter of merchandise trade in 2009, and eighth largest importer, thereby occupying only 1.7% and 2.6% shares of world merchandise exports and imports, respectively. Its shares in services are higher—it is the sixth largest exporter of services—but even here, its actual market shares are limited to 3.5%, in contrast to the EU which occupies 26.3% of the world market in services exporters or US shares amounting to 19.2% (impressive figures in their own right, but even more so if one takes into account how hard the EU and the USA have been hit by the global economic crisis).[3] If the primary explanation of India's rising status in the WTO were trade shares and economic weight, more serious contenders to a similar status would be China, Hong Kong, Mexico, and the East Asian newly industrialized countries (NICs). That India, along with Brazil, has come to acquire such a special position in WTO negotiations must have an alternative explanation.

The role of ideas: norms of liberalization

According to this argument, past Indian failures in the WTO were just a product of self-imposed and misguided preferences for protectionism. Either guided by the intrinsic rationality of economic and political liberalization (e.g. Kahler 1997) or driven by hegemonic imposition (e.g. Cox 1994), all developing countries today—including India—show an increasing policy convergence across issue areas. This policy convergence also translates into a more proactive and effective participation in the WTO. We find a similar set of arguments with respect to India's recent foreign policy successes in other issue areas as well. For instance, C. Raja Mohan argues:

> If a single image captured India's national strategic style, it was that of a porcupine—vegetarian, slow-footed and prickly. The famous defensiveness of the porcupine became the hallmark of India's approach to the world . . . India's engagement with the world since the early 1990s posits a fundamental change of course and a reconstitution of its core premises. Whether it was the de-emphasis of non-alignment or the new embrace of the US, or the attempts to rethink regionalism in the subcontinent and its environs, a radically different foreign policy orientation emerged by the turn of the millennium. (Mohan 2003: 260–3)

In other words, India is doing better in the WTO because its negotiators and people have finally embraced the processes of liberalization, and this is reflected in more rational and conciliatory strategies within the WTO.

Closer examination reveals that such arguments are flawed for two reasons. First, far from abandoning its 'prickly' negotiation style in the WTO, India continues to be a very tough negotiator in multilateral trade. In fact, even though its negotiation strategies have evolved over the years (as will be illustrated in the fourth section of this chapter), there remain some unmistakable continuities in negotiating style and substance. These are reflected in the continued and even more effective use of hard-line negotiation strategies, commitment to coalitions involving developing countries, and even allowing considerable free-riding within such coalitions.

Second, even though India has a reasonably successful programme of economic liberalization under way, this programme differs from the Latin American one in terms of its gradualism and restraint (Jenkins 1999; Kohli 2004). Further, normative commitment to this agenda is at best cautious at the government level and highly contested at the popular level. These reservations are reflected even in the negotiation positions adopted by the Congress government under Dr Manmohan Singh as Prime Minister and transcend party politics. In fact, over time, governments from the left to the extreme right have adopted very similar positions in the WTO. Interviews with senior bureaucrats in the national capital and Geneva reveal that the government's caution in trade negotiation reflects the popular suspicions of its populace. One mentioned India's 'strong colonial mindset' (interview, Geneva, May 2003) where the 'the spirit of liberalization has simply not seeped in' (interview, New Delhi, April 2004). A trade diplomat's eloquent statement captures the spirit of India's domestic political culture nicely: 'It is easier for our minister to come back home empty-handed as a wounded hero, rather than to come back with something after having had to make a compromise' (interview, Geneva, May 2003). However, could it be argued that India's successful emergence in the WTO is a product of neither a deep ideological conversion nor solely market size, but of domestic pressure groups?

Domestic politics

As per this set of explanations—again, well-rooted in international political economy—the persistence of caution in certain aspects of India's trade policy, as well as occasional bursts of liberalization in other issue areas, can be explained by examining the domestic political economy of particular interests. But this set of explanations, like the former two, finds only limited empirical support.

Decision-making on matters of trade policy in India takes place as a result of frequent consultation between the Indian mission to the WTO in Geneva and the Ministry of Commerce (MoC). The MoC in turn consults with various stakeholders, and receives inputs from apex-level organizations such as the Federation of Indian Chambers of Commerce and the Confederation of Indian Industry, as well as sector-specific organizations. The influence of business groups in trade policy making and trade negotiations is evident in certain niche sectors such as computing services. But all in all, particularly when compared with the role of interest groups in developed countries, the Indian state remains a remarkably effective gatekeeper for societal interests.

Evidence of the dominance of the state executive, particularly the MoC in the trade case, as the central agenda setter can be found in the stakeholder consultation process: the MoC decides whom to consult, when, and over what. Whilst maintaining links with relevant ministries over particular issue areas (such as the Ministry of Health over health services), the MoC remains one of the most powerful bureaucracies in the country. India's federal system further encourages disjointed decision making and thereby reinforces the dominance of the MoC. Parliamentary oversight exists, but remains limited (Sen 2003). Thus theories of domestic political economy provide only minimal insights into explaining the successes or failures of India's trade diplomacy.

Institution-specific explanations: learning to negotiate successfully

The previous section has illustrated that economic size/market potential provides only a necessary but not sufficient condition for India's rise in the WTO, and theories of domestic political economy and the role of ideas have only limited value. In this section, I propose an alternative explanation using negotiation analysis; having met the minimal condition of economic size, India's rise in the WTO can best be explained by analysing its negotiation process. Through decades of institutional learning and adaptation, India has successfully developed a set of negotiation processes that are particularly well suited to the WTO. We can operationalize the concept of negotiation process through several concrete variables; in this section, I focus on the three main variables of bargaining coalitions, negotiation strategies, and framing. Without having experimented with these aspects of negotiation process in the past, it is doubtful whether India would have managed to become an indispensable member of the key negotiation and decision-making small groups within the organization. It is also unlikely that it would have acquired the power to block in the organization, and thereby emerged as one of a group of four to six countries that must be on board for any deal to go through.

Coalitions

Admittedly, India's participation and leadership of coalitions involving developing countries is not new; the fact that it was one of the few developing countries present in the Green Room meetings of the GATT was a product of this leadership. But neither this leadership, nor the entry that it facilitated into Green Room meetings, translated automatically into greater influence in the WTO. It is only much more recently that India has learnt to form effective coalitions that have overcome the problems affecting the old coalition types.

The new coalitions, often led by India, are hybrids, which combine features of two different sets of coalitions of the past—issue-based and bloc-type—but also diverge from their predecessors.[4] Traditional bloc coalitions brought together a group of countries with a very diverse set of interests under the roof of a shared ideology or identity. Interests of members were log-rolled to constitute the collective agenda. Such coalitions proved especially prone to fragmentation, partly because outside parties were able to buy off members by appealing to their specific interests. The risk that the coalition might unravel if any concessions that were made also led leaders to pursue a strict distributive strategy (discussed below), show no flexibility in the negotiation process, and then collapse in the run-up to the endgame as individual members began to defect. The G10 coalition was a perfect example of this coalition type (see Box 18.3). In contrast, coalitions involving India in recent times have often used a specific issue area around which to converge. For instance, at Cancun, and in subsequent DDA negotiations, the G20 coalition—with Brazil and India at its helm—has focused on agriculture. It is not surprising that most of these coalitions have had a reasonably coherent agenda, particularly when compared with the bloc-type diplomacy of the 1980s.

Note, however, that recent coalitions also diverge considerably from their issue-based predecessors of the Uruguay Round. In the Uruguay Round, following the failures of the G10, and the successes of the Café au Lait and Cairns Groups, developing countries had shown a conversion (almost en masse with the exception of India) to so-called 'issue-based coalitions' which transcended North–South boundaries. Many of these coalitions were formed on some highly specific subsectors (such as air transport services, geographical indications, mode 4) or slightly broader but still issue-specific areas such as the Friends of Services and the Food Importers Groups (Narlikar 2003). Those dealing with specific subsectors often ended up facing the problem of limited collective weight. However, other issue-specific groups also showed problems of sustainability. They also ended up becoming increasingly vulnerable to fragmentation, particularly when they brought together countries with large diversified economies.

Recent coalitions of developing countries, including those in which India continues to act as leader, have overcome these problems by incorporating some ideational features as an additional cementing mechanism. As such, they combine features of the traditional bloc-type and issue-based coalitions. Even while focusing on a particular issue area and putting forward concrete proposals on it, they are often limited in membership to a subset of developing countries. The G20 provides one instance of such a coalition of developing countries focused on a specific issue. The first proposal by the G20, which was formed under a Brazilian and Indian initiative on agriculture, was signed by 20 members: Argentina, Bolivia, Brazil, Chile, China, Colombia, Costa Rica, Cuba, Ecuador, El Salvador, Guatemala, India, Mexico, Pakistan, Paraguay, Peru, the Philippines, South Africa, Thailand, and Venezuela. Unlike the old bloc-type coalitions, the G20 was not simply a blocking coalition but one with a proactive agenda. However, unlike the short-term issue-based coalitions of the Uruguay Round, it did not suffer from the problem of inadequate collective weight. It brought together most emerging powers—powers that we would expect to matter—with Brazil, China, India, Argentina, and South Africa as part of the core group. Further, by focusing on agriculture, it brought together countries with a shared understanding of the importance of this issue. As a result, the G20 has proved to be much longer lasting than the issue-based coalitions of the Uruguay Round. Other coalitions of developing countries in the Doha negotiations—in several of which India plays an important and often leading role—show a pattern similar to that of G20 in their constitution as well as their resilience (Ismail 2009; Narlikar 2009).

Based on its many and often difficult years of learning in the WTO, India has now learned that when building coalitions, careful selection of membership and a coherent agenda are key steps towards avoiding future fragmentation. Additionally, if the collective agenda is built around a an issue of considerable importance to all parties, it can provide an important method of offsetting bilateral deals that outside negotiating partners may offer. India recognizes that if the weakest members of the group are provided with some assistance from the leaders, the risk of their defection decreases. The G20 certainly attempts such strategies towards building cohesion, for instance by framing the agenda of the coalition so as to appeal to most of the members.[5] Brazil and India, in particular, have shown their willingness to bear the costs of coalition formation and conduct research initiatives,[6] but also to allow preferential market access to exports from the least developed countries (LDCs).[7]

Choice of negotiation strategy

The choice of negotiation strategy depends at least as much on domestic political culture and the coalitions that the country might be involved in, as it does on the individual negotiators. In the Indian case, negotiators have used what is known as a strict distributive strategy, i.e. they had very high opening demands, refused to make any concessions, and issued threats to the opponents. This strategy is not one that automatically generates successes. Coalitions which use such a strategy tend to attract divide-and-rule tactics from the outside party. Rather than giving in to the high demands of the coalition, the opponent prefers to buy off individual members of the coalition with bilateral deals. Should most coalition members defect in response to bilateral carrots and sticks, isolated members who continue to adhere to the hard line end up with few gains and only losses in the endgame (Narlikar and Odell 2006). The G10 provides an instance of all these at work in an inflexible bloc-type coalition, which collapsed in the endgame.

Interestingly, however, despite the risks involved, India has never quite abandoned its reliance on a strict distributive strategy; even more interestingly, the use of this distributive strategy has now begun to yield some pay-offs, including new allies within the developing world and rising power in the WTO. What is the explanation for the different outcomes resulting from the same negotiation strategy?

Even though India had relied on a 'just say no' strategy (Cohen 2001), recent years have given considerably greater bite to this strategy. The answer lies in the growing coherence of the coalitions that these countries have led, as discussed in the previous subsection. Constituting coalitions which combine features of issue-based and bloc-type coalitions, and further preserving the loyalty of smaller members that might otherwise defect through intra-coalition deals, Indian-led coalitions (such as the G20), and also others such as the G33, NAMA-11, Africa Group, and LDC group, show greater levels of stability. Coalitions which use a strict distributive strategy but collapse in the endgame end up with nothing, but coalitions which use a similar strategy while retaining their coherence have more possibilities before them. Depending on the nature of their demands, they can end up with the jackpot or deadlock in the negotiation.

For simplicity, assume that the negotiation proceeds in two stages (e.g. a key ministerial meeting could be seen as stage 1, and the negotiations following the meeting as stage 2, as was the case at Cancun and thereafter). In stage 1, the coalition credibly demonstrates that all its members are committed to the collective agenda; through some of the mechanisms discussed in the previous subsection, defections in favour of smaller side-deals are prevented. Following this demonstration at a ministerial meeting, we come to stage 2 of the negotiation. If the outside party perceives the costs of meeting the unified demands of the coalition to be small compared with the costs of deadlock, the coalition ends up with a deal that is highly favourable to itself. In contrast, however, if the coalition's demands are so high that meeting them will outweigh the costs of deadlock, then the negotiations end in impasse. This is particularly likely if the coalition comprises developing countries and is dealing with significantly powerful opponents, such as the EU or the USA, which have valuable BATNAs (best alternatives to negotiated agreements) that they can rely on should the multilateral negotiations fail. In either instance, however, if the coalition uses a strict distributive strategy in stage 1 and does not collapse through defections from members, the members cannot be easily ignored (Narlikar and van Houten 2006).

India, along with Brazil and other developing countries, made some important progress in stage 1 on the use of the strict distributive which is represented by the Cancun Ministerial. Since then, alone and via the coalition of the G20, it has stood firm in its refusal to cave in to the demands of the EU and the USA on agriculture. Having demonstrated a credible commitment to its position on agriculture, it is now seen (along with Brazil) as a veto-player—a Doha deal would be impossible without India on board.

Interestingly, even after having made it into the informal great power club within the WTO, India has retained a large part of its traditional Third-World-ist agenda rather than display socialization into a conformist agenda in line with that of the developed world. For instance, following the Mini-Ministerial in November 2005, Minister Kamal Nath stated: 'We have to ensure that whatever deal is re-calibrated to come up in Hong Kong meets the stated objectives of this Round. The test of this Round is whether it benefits those who earn a dollar a day or $5000 a month.'[9] This discourse has remained largely unchanged. In the make-or-break negotiations over the July Package of 2008, Minister Nath arrived at the meeting and stated: 'The position of developed counties is utterly self-righteous . . . This self-righteousness will not do. If it means no deal, so be it . . . I am obviously not here to hand around freebies without getting something in return'.[10]

Framing

As well as learning to build strong long-lasting coalitions and using negotiation strategies more effectively, the third explanation to rising Indian influence in the WTO lies at the ideational level. India, through participation in the organization over time, has learnt how to frame its demands in terms that appeal to particular constituencies (including other negotiators and particular constituencies within the opposing states), to fit well within the institutional context, and also to exploit the international context to its advantage. Such framing can be strategic or it might be driven by ethical concerns. Amongst methods used to legitimize the trade discourse, the most commonly used is that of fairness.

In the first almost forty years of their dealings with the WTO, India led developing countries in espousing a notion of fairness that emphasized the importance of equity rather than legitimacy, and outcomes rather than process (Franck 1996; Narlikar 2006). In fact, behind the refusal of developing countries to engage on a reciprocal basis within the GATT was a firm commitment to an equity-based notion of fairness; until the existing inequalities (some of which were seen to be reinforced by the institution of the GATT) were corrected, they could not be expected to make concessions to developed countries. This idea was borne out most clearly in the 1954 statement of Sir N. Raghavan Pillai, the Indian delegate to the GATT: 'Equality of treatment is equitable only among equals. A weakling cannot carry the same load as a giant' (cited in Kock 1969: 289).

Concretely, these demands for greater equity in the GATT were borne out in the call for special and differential treatment for developing countries that exempted them from the rules of liberalization that underlay the GATT system. Whether the logic behind such framing tactics was strategic, or a genuine ethical commitment to greater equity, is difficult to determine given that we see such a perfect correspondence between demands for GATT exemptions and the interests of developing countries who pushed for this agenda. These tactics generated only limited successes.

Following the launch of the Uruguay Round, many developing countries continued to appeal to fairness in the GATT, but now placed greater emphasis on fairness of process and legitimacy rather than equity. This change may have been partly a result of institutional learning within the GATT (and the failures of old Third World-ist coalitions and distributive strategies) or a result of changes at home where governments, under the impact of the debt crisis or through genuine enlightenment, increasingly began to give up old protectionist models of growth in favour of liberal economic models. Underlying this new ideological frame was a greater willingness to engage in reciprocal trade liberalization. But the gains from this pursuit of fairness in terms of legitimacy of process rather than distributive justice were few. In contrast, India's unbroken suspicion of reciprocal liberalization was vindicated, and a fairness discourse emphasizing issues of equity returned to prominence with the formation of the WTO and the recognition that the promises of the Uruguay Round had remained unfulfilled for developing countries.

After the formation of the WTO, when all the costs and limited benefits of implementing the Uruguay Round Agreements came to the fore, many developing countries recognized that even participating in the GATT in accordance with its own norms of liberalization, and having adopted notions of fairness framed as equal participation and process-based legitimacy, had yielded few gains. They updated their frames accordingly. For many developing countries, including the larger ones, this revision was a reversal from their discourse in the late 1980s and early 1990s; however, for India it was a logical continuation.

The new frame of fairness now focused on both the process and the substance of the negotiations. First, at the Seattle Ministerial Conference, the African Group of countries and a group of Latin American and Caribbean countries issued statements denouncing the process of negotiation from which most developing countries had been systematically excluded. The Indian-led Like Minded Group took up these issues as part of an agenda for institutional reform of the WTO which included greater transparency of meetings and open invitations so that members could self-select participation (interviews, Geneva, May 2003).

Second, in terms of substance, the Like Minded Group also became one of the first coalitions to bring equity back onto the agenda (Narlikar and Odell 2006). It focused on the so-called 'implementation issues' and argued that there was no question of launching a new round until the imbalances of the Uruguay Round were corrected. It brought back the demand for expanded special and differential treatment (SDT) arrangements that were of special relevance for its LDC members, and was supported in this call by the LDC grouping.[11] While making these demands negotiators from the group repeatedly referred to how they had kept their end of the Uruguay Round bargain, but the developed countries had not (interviews, Geneva, summer 2003). Whilst appealing to these notions of fairness, a Third World-ist tenor was evident in Indian claims. For instance, the Indian Commerce Minister Murasoli Maran denounced the Doha draft declaration in the following terms:

> . . . the draft Ministerial Declaration is neither fair nor just to the view points of many developing countries including my own on certain key issues. It is a negation of all that was said by a significant number of developing countries and least-developing countries. . . . The only conclusion that could be drawn is that the developing countries have little say in the agenda setting of the WTO. It appears that the whole process was a mere formality and we are being coerced against our will.[12]

In subsequent negotiations, India has continued to frame its demands with reference to fairer treatment for all developing countries. At the Hong Kong Ministerial Conference, Minister Kamal Nath stated:

> We need to finalize the proposal for duty-free quota-free access for exports of LDCs to developed country markets, without hedging. Developing countries too are ready to play their part, according to their abilities. India shall not be founding wanting in this respect.[13]

That this support goes beyond just rhetoric is suggested by some concrete actions that India has taken. At the Hong Kong Ministerial some developing countries protested against certain SDT provisions for the LDCs; India negotiators pointed out in private interviews that, irrespective of the costs to the country, India's long-standing position as a leader of the developing world would make it impossible for them to present any opposition to such proposals (interviews, New Delhi, January 2006). As well as coordinating positions across coalitions around ministerial conferences, and also supporting demands for preferential trade agreements (PTAs) by LDCs (as discussed in the previous subsections), India has provided technical assistance and preferential market access to LDCs in the run-up to the Hong Kong Ministerial and thereafter.

India's willingness to adhere to a discourse of fairness, and even bear costs for its weaker allies, provides an interesting contrast with its willingness to engage with the USA at the cost of other Third World allies on nuclear matters. However, this schizophrenia becomes less of a puzzle when we recall that India's rise in the WTO has come on the strength of its claim to leadership of several developing countries over time. If India were to abandon this informal constituency, its place in the various small-group meetings would become much more suspect. In contrast, India has developed its nuclear programme indigenously, and its nuclear diplomacy, particularly after the 1998 tests, has had little support from other developing countries. Its nuclear deal with the USA is not a result of its leadership of the Non-Aligned Movement, but a product of its effective diplomacy despite isolation from the North and

South. As a result, the India that pays such homage to questions of fairness and traditional Third World-ist alliances in the WTO, is also the India that goes it alone when negotiating with the USA on nuclear technology.

The burden of rising power

India is now in an indisputable position of central importance in the negotiation process, but an important caveat is in order at this point. The power to block, whilst an important step towards reaching one's foreign policy goals, does not necessarily translate into an ability to reach one's preferred outcomes.

In terms of actual outcomes, India's power to say 'no' has not produced the desired effects. Negotiations were 'suspended' in July 2006—an unexpected event for most negotiators and observers who had predicted a compromise in the form of a 'Doha-lite', and one that has postponed any gains that developing countries (including India) would have derived from the negotiation, besides undermining the credibility of the multilateral trading system. The deadlock was at least partly a result of the refusal of India to make any concessions even at this late stage of the negotiation. The US Secretary for Agriculture, Mike Johanns, made the following accusation after the breakdown of talks:

> Now advanced developing countries are world class competitors. This would be China, this would be India, this would be Brazil, this would be other countries around the world that quite honestly can compete with anybody very effectively. Yet in the proposal that they tabled, it essentially blocked 95 to 98 percent of their market. . . . So in the end, what we were faced with is this: we've got a very bold proposal already, we've announced our willingness to be flexible but we're still not seeing the market access that is necessary for world trade.[14]

The Indians did not deny these accusations, suggesting that the deadlock was a result of missing concessions rather than just misperceptions of each others' offers. Minister Kamal Nath is reported to have said at a press conference on 27 July: 'If the developed countries want to view this round as a market access round for themselves, which is going to impinge upon the livelihood of our farmers and is going to hurt our industry, then we made very clear there is and can be no further movement in these negotiations' (Mahapatra 2006).

In July 2008, India's negotiating behaviour revealed a similar pattern: its negotiation strategy remained strictly distributive, it continued to work closely with coalitions of developing countries, and it framed its demands in strongly developmentalist terms of fairness. The 2008 talks presented a moment in the negotiation process when the likelihood of an agreement was high, not least because of the US willingness to cap its trade-distorting agricultural subsidies at $14.5 billion. India firmly rejected this offer, and was especially vehement in its refusal to accept the compromise negotiated by Director-General Pascal Lamy on the Special Safeguard Mechanism in agricultural trade, which would protect developing country markets from import surges. In cooperation with China and its G33 allies, India demanded a lower 'trigger' mechanism (lower than the proposed 40% import surge over a three-year average), and also a higher level of percentage points by which countries using the Special Safeguard Mechanism could raise protectionist barriers. Attempts by its G20 ally, Brazil, to persuade India to compromise on these issues were rejected, and India's chief negotiator earned the dubious distinction of being branded 'Dr No' in the negotiation process (Beattie 2008). Since

July 2008, talks have rumbled along, but a conclusion of the deal was nowhere in sight at the time of writing this chapter (Summer 2011).[15]

The important lesson that emerges from these recent experiences is that the use of a strict distributive strategy, when accompanied by strong coalitions and smart framing devices, can gain developing countries a critical role in the process. This is no small achievement. But to use this position effectively to achieve outcomes, a strict distributive strategy must be accompanied by some integrative moves in the second stage. Resistance through strong coalitions is crucial in establishing the credibility of the leadership of a country/group of countries. But effective leadership—defined as success in achieving outcomes favourable for one's self and one's coalition—requires a willingness to make at least some compromise after having proved one's credibility as a powerful force. The pathway to real power—the power that goes beyond the power to block and actually facilitates outcomes that go in one's favour—lies in being able to use both these strategies with equal skill.

It is also worth recalling the schizophrenia in India's foreign policy. In the light of India's WTO encounters, its continued proclivity to 'just say no' becomes clearer. India has come to develop the potential of reformed bloc-type coalitions in the WTO after years of learning and adaptation within the institution. In contrast, the limitations of the Non-Proliferation Treaty have driven home a difference lesson to India, where the solution lies in bypassing the regime and developing parallel initiatives at a bilateral level. Admittedly, this is a tough balancing act to keep up for the diplomat. But for analytical purposes, the important point to note here is that India's instrumentality has been very institution- and regime-specific. Rather than act consistently as a status quo or a revisionist power, a challenger of the system or a conformer, India acts differently across regimes (Narlikar and Hurrell, work in progress).

Conclusion

This case study of India's rise in the WTO offers us three sets of conclusions. First, we find that India's rise is a product of negotiating behaviour learnt by engaging with the institution. Economic size provides a necessary but insufficient condition; other traditional explanations for India's rise in the WTO, including the role of domestic interests and ideational change, were found to be limited.

Second, pathways to power tend to be regime-specific; in fact, our case has emphasized the importance of behaviours that India has learnt by operating within the very specific institutional context of the WTO. As such, there is no reason to assume that its coalitions, negotiation strategies, and framing tactics in the WTO would translate automatically into other issue areas; indeed, it is unsurprising that India's foreign policy is schizophrenic given that pathways to power vary across institutions. Placed in this light, a general categorization of rising powers into BRICs and other such groupings becomes less meaningful; a more useful understanding would be provided by an examination of rising powers in different regimes and institutions.

Third, this chapter has analysed the process whereby India has managed to acquire its current influence in the WTO. However, we have also seen in this chapter that the power to say 'no' does not necessarily transform into the power to achieve one's preferred outcomes. India now finds itself in a position where it has credibly established itself as a major player in the WTO; even the most powerful members of the organization recognize that without India on board, no agreement will be possible. However, it has yet to use this power to more positive ends whereby it might achieve outcomes that go in its favour. By proposing a sequence of negotiation strategies, this chapter has suggested a way out of this dilemma.

 Key points

- India's emergence as a major player in the WTO is reflected in its participation in the negotiation processes of the organization, its use of the dispute settlement mechanism, and above all its proven ability to block the negotiations.

- Theories of domestic interest groups and ideational change do not explain India's rise in the WTO. Economic size provides a necessary and minimal condition for acquiring veto-player status, but not a sufficient one.

- India's effective use of the negotiation process, learnt after decades of participation within the GATT and the WTO, provides the central explanation for India's influence in this multilateral forum.

- 'Negotiation process' has been operationalized in this chapter using three variables: bargaining coalitions, negotiation strategies, and framing.

- This learning is institution-specific, which also explains the apparent schizophrenia in Indian foreign policy when we compare the issue areas of multilateral trade and nuclear policy.

- Answers to the question of which kinds of coalitions, strategies, and framing mechanisms have facilitated India's rise, and thereby which processes other rising powers might adopt, can be generalized as follows.

  - Hybrid coalitions, which combine features of bloc-type and issue-based coalitions, show greater stability and effectiveness.

  - A strict distributive strategy can improve the credibility of the coalition if and only if the coalition does not collapse in the endgame.

  - Framing the issue to fit the culture of the organization (e.g. fairness conceptualized as legitimacy of process as well as outcomes) can assist the state in legitimizing its demands.

- The power to block does not automatically translate into the power to achieve one's preferred outcomes. In fact, some of the strategies used to achieve veto-player status, such as a strict distributive strategy in the first phase of the negotiation, can result in deadlock and thereby pareto-inferior outcomes. To achieve an agreement in one's favour, the veto-player must learn to use an integrative strategy in the second stage of the negotiation.

 Questions

1. In what ways can India be described as a 'rising power'?

2. India's rise has been described as 'schizophrenic'. Discuss the contradictions in India's foreign policy. What explains these contradictions?

3. Trace and explain India's emergence as a major player in the WTO.

4. Does the influence of domestic pressures explain India's negotiation strategy in the WTO? What alternative or complementary explanations do you find useful?

5. To what extent is India's rise within the WTO a function of the specific features of the institution?

6. What is India's negotiation strategy in the WTO? Evaluate its successes and failures.

7. Trace the process whereby India has negotiated its rise in the WTO. What are its limitations?

8. Trace India's coalition patterns in the WTO. How far has participation in such coalitions been an effective bargaining tool in India's trade negotiations?

Further reading

Narlikar, A. (2005), *The World Trade Organization: A Very Short Introduction* (Oxford: Oxford University Press).
This book provides a short and accessible account of the WTO.

Hoekman, B. and Kostecki, M. (2001), *The Political Economy of the World Trading System: The WTO and Beyond* (Oxford: Oxford University Press).
This book provides an excellent in-depth analysis of the WTO agreements.

Gallagher, P., Low, P., and Stoler, A. (eds) (2005), *Managing the Challenges of WTO Participation: 45 Case Studies* (Cambridge: Cambridge University Press).
This collection provides some useful comparative insights into WTO participation by developing countries across issue areas.

 Web links

www.wto.org The WTO website provides easy access to the workings of the organization as well as updates on recent negotiations.

www.twn.sg The Third World Network is an NGO which presents news coverage and analysis of trade and development issues from a critical perspective.

 Visit the Online Resource Centre that accompanies this book for more information:
www.oxfordtextbooks.co.uk/orc/smith_foreign/

Rising Brazil and South America

ARLENE B. TICKNER

Chapter contents

 Reader's guide

This case study analyses the role of South America in Brazil's strategy to establish itself as a global player. The chapter begins with a general discussion of Brazilian foreign policy in order to situate the country's current bid for power within wider historical patterns of interaction with the world. Next, it evaluates the impact of more recent changes in global and domestic politics, including the end of the Cold War, globalization, the transition to democracy, and economic opening, upon Brazil's international relations and shows how they led to greater diplomatic assertiveness. The chapter goes on to trace the importance of South America for boosting Brazil's credentials as a middle power, considered crucial for recognition internationally, and for promoting national development, a long-standing feature of its foreign policy. Notwithstanding growing influence in South America and the strengthening of a subregional economic, political, and security bloc, the Brazilian case illustrates some of the dilemmas faced by emerging powers. First, greater subregional assertiveness has inflated expectations concerning Brazil's provision of goods to its South American neighbours. Second, despite Brazil's undisputed power, most of its partners in the subregion have been reluctant to acknowledge the country as leader.[1]

Introduction

Much ink has been spilled over what is no less than an 'extraordinary' transformation. Since the mid-2000s Brazil has accrued an impressive array of statistics and achievements that has won it increasing recognition as a global player. The fifth largest country and population in the world, the world's eighth largest economy, membership of BRIC (an acronym coined in

2001 by Goldman Sachs' chief economist, and expanded in late 2010 to add an 'S' for South Africa), the number one producer of sugarcane, coffee, beef, chicken, orange juice, and ethanol (and number two in soy), high economic growth rates and financial stability, one of the world's largest recipients of foreign investment, self-sufficient in energy, a leader in renewable/clean energy and in deep sea oil exploration, the Earth's greatest source of biodiversity and water supplies, a burgeoning middle class, and decreasing levels of poverty and inequality. Could the list of successes be any longer? How did a country typically known for its soccer stars, beaches, carnivals, samba, and *favelas* manage to be chosen seemingly overnight to host the UN Sustainable Development Summit in 2012, the Soccer World Cup in 2014, and the summer Olympic Games in 2016?

Luiz Inácio Lula de Silva (2003–2011), appropriately called 'the man' by US President Barack Obama during the April 2009 G20 summit in London, had something to do with it, as of course did his predecessor, Fernando Henrique Cardoso (1995–2003). While FHC (as he is referred to in Brazil) is largely credited with slaying hyperinflation and consolidating democracy, thus laying the foundations for the Brazilian boom, Lula, the charismatic ex-union leader, gave new meaning to the term 'presidential' diplomacy, rubbing elbows with both the leaders of the developed world in Davos, Switzerland, and representatives of the global South at the World Social Forum.

And yet, in a country with a long-standing diplomatic tradition, it would be a mistake to overestimate any president's agency in this process. A more institutionalist reading would suggest that Brazil's 'emergence' is simply the result of a century-long effort to gain international recognition, rooted in a sense of natural 'entitlement', given the country's size and continental nature.[2] According to this view, the strategy for achieving a larger global role also comes as little surprise, given that the main features of Brazilian foreign policy—including an active embrace of international institutions and norms, the peaceful resolution of conflicts, development, defence of sovereignty and non-intervention, the search for autonomy, alignment with both the developed and developing world, and gaining a seat in the UN Security Council as a permanent member—have remained unaltered for decades.

What is new, perhaps, is Brazil's relatively recent shift towards its own neighbours, and growing acknowledgment that international recognition largely hinges on greater regional power. Starting in the mid-1980s the country took steps to become closer to its historical rival, Argentina, when both underwent democratization. However, more extensive engagement with Latin America outside of Mercosur remained limited until the late 1990s. Since approximately 2000, Brazil has stepped in to mediate distinct political crises in South America and to lead the construction of a subregional order.

How and why South America became a key target of Brazilian foreign policy during the last decade is the central storyline of this chapter. Although a growing role in multilateral institutions and South–South relations constitute two other recent ingredients of Brazil's recipe for global ascent, the chapter will argue that achieving greater visibility and power in South America has been a key component of this strategy. As subregional interdependence has grown, trade relations have increased, and US influence has waned, the countries of South America have gradually assumed responsibility for enforcing governance, maintaining order and stability, and providing for security, albeit with important exceptions, such as Colombia's long-standing armed conflict. Although Brazil has aspired to spearhead such efforts, it has often underestimated the reluctance of some South American partners to acknowledge its

CHAPTER 19 RISING BRAZIL AND SOUTH AMERICA

369

leadership, as well as brushing off accusations of Brazilian 'imperialism'. Brazil has also had to contend with lingering US influence, especially in countries such as Colombia, and the preference of others for Venezuelan President Hugo Chávez's Bolivarian brand of revolutionary leadership. In part, Brazil's bid for global power hinges on its ability to secure South American recognition and to provide the economic and political goods need to bolster its foreign policy aspirations. On both counts, as the chapter will illustrate, success has been less than complete.

The chapter begins with a brief discussion of the main objectives and diplomatic style that have characterized Brazilian foreign policy throughout its independent history. Given the existence of historical trends in Brazil's international relations, the country's search for power in the region and the world cannot be fully understood in isolation from the ideas that have guided its foreign policy in the past. It then explores 'three pillars' (Soares de Lima and Hirst 2006) of more recent foreign policy efforts which began with President Fernando Henríque Cardoso and continued throughout Lula's two administrations. Next the chapter examines the role of South America in Brazilian foreign policy. To this end, it traces Brazil's rapprochement with Argentina, the establishment of the Common Market of the South (Mercosur) and the creation of South-American-wide initiatives such as the Union of South American Nations (Unasur). Subsequently, the question of whether or not Brazilian power and influence in the subregion has translated into leadership is addressed. The chapter concludes with a discussion of the potential obstacles to Brazil's current rise, including a brief discussion of current president Dilma Rousseff's (2011–2014) foreign policy.

Brazilian diplomacy: methods and mechanisms

Few would dispute that the Brazilian Ministry of Foreign Relations, Itamaraty, harbours one of the most effective and professional diplomatic corps in the world. The fact that Itamaraty has been largely in charge of steering Brazil's international course, and that it has enjoyed extremely high degrees of domestic legitimacy, makes the Brazilian case somewhat unusual compared with other countries. As a result, foreign policy exhibits a series of principles, objectives, and traditions that have remained largely unaltered throughout time and across governments of dramatically different ideological orientations.

Following independence, sovereignty and non-intervention became twin cornerstones of Brazil's stance towards the world. Although both principles have been a constant in the developing or post-colonial world, and for good reason, simple geography may explain Brazil's heightened sensitivity to them. Like the USA, its independent life began as that of a continental power. However, unlike its northern counterpart, the fact that the Brazilian state shared territorial borders with ten other South American countries (the entire subregion with the exception of Ecuador and Chile) made it acutely aware of the question of territoriality. European and then US interventionism in the hemisphere, which was palpable throughout the nineteenth and early twentieth century, only reinforced this feeling.

A second foreign policy principle, possibly an offshoot of Brazil's 'encirclement', is pacifism. For many, the image of the Baron of Río Branco, Minister of Foreign Relations between 1902 and 1912 has come to symbolize the country's insistence on the peaceful resolution of conflict

(Souza Costa Barros 1983). Contrary to the case of many other Latin American nations, where state consolidation processes coincided with prolonged and violent conflict, Río Branco is credited with successfully consolidating Brazil's national borders without spilling a drop of blood. The tendency to seek out negotiated settlements to conflicts and to eschew the use of force has been a constant of Brazilian foreign policy since the early twentieth century, suggesting that in many ways Brazil was practising 'soft' power long before the concept existed in the specialized literature on International Relations.

Respect for international law and the defence of multilateralism are a third mainstay of Brazilian diplomacy. Nonetheless, given the pre-eminence of sovereignty and non-intervention, the relationship has at times been uneasy. On the one hand, multilateral fora and appeals to the international rules of the game have provided sorely needed protection from great power influence. On the other, strict adherence to the principle of non-intervention has led Brazil to oppose international norms considered to reduce national sovereignty, or to critique their non-universal application, as occurred in the case of nuclear non-proliferation.

As in the case of other Latin American countries, during the early twentieth century the major objective of foreign policy was to consolidate, preserve, and defend Brazil's territorial integrity. However, beginning in the post-war period, development became a key objective, if not *the* objective, of consecutive Brazilian governments. In many ways, foreign policy became a direct offshoot of state development policy, shifting in response to changes in this realm. Between the 1950s and 1990s, this meant adopting international positions that reflected the thinking of the Economic Commission for Latin America (ECLA), and that favoured import substitution industrialization (ISI), active state intervention, protection of local industry, and strongly controlled exchange and foreign investment controls (see Box 19.1). As will be discussed subsequently, in the 1990s foreign policy underwent another noticeable transformation, largely in response to changes in the national development model.

In tandem with development, political autonomy became the other main objective of foreign policy. Under the centre-leftist leadership of Jânio Quadros (1961) and João Goulart (1961–1964), who was subsequently overthrown by a military coup, Brazil debuted its 'independent foreign policy'. Strong identification with the USA and the Western powers, prevalent until the end of the Second World War, was replaced by the search for independence from Washington and overtures towards the so-called 'Third World' (see Box 19.2).

The principles and objectives highlighted here have been inscribed within several competing foreign policy traditions also discernible since at least the end of the Second World War (Lafer 2002; Pinheiro 2004). First, Brazil's international relations have moved between pragmatic association with the USA as the quickest path to securing economic and political benefits, and diversification as the key to increased negotiating power and autonomy (Pinheiro 2004: 63). Although both closeness to the developed world and alignment with the developing countries, albeit to differing degrees, has been a permanent feature of Brazilian foreign policy (described in Chapter Eighteen as schizophrenic diplomacy), in combination the two traditions reflect the long-held belief that Brazil can act as a bridge between North and South (Soares de Lima 2008).

Second, a realist-based discourse about world politics, that is state-centric and power-based, and how best to insert Brazil into an anarchic and hostile international system and thus defend its national interest, has coexisted with 'Grotian' beliefs about the importance of norms and rules for promoting cooperation and forming an international society. The influence of

BOX 19.1 ECLA and dependency school thinking

The Economic Commission for Latin America (ECLA), created in 1948 (the Caribbean was added to its name in 1984), set out to explain underdevelopment in the region, and to design the domestic and foreign policy solutions needed to overcome it. ECLA-school thinking attempted to show that global factors, namely the international division of labour and the role occupied by the Latin American economies as primary goods exporters, produced asymmetrical relations between the large core countries and the nations of the periphery. Therefore it pointed to the need to implement inward-looking development strategies via ISI and to strengthen regional integration mechanisms in order to overcome existing sources of disadvantage in the world economy. The Commission also favoured active state intervention in the redirection of Latin America's productive process. According to this view, a strong national state capable of integrating distinct social groups and of keeping intrusive foreign actors at bay was indispensable to development.

ECLA established a roadmap for domestic economic, political, and social reform and for Latin American foreign policy during the 1950s and 1960s. The nationalist–developmentalist discourse that it espoused was most clearly visible in early developers such as Brazil, which became a 'model' for other countries in the region seeking to promote development and to enhance their autonomy *vis-à-vis* external actors, especially the USA.

Although they were influenced by ECLA in many ways, the diverse authors grouped under the dependency school label, many of them Brazilian in origin, were more assertive in arguing for the need for radical social change in Latin America. Dependency writers sought to explain economic underdevelopment at the periphery as the product of the specific nature of global capitalism, as well as examining the ways in which external dependency had moulded internal processes in ways that reinforced inequality and exclusion.

Fernando Henrique Cardoso[3] and Enzo Faletto spearheaded such efforts in their classic text, *Dependency and Development in Latin America* (1969). According to Cardoso, who went on to be elected President of Brazil in 1995, this work was less about dependency *per se*, and more about 'the variability of the forms of integration to the world market and on the existing alternatives for . . . economic growth, even when in situations of dependency' (Cardoso 2008: 381).

BOX 19.2 Autonomy

A key concern expressed within Latin America following the onset of the Cold War was related to the problem of autonomy. Between the 1950s and 1960s both the ECLA and dependency schools (see Box 19.1) shed light on how the global division of labour and the domestic manifestations of capitalism worked against the development potential of the state. Thus one of the main goals of regional foreign policy was to identify potential sources of economic and political autonomy, and to design effective strategies for achieving its full potential. Autonomy was considered an instrumental tool for practising Latin American international relations, given its role in safeguarding the region against the most noxious effects of the global system.

According to Brazilian Helio Jaguaribe (1979: 96–7), autonomy is a function of structural conditions that the author describes as 'national viability' and 'international permissibility', consisting of adequate human and material resources, the capacity for international exchange, local sociocultural cohesion, and the power to neutralize external threats. Technical–entrepreneurial autonomy and favourable relations with the core are also identified as prerequisites for autonomous action. Dependence had constrained the first goal by inscribing the Latin American countries into an unfavourable global division of labour. The latter entailed political strategies cognizant of established boundaries and rules of the game in Latin America's relations with the USA in exchange for US acquiescence in matters related to local development.

realism is visible not only in concern with Brazil's regional hegemony and the prevalence of balance-of-power perspectives in its relations with Argentina and Chile, but also in patterns of alignment with the USA, rationalized by Brazilian diplomats as a pragmatic and efficient way of defending the key national interest—development—given existing constraints and power differentials in the international system.

Charting a middle course between the competing and even opposing tendencies that characterize Brazil's diplomatic tradition has been Itamaraty's main challenge. Tellingly, the two most deeply rooted objectives of foreign policy, economic development and political autonomy, have underwritten both isolationist and insertion-based strategies, depending on the prevalent domestic development model and the political regime in place. In addition, although both have been present throughout the history of Brazilian foreign policy, different governments have assigned them varied causal weight—in other words, at times autonomy has been seen as the key for development, while on occasion greater development has been viewed to allow for more autonomy—leading to very different foreign policy orientations. In the case of relations with the USA, a similar tension is apparent and translates into relatively high levels of suspicion towards that country and its interventionist impulses, on the one hand, and consistent attempts to preserve fluid relations with Washington, on the other (Vigevani and Cepaluni 2007).

A final puzzle relates to the fact that Brazil has rarely had qualms about pursuing relations with governments considered 'unsavoury' by the rest of the world, or at least the developed West—the recent case of Iran and that of the South African apartheid regime in the 1980s come to mind—as long as 'strategic' national interests are at stake. In treating countries that are 'friends' and 'enemies', 'developed' and 'developing', and 'democratic' and 'non-democratic' equally, Brazil has also positioned itself as a 'neutral' or 'non-partisan' country capable of mediating myriad issues in the international arena.

Three keys to Brazil's rise

The continuities described in the previous section provide important background for coming to grips with the peculiarities of Brazilian foreign policy. Nonetheless, the proximate setting for the story of Brazil's rise was a combination of domestic and international factors, namely the transition to democracy, stagnation of the ISI development model (in place since the 1930s), domestic economic re-engineering, the end of the Cold War, and the intensification of globalization. Although twenty years of authoritarian rule in Brazil did not ostensibly modify the underlying principles, objectives, and traditions of the country's foreign policy, successive military governments were in practice defensive and isolationist, and sought to achieve 'autonomy through distance' (Soares de Lima and Hirst 2006; Vigevani and Cepaluni 2007), basically as a means of deflecting international criticism in many issue areas, including human rights and nuclear proliferation. In contrast, the post Cold War period and democratization set the stage for Brazilian acceptance and gradual embrace of core liberal values, rules, and norms, mainly related to democracy and neoliberal economics.[4]

Fernando Henrique Cardoso (FHC)is largely credited with setting the course for this change of strategy. During stints as Foreign Relations Minister (October 1992–May 1993) and Finance Minister (May 1993–April 1994), and two subsequent presidential administrations (1995–2003),

FHC argued that active insertion into the global economic and political order was a necessary precondition for democratic consolidation and for fighting Brazil's endemic high levels of inequality, both considered indispensable for national development. The change advocated during this period was largely a response to the rapidly changing global environment and the exhaustion of the domestic development model. At the same time, however, the basic tenets of Brazilian foreign policy were preserved.

'Autonomy through participation' (Vigevani and Cepaluni 2007; Hurrell 2008) was the foreign policy doctrine embraced by FHC, premised on the 'Grotian' idea that long-standing national interests such as development and autonomy could be achieved in a globalized and non-bipolar world by adjusting the domestic economic and political model to 'universal' (meaning Western) standards, diversifying external relations, and increasing Brazil's role in multilateral fora on a wide range of issues, including development, security, the environment, and democracy. While foreign policy during much of the Cold War had been characterized by a 'special relationship' with the USA, the post Cold War era gave way to accommodation and then outright assertiveness. The latter was boosted by the terrorist attacks of 11 September 2001 and the US-declared 'global war on terrorism', which created greater distance and higher levels of discrepancy between the two countries, especially in the security realm.

The role of South America

South America became an important prong of this strategy for several reasons (Rivarola 2008; Burges 2010; Sorj and Fausto 2011). First, the transition to democracy coincided with efforts to overcome historical tensions with Argentina (see next section), which also democratized in the mid-1980s. The underlying rationale for rapprochement was that bilateral economic integration and military cooperation would not only increase mutual reliance, thus eliminating past sources of tension, but also buttress the democratization process at home. Second, the subregion was largely viewed as a testing ground for Brazil's global insertion. As a result, efforts to promote trade liberalization with Argentina, and later, within the Common Market of the South (Mercosur), were considered fundamental to preparing the Brazilian productive sector, accustomed to high levels of state protection, for global competition. Third, as Brazil's global power aspirations grew, the consolidation of a South American bloc and of Brazilian influence became seen as a crucial step towards international recognition. Fourth, as US attempts to create a Free Trade Area of the Americas (FTAA) intensified in 1994, Brazil increasingly saw South America as an important corrective to increased US influence in the hemisphere.

Multilateralism

Although multilateralism has been a long-standing feature of Brazilian foreign policy, as mentioned previously, active participation in multilateral institutions became a second prong in the country's path towards global insertion and influence. In many ways, the UN Conference on the Environment and Development, held in Rio de Janeiro in 1992, constituted a turning point in the country's relations with the world and its embrace of international rules of the game (Rivarola 2008: 36). Previously, Brazilian governments had viewed multilateral negotiations on the environment with suspicion, fearing that the developed countries would use them to intervene in the Amazon, historically a constitutive part of Brazilian national identity and its sense of sovereignty, security, and territorial integrity. However, at the Earth Summit the link between development and environmental protection was introduced and exploited by Brazilian diplomats, setting the stage for future interventions on issues related to climate change, where the country has taken the lead in global negotiations.

Following a twenty-year absence during military rule, Brazil resumed and intensified its participation as a non-permanent member of the UN Security Council, taking on this role five times since the end of the Cold War (1989–1990, 1993–1994, 1998–1999, 2003–2004, and 2010–2011). In addition, the country has increased its involvement in UN peacekeeping missions, becoming active in over twenty since 1985. Gaining a permanent seat in the UN Security Council has become something of a Brazilian obsession since the mid-1990s (see Box 19.3). Indeed, participation in the UN Stabilization Mission in Haiti (Minustah) in 2004 became the cornerstone of the country's efforts to accredit its membership worthiness (see Box 19.4).

Although the Cardoso administration made important strides towards fulfilling Brazilian dreams of world status—a permanent feature of Brazilian self-imageries since the early twentieth century—Luiz Inácio Lula da Silva made the pursuit of global power the explicit goal of foreign policy (Herz 2011). One of the major dilemmas faced by the first Lula government (2003–2007) was how to reconcile the leftist discourse that got him elected with the domestic and international policies inherited from Cardoso, the continuation of which was considered crucial to keep the country on its path. One solution was to grant higher visibility to the 'Third World-ism' which had been prevalent in most periods of Brazilian foreign policy, but had occupied a lesser role during the Cardoso years. In doing so, a third prong was added to Brazil's strategy—South–South cooperation—through which alliances with like-minded countries were strengthened and social achievements at home, especially the reduction of poverty and inequality, could be showcased more forcefully in diverse multilateral scenarios. Thus Lula exploited the link between domestic policy and North–South relations more forcefully than his predecessor had done (Soares de Lima and Hirst 2006: 35–36).

BOX 19.3 United Nations Security Council

In an article published in *Foreign Policy* in March 2011, suitably entitled 'Let Us In', former Minister of Foreign Relations, Celso Amorím, sets forth Brazil's case for permanent membership of the UN Security Council (UNSC). The Brazilian government, along with other like-minded countries, including India, Japan, and Germany (the so-called G4), has long argued that the UNSC no longer reflects the global distribution of power. According to this view, the fact that the UNSC is not a representative organ also reduces the legitimacy of its decisions. According to Amorím, Brazil's admission promises to enhance the UNSC's effectiveness and credibility by incorporating the insights of emerging powers on myriad global problems and reducing the resistance of some countries to its 'power politics' strategies. In this vein, Brazil's geographical influence, which spans several continents, its leadership on issues such as climate change and the financial crisis, and its widespread recognition as a global interlocutor willing and able to speak to all parties to global conflicts constitute significant credentials for membership.

Amorín begins and ends the Brazilian case by noting that if US President Barack Obama supported India's bid for UNSC membership in November 2010, it would only be fair to support Brazil's as well, especially given the country's decision to not go nuclear. Lest the world misinterpret this gesture, what the Brazilian chancellor is suggesting is that the USA should reward such a decision instead of punishing it.

South–South cooperation

In keeping with Brazil's enduring goal of preserving an international climate favourable to domestic development, the country has been an active participant in multilateral trade negotiations conducted within the framework of GATT, and originally favoured the creation of the World Trade Organization (WTO) as a means of creating more effective rules to protect its weaker members. Indeed, in round after round of talks it became a self-appointed leader of the developing world, claiming the need for a trade regime sensitive to the vulnerabilities of the global South. As early as the Uruguay Round, begun in 1995, Brazil and India led those countries opposing tariff and non-tariff barriers to trade. However, in June 2003, with the creation of the India, Brazil, South Africa Dialogue Forum (IBSA) in Brasilia, efforts were made to consolidate this position, shared by India in particular, as intermediaries between the North and South. Although the three countries have sought to increase cooperation among themselves and with other nations from the South, from a Brazilian perspective the use of IBSA, and of the G20 as a global platform, has been one of its major attractions.

In this regard, IBSA's voice has been increasingly audible at the WTO negotiations and in discussions related to the 2008 global financial crisis. At the September 2003 conference in Cancun, the heads of government from the three countries played an active role in demanding that the countries of the North change their agricultural subsidies regimes. In general, IBSA has led developing countries, grouped together in the G20 (which Brazil was also active in creating), in pushing forward the South's agenda in multilateral trade talks.[5] Reform of the International Monetary Fund and the World Bank, mostly to reflect the growing importance of developing countries, has also been on IBSA's global agenda, as has democratization of UN decision-making mechanisms, especially in relation to the Security Council. Similarly, the UN Campaign against Hunger and Poverty, advanced by IBSA and the G20, can be read as an attempt to place the development agenda on the global trade table.

The role of South–South cooperation in Brazil's recent rise has also been visible in the country's interaction with Africa. Between 2000 and 2010 the number of Brazilian embassies on the continent doubled to 34, while during his two presidential periods Lula made 11 official visits to 25 different African countries.[6] In addition to promoting trade and investment, the Lula administration made use of expanded cooperation with the continent to showcase its own achievements in areas such as health, education, and agriculture. In fact, Africa has become the prime recipient of Brazilian cooperation assistance (Hirst *et al.* 2010: 33).

Why South America?

Brazil–Argentina: from rivalry to rapprochement

As mentioned previously, a key turning point in Brazilian recognition of South America's importance came after the transition to democracy and the adoption of a market-friendly development model. Integration between Brazil and Argentina, a first step in closing the gap with the rest of South America, was not only crucial for securing the economic liberalization and democratization processes under way in both countries, but also facilitated cooperation following a previous history of tense bilateral relations.

Power rivalry between Brazil and Argentina has deep historical roots including two wars in the nineteenth century and constant arms races, tension, and mistrust during the twentieth century. Following independence and the resolution of territorial disputes, Brazil viewed Argentina as a threat to its security mainly because of the country's search for hegemony in the Southern Cone. After the First and Second World Wars, in which Brazil actively supported the Allied powers and Argentina remained neutral, the two parted ways further as Brazilian foreign policy shifted towards a stronger alliance with the USA and Argentina opposed US interventionism in the region. Furthermore, Argentine efforts to sign trade, investment, and cultural agreements with neighbouring countries throughout the 1940s and 1950s were interpreted as an attempt to strengthen a Spanish-speaking block and thus isolate Brazil (Hilton 1985: 41).

After military coups removed civilian governments from power in Brazil in 1964, and Argentina in 1966 and 1976, national prestige and autonomy became closely tied to nuclear technology, which was viewed as the key to both regional influence and global recognition (Redick et al. 1994; Klepack and Neill 2000). Nuclear enmity, which had begun in the 1950s, reached a peak in the 1970s and 1980s. However, by 1985, when both countries had made the transition back to democracy, raging inflation, economic crisis, considerable foreign debt, and the need to exercise civilian control over the military—an immediate precondition for democratic consolidation—led the post-transition governments of José Sarney (1985–1990) and Raúl Alfonsín (1983–1989) to sign a first agreement—the Joint Declaration on Nuclear Policy of Foz de Iguaçu—to put an end to the nuclear race by increasing transparency and mutual inspection mechanisms.[7] A second Foz de Iguaçu agreement, signed in 1990 by President Fernando Collor de Mello (1990–1992) and President Carlos Menem (1989–1999) went on to ban the use of nuclear technology for military purposes, thus sealing a mutual commitment to its peaceful use.[8] In the years that followed, the two countries created the Brazilian–Argentina Agency for Accounting and Control of Nuclear Material (ABACC) and ratified both the 1967 Treaty of Tlatelolco, which provides for a nuclear-weapons-free zone in Latin America, and the 1968 nuclear Non-Proliferation Treaty (NPT).[9]

In tandem with bilateral agreements in the security realm, Brazil and Argentina agreed upon an ambitious agenda for economic and political cooperation, beginning with the 1986 Act for Argentine–Brazilian Integration and the 1988 Treaty on Integration, Cooperation and Development, both of which established concrete mechanisms for economic coordination and cooperation.[10] The comprehensive nature of these agreements, as well as their rapid timetables for implementation, pointed to the interest of both governments to lock them in place before domestic opponents, most significantly the military, could undo them.

From its inception, bilateral integration was viewed as the necessary starting point for a wider subregional process. Indeed, in 1991, only a few years after the Brazilian–Argentine accords were signed, the Common Market of the South (Mercosur) was created with the primary goal of eliminating trade barriers between the member countries (Argentina, Brazil, Paraguay, and Uruguay) and creating a common market by 1994. From a Brazilian perspective, Mercosur had many advantages (Pinheiro 2004: 63; Vigevani and Cepaluni 2009: 105). It facilitated a gradual process of economic opening and international insertion within a subregional bloc in which the Brazilian economy was dominant and relatively protected, thus constituting an effective instrument for addressing both the challenges of globalization and for promoting the country's influence in the region. Given Mercosur's basis in the concept of 'open regionalism', Brazil was also able to pursue a flexible route to trade liberalization and integration, characterized by minimal institutionalization and the preservation of protectionist measures that it allowed it to maintain and cultivate existing power differentials *vis-à-vis* other member countries.[11]

By 1998, Mercosur had signed a framework agreement with the other existing South American subregional bloc, the Andean Community of Nations (CAN), for the creation of a free-trade agreement between the two, and members of the CAN slowly became associate members of Mercosur. Although largely a statement of intent, which failed to materialize until 2004, and then only between some of the members, the move signalled the gradual emergence of South America as a discrete subregional unit.

As democratization, regional integration, and security cooperation between the members of Mercosur matured, and attempts to merge with the Andean countries progressed, the next 'logical' step in Brazilian foreign policy was to foster closer ties with South America as a whole. The fact that trade relations among Mercosur members took a temporary nosedive following the 1999–2001 financial crisis, which hit Brazil first and then Argentina even harder, added urgency to this process, as did the formal launching of the Free Trade Area of the Americas (FTAA) negotiations in 1998 at the Second Summit of the Americas meeting in Santiago, Chile. As mentioned earlier, the Brazilian government feared growing US dominance in the region, as it perceived had occurred with Mexico after the North American Free Trade Agreement (NAFTA) had come into effect in 1993. Therefore, although FHC participated in the FTAA negotiations, Itamaraty simultaneously attempted to mobilize the rest of South America around Brazilian interests, primarily the freedom to pursue development policies unfettered by a trade model similar to NAFTA (Sorj and Fausto 2011: 5). In this vein too, creating a distinctive South American process was viewed as an antidote to increased US influence if and when the FTAA became a reality.[12]

In light of the above, the Cardoso government actively cultivated the 'South American idea' in both domestic politics and foreign policy. In 2000, FHC hosted the first summit of South American presidents in Brasilia, confirming Brazil's vision of a 'division of power' in the Western hemisphere in which the US sphere of influence stopped at Central America and the Caribbean, and Mercosur's (and Brazil's) began in South America. The main by-product of this meeting was the Initiative for the Integration of Regional Infrastructure (IIRSA), which sought to go beyond simple trade relations by introducing a more strategic notion of subregional interaction, based upon the integration of the subregion's physical infrastructure. The aim of this project, in which Brazil has been the main protagonist, has been to build an extensive transportation, communications, and energy network across the subcontinent, thus linking together different parts of South America and promoting region-wide development. Thus the IIRSA satisfied the dual goal of enhancing Brazil's global insertion by fostering greater connectedness, and positioning the country as a subregional power.

In contrast with the Cardoso administration, for which South America was primarily a means to an end—upping the country's global competitiveness and consolidating its development model through increased regional trade—under Lula's leadership Brazilian foreign policy itself was 'South Americanized' (Gratius 2007: 14). In addition to pushing forward with his predecessor's subregional infrastructure and trade agenda, during the Lula government South America acquired important political overtones that were largely absent previously. The general shift towards centre-left and leftist governments in the subregion, and the ideological affinity between these and the Brazilian president, constituted one explanation for this trend.[13] Indeed, given the general 'presidentialist' quality of South American and Latin American relations, personal identification between political leaders was a key factor in shaping South American relations. Also, following the terrorist attacks of 11 September 2001 and the US declaration of a 'global war on terrorism,' the subregional security agenda, with the exception of countries such as Colombia, began to diverge significantly from that of the USA, and efforts to create greater 'breathing space' *vis-à-vis* Washington were stepped up.

In light of these changes, at the third summit of South American presidents, held in Cuzco in 2004, the South American Community of Nations (grouping together twelve countries, including Guyana and Suriname) was officially formed, and a statement of intent was signed whereby a subregional community was to be established along the lines of the EU, including a parliament and a shared currency and passport. In May 2008, its name was changed to Union of South American Nations (Unasur), a constitutive treaty was signed in Brasilia, and a permanent secretariat headquarters was stationed in Quito, Ecuador. Among Unasur's main objectives, strengthening political dialogue, securing regional cooperation and integration, and improving social indicators in the subregion stand out. Shortly after Unasur's creation, a political crisis in Bolivia posed the first challenge to its member states. In keeping with the organization's commitment to democracy, it successfully mediated an end to the violence which sought to remove President Evo Morales from power.

In parallel with efforts to strengthen South America as both a trading and a political bloc, beginning in 2007 the Brazilian government began to push for the creation of a security and defence arrangement (Moreira 2009). During Lula's second administration security and defence issues, which had been put on hold following the transition to democracy, acquired greater visibility. The salience of the Amazon as a potential source of global power and, in late 2007, the discovery of massive deep-sea oil reserves fed into this process, as did a growing domestic defence industry hungry for new export markets. The Brazilian president and his Minister of Defence, Nelson Jobim, launched the proposal to create a South American Defence Council (CSD) in February 2008, and efforts were made to sell the idea during the remainder of the year, both in the subregion and, tellingly, in Washington as well. The proposal was welcomed by the majority of countries (with the exception of Colombia, which finally came around), and in December 2008 the members of Unasur agreed to its creation. Among the Brazilian government's objectives in proposing the Council, the adoption of common positions on defence matters in international organizations—as had increasingly occurred with trade matters following the creation of Mercosur—the integration of South American defence industries, and the consolidation of a zone of peace were considered especially important for the pursuit of the country's goals internationally.

In the case of Unasur and the CSD, as in that of Mercosur, Brazil's strategy has followed a similar pattern of 'latent multi-institutionalization' (Flemes 2007). It consists of creating flexible alliances characterized by low levels of institutionalization, similar to the case of IBSA, whereby the country has been able to preserve significant degrees of autonomy and pursue the 'middle path' that has been Itamaraty's trademark for decades.

Power without leadership

Brazil's self-image *vis-à-vis* the world, as explained previously in this chapter, has revolved around being recognized as a 'big country' and assuming a global role consistent with its size and power. During the FHC and Lula administrations, in particular, Brazilian policy makers took important steps towards realizing this long-held goal. In myriad ways, gaining influence in South America has been at the core of this strategy. The subregion served as a testing ground for economic liberalization and political opening following the transition to democracy, safeguarding Brazil from the full-blown effects of a globalizing world. The consolidation of a South American 'idea' also underwrote a general plan to create a subregional trade, political, and security bloc 'led' by Brazil, and thus buttressing the country's global aspirations. In this sense, the capacity to demonstrate Brazil's ability to maintain order and stability, and to conduct South American affairs, was considered a crucial step towards acceptance as a global power. Indeed, since the mid-1990s, Brazil has weighed in on a number of subregional conflicts, beginning with the 1995 war between Peru and Ecuador, in which the country acted as a mediator.

The Lula government took steps towards even greater assertiveness, both regionally and internationally, while embracing more openly the concept of 'leadership'. Following the rupture of the WTO negotiations in Cancun in 2003, and Brazil's decision to lead the UN mission in Haiti, the country was increasingly hailed as an emerging leader. Indeed, by the early 2000s Brazil had accumulated uncontested power in South America, spearheading subregional integration, stepping up technical and financial cooperation, funding infrastructure projects, sharing intelligence gathering from its satellite monitoring system for the Amazon (Sivam), and becoming the greatest exporter of manufactured goods and source of foreign direct investment (Herz 2011). Importantly, Lula shifted from emphasis on trade, as highlighted by FHC, to building a political power base more suited to the country's global aspirations.

In keeping with this objective, efforts to intervene in distinct regional crises were also accelerated. In particular, the Brazilian government's decision to lead the peacekeeping operation in Haiti (Minustah) signalled a significant departure from the country's non-interventionist stance of the past, pointing to its willingness to become more involved in the maintenance of order and stability in its own hemisphere (see Box 19.4). In doing so, Lula promoted the idea of 'non-indifference' (Herz 2011) as an alternative to 'non-intervention', thus allowing the foreign policy establishment to reconcile the country's historic commitment to sovereignty and non-intervention with the need to 'prove' its readiness to assume the costs of leadership and to uphold 'universal' norms.

However, Brazil's political role in South America has been somewhat constrained. The country's activism in Haiti contrasts starkly with its lethargy towards its Colombian neighbour,

---

BOX 19.4 The Mission in Haiti

The UN Stabilization Mission in Haiti (Minustah)—the fifth in that country since the early 1990s—was created in June 2004, following an armed uprising that led to the departure of former president Bertrand Aristide from Haiti. Diplomatic and military coordination of the mission was split between several South American countries, most notably Brazil, Chile, and Argentina, highlighting a new phase in subregional coordination. In many ways, Haiti became a testing ground for South America's capacity to design solutions to regional problems independently of the USA. In the specific case of Brazil, leadership of Minustah has also served to reinforce the country's bid for a UN Security Council seat by showcasing its 'know-how' on matters related to humanitarian crises, its capacity to act as a 'peacekeeper', and its willingness to support multilaterally sanctioned actions (as opposed to the unilateralism and interventionism characteristic of the USA). Subsequent relief efforts following a devastating earthquake in January 2010 further confirmed the country's 'readiness' to assume the costs of global responsibility.

whose armed conflict is a prime candidate for subregional teamwork. South America's inaction in Colombia remains a major riddle that may be related to the strong US military presence there and to the Colombian government's strict alignment with Washington, at least until President Juan Manuel Santos took office in August 2010. Also, while it is true that during the Lula administrations the country became increasingly involved in subregional governance, it has been reluctant to shoulder the cost of integration and has exhibited low levels of commitment to the financial and institutional resources needed to support supranational efforts in South America (Sorj and Fausto 2011: 9).

The Brazilian case underscores the types of challenges, both material and ideational, faced by 'middle' or 'emerging' powers that aspire to power and leadership. Recognition at the global level often demands regional recognition first, especially in the case of countries such as Brazil that lack 'hard' power (Soares de Lima 2008). As this chapter has shown, Brazil's global insertion has been anchored largely in the construction of South America as a distinct geographical unit. While the subregion has generally embraced the South American 'idea', the majority of countries have been reluctant to support Brazil's bid for global protagonism.[14] Nor are they especially happy with what they largely perceive as Brazil's calculated use of South America as a springboard for global interests.

At the same time, moves to assert Brazilian power and leadership, especially during the Lula administration, have created expectations concerning the country's capacity and willingness to provide material resources such as investment, trade, and development assistance. Beyond Haiti, it is not clear whether the country is interested in committing significant resources to bolstering its leadership credentials, although this has changed somewhat in the past decade. Moreover, on key subregional issues, most visibly the Colombian armed conflict, the illicit drug traffic, and transnational organized crime, its capacity to become more involved has been limited.

Alongside the material sources of power, leadership is mostly the result of ideational factors such as recognition. Here, again, South American acceptance of Brazil's credentials ranges from tepid to cold, while suspicion of the country's hegemonic intentions is equally strong. Even though, as the chapter has illustrated, Brazil's particular model of diplomacy eschews 'raw' power and instead dictates that influence be sought out through 'consensus creation' (Burges 2008), what is perhaps most disconcerting from a South American perspective is the reluctance with which Brazilian policy makers have been willing to acknowledge their country's taste for power and influence! Tensions with neighbours such as Bolivia—which nationalized its natural gas industry in May 2006—and Paraguay—which has repeatedly accused Brazil of foul play in relation to their binational hydroelectric plant, Itaipú, one of the largest in the world—clouds this picture even further, as does lingering competition with Argentina.

In tandem with the lack of recognition, Brazil has had to contend with at least one other Latin American competitor for regional power and influence—the Venezuelan president Hugo Chávez. In coordination with Cuba, in 2004 Chávez launched the Bolivarian Alliance for the Americas (ALBA) on an aggressive anti-American anti-imperialist platform that has successfully attracted several like-minded partners.[15] Although the success of Chávez's diplomacy largely depends on the country's oil reserves, until now the Venezuelan leader has been much more willing (and capable, given the deterioration of democracy in that country) to dole out the resources needed to support his bid. On numerous occasions, President Lula walked a fine line between confronting Chávez, whose policies and proposals often strayed from his own, and coaxing him into the fold of the South American community. The March 2008 bombing of a FARC guerilla camp by Colombian armed forces in Ecuadorian territory constituted one such test, as did revelations in mid-2009 that the Colombian government of Álvaro Uribe (2002–2010) had negotiated an agreement with the USA whereby the US Southern Command would make use of five military bases in Colombia for counter-terrorism and counter-narcotics activities. Lula and Chávez were adamant in condemning both episodes, but at odds over the appropriate South American response to them.

Finally, although US power in the Western hemisphere is waning, predictions of complete decline seem far-fetched. Not only do countries such as Colombia and Peru maintain close bilateral ties with Washington, but also, on issues such as illicit drugs and organized crime, the USA continues to exert a tremendous degree of influence over regional policies. To a certain extent, strong and cordial bilateral relations between Brazil and the USA have acted to constrain Brasilia's potential subregional role, especially on matters related to security. While strong differences between the South American bloc and the USA came to light following 9/11, as in the case of Venezuela, and with few exceptions, Brazilian diplomats have been cautious of openly questioning Washington.

Conclusion

This chapter has evaluated the role of South America in Brazilian foreign policy and its recent bid for international recognition. Brazil has taken important steps towards accrediting its membership as a world player, and has made effective use of its diplomatic prowess, allowing it to exercise greater influence in the subregion and globally, especially in multilateral spaces, than its actual power would suggest. And yet, the country's strategic vision of its place in South America and the world is still rather foggy. On the one hand, Brazil has been unable to meet, or uninterested in meeting, some of the prerequisites of power, both material and social. These include the provision of economic and political goods to other South American countries, recognition of Brazilian leadership, and support of its aspirations beyond the subregion. On the other hand, it remains to be seen whether or not Brazil's particular brand of 'soft' power will be enough to consolidate its current strategy. Can Brazil rise *and* maintain strong and positive ties with the USA, and can it continue to reconcile its desire to be recognized as a 'big' country *and* to be a spokesperson for South America and the developing world writ large, constitute additional unanswered questions.

Although beyond the scope of this case study, the extent to which President Dilma Rousseff, who took office on 1 January 2011, will continue along the path set by her predecessors is unclear. As the chapter has argued, historically Brazilian foreign policy has adhered to a fixed set of objectives, most importantly economic development and political autonomy. Therefore it is to be expected that continuity will predominate over change.

As Brazil's international status expands, requests for 'goods' will only tend to grow. To the degree that active participation in global and regional security/stability problems is deemed necessary to defend Brazil's core foreign policy goals, it is to be expected that this strategy will be sustained. However, the announcement by the Rousseff government in early 2011 that Brazil is planning an exit strategy from Haiti could be read as a shift, albeit subtle, in the country's stance.

Finally, although hand-picked to succeed Lula, Rousseff's leadership style is dramatically different. Contrary to the Cardoso and Lula governments, during which foreign policy became heavily influenced by the Office of the President, Brazil's current chief of state lacks the political dexterity that both her predecessors made use of to engage personally with different leaders. While FHC gave greater attention to Europe and the USA in an effort to reduce the 'Third World-ism' characteristic of previous governments and earn Brazil a seat at the global negotiation table, Lula concentrated on the South, and reached out to regions, such as Africa, that had not been a priority in earlier periods (Gratius 2007). Lula used personal diplomacy to manage specific relations, especially those in South America (with like-minded leftist and centre-left governments), but also with countries such as Iran. How de-emphasis on presidential diplomacy might affect Brazil's subregional influence, especially given the emergence of other South American contenders—most notably Colombian president Juan Manuel Santos (2010–2014), who has employed tactics similar to those of Lula and FHC to carve out a larger role for that country—is worth considering.

 ## Key points

- The main features of Brazilian foreign policy, including diplomatic prowess, multilateralism, the acceptance of international norms, the peaceful resolution of conflict, development, and the defence of sovereignty and the non-intervention principle, have remained essentially unaltered over time.

- The search for autonomy has played a central role in Brazilian foreign policy, even in instances in which power itself has not been an explicit goal.

- Since the transition to democracy in the mid-1980s Brazil has actively pursued an enlarged role in regional and world politics and economic relations.

- Presidents Fernando Henríque Cardoso (FCH) and Luiz Inácio Lula da Silva (Lula) were largely responsible for creating an assertive foreign policy in South America, and for setting Brazil on its path towards regional power and global influence.

- The decision to take on the coordination of the UN peacekeeping mission in Haiti (Minustah) constituted a crucial step in Brazilian efforts to be recognized as an international player, to gain a permanent seat on the UN Security Council, and to consolidate the South American bloc.

- South–South cooperation, especially during the past eight years, has been another important component of Brazil's rise through, among others, the India, Brazil, South Africa Dialogue Forum.

- Brazil's South American strategy has largely entailed sponsoring subregional arrangements such as the Union of South American Nations and the South American Defence Council, characterized by low levels of institutionalization, which have allowed it to engage in other mutually reinforcing strategies at the international level.

- Although Brazil has increased its power and influence in South America, its neighbours have been reluctant to recognize the country as a subregional leader.

 ## Questions

1. What are the main historical pillars of Brazilian foreign policy?
2. How did the transition to democracy, the end of the Cold War, and the intensification of globalization change Brazil's foreign policy?

3. What factors explain South America's growing importance in Brazilian domestic and international politics?

4. Discuss the importance of the UN peacekeeping mission in Haiti (Minustah) for Brazilian foreign policy, both in South America and at the international level.

5. Brazil, along with its historical rival Argentina, forswore nuclear weapons as part of a rapprochement and bilateral integration process that was fundamental to the consolidation of a South American bloc. Do you think that Brazil reduced its chances of becoming a rising power in doing so (in contrast to India)?

6. What contradictions are observable in Brazil's South American strategy?

7. Do you think that being recognized as a leader is a necessary precondition for regional or global power?

8. To what extent has Brazil's strategy for achieving power at the international level been successful?

 ## Further reading

Burges, S.W. (2011), *Brazilian Foreign Policy After the Cold War* (Gainesville, FL: University Press of Florida.
Examines Brazil's peculiar style of regional leadership, described as 'consensual hegemony', based upon extensive interviews with Brazilian diplomats.

Council on Foreign Relations (2011), *Global Brazil and US–Brazil Relations*, Independent Task Force Report, No. 66 (Project Director, J.E. Sweig) (Washington, DC: Council on Foreign Relations).
Policy-relevant analysis of Brazil's shifting regional and global role and of its relations with the USA.

Roett, R. (2011), *The New Brazil* (Washington, DC: Brookings Institution Press.)
Traces Brazil's historical evolution into a regional power, linking domestic political and economic developments with the country's growing global insertion.

Rother, L. (2010), *Brazil on the Rise* (New York: Palgrave Macmillan).
A brief and readable account of Brazil's transformation which discusses economic, political, and cultural factors in accounting for the country's global rise.

Vigevani, T. and Cepaluni, G. (2009), *Brazilian Foreign Policy in Changing Times: The Quest for Autonomy from Sarney to Lula* (Lanham, MD: Lexington Books).
Analyses the role of autonomy, one of the main objectives of Brazilian foreign policy, in distinct governments following the transition to democracy.

 Visit the Online Resource Centre that accompanies this book for more information:
www.oxfordtextbooks.co.uk/orc/smith_foreign/

20

Australia and global climate change

MATT McDONALD

Chapter contents

 Reader's guide

This chapter analyses Australia's approach to global climate change, particularly its engagement with the global climate change regime. This case study highlights two key points. The first is that Australia's changing approach to international negotiations on climate change reflects a complex combination of domestic political considerations, the foreign policy orientation of governments, and the state of international negotiations. While at times Australia's position seems to reflect the ideologies of particular governments or domestic political constraints, at other times the Australian government's position seems to be strongly influenced by the state of international cooperation. The second point is that Australia's changing approach to climate change cooperation illustrates the profound challenges for the climate change regime generally. In particular, the Australian example suggests challenges for the climate change regime associated with different and changing sets of state interests, complex ethical questions, the power and institutionalized nature of existing political and economic arrangements, and the varying causes and effects of climate change in different places.

Introduction

Global climate change has emerged as one of the most significant challenges in world politics today. While uncertainty still surrounds the specific manifestations and time frame of effects, climate change has the potential to directly threaten or displace millions of people and undermine the livelihoods of millions more, and poses a long-term threat to the sustainability of life on the planet. While this is significant enough, climate change also constitutes a fundamental challenge for the core institutions and practices of world politics. The uncertainty associated with the effects of climate change undermines the impetus for a genuinely global response, while varying degrees of contribution to global climate change—and vulnerability to it—render attribution of responsibilities particularly difficult. And perhaps more than any other major international political issue, a transnational problem such as climate change illustrates the problems of a planet (arbitrarily) divided into state entities with exclusive territorial space.

While the increasing weight of scientific evidence has left little doubt as to the causes of climate change and its likely effects since it grabbed international attention in the 1980s, this has not translated into strong international action to respond to climate change. The much anticipated Kyoto Protocol of 1997 entailed a binding emissions reduction commitment for developed (so-called Annex 1) states, but subsequent political manoeuvring saw a diluted agreement that produced limited substantial effect on global emissions. This was even before the USA (the world's largest emitter of greenhouse gas emissions at the time) withdrew from the Protocol in 2001 under the Bush administration. The subsequent attempt to develop a post-Kyoto agreement in Copenhagen in 2009 failed, and at present there is little optimism regarding international agreement on a post-2012 climate regime, particularly one that involves binding emissions targets and the involvement of developing states.

This chapter focuses on engagement with the international politics of climate change, and the UNFCCC process in particular, by one state—Australia. As a relatively small international player with a tradition of multilateralism, Australia's (changing) approach to climate change provides us with crucial insights into the strength of the global climate change regime. The example of Australia also allows us to identify and explore some of the key dilemmas associated with responding to climate change. Fundamental dilemmas about climate change action in world politics—ethical complexities, international versus domestic considerations, and environmental versus economic concerns—have been central to the ebb and flow of both the climate change regime and Australia's approach to climate change in its foreign policy. While mapping and interpreting Australia's engagement with climate change in its foreign policy, then, this chapter also allows us insights into the challenges confronting the global climate change regime more generally.

This chapter proceeds in three parts. The first outlines the problem of global climate change and its likely effects, notes key complexities and dilemmas regarding climate change, and briefly maps the evolution of the climate change regime through the UNFCCC process. The second section discusses Australian considerations regarding climate change, ranging from domestic political concerns to international obligations and the ideology of particular governments. The final section maps Australian engagement with the UNFCCC process through four recent prime ministers: Hawke, Keating, Howard, and Rudd. Here we explore the role of different factors—domestic politics, international dynamics, and ideological orientation—in influencing their approach to the climate change regime.

Global climate change and the UNFCCC regime

Global climate change refers to the process wherein an increase in the volume of gases responsible for trapping heat in the Earth's atmosphere leads to an increase in the Earth's temperature, with follow-on effects for climate patterns and severe weather phenomena. These greenhouse gases[1] have increased in concentration significantly during the industrial era, primarily because of the burning of fossil fuels (for use in energy and transport, for example). The most recent (2007) synthesis report of the key international scientific body on climate change—the Intergovernmental Panel on Climate Change (IPCC)—concluded that global climate change is 'very likely' to have a human cause, and that temperatures were probably going to increase by 1.8–4°C by the end of the century. The report also noted that 11 of the hottest years on record had been in the 12 years leading up to 2007 (IPCC 2007).

While the science of climate change has strengthened on the causes of the problem, specific impacts are difficult to predict because much is still not known about how the ecosystem will respond to these temperature changes. Abrupt climate change scenarios such as the death of the Amazon rainforest, a transformation of monsoon patterns, or the shutting down of the global ocean currents system (popularized in the 2006 film, *The Day After Tomorrow*) have achieved some public and scholarly attention, even if they are unlikely in the near future. More commonly cited effects of the increase in global temperatures include rising sea levels, increasing intensity and frequency of severe weather phenomena such as cyclones and droughts, an increase in water-borne diseases, and changing rainfall patterns. Among the implications of these developments would be the inundation of low-lying coastal areas throughout the world, an increase in the displacement and destruction of communities, a reduction in arable land, a significant increase in instances of tropical diseases such as malaria, and significant species (biodiversity) loss. Aside from the threat to life, the UK's Stern Review of 2006 estimated that the costs of climate change could amount to 20% of global gross domestic product (Stern 2006).

While some debate exists over the specific nature of the effects of climate change and their time frame, there is a strong and ever-growing scientific (and political) consensus on the idea that climate change is happening and that it is human-induced. US President George Bush, for example, accepted the science of climate change in office even while withdrawing from the Kyoto Protocol, and the relatively conservative IPCC assessments have expressed less reservation about the likely causes and effects of climate change in each iteration of its reports over time.[2] Indeed, while perceptions of a genuine scientific debate about the realities of climate change persist in some countries, 97% of climate scientists surveyed for one 2010 international study indicated that they believed climate change to be happening and to be related to human activity (Anderegg *et al.* 2010).

However, as the movement towards international action on climate change demonstrates, even global acceptance of the science of climate change does not guarantee a concerted international response. Clear challenges here include the need for the political will to engage with an uncertain, long-term, and largely invisible problem, particularly when difficult changes or sacrifices are required of domestic populations. For some theorists, this difficulty is heightened in liberal democratic states with frequent elections and adversarial political systems, which arguably discourage policy makers from addressing long-term political issues (e.g. Doyle and Kellow 1995: 5–6, 130–3). The problem of global action on climate change is complicated further by a series of profound ethical questions. Core dilemmas arise from differentiated levels of responsibility for climate change, costs of mitigation action, and vulnerability to climate change. These ethical dilemmas are further complicated by the question of the nature of our obligations to other living beings or future generations, for example. Some of these dilemmas are outlined in Box 20.1.

BOX 20.1 Ethical dilemmas of climate change action

Historical or contemporary emissions?

Henry Shue (2011: 20) notes that the USA and European states combined were responsible for almost 60% of greenhouse gas emissions in the twentieth century. However, these states could feasibly argue that they did not know the effects of their actions on climate change for most of the twentieth century, even while benefiting from the development that the destructive processes of industrialization allowed. How convincing is that defence, and how (if at all) should that be taken into account when considering responsibility for climate change action?

Per capita or volume of emissions?

While some states produce a significant proportion of the world's contemporary greenhouse gases (for example, China and India produce approximately one-third of the world's greenhouse gas emissions (GGEs)), they produce significantly less per capita than other states (Australia or Canada, for example). In this sense, should there be an equal onus on all states to act, and if not, on what basis should differentiated action be agreed?

Differentiated vulnerabilities?

The UN Development Programme's 2007–2008 Human Development Report emphasized the vulnerability of populations of the developing world to climate change linked to both geographical location and capacity to respond to climate change. Effects will be worse in parts of the globe disproportionately inhabited by populations of the developing world (arid regions and areas near the equator, for example), while states of the developing world also have limited capacity for effective adaptation to manifestations of climate change. How do we make sense of these differentiated vulnerabilities, and how can we ensure that those least affected will act to help ensure the protection of those who will be most affected?

Luxury or survival emissions?

Agarwal and Narain (1991) suggest that a distinction should be made between GGEs in developed and developing states. In the former, emissions are often the result of individuals making unnecessary and unsustainable lifestyle choices (eating red meat or driving cars, for example), while in the latter emissions often result from attempts to ensure survival (slash and burn logging, for example). Does this distinction matter, and if so how should it be incorporated into a climate change agreement?

Future generations and other living beings?

Finally, how can we take account of the interests of those unable to contribute to debate about how we should act but who will be profoundly affected by the choices that we make regarding climate change? This applies to both other living beings and future generations. What obligations, if any, do we have to non-humans or future humans?

The ethical dilemmas associated with developing an international response to climate change have been central to debates over a climate change agreement. In the first instance, scientists who had identified climate change as a problem in the 1980s began to argue forcefully for international political action even when the science of climate change was less than certain. By 1991, an intergovernmental committee of state representatives was established to move towards an international agreement on climate change and emissions reductions—what was to become the UN Framework Convention on Climate Change (UNFCCC).

The UNFCCC was agreed in 1992 at the UN Conference on Environment and Development (UNCED) in Rio de Janeiro, and was signed by 154 states. While there was some disappointment that it stopped short of establishing binding emissions reduction targets at that initial stage, the UNFCCC provided a framework for negotiation as to what reduction targets for each state should be, how these should be monitored, and what time frames should govern these particular targets. In confronting some of the ethical complexities noted earlier, Article 3 of the UNFCCC stated that:

> Parties should protect the climate system for the benefit of future and present generations of human kind on the basis of equity and in accordance with their common but differentiated responsibility and respective capabilities. Accordingly, developed countries should take the lead in combating climate change and the adverse effects thereof.

Further, the 1992 UNCED (at which the UNFCCC was agreed) confronted the issue of lack of scientific certainty about the causes, dynamics, and effects of climate change by adopting the so-called 'precautionary principle'. Principal number 15 of the Rio Declaration noted that:

> Where there are threats of serious or irreversible damage, lack of full scientific certainty shall not be used as a reason for postponing cost-effective measures to prevent environmental degradation.

Therefore while the UNFCCC developed principles to guide cooperation on climate change, it was left to subsequent meetings of the UNFCCC to clarify what form agreement might take that could feasibly institutionalize these principles. While articulating a high-minded ideal, could the UNFCCC process end with an international agreement that a range of states saw as consistent with their perception of fairness, along with their own national interests? Clearly, this has been a challenge for the UNFCCC throughout its evolution (see Box 20.2).

The successful negotiation of the 1997 Kyoto Protocol (agreed at COP 3) seemed to suggest the possibility of international agreement on action on climate change consistent with the principles that underpinned the UNFCCC. After tense negotiations, it was agreed that Annex 1 (developed) states would commit to differentiated targets, with an average reduction target across these states of 5.2% of 1990 levels by 2008–2012. The restriction to developed states reflected both ethical and pragmatic concerns: it certainly appeared fair for developed states to take the lead, given both their overwhelming responsibility for the problem and stronger capacity to respond to it. But there was also recognition that asking developing states to make commitments might see negotiations descend into a broader (and unresolvable) North–South debate.

While promising much, however, controversy soon emerged over the deals that some states (including Australia) had achieved relative to others; the use of so-called flexibility mechanisms (carbon sinks and emissions trading) that could undermine the push for reductions; the long-term role of developing states in the agreement; and the relatively limited scale of global emissions reduction that it would achieve. And of course the withdrawal of the

BOX 20.2 The evolution of the UNFCCC

- **1988** World Conference on the Changing Atmosphere, Toronto: high-profile meeting of scientists. Recommends the reduction of CO_2 emissions by 20% by 2005.

- **1988** Intergovernmental Panel on Climate Change (IPCC) created to provide scientific advice on climate change to inform policy discussions.

- **1992** UNFCCC signed by 154 states at UNCED, Rio de Janeiro: aims to stabilize GGEs at 1990 levels by 2000. Enters into force 1994.

- **1995** UNFCCC Conference of the Parties (COP) 1, Bonn: states agree need for binding GGE reduction commitments for developed countries.

- **1997** COP 3, Kyoto: Kyoto Protocol agreed and signed. Commits Annex 1 (developed) states to average 5.2% reduction in GGEs from 1990 levels by 2008–2012.

- **2000** COP 6 (The Hague): talks collapse as the USA pushes for broad use of flexibility mechanisms (e.g. carbon trading and carbon sinks such as forest plantations) to avoid difficult reduction commitments.

- **2001** US President Bush announces American withdrawal from Kyoto Protocol.

- **2005** Kyoto Protocol enters into force after Russia ratifies.

- **2007** COP 13 (Bali): Bali Action Plan agreed, calling for long-term GGE reduction plan, measurable and verifiable national commitments, plan for involving developing countries, and agreement on assistance (technology transfer, adaptation) to developing countries.

- **2009** COP 15 (Copenhagen): no outcome achieved on post-Kyoto agreement.

Source: Bulkeley and Newell (2010: 20–1).

world's leading emitter—the USA—from the agreement in 2001 seemed to signal the death knell for the Protocol. Against expectations, Russia ratified the protocol in 2005 to ensure that it entered into force,[3] but the challenges that beset international agreement regarding the Kyoto Protocol have not been resolved in subsequent years and in subsequent negotiations. Indeed, the need to attempt to involve developing states responsible for an increasing share of GGEs, and to act quickly in light of recent scientific evidence on climate change, makes a post-Kyoto agreement a more challenging prospect for negotiators than its predecessor.

The following sections consider these challenges through analysis of the changing approach to climate change on the part of a single state—Australia. As a relatively small state with a broadly internationalist foreign policy tradition, the politics of Australia's engagement with the climate change regime gives us important insights into the ebb and flow of international cooperation on climate change.

Australia and global climate change

While climate change throws up a series of dilemmas and difficult choices in terms of the politics of a response, these dilemmas are particularly acute for a country such as Australia. They are associated with potentially conflicting interests regarding Australia's foreign policy traditions, economic interests associated with fossil fuel export and use, and the politics of domestic support/opposition.

In terms of foreign policy traditions, Australian governments have traditionally understood their national interests as being served through engagement with international society. Successive Australian governments have generally recognized the importance, for example, of making a contribution to addressing international problems and engaging actively in international institutions which attempt to develop rules and mechanisms for the management of global politics. This commitment has certainly ebbed and flowed at times. Ultimately, however, it has proved fairly resilient as a foreign policy orientation for a number of reasons. First, Australia's limited material capacity (as a country with a population of around 23 million) suggests that it has an interest in a rules-based international order. Drawing on the realist tradition in international relations thought, for example, we might argue that a commitment to the rules and norms of an international society is more likely to be characteristic of a smaller state that requires a rules-based order to protect it from the bare-faced use of military power in world politics (e.g. Kagan 2003). More positively, a case could be made that an active contribution to resolving international problems or managing international interaction might be seen as the best chance for a smaller state such as Australia to influence the broader dynamics of world politics.

While acknowledging the importance of the international distribution of power, however, such accounts do not take us far enough in understanding foreign policy orientation. Would we expect, for example, all states with similar material capacity—whether Thailand or Turkey, India or France, Burma or Bolivia—to behave in basically the same way? As has been argued in constructivist approaches to international relations (e.g. Katzenstein 1996; Weldes *et al.* 1999), an important dimension of foreign policy orientation is the role of identity—of who a particular nation-state community considers itself to be. In the Australian case, for example, policy-makers' representations of Australia as a 'good international citizen', playing an active role in world politics, reflect and reinforce a notion of who Australians are and what they value. In this sense, such representations arise from—and help constitute—a sense of Australians as willing to do their part to contribute to the effective management of global affairs and dynamics in a way that advances broadly liberal democratic values. Therefore Australia's core foreign policy traditions arguably predispose it towards engaging in 'middle power diplomacy'—a tendency to 'pursue multilateral solutions to international problems ... embrace compromise positions in international disputes, and ... embrace notions of "good international citizenship" to guide ... diplomacy' (Cooper *et al.* 1993: 19).

This idea has traditionally been applied to affluent countries with robust liberal democracies but limited material resources in world politics, such as Australia, Canada, and the Scandinavian countries. However, if their foreign policy traditions and interests predispose such states to an active role in tackling a global problem such as climate change, it does not always follow that domestic political considerations encourage such foreign policy activism across all issue areas.

In Australia, as in other 'middle power states', a robust and institutionalized environmental movement has drawn attention to the problems of climate change. Australia was home to one of the world's first Green political parties, which has grown in popularity and campaigns on a platform of strong action on climate change. Membership in environmental NGOs in Australia is also one of the highest in the world, and concern with the conservation of Australia's rich natural heritage has traditionally featured highly in national opinion polling in Australia (Hutton and Connors 1999). However, other domestic forces pull strongly in the opposite direction.

At the domestic level, Australia's role in developing a strong approach to cooperation on climate change is most obviously challenged by the scale of its current GGEs and its economic interests in the production and export of coal. Australians are among the largest per capita greenhouse gas emitters in the world, with particularly high emissions associated with transport and energy. The former has been linked to the size and limited population density of the Australian land mass, while the latter has been linked to the ready availability of coal to provide energy needs (Hamilton 2001). As such, any movement towards action on climate change that mirrors that undertaken by other developed states has tended to be viewed as posing a particular challenge for Australia. More directly, the size of Australia's coal industry suggests significant short-term economic interests in inaction on climate change mitigation and even in the failure of a global climate change regime. Australia is the world's largest exporter of coal, with coal exports constituting around 20% of total Australian exports, and the coal industry directly employing over 35,000 Australians. Other mining industries in Australia (aluminium and iron ore, for example) are also among Australia's largest revenue earners, yet are also high-emitting industries likely to be affected by domestic mitigation action.

Less directly, a strong Australian position on climate change is hampered domestically by the power and resonance of representations of a fundamental tension between economic prosperity (especially employment) and environmental preservation. While reconciling these imperatives is never straightforward, the idea of an inherent contradiction between the two is particularly prominent in Australian political and public debate, especially regarding climate change (Bulkeley 2001). Those opposing climate change mitigation action have focused overwhelmingly on the potential threat such action might pose to jobs and the economy, while justifications for action have focused significantly on how such action will *not* cause job losses or economic growth, certainly relative to the economic costs of climate change (e.g. Garnaut 2008).

A final point to note in illustrating the dilemmas associated with Australia's approach to climate change concerns Australian vulnerability to climate change. Both the 2007 IPCC assessment of climate change impact and vulnerabilities and the 2008 government-commissioned Garnaut Report on the costs and benefits of mitigation emphasized that while Australia had a strong adaptive capacity, it was particularly vulnerable to the impacts of climate change (IPCC 2007: Chapter 11; Garnaut 2008: Chapter 6). Of particular concern were potential increases in the number and intensity of tropical cyclones, the spread of diseases such as malaria and dengue fever, reduced rainfall and increased drought incidence in already arid areas in central Australia, significant species loss, a loss in tourism revenue associated in particular with bleaching coral on the Great Barrier Reef, and dangers to low-lying coastal areas as a result of sea-level rises. While contestable, some have also expressed concerns about a possible influx of 'environmental refugees' from poor, neighbouring small island states whose existence may be threatened by rising sea levels (e.g. Dupont and Pearman 2006).

Australia and UNFCCC

The potentially conflicting international and domestic concerns noted above are clearly not easily reconciled in Australia's case. Indeed, it might be suggested that Australia's (changing) approach to climate change in its foreign policy reflects these tensions and the relative weight given to some of these concerns over others as the UNFCCC—and of course the problem of climate change itself—has developed.

The Hawke government (1983–1992)

When global climate change found its way on to the international agenda in the late 1980s, the Australian Labor government of Bob Hawke embraced the issue. In 1989 Foreign Minister Evans—the intellectual force behind the concept of 'good international citizenship'—declared global climate change to be 'the biggest challenge facing mankind in this or any other age' (cited in McDonald 2005: 221). The Hawke government committed significant funding for scientific research into climate change, established a series of working groups composed of environmental NGO and industry representatives to discuss responses to climate change among other issues, and in 1990 adopted an interim planning target for the reduction of GGEs of 20% from 1988 levels by 2005. At the time, this was among the most significant reduction targets of any country in the world.

Therefore the position of the Australian government was a strong one in these early years. But how do we make sense of this position in terms of the varying impact of domestic and international considerations? At the domestic level, environmental concerns (particularly conservation concerns in Tasmania) had played a significant role in the election of the Hawke government in 1983. This ensured a government with some degree of sympathy for environmental considerations and heightened sensitivity to environmental lobbying. This period also coincided with a high point in international environmental concerns which had helped propel the broader international move towards action on climate change.

Arguably, international considerations also played a role in terms of the foreign policy approach adopted by the Hawke government. As Foreign Minister Evans (cited in McDonald 2005: 222) made clear in 1990:

> The approach we take to international environmental issues . . . is an integral part of the broader foreign policy interest we have in being—and being seen to be—a good international citizen.

Here, Australian activism on climate change could be linked to a concern with helping to shape the emerging global climate change regime and accruing reputational benefits in the process.

Finally, if more cynically, some might suggest that Australia's position simply reflected the fact that in this agenda-setting period, states could make grandiose statements about their commitments without undertaking substantive action on emissions reductions. This cynical interpretation could find support in the caveat attached to the government's interim planning target, which stated that:

> Australia will not proceed with any measures which have net adverse economic impacts nationally or on Australia's trade competitiveness, in the absence of similar action by major greenhouse gas producing countries (cited in McDonald 2011: 119).

Nevertheless, the position of Australia was seen as a strong and committed international voice on action to address climate change, manifested chiefly in its commitment to binding emissions reduction targets in the lead-up to UNCED in 1992. Indeed, the government's leading scientific organization even argued that the interim planning target adopted by the Hawke government was more significant than that necessitated by the science of climate change at the time (CSIRO, cited in McDonald 2005: 222).

The Keating government (1992–1996)

By the time UNCED was held in Rio de Janeiro in 1992, Bob Hawke had been deposed as leader of the Labor Party by deputy leader Paul Keating. As Treasurer, Keating had been committed to policies of economic rationalism, and was seen by many as a backward step on environmental issues. Regression in Australia's climate policy was not immediately apparent at UNCED in 1992, where the Australian delegation lobbied for the adoption of strong binding emissions targets and expressed disappointment that this was not agreed.

However, policy initiatives at the domestic level, and as international negotiations moved towards setting emissions reductions targets, suggested some retreat from international activism on climate change. The Keating government's domestic policies on climate change constituted relatively minor and fragmented initiatives, including calling on industry to reduce emissions 'wherever economically efficient' (cited in Hamilton 2001: 34). At COP 1 in Berlin in 1995—which was to identify the scope for an international agreement on emissions reductions—the Keating government began to side with the USA in calling for differentiated emissions targets for developed states (taking into account that it would be harder for countries such as Australia to reduce emissions than it would be for other developed states), and calling for the gradual involvement of developing states in the climate change regime.

Domestically, it could certainly be argued that the government's position reflected the ideological commitment to economic rationalism as well as the growing concerns of industry groups, who had begun to mobilize to draw attention to the potential impact of emissions reduction targets within Australia. Again, a cynical interpretation might suggest that it was when confronted with the move to binding emissions in UNFCCC negotiations that the government began to move away from earlier commitments to strong climate change action.

At the international level, however, Australia remained an engaged and constructive player in the global climate change regime. While pushing for differentiated targets and the inclusion of developing states in negotiations for the Berlin mandate, for example, the Keating government ultimately endorsed a mandate that did not fully recognize these concerns. For some analysts, this suggests that Australia did not dare 'take the blame for blocking consensus' (Oberthur and Ott 1998: 47). We might ask whether this reflects the extent of the government's commitment to 'good international citizenship', or the pressure imposed on a middle power state like Australia by strong international moves towards agreement?

The Howard government (1996–2007)

If the Keating government was in part constrained by the goal of being perceived to be a 'good international citizen', the same could not necessarily be said of the conservative Howard government elected to office in 1996. This government denigrated the notion of 'good international citizenship' as a 'trap for the ideologues and the naive', suggesting instead that Australia's foreign policy would be driven by the 'hard-headed' pursuit of the national interest (Downer 2002). And the prospects for an embrace of the climate change regime were arguably even less bright. In 1997 Prime Minister Howard argued that 'we should never have got aboard this particular truck [the UNFCCC] in the first place at the Rio Conference' (ABC Television 1997). In their analysis of the negotiation of the Kyoto Protocol, Oberthur and Ott argue that 'while Australia had certainly not been a climate activist under the previous [Keating] Labor government, the attitude of incoming Prime Minister Howard towards climate policy was almost hostile' (Oberthur and Ott 1999: 71).

At the COP 2 in Geneva in 1996, the Howard government certainly seemed to signal a shift to a hard-line stance on international action on climate change. Government representatives questioned climate science and specifically challenged the notion of IPCC findings informing UNFCCC discussions, a position shared only by the OPEC states and Russia. The government also challenged the need for binding emissions targets for developed states, and expressed regret that both the USA and the EU had supported this position (McDonald 2005: 225).

In the lead-up to COP 3 and associated negotiations for the Kyoto Protocol, the government began to argue forcefully for differentiated emissions reduction targets for developed states. The government argued that it should be granted more lenient targets because of its rapid population growth, reliance on primary industries and fossil fuels for transport, and reliance on the export of fossil fuels, particularly coal (Papadikis 2006: 267). Significantly, Prime Minister Howard argued:

> At Kyoto, I will just continue to put Australia's case . . . and if at the end of the day we are not successful in obtaining accommodation, well the arrangement will not be something that we can be part of (cited in Stevenson 2007).

Ultimately, the government was successful in making its case. While the average emissions commitment for developed states was a 5.2% reduction from 1990 levels by 2008–2012, Australia was granted an *increase* of 8% in emissions (the second-largest increase of any state). It was also successful in negotiating the inclusion of land-clearing in baseline emissions for 1990, in a move that would make it easier for Australia to meet its emissions targets given the reduction in land-clearing since 1990 (unrelated to government policy).

Given the concessions granted to the Australian government at Kyoto it may have been reasonable to expect that Australia would ratify the Kyoto Protocol. However, the Prime Minister began to argue that it was 'not in Australia's interests to ratify the Kyoto protocol . . . because the arrangements currently exclude both developing countries and the United States [and] for us to ratify would cost us jobs and damage our industry' (cited in McDonald 2005: 228).

Does this retreat from the climate change regime ultimately reflect the government's ideological commitments, dynamics of international engagement with the regime, or growing concerns about cost? Certainly, the Howard government had indicated an overarching commitment to the national interest relative to 'good international citizenship' that apparently enabled the retreat from multilateralism and middle power diplomacy. However, it is worth noting that even under the Howard government Australia remained engaged with the UNFCCC rhetorically until the Bush administration signalled that the USA would withdraw. Does this suggest that the government was at least partly concerned by perceptions of the legitimacy of its position, and may have been more constrained had the world's hegemon—and largest emitter of greenhouse gases—remained committed to climate change action? For some, this instance illustrates the primacy of the US alliance for the Howard government as a source of Australian security in a dangerous world. Some critics argue that the commitment to the US alliance influenced Australia's position on a range of issues, including its withdrawal from Kyoto, participation in a free trade agreement with the USA with deleterious economic effects for Australia, and, most controversially, Australian participation in military intervention in Iraq in 2003 (e.g. Matthews *et al.* 2007).

Domestically, the Australian government indicated that it was committed to economic growth and job protection over environmental concerns. Certainly, the importance of the coal industry for Australian exports alone suggested that Australia had much to lose from strong international climate action. While apparently illustrating a rational commitment to the pursuit of material interests, however, questions have also been raised about the closeness of government–industry relations in this period. For example, some policy insiders argued that high-polluting industry groups were granted unprecedented access to government climate policy discussions, and were central to government considerations (e.g. Hamilton 2001; Pearse 2005). Arguably, this was reflected in domestic climate policy, which reduced funding for climate research and investment in renewable energy technology while requiring only voluntary action from industry groups.

The Rudd government (2007–2010)

While the Howard government's position on protecting jobs and economic growth relative to acting on environmental issues seemed to resonate with many Australians throughout Howard's tenure as Prime Minister, climate change ultimately played a central role in his fall from power in 2007. Much of this relates to the rise and fall of international concerns about climate change over time, which subsequently impacted on Australian public opinion on climate change. The mid-2000s witnessed a resurgence of international concern about climate change, linked to the entry into force of the Kyoto Protocol (2005), severe weather events (Hurricane Katrina in 2005 and the Indian Ocean tsunami in 2004), the release of the Stern Review outlining global costs of climate change (Stern 2006), the success of former US Vice-President Al Gore's documentary *An Inconvenient Truth* (2006), the release of the latest IPCC assessment report (IPCC 2007) and the discussion of climate change as a global security threat in the UN Security Council (2007). More directly, Howard's government faced a Labor opposition leader in Kevin Rudd who supported ratification of the Kyoto Protocol and strong domestic action on climate change. For some, this was 'the world's first climate change election' (Rootes 2007).

After comfortably winning the 2007 election, Prime Minister Rudd ratified the Kyoto Protocol as a first order of government business and announced a raft of domestic policy initiatives on climate change. The Rudd government also committed itself to an active role in the development of a post-Kyoto international climate agreement. The Rudd government took one of the largest delegations of any country to the UNFCCC COPs in Bali (2008) and Copenhagen (2009), and in Copenhagen Kevin Rudd took on the role of 'friend of the chair' of the conference to attempt to broker an agreement. He had earlier announced that Australia was committed to an emissions reduction target of 5–15% reduction of greenhouse gas emissions (by 2020 from 2000 levels) depending on the position of other states. In justifying this commitment, Rudd declared that climate change was the 'greatest moral challenge of our time'.

While consistent with his electoral commitment to action on climate change and the domestic support for such action,[4] this position was also consistent with Kevin Rudd's stated commitment to middle power diplomacy. Rudd argued that Australia had been 'too quiet for too long across the various councils of the world', and that Australia would pursue an 'activist' foreign policy to contribute to the management of international challenges and act as 'a greater force for good in the world' (cited in Grattan 2008).

At the domestic level, the Rudd government's climate policy oriented around the Carbon Pollution Reduction Scheme (CPRS). The CPRS, which the government announced in 2008, involved both short-term (20% by 2020) and long-term (60% by 2050) emissions reduction commitment from 2000 levels, and this was to be achieved through a cap and trade scheme. Such a scheme entailed placing an upper limit on total emissions with allowances for businesses to trade in emissions credits or allowances within that cap. The government engaged in an extended period of consultation regarding the CPRS and attempted to pass the legislation twice in 2009. However, these attempts were unsuccessful, with the parliamentary upper house (the Senate) rejecting the legislation in August and December of that year.[5]

In April 2010, Prime Minister Rudd announced that the CPRS would be put on hold until the end of the Kyoto commitment period (post-2012). As talks in Copenhagen stalled just weeks after the Senate had rejected the CPRS for a second time, and the conservative opposition had elected a climate sceptic (Tony Abbott) as opposition leader who labelled the CPRS a 'great big new tax', Rudd became convinced that the time was not right to pursue this policy. Less than two months later, and amid declining popular support for the Prime Minister, Rudd had been deposed by his deputy Julia Gillard. His failure to meet words with deeds on climate change was seen by some as central to his political downfall (Rootes 2011).

Once again, how can we make sense of the role of different domestic and international considerations in impacting on the Rudd government's climate policy and the obstacles to it? International concerns about climate change had grown in the lead-up to Rudd's election in 2007, increasing domestic disquiet about the Australian government's disengagement from Kyoto under Howard. However, the failure of the Copenhagen talks in 2009 to achieve an agreement seemed to undermine a potentially powerful rationale for strong Australian action, while also pointing to the limits of Australian middle power diplomacy.

The domestic context was no less complex in this period. The government enjoyed relatively strong and consistent public support for action on climate change until late 2009, and in fact Rudd's failure to pass the CPRS legislation through the Senate was the result of opposition from an unusual coalition of opposing political parties. While support for the CPRS certainly waned under attacks of the policy on economic grounds, paradoxically it was Rudd's retreat from the CPRS that was seen as central to his steadily eroding public popularity in 2010. In a further paradox, the current minority Australian government under Prime Minister Gillard passed a wide-reaching carbon tax in the face of significant public opposition but support in the Senate.

Conclusion

The example of Australia's engagement with the climate change regime in its foreign policy illustrates a complex relationship between international dynamics, domestic politics, and the ideologies of different governments. It also illustrates the complexity and challenges associated with reaching international agreement on an issue like climate change with uncertain effects and complex ethical questions about responsibility for action. Therefore the case of climate change in Australian foreign policy raises important questions. First, and to turn to the themes of this book, how should we make sense of competing concerns and interests, and how does this challenge the way we generally think about the origins of foreign policy? While theories of foreign policy analysis often work with the idea that the national interest and foreign policy behaviour are the result of *either* external *or* domestic factors, this case reminds us that a complete picture of the origins and practices of foreign policy require attention to both domestic and international dynamics and the complex interaction between them. While this would paint a more realistic picture of state behaviour in international politics, however, this does not provide us with an easy set of tools for examining foreign policy.

Other core questions suggest themselves here regarding the prospects for the global climate change regime. First, to what extent is it possible to develop a strong international climate change regime when the politics of responding to climate change—and the strength of opposing positions on it—can be so divided in *one* country? From the origins of the regime to the present, Australia's position on the form of international cooperation and how Australia's commitment to climate change action should be reflected in domestic policy has altered significantly over time. This surely complicates any attempt to achieve global action on climate change. Second, and following from this, if a wealthy state with a disproportionate responsibility for global greenhouse emissions, a tradition of middle power activism, and vulnerability to climate change effects cannot commit itself to strong engagement with the climate change regime, what does this tell us about the chances for ensuring global participation in a climate change regime?

Australia is certainly an unusual case, with a disproportionately large contribution to greenhouse emissions and significant costs for adjusting to a low-carbon economy existing alongside a traditionally multilateral orientation in its foreign policy and vulnerability to manifestations of climate change itself. Yet we see combinations of these factors evident in states such as Canada and Norway, for example—countries with a reputation as 'good states' in the international system, but with high per capita emissions and some economic interest in the maintenance of fossil fuel economies. And we see radically changing approaches to climate change in foreign policy in the approach of the USA, for example, with different administrations exhibiting broad support (Clinton and Obama) or opposition (Bush Sr and Bush Jr) to international action on climate change at different times.

While posing challenges, such concerns do not mean that an international response to climate change is effectively doomed. The example of states such as Norway suggest that far-reaching commitment to climate change action can come from states with economic interests in maintaining current emissions and which may even benefit from the effects of climate change. And while becoming the largest gross emitter of greenhouse gases in the process of its continued economic development in recent years, China has simultaneously committed itself to renewable energy targets beyond that of many established developed states. What is also clear from the Australian example (especially 1995–1997) is that in instances where international concerns are high and international action on climate change has gained momentum, (smaller) states such as Australia have appeared compelled to engage constructively with the international regime. Therefore maintaining and strengthening global concern about the effects of climate change may be central to the prospects of overcoming the myriad difficulties associated with reaching an international climate change agreement.

Key points

- Cooperation on an issue like global climate change is particularly difficult given the different interests of states and the complex ethical and institutional questions of a response to it.
- Australia's position on climate change in its foreign policy has changed substantially over time and with different governments.
- The dilemmas of Australia's approach to climate change—and public debate surrounding that approach—can be viewed as a microcosm of broader global debate about climate change and the appropriate responses to it.
- Australia's approach to climate change has been influenced by a complex combination of factors relating to domestic political considerations, the ideologies of particular governments, and the development of the climate change regime itself.
- The challenges faced by Australia in developing a strong and effective response to climate change illustrate the problems facing the international climate change regime more broadly.

 Questions

1. What role does ideology play in influencing foreign policy decision making?
2. How important are domestic political considerations to foreign policy in an issue area like climate change?
3. Are states constrained by international norms and dynamics of cooperation associated with climate change?
4. What does 'middle power diplomacy' entail?
5. How has the climate change regime evolved, and why has it evolved in that way?
6. What are the core ethical complexities concerning climate change?
7. How successfully have ethical principles been incorporated into the climate change regime?
8. Will short-term economic interests always trump long-term environmental considerations?
9. Can transnational issues ever be effectively addressed in a world of states?
10. What hope is there for an effective international agreement on climate change?

 Further reading

Bulkeley, H. and Newell, P. (2010), *Governing Climate Change* **(London: Routledge).**
An excellent introduction to the history of attempts to manage global climate change and the actors involved in climate governance.

Cotton, J. and Ravenhill, J. (eds) (2011), *Middle Power Dreaming: Australia in World Affairs, 2006–10* **(Melbourne: Oxford University Press).**
An analysis of contemporary Australian foreign policy, drawing together leading researchers to explore core issues and relationships.

Doyle, T. (2000), *Green Power: The Environment Movement in Australia* **(Sydney: UNSW Press).**
An excellent discussion of the role of the environment in Australian politics, exploring the growth of environmental concerns and the extent of involvement of environmental groups in state decision making.

Dryzek, J., Norgaard, R., and Schlosberg, D. (2011), *The Oxford Handbook of Climate Change and Society* (Oxford: Oxford University Press).
A collection of contributions by some of the world's leading researchers on various dimensions of climate change, this volume explores questions of how climate change affects human systems, and how societies can, do, and should respond.

Gardiner, S., Caney, S., Jamieson, D., and Shue, H. (eds) (2009), *Climate Ethics: Essential Readings* (New York: Oxford University Press).
A collection of key papers exploring ethical questions arising from, and associated with, global climate change.

Hamilton, C. (2007). *Scorcher: The Dirty Politics of Climate Change* (Melbourne: Black).
A critical account of Australian climate policy, providing a detailed analysis of which actors have been considered in the Australian government's approach to climate change and which have been marginalized.

 Visit the Online Resource Centre that accompanies this book for more information:
www.oxfordtextbooks.co.uk/orc/smith_foreign/

Israeli–Egyptian (in)security: the Yom Kippur War

GARETH STANSFIELD

Chapter contents

 ## Reader's guide

This case study considers the Yom Kippur War of 1973, a key event in the intractable modern dispute known as the Arab–Israeli Conflict. In foreign policy terms, three questions stand out. Why did Egypt attack Israel in 1973? Why did Israel not take actions to prevent the attack from taking place? Did Egypt intend to inflict an absolute defeat on Israel, or merely force her to the negotiating table for domestic political reasons? In 1973, Egyptian military forces launched a devastating attack against Israeli forces stationed in the Sinai peninsula, but were subsequently overwhelmed by a highly effective Israeli counter-attack. The endgame of the conflict saw Egypt and Israel embark upon a peace process that culminated with the Camp David Accords, the relative normalization of the Egyptian–Israeli relationship, and the effective breaking of Egypt's alliance with other Arab states opposed to the existence of Israel. This chapter investigates the Yom Kippur War by first outlining the situation between Egypt and Israel following Israel's devastation of the Arab armies in 1967, which not only imbued the Israeli military establishment with a heightened sense of superiority, but forced Egyptian leaders to ask difficult questions about Egypt's position in the region and internationally. The second part of the chapter then develops several thematics that analyse the Egyptian move towards war in 1973 and the Israeli response. The chapter concludes with an assessment of the aftermath of the Yom Kippur War and the rapprochement between Egypt and Israel. Particular attention is paid to the 'cold peace' which characterized the relationship between 1979 and 2011, but which enabled the USA to provide the regime of Hosni Mubarak with significant military aid over this period. In view of the demise of the Mubarak regime in 2011, following the Egyptian episode of the wider Arab Spring, the chapter concludes by questioning the durability and sustainability of the 'cold peace' in a geopolitical environment radically different to that of the late 1970s.[1]

Introduction

It is impossible to exaggerate the effect of the Palestinian–Israeli dispute on the foreign policies of states of, and with interests in, the Middle East region. Indeed, it is the existence of Israel and the plight of the Palestinians that drives the foreign policies of Middle East states to such an extent that the conflict can be considered an *idée fixe* among foreign policy concerns. Quite simply, the failure to find a resolution acceptable to all parties involved in the immediate Palestine–Israel struggle, and by extension the wider Arab–Israeli conflict, is a festering sore inhibiting interaction between Israel and her neighbours. This dynamics of this problem are also not historical or unchanging. Indeed, following the changes brought about by the Arab Spring of 2011, the geopolitical sensitivities that existed between Israel and her neigbours became even more acute, as a new (or reformed) regime emerged in Egypt, the Ba'ath regime of Syria struggled to maintain its hold over the country, and the Palestinian leadership sought to advance its cause by demanding statehood more forcefully on the international stage and by appealing to the UN General Assembly in 2011. New problems also appeared for Israel, as states previously neutral on the issue of their treatment of the Palestinians adopted a more critical tone. In particular, the foreign policy of Turkey moved from being accommodating to Israel to being avowedly supportive, even protective, of the Palestinian cause following Israel's attack on Turkish-manned humanitarian vessels attempting to dock at Gaza. Such developments had wider international dimensions, with the USA caught between embracing the democratic developments in Arab states, yet needing to assuage Israel's fears of the posture of post Arab Spring governments towards them and the Palestinians. For President Obama, already looking towards the US presidential elections of 2012 and struggling with the global economic crisis and the unpopular deployment of US forces in Afghanistan, his natural tendency towards supporting the democratization efforts of Arab states was tempered by the need to maintain the domestic support of those significant components of the US electorate who are sympathetic to the Israeli cause. Furthermore, the EU and the USA viewed with alarm the rapidly deteriorating security situation in the eastern Mediterranean, as old political patterns unravelled and new ones emerged. These problems were not 'merely' on the ground, in the territories of Israel, Palestine, and the Arab states. They were also in, or beneath, the sea—new discoveries of very significant gas deposits in the eastern Mediterranean came at a time of global energy insecurity and, quite literally, poured fuel onto the fire of an already volatile geopolitical situation, as states began to position themselves to gain as much control of these offshore resources as possible.

Therefore the Arab–Israeli Conflict is not *only* about the plight of the Palestinians. Indeed, the conflict is multilayered and highly complex. More accurately, it is about how 'Palestine' is used and abused by Israel, Arab states, and regional states alike as they forward their own national interests in a highly unstable region. It is also about how international powers, including the USA, the EU, Russia, and China, situate themselves to promote their own national interests.

Thus the Arab–Israeli Conflict is multifaceted and, as such, needs to be disaggregated in order to rationalize the foreign policy actions of involved states. The conflict itself has a relatively recent starting point, which is the declaration of Israeli independence in 1948 (Sprecher and DeRouen 2005: 123). But this declaration was the outcome of several decades of activity, led by **Zionists**, who took the religious notion of a 'Return to Zion' and turned it into an ideologically driven political strategy (see Box 21.1). Having found support in Western capitals in the years following the First World War, most notably in London, the emergence of a Zionist state in Palestine was then given unstoppable momentum by the **Holocaust** committed by Nazi Germany against the Jews of Europe in the Second World War.

However, the problem was that the proposed 'homeland' was already the home of others—Palestinian Arabs—who could also prove their ancient tenure on the narrow strip of land between the River Jordan and the Mediterranean Sea. This competition over territory, rather than religiously based competition, is at the core of the conflict between Palestinians and Israeli Jews. Indeed, Jews, Muslims, and Christians had lived in relative harmony in Ottoman Palestine for centuries. Therefore the conflict that emerged in the twentieth century was distinctly modern. Indeed, there is little to suggest that Jews and Arabs should be 'in a fatal atavistic embrace based on **primordial hatred**' (Milton-Edwards and Hinchcliffe 2004: 22). Rather, 'modern hatreds' spawned by competition over territory and the sharpening of identities were then augmented by other differences, including those of religion.[2]

BOX 21.1 Zionism and the formation of the state of Israel

Zionism is the term given to the Jewish nationalist movement which emerged in Europe in the nineteenth century and sought the establishment of a Jewish state in the 'Land of Israel'. However, explanations about the origins of Zionism, vary, depending upon whether or not the Zionist cause is viewed sympathetically. Committed Zionists link modern Zionism to the 'historic longing of Jews to return to their biblical homeland', whereas others focus on Zionism as a modern ideology based upon self-identification rather than faith (Murphy 2005: 269–70). The chief architects of the modern Zionist project were based in Europe. Most notable of these was figures was Theodore Herzl, a Viennese journalist and sometime playwright, who in 1896 published a book called *The Jews' State: An Attempt at a Modern Solution to the Issue of the Jews* which called for the establishment of a Jewish state, preferably in Palestine (Dowty 2005: 36). Over the next twenty years, Zionists lobbied European capitals for support while European Jews, keen to escape from the heightened anti-Semitism that had become widespread in Russia in particular, began to settle in Ottoman Palestine. By 1914, an estimated 94,000 Jews had settled in what became Mandatory Palestine (about 13.6% of the total population), forming the basis of the 'Return to Zion' and the emergence of the Jewish state.

The making of Israel into a reality was given a significant boost during the First World War as the British sought to secure allies in their struggle to defeat the Ottoman Empire and to prevent the region falling under the dominance of Russia. As such, on 2 November 1917, British Foreign Secretary Lord Arthur Balfour noted in a letter to the head of the British Zionist Federation, Lord Lionel Rothschild, that Britain 'view with favour the establishment in Palestine of a national home for the Jewish people'. What became known as the 'Balfour Declaration' became policy when written into the British Mandate for Palestine by the League of Nations following the end of the First World War (Dowty 2005: 71).

The final spur for the establishment of Israel was the Holocaust committed by Nazi Germany against Jews and other peoples in the Second World War. Because of the Holocaust, Zionism became the tenet accepted by almost all Jews, and now the movement also benefited from support from the international community as sympathy towards the Jews for what they had suffered reached unparalleled heights. The passing of UN General Assembly Resolution 181 in November 1947 allowed for the partition of Palestine into Arab and Jewish states, but was resolutely opposed by the Palestinians and neighbouring Arab states. Fighting broke out at the end of 1947 and, on 15 May 1948, the Arab states sent military forces to Palestine, but to no avail. Israeli forces counter-attacked, carving out the boundaries of an expanded Jewish state and expelling some 600,000–750,000 Palestinians in the process.

The dispute became widened beyond the territorial setting of Palestine/Israel in 1948 when the state of Israel was declared and neighbouring Arab states attempted to destroy it. From then on, the confrontation concerned not only the future of Palestinians and Israelis. Once the conflict actually started, the importance of the plight of the Palestinians was often overshadowed by other, more regional, factors as the domestic conditions of combatant states fed into their foreign policy decision making, along with the influence of powers external to the region, most notably the USA and the USSR.

For Israel, its overwhelming foreign policy focus has always been the maintenance of its security. As such, the Israeli state prided itself upon having the most effective intelligence services and the most lethal military forces in the Middle East region. The names of Israel's **intelligence services**, especially **Shabak** (Shin Bet) and **Mossad**, became renowned with good reason as an omniscient guardian of the Zionist cause, watching Israel's Arab neighbours for signs of aggression and being ready to take pre-emptive (or at times preventive) action against them. The leading force among the Arab states opposed to Israel was Egypt. Clearly the pre-eminent threat, it had been a key player in the wars of 1948 and 1967 and its leaders remaining thunderously opposed to the very existence of the Zionist state. Yet Egypt, along with Syria and Jordan, had proved to be incapable of fielding military forces capable of even remotely matching those of Israel. Indeed, following their devastating defeat in the Six-Day War of 1967, Arab states seemed to be incapable of making anything other than hollow threats against the vastly superior military posture of Israel.

The foreign policy concerns of Arab states were of a different nature to those of Israel, and were fixated upon the existence of the Israeli state and the challenges it posed to the **legitimacy** and security of their often fragile regimes. Furthermore, in the competition that existed between Arab states for regional leadership, the actual fate of the Palestinians often became secondary to the desire to oppose Israel at any cost. The Palestinian exodus of 1948 also created serious domestic problems for neighbouring Arab states. In what Pappe refers to as the 'ethnic cleansing of Palestine', close to 800,000 people were uprooted, 531 villages destroyed, and eleven urban neighbourhoods emptied of their inhabitants between March and September 1948 (Pappe 2006: xiii). The magnitude of the subsequent Palestinian refugee crisis created serious internal problems for neighbouring states.

By the 1970s, three rounds of conflict had taken place between Israel and her neighbours (See Box 21.2), with Israel soundly defeating the Arab states in each episode in wars that emphasized the poor military organization of the Arabs and the preparedness of the Israelis. However, this was to change in 1973. The aim of this chapter is to provide an analysis of the war, and explain the reasons why Egypt and Israel acted in the ways they did. The chapter will then go onto consider why the two countries, after fighting each other to a standstill, then negotiated over the remainder of the decade a 'normalization' that had profound effects not only upon their own security but also on wider Middle Eastern concerns.

The legacies of the Six-Day War of 1967

The causal factors of the Yom Kippur War of 1973 can be traced to the aftermath of the previous Six-Day War of 1967, its territorial outcome, and the manner in which this war was conducted. This was the war that 'neither side wanted' (Shlaim 2000: 236). Following a series of

---

BOX 21.2 The the rounds of the Arab–Israeli Conflict

1948	War of Independence	War broke out on 15 May 1948 after the Israeli Declaration of Independence. Military forces from Egypt, Syria, Iraq, Jordan, and Lebanon were defeated by the IDF. Approximately 750,000 Palestinians were expelled. Greatly embarrassed Arab states; Israel viewed as being a part of a wider imperialist agenda; Israel sensitized to the regional threat ranged against it.
1956	Suez Conflict	President Nasser of Egypt's decision to nationalize the Suez Canal Company in July was an attempt to show Arab nationalist credentials and deal a blow against Western imperialism in the region. French, British, and Israelis cooperated against the Egyptians to recapture the canal, routing Egyptian forces in Sinai. Britain and France were forced to withdraw forces by US pressure. Nasser left in control of canal, but humiliated by military defeat.
1967	Six-Day War	In some ways inevitable as the culmination of unresolved Arab–Israeli disputes, and the peak of Arab nationalist sentiment. Arab war preparations prompted an Israeli pre-emptive strike on 5 June that largely destroyed the forces ranged against her. Israel occupied Sinai, the West Bank and Gaza, and the Golan Heights.
1973	Yom Kippur War	Egyptian and Syrian military attacks against Israel aimed to recapture the Golan Heights and Sinai. Initially successful, but then rebuffed by Israeli counter-attack.

skirmishes between Israel on one side and Syria, Jordan, and Palestinian guerrillas on the other, tensions escalated through a war of words over the summer months. President Nasser of Egypt, in an attempt to pressure Israel into not attacking Syria (with whom Egypt had an alliance), embarked upon a dangerous game of **brinkmanship** which included ordering troops into Sinai and closing the Straits of Tiran to Israeli shipping. However, Nasser not only failed to judge the response of the Israelis accurately, but his closure of the strategically important waterway and his attempts to challenge the Israeli Defence Forces (IDF) was intolerable to the USA. Recognizing that the IDF was more than capable of defeating the Arab armies, the USA effectively underwrote Israeli war plans by agreeing to the following: support of Israel at the United Nations, backing Israel in the event of Soviet intervention, and replenishing Israel's armouries if needed.

Israel needed no further encouragement. On 5 June 1967, a devastating surprise air strike was launched against Egyptian, Syrian, Jordanian, and Iraqi bases. In the first day of fighting, the Israelis had destroyed the air forces of the four Arab states, eliminating 400 enemy planes (the majority of which had not even managed to get airborne) and effectively handing victory to the IDF (Shlaim 2000: 241). Acting **pre-emptively**, Israel had secured a comprehensive victory through surprise and technologically superior forces. The Arab countries had lost for exactly the opposite reasons. They had acted in a predictable fashion, and were reliant on equipment that was obsolete in comparison.

The Six-Day War was undoubtedly a triumph for Israel. Large tracts of territory of strategic importance had been gained, including the Sinai peninsula, the West Bank and Gaza Strip, and the Golan Heights. Moreover, the defeat inflicted upon the Arab states had thrown their regimes into disarray. Their inability to return Palestinian land generated deep dissatisfaction within their domestic publics which questioned the very legitimacy of the regimes themselves (see Box 21.3).

For the Israelis, the comprehensive victory also brought subsequent complacency. With the prestige of the military at an all-time high, the Israelis began to perceive the threat against

---

BOX 21.3 Military governments in the Arab world

The emergence of the state of Israel in 1948 occurred at a time when Arab states were themselves only beginning to emerge from the shadow of colonialism. A common feature of these states at that time was the prevalence of military regimes. The military in Arab countries had begun to come to prominence from the mid-1930s, with coups in Iraq being the precursors for the taking of power by the military in other Middle East states after the Second World War. The new military regimes that took power in Iraq, Egypt, and Syria, in particular, did so through their being the most organized component of the state, and taking advantages of other weaknesses in society at large. However, they had to legitimize their positions quickly, and Israel was an ideal rallying point around which to achieve this and to deploy their armies to gain valuable foreign policy kudos. The relative strength of the IDF combined with the organizational weakness of many Arab armies meant that the rhetoric of the Arab military regimes was rarely matched by their actions in the field, beyond occasional local tactical successes or the early period of the Yom Kippur War.[i]

The relative longevity of the military–authoritarian Arab regimes led most commentators to view them as permanent fixtures on the map of the region. Indeed, the notion that the regimes of President Mubarak in Egypt, Colonel Gaddafi in Libya, or President Assad in Syria could ever be threatened by domestic pressures, let alone removed, was only ever entertained at the fringes of analysts' discussions. Therefore the sudden wave of protest across North Africa and the Middle East in 2011 was unexpected, not least by the regimes themselves. By the autumn of 2011, Tunisia, Egypt, and Libya had all seen a change of ruler, and Syria was in the throes of violent unrest with the majority of analyses pointing towards regime change happening sooner rather than later. Whether these changes proved to be significant structural democratic changes or would turn into 'old books in new covers', as was often mooted, remained to be seen. However, it was clear that the survivability, even existence, of the military–authoritarian Arab state could no longer be accepted as a constant of Middle East politics. The question that haunted Israel in particular, and also the USA to a significant degree, was: 'What would come afterwards?' While the military regimes were undemocratic with at best problematic human rights records, they had become known quantities in terms of their foreign policies and several, including Egypt and Libya, had developed good, even strong, security links with Western powers. Their rhetoric regarding Israel and Palestine was understood, as were their foreign policy actions in this theatre, and a clear if delicate status quo had emerged. The Arab Spring changed this cosy arrangement and paved the way for new populist forces to emerge either through the ballot box or through civil conflict. These new forces, whether Islamist or nationalist (Arab or country-based), would not necessarily be so accommodating towards Israel in the future, nor so ineffective.

[i] For an analysis of the role of the military in the political life of Middle East states (including Israel, in addition to Arab states) see Stansfield (2005).

them to be of a lesser magnitude than it once was. Field Marshal Mohamed El-Gamasy—one of the most senior Egyptian officials at the time of the war—noted that their '[m]orale was high and Israel felt absolutely certain of its military might; its senior officers were confident to the point of arrogance and conceit' (El-Gamasy 1989: 78). This point is echoed by US military analysts Anthony Cordesman and Abraham Wagner who noted that '[t]he Israeli victory in 1967 was so sweeping that it is understandable that Israel did not follow its victory with a searching examination of its remaining military weaknesses' (Cordesman and Wagner 1990: 17).

For Egypt, the defeat of 1967 prompted a re-evaluation of the status of their military strength and tactics, but more importantly a consideration of their political and economic standing. Important military lessons were learned and new strategies that would have profound implications for Egypt's relationship with other Arab states were planned. Both dynamics would feed into a new policy direction from Egypt—one that would be more aggressive and seek to beat the Israelis at their own pre-emptive game.

Why did this move towards developing a more effective strategy against the Israelis take place? It certainly was not driven by any deeply held notion of solidarity with the Palestinians —beyond the usual references in pan-Arab-coloured public pronouncements. Rather, the changes that occurred within Arab capitals were driven by domestic pressures and the need to enhance the security of regimes themselves struggling to maintain their hold on power.

International actions (or, more accurately, inactions) were the final catalyst that brought about the Egyptian pre-emptive strike against Israel in 1973. In 1971 the Palestinian leadership, in the form of the Palestinian Liberation Organization (PLO), now led by Yasser Arafat, was forced to move its command structure from Jordan to Lebanon, following failed attempts by other Palestinian parties to overthrow the Jordanian monarchy as a first step in creating a more radical front by which to challenge Israel (Smith 2005: 227).[3] In what became known as the Jordanian Civil War, which raged in August and September of 1970, King Hussein crushed the rebellious Palestinians and forced their political parties to relocate to Lebanon.

This event had serious ramifications for how the Arab–Israeli Conflict would proceed henceforth.

- First, the Jordanian government would place the stability of the regime above any notion of Arab solidarity with the Palestinian cause, such that Jordan was never again to confront Israel directly. This move illustrates how domestic considerations are often more powerful drivers of foreign policy direction than **pan-Arab loyalties**. The retirement of Jordan from the struggle with Israel would force other Arab states into considering their own, now further exposed, situation *vis-à-vis* their neighbour.

- Second, the expulsion of Palestinian parties, most notably the PLO (which had been involved in only a limited way in the struggle against the Jordanian monarchy), brought Lebanon directly into the conflict and thereby heightened significantly the potential for Syria and Israel to come into violent disagreement.

- The third dynamic to occur at this time (although not related to the Jordanian Civil War) was the death of President Nasser of Egypt. Nasser, who had only just successfully negotiated a ceasefire with Israel, was succeeded by Anwar Sadat—a figure known for his rampant animosity toward Israel.

The Egyptian build-up to war in 1973 and Israel's failure to react

The reaction of the Egyptian government and military to their drubbing of 1967 was not a particular secret. Indeed, the build-up to war in 1973 was clear enough—and not merely with the benefit of hindsight. Two sets of questions emerge when considering the immediate pre-war environment.

● Why did Egypt decide to go to war against Israel in 1973? Without Jordan and a wider Arab alliance, how could any attack be considered 'Arab'? Was it more 'Egyptian', and undertaken merely to avenge their earlier defeat? Was it to recapture lost territories? Or was there still some consideration of fighting on behalf of the Palestinians?

● Why did Israel, clearly aware of the rising threat, choose inaction rather than the previous policy of pre-emption that had been so successful six years earlier?

The Egyptian position was complex. Of course, issues of national pride fed into the desire to avenge the defeat of 1967, but there also were more pressing issues to be faced. The Egyptian economy was in a terrible state, in large part due to the low levels of support and investment coming particularly from the USA. The regime itself was deemed to be weak and in need of showing its strength in terms not only of fighting Israel, but also of improving the internal characteristics of the state. Also, the Egyptian leadership viewed with concern the possibility of Egypt being dragged into a war against Israel if Syria chose to launch a pre-emptive attack.

However, while there were many factors to take into account, one aspect of Egypt's posture was easy enough to understand: President Sadat had made clear his country's intention of ending the stalemate of 'no peace, no war' that had existed between Egypt and Israel since the Six-Day War of 1967, and creating favourable political conditions through which territories lost to Israel would be returned. Indeed, statements made by Sadat from 1971 onwards certainly indicated that the Egyptian president had a mind to go to war, yet Israeli observers remained distinctly uninterested when faced by even the most belligerent of outbursts. The fact that Sadat had also actively been seeking to negotiate with Israel, via US National Security Advisor Henry Kissinger, as late as February 1973 (the approaches were rebuffed by Israel) should have at least forewarned Israeli analysts that the Egyptian president was of a mind to regain control of territory lost in 1967, and if a diplomatic solution was not possible, then the only option left would be military (Bar-Joseph 2006: 546). The evidence of Egyptian war-planning taking place, even months before the event, was clear and based upon facts gained by the intelligence services rather than inferences derived from other events, leading Uri Bar-Joseph too conclude that '. . . months before the war started Israel had much of the relevant information about Egypt's and Syria's war preparations and at least one warning about their intention to launch the war soon; from September 1973, as war preparations accelerated, concrete information about them started to flow' (Bar-Joseph 2000: 14). Why, therefore, did the Israelis act as though nothing was untoward?

The answer lies in a combination of endogenous and exogenous factors. In terms of the former, Israel suffered from a dose of overconfidence. Benefiting from the overwhelming defeat of the Arab armies in 1967 and the subsequent unwillingness of Israel to negotiate any form of normalization, Israelis viewed the period between 1967 and 1973 as being particularly 'good years' (Handel 1977: 481; Lochery 2004: 101). The comprehensive defeat of the Arab armies also promulgated a view within the Israeli military that the Arabs, while continuing to be antipathetic toward Israel, did not have the organizational or technical wherewithal to defeat her—as one Arab writer from the Egyptian Air Force noted '[t]he Israeli's false victory in the Six-Day War confirmed their assumption of continuing Arab disunity and incompetence . . . [t]he possibility of an early Arab revival was just not credible to the Israelis, and for this arrogance, they were to pay a heavy price in the fourth round [the Yom Kippur War] of October 1973' (Anwar 1986: 5–6). This selective blindness to the growing threat was further deepened by exogenous factors such as advice given by the USA to Israel. Fearing the alignment of Egypt and Syria with the Soviet camp, the USA adopted a policy of not pressurizing Israel into negotiations with Arab states, and instead encouraged her to remain intransigent. With the confidence given by overwhelming victory and enjoying superpower support, it is perhaps understandable why Israeli foreign policy makers did not take the threats against them seriously in the early 1970s.

However, the failure of the Israelis to react cannot be explained merely by ineptitude and an unwillingness to see facts that did not fit preconceived patterns. Credit also has to be given to the Egyptian war-planners for successfully concealing their intentions through **deception** and **secrecy**. In Egypt, and particularly around the Suez Canal, a heightened pattern of military activity was maintained, including calling up reservists 22 times in the summer of 1973 alone, and continually moving bridging equipment backwards and forwards to the Suez Canal area to such an extent that Israeli intelligence believed the pattern to be unexceptional. Indeed, Israel viewed such manoeuvres as merely activities to maintain the morale of the army (Boyne 2002: 11). Sadat also expelled Soviet advisors working with the Egyptian military establishment, leading Israeli analysts to conclude that no invasion was imminent as such a complex initiative would need external professional advice. Lastly, the Egyptian command gave considerable thought to what would be the ideal date for the operation to retake Sinai, settling on 6 October. This date was of crucial importance for several reasons. First, the cycle of the moon was at its most opportune for building up the invasion force and, second, 6 October was the Jewish religious holiday of Yom Kippur and was also in the period of Ramadan for that year. Therefore the Israelis would be at their most exposed because of their own holiday period and their belief that no attack would occur during the religious holiday of their opponents (Cochrane 1998: 10). Yet none of these facts were based upon any particularly secret pieces of knowledge, and could have been discerned by Israeli analysts tasked with '**red-team' thinking** (i.e. acting as an opponent would act).

These outlooks, combined with the fact that Arab leaders regularly made threats against Israel that never materialized, blinded the Israelis to the reality that the Egyptian and Syrian governments—driven by powerful domestic dynamics and damaged national pride—were intensifying their military preparations. In some ways, Israel's unwillingness to see the threat rising from Arab states was driven by the fact that, quite simply, war was not planned for. There was, within Israeli military circles, a realization that the threat from Arab regimes had not conveniently evaporated, but they believed that it would have to be faced down much later in the decade. Various defence-related policies associated with this mindset, including the levelling off of the military budget, a reduction of compulsory military service, and the retirement of many senior officers, placed the Israeli military at a further disadvantage for fighting a war in 1973 (Handel 1977: 484). This approach to 'the next conflict' was also driven by the earlier experience of the 1967 War, which many Israeli planners viewed as the outcome of military preparations that developed a momentum that could only result in war—i.e. to mobilize too soon was to engage in a **self-fulfilling prophesy**. But this dynamic is not something unique to this situation—indeed, 'not desiring war', leading to policy makers being 'unable to visualize war' in the immediate term, is something that appears regularly in other conflicts and nearly always benefits the opponent, which is exactly what happened in 1973.

The final move towards war occurred when Israel annexed a large area of Sinai in defiance of UN Security Council Resolution (SCR) 242, with the USA doing nothing to prevent it. Recognizing that Israel could only be forced to return the lost territories by military action rather than diplomatic pressure, Egypt and Syria moved to attack Israel in order to force the USA to become involved in the conflict and thereby return negotiate the return of Sinai and the Golan Heights (Stein 1999: x). Sadat made the decision to go to war as early as November 1972, with the military plan being a swift attack aimed at establishing a bridgehead on the east bank of the Suez Canal and posing a threat to Israel that could not be ignored. From this position of strength, negotiations could then take place that would signal the end of the stalemate. Other alternatives, such as a return to the war of attrition, were not seriously entertained as this would expose the Arab states to the far superior military forces of Israel once the element of surprise had been lost (Cochran 1989: 9).

The attack, codenamed Operation Badr, commenced on 6 October 1973, with Syrian troops attacking through the Golan Heights and Egyptian forces crossing the Suez Canal and advancing into Sinai. Under cover of a massive artillery bombardment, 8000 Egyptian infantrymen crossed the Suez Canal and succeeded in establishing bridgeheads of around seven miles into Sinai. The Egyptians and Syrians had, to a considerable degree, nullified Israel's technological superiority with Soviet-supplied air-defence systems and their armies had a new grit and determination instilled in them through a training regime designed by Soviet advisors. However, Sadat's limited strategic objectives meant that Egypt failed to exploit Israel's weakness of fighting on two fronts (in Sinai and on the Golan); once Israel had completed its counter-attack against the Syrian advance, her forces were then thrown against the now stationary Egyptian positions (Stein 1999: 74–5). The Arab successes were short-lived. Israel counter-attacked, held the Syrian forces, and even managed to push back the Egyptian forces across the Suez Canal and then occupy its western bank.

While Israel had technically 'won', the myth of the invincibility of the Israeli army had been shattered by the Arab forces' lightning attack. Furthermore, Sadat had succeeded in ending the stalemate that had had such a negative impact upon Egypt's domestic conditions, with the USA itself keen to open discussions about returning territory taken in 1967. Henry Kissinger, now US Secretary of State and National Security Advisor, brokered negotiations between Israel, Syria, and Egypt which saw agreement reached over an Israeli pullback on the Golan Heights and in the Sinai (Smith 2005: 228). Israel, even if able to claim a victory of sorts, was profoundly shocked by the fact that it had very nearly suffered a catastrophic defeat, and fears were again raised about the vulnerability of Israel and the threat of annihilation that was still perceived to hang over the the Israeli nation. For new Israeli Prime Minister Yitzhak Rabin, faced with this sudden exposure of Israel's vulnerability, the idea of withdrawing from the Golan Heights and the West Bank was simply not an option, irrespective of what UN SCR 242 required or Kissinger expected. Instead, Rabin sought to remove from the equation the threat posed by Egypt, which would thereby allow pressure to be exerted upon Syria and Jordan. Therefore this strategy meant negotiating with Sadat.

The road to Camp David: explaining Egypt's disengagement

At first sight, it would seem unlikely that a leader like Anwar Sadat would negotiate with Israel—after all, Sadat's sentiments towards Israel were well known and deeply rooted. Therefore the question to ask is: Why did Egypt, under Sadat, undertake a **policy shift** (Holsti 1982) *vis-à-vis* Israel after the Yom Kippur War? Why did Egypt make a distinct departure from the Arab policy of 'no recognition, no negotiation, no peace', to recognizing, negotiating, and then making peace with Israel? In so doing, Sadat eradicated any claim to Arab unity in the struggle against Israel, or towards supporting the Palestinians. The disengagement of forces and normalization of relations proceeded throughout the 1970s and culminated with a visit by Sadat himself to Jerusalem in 1977, and then the signing of the Camp David Accords in 1979.

There is no single explanation that satisfactorily accounts for Sadat's policy shift. The conventional approaches focus upon cognitive, class, and structural explanations (Karawan 2005). The first of these consider the person of Sadat, and how considerations of his own identity somehow fed into the overall foreign policy decision-making process of the Egyptians. Exponents of this explanation contend that Sadat saw himself principally as an Egyptian, rather than as an Arab, which gave him the flexibility necessary to negotiate a settlement in the interests of Egypt rather than following the more absolute requirements of the pan-Arab movement. The explanation is persuasive when the situation is considered from the perspective of the man himself, who reflected that '[i]t is not conceivable that the fate of my country should be dependent on the consent of other Arabs' (Dishon 1978: 13–15). Yet Sadat's change of mind seems convenient, particularly when his previous position of refusing to negotiate with Israel under any circumstances is taken into account.

The second of the 'conventional' explanations focuses upon class-based politics within Egypt itself. This explanation places the demands of Egypt's expanding bourgeoisie centre stage and contends that, as a 'hegemonic class block', they brought about a policy shift that maximized their class interests by realigning Egypt with the USA (Amin 1985; Imam 1986; Karawan 2005). However, this explanation oversimplifies the nature of economic development in Egypt, particularly in terms of its portraying the middle class as a hegemonic actor. Furthermore, in keeping with the practice of authoritarian regimes, the levers of economic development in Egypt were very much in the hands of the regime, and not elsewhere within financial or mercantile circles. Hence, it is unlikely that a bloc capable of influencing foreign policy so profoundly that had not been created by the regime itself could emerge within Egyptian society.

The concluding part of the trio of conventional explanations focuses upon the involvement of external powers, and particularly upon Egypt's need to comply with US strategy. This explanation places centre stage the desire of the USA to end the Arab–Israeli dispute, which it wished to do in order to promote its economic interests in the region. In this scenario, US support for Israel, the manipulation of Sadat by the CIA, and US influence on the actions of the International Monetary Fund (IMF) in Egypt all served as tools to push Egypt into effecting a policy shift (Karawan 2005). However, while such explanations are attractive, particularly to those who favour interpretations that illustrate the omnipotent presence of the USA in the affairs of the Middle East, they do perhaps give too much credence to the efficacy of broad policy strategies pursued by outside powers. The exercise of such leverage by the USA would have required considerable penetration of the Egyptian economy, which was simply not the case in the 1970s (Karawan 2005: 327).

No single reason adequately explains why Egypt changed its policy toward Israel following the Yom Kippur War. Rather, it is likely that some amalgam of the three explanations formed a context within which Sadat's course of action became perceived to be the most advantageous for Egypt at that particular moment in time. Sadat, faced with considerable socio-economic problems within the state and keen to exploit the advantages gained during the military actions of 1973 that could see a re-alignment with the USA, chose to pursue an 'Egypt-first' policy at the expense of Arab unity. It is only conjecture, of course, but while it does not answer conclusively *why* Egypt disengaged from the Arab–Israeli Conflict, it does at least emphasize the multifaceted pressures that influence foreign policy decision making, particularly in highly volatile situations.

One contextual factor should be seen as crucial when viewing Egypt's policy shift, and it is common to all the above explanations. The regime needed to contain threats emerging towards it from *inside* Egypt. In other words, the foreign policy shift was driven by the domestic need to maintain the regime. By far the most problematic issue for Sadat to tackle was that of poverty in Egypt's urban centres, which would lead to an associated expansion of Islamist movements. Sadat's foreign policy shift was successful in two ways. First, it allowed him to claim victory for regaining control of Sinai. Second, it normalized trade with Israel and the USA and saw the IMF grant loans to the government, thereby lessening the socio-economic problems afflicting the majority of Egypt's population. The policy also had a further beneficial domestic aspect as it allowed the military budget to be cut, with resources again refocused on alleviating socio-economic problems. If the period between 1974 and 1979 is considered, the financial benefits of the foreign policy shift are clear to see: military expenditure (relative to GNP) declined from 52.4% in 1975 to 13% in 1979, US aid rose from $250 million in 1974 to $2.2 billion in 1979, and revenue from the Suez Canal and oil rose from $0.8 billion in 1974 to $3 billion in 1979 (Karawan 2005: 332; see also Aly 1988: 65). The results of these huge influxes of revenue were improved employment, reduced socio-economic tensions, and, ultimately, improved regime security.

Egypt's final disengagement from the Arab–Israeli Conflict came about following the failure of the USA to broker a final solution to which all Arab states and Israel would subscribe. With the election of Jimmy Carter as US President in November 1976, a new approach was pursued which was to find a comprehensive solution to the conflict, rather than the approach pursued by Kissinger of seeking to build confidence through a series of agreements of limited scope. By definition, such a solution would have to identify a solution to the underlying problem of the Palestinian question. On this task, the conference ultimately failed. The PLO could not accept any solution unless the Palestinian right to statehood was agreed beforehand—something that the USA could not support because of Israel's objections. This obdurate Israeli position was further strengthened by the rise of the right-wing Likud Party and Rabin's replacement by Menachem Begin—a figure who had continually advocated the need for Israel to invade the West Bank in order to fulfil the Zionist goal of governing the land of ancient Israel (Smith 2005: 229).

For Sadat, however, the notion of remaining hostile to Israel because of the PLO was no longer acceptable. Instead, he remained committed to pursuing a policy which would disengage Egypt from a conflict that, with the ascension of Begin, looked as if it had every potential to become even more destabilizing. On 9 November 1977, the Egyptian President announced that he would be prepared to visit Jerusalem in search of peace, if an invitation was extended to him by the Israelis. Within the same month, Sadat was in Jerusalem to begin negotiations that would lead to him and Begin signing the Camp David Accords on 17 September 1978, followed by the Egyptian–Israeli peace treaty of March 1979. The treaty returned Sinai to Egypt, but brought with it vociferous criticism of Egypt from Arab states who believed that Egypt's accommodation with Israel would allow the latter to consolidate its hold over other territories occupied in 1967, and to pose a far more dangerous threat to the states still confronting her.

This 'cold peace' remained in place until the fall of the regime of President Mubarak in 2011. The weakening of the regime's grip on Egyptian society allowed the murmurings of discontent concerning Egypt's relationship with Israel to grow into vocal demonstrations, spurred on by the involvement of groups such as the Muslim Brotherhood, with anti-Israeli slogans being a common feature of the demonstrations across the country. The situation moved from being vocal to being violent in August 2011 when Egyptian-based guerrillas undertook several attacks against a range of targets in southern Israel, killing six civilians, a soldier, and a policeman. The situation deteriorated further following the killing of five Egyptian soldiers by Israeli soldiers pursuing guerrillas over the border. By the end of August 2011, the relationship between Cairo and Tel Aviv was at its lowest ebb since the end of the Yom Kippur War over thirty years before. Diplomatic relations were broken following the storming of the Israeli embassy in Cairo in September, resulting in the evacuation of the Ambassador and his staff. As post-Mubarak Egypt struggles to satisfy the demands of the wider population, and with the Egyptian economy showing no indication of improving in the near future, the EU and USA remained keenly aware of the possible trajectories that Egypt could take in the future—including further revolution and the possible emergence of political forces, whether from the Muslim Brotherhood, nationalist groups, or the military, none of which would have an immediate or obvious interest in re-establishing the truce with Israel which had been a cornerstone of Middle East politics since 1979.

Foreign policy thematics

The narrative of the Yom Kippur War and the subsequent disengagement has raised several issues relating to the foreign policies of Egypt and Israel, in particular, in an attempt to build an understanding of why certain foreign policy actions are taken when contextual and/or historical circumstances suggests that different courses of action were more likely or more appropriate. The environment in which Egypt and Israel constructed their foreign policies is multilayered and fiendishly complex, yet some themes remain clear to see.

Contextual complexity

Perhaps most obviously, the wider Arab–Israeli Conflict illustrates the **power of symbolism** and the ties of religion and ethnicity in foreign policy construction, even when states may not be affected directly by the 'core' dispute (the Palestine–Israel conflict over territory) itself. Furthermore, the case study illuminates the complexity of considerations that may underlie foreign policy decisions. The relationship between the Arab–Israeli Conflict and the foreign policy orientations of Middle East regional states was and remains far from straightforward. The displacement of Palestinians from territories west of the Jordan to the attenuated territories of the West Bank and Gaza, or into neighbouring Arab states such as Jordan, Egypt, or Syria, or further afield into a global diaspora presented complex dilemmas for Middle East states. For Arab states, it was not simply a case of supporting, or being seen to support, the Palestinians in their struggle against invading Zionists. They also had to find ways of managing refugees in their midst who threatened to destabilize their own often fragile regimes. Furthermore, they also had to identify strategies by which the USA, with its strong and deep-rooted support of Israel, could be engaged without empowering, or legitimizing further, Israel itself. For Israel, the problem was not simply one of securing the state against Palestinian groups. It was one of existing in an environment of enemies, speaking words of annihilation that struck deep in the collective mindset of a people traumatized by the Holocaust.

The 'localization' of foreign policy

Within the wider Middle East, the regional security system became dominated totally by considerations regarding the presence of the Israeli state. Israel's foreign policy was, and remains, wholly concerned with the absolute primacy of its national security (Heller 2000: 14). From the perspective of Israelis, with their historical memory reaching back millennia to include the enslavement in Babylon by Nebuchadnezzar, to the state-sponsored violence committed against Jewish communities in Europe during the nineteenth century, and culminating with the Holocaust, there exists a 'profound sense that at any given moment, the Jewish people may be annihilated' (Gordon and Arian 2001: 199). This sense is so deep that it indelibly colours Israeli foreign policy making.

Meanwhile, foreign policy concerns in Arab capitals were of a distinctly different nature to those that were occurring in Israel. While Arab capitals spoke seemingly in unison against the presence of Israel, a difference needs to be recognized between what Shlaim (1996) refers to as the 'rhetorical and operational levels of Arab foreign policy'. For Arab states, the 'official' rationale for the conflict with Israel was one of defending Arab nationalist pride. But each Arab state also had its own less publicized reasons for opposing Israel. Arab regimes, in states emerging from under the shadow of colonial masters who had only recently departed into a new and uncertain post-colonial age, enjoyed only precarious levels of internal stability and popular legitimacy. Challenges existed from Islamists, communists, other political movements (such as Ba'athism), and groupings within the military establishment itself. Combined with these internal problems of stability was an Arab 'regional' geopolitical competition, itself a reaction to the effects of imperialism that remained all too raw. By the mid-twentieth century—just as Zionism was succeeding in carving out its territorial manifestation in Palestine—Arab nationalism had emerged as the major political force in the political life of Arab states. The presence of the new Israeli state provided regional Arab states with a focal point for action, and success against Israel, in the name of the deposed Palestinians, would equate to that state being able to claim the accolade of being at the vanguard of Arab nationalism.

The 'theory of surprise'

In terms of analysing foreign policies, the Yom Kippur War opens a window onto one of the most challenging problems foreign policy makers have to contend with—and one that academics struggle to incorporate into their theoretical models. This problem relates to the specifics of the operational environment in which decision and policy making takes place, and why policies are followed that run counter to the information available at the time. In what Michael Handel, in a study addressing Israeli policy making, refers to as 'the theory of surprise', he notes that '[i]n almost all cases of strategic surprise, intelligence officers familiar with surprise theory and decision makers who had in their possession all the necessary data failed to arrive at the correct conclusions' (Handel 1977: 462). Therefore the problem is not necessarily one of *not* having enough information on which to make a decision, but failing to act upon the information available, with 'noise' prevailing over 'signals', 'inertia' over 'openness', and 'wishful thinking' over 'realism' (Wasserman 1960: 156–69; Wohlstetter 1962). At repeated intervals, and especially with reference to Israeli policy, we see examples of the 'theory of surprise' in action.

Inertia in foreign policy

In some quarters of the defence analysis community, Israel is admired. It is admired for the manner in which its armed forces are trained and the ruthlessness with which they go about their business. Indeed, if the professionalism of the military is to be judged, then there would be few militaries in the Middle East or globally that could match the standing of the IDF. However, the example of Israel also illustrates that military might is not everything. Israel has suffered many setbacks and problems since its inception in 1948, and these can be traced to considering future scenarios by the evidence of what has gone before. Of course, this tendency is common to governments the world over, and not just in the foreign policy sphere, but it is particularly telling in the case of Israel's foreign policy as the stakes for the state are so high. A pattern can be seen, from 1948 through to the most recent Israeli invasion of Lebanon in 2006 (see Hilsum 2006), whereby the readiness of the armed forces, and the outlook of foreign policy makers, view current events through the lenses of lessons learnt from the most recent conflict rather than basing policies upon analyses grounded in a realistic analysis of the contemporaneous facts.

This pattern begins in 1948, with an Israeli military victory achieved against seemingly overwhelming odds. The result certainly buoyed the Israeli military and political establishment, but it also imbued it with a heightened fear and mistrust of Israel's Arab neighbours. This outlook was largely responsible for the rapid expansion of the Israeli military and the political desire to secure the state, through war if necessary. With so many potential conflict triggers in place, it was only a matter of time before Israel reacted with overwhelming force against the combined Arab armies of Egypt, Syria, and Jordan in the summer of 1967, when President Nasser of Egypt sent troops into the Sinai Peninsula in May, and Syria became involved in skirmishes with Israel earlier in the year (Smith 2005: 224). With vastly superior air capabilities, the Israelis destroyed the opposing armies in a rout that was so complete that a new air of superiority—perhaps of complacency—replaced that of fear which had previously reigned within Israeli defence and foreign policy circles. But this complacency almost led to the destruction of Israel in the war of 1973. Even when Israeli intelligence could see the mobilization of the militaries of Arab states, the government still refused to act on the information that had been assembled. Following the Yom Kippur War and the subsequent disengagement with Egypt, the nature of the Arab–Israeli dispute changed significantly, as Arab states realized that without Egypt no meaningful 'regular' military threat could be assembled that had a chance of defeating Israel. There-fore, Arab and Islamic states—most notably Syria, Iraq, and Iran—increased their spon-sorship of non-state actors in Palestine and Lebanon, meaning that groups such as Hizbollah, Islamic Jihad, and Hamas took up the struggle against Israel. Even though the nature of the threat had changed, Israel continued to view regular military might as being its main defensive tool, leading it into two disastrous invasions of Lebanon in 1982 and 2006 (see Box 21.4).

BOX 21.4 The Arab–Israeli Conflict beyond 1979

1981	Israeli pre-emptive strike against Iraq	Israeli airforce attacks Iraq's Osirak (Tammuz) nuclear reactor near Baghdad.
1982	Israeli invasion of Lebanon	PLO units based in south Lebanon had opened attacks against Israel, with IDF units responding. Israel invaded Lebanon in June, reaching Beirut and placing it under a blockade. IDF combined forces with Christian Phalangists against PLO and Lebanese National Movement. PLO evacuation to Tunis, followed by massacre of Palestinians by Israelis and Phalangists at the Sabra and Shatilla refugee camps.
1982–2000	Israeli occupation of Lebanon	Israeli occupation of southern Lebanon. Israeli retreat hastened by Hizbollah actions.
1987	First *intifadah*	Mass Palestinian uprising lasting until 1993. Over 1000 Palestinians killed.
1991	Iraq attacks Israel	Saddam regime of Iraq launches 39 SCUD missiles at Israel in a bid to provoke Israeli response.
1993	Oslo Accords	Signing of the 'Declaration of Principles' in Oslo between PLO and Israel.
1994	Jordan peace treaty	Peace treaty signed between Jordan and Israel in October ending hostilities.
2000	Al-Aqsa *intifadah*	Deterioration following the failure to implement the Oslo Accords.
2010	Arab Spring in Tunisia	Demonstrations in December 2010 lead to the overthrow of President Ben Ali in January 2011, as the first episode in the Arab Spring.
2011	Arab Spring in Egypt	President Hosni Mubarak resigns on 11 February following nationwide protests.
2011	Arab Spring in Syria	Demonstrations commence in March. Ongoing in autumn.
2011	Palestinians demand statehood	Palestinian leader Mahmoud Abbas submits bid to UN General Assembly in September, demanding recognition of a Palestinian state. Opposed by Israel, and vetoed by the USA.

Conclusion

This chapter has exposed at least some of the reasons why Egypt and Israel pursued the foreign policies they did between 1967 and the end of the 1970s. The struggle in which the two were embroiled—the Arab–Israeli Conflict—was one of the most destabilizing in the world at that time, with a multitude of dynamics making the stakes for the combatants of such a nature that defeat could equate to either absolute destruction (in the case of Israel) or regime change (in the case of Arab states). This makes the policy decisions of Israel in 1973 and Egypt all the more surprising, at least at first glance.

The case study of the Yom Kippur War of 1973 illustrates that foreign policy decisions are not always dictated by logic or by the facts. Even when Egypt's military posture had turned distinctly threatening, with its president openly speaking of retaking Sinai, and its military reorganizing and re-training with advanced equipment, Israeli policy makers remained distinctly uninterested in the notion of launching a pre-emptive attack, as they had done so successfully only six years previously. Why this was the case is not difficult to answer, with a collective complacency following a spectacular victory being largely to blame, in addition to an 'institutional' inflexibility of successive governments and policy makers to react to situations that they have not planned for in the time frame available.

An analysis of the post-war period, in the remainder of the 1970s, illustrates that foreign policy does not have to match the sentiments of a country's rhetoric. Primarily for domestic socio-economic reasons, Egypt withdrew its support of the wider pan-Arab nationalist ideal. It then managed to carve out a peace agreement with Israel that resulted in the rest of the Arab world treating Egypt as a pariah, but that ultimately benefited Egypt (and the ruling regime) through the improvement of its economy and the wider support it received from the USA and other Western powers.

The case study also sheds light on the multilayered nature of foreign policy problems, and the intricacies of making sense of the foreign policies of a range of actors. Especially in this period of as yet unclear change being brought about by the Arab Spring and the realignment of the politics of the Middle East, the interplay of the national interests of states inside and outside the region, combined with the pressure brought to bear on regimes by domestic populations which may have radically different outlooks (and this refers to the USA as much as it does to Egypt and Israel), (in)security in the Middle East is clearly a subject that remains as critical to global security as it was during the Yom Kippur War.

 Key points

- Although they are related, there is a difference between the Arab–Israeli Conflict and the dispute between Palestinian Arabs and Israeli Jews. While the latter is often used as a pretext for actions taken by Arab states against Israel, and vice versa, the causes behind conflicts such as that of 1973 are often distant from resolving the Palestinian question.

- The 1973 War can best be understood as a product of the Six-Day War of 1967, in terms of both how Israel viewed her neighbours and how Egypt in particular chose to redress the strategic imbalance produced by the war.

- States do not always act rationally, even when aware of situations developing around them. The Israeli government was aware of the threat and capabilities of Egypt in particular in 1973, yet did not respond to this.

- Egypt's support of a pan-Arab position proved to be less important than the need to manage domestic pressures. The 1973 War was as much about allowing the Egyptian government to manage its domestic concerns as it was about redressing the strategic balance with Israel.

- Israel's overwhelming security outlook remains dominated by its fear of existential threats. This is rooted in ancient as well as modern Jewish history and continues to condition Israel's posture today. However, 1973 proved that Israel suffers from problems of policy inertia as much as other states.

- Although the 1973 War was a 'regional' conflict involving two neighbours, the role of superpowers (and especially the USA) remained crucially important. It was US actions that led Egypt into believing that it needed to attack Israel in 1973, and then to distance itself from other Arab states in the post-war period.

 ## Questions

1. Is it possible to explain Israel's foreign policy outlook by reference to existential threats?

2. Why were Arab states so determined to remove the state of Israel from the map of the Middle East?

3. What do you think were the policy objectives of the Egyptian government in attacking Israel in 1973?

4. How satisfactorily does the notion of 'inertia' explain Israel's failure to respond to the threat posed by Egypt and Syria from 1972 onwards?

5. If you were the prime minister of Israel following the events of 1973, how would you view Israel's position in the region, and how would you choose to respond to the threat ranged against you?

6. If you were the leader of a neighbouring Arab state following the events of 1973 (for example, King Hussein of Jordan or President Sadat of Egypt), how would you consider the security of your regime?

7. Can Israel's future only be secured by pursuing foreign policies built around pre-emptive or even preventive action, such as 1973 or the bombing of Osirak?

8. To what extent was the USA responsible for the outbreak of war in 1973?

 ## Further reading

Dowty, A. (2005), *Israel/Palestine* **(Cambridge: Polity Press).**
A recent account of the origin and history of the Palestine–Israeli dispute. Perhaps more sympathetic to the Israeli position, this remains one of the best short analyses available.

El-Gamasy, M.A.G. (1989), *The October War: Memoirs of Field Marshal El-Gamasy of Egypt.* **(Cairo: International Press). Translation of** *Mudhakkarat al-Gamasi: Harb Uktubar 1973* **(Cairo: American University of Cairo Press).**
Fascinating account written by one of the principle Egyptian architects of the 1973 War.

Lochery, N. (2000), *Why Blame Israel?* **(Cambridge: Icon Books).**
Pro-Israeli account of the position of Israel in the Middle East, and why Israel acts in the way that it does.

Pappe, I. (2004), *A History of Modern Palestine: One Land, Two Peoples* **(Cambridge: Cambridge University Press).**
Comprehensive history of modern Palestine.

Shlaim, A. (2001), *The Iron Wall: Israel and the Arab World.* **(New York: W.W. Norton).**
Perhaps the leading account of Israel's relationship with the Arab world.

Smith, C. (2010), *Palestine and the Arab–Israeli Conflict: A History with Documents* **(7th edn) (New York: Palgrave Macmillan).**
Highly detailed account of the Arab–Israeli Conflict, complete with important documentation.

Web links

www.chathamhouse.org.uk Royal Institute of International Affairs

http://www.tau.ac.il/jcss/ Jaffee Center for Strategic Studies

http://www.sis.gov.ps/english/index.html Palestinian National Authority information service

http://www.mfa.gov.il Israeli Ministry of Foreign Affairs

http://www.sis.gov.eg Egypt State Information Service

 Visit the Online Resource Centre that accompanies this book for more information:
www.oxfordtextbooks.co.uk/orc/smith_foreign/

22 Blair's Britain and the road to war in Iraq

TIM DUNNE

Chapter contents

 Reader's guide

This case study is about Blair's decision to go to war in March 2003: How did the then prime minister end up in a situation where he went to war without the backing of the UN Security Council and with his cabinet and the country being deeply divided? The narrative begins with the early policy statements of the first Blair administration (1997–2001), which raised expectations that the Labour government was about to plot a new course for Britain based around an internationalist set of commitments. The second part of the chapter considers the strategic dimension of the Blair effect: How far were the values consistent with Britain's status as a regional great power? Then, in the main body of the chapter, the explicit focus is on the diplomacy of disarmament inside the UN Security Council through 2002 and the wider impact that the Iraq War had on British domestic politics. In both domains, the government was unable to deliver on its promise to bridge the transatlantic divide that had opened up over Iraq. What influence did Britain exert on the course of events once it became clear that the USA was preparing for a military solution? And did the UK get a sufficient return for its risky decision to join the coalition of the willing?[1]

Introduction

In the days immediately following the attacks on the World Trade Center and the Pentagon, it became clear that Tony Blair had become a highly influential world leader. The *Washington Post* described him as one of the few political figures who, in these troubled times, had managed to break through 'the world's stunned disbelief' (Seldon 2005).

By late 2001, it did indeed seem that all was for the best in Blair's world: the government had just won a 167-seat majority in the general election; the economy was in robust shape and public services were beginning to get the investment needed to meet the public's expectations; the Prime Minister's grip on Parliament and his party was vice-like and the only 'opposition' he had to contend with was from his neighbour (and successor) in No. 11 Downing Street. As he delivered his 2001 Leader's Speech at the Labour Party conference, Blair's power was at its zenith. And his message? It was not the delivery of public services or the importance of being a player in Europe while retaining Britain's sense of identity. Instead, Blair led on the opportunities that 9/11 presented for a new world order. In a spirited oration, he concluded that, by harnessing the power of community, the time had come to 're-order this world around us'.

Looking back on Blair's decade in office, the obvious question is: 'Where did it all go wrong?' The one-word answer favoured by the media and large sections of public opinion is 'Iraq'. Blair's gamble was that, by giving unconditional support to Bush, he would be able to influence the course of American **grand strategy**. The key to managing the American response to the terror attacks was, he believed, to gain the backing of the UN Security Council (UNSC) as well as a wider coalition in favour of the wars against Afghanistan and Iraq. As America rushed to war in early 2003, the coalition was in tatters and Britain was virtually alone in providing significant military support to the USA in a disastrous campaign to remove Saddam Hussein and the Ba'ath Party from power. While that part of the mission was accomplished, the other stated goals of economic reconstruction and democratization appear more distant than ever. Many knowledgable practitioners were right to think that the situation was going to get worse before it got better, with 2007 as the low-point in terms of death and destruction.

There is a danger in thinking that Britain has *one* foreign policy. As Williams (2005) argues, there are several foreign policies covering a wide spectrum of issues and regimes. Nevertheless, while this point is well made, one of the intriguing aspects of the Blair decade was the emergence of a doctrine of **liberal interventionism**. Such a doctrine developed out of the quest for moral progress in a world in which there are many enemies of liberalism. In this respect, Iraq was not an aberration. The path to war was laid by missionary-like distinctions between moderate or fundamentalist religions, tolerant or despotic governments, societies committed to eradicating the threat of terrorism and those geared towards nurturing and protecting them. While many individuals and non-governmental organizations may have a great deal of sympathy with internationalist causes, the danger with trying to make the world a better place is that 'the tests are likely to be regular' (Freedman, cited in Seldon 2005: 303). Regular they were. In the Blair decade, British troops were despatched on enforcement missions to Afghanistan, East Timor, Iraq (the aerial bombings in 1998), Kosovo, Sierra Leone, and the Democratic Republic of Congo (a small contingent deployed in 2006).

To understand how the Iraq decision came about, it is necessary to turn the clock back to 1997. It is here that the 'mission' for UK foreign policy first saw the light of day. On 2 May 1997 the new Labour Foreign Secretary, Robin Cook, threatened an assault on the Foreign and Commonwealth Office (FCO) establishment. In a manner that came to symbolize Labour in power, Cook turned his opening speech about UK foreign policy into a media spectacle. The cameras were brought into the imperial chambers, the spotlights were turned on, and Cook delivered a 'mission statement' for the organization. Beneath the fanfare, many of his arguments resonated with the traditional pragmatism associated with the FCO such as the importance of national security and promoting economic goals. What sounded strange was the idea that Britain should have an 'ethical dimension' to its foreign policy. This Labour government, Cook went on to say, 'does not accept that political values can be left behind when we check in our passports to travel on diplomatic business'.

Unsurprisingly, the following day's newspaper headlines were dominated by the apparently novel idea that Britain was going to have an 'ethical foreign policy'. Notice that, already, the media had elided the difference between an ethical 'dimension' to foreign policy and an ethical foreign policy *per se*. No matter, Cook's phrase 'released a cosmopolitan genie from the official UK foreign policy bottle' and however hard his subsequent successors as Labour foreign secretaries tried—and Jack Straw certainly tried—they did not succeed in putting it back in (Williams 2005).

Blair was said to be annoyed that Cook's speech had been delivered without his knowledge of the content (Kampfner 2004).[2] Indeed, if you compare the Prime Minister's first speech on foreign affairs delivered at the Lord Mayor's banquet a few months later, there were important differences, not least in terms of the priority Blair assigned to the relationship with the USA (Blair 1997). Cook did not mention the Atlantic ally in the mission statement; Blair, on the other hand, described it as being of critical importance to British security and identity.

A great deal of the content of UK foreign policy over the ten-year period is prefigured in these two speeches by Cook and Blair. From the outset, it is clear that Blair intended to take a highly active role in foreign policy making. By putting ideas and values at the heart of British foreign policy, and hitching these to Britain's significant diplomatic and military power, the risks of costly entanglements were there from the beginning. The early speeches also reveal the tensions between wanting to be a 'good citizen' on the global stage by following the rules, yet at the same time pressing for solutions to intractable problems even if this meant acting outside the accepted norms of international conduct.

When the storm clouds were gathering over Baghdad, these tensions began to unravel. Ministers resigned, there were public rows with other European leaders, and poll data showed that a plurality of ordinary British voters opposed war without a second resolution and proof that Iraq was hiding weapons of mass destruction.

This chapter reconstructs the dramatic struggle the British Prime Minister was waging in order to ensure that the war was both lawful and attained a high degree of domestic **legitimacy**. To do this, the chapter poses a number of questions about the policy position taken by the UK government in the period from 9/11 to early 2003. Was Blair realistic in thinking that the military activism of the USA could be reconciled with the slow negotiations of the UNSC? Could the transatlantic rift have been anticipated? Most significantly of all, after a second UNSC resolution was not forthcoming, was Britain in a position to derail the American train from its rush to war? In persuading the British people—and his colleagues in Westminster—to join the US-led mission, what was Blair able to negotiate with the USA in return for this heroic (tragic?) act of loyalty?

It is impossible to answer such questions without engaging with ideas and theories found in the foreign policy literature. This is a case study which has **leadership** at the heart of the matter. There are two important dimensions to judging Blair's conduct. First, did he allow decision making to be adequately scrutinized by advisers or more broadly by governmental committees? Second, independently of the process of government, did the UK have sufficient international standing to make a real difference? The importance of this issue is such that the chapter begins with an analysis of **agency**, or the capacity of the state to mobilize power and resources to affect change in the world. Finally, to understand how it was judged to be in Britain's interests to go to war it is necessary to engage closely with the conception of a shared Atlanticist identity that was shaping perceptions at the heart of the Labour government (Dunne 2004). Viewing the bonds with America in these terms helps to explain why the Prime Minister did not extort a higher price for his loyalty.

UK foreign policy: agency and commitments

One of the first questions students of foreign policy need to address concerns the power of the actor in question. In the case of the UK, the answer to this question is not self-evident. Writing at the turn of the 1990s, Steve Smith rightly noted that the country defies easy classification into the kinds of categories favoured by foreign policy analysts (Smith 1991). These interdependences include membership of 120 international institutions (Williams 2005: 29), permanent membership of the UNSC, and one of the 'big three' states in the EU. Recognized membership of the nuclear club is also, some would argue, an indicator of high status in world politics. Yet, as we shall see below, Britain's capacity to get its way in the world is highly constrained.

Three faces of power

When Blair talked about Britain's capability he employed the useful term **pivotal power**. By pivotal, Blair meant a country 'that is at the crux of the alliances' that 'shape the world and its future'. Projecting the term into the language used in International Relations to categorize states, one could argue that pivotal powers claim the same rights and responsibilities as great powers, albeit in a domain that is restricted. Pivotal powers are regional great powers with the capacity to project their military forces in their near-abroad. This sets them apart from the category of middle powers who make no corresponding demand to be serious military players in their region. Examples of other pivotal powers include Australia, Brazil, Israel, India, Indonesia, Iran, France, Japan, Nigeria, South Africa, and Turkey.[3]

Even a realist would admit that **hard power** capability is only a necessary condition for influence—it is certainly not sufficient. Given the UK's relative decline as an economic and military power since 1914, an analysis which only addressed hard power would inevitably conclude that Britain is a significantly diminished player on the world stage. Historians of the decline thesis often point to the Suez crisis of 1957 as a symbolic moment when a once-global power realized it could no longer flex its military muscle without the support of the Americans.

While material power has been in decline since the Second World War, foreign policy traditionalists would claim that Britain has maintained its influence through the skilful mobilization of **soft power** resources (Nye 2004). These include the extensive diplomatic network; the wealth of experience in international relations that comes from being a former imperial power; the importance of London as a financial centre; the private school and university system which indirectly socializes many of the next generation of world leaders; the importance of English as a world language; and membership of powerful international institutions (the EU, the UNSC, NATO, and the Commonwealth). By pulling on the levers of soft power, Britain has been able to 'punch above its weight', to invoke Douglas Hurd's worn-out phrase.

Liberals are drawn to soft power levers just as realists focus on material or brute power. Constructivists, on the other hand, argue that the only durable way to get others to do what you want is to wield **legitimate power**. Coercion is costly in terms of human life and resources. Bribery is simply expensive and its results are short-lived. Stable compliance comes from locking others into a normative context that they believe to be morally right, thus shaping their identity and enabling a recalibration of their interests. It is hard to see how measures like the legalization of the Human Rights Act—during the first Labour government—helped to advance the national interest in a conventional sense. Instead, institutionalizing human rights principles was an indicator of the emergence of a social identity which owed more to social democratic values and less to an imperialist past. The fact that, post 9/11, many core human rights values have been under threat from the Labour government suggests that internationalist norms are not deeply embedded in the habits and practices of the British state (Dunne 2007).

Later in the chapter, it will be argued that the UK *could* have exerted considerable influence on the direction of US policy—thereby defying the 'poodle' image beloved by cartoonists (Figure 22.1).

The Prime Minister could have made a second UN resolution a red-line issue that the UK would not cross under any circumstances. Without a clear resolution which explicitly authorized military force to disarm Iraq, he could have pulled British forces out of the warfighting campaign while at the same time providing diplomatic and logistical support to the USA. Such a role was mooted by Secretary of Defense Donald Rumsfeld who, when questioned on 11 March 2003 about the difficulties the UK was having over Iraq, noted that the situation for the UK was 'unclear' and, if necessary, the USA would go it alone. The response from Secretary of Defence Geoff Hoon the following day was to reiterate the British government's commitment to forcibly disarm Iraq even without a second resolution. Would a better alternative have been to use Rumsfeld's intervention as a moment to pull British forces back from the brink of war, and to see whether others in the US administration bought the Defense Secretary's line that the USA could in fact 'go it alone'?

Goals and commitments[4]

The above discussion has focused on the many levers of power that the UK government is able to pull to effect change in world politics. What, then, of the goals that these capabilities are designed to deliver?

The first commitment underpinning Labour's strategic foreign policy goals is **multilateralism.** This goal has a principled as well as a prudential basis. Multilateralism is consistent with Labour's long-standing belief in internationalist values and the institutions which support them. Also, given the country's dynamic soft power capability, it made sense to harness the country's diplomatic resources in order to shape the rules-based international order.

Alongside multilateralism, and sometimes in tension with it, the Labour governments under Tony Blair (1997–2007) and Gordon Brown (2007–2010) demonstrated the clear view that the UK's interests were best served by maintaining a **special relationship** with the USA. Whether or not this sense of diplomatic intimacy is shared on both sides of the Atlantic is an

Figure 22.1 Tony Blair on a leash.

Source: www.CartoonStock.com

issue which historians have long contested: suffice it to say that there is far greater noise about the special relationship in Britain than there is in Washington DC. In the literature on the special relationship, it is possible to distinguish a narrow and a wide conception. The narrow view is based on close defence cooperation, including the sharing of weapons technologies and the pooling of information by the intelligence services of the two countries. The wide view goes beyond military cooperation—what defines the special relationship are the shared values and connected histories. What does this mean in terms of policy formulation? The degree of trust that the USA accords Britain is such that it enables the junior partner to exercise a degree of influence in return for its loyalty.

What is striking about the Atlantic alliance during the Blair years is the disjuncture between the extremely close personal relationship he established with George W. Bush—aided in part

> ## BOX 22.1 **Ending the special relationship the** *Love Actually* **way**
>
> Context: Press conference in 10 Downing Street after discussions between the new British Prime Minister and the President of the United States.
>
> [Question]. Mr President, has it been a good visit? [President]. Very satisfactory indeed. We got what we came for and our special relationship is still very special.
>
> [Prime Minister addresses question]. I love that word 'relationship'. Covers all manner of sins, doesn't it? I fear that this has become a bad relationship. A relationship based on the President taking what he wants and casually ignoring all those things that really matter to Britain. We may be a small country but we're a great one, too. The country of Shakespeare, Churchill, the Beatles, Sean Connery, Harry Potter. David Beckham's right foot. David Beckham's left foot, come to that. And a friend who bullies us is no longer a friend. And since bullies only respond to strength, from now onward, I will be prepared to be much stronger. And the President should be prepared for that.
>
> *Source*: Reprinted by permission of the Peters Fraser and Dunlop Group on behalf of Richard Curtis.

by the shared Christian convictions[5]—and the uncomfortable tensions which exist between their respective political parties. In the virtual realm, the YouTube sketch of the two leaders singing 'Endless Love' was much closer to the mark than the fraught Anglo-American press conference featured in the film *Love Actually* (see Box 22.1).

The third goal framing UK foreign policy was a commitment to **neoliberal** views of political economy. Internationally, this meant supporting the position on trade, economic development, and aid taken by key international institutions such as the World Bank and the World Trade Organization. From his earliest interventions in foreign policy, Blair took on board the realities of globalization and the need for the UK to steer a course between succeeding in the global marketplace while maintaining sufficient welfare provision to protect communities from the consequences of economic failure. Domestically, modernization meant applying a new regulative framework to the public sector, including the FCO and the Ministry of Defence (MoD). This prompted the former head of the diplomatic service, John Coles, to observe that 'the priority accorded to issues of management and administration detracted from the time ministers and civil servants had to engage in strategic reflection about foreign policy' (Williams 2005: 31).

Putting morality at the heart of British foreign policy remained a consistent commitment during the last decade. In the language used by Robin Cook in the 1997 FCO mission statement, he and the Labour leadership wanted a different kind of identity for Britain. Instead of being regarded as a declining imperial power which had little influence beyond the Commonwealth, Cook and Blair were agreed that Britain needed to become 'a force for good in the world' promoting human rights, tackling debt among the poorest nations, and supporting progressive multilateral initiatives such as the International Criminal Court and the Kyoto Protocol on climate change. The fourth framing commitment was, in other words, that Britain had to be a so-called **ethical state.**

The missionary-like commitment to promoting good over evil led the *Economist* to amend Dean Acheson's famous quip and reformulate it along the lines that Britain had indeed lost an empire but it had found Tony Blair (Williams 2005: 165). Behind the quip lies a serious point: the former prime minister was engaged with foreign policy issues from the outset despite showing little knowledge of, or interest in, world politics prior to 1997. This fact makes a

BOX 22.2 The ethical state debate

The altered language of foreign policy that accompanied the arrival of 'New Labour' in power generated a significant academic debate about the possibilities and perils of exporting ethics. Such claims provoked a backlash in the right-wing press who preferred the familiar path of the national interest. Former practitioners partly endorsed the idea that this was a risky strategy while at the same time implying, somewhat contradictorily, that the pragmatic approach associated with the tradition of the FCO had always sought to try and make the world a more civilized place.

The academic debate on the 'ethical foreign policy' took a different form. Early interventions concurred that the political debate was misconceived: all foreign policies are ethical in that they are driven by moral commitments. Recall how classical realists understood that the primacy of national security was, first and foremost, a commitment to the nation as the source of value. Even arch-pragmatists with their cost–benefit calculus are slaves of an ethical theory of sorts, in this case a crude form of utilitarianism.

While all agreed that the government had no choice but to have an ethical foreign policy, a significant chasm opened up in terms of evaluating whether or not they had made progress towards their stated goals. On one side were those who believed that states should strive to be 'good international citizens', but that this was often compromised by the fact of value pluralism and the degree of contestation over the meaning and priority accorded to principles of justice (Dunne and Wheeler 1999). A broad commitment to social democratic values in foreign policy does not provide a clear guide as to how to resolve a number of moral dilemmas. For example, does supporting equality entail privileging the substantive rights of individuals over the procedural rights of states? Or, under what circumstances are institutional inequalities reasonable—for instance, in the nuclear Non-Proliferation Treaty or in terms of the veto power of the five permanent members of the Security Council? One way to reconcile such tensions endorsed by advocates of the 'good state' is to allow governments to make decisions that are at odds with cosmopolitan values *only* when their vital interests are not threatened.

By engaging with the Labour government's declaratory policy, advocates of good international citizenship risked becoming apologists for those in power. Writers such as Mark Curtis adopt a more radical position: Britain is an 'outlaw state' and all claims to be ethical are a chimera. The truth, for Curtis, is that there was never an intention to chart an ethical course in British foreign policy (Curtis 2003). Elsewhere, he argues that 'violating international law has become as British as afternoon tea' (Curtis 2003: 7). Yet what critics never adequately appreciate is that international legal rules are enabling of certain policies thought to be unconscionable such as the arms trade.

mockery of the media line that the ethical foreign policy died a death when Robin Cook left the ministry at the end of the first Labour administration. Box 22.2 highlights the academic debate triggered by Labour's mission statement and the wider question about whether states can be progressive change agents in world politics.

Given these commitments, what was Britain going to do when brutal dictators such as Slobodan Milosevic decided to turn the brutish power of the state against a particular ethnic grouping among its own population? By early 1999, it was clear that the answer was that Britain was prepared to fight alongside NATO partners in a humanitarian war. Not only did the armed forces engage in the intense waves of aerial bombings, but in April 1999 Blair used an invitation from the Economic Club of Chicago to identify 'the circumstances in which we should get actively involved in other people's conflicts' (Blair 1999). The subtext of the speech was to remind the US political elite of their responsibility to act militarily when a humanitarian emergency was unfolding. (An excerpt from Blair's speech can be found in Chapter Twelve, Box 12.2.)

In today's world, the Prime Minister argued, countries 'fight for values, not for territory'. More precisely, he went on, we must be prepared to act forcibly when genocide or ethnic cleansing had occurred, when refugee flows threaten international peace and security, and to deal with 'undemocratic' and 'barbarous' regimes. Since **humanitarian intervention** breached the norm of non-intervention (article 2.4 of the UN Charter), Blair recognized the crucial significance of establishing a shared consensus about the determination of legitimate conduct. He came up with the following 'five considerations'.

1. Are we sure of our case?
2. Have we given diplomacy every chance?
3. Can military force be successful? Are there military options that are viable?
4. Are we in it for the long term?
5. Is our own national interest at stake?

This list chimes with a great deal of contemporary thinking on the just war doctrine (Walzer 1992). However, there is one important difference—nowhere did Blair admit the need for military action to have 'right authority' by which advocates of just war mean prior authorization from the appropriate international organization(s).[6]

The Kosovo case stimulated a heated debate about the former prime minister's crusading approach to international relations (Booth 2001). Internationally, it triggered a fierce argument as to whether humanitarian intervention can be regarded as a general right or duty (Wheeler 2000; Holzgrefe and Keohane 2003). The fact that China and Russia threatened to block a resolution legitimating armed intervention, was to Cook and Blair an 'unreasonable' use of their UNSC veto power. As Blair was to argue over Iraq, it would be wrong for the UNSC to be paralysed from acting simply because a permanent member took the decision to block the resolution regardless of its wording.

The road to war

Towards the end of his first term in office, Tony Blair had established himself as an important international statesman. Relations with other European states were more constructive than they had been during the previous four Conservative administrations. He had led the pro-intervention debate over Kosovo, and sought to galvanize world opinion around values of justice and fairness in relation to the environment and global poverty.

9/11 and the new world order

Then came 9/11. While the US President appeared uncertain as to how to respond to the attacks on the Twin Towers and the Pentagon, Prime Minister Blair instinctively found the right words to describe the shared sense of outrage and the concomitant duty to stand 'shoulder to shoulder' with the USA in its hour of need. For Blair, 9/11 had changed the terms of the debate about security threats: 'potential threats had to be dealt with before they became actual' (Freedman 2004: 38). Shortly after 9/11, Blair delivered one of his most powerful speeches on foreign policy at the Labour Party conference in Brighton. It advanced the idea of the 'power of community' both domestically and internationally. In a rhetorical flourish, the Prime Minister urged his party faithful to seize the moment: 'the kaleidoscope has been shaken. The places are in flux. Soon they will settle again. Before they do, let us re-order this world around us' (Blair 2001). Many critics pointed out that this level of normative ambition far outstripped Britain's capability to bring about those ends.

In the immediate post-9/11 period both Bush and Blair were strengthened domestically by their close cooperation on international issues. The US media increasingly viewed Blair as an important player in internal Bush administration debates about how to respond to the al-Qaeda attacks. As has been well documented (Woodward 2002), the period from 9/11 through 2002 saw the US position hardening on the need to eliminate the threat that Iraq posed. After the defeat of the Taliban, the neoconservatives increasingly viewed Iraq as the next front in the War on Terror.

Cheney and other leading neocons had hoped that Saddam Hussein would be overthrown in the period following the first Iraq War. Instead, the Iraqi President remained in complete control of the regime despite a highly intrusive monitoring of Iraqi military capabilities in line with UNSC resolution 687 of April 1991. This resolution linked a cessation of hostilities to the elimination of weapons of mass destruction (WMDs) and missiles with a range of more than 150 kilometres. The regime tasked with overseeing the policy of disarmament was the UN Special Commission (UNSCOM). From 1991 to 1997, UNSCOM uncovered significant stock-piles of chemical and biological weapons. By the end of 1997, this policy of containment combined with coercion (resolution 687 allowed 'all necessary means' to be used) was begin-ning to fray: Iraq was subverting UNSCOM's activities and leading states on the UNSC were increasingly unsupportive. One year later, the head of UNSCOM, Richard Butler, reported Iraq's continued non-compliance to the UNSC. Inspectors were withdrawn and the USA and the UK prepared for Operation Desert Fox—coordinated waves of air strikes against Iraqi mili-tary targets.

Well before the al-Qaeda attacks on America, the policy of containment and sanctions against Iraq was increasingly regarded as ineffectual and disreputable. As the President later observed, after September 11 'the doctrine of containment just doesn't hold any water' (Freedman 2004: 16). The agenda had moved on—prevention was the new strate-gic narrative. In this spirit, Vice-President Cheney formulated the so-called 'one percent doctrine' meaning that if there is only a one percent chance that the USA might be at-tacked then it has to respond militarily to such a potential threat (Suskind 2006). As Presi-dent Bush noted, 'facing clear evidence of peril, we cannot wait for the final proof—the smoking gun—that could come in the form of a mushroom cloud' (Freedman 2004: 17). Week by week, it was becoming apparent to decision makers in Washington and London that the policy of containment had to make way for a policy of removing the threat altogether.

2002 policy options

During the crucial twelve months after 9/11, Blair and his foreign policy team visited Bush and his administration on three occasions—Washington in September 2001, Crawford in April 2002, and Camp David in September 2002 (see Box 22.3).

BOX 22.3 The road to war: a timeline

2001

11 September 2001	American Airlines Flight 11 crashes into the north tower of the World Trade Center in Manhattan just before 9.00 a.m. Fifteen minutes later, United Airlines flight 175 hits the south tower.
12 September 2001	Bob Woodward, in *Plan of Attack*, notes that both Donald Rumsfeld (Secretary of Defense) and Paul Wolfowitz (his deputy) raised the issue of broadening the military response from al-Qaeda to Iraq.
28 December 2001	General Tommy Franks, head of US Central Command, briefs President Bush on Pentagon planning for the Iraq War.

2002

29 January	Bush's first State of the Union address lists Iraq as one of the 'axis of evil' who threaten world order through their attempts to acquire WMDs and who sponsor terrorism.
1 June	At an address given at West Point, Bush argued that 'shadowy terrorist networks' could not be deterred. For this reason, 'we must take the battle to the enemy, disrupt his plans, and confront the worst threats before they emerge'. Our security means we have 'to be ready for pre-emptive action when necessary'.
12 September	Bush goes to the UNSC and urges them to enforce Iraq's compliance with previous disarmament resolutions. If the UN was not prepared to act, it should stand aside as the USA acts.
22 September	Gerhard Schröder wins the German election on a platform of withholding German support for the war.
24 September	UK Government publishes dossier on Iraq's WMD capability. Dossier claims that Iraq could produce nuclear weapons within one to two years. Includes the claim that Iraq could launch chemical or biological weapons within 45 minutes of the order being given (see Box 22.4).
10 October	The US Congress authorizes Bush to use armed force against Iraq in order to (1) defend US national security, and (2) enforce all relevant UNSC resolutions regarding Iraq.
8 November	UNSC unanimously approves resolution 1441 countersigned by the USA and the UK. The resolution gives Iraq 'a final opportunity to disarm', warning that 'serious consequences' would follow if Iraq continued violations of UNSC resolutions.
18 November	Hans Blix leads UNMOVIC (UN Monitoring, Verification, and Inspection Commission) team back to Baghdad to start their mission.

(Continued)

7 December	One day before the UN deadline, Iraq deposits its 12,000-page dossier indicating it had disarmed.
19 December	Following concerns raised by both Hans Blix (head of UNMOVIC) and Mohamed El-Baradei (head of the International Atomic Energy Agency), US ambassador to the UN, John Negreponte, says that Iraq is in 'material breach' of 1441.
2003	
9 January	Blix reports to the UNSC that no 'smoking gun' had been found, though there were aspects of Iraqi non-compliance including disclosing the names of key scientists.
27 January	Sixty days after the resumption of inspections, Blix tells the UNSC that Iraq 'appears not to have come to a genuine acceptance' of 'the disarmament which was demanded of it'. There were gaps which Iraq ought to have resolved by now, but UNMOVIC's information is, according to Blix, too incomplete to conclude that Iraq possessed prohibited weapons.
28 January	President Bush gives his second State of the Union address. The speech claims that British intelligence reveals that Iraq recently acquired significant quantities of uranium from Africa. 'Trusting in the sanity and restraint of Saddam' is not an option and is not a strategy, Bush declared.
31 January	Meeting between Bush and Blair in Washington. Blair allegedly tells Bush he is 'solidly' behind US plans to invade Iraq despite doubts about the legality of such action expressed by the Attorney General.
3 February	A briefing document produced by No.10 staff sets out the 'concealment' charge against Saddam Hussein. Cambridge academic Glen Rangwala notices that large sections have been copied from a 2002 article published in *Middle East Review of International Affairs*.
5 February	US Secretary of State Colin Powell presents the US case against Iraq to the UNSC.
9 February	The French and German governments set out a proposal to increase the number of inspectors.
14 February	Blix reports that there continues to be more cooperation with the weapons inspectors in terms of 'process' than 'substance'.
15–16 February	Anti-war demonstrations in several cities around the world; one million in London and Glasgow organized by Stop the War Coalition.
1 March	Turkish Parliament votes to refuse the USA a base in southern Turkey from which it could launch a second front against the Iraqi army.
7 March	Blix and El-Baradei report that Iraqi cooperation had increased since January and that, for the remaining disarmament tasks to be met, the process will take several months. In the UK, the Attorney General presents equivocal advice on the legality of the war.

10 March	President Chirac declares that France will oppose any move within the UNSC to pass a resolution enabling war.
11 March	Secretary of Defense Donald Rumsfeld admits that the situation for the UK without a second resolution was 'unclear'. The implication was that the USA was prepared to go it alone.
17 March	The Attorney General gives his legal advice to the Cabinet stating that the war would be legal even in the absence of a second resolution.
	Robin Cook resigns from the government in order to distance himself from a war that lacked 'international authority' and 'domestic support'.
	Back in New York, the attempt to secure a second resolution authorizing force collapses when it becomes clear that there is no majority for such action in the UNSC and, if there were, France would use its veto.
18 March	Debate in the UK Parliament. The Prime Minister argues that 'our legal base' is disarmament as set out in 1441: 'I have never put our justification for action as regime change.' With the support of the Conservative Party, Blair defeats an anti-war motion. 139 Labour MPs voted for the motion and against the Prime Minister.
19 March	Operation Iraqi Freedom begins with decapitation strikes against Iraqi military targets.

At what point did Blair know that the USA had decided to take military action against Iraq? And crucially, when did he give an assurance to Bush that Britain would also participate in the ground offensive? What conditions were sought by British policy makers for this unstinting support?

No one is better placed to judge the timing of the British 'decision' than Christopher Meyer, the UK Ambassador to Washington throughout the diplomatic crisis. According to him it was during a series of meetings in 2002 that an understanding developed that the UK would participate in the coming war.[7] A key date in this respect concerns the meeting between Bush and Blair in Crawford, Texas, on 6 April 2002. Classified Cabinet Office documents leaked to the press record that Blair told Bush at the Crawford meeting in April that:

> The UK would support military action to bring about regime change, provided that certain conditions were met: efforts had been made to construct a coalition/shape public opinion, the Israeli–Palestine crisis is quiescent, and the options for action to eliminate Iraq's WMD[s] through UN weapons inspectors had been exhausted (Meyer 2005: 246).

In a speech the following day given in the Presidential Library at Texas A&M University, the Prime Minister set out his unflinching support for the US position. When America is fighting for democratic values 'we fight with her', Blair said.

Given how critical UK support was for the American-led war, this was a moment to put the special relationship to the test. To what extent did the diplomacy over Iraq illustrate that London was able to exert 'influence' over Washington in return for fighting 'with her'.

Which of the 'conditions' noted by the UK Ambassador were met and which were side-lined? Of the three conditions, gaining UNSC backing was the most significant in the eyes of the British executive. Blair and his team of advisers threw their diplomatic weight behind an initiative to multilateralize the decision-making process. Going through the UNSC would be deemed reasonable by most world leaders—the heavyweight neocons in the Bush administration did not see it this way. It had become a *leitmotif* of their cause that America does not need anyone's permission before it uses military force. In order for Blair's initiative to work, he had to bolster the more moderate voices in the administration, such as Secretary of State Colin Powell, who were up against the powerful neocon grouping in the Pentagon (supported by Cheney).

The British government have tried to take the credit for persuading Bush to go the UN route. However, according to Meyer, a private meeting between Powell and Bush on 5 August appears to have been 'decisive' (Meyer 2005: 250). Either way, the multilateral preferences of the State Department and the British government had prevailed over the Cheney–Rumsfeld preference to keep the UN at arm's length.

At the strategic level, Blair saw the issue in plain terms: commit the military to the forcible removal of Saddam Hussein or allow the USA to go it alone. As is often the case in international politics, neither choice was without significant costs. A war of regime change would be fought in the teeth of international and domestic opposition. Allowing the USA to go it alone undermined the bilateral relationship which had been the key-stone of UK foreign policy for most of the post-1945 period. Blair concluded that join-ing the US-led war was the right path to follow, and that decision was endorsed by Parliament.

Were these the only policy options? Would it have been possible to defer a decision to sup-port the USA militarily until Blair was certain that there was wide international support for such action? If this support was not forthcoming, could the UK have opted out of the decapi-tation phase while offering significant military assistance in the reconstruction phase? Experts located in Washington think-tanks argued that there was a window of opportunity for the UK to explore an alternative policy. This window was opened up when Rumsfeld let slip, on 11 March, that the British position was 'unclear' and that America was becoming impatient with the endless rounds of diplomacy in New York.

'Britain opting out', noted Ken Pollock from the Brookings Institute, 'would have radically changed the course of the war' (interview, 6 June 2007). The timing of the war would, in his view, have been slowed down. Moreover, the likelihood of Italy and Spain joining the coali-tion of the willing would have been very remote without at least one of the 'big three' being on board. It is even conceivable, Washington insiders claim, that in the absence of military support from Europeans—allied with the refusal of Turkey to allow its bases to be used—the USA might not have have been prepared to 'go it alone'. The damage such untrammelled unilateralism would have done to transatlantic relations would be a cause for concern even among the neocons.

While it would have been diplomatically very difficult for Britain to change tack as late as March 2003, the multilateralists in the British and US governments should have bargained harder. The combined power of Powell in the State Department and Blair in Downing Street was enough to insist that the administration engage in more robust planning for the post-war reconstruction and stabilization phase of Operation Iraqi Freedom.

Inside the UNSC

There followed frantic months of diplomatic negotiations in order to come up with a Security Council resolution (UNSCR) that was both robust and fair, such that it could retain the support of all permanent and non-permanent members on the Council. UNSCR 1441 stipulated that Iraq must comply with previous Security Council resolutions and disarm. If it failed to do so 'serious consequences' would follow. To establish whether Iraq had taken up the final opportunity to disarm, the Security Council mandated an inspections team (UNMOVIC) to be sent to Iraq to intrusively monitor Iraq's WMD capability.

How far was the UK 'condition' of allowing inspectors to assess Iraq's compliance or non-compliance met? There is no easy answer to this question as there were too many ambiguities in the process. Was the mission of the inspectors to find whatever capability Iraq had, or to verify the Iraqi disclosure demanded by 1441? If nothing was found, does that mean that Iraq has fully disarmed, or cleverly concealed its stockpiles? And if the inspectors deemed Iraq to be in partial compliance, would this be a reason for peace or war? Was a follow-up resolution required before military action could be taken?

In the aftermath of 1441, the greatest risk lay with the possibility that the inspectors' reports would become the site of a battle between the coalition of the willing and the coalition of the unconvinced. Was it ever realistic to think that any empirical claim, or even proof, as to what capability Saddam possessed would be evaluated according to the same criteria? Such a conundrum was encapsulated in Donald Rumsfeld's dismissal of cautious UNMOVIC reports: an 'absence of evidence', he argued, was not the same as 'evidence of absence'.

Ambiguities about how to interpret what was 'there' were heightened by the radically opposed understandings about what 1441 permitted if WMDs were found. For the USA and the UK, UNSCR 1441 was a 'trigger' resolution, meaning that if Iraq was found to be in 'material breach' of the resolution, war would follow. Other members of the Security Council took a different view. Evidence of WMD capability suggested that the inspections were working, and that the inspectors should be given more time to finish the job. Decision makers in London and Washington viewed further rounds of inspection as a return to the failed policy of containment. The truth was that no evidence was going to be regarded as neutral by either the USA–UK axis or France–Germany–Russia (the so-called *non-nein-nyet* states) and the rest of the Security Council. War remained a possibility even if Iraq responded to 1441 by disarming and asking the Americans to take 'yes' for an answer.

Spinning the threat

Apart from scrutinizing the **special relationship**, the road to war raises important and controversial questions about the 'reality' of the threat posed by Iraq, how this was sold to the British public, and the processes by which intelligence estimates were mobilized in favour of the line being taken by Blair internationally. As we have seen, the former Prime Minister ultimately made the case for war on the basis of Iraq's capability *and* the fact that there was good reason to impute an intention on the part of Saddam Hussein to threaten international peace and security. Indeed, given that the military action was in part justified by prevention, it was vital that the public understood the nature of the threat and why the coalition of the willing had to act.

In September 2002, members of Blair's inner circle—including his press secretary Alastair Campbell and one of the Prime Minister's foreign policy advisers David Manning—published an assessment of 'Iraq's weapons of mass destruction'. Several times, including in the foreword by Blair, the dossier noted that Iraq's WMDs could be ready to deploy 'within 45 minutes of an order to use them' (UK Government 2002: 4). This claim became notorious for two reasons.

BOX 22.4 The 45-minute claim

It would be naïve to expect politicians to be indifferent to the possibilities of shaping public opinion. In his biography of Blair, Anthony Seldon refers to his 'hubristic belief' in his own powers of persuasion (Seldon 2005). The September 2002 dossier on *Iraq's Weapons of Mass Destruction* illustrates the difficulty of staying on the right side of the line between persuasion and propaganda. As a former chair of the Joint Intelligence Committee, Pauline Neville-Jones, put it, 'the dossier required the JIC to shift from evaluating to make that case' (Freedman 2004).

At the outset, one of the difficulties with the dossier is that its ownership is obscure. The report draws on a variety of intelligence sources, including the Secret Intelligence Services (SIS), the Government Communications Headquarters (GCHQ), the Security Service (MI6), and the Defence Intelligence Staff (DIS). The heads of these various agencies sit on a key Cabinet Committee called the Joint Intelligence Committee (JIC) chaired by Sir John Scarlett. The committee provides advice and analysis to the Prime Minister on a range of international issues and concerns.

The foreword to the September dossier was written by the Prime Minister, though the original draft was by Alastair Campbell. It contained 'the 45-minute claim' which was repeated a further three times in the document, despite being based on only a single uncorroborated source (para. 70, Foreign Affairs Committee, June 2003). The following day, newspaper headlines drew the inference that Saddam Hussein could launch strategic chemical or biological weapons with in 45 minutes. Yet the intelligence assessment of Iraq's WMD capability referred only to battlefield weapons. This initial omission—and subsequent failure to clarify—generated a misleading impression.

On 29 May 2003, the BBC *Today* programme ran an interview with its security correspondent Andrew Gilligan. In the course of a short two-way conversation with John Humphrys, Gilligan alleged that an 'intelligence source' had claimed that the September dossier had been 'sexed up' to make it less equivocal. He highlighted the 45-minute claim as a basis of concern among the intelligence community. Gilligan's source was David Kelly, an MoD adviser on biological weapons and expert on Iraq's capability. Kelly had met Gilligan but denied commenting on the 45-minute claim. No.10 and the MoD were keen to 'out' the source in order to bolster their own credibility. The process by which this occurred was unfortunate: the media were not told the source for Gilligan's story but instead were allowed to guess the person's name. The combination of the allegations laid at Kelly's door, the lack of protection given to him by the MoD, and the intense media pressure, were all contributing factors to him taking his own life on 17 July 2003.

The public outcry created by his death led the Prime Minister to set up an inquiry into the circumstances that had brought it about. The Hutton Inquiry had narrow terms of reference: 'The question of whether the information in the September dossier was unreliable was an irrelevance; if the JIC had approved and the government believed it was reliable, then it could be taken as reliable by the inquiry' (Doig 2005: 117). Hutton concluded that the document had not been 'sexed up' and that the 45-minute claim had not been inserted by the Prime Minister's press secretary Alastair Campbell. Following the publication of the inquiry, Gilligan resigned as did Greg Dyke, the Director-General of the BBC.

On 12 October 2004, UK Foreign Secretary Jack Straw told the House of Commons that the head of M16 had withdrawn the 45-minute claim.

First, it later transpired that the dossier did not stipulate that this applied to battlefield weapons which could not have an offensive capability. Second, when doubts about this claim were aired by a BBC journalist, a major confrontation began between the BBC and the government, a battle whose significance was heightened by the tragic death of the WMD adviser Dr David Kelly who had been an MoD employee. (See Box 22.4.)

The errors underpinning the presentation of the 45-minute claim were not the only examples of the misuse of intelligence information. In February 2003, a second dossier was published with the aim of providing Parliament and the British public with 'further information' about, in the Prime Minister's words, 'the infrastructure of concealment'. The document had not been cleared by the Joint Intelligence Committee (JIC) or the FCO. It included text taken from an article by Dr Al-Marashi without his permission either being sought or granted. In its July 2003 report, the Foreign Affairs Committee noted that the effect of the dossier was to undermine the credibility of the government's case for war.

Alastair Campbell later confirmed to the Select Committee that the February dossier had been a 'cock-up' and that he had apologized to the Chief of the Secret Intelligence Service and the Chair of the JIC. The embarrassment of the February dossier did not shake the Labour leadership's unstinting belief that Saddam Hussein had WMDs and that either the UNMOVIC inspectors would find the weapons *or* he was engaged in an elaborate process of concealment. As the former Prime Minister told the House of Commons on 5 February 2003, 'it is perfectly obvious that Saddam has them' and that he was refusing to put them beyond use.

Not everyone who saw the intelligence information agreed with Blair. Robin Cook, leader of the House of Commons during the build-up to the Iraq War, had access to the intelligence reports produced by the JIC. Cook was sceptical that Iraq constituted a current and serious threat to UK national security; in fact, he believed that Saddam had no 'usable' WMDs. The French President, who was also sceptical of the case, admitted that his intelligence services also had estimates of Iraq's WMD capacity though he chose not to attach too much credibility to these sources. Instead, he followed Clausewitz's dictum that 'many intelligence reports in war are contradictory; even more are false, and most are uncertain' (Jervis 2006).

Long after the cessation of the ground offensive, the quest for proof that the weapons existed took another twist. In June 2003 a US-led team was despatched to search for the WMDs that UNMOVIC failed to locate. Months later, David Kay, the head of the group, told a US Senate hearing that his survey group had not uncovered any stockpiles of WMDs. In a devastating appraisal of the intelligence information, Kay noted that 'we were almost all wrong'. Contrast this with the confidence prior to the war expressed by CIA leader George Tenet who sought to reassure the President with the phrase it was 'a slam dunk case'. In spinning the threat in late 2002, Bush and Blair had left themselves exposed to the charge that they sold their publics a false prospectus for war.

Explaining the errors

In the last instance, the British public ought not to have been surprised that Tony Blair tried to persuade them of the 'fact' that the Ba'athist regime in Iraq posed a threat to its people, to the region, and potentially beyond. All attempts to avert a *potential* threat require strong and persuasive rationales. The question, in this case, is whether the Prime Minister and members of his inner circle of advisers and officials misrepresented intelligence assessments as though they were the same as threat assessments (Freedman 2004: 36). The insertion into the September dossier that Iraq's threat was 'serious and current', and the many expressions of certainty that Iraq *had* WMD capability, implied that these claims were securely grounded in intelligence information. They were not. Even if there was no intention to deceive, as the Prime Minster persistently reminds the British public, this was a significant failure of leadership.

The extent to which the intelligence community in the UK were complicit in this process needs to be considered. There existed inside the secret intelligence service a preconceived belief that Saddam had sought WMDs before the Gulf War and tried to develop them afterwards; therefore rational and coherent. Into this general hypothesis, various details from Western intelligence agencies were inserted. Each new piece of information 'that *could* be interpreted as showing that Iraq had active programmes was interpreted in this way' (Jervis 2006: 22).

Besides the tendency to join up the dots in the intelligence information that fitted a preconceived picture, the information presented to decision makers was inadequately scrutinized. There was an active search for leads that confirmed the existence of WMD capability and intent, and there was a downplaying of negative evidence. Critics of the intelligence community argue that they allowed their work to be politicized; the more cautious charge made by Hans Blix was that there was a 'deficit of critical thinking' on the part of the intelligence agencies (Blix 2005).

This deficit came about because of **groupthink**. In its original academic formulation (Janis 1982), groupthink captures the tendency for tightly knit groups to seek converging opinions and approval. Members of the group avoid challenging the consensus, preferring to adopt strategies of affirmation. Evidence that groupthink was operational in this case can be gleaned from the carefully worded conclusion of the Hutton Inquiry that the Prime Minister may have 'subconciously influenced' those drafting the document with his request for a document that was 'consistent with the available evidence' but at the same time was 'as strong as possible in relation to the threat' (Freedman 2004: 27).

The tendency of decision makers to seek convergence is such that all governments need institutional mechanisms and procedures in which unity can be punctured and criticisms can be ventured. Cabinet committees exist to provide this scrutiny. Unfortunately, under Blair, both the full cabinet and the committees were stripped of their power. In place of the formal committee structure, Blair preferred an informal style of leadership based around a charmed circle of advisers holding meetings in the 'den' at No.10. Minutes were seldom taken. Often individuals would not be present for the entire meeting. The casual politics of the 'denocracy', as Seldon calls it, explains how it was that the Attorney General's advice on the legality of the war was never put before a full cabinet meeting. Evidence gathered by the Hutton Inquiry provides further weight to the view that formal government processes were not operational through 2002 and early 2003.

The disunity over the interpretation of 1441 ramped up the need for a second UNSC resolution which unambiguously declared that Iraq had not taken the final opportunity to disarm and that 'all necessary means' were now required. It was also made apparent to Tony Blair in a memorable live BBC *Newsnight* broadcast that a second resolution would go a long way towards tempering domestic concerns about the impending war. When the US President understood the dilemma his friend faced, he was prepared to override Cheney and others who were opposed to going for a second resolution. To which Bush replied: 'if that's what you need', we will 'go flat out to try to help you get it' (Seldon 2005: 590). Whether this was in fact the case has been doubted by British writers. Either way, when it became clear that France and Germany were not going to support regime change, the USA and the UK regrouped outside the Council, declaring that it was them and not their opponents who were acting in support of the United Nations.

Back in London, the Chief of Defence staff needed a ruling that the war was legal. Previous advice given by the Attorney General indicated that a second resolution was vital in order to dispel doubts about the legality of war. Despite the collapse in negotiations in New York, the Attorney General revised his opinion and gave military action his cautious support. In a secret memo of 7 March 2003, he noted that 'a reasonable case can be made that resolution 1441 is capable of reviving authorisation in 678 without a further resolution' (Goldsmith 2003). This prompted the immediate resignation of the deputy legal adviser to the Foreign Office, Elizabeth Wilmshurst. In her words, 'an unlawful use of force on such scale amounts to the crime of aggression'.

The former Prime Minister's apparent willingness to countenance war where the legal basis is doubtful is one of the most damaging aspects of the case. However, it is overshadowed by the charge that Blair held a strong diplomatic hand during the crisis but played it poorly. Efforts to multilateralize the conflict came to a halt by about December 2002 as the US government had already decided that Iraq was in 'material breach' of disarmament resolutions. Yet, even as it grew more likely that the coalition of the willing was going to be a narrow one (in the sense of significant troop deployments), Blair still had a final card to play: he should have coordinated more closely with Colin Powell to ensure that a higher priority was placed upon post-war planning.

Conclusion

This chapter has considered the choices made by the Prime Minister Tony Blair as the storm clouds gathered over Iraq between 9/11 and early 2003. Controversy over the decision still rages, as the oral evidence surrounding the Chilcot Inquiry makes clear (see 'Further reading').

The framing question underpinning this case study has been why Blair pledged his active support for military action (including the issue of the timing of this support). One answer, familiar to historians of the special relationship, is that Blair was looking to influence the Americans. Having a seat at their table gave him an opportunity to reinforce the State Department's preference for building a broad coalition prior to military action being taken. Bush's decision to go the UN route was a partial victory for British diplomacy—it was, after all, one of the 'conditions' for ensuring we would be standing side by side when the shooting started. It was only partial for the reason that the divisions between France, Germany, and the USA proved unbridgeable.

Britain's second condition—bringing back weapons inspectors—backfired spectacularly. A leaked confidential Downing Street memo of 23 July 2002 records the Foreign Secretary's view that the intelligence case was 'thin'. From that moment on, it was vital that the intelligence case became sufficiently robust to deliver domestic and international support for the war. As it turned out, allegations that Iraq posed a threat to its neighbours and to regional and international security proved as unpersuasive to President Chirac as it did to large sections of the UK public.

While the intelligence condition backfired, the third—the Middle East roadmap—was still-born. The position of both George W. Bush administrations was consistently hostile to the idea of an independent Palestinian state, while supporting the Israeli programme of building settlements on Palestinian lands. It was never realistic to believe, as Blair hoped, that a solution to the Palestinian problem was important to the USA. This prompted the British Ambassador to Washington to ask, incredulously: 'when is a condition not a condition?' (Meyer 2005: 247).

Beyond the Atlantic alliance, what was the Blair effect on British foreign policy? The humanitarian disaster created by the Iraq War buried any credible claim for Britain being a good international citizen, despite the leadership Blair and his successor Gordon Brown showed over debt relief for the poorest African nations. It is unlikely that Britain can rebuild itself as an ethical state until it shows fidelity to the rules and institutions of international society. The power of community, so valued by Blair, means following the rules even when these are potentially at odds with your strategic vision. Far from re-ordering the post-9/11 world along progressive lines, the Blair effect in foreign policy was to lend legitimacy to US interventionism as well as fanning the flames of instability and injustice in the Middle East.

 Key points

- The arrival of the Labour government in May 1997 suggested the possibility of a new course for UK foreign policy, particularly in relation to the 'ethical dimension'.

- Continuities with previous governments remained, however, particularly in relation to the importance the UK Prime Minister attached to the special relationship.

- From post-9/11 to March 2003, it became clear that many of the goals pursued by Britain were in tension with one another. Following a brief moment of unity in the Security Council in November 2002, a division opened up between Britain's European allies and the USA.

- The government, reflecting the strong convictions of the Prime Minister, has been committed to an interventionist foreign policy over the past decade.

- The policy choice made by Blair was to stay close to the USA in order to ensure that the world's hegemonic power went the UN route. This was initially a success. But by March 2003, the UNSC was unable to agree a second resolution and the war was fought without explicit authorization.

- Blair's two other conditions—to ensure that intelligence information is public and convincing, and that the US administration takes seriously the need for progress on the Palestine–Israeli crisis—were not met.

- Were there other choices that could have been taken? As the US position hardened at the end of 2002, the Prime Minister should have coordinated more closely with the US State Department such that more attention was given to post-war planning.

- When it became clear, in March 2003, that the USA was past the point of no return in terms of war planning, the UK should have remained on the sidelines in the absence of a second UNSC resolution. At best this might have prevented the war altogether; at worst, it would have slowed the timetable for war. Set against this, if the USA went alone, the implications for future transatlantic relations could have been very negative.

 Questions

1. Knowing that your key ally had decided to go to war, if you had been Prime Minister, would you have taken the same strategic decision? If not, evaluate the likely consequences of your chosen path.

2. What are the key commitments underpinning UK foreign policy during the Blair decade? Are they coherent?

3. Does Britain have to choose whether it is to be intimately connected with either the USA or Europe?

4. What does the Butler Inquiry tell us about the use of intelligence assessments by the UK government as the storm clouds gathered over Iraq? What does the Chilcot Inquiry tell us about the legal arguments presented by the Attorney General (Lord Goldsmith) and how these impacted upon the Blair government's policy options?

5. How far has 9/11 changed the calculation of risk in terms of potential threats to national and international security?

6. Has Blair been the 'foreign secretary' throughout his premiership? Is such involvement of the executive in international affairs routine or anomalous? Evaluate the advantages and disadvantages of prime ministerial activism in this domain.

7. Why do states find it so hard to practise ethical statecraft? Is the failure rooted at the individual level (leadership), the state level (nationalism), or the international level (the problem of anarchy)?

8. Where do you think Britain falls on an analytical continuum with 'outlaw state' at one end and 'ethical state' at the other?

 Further reading

Curtis, M. (2003), *Web of Deceit: Britain's Real Role in the World* (London: Vintage).
Takes a highly critical view of Labour in power, showing the negative humanitarian impact of the arms trade and other pro-capitalist initiatives pursued during the Blair decade.

Freedman, L. (2004), 'War in Iraq: Selling the Threat', *Survival*, 46: 7–50.
A comprehensive and measured article on the intelligence debate leading up to the war.

Goldsmith, P. (2003), 'Iraq: The Legal Case', *Guardian Unlimited*, 25 April 2007.
Advice on the legality of the war given by the Attorney General on 7 March 2003.

Hill, C. (2003), *The Changing Politics of Foreign Policy* (Basingstoke: Palgrave Macmillan).
The best single authored work on foreign policy; examples are frequently drawn from the British case.

Kampfner, J. (2004), *Blair's Wars* (London: Free Press).
A lively account of Blair's military interventions. The narrative very much takes the line pursued by Robin Cook.

Lawler, P. (2004), 'The Good State: In Praise of "Classical" Internationalism', *Review of International Studies* 31: 427–99.
An excellent account of the theoretical issues at stake in the ethical foreign policy debate.

Meyer, C. (2005), *DC Confidential: The Controversial Memoirs of Britain's Ambassador to the U.S. at the Time of 9/11 and the Iraq War* (London: Weidenfeld & Nicolson).
An extremely lively and readable account of Blair and his team during their many visits to Washington.

Ralph, J. (2010). 'After Chilcot: The "Doctrine of International Community" and the UK Decision to Invade Iraq', *British Journal of Politics and International Relations*, 13: 304–25.

Seldon, A. (2005), *Blair* (London: Free Press).
An outstanding biography—draws on a phenomenally large range of sources (kept confidential).

Williams, P. (2005), *British Foreign Policy Under New Labour 1997–2005* (Basingstoke: Palgrave Macmillan).
An unrivalled account of UK foreign policy during the first two New Labour administrations.

Wheeler, N.J. and Dunne, T. (2004), 'Moral Britannia? Evaluating the Ethical Dimension in Labour's Foreign Policy', Foreign Policy Centre paper.

 ## Web links

There have been three government-led inquiries into Britain's role in the Iraq War.

http://www.the-hutton-inquiry.org.uk The Hutton Inquiry was tasked with investigating the death of scientist Dr David Kelly.

http://www.archive2.officialdocuments The Butler Inquiry was set up to investigate the accuracy of intelligence on Iraqi WMDs.

http://www.iraqinquiry.org.uk/about.aspx The Chilcot Inquiry (or Iraq Inquiry) had a broader remit to focus on policy. It considered the UK's involvement in Iraq to establish 'what happened and to identify the lessons that can be learned'. Witness testimony was broadcast live over the internet and the transcripts used here are available on the same website.

 Visit the Online Resource Centre that accompanies this book for more information:
www.oxfordtextbooks.co.uk/orc/smith_foreign/

23

Energy and foreign policy: EU–Russia energy dynamics

AMELIA HADFIELD

Chapter contents

 Reader's guide

This chapter examines a sector that has long been vital to the progress of human society but has only recently come to prominence as a foreign policy factor. Energy represents a source of control for those capable of accessing and selling it, a security issue for both suppliers and buyers, and a foreign policy tool wielded by state actors. While energy has the capacity to maintain stability and generate interdependence between exporting and importing states, the January 2006 'gas spat' between Russia and Ukraine demonstrates energy's ability to generate deep insecurities between sovereign and commercial actors, and in the process reshape the geopolitical terrain of the developed West and key actors on its peripheries.[1]

Introduction

Energy security appears to be something of a new addition to the foreign policy agenda. However, natural resources have long enjoyed a history of influence, stimulating the expansion of European power, provoking state rivalries in the form of 'resource wars', and generating geopolitical structures of power, war, and trade. In developing countries, such as Sierra Leone and Nigeria, access to natural resources like oil and diamonds has produced scarcity and bloodshed. In more developed actors, like Canada, the US and Norway long-term access to reliable energy resources has increased the level of political, economic, and societal progress, but it has also highlighted the vulnerability in their dependence upon natural gas and oil, and underlined energy as a strategic resource. Therefore the significance of natural resources is 'largely rooted in the political and economic vulnerabilities of resource dependent states' (Le Billon 2004). As will be seen, **energy dependence** can take many forms.

Natural resources possess particular geographic, historic, and even social attributes which shape their role in the social practices of peacetime and direct their use in times of war. The value placed upon a resource like oil is as much a social construction as a market indicator. As such, energy products operate on a wide spectrum of material and constructed understandings, combining the practical issues of access with perceptions of vulnerability and sensitivity that are inherent in the politics of access. This combination, plus the unequal distribution of energy reserves across the globe, is what makes energy a strategic resource.

Before accepting energy as a foreign policy factor, two aspects need to be considered: first, the inherently sovereign attributes of energy; second, energy's ability to dramatically transform the fortunes of states. Tackling the former, it is clear that energy resources are a strategic *national* asset, consolidating the domestic and foreign status of a given state. This is because energy resources are inherently **territorialized**, meaning that they constitute the very material of a country, giving greater definition to both the physical contours and political boundaries of a state. In addition, the revenue raised by the sale of energy exports usually outweighs that of any other national industry. Politically and economically, energy raises a number of 'sovereign stakes' regarding its ownership, access, transport, and sale. As such, both muscular petro-states and hyper-dependent countries (the 'haves' and the 'have nots') are compelled to rank energy policy highly within their sovereign prerogatives. Natural resources are capable of providing states with internal order and external influence, and thus are a source of relative power. Built into the fabric of modern state infrastructure and quintessential to international political economy, energy has emerged as both a foreign policy issue and a foreign policy instrument that states are prepared to use in pursuit (or defence) of their national interest.

Second, states run serious risks in becoming dependent upon the role that natural resources play in raising or diminishing national revenue. If energy resources are well managed, as with exporter states like Norway, Qatar, and Canada, the significant revenue raised from their sale can usually be reinvested for the benefit of the state. However, the poor management of energy resources can produce a number of damaging trends, including commercial mismanagement and radical privatization or nationalization of parts of the energy industry, as with Russia and Venezuela. Alternatively, rampant corruption by governments or extortion by local militia can provoke small- and large-scale strife (or 'petro-violence'), as in Nigeria, Sudan, and Colombia. For many countries, plentiful energy resources have been a curse rather than a blessing (Yergin 1991).

All states now face precisely these same issues of sovereign assets, commercial access, and increasing dependency (upon supply or demand). As Robert Skinner describes it:

> The global energy supply system is a vast, inertia-ridden complex of large, fixed assets that take years to plan, sanction and construct, and they tend to be in place for decades. This long-term business must operate within a political context manifestly driven by short-term concerns and developments. Government policies affect energy supply and demand, but not as quickly as politicians might like . . . governments tend to be slaves to the 'urgent' rather than to the important, where urgency is largely determined by special elites and interests (Skinner 2006: 2–3)

In an attempt to find solutions, energy issues have gradually featured as foreign policy issues on both sides of the Atlantic, and elsewhere. Yet 'who' is actually acting when it comes to energy? Essentially, responsibility for energy is divided between the public and private sectors. In the public sector, this includes governments and state energy enterprises owned or controlled by governments. In the private sector, this includes private companies (e.g. BP, Royal Dutch Shell, Total, Q8, Exxon Mobil, Texaco). In addition, there are a few international organizations, representing exporters (OPEC), importers (IEA), and some representing both (European Commission, Energy Charter Conference, WTO). For foreign policy students, this means incorporating a new group of foreign policy actors, which effectively widens the foreign policy terrain. Alongside traditional state actors (themselves divided into exporters, importers, and transit states), energy policy is affected by non-state actors from both the public and private sectors. Taken together, the foreign energy policies of states are a complex mix of 'national interest' of the public sector and 'business interests' which may not always sit easily within the national goals of a given state.

Nowhere are the *dramatis personae* of energy more confusing than in the EU itself. **Competence** (authority) over energy issues is divided between the European Commission and EU member states. As of 2009, the European Commission has competence in issues where energy relates to external and internal trade, environmental requirements (climate change and sustainable development), and various aspects of competition (anti-trust) and aspects of investment, Member states dominate other commercial aspects, including investment. In days before the gas spat, the uneasy division of labour between the Commission and Member States led some observers to suggest that sourcing of their energy supplies and most crucially their choice of energy mix and the uneasy division of labour between Commission and member states suggests that as a whole 'the Union suffers from having no competence and no community cohesion in energy matters' (Commission of the European Communities 2000: 28). However, with the Sept 2011 Commission strategy, entitled 'The EU Energy Policy: Engaging with Partners Beyond our Borders' entitles the Commission to Scrutinize, and possibly negotiate energy security contracts entered into between MS and third parties. Change in this area was sparked by the shock of the January 2006 gas stoppage which compelled European actors to consider the possibility that energy security may require a collective solution. More recently, as noted by Jan Frederik Braun, 'a conspicuous change in European primary law has been the inclusion of a specific chapter on energy' (Braun 2011) (Box 23.1), Art. 194(1) of the Treaty on the Functioning of the European Union (TFEU or 'Lisbon Treaty'), which establishes the four main aims of the EU's energy policy:

- to ensure the functioning of the energy market;
- to ensure the security of supply in the EU via increased solidarity;
- to promote energy efficiency, energy saving, and to develop new and renewable forms of energy;
- to promote the interconnection of energy networks.

The role of energy in foreign policy

Before exploring the key details of the case study at hand, a few final points remain in order to place energy correctly within the dynamics of foreign policy. First, what is the role of energy

BOX 23.1 Energy provisions in the TFEU (Lisbon Treaty)

The main aims of the Ell's energy policy, including a functioning energy market, enhanced energy security, energy efficient, emphasis on renewables and the interconnection of energy networks, as stipulated in Art. 122(1) of the TFEU, are to be executed in a spirit of solidarity, whereby :

> [w]ithout prejudice to any other procedure provided for in the Treaties, the Council, on a proposal from the Commission, may decide, in a spirit of solidarity between the Member States, upon measures appropriate to the economic situation, in particular if severe difficulties arise in the supply of certain products, notably in the area of energy.

On the one hand, this provision confirms the Union's competence to adopt preventive measures to avoid security threats and may provide a basis for political backing for more far-reaching preventive measures in the future. However, with no legal obligation on the member states, solidarity remains weak. A prime example in this regard is Regulation No. 994/2010/EU on the security of gas supply that was adopted at the end of 2010. This Regulation was proposed largely in response to episodes like the Ukraine–Russia dispute, where the solidarity aspect had to be improved. While leading to a more harmonized and consistent implementation of measures for the security of gas supply and to a higher degree of preparedness in most member states, it achieves little regarding solidarity amongst the member states beyond what could already be done on a voluntary, bilateral basis.

Besides being a dedicated title in the Treaty, energy constitutes a horizontal policy issue. In this regard, the EU's energy policy is a component of other policy areas, such as:

- *foreign policy* (e.g. linked to technological innovation and developing long-term relationships with supply and transit countries through a 'package approach');
- *environment/climate change* (e.g. a key element in reducing CO_2 and stimulating investments in renewables);
- *competition* (e.g. access to affordable energy resources for ensuring the international competitiveness of European industries).

Despite its cross-cutting sectoral nature, the legal base used for negotiations in the Union's external dimension of the energy policy formally falls within Art. 194 of the TFEU. Yet there still seems to be a certain ambiguity about which Treaty legal base to use in external action on energy and where to draw the line in the mix of the competences of the EU and the member states. Moreover, this is accompanied by a rather hybrid negotiating format.

Source: Braun, J.F. (2011), 'EU Energy Policy Under the Treaty of Lisbon Rules Between a New Policy and Business As Usual, European Policy Institutes Network, Working Paper 31, February 2011' (http://www.epin.org).

within domestic and foreign policy? Simply put, energy indicates national prosperity and underwrites national security. States now desire energy security in the same sense that they desire military and economic security. **Energy security** can be understood as 'assurance of the ability to access the energy resources required for the continued development of national power . . . and adequate infrastructure to deliver these supplies to market' (Kalicki and Goldwyn 2005: 9). On closer inspection, one sees that energy security means different things to different actors. For the majority of importer states in Europe, energy security means **security of supply**, in which the consistent delivery of affordable energy sources is paramount. For exporter states like Russia, **security of demand** requires access to a developed and reliable market for the long-term sale of energy products (Hadfield, in Bisley and Beeson, 2012). For

---

BOX 23.2 Security of supply: all in your head?

The phrase 'security of supply' embraces a hard and a soft concept: the economic fact of a quantity of a good or service delivered at a price and the psychological notion of security, which is a feeling . . . One country can be entirely dependent in imports yet feel secure. Another can rely only partly on imports yet feel this constitutes a major vulnerability. Supply quantity and the degree of dependence can remain unchanged, yet the feeling of insecurity can increase or decrease with time. It becomes clear that the particular political relationship between the trading parties defines the sense of security of that trade . . . It might be concluded based on recent developments that one of the sources of insecurity is the rhetoric and signals from political leaders and how the media portrays these. (Skinner 2006: 6).

---

both sides, energy assurance can be swiftly undermined by price shocks and unexpected reductions or stoppage of supplies (see Box 23.2).

Second, what are the main concerns of states when energy features in their foreign policy? States have *economic concerns* about maintaining supply and demand between exporters and importers respectively, and attempt to minimize any energy disruptions or shortages on the premise that such energy shocks could undermine their economic well-being. In addition, states have *political concerns* about the potential leverage exercised by exporter states over both importer states and **transit states** (countries across whose territory energy is transported) due simply to their dominant position as energy suppliers. Political and economic concerns about the supply and demand of energy resources are strongly connected. Anxieties over political leverage often spill over into discussions about security of supply; debates about reliable buyers and sellers are frequently couched in the language of foreign policy leverage. Students of foreign policy should not be surprised at the complexity or content of such disputes, as states frequently 'use the instruments of economic policy to pursue political objectives as well as economic ones' (Bayne and Woolcock 2003: 11). What is surprising is that states themselves have been caught on the back foot in appreciating the role of energy as a salient foreign policy issue, and for the most part have been unhurried in concocting solutions to address both the economic and political components of energy security.

Third, accepting that natural resources form part of the raw material of national power, we need to determine the various functions of energy as a foreign policy tool. Christopher Hill suggests that the foreign policy instruments available to policy makers are the combined result of resources, capabilities, and varying levels of power and influence available at a given time. These instruments can be ranked on a **continuum of power**, a spectrum denoting the actual 'means' that a state can use to achieve its desired ends (Hill 2003: Chapter 6; see also Chapter Eight of this volume). As will be explained, energy can feature in a variety of places on this continuum, from the hard edge of physical coercion to the softer features of political culture and diplomacy.

As a foreign policy tool for exporters, energy frequently takes the shape of diplomacy (OPEC), embargos (Organization for Arab Petroleum Exporting Countries in 1973), and in some cases coercion (Russia). For importers, energy is rather different. Without the existence of natural energy resources, importers lack the specific leverage that comes with possessing vast supplies of gas and oil. However, importers do possess large markets, without which the reciprocal exporter–importer relationship would quickly founder. For importers, energy has been used in pursuit of soft power objectives, as with the EU's recent overtures to members of the Commonwealth of Independent States (CIS) and less successfully to Russia. It has also operated as the hard edge of political sanctions (Iraq) and economic embargoes (Iran). Ultimately, when market incentives fail or are threatened significantly, energy can feature as a proximate cause of fully fledged military presence, including the USA's historic and recent activities in the Middle East and Persian Gulf.

The present case study examines the foreign policy decision by Russia in 2006 to stop the flow of natural gas to the Ukraine and the serious impact this had on Europe. If the overall impact of the decision can be said to have had a 'targeted, coercive, often immediate and physical' impact, then the stoppage of gas is a good example of energy hard power. Alternatively, the stoppage may have been used by Russia as a form of diplomatic compellence after previous negotiations had failed. Or, like the EU's own approach, the decision could have been taken to induce change that was ultimately 'indirect, long-term . . . [operating] more through persuasion than force' (Hill 2003: 135). All these possibilities will be considered in greater detail.

Accepting that energy influences foreign policy is a good first step. But then what? For foreign policy makers, the question is not merely an appreciation of the multisectoral nature of energy as a policy area, but its placement within the sequence of national interests and its ability to mediate the overall foreign policy stance of the state or region. As US analysts have recently pointed out, 'energy policy is an important goal in its own right, but it becomes critical when viewed against the broader canvas of foreign policy and economic development' (Kalicki and Goldwyn 2005: 14).[2]

Energy in post Cold War reform

The break-up of the Soviet Union was instrumental in realizing the foreign policy potential of energy in Europe. It was also crucial in underwriting Europeans' ambitions to construct a common European energy policy, with internal and external components.

The original European initiative was one of deep engagement with Russia in order to minimize the potential political chaos and economic disarray emerging from the collapse of communism in Eastern Europe. Focusing on Russia, the newly emerging CIS, and especially the Central and Eastern European (CEE) states in between, the EC used a mixture of economic and political support to diminish incidences of post Cold War instability, assisting their gradual emergence into the structure of democratic capitalism (Haggard and Moravcsik 1993). Urged on by a newly unified Germany, and despite the misgivings of Britain, the EC elected to deal with its new neighbours using multilateral projects in which economic aid would ensure that political reforms would be both multisectoral and permanent. As the catalyst of such reforms, Russia was the EC's main focus and in 1989 received a full 30% of EC aid.

Multilateral aid schemes for Central and Eastern Europe included PHARE in 1989 (Pologne, Hongrie Assistance à la Reconstruction Economique) and TACIS in 1991 (Technical Assistance to the CIS). Launched by the EC and the European Bank for Reconstruction and Development, these projects represented the EC's first decisive engagement with Eastern Europe and Russia in the post Cold War era. TACIS, with its wider geographical coverage and substantial aid package, operated as a vehicle for broad East–West regional reform, committing €4221 million to Russia and the CIS states between 1991 and 1999 (see TACIS Home Page, Europa Website). As well as issues of nuclear safety, the Regional Cooperation Programme of TACIS focused on the access and transit of energy, through the INOGATE energy initiative (Interstate Oil and Gas Transport to Europe).[3]

INOGATE's central goal was largely technical in nature. Drawing upon comprehensive Western investment and the provision of targeted technical assistance, it aimed to overhaul ageing ex-Soviet transmission systems in order to help support the regional integration of pipeline systems between east and west, and ultimately to guarantee a reliable supply of oil and gas to European markets. Indirectly, INOGATE served as a catalyst for stimulating private investment to support Europe's vast energy infrastructure. Western European energy companies did indeed demonstrate interest in the investment opportunities presented by ex-Soviet energy industries, hoping to capitalize on their dramatic restructuring from state control to private commercial entities. However, INOGATE could not provide a sufficiently robust forum to deal with the multitude of legal and regulatory issues that had arisen in the wake of increased Russian gas exports penetrating the European energy market.

The European Energy Charter (EEC) was signed in 1991 to help set the political context of tackling East–West energy issues. Operating solely as a political declaration, the EEC was inspired by the general logic of establishing closer economic relations with Russian and former Soviet energy suppliers, with the goal of creating a reliable framework of hydrocarbon trade and transit across Europe. As expected, both the upsurge of free-market principles and the need to guarantee security of supply led to the binding multilateral **Energy Charter Treaty** (ECT) of 1994. The ECT's aim was to create a series of binding obligations on the trade, transit, and investment of energy goods, culminating in a framework of East–West energy cooperation resting on liberal market principles. Therefore the goal was a predictable and enforceable framework that would bring stability and clarity to all aspects of Europe's unwieldy energy industry, especially the tricky overlaps between state and non-state energy actors.

The political significance of energy during these momentous post Cold War years cannot be underestimated. As the dominant industry in Russia and the CIS countries, reforms to the energy sector could feasibly trigger reforms in the wider economic structure. Such reforms stood a real chance of coming to fruition if the ECT—as a vehicle that codified liberal ideology on trade and investment in energy—could be agreed to by as many European states as possible. Thus the political significance of the ECT lay in its recognition of energy as a key feature of the national infrastructure of every European country. More importantly, the ECT acknowledged energy as a *policy area* capable of entangling sovereign principles and issues of national ownership with private sector ambitions relating to trade and investment. Therefore, for the purposes of this chapter, the ECT is an important watershed in understanding energy as a central feature in the composition of post Cold War statehood—one factor that could subsequently affect the foreign policies of eastern and western states.

The ECT represented one of a number of assorted overtures made to Russia and Eastern Europe by the EU. The overall goal of these initiatives was to bolster the economic efficiency and competitiveness of post-Soviet economies, making them capable of supporting widespread political reforms. Over the long term, such restructuring trends became even more ambitious in attempting to export eastward the process of European integration. As such, a number of foreign policy instruments were constructed by the European Council, including a number of Common Positions and Joint Actions agreed between the EU, CIS, and CEE states. Keen to identify Russia and the Ukraine as key strategic actors in the impetus of East–West reforms, the Council also crafted a Common Strategy for each in 1999.

However, the late 1990s saw the first setbacks in the reforming ambitions of the EU. The efficiency of the EU's Common Strategy for Russia was ultimately thwarted by its own scope. Instead of focusing on a few manageable, goals, it attempted to do too much at once, making any reforms difficult to determine.[4] More distressing was the stalled status of the ECT, which Russia, as the key player, had signed but now refused to ratify, a situation which still exists.[5]

In an attempt to revive the flagging East–West energy dialogue in a climate of growing Russian distrust of Western motives, the **EU–Russia Energy Dialogue** was launched in 2000. For the past decade, the Dialogue has operated as a bilateral foreign policy forum designed to increase long-term reform and promote reliability in Russia's public and private sector. Judging the Dialogue's overall success is tricky. It has generated some cooperation in a few key areas: East–West electricity grid collaboration, energy efficiency, nuclear safety, and environmental protection. It also functions as an auxiliary of other EU foreign policy initiatives with Russia. However, despite annual EU–Russia summits and its own annual synthesis reports, the EU–Russia Energy Dialogue has not solved the outstanding energy security issues still plaguing the EU–Russia relationship.

Most recently, and perhaps most damaging, persistently differing views by Gazprom regarding the *finalité* of the liberalization process of European and Russian energy markets, along with trade and transit issues and an incorrect legal interpretation of key ECT articles on the treatment of national and foreign investors, ultimately led to Russian termination of its provisional application of the ECT in August 2009. As a result, while the ECT's legal status is unaffected, its broader effectiveness in terms of promoting East–West energy cooperation is coming under political scruting. (Amkhan and Hadfield 2011). (See Box 23.3.)

As regards the EU–Russia Dialogue, the termination of the ECT can also be considered a further failure of the two sides to at least understand the needs and perspectives of the other. Russia stands opposed to what it perceives as an unwelcome imposition of a generic EU-style model of liberalization targeted at itself and its neighbours. Russian reform preferences take the shape of a gradual reduction of subsidized oil and gas to its neighbours, coupled with implicit foreign policy signals to encourage them to remain politically committed to Kremlin perspectives. As a result, Russian foreign energy policy has developed into a potent mix of *political **revanchism*** (policies directed at the recovery of territory and power) and *quasi-liberal economic adjustments*. Indeed, some would argue that Russian energy foreign policy and

BOX 23.3 Gazprom and the Energy Charter Treaty

Amongst Gazprom's long-standing misgivings about ratifying the ECT is the argument that doing so would diminish Gazprom's monopolistic position in Russian energy markets by eventually obliging Russia to open its pipeline network to transport cheaper gas and oil from Central Asia (i.e. Turkmenistan and Kazakhstan) via the process of third-party access. From Gazprom's perspective, the ECT obliges them to grant to a third party access to the Russian pipeline system wherever there is available capacity in a given gas or oil pipeline (which is generally abundant). However, such claims are based on incorrect readings of the ECT's provisions, which specifically *exclude* mandatory third-party access to pipeline systems (i.e. when a third party requires access to the extra capacity that generally exists in most pipelines). Russia's withdrawal of its provisional application of the ECT in 2009 created various shock waves in both energy and legal communities. Equally, recent cases of investors suing Member States under the ECT continue to bring it to prominence. Ultimately, Russia remains an ECT signatory, as does the EU (as an Economic Integration Organization).

oil–gas spat outcomes are nothing new: 'The recent "gas war" between Ukraine and Russia does not reflect a policy change in Moscow. Russia has used its energy power in an attempt to influence the foreign and security policies of its neighbours since 1990' (Smith 2006: 1). However, EU foreign policy has yet to fully acknowledge the implicit foreign policy factors inherent in energy security, and still operates on the traditional arguments for liberalized markets and EU-style governance. Despite a few areas of progress, the overall trend since 2000 has been an increase in incidents where actions by one side are perceived by the other as interference at best and hegemonic at worst.

As a result, the Dialogue has effectively promoted only dialogue, rather than viable progress on energy security. Unfortunately, during this same period, Europe's dependence on imported Russian gas has only increased. Heavily conditioned by the increasing salience of energy security, as well as the rising sense of importer and exporter identities characterizing both sides, the political relationship between the two has become far shakier.

Pre-crisis

Despite the advantages of seeking a mutually beneficial relationship, by 2005 the EU and Russia were visibly divided on key energy issues. For Russia, disenchantment with the ECT (seen as counter to Russian interests) and a lacklustre attitude to EU initiatives suggested a new trend of foreclosing on multilateral projects in order to operate on its own terms.

The aspects of power inherent in Russian energy are threefold (*Economist* 2007: 37–9). First, ownership and access to its vast energy resources: Russia is the world's largest gas producer and exporter (with roughly one-third of the world's total) and second-largest oil exporter. The vast majority of Russian gas activity is conducted by the Russian state-owned company Gazprom. Second, pipeline ownership: pipelines within Russia are owned outright by another Russian state-owned company, Transneft. Ownership of the other dozen or so pipelines connecting Russia to the Caspian, the Baltic region, and Europe itself are divided amongst the states (or state enterprises) across which the pipelines run.[6] Third, long-term contracts which lock in Russian exports to a guaranteed set of European importers. The gas spat was the undiplomatic outcome of differing perceptions on the long-term Ukraine–Russia gas contract.

With all three components in place, the economic side of Russian energy presents serious monopolistic challenges from the European perspective. State companies like Gazprom, Transneft, and the oil company Rosneft are generally assumed to be 'highly influential agent[s] of government oil [and gas] policy' (Gorst 2004: 1). But transforming Russia from a market behemoth of reserves, pipelines, and contracts into a rogue state requires an additional variable—the visible use of energy as a means of achieving explicitly political ends. Therefore a decent analysis of Russia's role as a foreign policy maverick must spring from an appreciation of the multiple roles that energy plays in Russian economic power and the crucial addition of the political element. On its own, Russian energy dominance is a *necessary* but insufficient explanation for alleging that energy is a tool of Russian foreign policy. However, the addition of an external *political goal* represents a *sufficient* factor. Once these two are brought together in the political context of foreign disputes, the alleged foreign policy component of Russian energy can be argued to exist. As a result, external perceptions of Russian actions may well work inductively (in bottom-up fashion) from specific foreign policy incidents in which energy features to a more general assumption that the Russian state has become a maverick in its coercive use of energy dominance to force political compliance in its immediate neighbourhood, and possibly further afield.

The aspects of power inherent in European energy are far more diffuse and cannot rival the sheer concentration of Russian assets. Whilst some key states like Norway, and to a lesser extent Britain, currently enjoy a favourable energy security situation thanks to regional (if diminishing) reserves in the North Sea, the vast majority of European states possess no notable energy reserves. All they can hope for is unproblematic uninterrupted supplies from external, mainly Russian, reserves. There have been only limited attempts to explore shared ownership of Russian-owned pipelines transiting states outside Russia, or to construct a decent project by which European investment could revitalize the ageing energy infrastructure in Russia itself. Europe's own pipeline project—Nabucco—is an ambitious consortium project designed to reach 3300 kilometres from the Black Sea (with further Caspian links) to Austria via Hungary, Bulgaria, and Romania, bypassing Russia in the process. With stop–start approaches and a host of political uncertainties, Nabucco is arguably still closer to a pipe dream than a pipeline.

Europe's sole remaining area of leverage is as the world's largest energy market. Europe possesses a multitude of national and commercial customers (in France, Germany, Austria, and Italy) who so far remain reliable buyers of Russian exports and are happy to grant Russia direct access to their domestic markets. The 2004 round of EU enlargement included states that are even more heavily dependent on Russian gas. If European buyers in this market were to act in concert politically—either within EU perimeters, or in a separate political forum—their combined leverage could prompt serious security of demand issues in Russia. However, European buyers have been both reassuringly loyal to their Russian sellers individually and predictably unable to summon the collective political will to act in concert. Indeed, Germany and Hungary have respectively signed and signalled approval for new pipeline deals with Russia.[7]

In addition to energy power in the form of reserves, pipelines, and contracts, foreign policy leverage for Russia and Europe is located in post-enlargement European geopolitics itself. Here, continental tussles are complicated by the visible desire of each side to co-opt the buffer zone of *non-EU* countries between Moscow and Brussels, including Ukraine, Georgia, Belarus, and Moldova, plus the Caspian cousins. More than just pipelines transit this region; these states are in the uncomfortable position of being both a Western laboratory for the external dimensions of EU integration and an Eastern testing ground for Russian revanchism. Therefore it is unsurprising that Ukraine, as the political fulcrum of this zone, was also the site of a foreign policy contest between Russia and also the EU, with energy as the key medium.

A few key contributory elements need to be borne in mind. First, the majority of European countries are heavily dependent upon energy imports. Although figures vary widely in this respect, average estimates suggest that Europe—and by extension the political unit of the EU—is roughly 30–50% dependent on Russian gas for its total imports and 26–30% dependent upon Russian oil.[8] Second, the EU depends on the crucial role played by key transit countries, across which gas pipelines run. With two major pipelines running across its territory, Ukraine is of greatest strategic importance because of its ability to connect Russia to markets in Germany, Austria, Italy, Slovenia, and Croatia. Third, as a transit country and a major gas importer, Ukraine

Map 23.1 Existing and planned natural gas pipelines to Europe.

Source: Energy Information Administration.

is itself dependent upon Russia for the revenues it charges Russia for gas crossing its territory en route to Europe (see Map 23.1). Ukraine is also dependent upon European markets to keep its transit relationship with Russia healthy, and finally it is dependent upon Russia for its own domestic gas imports. The scope of all such dependencies must be borne in mind by foreign policy students in assessing any foreign policy incidents that involve energy.

In late 2004, friction arose between Ukraine and Russia over Ukraine's inability to pay for Russian gas. Previous Ukrainian debts had been dealt with by Russia reducing its supplies to Ukraine in order to restore 'payment discipline', but this tactic began to result in 'unauthorised

BOX 23.4 East–west geopolitical friction?

Apart from the EU–Russia Energy Dialogue, there are two other significant Commission-led projects involving the energy-exporting southern and eastern peripheries of the EU. The first was the Euro-Mediterranean Partnership (EMP), a broad framework geared at enhancing the EU's relationship with North African and Middle Eastern states along political, economic, and social lines. Drawing the 'partner countries' of this region into the projected 2010 free trade area, the EMP aimed to bolster economic development and integration, investment, and employment, 'all of which will contribute to a stable political environment in which energy supply projects can flourish' (Gault 2004: 177). EMP partner states, along with an eastern arc of CIS states, have now been subsumed into the second and more ambitious and possibly more vigorous European Neighbourhood Policy (ENP), which is a regional project aiming to prevent post-enlargement fault lines from undermining European stability and security. Energy is a key feature of ENP Action Plans which are agreed bilaterally between the EU and its ENP partners, and at least within the ENP is an issue area treated in a more holistic sense as impacting on political, economic, and security spheres. The ENP has sparked particular East–West controversy. The EU's perspective is to build a ring of friends to enhance the security and stability of wider Europe by encouraging key reforms in its new neighbours. Russian motives appear to have more to do with an older sense of entitlement, and its security ambitions appear clearer than Europe's. As one Russian commentator put it: 'The West is doing this under the banner of democratisation, and one gets the impression we are doing it only for the sake of ourselves . . . Our activeness is following too openly Russian interests. This is patriotic but not competitive.' (Constantion Kosachev, cited in Popescu 2006). Russia is further puzzled as to why their former satellite states who 'enjoy more benefits from cooperation with Russia' (Popescu 2006) would want to 'enter into the straitjacket of European institutions and to fall under the diktat of Brussels' (Kosachev, cited in Popescu 2006).

diversions of the volumes in transit to European countries' (Stern 2006: 2). Ukraine's steadily rising debt with Russia was written off in 2004 by a Ukrainian agreement to receive Turkmen-sourced gas for its own markets and to transit Russian gas reliably to Gazprom's customers in Europe at established volumes and prices. Driven by an undercurrent of dramatic political events, energy relations between Ukraine and Russia then worsened throughout 2005. From a Foreign Policy Aanalysis perspective, each of these developments can be seen as simple tit-for-tat retaliations, worsened by inadequate information and compromised decision making which ultimately prompted stand-offs and dramatic gestures by both sides. (See Box 23.4.)

During these various tussles, it should be noted that Russia acknowledged the risk (if not the impact) that a shortfall would cause to European customers. Similarly, Ukraine was aware of its strategic location as the pivot between Russian supplies and European buyers. However, instead of successfully using its position to its advantage, Ukraine found itself pinned uncomfortably between two different pricing systems: a lower subsidized Russian gas price specifically for CIS customers of around $50 per thousand cubic metres and higher non-subsidized European market prices at $230. Ukraine's original tactic in 2005 was to cut itself a deal by charging Russia European-level transit tariffs for gas bound for Europe (thereby increasing its national revenue). However, this backfired when Russia insisted that Ukraine could certainly charge Russia higher transit tariffs, but only if Ukraine agreed to pay these same higher prices for its *own* domestic imports, which would make a significant dent in its national revenue. Western pressure from the EU and WTO had been placed on Russia to eradicate subsidies, so the move was not altogether unexpected. Ukraine argued that the proposed fivefold increase in gas prices was too steep to manage all at once. A transition period was needed to avoid instability in its industry and economy. With the global increase of energy already intensifying the debate on gas prices, the Russian announcement that it was prepared to shut off gas to Ukraine 'provoked alarm in Western Europe' and anger in Kiev (Buckley *et al.* 2005).

Therefore the foreign policy dilemma prior to the January 2006 gas spat was the dilemma of who would blink first. Would Gazprom stick to its demand of European market prices? Or would Ukraine view the price hike as 'a provocation' and refuse to acquiesce (Buckley and Parker 2005)? Ukraine appeared to have three options. First, it could barter its way out of paying European market prices if it conceded to Gazprom's 2004 demand for an 'equity stake' in the Ukrainian pipeline network. In other words, Ukraine would have to weigh up the value of retaining pipeline ownership versus the revenue gained by keeping prices low. Second, it could continue to demand increased **transit tariffs** for Russian gas exported to Europe, the high revenue of which could feasibly offset the increased costs of its own imports. Third, Ukraine could consider illegally tapping into Russian exports to feed its own markets. This could cause a major disruption in the supply to Europe, with the probable result of both Russia and Europe calling into question Ukraine's reliability as a transit country.

Russia's options, via Gazprom, were a mirror image of Ukraine's three problems. As argued, Russia could negotiate with Ukraine for a stake in the Ukrainian pipeline in exchange for operating at lower subsidized prices. Second, it could insist that Ukraine operate at the higher European market prices for both its own Turkmen-sourced domestic gas and Europe-bound gas. Alternatively, Gazprom could simply shut off the supply of gas to Ukraine to signal displeasure with the pricing arguments and to demonstrate its superior leverage. However, this choice came with the obvious consequences of a dramatic reduction of Russian gas to key European markets and a damaged reputation as a reliable supplier. If Gazprom had a foreign policy ace up its sleeve, it would have been the threat to alter the route of its Russian gas to Europe by opting for another pipeline.

Security of supply crisis

Two events contributed to the security of supply crisis, one remote, and one proximate. The **remote cause** of the crisis was political. With the extension of the East–West tension of ideas, norms, values, and development discussed above, the 'Orange Revolution', which began in November 2004, represented a vigorous undercurrent of worsening political relations between Ukraine and Russia and enhanced dialogue with the EU. Since 1998 Ukraine had entered into a number of bilateral relationships with the EU including its own Common Strategy. Along with various bilateral agreements on science and technology, trade, steel, textiles, and nuclear energy, these agreements allowed Ukraine to engage in enhanced political dialogue with the EU on issues of economic and legislative collaboration, trade, and investment. This relationship was further bolstered by the 2004 European Neighbourhood Policy (ENP) Action Plan for Ukraine which, counter to the assessment of Brussels, saw EU membership as the ultimate goal.

The sum total of these engagements with the EU was a tacit rejection of Russian leadership in favour of EU-led transformation, a view which strengthened throughout 2004. Pro-Western sentiment reached its zenith in the **Orange Revolution** of November 2004–January 2005 when popular discontent erupted over the outcome of the presidential election between Kremlin-backed President Viktor Yanukovich as the chosen heir of outgoing president Leonid Kuchma and the pro-Western incumbent, Viktor Yushchenko. Yushchenko, as leader of the Our Ukraine Bloc whose campaign colour was orange, had campaigned on a platform of greater independence from Russia. Opting for greater allegiance with Moscow, Yanukovich won the count on 21 November 2004. However, the election was beset by voter intimidation, corruption, and instances of electoral fraud (upheld by international election monitors), which promptly instigated an enormous parliamentary and then popular outcry. Popular re-action against Kremlin interference spilled out into the streets in both violent demonstrations and protracted peaceful protests, frequently numbering in the hundreds of thousands and lasting for weeks. The Yanukovich government conceded to the recount ordered by Ukaine's Supreme Court on 26 December 2004, which subsequently saw Yushchenko emerge as the winner with 52% of the vote. His inauguration took place in Kiev on 23 January 2005. The Orange Revolution catapulted Ukraine, with all its strategic and symbolic weight, towards the West. In its political outlook and future ambitions, Kiev now leaned visibly closer to Brussels (and even Washington) and further from Moscow. Throughout 2005, Ukraine agitated publicly on a pro-EU platform for membership of both NATO and the EU. Neither outcome was particularly easy for Moscow or the vocal minority of pro-Russian Ukrainians to swallow (Coronakis 2006).

The roots of the **proximate cause** of the gas crisis were ostensibly commercial, and have been outlined above. The crunch came at the end of December 2005. Gazprom had made clear that while neither it nor the Kremlin were willing to budge on the $230 price, the company would grant a substantial loan of $3.6 billion to Ukraine to assist it to meet this price. The subsequent offer by President Putin that the increased gas price could be suspended for three months before the final transition was meant to be conciliatory (Buckley and Parker 2005). Neither overture was understood as such in Kiev, which viewed the offers as a way of becoming permanently ensnared in Gazprom's ambitions. Both were rejected. Gazprom, in a televised broadcast that showed Gazprom technicians shutting down key pipelines, then stopped gas supplies to Ukraine on the morning of 1 January 2006 (Stern 2006: 7). Both the act and its coverage transformed the understanding of gas-spat tactics into a broader strategy of using energy leverage as a form of foreign policy to bring about a change in behaviour of another actor.

What remains unclear of course is *which* gas. Did Gazprom switch off gas destined only for the Ukrainian domestic market in order to make a local point? Or, in a gesture of continental proportions, did it switch off both domestic *and* transit gas? Whatever the choice, European countries could hardly fail to miss the point: Hungary, Austria, Slovakia, Romania, France, Poland, and Italy lost between 14% and 40% of their deliveries (BBC News Website 2006). Europeans, witnessing both Gazprom's own actions and the physical impact of the stoppage, believed it to be a Kremlin-approved tactic, heralding an epoch in which Russia would not hesitate to use its energy clout for political dominance.

However, Russia saw things differently. Arguing that it had not failed to supply its contractual volumes to Europe, Gazprom contended that European gas was still running through Ukrainian pipelines and that any shortfall was due to illegal taking by the Ukrainian gas company Naftogaz. In a less than clear fashion, President Viktor Yushchenko then rebuffed these accusations, arguing that Ukraine was entitled to 15% of transit gas (Stern 2006: 8).

To mitigate the damage to its reputation as a reliable supplier, Russia began pumping additional volumes to restore the balance on 2 January. Normal supplies to Europe were restored by 4 January. Both allegations of Ukrainian illegal takings and Gazprom's own assertions of not having compromised its European customers continue to bedevil the details of the New Year's Day gas crisis, and have subsequently clouded both Russian–Ukraine and EU–Russia relations.

Europe: post crisis

For Europe, there were three major outcomes to the gas spat. First, a hardening of perceptions in the West: within the arena of energy supply and demand, the gas stoppage left Europeans with serious concerns about Gazprom's reliability in general, and Russia's use of its energy leverage over European markets in particular. Coupled with the pro-Western changes in Ukraine, judged to be antithetical to Russian interests, further anxieties arose as to the actual foreign policy content of Russian energy clout. In other words, the timing of the gas difficulties between Ukraine and Russia came so closely on the heels of a political shift away from Kremlin ideologies that it was difficult not to see the Kremlin-sanctioned gas stoppage as anything other than retaliatory tactics. Today, these perceptions remain in place throughout much of Europe.

Second, the gas stoppage dramatically exposed the scope and intensity of Europe's reliance on Russian gas imports. The political impact was even greater, demonstrating a major gap in the EU's ambitions to complete its marketplace—namely the absence of a decent external energy policy to deal both economically and politically with such a crisis. By the end of January 2006, the majority of Europeans were aware that 30–50% of Europe's total gas imports come from Russia, a full 90% of which crossed Ukraine by pipeline. American perspectives indicated that if gas spats were to become the norm, 'the energy policies of the Kremlin are a danger to Europe and particularly to the independence of Central Europeans . . . [and] are also not in the long-term interest of Russia itself' (Smith 2006: 1).

Third, in an attempt to redress the absence of an energy policy, the EU was compelled to react. It did so quietly to begin with. No denunciations of Russian actions emerged from the Council, only a welcome of the agreement reached between Russia and Ukraine by Common Foreign and Security Policy (CFSP) High Representative Javier Solana on 4 January. However, on the same day Energy Commissioner Andris Piebalgs indicated in a press conference that 'Europe needs a clearer and more collective and cohesive policy on security of energy supply . . . security of energy supply is only really considered at national Member State level; but in reality we need a much greater European-wide approach on this issue' (Piebalgs 2006).

The next step was the Spring Council Session, which agreed to develop 'a common foreign and trade policy approach in support of energy policy objectives'. In relation to Russia, the Council determined that it should pursue Russian ratification of the ECT, and that the EU–Russia Energy Dialogue should be 'revitalised and become more open and effective in support of EU energy objectives' (Council Secretariat 2006: 5–6). In the familiar turf battles between Council and Commission, the Council rebuffed the argument by Commission President José Manuel Barroso to bestow enhanced energy competences on the Commission. While shying away from a fully **communitarized** energy policy, the Council did invite both the Commission and Javier Solana as the CFSP High Representative to coordinate the newest form of EU foreign policy—**external energy relations**. Solana had already identified energy dependence as a key point in his European Security Strategy of 2003; now it was the turn of the Council-endorsed Commission to become the architect of an external energy policy.

The European Commission produced an avalanche of energy policy papers in the wake of the gas crisis. The March 2006 Green Paper called for an EU-wide energy strategy that dealt with third-country foreign policy issues implicit in security of supply issues. January 2007 yielded another suite of energy papers on market liberalization and energy efficiency, and a second major paper entitled 'An Energy Policy for Europe', outlining sustainability, security of supply, and competitiveness as the new three pillars of EU energy policy. At the national level, energy now dominates every major agenda. Therefore the EU is clearly aware of the implications of energy security, but now needs both the political will and a robust EU–Russia agreement to transform ideas into actions.

Ukraine: post crisis

For Ukraine, the outcome was complex. On the energy front, Gazprom and Naftogaz signed a five-year contract on 4 January that contained many uncertainties; cheaper Turkmen gas appeared to be the new source for Ukraine's domestic market, but still charged at higher, though unconfirmed, rates. The ensuing weeks and months were unkind to the political stability of the new Yushchenko government, which lost a vote of no confidence and became mired in a constitutional crisis. The Yanukovich-led opposition moved swiftly to use the gas contract as a fillip for re-election based on cutting a fairer deal with Gazprom. Despite the assurances given by President Putin immediately after the crisis that Gazprom would continue to meet its commitments to Ukraine on terms he declared 'absolutely reasonable and mutually profitable', and Yushchenko's own confirmation that Ukraine would not violate the contract, deep unease remained in Ukraine over its situation (Buckley and Warner 2006). The unease remains. The leader of Ukraine's parliamentary opposition, Yuliya Timoshenko, wrote in early 2007 of her country's nervousness over Russia's future objectives. While its political goals seem to spring from 'a remorseless imperial tradition' with expansionist motives, Russian economic growth is argued to be precariously balanced on high energy prices, with the EU still too divided to assert a common position (Timoshenko 2007: 69–72). Timoshenko has two conclusions. First, Ukraine's future lies with the EU. Second, the EU needs a common policy to adequately tackle the myriad foreign policy challenges posed by Russia: 'If there is one country toward which Europeans—and indeed, the entire West—should share a common foreign policy, it is Russia.' (Timoshenko 2007: 74). (See Box 23.5.)

Foreign policy perspectives

In every foreign policy crisis there are at least two major actors, and as such more than one way to understand the story. The same is true for the present case. From the Russian perspective, the suggestion that the gas stoppage constituted a politically motivated punishment designed to place Ukraine under severe economic stress was rejected outright. Assertions

BOX 23.5 Energy supply disruptions

The 2006 gas spat was not a solitary case. Since the dissolution of the Soviet Union, several post-Soviet countries have faced energy supply disruptions. Some have occurred because of technical problems, but others have been interpreted as Russian attempts to express their disapproval of the domestic or foreign policy proclivities of a given country: *'Russia has a track record of turning off the energy taps during disputes with neighbours; though in each case it has cited technical or commercial reasons'* (Zhdannikov 2007).

Many of these disruptions have been in the Baltic states. There were several oil and gas spats during the 1990s as these states progressed from achieving independence to demands to remove Russian military forces, to eventual preparation for EU membership. Other disruptions were connected with Russian attempts to gain control over domestic facilities and infrastructure. If these attempts were unsuccessful and assets were sold to non-Russian firms, Russian firms simply cut off supplies to the facilities. The case of the Lithuanian oil refinery, Mazeikiai, which underwent nine oil disruptions between 1998 and 2000, whilst it attempted to conclude its sale to a US company, is a clear example. In 2007 Estonia, in the throes of domestic discontent about the relocation of a Soviet war memorial in Tallinn, faced protracted disruptions of oil and steam coal supplies from Russia, which in turn alleged that there were technical problems with the pipeline and shortage of wagons for coal shipment.

Spats have also involved Ukraine and Belarus; the latter had a severe impact on Polish supplies and minor shortages affected Germany too. Other disruptions of oil supplies to Slovakia and the Czech Republic via the Druzhba pipeline occurred in 2008, with 2009 gas crises affecting most of the EU countries importing Russian gas, culminating in a complete cut-off of supplies for 13 days. The magnitude of the 2009 gas spat was far larger than previous ones, and had a profound impact on many European countries. In the Balkans it caused a humanitarian emergency, and in Hungary and especially in Slovakia it caused significant economic losses due to limitations on the biggest gas consumers. The crises also fully revealed the lack of supplier diversification in Central, Southern, and Eastern Europe, as well as a lack of infrastructure (e.g. mutual interconnections), and starkly highlights the reality of their dependence on Russia. Both Russia and Ukraine continue to deny responsibility for the event, in a scenario reminiscent of the 2006 gas crisis.

However, there were benefits in that the 2009 gas crisis accelerated the view of energy by EU policy makers as a strategic commodity, *and* a subject of EU foreign policy. None of the previous disruptions of supplies from Russia had had such an impact on mutual relations. From the European perspective, attempts to diversify its suppliers and transit routes once again illustrate Russia as an unreliable supplier and Ukraine as an unreliable transit state, prompting a number of outcomes—the revived South Corridor pipeline project, intensified relations with Caspian regions, focus on the development of Europe-based shale gas production, and the conclusion of a series of wide-ranging energy legislations (see Box 23.1), including the priorities of the 2011 Hungarian and Polish presidencies of the EU.

'UPDATE 3—Russia to cut Estonia fuel transit amid statue row', Wed 2 May 2007, Dmitry Zhdannikov (Reuters) (http://uk.reuters.com/article/2007/05/02/estonia-russia-protest-idUKL0271267920070502)

that Gazprom is in reality a surrogate Kremlin operative in Ukraine (and elsewhere) have been parried by argument that the company has made no explicit political demands of the Ukrainian government (Stern 2006: 12). Ukrainians themselves believed that the gas agreement signed with Gazprom on 10 January 2006 was not the work of Russian leverage but the result of poor negotiating skills of President Yushchenko, which explained the vote of no confidence in his government within days of its signing. By 2010 however, the game had changed completely. Yushchenko and Timoschenko were out, and pro-Russian Viktor Yanukovych was in, as President. Worse was to follow (Timoshenko initially challenged the outcome, claiming that the election was rigged). In october 2011, Julia Timoshenko was convicted in a Ukrainian court of abuse of office in brokering a ten-year contract gas with Gazprom in the wake of the 2009 gas spat with Russia. Her conviction was roundly condemned by a variety of international actors, including the EU. As argued by Michael Emerson, 'Ukraine's Orange revolution became a sad spectacle. Its foundations in a vibrant civil society were real. It foundered on irreconcilable competition and disagreement between its two leaders, Yushchenko and Timoshenko, which led to dysfunctional chaos between the institutions of democractic governance, compounded by failure to do anything about endemic corruption' (CEPS 2011: 2).

From Russia's perspective, the gas spat incident was a clear case of Ukrainian illegal taking of transit gas bound for Europe, which undermined Russia's reputation as a reliable supplier. Therefore Gazprom's objective is to prevent future problems by developing a more robust relationship with Ukraine using set prices and guaranteed volumes based on the European price range—a system that has been extended to all CIS countries in order to operate as a coherent market. In addition, it will launch enterprises that lessen the transit weakness of European gas, such as the Nord Stream pipeline agreement with Germany. Purchasing increasing amounts of European energy assets and signing further long-term contracts (as with Gaz de France) to guarantee security of demand will also avoid future disruptions. In reaction to Europe's growing anxieties over security of supply, Gazprom argues that it has an equal right to be concerned with security of demand, particularly in light of European statements about looking elsewhere for other gas suppliers after years of reliable Russian supply. From this view, Europe is 'generating an insecurity of demand for its [energy] supplies' (BBC World, 24 April 2007).

From the European perspective, having lost the political battle to retain Ukrainian sympathies, Russia had used its state energy company Gazprom to coerce Ukraine back into the fold of Russian influence. This was a trend that appeared to have begun earlier than the spat itself, with the resignation of Andrei Illarionov, chief economic adviser to President Putin, who argued that Russia was 'no longer free' and pointed to the 'state's increasing tendency to use energy as a "weapon" in relations with other countries' (Buckley 2005). Opinions on the coercive element present in Russia's energy tactics were strengthened after the spat when Russia induced similar price rises in countries that were perceived to have moved in a pro-European direction, including Armenia, Azerbaijan, Georgia, Moldova, Latvia, Lithuania, and Estonia, and as of 2007 Belarus.[9]

Forceful statements by Gazprom in spring 2006 that it could easily afford to switch its supplies to Asian markets further rattled EU member states. Equally terse statements by President Putin about the central role of energy resources in a renewed Russia demonstrated to EU governments an increasing element of realpolitik in Russian foreign policy. Coupled with Russia's apparent willingness to use its energy dominance to pursue both economic and political objectives, energy as an instrument of Russian foreign policy has taken up residence as an axiom of Western thinking. Recriminations have continued. In the year following the gas spat, Russia's disagreements over energy costs with its former Soviet states have ballooned into the accusation 'that Russia is using energy exports as a political weapon' on both its immediate neighbours and a visibly dependent EU (BBC World, 24 April 2007). From Timoshenko's perspective, Putin's 'use of energy to bully Russia's neighbours' extends not only to Ukraine but indeed to all of Europe (Timoshenko 2007: 76). Overall, EU perspectives indicate that Russia's reputation as a solid energy supplier has been seriously tarnished by its indiscreet deployment of coercive energy tactics.

BOX 23.6 Addressing European energy security

John Gault argues that reliance upon energy imported from key peripheral areas (namely Russia, the Caspian, North Africa, and the Middle East) has important implications for European security. He makes a number of suggestions for easing European energy dependency and assisting in the greater goal of strengthening European energy security.

- 'New production capacities in the periphery regions [must] be developed in a timely manner along with adequate transportation systems to delivery the energy to European markets. European security then requires that the likelihood of interruptions to such supplies is minimized, and, in the event of an interruption, that the consequences for European consumers are moderated.

- Oil and gas production capacities in countries neighbouring Europe are being enlarged, and transportation systems are being planned and constructed to provide additional supplies to Europe.

- For the most part, private companies from both importing and exporting countries . . . are making these investments, often as joint ventures.

- A continuous flow of energy from the periphery countries to Europe will depend, ultimately, upon steady improvements in the quality of life and the comprehensiveness of political participation in the periphery countries themselves.' (Gault 2004: 170)

The foreign policy dilemma here is acute. The two sides must come to a more comprehensive agreement in which energy features prominently and permanently as a policy issue, not a foreign policy tool. Or else they must continue to look elsewhere, running the risk of creating an 'energy security dilemma' in the mutual preparations to replace each other, thereby generating even greater instability (Monaghan and Montanaro-Jankovski 2006: 8). The EU–Russia relationship is not only interdependent quantitatively in terms of energy, trade, and investment, but relies on political reciprocity for viable future developments. While the EU–Russia Energy Dialogue has so far failed to produce any guarantees, it is clear that neither side can afford to lose the other as a key element of its overall security.

After the withdrawal of the Energy Charter Treaty, the EU–Russia Energy Dialogue continues within other broad platforms of mutual cooperation including the EU–Russia Strategic Partnership. However, at the moment the most comprehensive framework for cooperation is the EU–Russia Common Spaces covering the following four fields: the Common Economic Space (including energy), the Common Space of Freedom, Security and Justice, the Common Space of External Security, and the Common Space of Research and Education. Whilst both sides clearly view the critical need to address the myriad aspects that constitute energy security, none of these platforms is legally binding and they serve only as a lukewarm framework for dialogue. (See Box 23.6.)

Conclusion

Acknowledging the role of energy in national and international dynamics suggests that something of a paradigm shift is needed in the construction and conduct of foreign policy. Kalicki and Goldwyn suggest that all states:

> . . . must evolve from a more traditional foreign policy view, preoccupied with military secu-
> rity issues and relatively disconnected from the world of resource and economic forces, to a
> more modern view that addresses economic and political factors and recognizes that world
> events are determined far more by the flow of resources—human and material—than by the
> flow of officials and diplomats, or even soldiers. (Kalicki and Goldwyn 2005: 14)

The validity of this suggestion rests in large part upon the central role played by energy for a number of key states. It assumes that the foreign policies of key exporting states should swiftly be overhauled and that the terrain of importing states has shifted radically to absorb these new orientations. While energy is a key facet of foreign policy, it is not yet a predominant feature. Indeed, what we know about the role of energy within foreign policy is that it gener-ally features sporadically. As yet, for both major exporting and importing states, energy does not *dominate* to the extent that it *dictates*. Rather, energy has reoriented what constitutes political power, and has highlighted a new form of vulnerability. Both changes indicate that energy needs to be accommodated within the broad perimeters of foreign policy issues, but not to the detriment of other forms of national power. Energy will not displace traditional military force; and foreign policy itself has long incorporated the resource flows that Kalicki and Goldwyn mention. Plenty of imbalances between major powers will continue without energy being factored in. Common-sense counterfactuals produce numerous examples where foreign policy clashes would occur without the trigger of energy.

However, energy is undoubtedly a key **mediating factor** through which national and regional power is affected and by which influence is made, and felt. As such, students of foreign policy should expect two things. First, that major foreign policy clashes in which energy is a *central feature* will remain sporadic. This is simply because energy is not yet a structural feature; it is still a function of remote, rather than proximate, geopolitical shifts. Gas spats are as yet a rarity. Indeed, the EU's own scramble to produce an energy stance with foreign policy features indicates that energy has not yet been structurally incorporated into foreign policy frameworks, as per the suggestion by Kalicki and Goldwyn. Second, major foreign policy clashes in which energy operates as a proximate problem will remain a **key international feature**, qualifying and conditioning issues from national interest to regional influence. Thus EU–Russia foreign policy on issues like the US missile defence shield, influence in Central Asia, and even democracy in Russia itself will arguably incorpo-rate dynamics of European energy dependence. A good example was the May 2007 EU–Russia Summit in Samara, in which energy featured among a host of other issues (including visas, the role of Kaliningrad, cross-border cooperation, research, trade, policy, and climate change) but with the power to condition responses on both sides (Emerson 2007: 1). There-fore energy should be regarded as a new and important conduit, but one in which tradi-tional forms of power will continue to make predictable appearances.

Since the end of the Cold War, energy has become an implicit part of the external composi-tion of European states and the foreign policy stance of Russia. In its ability to institute and affect key political and economic norms, energy is now understood by both the EU and Russia as a key medium by which to secure continental stability, and even dominance, and as such is something of microcosm for the foreign policy ambitions of both. This is the case simply be-cause the political content of energy supply is inseparable from the economic imperatives of demand. A collective EU solution is certainly feasible, but it will have to incorporate political instruments capable of dealing with commercial dynamics and foreign policy demands. This may also require the EU to think more strategically of itself as a foreign policy actor. At present, the EU has opted for a diplomatic, even diluted, route regarding its collective foreign policy stance on Russia, and remains divided at the national level over the right to procure Russian energy. Some view this lack of coordination as a weakness. Timoshenko, for example, argues that 'western European countries have been far too circumspect in their criticism and too anxious to make separate deals that will supposedly guarantee their national supplies of energy' (Timoshenko 2007: 76) (as evidenced by the May 2007 deal between Gazprom and the Central European Gas Hub, owned by OMV, an Austrian energy group). On the other hand, factoring in dominance and weakness, vulnerability and sensitivity, is a pragmatic foreign policy stance. Until EU member states are prepared to overhaul or shift their energy competence, they will continue to struggle to find a political solution which 'divides the risks of any possible energy blockade equally among all Europeans' (Timoshenko 2007: 77). Further, any decent European energy policy will need to incorporate both specific energy policies and foreign policy instruments. As Gault argues, 'ultimately energy security is inextricable from broader economic and foreign policy challenges and solutions' (Gault 2004: 170).

 ## Key points

- Energy resources possess inherently sovereign attributes. In addition, the presence of energy resources has the ability to dramatically transform the fortunes of states.

- When considering the role of energy in foreign policy, foreign policy students must bear in mind three changes: states as energy actors (exporters, importers, and transit states), important non-state actors from both the public and private sector, and the robust presence of elite and business interests within the national interest.

- Energy security incorporates the dynamics of supply and demand, incorporating both public and private sector actors, comprehensively mixing national interests and foreign policy decision making with market forces.

- The break-up of the Soviet Union was instrumental in unlocking the foreign policy potential of energy in Europe. It was also crucial in underwriting European ambitions to construct a common European energy policy. The best example of this is the Energy Charter Treaty (1994), whose aim was to create a series of binding obligations on the trade, transit, and investment of energy goods, culminating in a framework of East–West energy cooperation, resting on liberal market principles.

- Aspects of power inherent in Russian energy consist of ownership and access to its vast energy resources, pipeline ownership, and long-term contracts. European assets are far less concentrated and its energy policy is less centralized.

- European countries are heavily dependent upon Russian energy imports. As a key transit country, Ukraine is of strategic importance, and is itself reliant upon Russia for both gas imports and transit tariffs.

- The proximate cause of the energy spat was a dispute in pricing between Gazprom of Russia and Ukraine; the remote cause was the governmental upheaval in Kiev when the 2005 election saw the country adopt a visibly pro-Western stance.

 ## Questions

1. Who are the key actors in European energy security?
2. Explain what factors make energy a strategic resource.

3. What is the role of energy within national and foreign policy and what are the main concerns of states when energy features in their foreign policy?

4. What was the political significance of energy during the immediate post Cold War years and what East–West forms of cooperation were attempted?

5. What were the major causes of the gradual falling-out between Russia and the EU, and what role did energy play?

6. What were the proximate and remote causes of the January 2006 gas spat between Ukraine and Russia?

7. Compare the perspectives of the EU with that of Russia and Ukraine as to the reasons behind the stoppage of gas.

8. What components will an effective EU energy policy require?

 Further reading

Kalicki, J.H. and Goldwyn, D.L. (2005), *Energy and Security. Toward a New Foreign Policy Strategy* (Washington, DC: Woodrow Wilson Centre Press and Baltimore, MD: Johns Hopkins University Press).
An American output, arguing for a holistic appreciation of the role of energy in foreign policy, with some good chapters on each region of the world.

Müller-Kraenner, S. (2008), *Energy Security* (Penguin Group).
An accessible introduction into the characteristics of the global energy system and energy security.

Pascual, C. and Elkind, J. (2009), *Energy Security: Economics, Politics, Strategies, and Implications* (Penguin Group).
A comprehensive and technical introduction to the tripatite components of energy security.

Prozorov, S. (2006), *Understanding Conflict between Russia and the EU: The Limits of Integration* (Baskingstoke: Palgrave Macmillan).
A well-researched overview of the various conflicts between Russia and the EU including integration, enlargement, sovereignty, and identity, situated in key IR perspectives.

Spykman, N.J. (1944), *The Geography of the Peace* (New Haven, CT: Yale University Institute of International Studies and New York: Harcourt Brace).
From one of the earliest institutes of international studies for promoting training in IR, Spykman's work is a seminal mid-century geopolitics perspective, giving an insight into both the role of Eurasia and the use of energy (coal and iron) in foreign policy which is still relevant.

Yergin, D. (2011), *The Quest: Energy Security, and the Remaking of the Modern World.*
A strong new addition by the US doyen of energy security.

Youngs, R. (2009), *Energy Security: Europe's new foreign policy challenge* (Penguin Group).
A comprehensive evaluation of the EU's perspective on energy security.

 Visit the Online Resource Centre that accompanies this book for more information:
www.oxfordtextbooks.co.uk/orc/smith_foreign/

New actors, new foreign policy: EU and enlargement

LISBETH AGGESTAM

Chapter contents

 ## Reader's guide

The foreign policy of the European Union (EU) challenges many of the assumptions of traditional foreign policy analysis in terms of actorness and power. The EU is not a state and its foreign policy is closely connected to the exercise of soft power. In this sense, the EU represents a new kind of actor in world politics and signifies a deeper transformation of foreign policy in Europe. The EU has had a profound influence on the reshaping of European order after the end of the Cold War by extending EU membership to an ever-increasing number of countries. Therefore EU enlargement is widely seen as the most important foreign policy instrument of the EU. This chapter examines a decision with far-reaching implications for European international relations, namely the 'Big Bang' enlargement of the EU, which involved its expansion from fifteen to twenty-seven members between 2004 and 2007. It is an interesting case for examining the complexity of the EU as an international actor. It highlights the significance of European norms in reshaping member states' interests and the supranational role of the European Commission in framing and implementing the decision to enlarge the EU. However, despite the successful outcome of enlargement of the EU in 2004 and 2007, this powerful instrument of EU foreign policy may be less available in the future. Therefore this chapter ends by looking at EU foreign policy beyond enlargement and asks whether the European Neighbourhood Policy (ENP) represents an alternative.

Introduction

The reshaping of Europe since the end of the Cold War in 1989 is not the result of the concert-like machination of a few dominant great powers. One of the novel features of the emerging European order is the role played by the EU, not through the projection of hard power, but through the power of attraction. By offering the prospect of EU membership, the EU has been able to fundamentally shape the norms of domestic and international behaviour to ensure peace and stability in Europe. The EU represents a new kind of actor in world politics and signifies a transformation of foreign policy in Europe. Given that the EU is not a state, it is often referred to as a new 'sui generis' (unique) actor. However, the precise characteristics of the EU as a power are contested (Manners 2002; Hyde-Price 2006; Sjursen 2006a; Aggestam 2008; Toje 2011).

This chapter examines the historic decision to enlarge the EU in 2004 and 2007. Enlargement is an interesting case study of EU foreign policy, as it is widely considered to be the most powerful instrument that the EU has at its disposal (Sedelmeier 2010; Smith 2004). The fifth enlargement was the biggest ever, with the entry of ten new members in 2004 and a further two joining in 2007 (see Map 24.1). Hence, it is known as the Big Bang enlargement. However, the decision to enlarge was not a given from the start and demonstrates the complexity of the EU as a foreign policy actor. What is interesting is that while initially member states were deeply divided (Sjursen 2006a), in the end they reached a consensus that a Big Bang enlargement was the best outcome to ensure peace and stability in Europe. This raises a number of pertinent questions: What motivated this decision? Were decision makers swayed by normative considerations based on European identity and values, or by geostrategic calculations and material interests? How significant were particular individuals, institutions, and governments in the decision-making process?

Three of the largest EU members—Britain, France and Germany—held distinctively different views on enlargement regarding its implications for their own national interests, shifts to the existing balance of power within the EU, the impact on the functioning of EU institutions, and the future of the integration process (Aggestam 2004). Reunified Germany quickly emerged as a strong proponent of a simultaneous widening and deepening of the process of European integration. France, on the other hand, whilst not rejecting enlargement *per se*, stressed the importance of ensuring that enlargement did not threaten further integration towards the political project of a *Europe puissance* ('European power'). Britain, in turn, viewed the prospect of enlargement as an opportunity to put a brake on the deepening process of European integration to ensure the emergence of a looser and more flexible union.

Significantly, while all three governments held strong views on enlargement, rooted in their own vision of a future European security architecture, they chose to multilateralize their policies through the EU. They agreed to delegate substantial powers to the European Commission, allowing it to set the agenda, frame the issues, and implement decisions on this controversial topic. In fact, the Commission came to exercise a policy-making role far beyond that usually associated with the bureaucratic apparatus of an international organization and ended up playing a leading role in the policy process. Thus the

Map 24.1 EU member states before and after the Big Bang.

decision to enlarge the EU cannot be understood merely as a result of intergovernmental bargaining between member states, or simply as a result of supranational leadership of the policy process. Hence this case focuses on both of these levels in the decision-making process.

The chapter ends by considering whether the decision for a Big Bang enlargement sets a precedent for the future. In other words, will the EU continue to rely on the instrument of enlargement to achieve influence in foreign policy? The queue for EU membership remains long. Several countries have declared their ambitions to become EU members in the future. Croatia has completed its accession negotiations with the EU and is set to become the 28th member in 2013. However, there is considerable evidence suggesting that future decisions on EU enlargement will be harder to achieve. Hence this chapter will conclude with an analysis of the EU's attempt to develop alternative foreign policy instruments to exert influence in wider Europe.

EU foreign policy

The European Union is often regarded as a *sui generis* actor in the international system because it does not fit traditional conceptions of foreign policy, power, and agency in the international system. This problem of how to conceptualize the EU as an actor has generated considerable academic interest (Bretherton and Vogler 2006; Dunne 2008; Bickerton 2011; Hill and Smith 2011; Thomas 2011) with some making the case that Foreign Policy Analysis in Europe demands a more distinct, less American-oriented approach (Manners and Whitman 2000; Larsen 2009). EU foreign policy, particularly on enlargement, challenges traditional mainstream conceptions of the inside–outside of foreign policy, the nature of foreign policy actorness, and the relevance of ideational versus materialist power.

To begin with, foreign policy is normally seen as the exclusive prerogative of states, yet the EU has explicitly made claims since the Maastricht Treaty of 1993 to a common (as opposed to a single) European foreign and security policy (CFSP). EU member states still pursue national foreign policies, but nevertheless have made far-reaching commitments to coordinate their policies through common institutional structures at the European level that go beyond established forms of foreign policy cooperation (Wong and Hill 2011). The Lisbon Treaty, ratified in 2009, significantly strengthens the institutional framework of European foreign policy making (see Box 24.1).

BOX 24.1 The Lisbon Treaty: enhancing EU actorness

A major part of the Lisbon Treaty is devoted to reforming EU foreign policy to increase its international coherence and effectiveness. Some of these reforms are as follows.

- **External action** The Common Foreign and Security Policy (CFSP) and EU external relations (enlargement, development, trade) are drawn closer together by abolishing the previous pillar structure of the Union. This is to ensure a more effective working relationship between the Council and the Commission.

- **Legal personality** The Union can sign treaties and international agreements—a clear example of the new kind of actorness that the EU represents in world politics.

- **President of the European Council** This post was created to provide a more singular external representation of the European Council on the international stage. As such, the President can act on behalf of heads of state and governments of EU member states in the international arena.

- **High Representative of the European Union for Foreign Affairs and Security Policy** This is the hub of EU foreign policy making to ensure greater harmonization between national foreign policies. The role also includes the post as Vice President of the Commission to achieve greater consistency between various external policies. However, there still remains a European Commissioner in charge of EU enlargement policy and the ENP.

- **European External Action Service (EEAS)** The Lisbon Treaty gives birth to an embryonic European diplomatic corps to assist the High Representative and to streamline EU external services. Officials are drawn from the Council, the Commission, and diplomats seconded from EU member states.

- **Solidarity and mutual assistance** There are clauses in the Lisbon Treaty that call on EU member states to aid each other in the case of armed aggression, terrorist attacks, and major disasters. Importantly, it is left to member states to decide what kind of assistance will be provided. This is an important addendum for those states which still claim to be non-aligned.

For a more detailed overview of the Lisbon Treaty reforms, see Whitman and Juncos (2009).

The Lisbon Treaty aims to provide the EU with greater coherence as an international actor. Although the Lisbon Treaty formally dissolves the pillar structure of the Union, the different fields of policy making remain distinctive in terms of supranational and intergovernmental procedures. In the areas of external economic relations, such as trade, aid, and enlargement policy, member states have delegated significant functions to the European Commission (EC), the European Parliament (EP), and the European Court of Justice (ECJ). However, foreign affairs and security policy remain essentially intergovernmental. EU member states have committed themselves to speaking with 'one voice' on a range of foreign policy issues, for instance on the Middle East peace process, and at international institutions like the UN General Assembly. Over the last decade, the EU has also developed a Common Security and Defence Policy (CSDP). In December 2003, member states agreed a European Security Strategy (ESS), which has given a further fillip to the long-running debate on how best to conceptualize the EU, and whether the concept of 'civilian power' is still relevant. The EU has dispatched a number of civilian and military CSDP missions around the world to undertake peacekeeping, crisis management, and humanitarian operations. Nonetheless, despite these advances in European integration, it is important to acknowledge that EU foreign policy continues to suffer from divisions on many levels of policy making that undermine the ambition to speak with one voice. The EU's response to the Arab Spring and the Libyan crisis in 2011 is a testimony of that.

EU enlargement involves all the EU's policy areas and has a strong element of constitutive policy in the sense that it profoundly affects the EU's core structures, policies, budget, and decision-making processes. Externally, enlargement has major implications for the Union's global presence, expanding its network of international interests and generating heightened expectations about the EU's future responsibilities for international peace, security, and prosperity.

EU enlargement raises important questions about the nature of power in the contemporary international system. It can be viewed as an attempt to extend the post-war West European 'security community' (Deutsch 1957). As early as the 1970s, François Duchêne (1973) argued that the then EC represented a new form of international actor, which he designated a 'civilian power'. Drawing on liberal notions of economic interdependence and the domestication of international politics through the observance of common rules, he argued that the emerging European civilian power could tame anarchy and facilitate the peaceful resolution of disputes in ways that traditional military powers could not.

The concept of civilian power has provided the starting-point for other analysts who have argued that the EU is a distinctive international actor because it 'exercises influence and shapes its environment through what it is, rather than through what it does' (Maull 2005: 778) (on normative power, see Manners 2002). In contrast with previous hegemons and empires, who have sought to promote their own values and project a favourable image of themselves on the basis of their hard power, the EU, it is argued, has been able to reshape post Cold War European order through the power of attraction and magnetism as a civilian power. Much of the EU's power derives from its normative appeal as the institutional embodiment of peace and reconciliation, democracy, the rule of law, respect for human rights, liberty, and solidarity—all of which are part of the treaties and agreements that make up the *acquis communautaire*. However, the EU's conditionality clauses that underpin the accession process can imply an element of coercion that should not be overlooked (Vachudova 2005; Epstein and Sedelmeier 2009). It involves a degree of interference in the domestic affairs of candidate countries that sits uneasily with traditional principles of non-interference in the internal affairs of sovereign states. Above all, it demonstrates a new kind of foreign policy in which the domestic and international domains increasingly overlap.

The Big Bang enlargement

The decision to enlarge the EU with a large number of new members is an interesting case study, as it demonstrates the complexity and multi-faceted nature of EU foreign policy making. Although the governments of EU member states were crucial in the decision-making process, the case also reveals the critical role played by new institutional actors, such as the European Commission and the presidency of the EU. The case also demonstrates how interlinked material and ideational factors are in explaining EU enlargement. Material interests, security, and geopolitical considerations were clearly at play, as well as conformity to norms, rules, and identities. In this sense, it could be argued that both a rationalist and constructivist foreign policy analysis would be able to provide convincing, if rivalling, explanations of EU enlargement. The following analysis will show the interplay of these factors in four phases of the process that eventually led to the decision to enlarge the European Union with twelve new members.

The key dilemma: widening versus deepening European integration

Despite the intoxicating mood of euphoria that accompanied the end of the Cold War, the new democracies' call for a 'return to Europe' was not reciprocated with immediate enthusiasm by the EU. Instead, EU member states seemed disoriented by the speed of change as communist regimes fell like skittles, the Warsaw Pact dissolved, the Baltic states broke from the Soviet Union, Germany reunified, Yugoslavia descended into war and conflict, and—most dramatically of all—the USSR ceased to exist. With no blueprint to go by, governments in Western Europe reacted in an ad hoc and piecemeal manner, often returning to traditional national foreign policy roles and visions of Europe (Niblett and Wallace 2001).

Yet at the same time, the early 1990s were marked by great strides forward in the process of European integration, which in many respects constituted the high tide of supranationalism: the internal market was completed by 1992, and in the same year the Maastricht Treaty establishing the European Union and setting out the timetable for monetary union was negotiated. This reflected a widely held view—underwritten by a powerful constituency consisting of the Commission, France, and Germany—that widening should not be at the expense of deepening. Indeed, a deepening of the European integration process was considered crucial to the creation of a stabilizing core for post Cold War Europe. Above all, deepening addressed a central concern of the French, which was to anchor a reunified Germany firmly within a more integrated European structure. French decision makers were determined to consolidate their institutionalized partnership with Germany prior to any enlargement of the Union, fearing that Germany's geopolitical interests would push its government to develop close partnerships with its neighbours in *Mitteleuropa*. In this way, French decision makers hoped that, in cooperation with their German counterparts, they would provide strategic leadership for Europe and constitute its core within a Europe defined by 'concentric circles' of integration.

The idea of a European confederation transcended the contradiction between deepening and widening, thereby combining *Petite Europe* and *Grande Europe* within a single overarching framework (Mitterrand 1991). Although enlargement was seen by French policy makers as a distant prospect, they did not deny that it was a long-term historical responsibility and political necessity. But they insisted that enlargement could not be done on the 'cheap' as this would threaten the *acquis* and thus the effective decision making of the Union, thereby undermining its capacity to act as a stabilizing core of the new Europe. There was pronounced fear in Paris that enlargement would dilute the Union into a loosely articulated 'European space'. Hence membership of the European Union was not deemed to be immediately accessible for everyone and could only take place after candidate states had accepted all the clauses of the Maastricht Treaty (Aggestam 2004: 174).

The idea of concentric circles became firmly established in the European Commission, with the Commission President Jacques Delors, a former French socialist colleague of Mitterrand, adding texture and detail to Mitterrand's rather abstract conception of a European Confederation. The Commission, perceiving itself to be the institutional guardian of the 'idea of Europe', also adopted the position that widening must not be at the expense of deepening'. An integrated EU, it was argued, would be at the centre of the new Europe, followed by a ring of prosperous and small members of the European Free Trade Association (EFTA). The Central and Eastern Europe countries (CEECs) would occupy the next ring, linked by Europe association agreements, while a looser ring would include the Soviet Union. These concentric circles would allow the Community to proceed with economic and political integration in the core, while strengthening its relations with its European neighbours without offering them immediate membership of the EU (Smith 2005: 273).

While France did not have vital national interests in Central and Eastern Europe, Germany—a country situated at the heart of Europe and therefore bordering directly onto a number of countries in the post-communist East—was acutely affected by the end of Cold War bipolarity. For German decision makers—following their rapid absorption of East Germany—both the deepening and the widening of the EU were seen as central foreign policy objectives, providing the solution to the dilemmas of their *Mittellage* ('central geographical location'). Therefore widening of the EU and deepening of the integration process were seen as complimentary processes rather than 'either–or' choices. Thus the German government quickly emerged as a leading proponent of 'deepening' (to address fears about reunited Germany's new-found sovereignty), as well as an advocate of enlargement of the Union to the east. The preamble of the German Constitution commits the Federal Republic to the goal of building a peaceful and stable European order. Germany's 'politics of responsibility' coincided with its national economic and strategic interests in stabilizing its eastern neighbours. This notion of 'stability transfer' was designed to serve German national interests by surrounding it with allies and partners, and drew on Germany's own experience of post-war *Westbindung*. The commitment of German decision makers to EU enlargement was based on the belief that if 'we do not export stability now, we will be subject to instability sooner or later' (Rühe 1994: 7). However, Germany's national interests led them to advocate a limited round of enlargement, primarily focused on the 'Visegrad' countries (the Czech Republic, Hungary, Poland, and Slovakia) to its immediate east.

In contrast with Germany, the UK did not have any direct and immediate interests at stake in Eastern Europe beyond that of the geopolitical stability of post Cold War Europe.

Nonetheless, the British government quickly emerged as a champion of an early enlargement of the EU, an organization it valued above all for its role in creating a continental free-trade market. From the perspective of the British government, the choice of widening and deepening presented no dilemma whatsoever. On the contrary, the British government under John Major explicitly argued that enlargement should take priority over deepening, because any further deepening of European integration would make it more difficult for the CEECs to join. Indeed, enlargement was welcomed by the British government as a means of watering down the federalist impulses of some EU member states and making the Union more flexible. Thus the British government saw the end of the Cold War as providing a window of opportunity for championing a new course for the EU—one that would embody a distinctly British vision of a wider, more outward-looking Union (Aggestam 2004: 127).

The lack of a coherent message from EU member states because of competing foreign policy perspectives, along with the perception that enlargement was not an immediate priority for the EU given the focus on implementing the Maastricht Treaty, was deeply disappointing for the new democracies from the post-communist East (Hyde-Price 1996). The CEECs had hoped that their aspirations to join the EU would be met with the same commitment and decisiveness that characterized the negotiations leading to membership for the post-authoritarian regimes of Greece, Portugal and Spain, where the criteria for membership had clearly been formulated in terms of political considerations to consolidate democracy and stability in these countries (the democratic peace argument). However, the scale and complexity of the challenge presented by future membership of the new democracies from Central and Eastern Europe led the EU to spell out explicitly and in considerable detail its expectations of the aspirant countries. The first step consisted in detailed negotiations leading to so-called Europe Agreements covering a range of economic and political policies.

The whole idea of concentric circles collapsed under the pressure of events that followed. The EFTA countries quickly swallowed their reservations about sovereignty and sought greater influence by becoming full members of the EU. Consequently, in January 1995, Austria, Finland, and Sweden joined the EU, which welcomed them with open arms as stable democracies and net contributors to the EU budget. However, the eastern enlargement of the EU would impose substantial new costs on the Union's budget, a prospect that few member states relished. Nonetheless, as the Balkans descended into war and conflict, many EU members recognized the implicit connection between enlargement and security. In order not to compound the disappointment felt in the CEECs by the tardy pace of their 'return to Europe', EU member states recognized that they had to send a clear political signal to the CEEC that their future membership of the Union was firmly on the EU agenda.

Deciding on the membership criteria

For the new democracies of Central and Eastern Europe, 'returning to Europe', by which was meant joining the EU, was their principal foreign policy objective. The transformation of their moribund political, economic, and social systems after the collapse of communism was explicitly framed in terms of their commitment to core European values. In so doing, they hoped to use a form of moral leverage to make it more difficult for the West Europeans to avoid making a firm commitment on EU membership (Hyde-Price 1996; Schimmelfennig 2003).

Therefore the EU faced a difficult balancing act: on the one hand providing the necessary incentives for painful transformation of post-communist polities and economies, and on the other avoiding deepening the sense of frustration and disappointment that was already emerging in CEECs. Against the backdrop of continuing conflict in the Balkans, and in order to enhance the EU's power of attraction in the post-communist East, it became clear that the EU needed to send out, if not a precise timetable for membership, a clear political signal that enlargement was on the agenda.

With these considerations in mind, the Commission proposed to the European Council meeting in Copenhagen in 1993 that a clear membership commitment be made to signatories of Europe Agreements. This, it was argued, would boost the reform process in the CEECs, thereby contributing to the peace and security of Europe. Consequently, at Copenhagen, the Union specified three key conditions for future membership: (i) applicants had to be democracies with (ii) functioning market economies which could compete in the single market, and (iii) they had to have the ability to take on all the obligations of membership including the adherence to the aims of political, economic, and monetary union (the *acquis*). These 'Copenhagen' criteria were not novel in themselves, but this was the first time they had been adumbrated so explicitly. Their intention was to ensure that widening and deepening would be pursued in parallel (European Council 1993: 13).

The Copenhagen criteria were initially directed at the six countries that had already concluded, or were currently negotiating, Europe agreements (Bulgaria, the Czech Republic, Hungary, Poland, Romania, and Slovakia). However, almost before the ink was dry on the Copenhagen document, new aspirants for membership were queuing at the EU's doors, spurred on by further tectonic shifts in the European political and security landscape. Consequently, within a year of the Copenhagen Council meeting, both Malta and the Republic of Cyprus (who had already applied for membership in 1990) were recognized as applicants, and four newly independent countries—Estonia, Latvia, Lithuania, and Slovenia—were able to begin negotiations for Europe agreements, thereby joining the queue for future membership. (See Box 24.2.)

The inclusion of two Mediterranean 'orphans', Cyprus and Malta, amongst the applicant countries was politically significant, and reflected concerns about the shifting balance of influence between EU member states—above all, France and Germany. France and the other southern European EU member states bordering the Mediterranean were worried that the opening to the CEECs would shift the EU's interests and concerns northwards and eastwards, thereby enhancing the geopolitical weight of united Germany. The launch of the 'Barcelona process' was one response to this; the other was the inclusion of Cyprus and Malta in accession negotiations. The negotiation of Europe Agreements with the three Baltic states and Slovenia was also a setback for the German government, which tended to favour a more limited enlargement involving the Visegrad countries of East Central Europe, thereby stabilizing the Federal Republic's immediate neighbourhood. Whilst this was disappointing to the Visegrad states, who had otherwise hoped for early membership, it reflected a suspicion that once Germany's direct interests had been satisfied, the drive for further enlargement would weaken.

As political momentum for a large enlargement grew, so did French concerns that this would entail serious financial costs and prevent the further deepening of the integration project. Worries that the *acquis communautaire* would gradually be watered down, given the

BOX 24.2 The Big Bang enlargement: from Europe agreement to application and accession

	Association/Europe agreement	Application	Accession
Bulgaria	1993	1995	2007
Cyprus	1972	1990	2004
Czech Republic	1993	1996	2004
Estonia	1995	1995	2004
Hungary	1991	1994	2004
Latvia	1995	1995	2004
Lithuania	1995	1995	2004
Malta	1971	1990	2004
Poland	1991	1994	2004
Romania	1993	1995	2007
Slovakia	1993	1995	2004
Slovenia	1996	1996	2004

pressures of absorbing a large group of new members, and that the EU would revert to little more than a free-trade area with weak decision-making capabilities led French officials to underline the importance of institutional change to meet the demands of enlargement. In the face of perceived British intransigence on deepening the integration process, the French began to advocate 'reinforced cooperation', which would allow those member states who could and wished to move ahead with further integration to do so. In addition, the French successfully persuaded other members to agree a list of progress and convergence criteria as a means of objectively measuring how ready a country was to take on the responsibilities and commitments of EU membership.

Not such a 'soft power': applying political conditionality

To the dismay of applicant countries from Central and Eastern Europe, the Copenhagen criteria proved far from being vaguely formulated conditions that could be quickly and painlessly met. On the contrary, the European Commission took the task of specifying their intentions very seriously and ended up producing thousands of pages of legislation for the candidates to implement and proposing some very detailed institutional changes. Potential joiners have to show that they have the administrative capacity to apply EU rules properly and the political will to do so (Grabbe 2006). (See Box 24.3.)

BOX 24.3 EU policy making and enlargement

Prospective members submit applications to the EU Council of Ministers. The European Commission thereafter evaluates and makes a formal opinion on candidates. A unanimous Council decision is required to start accession negotiations. The first phase of accession negotiations is conducted by the Commission, and involves a detailed scrutiny of the candidates' ability to apply to the *acquis* and identifies controversial issues for negotiations. On the basis of a common position adopted by the Council and the Commission, the Council Presidency conducts bilateral accession negotiations. To endorse the accession treaties, a favourable decision has to be taken by the Council (unanimity), the Commission, and the European Parliament (simple majority). Finally, the accession treaties need to be ratified by applicants and EU member states (Sedelmeier 2005a: 404).

What political conditionality meant in practice was that the Commission was able to exert powerful pressure on candidates to undertake a host of legal and institutional changes, affecting a broad range of issues from their macro-economic policies to their treatment of minorities and judicial reforms—in many ways extending beyond the remit of the *acquis* itself. The Commission was also not adverse to singling out good performers and shaming the laggards. This demonstrated that the EU was not just a toothless 'soft power', but willing and able to use power coercively by threatening to withhold the carrot of future membership. In this way, the EU actively used political conditionality to influence applicant countries. This went beyond merely enforcing the *acquis*, and included strong criticism of domestic political processes and outcomes. For example, during negotiations on the Pact for Stability (a multilateral negotiating framework designed to address potential causes of conflict and insecurity which the EU sponsored between May 1994 and March 1995), the CEECs were urged to conclude 'good neighbourly' agreements with each other on borders and treatment of minorities (Smith 2005: 279). The EU exerted direct pressure on Hungary, Romania, and Slovakia to resolve disputes over Hungarian minorities, and on the Baltic states to improve their treatment of their Russian minorities.

From the start, the Commission was tasked with the critical role of evaluating each membership application to see how well applicant countries performed in fulfilling the Copenhagen conditions, which was the pre-condition for starting membership negotiations. Each application was to be judged on its own merits, thereby differentiating between applicant countries and providing an additional spur to progress by the laggards. However, differentiation created a new political dilemma between inclusion and exclusion dilemma. Rejecting or delaying an application could have destablizing effects on the country concerned, isolating it from the benefits of EU membership and paradoxically insulating it from further EU pressure. Countries whose application was rejected or delayed might become alienated from the EU, thereby reducing the Commission's leverage on that state, and undermining the grand strategy of using enlargement to project peace and security into the post-communist East.

The inclusion–exclusion dilemma increasingly came to haunt EU deliberations. Debates over the implications of the Commission's strategy of differentiating between applicant countries eventually led EU member states to opt for an inclusive accession process and open negotiations with all the applicants (Smith 2005).

By the late 1990s, significant momentum had built up behind the enlargement process. This in turn led to a shift in the terms of the debate on the widening versus deepening dilemma. An Intergovernmental Conference (IGC) was held in 1996–1997 aimed at reforming the EU treaties and thus preparing the Union for enlargement, principally by expanding the use of qualified majority voting and streamlining the EU's institutions. The IGC negotiations witnessed renewed skirmishing over the future of European integration, with France and Germany seeking to exercise their traditional leadership role and insisting that widening and deepening must go hand in hand. If not, they threatened, they might be tempted to move ahead independently in order to establish a core Europe. However, by the time the IGC concluded in Amsterdam, a pragmatic compromise had emerged which left key unresolved issues for the subsequent IGC. This compromise was important because it signalled that the enlargement process was now irreversible and unstoppable. For the time being, it seemed, widening was to take precedence over deepening, thereby reinforcing the momentum that was building behind the enlargement bandwagon. (See Box 24.4.)

A month after the IGC concluded in Amsterdam, the European Commission published its opinions on the membership applications. In a wide-ranging report entitled 'Agenda 2000', the Commission recommended that membership negotiations be opened with only six countries: Cyprus, the Czech Republic, Estonia, Hungary, Poland, and Slovenia. Although no candidate country met all the membership conditions, it was argued that these six states came closest to doing so. The other five CEECs were too far behind in the reform processes; in particular, Slovakia was singled out as the only country which did not meet the required political conditions. For example, throughout Vladimir Meciar's term in office in Slovakia (1992–1998) the EU had issued numerous warnings that Slovakia must develop more robust and transparent democratic norms before it could join the EU. The decision to include Estonia and Slovenia alongside Germany's regional neighbours in the Visegrad group was influenced by NATO's decision in June 1997 to offer membership to these three countries alone; the EU wished to signal that enlargement would extend beyond East Central Europe. Consequently, in December 1997 the Luxembourg European Council endorsed

---

BOX 24.4 The criteria for EU membership

The criteria for EU membership have been defined in a number of Treaty texts and declarations.

THE TREATY OF ROME 1957 'Any European state may apply to become a member of the Community' (Article 237).

THE COPENHAGEN EUROPEAN COUNCIL 1993 A functioning market economy with the capacity to cope with competitive pressures and market forces inside the EU; stability of institutions guaranteeing democracy, the rule of law, human rights, and respect for and protection of minorities; and the ability to take on the obligations of EU membership including adherence to the aims of economic and political union (the *acquis*).

THE AMSTERDAM TREATY 1999 Any European state that respects the principles of liberty, democracy, respect for human rights and fundamental freedoms, and the rule of law, may apply to become a member of the Union (Articles 5 and 49).

THE HELSINKI EUROPEAN COUNCIL 1999 Candidate countries must demonstrate 'good-neighbourliness' by resolving outstanding border disputes peacefully, if necessary through arbitration by the International Court of Justice.

the Commission's recommendation for negotiations to start with the so-called 'Luxembourg Six' (European Council 1997).

Widening takes precedence: strategic security considerations

By the late 1990s, the political momentum for EU enlargement had become irresistible. The enlargement bandwagon benefited from two contingent factors: first, a series of pro-enlargement presidencies, and second, the Kosovo War. Serendipitously, in the late 1990s the rotating presidency of the EU was held by a string of pro-enlargement governments: first the UK in the first half of 1998, followed by Austria and then Germany in early 1999. In the case of the British presidency, not only was the UK a traditional advocate of enlargement, but New Labour had won a stunning electoral victory the previous year, and Tony Blair was keen to demonstrate his government's new-found commitment to being 'at the heart of Europe'. Therefore it was with evident delight that Prime Minister Blair was able to announce in March 1998 that membership negotiations would formally begin with the 'Luxembourg Six'.

The opening of accession negotiations with the Six was accompanied by a decision to draw up annual Accession Partnerships with all the applicant countries, listing the objectives that the EU wanted each applicant to meet. The aim in doing so was to address the potentially destabilizing implications of the inclusion–exclusion dilemma by maintaining pressure on the applicant states to carry out the desired reforms, whilst dangling the carrot of formal accession negotiations if they made satisfactory progress. This strategy proved highly successful: for example, both Latvia and Lithuania, concerned that they had fallen behind Estonia, made extraordinary progress in meeting the conditions, whilst elections in Slovakia in September 1998 brought down the Meciar government and opened the door for rapid progress towards accession. At the end of 1998, three more CEECs and Malta moved closer to beginning accession negotiations, leaving Bulgaria and Romania trailing behind.

The German EU presidency in the first half of 1999 also accelerated the momentum towards enlargement. As in the case of the UK, an election in the previous year had brought to power a 'Red–Green' coalition led by Chancellor Gerhard Schröder. His administration was keen to shed the image of *Geo-Klientelismus* that was associated with Chancellor's Kohl's focus on Germany's immediate neighbourhood in East Central Europe, and spoke more positively of a wider circle of enlargement encompassing both the Baltic states and much of southeast Europe, possibly including Turkey. This shift in German thinking towards a larger round of enlargement was reinforced by the Kosovo War, which gave added weight to the geostrategic considerations which had always favoured EU enlargement. Renewed conflict in the Balkans underlined the importance of avoiding alienating Bulgaria and Romania, particularly in the light of the crucial support they provided to NATO during Operation Allied Force. The geostrategic dangers posed by the inclusion–exclusion dilemma were explicitly addressed by Tony Blair, who argued that 'Events in Kosovo also bring home to us the urgency of enlargement . . . I do not underestimate the difficulties involved in extending enlargement to these countries . . . But I do believe we have a moral duty to offer them the hope of membership of the EU . . . the inestimable advantage of political stability of the continent' (Blair 1999).

In the wake of the Kosovo War and the successive pro-enlargement EU presidencies, the Commission adopted a new position. In October 1999 it recommended on political and security grounds that the EU open negotiations with all the applicant countries (except Turkey), arguing that enlargement was a political imperative if the EU was to make a decisive contribution to stability and prosperity in Europe. The Commission justified its recommendation by arguing that the applicant countries met the political conditions for membership (which were described as the most important of the Copenhagen criteria), even if their record in meeting the other conditions was patchier (Verheugen 1999). Prioritizing the political criteria also provided a convenient way of side-stepping Turkey's membership application, because it could be argued that Turkey did not yet meet the political conditions and therefore would only be offered negotiations leading to an Accession Partnership.

After a string of pro-enlargement presidencies, the French found their room for manoeuvre significantly constrained when they took over the presidency in the second half of 2000. Although French decision makers accepted the principle of enlargement, they were determined to ensure that EU institutions and decision-making processes were reformed prior to enlargement taking place. They succeeded in securing agreement at Nice on a complex compromise arrangement on how votes were to be distributed in both the European Parliament and Council of Ministers in an enlarged EU of 27 member states. The problem with the Nice Treaty was that its voting system was not transparent and, above all, it made it possible for minority coalitions to block decisions. Mutual dissatisfaction with the compromise hammered out at Nice led to Franco-German agreement to establish a Convention which would agree a 'Constitution for Europe', reforming EU institutions and deepening the integration process. As Germany was a founding member of the European Union and a leading proponent of multilateral cooperation and integration in Europe, German policy makers found themselves increasingly torn between their advocacy of enlargement and their desire to preserve the effectiveness of a more exclusive and homogeneous European Union. Thus the Red–Green coalition government became more insistent that the EU had to conduct root and branch institutional reforms before enlarging its membership. This concern with ensuring the continued deepening of EU integration process and the efficacy of its decision-making processes in tandem with enlargement brought the German government much closer to the position of their French counterparts (Aggestam 2004: 223).

By this stage in the enlargement process, the Commission concluded that it could not make a convincing case that some of the eight CEE candidates were more ready to join than the others. Poland, in particular, presented the Commission with a major dilemma. Its pre-accession strategy proceeded in fits and starts, sometimes keeping in step with the other candidates but more often than not falling behind. The Commission was sorely tempted to threaten Poland with a delay in its accession in order to force it to get its act together, but Warsaw never dropped far enough behind the other candidates to make the threat credible. And Poland had powerful backers in Germany, who for a mix of historical, political, and strategic reasons were committed to Polish EU membership (Grabbe 2004: 14).

Differentiation or not? Copenhagen revisited

By 2000–2001, the big question facing the EU was how many countries would conclude negotiations by the 2002 deadline that had been set. Support for a Big Bang enlargement involving ten candidate countries grew among many informed observers, though this proposition had only limited support among member states. Proponents of a Big Bang argued that taking in ten countries together would leave fewer on the outside (thus minimizing the problem of exclusion) and necessitate only one large-scale adjustment by the EU. However, a Big Bang enlargement would also risk disappointing the front-runners (who would then have to wait for the laggards to catch up), and could reduce the pressure on all of them to undertake unpopular reforms (Smith 2005: 283). In addition, according to Eurobarometer polls there was little support for a Big Bang enlargement among the publics of the member states.

Thus the key question of how and when to enlarge was still left hanging—indeed, purposely so, given the unresolved issues raised by the dilemma of differentiation discussed above. Nonetheless, in February 2000 formal membership negotiations were initiated with the 'Helsinki Ten'. As policy makers grappled with the dilemma of differentiation and the debate over a Big Bang enlargement gathered pace, advocates of the political project of an integrated EU became more outspoken. Underlining these criticisms of a Big Bang was the fear that enlargement would turn the EU into little more than a glorified free-trade area.

At this sensitive juncture in the debate, it was once again the Commission that was able to frame the policy agenda. The Commission eventually joined the Big Bang bandwagon in 2001, thus throwing its considerable weight and authority behind this option. The Commissioner for Enlargement, Günter Verheugen, maintained that ten countries could join the next enlargement round—in other words, all the existing candidates except for Bulgaria and Romania. He urged more political support for what he described as a historic process, and argued that a Big Bang would be preferable to a small first wave because it would avoid cutting off countries from their neighbours (Verheugen 2001). The terrorist attacks of 9/11 also served to reinforce the security rationale for the Big Bang option, with the Commission declaring that 'a strong and united Europe is more important than ever before, against the background of the terrorist attacks of 11 September' (European Commission 2001).

The Commission's progress report stating that ten countries were ready to join received a mixed response among politicians in member states. Hubert Védrine, France's then foreign minister, publicly questioned the Commission's methodology for assessing the candidates' readiness to join (Védrine 2001). But given that member states had in part delegated the management of the enlargement negotiations to the Commission, it was too late in the process to raise these concerns (Grabbe 2004: 13).

In the second half of 2002—nine years after the historic decision in Copenhagen to specify criteria for membership—the Danes once again held the EU presidency. For Danish Prime Minister, Fogh Rasmusson, the stakes were high. A failure to conclude the enlargement negotiations in Copenhagen would potentially postpone it for a substantial period of time, given the EU's exceptionally busy agenda for the next few years (yet another IGC and controversial budget negotiations). In October 2002, the Commission declared that the ten candidate countries would be able to assume the obligations of membership from 2004. To meet the deadline, the last two months of 2002 involved intense negotiations, particularly in the fields of agriculture and finance. Finally, however, and to the relief of all involved, the deal was done at the December 2002 Copenhagen European Council—the ten countries would accede to the EU on 1 May 2004.

As for Bulgaria and Romania, the Copenhagen European Council stated that 'depending on further progress in complying with the membership criteria, the objective is to welcome Bulgaria and Romania as members of the European Union in 2007' (European Council 2002: 4). This constituted a remarkable turnaround, because previous European Councils had been very reluctant to set a definite date for the accession of specific candidates. Reverting to traditional arguments about spheres of influence, France in particular warned of the dangers of leaving Bulgaria and Romania out of the forthcoming enlargement round. Ironically therefore, given its initial reservations about enlargement, France ended up playing a leading role in persuading reluctant members—notably Germany—to accept a Big Bang enlargement that would result in twelve new EU member states.

Beyond enlargement: EU foreign policy in the neighbourhood

Ironically, although the Big Bang enlargement can be seen as a successful outcome of EU foreign policy in shaping European order after the end of the Cold War, it also raises serious questions about the future prospects of enlargement. The normative commitment to enlargement is still there in principle, but the conditions on which future decisions will be taken have changed profoundly. The latest enlargement with twelve new EU members has raised serious question about the EU's 'absorption capacity', i.e. the EU's ability to remain coherent and cohesive with the ever-increasing diversity that each enlargement brings. It is widely recognized that a feeling of 'enlargement fatigue' has taken hold in large sections of European elites and public opinion, and that the 'permissive consensus' (Hooghe and Marks 2008) on enlargement no longer holds (Hillion 2010). The difficult negotiations over institutional reforms that resulted in the Lisbon Treaty and the economic recession do not whet the appetite for future enlargements at present. At the same time, it is also clear that the normative appeal of the EU may be waning in an increasingly multipolar world with rising new powers. These developments raise some serious questions about the EU's ability to exercise power in its foreign policy through enlargement. This section will briefly discuss some of the challenges lying ahead in EU foreign policy by analysing prospects for future enlargements, primarily towards Southeastern Europe, and the alternative offered by the so-called European Neighbourhood Policy (ENP).

The carrot of enlargement is still a powerful instrument in EU foreign policy for shaping developments in the Balkans, a region that in so many ways has been a test case and constitutive to the development of EU foreign policy. The EU affirmed its normative commitment to extend membership to the Balkan countries at a European Council meeting in Thessaloniki in June 2003. Since then, Croatia has completed its accession negotiations and is likely to join in 2013 if ratification of the accession treaty is approved by all EU member states. The prospect of enlargement for the remaining Balkan countries (Albania, Bosnia Herzegovina, Kosovo, Serbia, Montenegro, Yugoslav Republic of Macedonia) is blighted by serious obstacles, some of which are internal to these states themselves, but also because of divisions among EU member states (particularly on Kosovo). Maintaining the prospect of EU enlargement as credible leverage to influence developments in the region is a precarious balancing act for the EU. Again, the role of the European Commission is critical in keeping the momentum going in the negotiations with potential and candidate countries (see Map 24.2).

The longest-standing applicant for EU membership is Turkey, who first applied in 1987. Turkey became an official candidate in 1999 and started negotiations in 2005. By 2011, only one out of thirty-three chapters has been closed in the negotiations. As in the case of the

Balkans, the geostrategic imperatives for enlargement are considerable. However, the question of Turkish membership is highly divisive among EU member states. Turkish membership is challenging for a number of reasons related to the large size of Turkey, its socio-economic composition, its religion, and, not least, conflicting issues with some of its neighbours over Cyprus. Significantly, both the French and German governments have officially stated their reservations and signalled that they would prefer a solution in which Turkey is granted the status of 'privileged partnership' rather than full EU membership (Rahigh-Aghsan 2011; Schimmelfennig 2011).

The question about what kind of relationship the EU should build beyond enlargement became a pressing issue as soon as the decision for a Big Bang enlargement had been taken. There was a concern that eastern enlargement could create new divisions in Europe between insiders and outsiders, triggering instability and a growing sense of insecurity in the countries bordering the European Union. Hence, European policy makers were keen to develop an instrument whereby the EU would be able to shape and influence its immediate neighbourhood without promising EU membership (Whitman and Wolff 2010). The European Security Strategy of 2003 explicitly states that one of the aims of EU foreign and security policy is to build 'security in the neighbourhood'. A year later, the European Neighbourhood Policy (ENP) was set up with the aim of creating a ring of well-governed neighbours surrounding the EU from North Africa, through the Middle East, to Eastern Europe and the Caucasus (see Map 24.2).

The ENP is built on liberal ideas that increasing mutual interdependence and the normative attraction of the EU will foster prosperity, stability, and security. In many ways, the ENP is symptomatic of how the EU pursues its interests and exercises power in foreign policy, which can be characterized as a form of 'milieu-shaping' (Wolfers 1966) and 'structural power' (Keukeleire and MacNaughtan 2008). The emphasis is on material assistance and a preference for soft power mechanisms rather than coercive elements. The Action Plan that the EU negotiates individually with each country sets out benchmarks to consolidate democracy, good governance, rule of law, and public administration in return for greater access to the European market. But in contrast to the strong conditionality that the EU enlargement process entails, the incentive structure is markedly different in ENP as it does not promise membership. Each individual country decides in negotiations with the EU what to include and the level of ambition in the Action Plan. Hence, there is a high degree of differentiation between ENP countries.

The EU has also become increasingly involved in what is normally perceived as more traditional foreign and security policy, such as diplomatic mediation and crisis management operations in the neighbourhood. The EU's mediation efforts in ending the Georgian War of 2008 and its aftermath is evidence of its growing ambitions in undertaking these types of missions. The combined development of the ENP and the Common Security and Defence Policy (CSDP) demonstrates the presence of the EU as an actor in the neighbourhood. However, many analysts question whether the EU has been successful in turning this presence into power (Barbé and Johansson-Nogués 2008; Edwards 2008; Bicchi 2010; Popescu and Wilson 2011). In Eastern Europe, the democratic transition has stalled in favour of more autocratic regimes. The EU's response to the Arab Spring of 2011 and the democracy movements in North Africa and the Middle East was fragmented. The single voice of the EU High Representative, Catherine Ashton, was simply drowned in the cacophony of voices from EU member states. This raises some serious questions about the effectiveness and coherence of EU foreign policy beyond enlargement.

Map 24.2 European Neighbourhood Policy.

Conclusion: the transformative power of the EU

The Big Bang enlargement of 2004–2007 will no doubt go down in the history books as an impressive achievement. Fifteen years after the end of the Cold War bipolarity, European order was fundamentally reshaped, with the EU playing a major role in this reshaping process. However, this was not a self-evident outcome at the start of the 1990s. On the contrary, as this chapter has demonstrated, the decision to open the EU up to such a large group of new members was reached only fitfully and incrementally, and was deeply contested at crucial conjunctures given its implications for existing member states who had asymmetrical sets of material and geostrategic interests.

However, one thing they did agree on in principle was the moral imperative to enlarge as enshrined in a number of EU treaties (see Box 24.5). That member states felt constrained by this normative commitment is of considerable significance. From a purely materialist point of

---

**BOX 24.5 Landmark agreements in the history
of the Big Bang enlargement**

1957 Rome Treaty stipulating any European state can apply for membership

1993 Copenhagen European Council (defining membership criteria)

1994 Essen European Council (agreement on pre-accession strategy)

1997 European Commission publish Agenda 2000

1997 Luxembourg European Council (decision on the six candidates for accession negotiations)

1998 Start of accession negotiations with first five CEECs and Cyprus

1999 Helsinki European Council (decision to start negotiations with three more CEECs and Malta)

2002 End of accession negotiations for ten countries

2004 Accession of Poland, Hungary, Czech Republic, Slovakia, Estonia, Latvia, Lithuania, Slovenia, Cyprus, and Malta

2007 Second phase of accession of Bulgaria and Romania

---

view, it is not at all obvious why the EU should shoulder the considerable costs involved in accepting new members from regions much poorer and less developed than the EU's West European heartlands, particularly as doing so would have severe repercussions on the effectiveness of the EU itself. The fact that EU member states should feel such a sense of obligation is noteworthy and gives credence to the social constructivist argument that identity and the way it informs interests is a major explanatory variable in the case of enlargement. Although the member states sought to lessen the negative effects of enlargement, notably through applying political conditionality, they were eventually prepared to accept the risks that enlargement would entail. They did so because they shared a strong sense of responsibility for peace and security in Europe, and thought that, at the end of the day, enlargement was the best way to achieve this strategic imperative.

Moreover, despite the fact that enlargement was deeply divisive, EU member states largely delegated the negotiation and framing of this issue to the European Commission. The Commission played a decisive role, particularly towards the end of the process when the enthusiasm of member states, among both the governing elite and the general public, started to wane. In so doing, the Commission acted as a crucial policy entrepreneur (Sedelmeier 2010). Although the EU heads of state and government took the key decisions at critical moments—such as starting negotiations with just six countries in 1998, or setting the final entry date for 2004—these steps were all shaped by input from the Commission. The Commission kept the momentum up, ensuring progress towards the goal of enlargement even when there was little political impetus from EU governments.

These two points—the normative commitment to enlarge, and the significant role played by the European Commission—illustrate how far the foreign policy process in Europe has been transformed over recent decades. The challenge for the future will be that the fifth enlargement will still leave numerous 'European' states on the outside, many of whom have already expressed their desire to join the EU. Ultimately, this raises fundamental and unresolved questions about the borders of Europe and the problems of inclusion–exclusion, and, last but not least, how the EU can exert influence when the prospect of EU membership—one of the most powerful and successful instruments in its foreign policy—is no longer available.

 Key points

- The EU is a *sui generis* foreign policy actor, which poses significant conceptual and theoretical challenges to conventional conceptions of agency and power in FPA.

- EU enlargement is the most powerful instrument of EU foreign policy, enabling the Union to play a significant role in the reshaping of European order after the end of the Cold War.

- Enlargement increases the EU's global presence, but it also affects the EU's internal coherence and effectiveness as an actor. The reforms in the Lisbon Treaty of 2009 seek to address these issues.

- The decision for a Big Bang enlargement was only reached incrementally. Differences over the 'how and when' of enlargement were contested, given the asymmetrical sets of material and geostrategic interests of member states and their differing visions of Europe. These differences were particularly pronounced between Britain, France, and Germany, the three largest EU member states.

- Enlargement is significant because it is an example of a foreign policy decision that reflects social constructivist arguments about collective identity and rule-based action. The overwhelming moral imperative to enlarge, rooted in the Rome Treaty, meant that enlargement *per se* was never seriously questioned.

- EU member states delegated large parts of the policy process to the European Commission, which played a leading role in framing and implementing the policy on enlargement at critical junctures.

- The Commission was able to exert a powerful influence on the candidate countries by using political conditionality to encourage a host of legal and institutional changes to be undertaken prior to membership, clear evidence of a type of foreign policy where the domestic and international domains increasingly overlap.

- Throughout the decision-making process, EU member states grappled with a major paradox: enlargement was meant to project stability and cooperation into Central and Eastern Europe, but enlargement would draw new lines of inclusion and exclusion in this region. This dilemma is important in explaining why in the end EU member states opted for an inclusive Big Bang in 2004, including Romania and Bulgaria in 2007.

- The decision on the fifth EU enlargement has not settled the question about the borders of Europe. The EU faces a huge task of seeking to shape developments in its 'new neighbourhood' without being able to use the leverage of promise of future membership.

 Questions

1. Assess the relative impact of member states and the Commission in framing the agenda on EU enlargement.

2. Why is the concept of 'foreign policy' problematic in the case of EU enlargement?

3. In your view, which approach best explains the EU enlargement process: a social constructivist approach based on norms and identities, or a rationalist approach focusing on material interests and strategic calculations?

4. Why was the Big Bang adopted in preference to other options for enlarging the EU?

5. Did the application of political conditionality in the accession process represent a form of power coercion?

6. How did the debate on inclusion–exclusion shape the decision on enlargement?

7. How did differing national interests shape British, French, and German attitudes to enlargement in the early 1990s?

8. What impact will the inclusion of twelve new members in the EU have on its external relations and its ambitions to speak with 'one voice' in international affairs?

9. Discuss the borders of Europe and whether there are limits to EU enlargement.

10. Does the European Neighbourhood Policy (ENP) offer an effective alternative instrument for shaping relations with countries bordering the EU?

 Further reading

Bretherton, C. and Vogler, J. (2006), *The European Union as a Global Actor* **(London: Routledge).**
A central text in the conceptualization of the EU's international role, combining a constructivist approach with extensive empirical research.<BIP

Grabbe, H. (2006), *The EU's Transformative Power: Europeanization through Conditionality in Central and Eastern Europe* **(Basingstoke: Palgrave Macmillan).**
Provides a detailed study of how and to what effect the EU applied the principle of conditionality in the enlargement process, written by an academic with practical experience inside the European Commission.

Hill, C. and Smith, M. (ed) (2011), *International Relations and the European Union* **(Oxford: Oxford University Press).**
This book provides for an authoritative account of the multi-faceted nature of EU external relations in the international system.

Sjursen, H. (ed.) (2006), *Questioning EU Enlargement: Europe in Search of Identity* **(London: Routledge).**
A comparative country-specific analysis of how EU enlargement was understood within a number of EU member states.

Smith, K.E. (2004), *The Making of EU Foreign Policy: The Case of Eastern Europe* **(Basingstoke: Palgrave Macmillan).**
This book explicitly argues that enlargement is a case of EU foreign policy.

Vachudova, M. (2005), *Europe Undivided: Democracy, Leverage, and Integration after Communism* **(Oxford: Oxford University Press).**
Brings a nuanced understanding to the passive–active leverage of EU power in the enlargement process.

 Visit the Online Resource Centre that accompanies this book for more information:
www.oxfordtextbooks.co.uk/orc/smith_foreign/

Glossary

Acquis communautaire: EU terminology for the entire body of European law, including all the treaties, regulations, and directives passed by European institutions.

Active learning: active learning exercises put the student in the centre of the learning process. Listening to a lecture and simply taking notes is a passive learning experience. A case discussion that requires participation and involves the entire class in analysis and evaluation of a complex policy situation is an active learning experience.

Actor: can be an individual but also a group, an organization or a collective entity such as the state, as long as such entities can be said to have agency.

Actor-general theory: theory that explains the behaviour of actors in general, such as game theory.

Actor-specific theory: theory that explains the behaviour of specific actors, such as Foreign Policy Analysis theory. This type of theory may be generalizable, but under specific scope conditions for applicability. Actor-specific theory is a form of middle-range theory, in that it is more generalizable than insights derived from case studies, but on the other hand, has more severe scope conditions constraining its generalizability than actor-general theory. However, given its nature, actor-specific theory allows for richer explanation and even prediction of the foreign policy behaviour of particular entities than does actor-general theory.

Agency: the capacity an actor has to effect change. To use the analogy from card games, agency refers to how you play your hand (whereas structure is the hand you are dealt).

Agency–structure problem: refers to the question of how human actors are related to social structures, and vice versa, and what the implications of this relationship are for social scientific research.

Agenda setting: occurs when media reports direct people to think about certain issues, and not others.

Agenda setting, priming, and framing: terms used to refer to key processes by which the media influence audiences.

Agents and structures: when studying the world around us, we can think of it as being constituted by agents (decision makers, presidents, states as actors) and structures (a distribution of military capabilities, a structure of meaning). If much of traditional FPA examines agents, then a constructivist study of foreign policy would emphasize the interaction between agents and structures (see below, 'mutual constitution').

Aggressive neorealism: a theory claiming that the structure of the international system encourages states to maximize their share of world power, including the pursuit of hegemony, which tends to intensify security competition. Also goes by the name of offensive realism.

Analogical reasoning: reasoning based on simple analogies. Used by political leaders to make a complex world somewhat simpler, by drawing one-to-one comparisons.

Anarchy: a term that realists and neorealists use to indicate that international politics takes place in an environment that has no overarching central authority which can compel states to comply with the rules.

Asian values: a phrase that was particularly popular among some East Asian leaderships in the late 1980s and early 1990s. It conveyed the idea that human rights were not universal in nature but were subject to cultural interpretation. Asian values attached primacy to the community over the individual.

Balance of power: policy that seeks to ensure an equilibrium of power in which no single state or coalition of states is in a position to dominate all the others.

Balance of threat: a realist theory explaining strategic reactions to a rising and potentially threatening hegemonic state.

Ballistic missile: a missile designed to follow a suborbital flight path to deliver a warhead to a predetermined target.

Behaviouralism: a movement in the USA, initiated just prior to the Second World War and culminating during the first two decades after the war, whose proponents argued that the social sciences, including IR, could move forward only by modelling themselves on the natural sciences. More specifically, this meant an emphasis on a theoretically grounded empiricism (with an emphasis on quantitative methodology) in contrast with descriptive, historical, and normative scholarship.

Beltway: The Capital Beltway is the American inter-state freeway that encircles Washington DC, passing through Virginia and Maryland.

Bipolarity: an international system shaped by the power of two major states, or superpowers.

Bounded rationality: this is an understanding of rationality which assumes that it is not possible for humans to attend to everything simultaneously or to calculate carefully the costs and benefits of alternative courses of action; attention is a scarce resource. Organizational and group environments provide simplifying shortcuts, cues, and buffers that help policy makers decide.

Brinkmanship: when attempting to force a particular situation, a tactic that has often been pursued in the context ofMiddle East politics is that of brinkmanship. In order to achieve an advantageous outcome, a situation is pushed to the very limit—often to the point of disastrous military conflict—in order to force an opponent to back down. Brinkmanship can and has worked, such as in the conflict between Egypt and Israel, but is a very dangerous strategy to pursue, as Saddam Hussein found out in the run up to war with the USA in 2003.

Bureaucratic politics: an approach that focuses on governmental behaviour in terms of the individual decision makers who make policy and who do so as players in a central and competitive bargaining game.

Capabilities: operationalized resources, i.e. attributes such as population and size turned into usable assets such as technology and wealth.

Civilian power: uses non-military means in its foreign policy and favours international structures for regulating international action. Duchêne famously coined the phrase for the EU which he saw as an exemplar of a new stage in political civilization, domesticating international problems through structures of contractual politics.

Classical realism: all realist writings before the publication of Waltz (1979).

CNN effect: a term that has come to be used to describe circumstances in which news media coverage directly affects foreign policy decision making, causing policy makers to pursue a course of action which, in the absence of media pressure, they would not have embarked upon.

Coalition: a group of countries which seek to defend a common position in an international negotiation through explicit coordination.

Coercive diplomacy: the threat of punishment to force an adversary to undo an action already taken.

Cognitive and psychological approaches: cognitive approaches in IR refer to the faculty of knowing in human consciousness (how the mind works), including learning processes and the formation and structure of belief systems, whereas psychological approaches are broader in scope, including a focus on perceptions, motivational factors, and personality traits.

Cognitive bias: a term referring to distortions in the human mind which lead to perceptions and judgements that deviate from 'reality'.

Cognitive consistency: a theory produced by cognitive psychologists, which argues that people strongly prefer consistency, are made uncomfortable by dissonant information, and consequently discount inconsistent information to preserve their beliefs.

Cold War: the intense period of ideological animosity between the USA and the Soviet Union which lasted from the mid-1940s to the early 1990s.

Communicatively rational: an understanding of rationality which assumes that humans are deeply social, and that they 'decide' by deliberating with others. Communicatively rational agents do not so much calculate costs and benefits, or seek cues from their environment, as present arguments and try to persuade and convince each other. Their interests and preferences are open for redefinition.

Communitarianism: emphasizes how the community, often defined in terms of geography, is a source of identity, values, and obligations; in relationship to questions of international politics, a central claim is that because the 'local' community (frequently a shorthand for the state) has its own distinctive values, traditions, and beliefs, it should have autonomy and sovereignty.

Competence: legislative power to act conferred upon a given actor by a specific treaty.

Complex interdependence: a term coined by Robert O. Keohane and Joe S. Nye. It refers to the end of a simple model of world politics in which interactions were dominated by sovereign states. The new pattern of relations among advanced countries takes place between state agencies, firms, and international organizations. In contrast with the earlier literature on transnationalism, complex interdependence is less about the eclipse of the sovereign state and more about the complex institutional process of governance in an interdependent world.

Conceptual model: a theoretical construct used to facilitate the reasoning of a complex framework of processes.

Concert of Europe: a series of meetings between the great powers of Europe initiated by Britain, Austria, Russia, and Prussia, and conducted between 1815 and 1822.

Convention on Certain Conventional Weapons: the Convention on Certain Conventional Weapons (CCW) was concluded on 10 October 1980 and entered into force on 2 December 1983. It consists of a convention and protocols that ban or restrict the use of certain kinds of weapons. These weapons are considered to cause unnecessary suffering to soldiers or civilians. The convention was reviewed in 1996 and in 2001. Individual states have to ratify or accede to the Convention and to each Protocol.

Cosmopolitanism: the belief that all peoples are of equal moral worth and that we should not let territorial boundaries define the limits of our identification, our solidarity with others, and our obligations to peoples.

Counterfactual: to ask a counterfactual is to engage in a thought experiment: in the absence of the causal factor you think was important, would the outcome nonetheless have been the same? If the answer could plausibly be 'yes', then you should also test for the importance of these other factors.

Decision-forcing cases: these are usually short stories or descriptions about policy situations in need of a solution. These cases present the facts from different perspectives and students are asked to make a decision. A good retrospective case may include many decision-forcing situations.

Defensive cognitions: forms of behaviour or phraseology activated to 'defend' oneself from an unpleasant or dissonant thought.

Defensive neorealism: a theory claiming that structural factors limit how much power states can possess, which helps dampen security competition.

Defensive realism: a structural realist theory that views states as security maximizers.

Democratic peace thesis: a central plank of internationalist thought which maintains that liberal democracies *tend* not to make war on fellow democracies. Some advocates go further and argue that democratic states are more peace prone *per se*.

Deterrence: a policy that discourages aggression by threatening to punish another state if it undertakes certain actions deemed to be unacceptable.

Distributive negotiation strategy: a set of tactics used for claiming value from others, when one party's goals are partly in conflict with those of the other. Tactics include very high opening demands, refusal to make any concessions, exaggerating one's minimum needs, and issuing threats. For a detailed analysis, see John Odell (2000) *Negotiating the World Economy* (Ithaca, NY: Cornell University Press).

Doha Development Agenda: a new round of trade negotiations that was launched at the Doha Ministerial Conference of November 2001. The round is also known as the Development Round, given its attempts to address the concerns of developing countries. Twenty-one subjects are listed in the Doha work programme, and include negotiations over the highly contested issue of agriculture. It was due for completion by January 2005, but has run into recurrent deadlock. As of October 2011, the round was nowhere near completion.

Economic statecraft: the use of economic tools and relationships to achieve foreign policy objectives.

Elite model: a theoretical position, in opposition to the pluralist model, which argues that both media and public opinion are overwhelmingly influenced and shaped by the interests of elite groups in society. As a consequence, media and public opinion remain unable to influence political and economic processes.

Endogenize: to endogenize interests or identity means to examine and study their development; they are not assumed or taken as given. Constructivists endogenize the process of interest and identity formation.

Energy dependence: a situation in which the energy needs of a given actor (usually a state) can no longer be met indigenously through national energy sources. This obliges the actor to depend upon the import of energy products from other exporters.

Energy security: the combination of demand and supply pressures linking exporters and importers, both of whom ultimately have the same goal, namely to ensure access to, transport of, and a market for energy resources required for the long-term and stable development of national power.

Episodic news: a term used to describe news media reports that are framed in terms of immediate events and without broader context. A news report detailing the progress of US troops during the 2003 Iraq War but providing no broader contextualization (e.g. the justification and rationale for the military action) could be described as *episodic*.

Epistemology: epistemology addresses 'how we come to know' in the study of foreign policy. Do we seek to uncover law-governed causal processes (positivism)? Or do we instead ask what makes such processes possible in the first place (interpretive modes of understanding)?

Ethics: concerns the values of actors, including what kinds of actions are right or wrong, what is a good life and how to live it, what our obligations and responsibilities are to others, and the application of moral rules and ethical principles to concrete problems and situations.

Exogenize: To exogenize interests or identity means that their development lies outside the scope of one's research; they are simply assumed or taken as given. Rational choice scholars typically exogenize interest formation.

External other: the opposite or antithesis of the self. States often refer to an external other (e.g. a totalitarian and communist Soviet Union) as a means to get at, or reinforce, a sense of the self (e.g. a democratic and capitalist USA).

Financial sanctions: restrictions on the movement of money into a target country.

Foreign policy: the sum total of decisions made on behalf of a given political unit (usually a state) entailing the implementation of goals with direct reference to its external environment. Foreign policy *inputs* are those many factors that influence foreign policy decision making, whilst the observable *outputs* of foreign policy are a feature of state (and non-state) behaviour within the international system.

Foreign Policy Analysis: the subfield of International Relations that seeks to explain foreign policy, or, alternatively, foreign policy behaviour, with reference to the theoretical ground of human decision makers, acting singly and in groups. The subfield has several hallmarks:

- a commitment to look below the nation-state level of analysis to actor-specific information;
- a commitment to build actor-specific theory as the interface between actor-general theory and the complexity of the real world;
- a commitment to pursue multicausal explanations spanning multiple levels of analysis;
- a commitment to utilize theory and findings from across the spectrum of social science;
- a commitment to viewing the process of foreign policy decision making as important as the output thereof.

Foreign policy behaviour: the observable artefacts of foreign policy; specific actions and words used to influence others in the realm of foreign policy; may include categorization of such behaviour, such as along conflict cooperation continua, which categorizations could be used to construct data, such as event data. Foreign policy behaviour may include behaviour that was accidental or unintended by the government, and in addition decisions to do nothing may not leave any behavioural artefact; thus there is slippage between the concept of foreign policy and the concept of foreign policy behaviour.

Framing: refers to the specific properties of news text (i.e. the selection of language, facts, and images) that encourage readers/viewers to think about issues in a particular way.

Fundamental attribution error: the tendency of people to over-emphasize dispositional explanations for behaviours observed in others while under-emphasizing situational explanations (social and environmental forces).

Globalization: a term used to describe processes of economic, cultural, and political integration between states which have reduced the significance of geographical separation and generated greater levels of interdependence between states around the world.

Grand strategy: the overall vision of a state's national security goals and a determination of the most appropriate means to achieve these goals.

Great Society: the series of anti-poverty and society improvement laws introduced during the Presidency of Lyndon Johnson. They including the Economic Opportunity Act of 1964, Medicare and Medicaid, and environmental protection acts.

Groupthink: a concept used to describe the failure of small decision units to meet the criteria of optimal decision making by their tendency, under certain conditions, to reach a decision too quickly as a result of premature consensus seeking.

Gulf War of 1990–1991/Operation Desert Storm: the war launched by President George Bush Sr to reverse Iraq's invasion of Kuwait in 1990. The US-led multilateral coalition ejected Saddam Hussein's military from Kuwait but President Bush and his advisers decided against attacking Baghdad to remove Saddam Hussein from power. Operation Iraqi Freedom of 2003 was, according to some, an attempt to finish what was not done by Operation Desert Storm.

Hard power: a concept intimately connected with realist thinking on foreign policy. Hard power denotes the material capabilities of a state—its size, population, wealth, and, crucially, its military capacity.

Hegemonic stability: a realist theory explaining the emergence and stability of international orders backed by a single dominant power.

Heuristics: the rules or indicators which leaders use in order to test the propositions embedded in their own schemas (e.g. 'rules of thumb').

Hindsight bias: the inclination to view things that have already happened as being relatively inevitable and predictable (also known as the 'I knew it all along' effect).

Holocaust: the Holocaust refers to the killing of some six million Jews and other target groups in the Second World War as part of a systematic policy of genocide followed by Nazi Germany. The genocide occurred in several stages, culminating with the concentration and extermination camps.

Human security: a people-centred approach that identifies individuals rather than states as the referent object of security and considers a range of issues such as health, employment, and sustainable development.

Humanitarian intervention: the use of force by a state or group of states aiming at stopping or preventing a humanitarian emergency. In cases of humanitarian intervention, permission for the use of force has not been granted by the government who has jurisdiction over the territory.

Humanitarianism: the goal of providing life-saving relief to people in need, often in far-away places.

Humanity: concerns the claim that all individuals possess basic inalienable rights and is a foundation for a general commitment not to distinguish individuals on the basis of their nationality, religion, ethnicity, or other markers.

Identity: identity is a sense of community and 'we-ness'. It tells us who we are. While one can talk of individual identity, in foreign policy it is more typical to talk of state or national identity.

Implementation: the translation of decisions into actions and impact; a 'boundary' process which connects actors to their environments via the pursuit of foreign policy.

Indexing hypothesis: Bennett's (1990) widely adopted theoretical framework that explains the tendency of US journalists to defer to, or *index the news to*, official US government sources when defining the news agenda and framing news stories.

Influence attempts: the use by a government or governments of economic, military, or diplomatic measures to affect the behaviour or capabilities of a target state.

Infotainment: a form of news that merges the traditional style of hard factual reporting about matters of political importance with *softer* news about, for example, celebrities and gossip.

Instrumentally rational: an understanding of rationality which assumes that actors know what they want and bargain to get it. Bargaining means that individuals make concessions at the levels of strategy and tactics, while protecting their core interests. Instrumentally rational agents carefully calculate and seek to maximize given interests.

Instruments: the specific options available to policy makers for exerting influence on other actors in the international system.

Integrative negotiation strategy: a set of tactics used to achieve goals that are not in fundamental conflict. Tactics include sharing information relatively openly, proposing an exchange of concessions that might benefit more than one party, and reframing the issue space itself to ease an impasse (Odell 2000).

Intelligence services: in order to inform policy and to take action against threats against the state when the civil or military organizations are unable to act, governments rely upon a range of agencies that form the intelligence service. Such services usually operate in a covert fashion, with the identities of employees remaining secret in order to facilitate the accumulation of information by means of espionage and interception, and to prevent the service itself from being infiltrated by foreign organizations.

Intercontinental ballistic missile: a missile with a range of more than 5500 kilometres designed to deliver nuclear warheads from one continent to another.

Intergovernmentalism: decision making within international organizations taken by governments on the basis of collective action. Within the EU, this would suggest that national governments control the level and speed of European integration.

Intermediate range ballistic missile: a missile with a range of 3000–5500 kilometres designed to deliver nuclear warheads.

International Criminal Court: the ICC was established by the Rome Statute of the International Criminal Court in July 1997. The International Court tries people for genocide, crimes against humanity, and war crimes. It is a court of last resort—if a case is investigated or prosecuted by a national judicial system, it will not act unless the national proceedings are not genuine.

Interpretive: an interpretive epistemology emphasizes the role of background knowledge—often social discourses—in making possible certain courses of action. The focus is understanding and the recovery of meaning, not causal explanation. Many, if not most, European constructivists are interpretive in epistemological orientation.

Investment restrictions: restrictions on the ability of private firms to set up manufacturing, service, or extractive facilities in a target country.

Leadership: the term can apply to either individuals and their particular characteristics—whether it be 'tough' or 'charismatic' or 'weak'—or leadership in the international system. In the case of the latter, leadership is often connected with the capacity of a so-called hegemonic state to shape the rules and institutions of international society.

Legitimacy: there is a an irreducible moral and social basis to legitimacy. An actor who possesses legitimacy is able to persuade others to do what they want without resorting to side-payments or coercion (both more costly in the long run).

Levels of analysis: one can study and seek to explain foreign policy by considering factors operating at various levels, including the individual, societal, state, or international system. For example, if the object of analysis (or explanandum) is the behaviour of the state, explanation can proceed in terms of factors on the individual level, the state level, or the international level.

Liberalism: a philosophy stressing the significance of individual rights, markets, and representative government. In foreign policy analysis, it emphasizes the central role, in the making of policy, of civil society and economic development based on individual rights, and the notion that the modern liberal state will bring peace and prosperity, and that relations between such states will be collaborative and cooperative.

Liberal 'imprudence': the idea that liberal foreign policy is susceptible to mood swings between excess interventionism and isolationism.

Liberal peace: the peace among established liberal republican democracies.

Logic of appropriateness: in contrast with the logic of consequences (see below), a term used to describe the logic underlying actions taken with reference to rules and norms that define what is deemed to be proper and legitimate behaviour.

Logic of consequences: a term used to describe how actors make decisions by rationally calculating which action maximizes their interests. See also 'logic of appropriateness'.

Mechanisms: mechanisms operate at an analytical level below that of a more encompassing theory, increasing its credibility by rendering more fine-grained explanations. By linking initial conditions and a specific outcome, mechanisms connect things. In many analyses of foreign policy, decision-making processes are the mechanism connecting initial conditions (constellations of interest and power) and outcomes.

Medium range ballistic missiles: a missile with a range of 1000–3000 kilometres designed to deliver nuclear warheads.

Middle power: a state that is not a superpower, or a great power, but still has some influence internationally and especially regionally.

Monetary sanctions: the buying or selling of another country's currency in order to influence its economy and eventually its foreign or domestic policies.

Mossad: Mossad literally means 'Institute' and is an abbreviation of the 'Institute for Intelligence and Special Operations'. Mossad is one of the most famous intelligence agencies, alongside the CIA of the USA, the Secret Intelligence Service (MI6) of the UK, and the KGB of the former USSR. Its task is to operate beyond the borders of Israel in information gathering, counter-terrorism, and covert actions.

Most-favoured nation trading status: one country will offer another the lowest levels of tariffs it has agreed with any third country. The country awarded MFN status will not be treated worse than any other trading partner.

Multilateralism: the process by which ends are sought through cooperation, or at least negotiation, at times by ad hoc processes but usually in the context of an international organization.

Multipolarity: an international system shaped by the power of three or more major states.

Mutual constitution: the constructivist response to the agent–structure problem. Instead of focusing just on agents or just on structure, constructivists argue that social reality emerges from a process of interaction—'mutual constitution'—between agents and structures. The latter are typically conceptualized as social in nature (norms or discourses).

National security: realists argue that national security is the first goal of statecraft. In essence, national security relates to the notion of protecting and ultimately securing the physical survival of the nation-state from external threats.

Neoclassical realism: a version of realism which combines systemic factors, such as the international distribution of power as emphasized by neorealists, with domestic (or unit level) factors, such as how power is perceived and how leadership is exercised.

Neoconservative: those who believe that the USA should pursue a 'tough foreign policy on behalf of morality'. Neoconservatives insist on distinguishing between good and bad states in the international arena, with the USA spearheading the good to change or remove the bad. They also believe that the USA should strive to remain pre-eminent militarily and are strong advocates of higher defence budgets. Willingness to use military force to attain American goals as well as a suspicion of international institutions are the other trademarks of neoconservative foreign policy thought. Together, these four tenets form a coherent but controversial theory of the USA's role in the world.

Neoliberal institutionalism: a theory rejecting the assumption that states are the only important actors on the international stage (as neorealists claim), suggesting instead that non-governmental organizations may also have effects on patterns of international behaviour, and thus that they can serve as a valuable foundation for international cooperation. Also know simply as neoliberalism.

Neorealism: a reaction to and development of realism, claiming against the latter that it has failed to understand that international politics should foremost be understood as a system with a precisely defined structure, and that it is this structure—rather than the principles of human nature, interests defined in terms of power, and the behaviour of statesmen—that constrains and hence explains the behaviour of states. For this reason it is also known as structural realism.

Neuroeconomics: an interdisciplinary field of research that combines neuroscience, economics, and psychology to study decision making.

Normative: a term used to indicate ethical or moral discussion about how things *should* be, as opposed to how things actually *are*.

NSC-68: often seen as the blueprint for America's containment policy, National Security Council document no. 68 was written in 1950 by a team chaired by Paul Nitze. It assessed the Soviet threat and stressed the need for a US military build-up and the use of military means to counter Soviet expansionism wherever it occurred. It is usually contrasted with the more political–diplomatic approach to containment advocated by George Kennan, Nitze's predecessor in the Office of Policy Planning in the Department of State.

Offence–defence balance: the costs of defending territory minus the costs of conquering an enemy.

Offensive power: military strength used to attack an enemy.

Offensive realism: a structural realist axiom that views states as power maximizers.

Operation Anadyr: during the Cuban missile crisis, this is the secretive operation in which Soviet missiles were delivered to Cuba, eluding all methods of detection until missiles were deployed in the field.

Operation Iraqi Freedom: the war launched by the United States and the United Kingdom in March 2003 against Iraq in order to depose Saddam Hussein. The primary justification for the war was Saddam Hussein's refusal to give up weapons of mass destruction, which the US was afraid he might share with terrorists. It is now known that these allegations were false.

Organizational behaviour: the view, inspired by organizational theory, that governmental behaviour does not conform to the notion of a unitary and rational decision maker, but rather takes the form of outputs of large organizations functioning according to standard patterns of behaviour.

Ottawa Process: the negotiation process that was launched in Ottawa in 1996 and led to an international treaty banning the use and trade of landmines.

Overstretch: the tendency of a country to take on foreign policy commitments which it cannot sustain over an extended period.

Pan-Arabism: closely related to Arab nationalism, pan-Arabism is the belief in the unified nature of the Arab world, and the need for Arabs to act in a coordinated manner against external threats—most notably that posed by Zionism. Pan-Arabism tends to be secular and nationalist, unlike pan-Islamism which is also a feature of Middle East political life. The struggle between pan-Arabism and pan-Islamism is likely to become a defining feature of Middle East politics in the forthcoming decades.

Pivotal power: Blair's term to describe Britain's position 'at the crux' of several alliances and institutions that shape world order.

Pluralist model: a theoretical position, in opposition to the elite model, which argues that power is sufficiently distributed throughout society so that both media and public opinion are independent of political and economic groups. Consequently, media and public opinion are able to influence political processes.

Political conditionality: setting out conditions to be fulfilled in a 'carrot-and-stick' approach, i.e. promising benefits in case of compliance and suspension or termination of the process in case of non-compliance. EU enlargement is an example of this process where strict conditions were set and progress towards meeting them was critically evaluated on the road to membership.

Positivism: a positivist epistemology argues that the social world can be studied with tools borrowed from the natural sciences. Thus a scholar searches for general laws and regularities, and embeds the analysis in the language of variables. The focus is causal explanation, not the inductive recovery of meaning.

Power of attraction: liberal-inspired idea that the EU, based on its normative and soft power appeal, will be able to draw states into a 'civilizing process' with the promise of EU membership.

Power transition: a realist theory of war between a rising challenger and declining dominant state.

Preventive war: a war initiated by A against B to prevent B from posing serious threats to A in the future. To be distinguished from pre-emptive war in which A starts a war first against B upon discovering that B is planning an imminent attack against A.

Priming: refers to the process by which media direct people to judge their political leaders according to particular issues.

Primordial hatred: the origin of conflict between groups is a subject of considerable debate in the academic literature. The poles of the argument revolve around those who consider differences to be grounded in ancient times and perhaps linked to notions of ethnicity—these are primordialists—and those who contend that group identities and therefore differences between groups are modern constructs.

Probability estimate: an analytically derived expectation on the consequences of action in rational decision making.

Procedural criticism and influence: a term used to define the level or extent of media criticism and influence whereby media reports criticize the way in which a particular policy is being pursued and whether that policy will work. Procedural criticism is distinct from substantive criticism which relates to the underlying justification or rationale for a policy. An example of procedural criticism would be a news story that criticized the use of cluster bombs during the 2003 Iraq War, but did not question the validity of military action in the first instance.

Process theory: these theories are more attractive to policy makers because they introduce ways to structure and manage the policy process and achieve policy goals.

Process tracing: this is a technique used to trace the operation of the causal mechanism(s) at work in a given situation. One carefully maps the process, exploring the extent to which it coincides with prior, theoretically derived expectations about the workings of the mechanism.

Project for the New American Century: a small but influential think tank set up by William Kristol in 1997 to give voice to a vision of American foreign policy that would allow it to remain the pre-eminent power.

Widely construed as the reference site for neoconservative foreign policy thought.

Public sphere: a term used to refer to any network by which *public* issues can be debated. In modern society, the mass media is a central component of the public sphere containing news, current affairs programming, and opinion which help to facilitate public debate and opinion formation.

Rally round the flag effect: a nationalist response to economic sanctions; the tendency for governments and their populations to unite in resisting economic sanctions.

Rational choice: on the most general level, a methodological approach that aims to explain both individual and collective outcomes in terms of individual goal-seeking under constraints.

Rational decision making: the cognitive process of decision making that is based on logical analysis.

Reaganite foreign policy: an approach to foreign policy that privileges moral argument, military might, promotion of democracy and individual liberty, and using all these resources to confront America's adversaries. Neoconservatives believe this was how President Ronald Reagan (1981–1989) dealt with the Soviet Union. He was not afraid to characterize the latter as an 'evil empire' and the massive increase in military expenditure during his administration helped bring about the collapse of the Soviet empire.

Realism: in its twentieth century form, the claim that at the core of state behaviour lies the concept of interest defined in terms of power. In the view of realists, the world is a most dangerous and insecure place, and will remain so; hence the prime consideration of the state is the constant pursuit of its own self-interest, which can only be done in terms of the exertion of power in defence of its security. Given the nature of humans and the anarchy characterizing the international system, this means that military might is what counts, not cooperation through international law or organizations.

Red-team thinking: in order to provide a more nuanced understanding of how an opponent will act in any given situation, security and military agencies engage in 'red-team thinking', whereby a team is given the responsibility to consider a situation from the viewpoint of the opponent.

Regimes: international social institutions that are based on agreed norms, rules, principles, and decision-making procedures, governing the interactions of states and non-state actors in selected issue areas, such as energy, the environment, and human rights.

Research cases: in these cases the answers are usually provided. There is some space for discussion but that usually involves the evaluation of the contending theories used to explain the policy or an evaluation of the findings themselves.

Resources: the elements, deriving from history and geography, which determine the limits of a country's impact on the world.

Responsibility to protect: the legal and ethical basis for humanitarian intervention by external actors in a state that is unwilling or unable to fight genocide, massive killings, and other massive human rights violations. The principle of responsibility to protect holds that if a particular state is unwilling or unable to carry out its responsibility to prevent such abuses, that responsibility must be transferred to the international community. This community will seek first to solve problems primarily via peaceful means but will, as a last resort, use military force.

Retrospective cases: these cases provide comprehensive stories or histories of issues and events with an emphasis on the personalities and the conflicts that helped to define that event.

Security dilemma: a realist theory about how group efforts to provide security under anarchy can spark spirals of conflict.

Security of demand: a central requirement of exporter states to ensure permanent access to a developed and reliable market for the long-term sale of energy products.

Security of supply: a central requirement of importer states who are generally dependent upon natural gas and oil in which the consistent delivery of affordable energy sources is key.

Self-help: according to realist theory, the basic principle of action in an anarchical environment is self-help. Each state must take care of itself.

Shabak: usually referred to in English as Shin Bet, or the Israeli Security Service, Shabak is the internal security service of Israel, roughly equivalent to the UK's MI5 and the USA's FBI.

Sinatra doctrine: the phrase 'Sinatra doctrine' refers to a Soviet leadership decision announcing that the countries of eastern Europe could reform 'doing it their way'. This phrase, drawn from a well-known song of the late Frank Sinatra, 'I did it my way', implied the end of Soviet intervention in these countries.

Smart sanctions: economic sanctions precisely targeted to affect the economic conditions of a particular segment of the population of a target country, usually the governmental elite.

Social contract: originally concerns the kinds of rights that individuals are willing to give up, frequently to the state or some other legitimate authority, in return for protections and stability.

Social constructivism: a meta-theory claiming that the social domain does not exist in nature but is constructed through ongoing processes of social interaction and the transmission of social meanings.

Social discourses: discourses are broad structures of meaning that make possible human–state agency in foreign policy. For example, the discourse on terror in the USA after 11 September 2001, has made possible certain kinds of American foreign policy actions. Discourse analysis is a key method used by interpretive IR theorists including constructivists and post-structuralists.

Social norms: social norms are shared, collective understandings that make behavioural claims on actors. Norms have a quality of 'oughtness'—this is the way that something should be done.

Soft balancing: a realist theory built on balance of threat theory, which explains constraint actions against a unipole.

Soft power: indirect influence over political bodies through personal relationship building and through cultural and ideological means. Soft power can be distinguished from more directly coercive exercises of power, such as military action (hard power) or economic incentives.

Scope conditions: the conditions that must be present in the real world for a given theory to apply.

Strategic balance of power: a central concept in the (neo)realist theory of international relations, which refers to the parity that exists between competing forces in the international system.

Strategic–relational approach: a type of systems approach which understands foreign policy behaviour as the product of a dialectical interplay between the actor's own strategy, its context, and its ideas.

Structural linkage: the promotion of economic relationships over an extended time period to transform political interests in a target state in a manner preferred by the sanctioning state.

Structure: a term often used in IR theory but one with various meanings, primarily because it is not observable in social life. Often defined as something that exists independently of actors but which is an important determinant of the nature of the actions performed by actors, since it ties together the various elements of the social system.

Substantive criticism and influence: a term used to define the level or extent of media criticism and influence whereby media reports criticize the fundamental justifications of a policy. Substantive criticism is distinct from procedural criticism which relates to the way in which a particular policy is being pursued and whether it is likely to work. An example of substantive criticism would be a news report questioning the moral, legal, or practical justification for a particular war.

Substantive theory: these are more academic theories that help us understand major foreign policy issues, provide descriptions of foreign policy instruments, and introduce us to foreign policy strategies.

Sui generis actor: description of the unique composition and actorness of the EU, combining a mixture of supranational and intergovernmental characteristics—clearly not a federal state but more than a traditional organization or confederation.

Supranationalism: where international institutions enjoy significant independence from member states. In the EU, supranational decisions are mainly taken by institutions such as the European Commission, the European Court of Justice, and the European Parliament. These bodies have authority over member states.

Tactical linkage: the promotion or denial of economic relationships to influence specific politics of a target country.

Teaching cases: these policy stories provide a comprehensive description of a policy issue, debate or event that places an emphasis on personalities, drama, and whenever possible quotes from the critical actors in the case. These cases do not include the application of theories or the detailed discussion of theoretical literature. The analysis is done during the teaching. Through questions and responses the students discover the answers and reach a better understanding of the policy situation.

Thematic news: a term used to describe news media reports that are framed in terms of the broad context surrounding an issue. For example, a news report on the 2003 Iraq war could be described as thematic if it dealt with the background to the conflict including possible causes and debate over the justification for the war.

Trade restrictions: cutting off imports or exports to influence the behaviour or capabilities of a target state.

Transit: the activities involved in transporting energy to a third party.

Transit states: states through whose territory energy resources cross.

Transit tariffs: payments received by the transit state (or operators of the transport facilities within that country) in exchange for transiting energy across the territory of the transit state.

Unipolarity: an international system shaped by the power of one major state, or unipole.

Universalism: the fact or condition of being universal in nature or scope. As applied to human rights, it means that we all have the same rights simply because we are human beings.

Uruguay Round: the last round of trade negotiations in the GATT. The negotiations continued for eight years, from 1986 to 1994, making it the longest round of trade negotiations in the history of the GATT. The protracted negotiations were over a very wide set of issues, including trade-related intellectual property rights (TRIPs), trade-related investment measures (TRIMs), and trade in services, and the creation of a stronger Dispute Settlement Mechanism. The round was completed in April 1994 at the Marrakesh Ministerial Conference. The Uruguay Round also saw the creation of the World Trade Organization.

Zionists: the term 'Zionist' was originally a term used to denote those who supported 'Zionism'—a nationalist project to establish a Jewish state in Palestine. The Zionist movement can be traced to the late nineteenth century among the European Jewish community. Since the formation of Israel in 1948, the term 'Zionist' has commonly been used in a pejorative sense to include non-Jews whose actions are deemed to support the Zionist project.

Endnotes

Chapter 1

1. Sections of this paper were previously published and reprinted by permission, including the introductory chapter of *Foreign Policy Analysis: Classic and Contemporary Theory* (New York: Rowman & Littlefield, 2007) which drew upon 'Foreign Policy Analysis Yesterday, Today, and Tomorrow' (with Christopher Vore; *Mershon International Studies Review*, Vol. 39, Supplement 2, 1995, 209–239), and 'Foreign Policy Decision-Making: A Touchstone for International Relations Theory in the Twenty-first Century', in Richard C. Snyder, H.W. Bruck, and Burton Sapin (eds), *Foreign Policy Decision-Making (Revisited)* (New York: Palgrave-Macmillan, 2002, 1–20).

Chapter 2

1. Here I follow Gilpin (1996: 7–8). See Donnelly (2000: 7–8) for a good list of representative defining assumptions of realism.

2. For further discussion, see Wohlforth (1993: Chapter 9).

Chapter 3

1. I thank Johanna Fine and Dessi Kirilova for excellent research assistance, and Makael Burrell and Geoffrey Carlson for helpful editorial suggestions.

2. One can further describe and code these four elements: market and private property economies; polities that are externally sovereign; citizens who possess juridical rights; and non-unitary and representative ('republican') government. The latter includes the requirement that the legislative branch has an effective role in public policy and is formally and competitively elected. Furthermore, before the modern era of universal suffrage, one should take into account whether male suffrage is wide (i.e. 30%) or open to 'achievement' by inhabitants (for example, poll-tax payers or householders) of the national or metropolitan territory and whether female suffrage is granted within a generation of its being demanded. The representative government should be internally sovereign (including especially over military and foreign policy decision-making).

3. The actual rights of citizenship have often been limited by male suffrage or property qualifications, but liberal regimes harboured no principle of opposition to the extension of juridical equality and as pressure was brought to bear they progressively extended suffrage (Huntington 1981b).

4. The sources of classic laissez-faire liberalism can be found in Locke, *The Federalist Papers*, Kant, and Nozick (1974). Expositions of welfare liberalism are in the work of the Fabians and Rawls (1971). Gutmann (1980) discusses variants of liberal thought. Uncomfortably paralleling each of the high roads are 'low roads' which, while achieving certain liberal values, fail to reconcile freedom and order. An overwhelming terror of anarchy and a speculation on preserving property can drive laissez-faire liberals to support a law-and-order authoritarian rule that sacrifices democracy. Authoritarianism to preserve order is the argument of Hobbes's *Leviathan*. It also shapes the argument of right-wing liberals who seek to draw a distinction between 'authoritarian' and 'totalitarian' dictatorships. The justification sometimes advanced by liberals for the former is that they can be temporary and educate the population into an acceptance of property, individual rights, and, eventually, representative government (Kirkpatrick 1979: 34–45). Complementarily, when social inequalities are judged to be extreme, the welfare liberal can argue that establishing (or re-establishing) the foundations of liberal society requires a non-liberal method of reform, a second low road of redistributing authoritarianism. Aristide Zolberg reports a 'liberal left' sensibility among US scholars of African politics that justified reforming dictatorship (Zolberg 1969: viii). And the argument of 'reforming autocracy' can be found in J.S. Mill's defence of colonialism in India.

5. Streit (1938: 88, 90–92) seems to have been the first to point out (in contemporary foreign relations) the empirical tendency of democracies to maintain peace among themselves, and he made this the foundation of his proposal for a (non-Kantian) federal union of the fifteen leading democracies of the 1930s. D.V. Babst (1972: 55–58) performed a quantitative study of this phenomenon of 'democratic peace', and R.J. Rummel (1983: 27–71) did a similar study of 'libertarianism' (in the sense of laissez-faire) focusing on the post-war period. I use 'liberal' in a wider (Kantian) sense in my discussion of this issue (Doyle 1983a: 1997). More recent work supporting the thesis of democratic peace is discussed in Zeev and Abdolali (1989), O'Neal *et al.*

(1996), and Rousseau (2005). A valuable survey of the debate on the empirical evidence for the democratic peace, assembling much of the best of the criticism and responses to that criticism, can be found in Brown et al. (1996).

6. I follow the same coding that I used in Doyle (1997: 264) including all states listed by Freedom House as 'Free' and those scoring 4 or less on the political scale and 5 or less on the civil liberties scale as 'Partly Free' (http://www.freedomhouse.org/).

7. Babst (1972: 56) made a preliminary test of the significance of the distribution of alliance partners in the First World War. He found that the possibility that the actual distribution of alliance partners could have occurred by chance was less than one percent. But this assumes that there was an equal possibility that any two nations could have gone to war with each other; and this is a strong assumption.

8. There is a rich literature devoted to explaining international cooperation and integration. Karl Deutsch (1957) develops the idea of a 'pluralistic security community' that bears a resemblance to the 'pacific union', but Deutsch limits it geographically and finds compatibility of values, mutual responsiveness, and predictability of behaviour among decision makers as its essential foundations. These are important, but many states sharing these characteristics have gone to war with each other. The particular content of liberalism appears to be more telling. Joseph Nye (1971) steps away from the geographical limits set by Deutsch and focuses on levels of development, but his analysis is directed towards explaining integration—a more intensive form of cooperation than the pacific union.

9. With 'imprudent vehemence', Hume referred to the English reluctance to negotiate an early peace with France and the total scale of the effort devoted to persecuting that war, which together were responsible for over half the length of the fighting and an enormous war debt. Hume, of course, was not describing fully liberal republics as defined here, but the characteristics he describes do seem to reflect some of the liberal republican features of the English eighteenth-century constitution (the influence of both popular opinion and a representative, even if severely limited, legislature). He contrasts these effects with the 'prudent politics' that should govern the balance of power and with the special, but different, failings characteristic of 'enormous monarchies'.

10. For a discussion of the historical effects of liberalism on colonialism, the US–Soviet Cold War, and post-Second World War interventions, see Doyle (1983b) and the sources cited therein.

11. The arguments in Chan (1984) and Weede (1984) support the conclusions reached by Small and Singer (1976). Both counter Rummel's (1983) view that libertarian states are less prone to violence than non-libertarian states, which he based on a sample of data from 1976–1980 which were not representative of the war-year data of 1816–1980 of Chan or the 1960–1980 data of Weede.

12. However, there are serious studies showing that Marxist regimes have higher military spending per capita than non-Marxist regimes (Payne 1986). But Stanislav Andreski (1980) argues that, because of their domestic fragility, (purely) military dictatorships have little incentive to engage in foreign military adventures.

13. This does not necessarily mean that the non-liberals are strategically inferior or less capable of mobilizing the resources needed to win. Non-liberal Russia bore the burden of both those sets of victories. The liberal advantage in the First and Second World Wars was in not fighting each other and being resistant to defection to the non-liberal camp. For recent work on the wider debate on whether democracies attack dictators or dictators attack democracies see Reiter and Stam (2003), but the nineteenth-century colonial record also needs to be included.

14. The following paragraphs build on arguments presented in Doyle (1997).

15. Memoranda by Mr Eyre Crowe, 1 January 1907, and by Lord Sanderson, 25 February 1907, in Gooch and Temperley (1928: 397–431).

16. John L. Gaddis has noted logistical differences between laissez-faire and social welfare liberals in policy towards the Soviet Union. In US policy, until the advent of the Reagan administration, the fiscal conservatism of Republicans led them to favour a narrow strategy, and the fiscal liberality of Democrats led to a broader strategy (Gaddis 1982).

17. Gladstone had proclaimed his support for the equal rights of all nations in his Midlothian speeches. Wilfrid Scawen Blunt served as a secret agent in Egypt, keeping Gladstone informed of the political character of Arabi's movement. The Liberal dilemma in 1882—were they intervening against genuine nationalism or a military adventurer (Arabi)?—was best expressed in Joseph Chamberlain's memorandum to the Cabinet, 21 June 1882, excerpted in Garvin and Amery (1935: 448). See also Mansfield (1971: Chapters 2 and 3), Hyam (1976: Chapter 8), and Tignor (1966).

18. During the Alliance for Progress era in Latin America, the Kennedy administration supported Juan Bosch in the Dominican Republic in 1962 (Bundy 1975).

19. See Huntington (1981b) and Quester (1980) for argument and examples of the successful export of

liberal institutions in the post-war period. A major study of the role of democratic expansion in US foreign policy is given by Smith (1994).

20. In 1851, the liberal French historian Guizot made a similar argument in a letter to Gladstone urging that Gladstone appreciate that the despotic government of Naples was the best guarantor of liberal law and order then available. Reform, in Guizot's view, meant the unleashing of revolutionary violence (Magnus 1954: 100).

21. Kirkpatrick (1979) points out our neglect of the needs of the authoritarians. Theodore Lowi (1963: 699) argues that Democratic and Republican policies towards the acquisition of bases in Spain reflected this dichotomy. In other cases where both the geopolitical and the domestic orientation of a potential neutral might be influenced by US aid, liberal institutions (representative legislatures) imposed delay or public constraints and conditions on diplomacy that allowed the Soviet Union to steal a march. Warren Christopher has suggested that this occurred in US relations with Nicaragua in 1979 (Christopher 1982: 998).

22. Ideological formulations often accompany these policies. Fear of Bolshevism was used to excuse not forming an alliance against Nazi aggression with the Soviet Union in 1938. And Nazi and fascist regimes were portrayed as defenders of private property and social order. But the connection that liberals draw between domestic tyranny and foreign aggression may also operate in reverse. When the Nazi threat to the survival of liberal states did require a liberal alliance with the Soviet Union, Stalin became for a short period the liberal press's 'Uncle Joe'.

23. Fukuyama's (1989) argument is more sophisticated than it has often been portrayed. Making related arguments about the end of war are John Mueller (1989) and Rudolph Rummel (1983). Katherine Barbieri (2003) criticizes the simple 'trade produces peace' thesis.

24. Of course, the individual subjects of autocracies do not lose their rights. It is just that the autocrats cannot claim legitimately to speak for their subjects. Subjects retain basic human rights, such as the rights of non-combatants in war. The terror bombing of civilians—as in the bombings of Dresden, Tokyo, Hiroshima, and Nagasaki—constitute, in this view, violations of these rights and of liberal principles and demonstrate weaknesses of liberal models in these cases.

25. These three points are developed in Doyle (1983a, 1983b, 1997).

26. There are other liberal views that reject attempts to expand the liberal pacific union (e.g. Rawls 1999).

27. Multilateral management is important and far from automatic, and liberal peace is not the same as inter-liberal cooperation. Current inter-liberal pacification is, of course, compatible with considerable competition and failure to achieve the mutually beneficial outcomes that long-term peace will require. For strategies of cooperation see the studies by Ruggie (1993) and Martin (1992).

28. The review essay by Wade (1992) effectively makes this case. Interestingly, Fukuyama's book also stresses this latter more complicated perspective on development; his article lends itself to the more libertarian interpretation of economic development.

29. The classic liberals also give mixed advice on these matters. Kant argued that the 'preliminary articles' from his treaty of perpetual peace required extending non-intervention by force in internal affairs of other states to non-liberal governments and maintaining a scrupulous respect for the laws of war. J.S. Mill, on the other hand, while condemning interventions for profit or to spread ideas, listed numerous justifications for intervention, including ending destructive civil wars and establishing a beneficent empire (see Doyle 2009).

30. Michael Reisman (1984) suggests a legal devolution of Security Council responsibilities to individual states. Oscar Schachter (1984) argues that such rights to intervene would be abused by becoming self-serving. For a carefully reasoned revival of moral arguments for just war criteria, see Walzer (1977). The policy of sanctions against South Africa, designed to undermine the domestic system of apartheid, is an earlier instance of these efforts.

31. Lesser violations of human rights (e.g. various lesser forms of majority tyranny) can warrant foreign diplomatic interference. The two severe abuses of liberal respect call for something more. Of course, the two severe abuses also tend to go together. Democratic resistance to authoritarian or totalitarian governments tends to result in the government inflicting severe abuses of human rights on the democratic resistance. Governments that systematically abuse the rights of their citizens rarely have widespread popular support. But they need not go together; hence their independence as criteria and one further constraint. Although the only popular movements for which one might justly intervene need not be democratically liberal, by these standards it would clearly be wrong to intervene in favour of a popular movement committed to a political programme that would involve the systematic abuse of basic 'objective' human rights. On some of the dangers of democratization for peace see Mansfield and Snyder (1995), and for another interpretation of the data see Rousseau (2005).

Chapter 4

1. At a recent seminar, Kenneth Waltz maintained that NATO's years were still numbered.

2. In an influential article called 'Back to the Future' John Mearsheimer (1990) outlined a bleak prospect for Europe after the Cold War, where European states would return to nuclear armed rivalry. On the other hand, Waltz maintained that on the strategic and systemic level, nothing had changed as strategic nuclear weapons remained in place.

3. Arguably some of the integration theories of the 1950s—most notably Ernst Haas's writings on neofunctionalism and Karl Deutsch's writings on security communities had focused on what was later to develop into constructivist issues of identity and changed practices (see, for example, Adler 2002). Casper Sylvest has also suggested that Hertz was in fact a social constructivist (Sylvest 2009), and Tim Dunne has argued that there are similarities between constructivism and the English School (Dunne 1995).

4. Karl Deutsch and his associates were arguing in the 1950s that increased trans-border interactions would gradually lead to 'mutual sympathy and loyalties . . . trust and mutual consideration' (Deutsch *et al.* 1957: 36) which would produce new identities (a 'we-feeling'). Deutsch argued that a so-called 'security community' might result, which would be characterized by 'dependable expectations of peaceful change' (Adler and Barnett 1998: 34).

5. I have explored this question by focusing on Social Identity Theory as an agent-level theory that can explain how and why norms change (see Flockhart 2006).

6. For a more thorough analysis of the identity constructions and role perceptions in NATO, see Flockhart (2011).

7. This was the wording in the London Declaration issued at the NATO Summit.

Chapter 7

1. I deliberately exclude 'reasonable' from these minimal requirements of rationality because it has much broader and deeper requirements. What 'reasonable' means is both culturally and situationally specific and a contested concept.

2. In the technical language of decision theory, decision makers should perform regular Bayesian updating of subjective probabilities, maximize expected utility in multi-attribute choice tasks, and quickly converge on equilibrium solutions to game-theoretic problems (see Tetlock 2006).

3. People pay inadequate attention to the base rates of occurrence in estimating probabilities. They often attach high probabilities to low-probability events.

4. This view of two operating systems is challenged by Glimcher (2002) who argues that there is no evidence that there are two fully independent systems, one emotional and the other computational, operating inside the brain. He finds within the brain of rhesus monkeys a remarkably economic view of the primate brain in which the final stages of decision making seem to mirror a utility calculation.

5. This summary draws on an informal presentation given by Daniel Kahneman at the Munk School at the University of Toronto on 16 February 2007.

6. Responses were monitored by functional magnetic resonance imaging (fMRI) during the experiment. Activity was strongest in the interior ansula, the part of the brain consistently associated with negative emotional responses. Activity in this part of the brain was even stronger when people thought that the offer was coming from a human partner rather than from a computer (Cohen 2005: 14).

Chapter 8

1. We are most grateful to Matthew Ham for assistance with the figures in this chapter.

2. This terminology, offensive to modern eyes in its routine misogyny, was wholly routine in Kennedy's era.

Chapter 9

1. For further information on critical approach see M. Rupert, 'Marxism and Critical Theory' in T. Dunne, M. Kurki, and S. Smith (eds), *Theories of International Relations: Discipline and Diversity* (Oxford: Oxford University Press, 2007).

Chapter 10

1. For a feminist account of security, see Enloe (1989) and Tickner (2004).

2. For a general overview of the field of security studies, see Walt (1991), Baldwin (1995), and Collins (2007).

Chapter 11

1. This and the following section draw heavily on Mastanduno (1999–2000: 301–15).

Chapter 14

1. Materials supplementary to the text were provided by Lara Silver, doctoral research student at the University of Kent at Canterbury.

2. Material for this chapter is drawn from Graham Allison and Philip Zelikow, *Essence of Decision: Explaining the Cuban Missile Crisis* (2nd edn) (New York: Longman, 1999). Grateful thanks to Longman

for permission. The author also wishes to express special thanks to Minh Ly and Ali Wyne for assistance in the preparation of the chapter.

3. These sources include: A. Fursenko and T. Naftali, *One Hell of a Gamble': Khrushchev, Castro and Kennedy 1958–1964* (New York: W.W. Norton, 1997); A.I. Gribkov, 'The View from Moscow and Havana', in A.I. Gribkov and W.Y. Smith (eds), *Operation Anadyr: U.S. and Soviet Generals Recount the Cuban Missile Crisis* (Chicago: Edition q, 1994); various CIA estimates, many reprinted in *CIA Documents on the Cuban Missile Crisis;* US Congress, House Appropriations Committee, Subcommittee on Department of Defense Appropriations, *Hearings, 88th Cong., 1st sess., 1963; Department of Defense, Special Cuba Briefing,* 6 February 1963; US Congress, Senate Armed Services Committee, Preparedness Investigating Subcommittee, *Interim Report on Cuban Military Buildup,* 88th Cong., 1st sess., 1963.

4. Ballistic missiles are classified according to their range: MRBMs (1000–3000 km or 620–1825 miles); IRBMs (3000–5500 km or 1865–3420 miles); and ICBMs (more than 5500 km or 3420 miles).

5. In his memoirs, Khrushchev recalled, 'While I was on an official visit to Bulgaria [14–20 May 1962], one thought kept hammering at my brain: What will happen if we lose Cuba?' (Khrushchev 1970: 493).

6. The Committee on the Present Danger used the phrase to describe the threat to the United States from American policies of the late 1970s and early 1980s.

7. Khrushchev certainly needed a success. As the historian James Richter observed, 'Khrushchev's domestic position set the stage for his foreign policy behavior. He needed a foreign policy success more than ever. The mounting difficulties in his domestic programs discredited his arguments that he could lead the Soviet Union to a rapid victory over the United States in the economic competition, even as the increased strains on capital investment reinforced his incentive to save on defense spending' (Richter 1994: 128).

8. The following draws upon the Afterword by R.E. Neustadt and G.T. Allison to R.F. Kennedy, *Thirteen Days: A Memoir of the Cuban Missile Crisis* (New York: W.W. Norton, 1971).

9. M. Dobbs, *One Minute to Midnight: Kennedy, Khrushchev, and Castro on the Brink of Nuclear War* (New York: Knopf, 2008), 39–40.

10. Dobbs 2008: 91–4.

Chapter 16

1. Drolet (2007) suggests that the neoconservatives' domestic and foreign policy agendas are intimately linked. For him, the external danger and evils identified by the neoconservatives are integral to the success of America's internal moral regeneration. Stelzer (2004) and Fukuyama (2006) make a stronger separation.

2. The Team B phenomenon was very much in evidence in the lead-up to Operation Iraqi Freedom. The Office of the Vice-President and the Department of Defense consistently second-guessed CIA estimates of Saddam Hussein's WMD capabilities and his links to al-Qaeda. See Suskind (2006) and Mann (2004).

Chapter 18

1. Research for this paper is based on a three-year Nuffield Foundation project on Emerging Powers in International Regimes. The author is indebted to the Foundation for its support, and also thanks Dr. Andrew Hurrell for extensive and invaluable discussions on the subject. A part of the argument developed in this paper was first explored in A. Narlikar and A. Hurrell, *Negotiating Trade as Emerging Powers*, IRIS Working Paper, 2003/023, International Institute of Stavanger, Norway, 2007. Early versions of this argument were presented at the International Research Institute of Stavanger and POLSIS Department Seminar, University of Birmingham. The author is grateful to the participants at both seminars for helpful feedback.

2. The term BRICs first appeared in the Goldman Sachs study by Wilson and Purushothaman (2003), and refers to the rising powers of Brazil, Russia, India, and China.

3. *International Trade Statistics 2010;* www.wto.org/english/res_e/statis_c/its2010_e/its2010_e.pdf, accessed 24 September 2011. Note that these figures exclude intra-EU trade.

4. Narlikar (2003) makes a distinction between two types of coalitions—bloc-type and issue-based. First, blocs are formed against a backdrop of ideational or identity-based factors, whereas the latter type of coalition involves an instrumental convergence of countries around a shared issue of concern. Second, blocs bring together like-minded countries that try to coordinate positions across issue areas and over time, whereas issue-based coalitions are formed against a specific threat and tend to dissipate after the threat is gone.

5. Whilst at the Cancun Ministerial Conference, the author asked several smaller members of the coalition why they would not defect in favour of a deal, perhaps in the form of a Preferential Trade Agreement with the United States or the EC. Several of the respondents pointed out that the collective gains to be had from the G20 agenda would so significantly outweigh the benefits of any bilateral deals that

defection from the coalition would be irrational. (Interviews, Cancun, 10–14 September 2003.)

6. Whilst at the Cancun ministerial conference, the author asked several smaller members of the coalition why they would not defect in favour of a deal, perhaps in the form of a Preferential Trade Agreement with the US or the EC. Several of the respondents pointed out that the collective gains to be had from the G20 agenda would so significantly outweigh the benefits of any bilateral deals that defection from the coalition would be irrational. Interviews, Cancun, 10–14 September 2003.

7. In the case of the Like-Minded Group India organized weekly meetings to discuss concerns of members; Brazil spent a great deal of effort coordinating with other countries as well as NGOs on TRIPS and public health; the G20 was formed on the initiative of Brazil, China, and India. Brazil and India drafted the first G20 text together, and subsequently got Chinese support for it; in post-Cancun negotiations Brazil and India continued to take the lead in organizing meetings, conducting research on the implications of various proposals, and acting as spokesmen for the group.

8. As part of signalling their commitment to the LDC counterparts, India has not attempted to restrict this market access on a product-specific basis to reduce the costs of such free-riding. (Interview with a senior official in the Ministry of Commerce, New Delhi, 10 April 2006.)

9. Third World Network information service, 10 November 2005, accessed on 7 August 2006 at http://www.twnside.org.sg/title2/twninfo297.htm .

10. TNC Meeting, Statement of Shri Kamal Nath, 23 July 2008, accessed at www.wto.org/english/tratop_e/dda.../meet08_stat_ind_21jul_e.doc on 24 September 2011.

11. WT/GC/W/442, Proposal for a Framework Agreement on Special and Differential Treatment, 19 September 2001.

12. Statement by H.E. Mr Murasoli Maran, India, WT/MIN(01)/ST/10, 10 November 2001 (www.wto.org).

13. Statement by H.E. Mr Kamal Nath, India, WT/MIN(05)/ST/17, 14 December 2005 (www.wto.org).

14. Press Release, US Mission to the UN, Geneva, 24 July 2006 (http://geneva.usmission.gov/Press2006/0724Doha.html accessed 7 August 2006). See also Schwaab (2011) for a scathing assessment of the role of the rising powers in the Doha negotiations.

15. The costs of no agreement are not just the delayed benefits of the round for all the members of the WTO, but also the credibility of the multilateral trading regime. The dangers of protectionism are high, particularly in the uncertain and difficult economic situation triggered first by the global financial crisis of 2008, and then by the evolving sovereign debt crisis of 2011. The Doha Development Agenda (DDA) offers an invaluable insurance policy against further protectionism, as well as several other important benefits (see Bhagwati and Sutherland 2011). As this chapter has argued, India must accept a fair share of the blame for the Doha deadlocks and the resulting dangers of non-agreement. Importantly, however, India is not the sole culprit. While a full account of this cannot be developed in this chapter because of limitations of space, other parties which share equal responsibility (albeit in different phases of the negotiation) are the established powers (especially the United States and the EU) as well as other rising powers and coalitions of developing countries.

Chapter 19

1. I thank José Luis Bernal and Saúl Mauricio Rodríguez for their assistance in conducting research for this chapter, and Mônica Herz for providing helpful comments on earlier drafts.

2. Brazilian exceptionalism is rooted in the fact that its identity and culture have always been different from those of its 'Latin American' neighbours, a term that Brazilian elites and intellectuals have long rejected. Not only is it the only Portuguese-speaking country in the region, but it was founded as a monarchy and not a republic, as occurred elsewhere.

3. See Hurrell (2010) for a comprehensive treatment of Fernando Henrique Cardoso's thinking about world politics.

4. Brazil was a latecomer in adopting neoliberal reform, and it never completely embraced the 'Washington Consensus' formula for macro-economic stabilization, including reduced state intervention in the economy, privatization, and economic opening.

5. For an in-depth analysis of India's role in this process, see Chapter Eighteen.

6. Growing ties with Africa have been rooted in appeals to Brazil's shared identity with the continent; the country hosts the world's second-largest Afro-descendant population after Nigeria.

7. The 1982 Falklands/Malvinas war, provoked by the Argentine invasion of the Falkland Islands and declaration of war against the United Kingdom, had the unintended consequence not only of hastening military rule in Argentina but also of bringing the two countries closer together.

8. Collor de Mello adopted much stronger measures than those of his predecessor to restrict the Brazilian nuclear technology programme, while also publicly denouncing secret plans on the part of the military to develop a nuclear bomb.

9. Nevertheless, Brazil's nuclear intentions, especially following Lula's election, are unclear. The Brazilian president's announcement in July 2007 that the country would build a nuclear submarine with French technology aroused suspicion, as did his critiques of the NPT.

10. In the 1980s Brazilian trade with the rest of South America was minimal, reflecting the inward-oriented development model prevalent in most of Latin America at the time. However, economic liberalization throughout the subregion led to important shifts in trade patterns. For example, Brazilian trade with Argentina increased nearly fivefold between 1990 and 1995 as a result of the bilateral agreements signed between the two countries.

11. For an in-depth discussion of 'open regionalism' in the context of the Southern Cone, see Phillips (2003).

12. By the 2005 Summit of the Americas meeting, the agreement was virtually dead, in no small measure due to South American opposition.

13. The 'wave' began with Hugo Chávez in Venezuela (1999) and continued with the election of Néstor Kirchner in Argentina (2003), Lula in Brazil (2003), Evo Morales in Bolivia (2006), Michelle Bachelet in Chile (2006), Rafael Correa in Ecuador (2007), Cristina Fernández de Kirchner in Argentina (2007), and Fernando Lugo in Uruguay (2008).

14. Countries such as Argentina (and Mexico) have openly opposed Brazil's bid for a permanent UN Security Council seat.

15. To date, the members of ALBA are Venezuela, Cuba, Ecuador, Bolivia, Nicaragua, Saint Vincent and the Grenadines, Antigua and Barbuda, and Dominica.

Chapter 20

1. The key human-induced greenhouse gas is carbon dioxide, but methane, nitrous oxide, and other gases also contribute to climate change.

2. There have been four integrated IPCC assessment reports on the science of climate change (1990, 1995, 2001, and 2007), with a fifth scheduled for 2014.

3. To come into effect, the Kyoto Protocol had to be ratified by fifty-five countries, together producing at least 55% of the world's 1990 carbon dioxide emissions. Russia's ratification took the Protocol over the latter threshold.

4. A 2007 Australian Election Study showed that 66% of Australians supported participation in the Kyoto Protocol (Tranter 2011: 88).

5. Green senators opposed the CPRS as inadequate, while several Conservative senators opposed it as a potential threat to jobs and economic growth.

Chapter 21

1. Thanks to Tim Dunne and Lise Storm for reading earlier versions of this chapter.

2. Readers interested in understanding more about the relationship between 'modern hatreds' and 'ancient hatreds' should read Kaufman (2001).

3. These parties included the Popular Front for the Liberation of Palestine led by George Habash and the Popular Democratic Front for the Liberation of Palestine led by Nayif Hawatmah.

Chapter 22

1. Thanks to Jocelyn Vaughan and Lara Silver for their assistance in preparing the first edition of this chapter. Paul Williams and my fellow editors provided very helpful comments on earlier drafts. The chapter builds on previous work in this area which was co-authored with Nick Wheeler; as ever I am grateful for the knowledge he generously shares. The incorporation of insights from policy planners was made possible by an ESRC knowledge transfer grant. Part of the activity associated with the grant included a seminar on UK foreign policy at the Royal College of Defence Staff—many thanks to the invitees for their input into these questions.

2. Kampfner's claim is challenged by Seldon. On this and many other issues, there are contradictory statements in the public realm, reflecting the bipolar nature of elite opinion in relation to the Blair years.

3. This list assumes that China, the United States, and Russia are great powers with global reach (while recognizing that the United States is, strategically speaking, first among equals).

4. This section draws heavily on the excellent discussion in Williams (2005: 28–9). For an alternative view, see Curtis (2003: 276). Here, he argues that the 'twin goals' of UK foreign policy are to maintain Britain's great power status and to ensure that the international political economy functions 'to benefit Western businesses'.

5. It is worthy of note that Anthony Seldon's authoritative biography includes a chapter on 'God' (Seldon 2004).

6. I am grateful to Nick Wheeler for pointing this out.

7. It is worth noting that Meyer wisely resists talking about the 'road to war' being inevitable. The road, to him, looked 'anything but straight or the destination preordained' (Meyer 2005: 238).

Chapter 23

1. Thanks as ever are due to Adnan Amkhan for his insights on the Energy charter Treaty, particularly the ticklish subject of Russian withdrawal of provisional application of the ECT.

2. Students need to bear in mind that a key feature of energy security (including energy efficiency) is its impact on the environment. The Kyoto Protocol has demonstrated the dilemma that states face in their increasing dependence upon hydrocarbons with incontrovertible evidence of hydrocarbon damage to the global environment via carbon dioxide emissions. More than ever before, states must consider a collective approach to regulating energy use, deciding on appropriate energy resources, and environmental obligations.

3. In this chapter a legalistic distinction must be drawn between what constitutes transit and transport. The former applies to the countries through whose territory energy is transported to a third party. However, the latter applies to any form of energy transport.

4. As a foreign policy instrument, however, the Common Strategy—and the earlier 1997 Partnership and Cooperation Agreement (PCA)—allowed the European Union to successfully establish permanent dialogue with its two key Eastern players.

5. While Russia did not ratify the ECT, it did apply it provisionally in accordance with Article 45 ECT until terminating its provisional application of the ECT in 2009.

6. A current issue of dispute is the recent statement that non-Russian pipeline infrastructure may be solicited by Gazprom despite the monopolistic lock which Transneft has on Russian pipelines, effectively barring any Western investment.

7. In 2006, former German Chancellor Schröder and Russian President Putin agreed to the Nord Stream Pipeline which will extend from Russia to Germany via the Baltic Sea, bypassing Eastern European transit countries. Hungarian Prime Minister Gyurcscany in March 2007 supported the proposed extension of Russia's Blue Stream pipeline from Turkey to Hungary.

8. Average import figures are difficult to determine because of their innate fluctuations and the different dependencies of various European states. Norway and Algeria constitute Europe's other major gas suppliers; Norway, Saudi Arabia, Libya, and others constitute its oil suppliers.

9. The embargo tactic has been visibly expanded throughout 2006, with Russia now banning the import of Moldovan meat products, plants, and wines, Georgian wines, plants, and vegetables, and Polish meat and plant products. As leading suppliers to the Russian market, various commentators, along with various EU member states, have suggested that 'these bans are politically motivated, aiming to damage the economies of . . . pro-Western countries that Moscow regards as disobedient' (Soccor 2006).

Bibliography

ABC Television (1997), 'The Hot Debate', *Four Corners, ABC Television*, 18 August (http://www.abc.net.au/science/news/eureka/transcripts/hot.htm).

Achen, C.H. (1975), 'Mass Political Attitudes and the Survey Response', *American Political Science Review*, 69: 1218–31.

Adler, E. (1997), 'Seizing the Middle Ground: Constructivism in World Politics', *European Journal of International Relations*, 3: 319–63.

Adler, E. (2002), 'Constructivism and International Relations', in W. Carlsnaes, T. Risse, and B.A. Simmons (eds), *Handbook of International Relations* (London: Sage), 95–118.

Adler, E. (2008), 'The Spread of Security Communities: Communities of Practice, Self-Restraint and NATO's Post Cold War Transformation', *European Journal of International Relations*, 14, 195–230.

Adler, E. and Barnett, M. (eds) (1998), *Security Communities* (Cambridge: Cambridge University Press).

Adler-Nissen, R. (2008), 'The Diplomacy of Opting Out: A Bourdieudian Approach to National Integration Strategies', *Journal of Common Market Studies*, 46: 663–84.

Agarwal, A. and Narain, S. (1991), *Global Warming in an Unequal World: A Case of Environmental Colonialism* (New Delhi: Centre for Science and the Environment).

Aggestam, L. (2004), *A European Foreign Policy? Role Conceptions and the Politics of Identity in Britain, France and Germany* (Edsbruk: Akademitryck).

Aggestam, L. (ed.) (2008), 'Ethical Power Europe?', Special issue, *International Affairs*, 84(1).

Alden, C. (2007), *China in Africa* (London: Zed Books).

Allison, G.T. (1971), *Essence of Decision: Explaining the Cuban Missile Crisis* (Boston, MA: Little, Brown).

Allison, G.T. and Halperin, M.H. (1972), 'Bureaucractic Politics: A Paradigm and Some Policy Implications', *World Politics*, 24: 40–79.

Allison, G., and Zelikow, P. (1999), *Essence of Decision: Explaining the Cuban Missile Crisis* (2nd edn) (New York: Longman).

Almond, G.A. (1950), *The American People and Foreign Policy* (New York: Praeger).

Almond, G.A., and Verba, S. (1963), *The Civic Culture: Political Attitudes and Democracy in Five Nations* (Princeton, NJ: Princeton University Press).

Aly, A.M.S. (1988), 'Egypt: A Decade After Camp David', in W. Quandt (ed.), *The Middle East: Ten Years After Camp David* (Washington, DC: Brookings Institution), 63–93.

Amin, S. (1985), 'Ta'ammulat Hawla Tabi'at al Ra'smaliyah fi Misr' [Reflections on the Nature of Capitalism in Egypt], *al-Tali'ah [The Vanguard]*, August: 96–118.

Anderegg, W., Prall, J., Harald, J., and Schneider, S. (2010), 'Expert Credibility in Climate Change', *Proceedings of the National Academy of Sciences of the United States of America*, 107: 12,107–9.

Anderson, C.A. (1983), 'Abstract and Concrete Data in the Perseverance of Social Theories: When Weak Data Lead to Unshakeable Beliefs', *Journal of Experimental and Social Psychology*, 19: 93–108.

Anderson, C.A., Lepper, M.R., and Ross, L. (1980), 'Perseverance of Social Theories: The Role of Explanation in the Persistence of Discredited Information', *Journal of Personality and Social Psychology*, 39: 1037–49.

Anderson, P. (1987), 'What Do Decision Makers Do When They Make a Foreign Policy Decision? The Implications for the Study of Comparative Foreign Policy', in C.F. Hermann, C.W. Kegley, and J.N. Rosenau (eds), *New Directions in the Study of Foreign Policy* (Boston, MA: Allen & Unwin), 285–308.

Andreski, S. (1980), 'On the Peaceful Disposition of Military Dictatorships', *Journal of Strategic Studies*: 3: 3–10.

Andriole, S.J., and Hopple, G.W. (1981), 'The Rise and Fall of Events Data: Thoughts on an Incomplete Journey from Basic Research to Applied Use in the US Department of Defense', unpublished paper (Washington, DC: US Department of Defense).

Anwar, T. (1986), *The Ramadan War, 1973*, Air War College Research Report (Maxwell Air Force Base, AL: US Air Force Air University).

Aradau, C. (2008), *Rethinking Trafficking in Women: Politics Out of Security* (Basingstoke: Palgrave Macmillan).

Aron, R. (1966), *Peace and War: A Theory of International Relations* (Garden City, NY: Doubleday).

Ashley, R.K. (1976), 'Noticing Pre-Paradigmatic Progress', in J.N. Rosenau (ed.), *In Search of Global Patterns* (New York: Free Press), 150–7.

Ashley, R.K. (1981), 'Political Realism and Human Interests', *International Studies Quarterly*, 25: 204–36.

Ashley, R.K. (1987), 'Foreign Policy as Political Performance', *International Studies Notes*, 13: 51–4.

Ashley, R.K. (1987), 'The Geopolitics of Geopolitical Space: Toward a Critical Social Theory of International Politics', *Alternatives*, 12:403–34.

Ashley, R.K. (1989), 'Living on Border Lines: Man, Poststructuralism, and War', in J. Der Derian and M.J. Shapiro (eds), *International/Intertextual Relations: Postmodern Readings of World Politics* (Lexington, MA: Lexington Books), 259–321.

Axelrod, R. (ed.) (1976), *Structure of Decision* (Princeton, NJ: Princeton University Press).

Axworthy, L. (1996), Address at the Closing Session of the International Strategy Conference Towards a Global Ban on Antipersonnel Landmines, Ottawa, 5 October.

Babst, D.V. (1972), 'A Force for Peace', *Industrial Research*, 14: 55–8.

Bailey, T.A. (1948), *The Man in the Street: The Impact of American Public Opinion on Foreign Policy* (New York: Macmillan).

Baker, J.A., III (2006), *The Iraq Study Group Report* (New York: Vintage Books).

Baldwin, D.A. (1985), *Economic Statecraft* (Princeton, NJ: Princeton University Press).

Baldwin, D.A. (1993), 'Neoliberalism, Neorealism, and World Politics', in D.A. Baldwin (ed.), *Neorealism and Neoliberalism: The Contemporary Debate* (New York: Columbia University Press), 3–25.

Baldwin, D.A. (1995), 'Security Studies and the End of the Cold War', *World Politics*, 48: 117–41.

Banchoff, T. (1999), 'German Identity and European Integration', *European Journal of International Relations*, 5: 259–90.

Banerjee, S. (1991), 'Reproduction of Subjects in Historical Structures: Attribution, Identity, and Emotion in the Early Cold War', *International Studies Quarterly*, 35: 19–38.

Banks, A. and Overstreet, W. (1983), *A Political Handbook of The World* (New York: McGraw-Hill).

Bar-Joseph, U. (2000), 'Israel's 1973 Intelligence Failure', in P. Kumaraswamy (ed.), *Revisiting the Yom Kippur War* (London: Frank Cass), 11–35.

Bar-Joseph, U. (2006), 'Last Chance to Avoid War: Sadat's Peace Initiative of February 1973 and its Failure', *Journal of Contemporary History*, 46: 545–56.

Barbé, E. and Johansson-Nogués, E. (2008), 'The EU as a Modest "Force for Good": The European Neighbourhood Policy', *International Affairs*, 84: 81–96.

Barber, J.D. (1972/1985), *The Presidential Character: Predicting Performance in the White House* (Englewood Cliffs, NJ: Prentice-Hall).

Barbieri, K. (2003), *The Liberal Illusion: Does Trade Promote Peace?* (Ann Arbor, MI: University of Michigan).

Bargh, J.A. and Chartrand, T.L. (1999), 'The Unbearable Automacity of Being', *American Psychologist*, 54: 462–79.

Bargh, J.A., Chaiken, S., Raymond, P., and Hymes, C. (1996), 'The Automatic Evaluation Effect: Unconditional Automatic Attitude Activation with a Pronunciation Task', *Journal of Experimental Social Psychology*, 32: 104–28.

Barnet, R. (1968), *Intervention and Revolution: The United States in the Third World* (New York: Meridian).

Barnett, M. and Duvall, R. (2005), 'Power in International Politics', *International Organization*, 59: 39–75.

Barnett, M. and Finnemore, M. (2004), *Rules for the World: International Organizations in Global Politics* (Ithaca, NY: Cornell University Press).

Baum, M.A. and Groeling, T.J. (2010), *War Stories: The Causes and Consequences of Public Views of War* (Princeton, NJ: Princeton University Press).

Bayne, N., and Woolcock, S. (2003), *The New Economic Diplomacy: Decision-Making and Negotiation in International Economic Relations* (Aldershot: Ashgate).

BBC News (2006), 'Russia Vows to End Gas Shortage', 2 January (http://news.bbc.co.uk/1/hi/world/europe/4575726.stm)

BBC News (2009) 'Czechs Apologise for Hoax EU Art', 15 January (http://newsvote.bbc.co.uk/mpapps/pagetools/print/news.bbc.co.uk/2/hi/europe/7830498.stm?ad=1) (accessed 6 September 2011).

Beal, R.S., and Hinckley, R. (1984), 'Presidential Decision-making and Opinion Polls', *Annals of the American Academy of Political and Social Science*, 472: 72–84.

Beattie, A. (2008), 'Expectations Low as Doha Trade Talks Commence', *Financial Times*, 22 July.

Beer, F.A. (1981), *Peace Against War: The Ecology of International Violence* (San Francisco, CA: W.H. Freeman).

Belasco, A. (2011). *The Cost of Iraq, Afghanistan, and Other Global War on Terror Operations since 9/11*, Congressional Research Service, Washington, DC (http://www.fas.org/sgp/crs/natsec/RL33110.pdf).

Bennett, A. and George, A. (2005), *Case Studies and Theory Development in the Social Sciences* (Cambridge, MA: MIT Press).

Bennett, W.J. (2002), *Why We Fight: Moral Clarity and the War on Terrorism* (New York: Doubleday).

Bennett, W.L. (1990), 'Toward a Theory of Press–State Relations in the United States', *Journal of Communication*, 40: 103–25.

Bennett, W.L., Lawrence, R.G., and Livingston, S.L. (2006), 'None Dare Call it Torture: Indexing and the Limits of Press Independence in the Abu Ghraib Scandal', *Journal of Communication*, 56: 467–85.

Berenskoetter, F. (2010) 'Identity in International Relations', in R.A. Denemark (ed.), *The International Studies Encyclopedia* (Oxford: Blackwell; Blackwell Reference Online).

Berger, P. and Luckmann, T. (1966), *The Social Construction of Reality* (Harmondsworth: Penguin Books).

Bergsten, C.F., Berthoin, G., and Mushakoji, K. (1978), 'The Reform of International Institutions' (Triangle Paper 11), in *Trilateral Commission Task Force Reports 9–14* (New York: New York University Press).

Berlin, I. (1969), *Four Essays on Liberty* (New York: Oxford University Press).

Berlin, I. (1992), 'On Political Judgment', *New York Review of Books*, 43: 26–30.

Berlin, I. (1997), 'The Hedgehog and the Fox', in *The Proper Study of Mankind* (New York: Farrar, Strauss, and Giroux), 436–98.

Bhagwati, J., Sutherland, P., *et al.* (2011), *The Doha Round: Setting a Deadline, Defining a Final Deal. Interim Report* (http://www.number10.gov.uk/wp-content/uploads/doha-round-jan-2011.pdf).

Bicchi, F. (2010), 'The Impact of the ENP on EU–North Africa Relations: The Good, the Bad and the Ugly', in R.G. Whitman and S. Wolff (eds), *The European Neighbourhood Policy in Perspective: Context, Implementation and Impact* (Basingstoke: Palgrave Macmillan).

Bickerton, C. (2011), *European Union Foreign Policy: From Effectiveness to Functionality* (Basingstoke: Palgrave Macmillan).

Billings, R. and Hermann, C.F. (1994), 'Problem Identification in Sequential Policy Decisionmaking', paper presented at the 35th Annual Conference of the International Studies Association, Washington, DC, 28 March–1 April.

Bilmes, L. and Stiglitz, J. (2006), 'The Economic Costs of the Iraq War: An Appraisal Three Years after the Conflict', working paper (http://www2.gsb.columbia.edu/faculty/jstiglitz/Cost_of_War_in_Iraq.pdf).

Blair, T. (1997), 'The Principles of a Modern British Foreign Policy', speech at the Lord Mayor's Banquet, London, 10 November.

Blair, T. (1999), 'Doctrine of the International Community', speech at the Economic Club of Chicago, 22 April.

Blair, T. (1999), 'The New Challenge for Europe', speech at the ceremony to receive the Charlemagne Prize, Aachen, 13 May (www.fco.gov.uk/news/speechtext).

Blair, T. (2001), 'Let Us Reorder the World Around Us', speech to the Labour Party Conference, Brighton, 2 October.

Blieker, R. and Hutchinson, E. (2008), 'Fear No More: Emotions and World Politics', *Review of International Studies* 34: 115–35.

Blix, H. (2005), *Disarming Iraq* (London: Bloomsbury).

Bobrow, D.B., Chan, S., and Kringen, J.A. (1979), *Understanding Foreign Policy Decisions: The Chinese Case* (New York: Free Press).

Bock, P.G., and Berkowitz, M. (1966), 'The Emerging Field of National Security', *World Politics*, 19: 122–36.

Booth, K. (2001), *The Kosovo Tragedy: The Human Rights Dimensions* (London: Frank Cass).

Booth, K. (2005) (ed.), *Critical Security Studies and World Politics* (Boulder, CO: Lynne Rienner).

Bornstein, D. (1999), 'A Force Now in the World, Citizens Flex Social Muscle', *New York Times*, 10 July: B7.

Boyne, W. (2002), *The Two O'Clock War: The 1973 Yom Kippur Conflict and the Airlift that Saved Israel* (New York: St. Martin's Press).

Boynton, G.R. (1991), 'The Expertise of the Senate Foreign Relations Committee', in V.M. Hudson (ed.), *Artificial Intelligence and International Politics* (Boulder, CO: Westview Press), 291–309.

Braun, J.F. (2011), 'EU Energy Policy Under the Treaty of Lisbon Rules Between a New Policy and Business as Usual', European Policy Institutes Network Working Paper 31, February 2011 (http://www.epin.org).

Brecher, M. (1972), *The Foreign Policy System of Israel: Setting, Images, Process* (London: Oxford University Press).

Brecher, M. (1974), *Decisions in Israel's Foreign Policy* (London: Oxford University Press).

Bremer, S.A. (1993), 'Democracy and Militarized Interstate Conflict, 1816–1965', *International Interactions*, 18: 231–49.

Breslauer, G.W. and Tetlock, P. (1991) (eds), *Learning in US and Soviet Foreign Policy* (Boulder, CO: Westview Press).

Bretherton, C. and Vogler, J. (2006), *The European Union as a Global Actor* (London: Routledge).

Brighi, E. (2005), 'Foreign Policy and the International/Domestic Nexus: The Case of Italy', unpublished PhD thesis, London School of Economics and Political Science.

Brock, G. and Brighouse, H. (eds) (2005), *The Political Philosophy of Cosmopolitanism* (Cambridge: Cambridge University Press).

Broderson, A. (1961), 'National Character: An Old Problem Revisited', in J.N. Rosenau (ed.), *International Politics and Foreign Policy* (Glencoe, IL: Free Press of Glencoe), 300–8.

Brodie, B. (ed.) (1946), *The Absolute Weapon* (New York: Harcourt Brace).

Brookings Institution (2011). *The Iraq Index* (http://www.brookings.edu/saban/iraq-index.aspx) (accessed 26 August 2011).

Brooks, S. (2005), *Producing Security: Multinational Corporations, Globalization, and the Changing Calculus of Conflict* (Princeton, NJ: Princeton University Press).

Brooks, S.G. and Wohlforth, W.C. (2008), *World Out of Balance: International Relations and the Challenge of American Primacy* (Princeton, NJ: Princeton University Press).

Brown, M., Lynn-Jones, S., and Miller, S. (eds) (1996), *Debating the Democratic Peace* (Cambridge, MA: MIT Press).

Brummer, K. (2011). 'FPA and the Global South', research paper presented at the International Studies Association Annual Conference, 'Global Governance: Political Authority in Transition', Montreal, Canada, 16–19 March 2011

Brysk, A. (1993), 'From Above and Below: Social Movements, the International System and Human Rights in Argentina', *Comparative Political Studies*, 26: 259–85.

Buckley, N. (2005), 'Putin's Chief Economic Adviser Quits', *Financial Times*, 28 December.

Buckley, N. and Parker, G. (2005), 'Ukraine Rejects Moscow Gas Loan Offer', *Financial Times*, 30 December.

Buckley, N., and Warner, T. (2006), 'Kiev Turmoil Raises More Doubts Over Gas Deal', *Financial Times*, 12 January.

Buckley, N., Minder, R., and Olearchyk, R. (2005), 'Russia Prepares to Turn off Gas to Ukraine', *Financial Times*, 30 December.

Bueno de Mesquita, B. and Lalman, D. (1992), *War and Reason: Domestic and International Imperatives* (New Haven, CT: Yale University Press).

Bulkeley, H. (2001) 'No regrets? Economy and environment in Australia's domestic climate change policy process', *Global Environmental Change: Human and Policy Dimensions*, 11: 155–69.

Bulkeley, H. and Newell, P. (2010), *Governing Climate Change* (London: Routledge).

Bull, H. (1977/1995). *The Anarchical Society* (New York: Columbia University Press).

Bull, H. and Watson, A. (eds) (1982), *The Expansion of International Society* (Oxford: Clarendon Press).

Bulmer-Thomas, V. (2006), 'Blair's Foreign Policy and its Possible Successor(s)', Chatham House Briefing Paper, December (http://www.chathamhouse.org/publications/papers/view/108365).

Bundy, McG. (1988), *Danger and Survival: Choices about the Bomb in the First Fifty Years* (New York: Random House).

Bundy, W.P. (1975), 'Dictatorships and American Foreign Policy', *Foreign Affairs*, 54: 51–60.

Burges, S.W. (2008), 'Consensual Hegemony: Theorizing Brazilian Foreign Policy after the Cold War', *International Relations*, 22: 65–84.

Burges, S.W. (2010), 'Brazil as Regional Leader: Meeting the Chavéz Challenge', *Current History*, 109: 53–9.

Butler, J. (1990), *Gender Trouble: Feminism and the Subversion of Identity* (London: Routledge).

Buzan, B. (1991), *People, States, and Fear: An Agenda for International Security Studies in the Post-Cold War Era* (2nd edn) (Boulder, CO: Lynne Rienner).

Buzan, B. and Hansen, L. (2009), *The Evolution of International Security Studies* (Cambridge: Cambridge University Press).

Buzan, B., Wæver, O., and de Wilde, J. (1998), *Security: A New Framework for Analysis* (Boulder, CO: Lynne Rienner).

Byers, M. (2003), 'The Laws of War, US-Style', *London Review of Books*, 20 February.

Callahan, P., Brady, L., and Hermann, M.G. (eds) (1982), *Describing Foreign Policy Behavior* (Beverly Hills: Sage).

Camerer, C., Issacharoff, S., Loewenstein, G., O'Donoghue, T., and Rabin, M. (2003), 'Regulation for Conservatives: Behavioral Economics and the Case for "Asymmetric Paternalism" ', *University of Pennsylvania Law Review*, 151: 1211–54.

Camerer, C., Loewenstein, G., and Prelec, D. (2005), 'Neuroeconomics: How Neuroscience can Inform Economics', *Journal of Economic Literature*, 43: 9–64.

Campbell, A., Converse, P.E., Miller, W.E., and Stokes, D.E. (1964), *The American Voter* (New York: John Wiley).

Campbell, D. (1998), *National Deconstruction: Violence, Identity and Justice in Bosnia* (Minneapolis, MN: University of Minneapolis Press).

Campbell, D. (1992), *Writing Security: United States Foreign Policy and the Politics of Identity* (Manchester: Manchester University Press).

Canadian Department of Foreign Affairs and International Trade Report, 'Freedom from Fear: Canada's Foreign Policy for Human Security' (http://pubx.dfait-maeci.gc.ca/00_Global/Pubs_Cat2.nsf/4d5c1b5e541f152485256cbb006bb5ff/56153893ff8dfda285256bc700653b9f?OpenDocument).

Cantril, H. (1967), *The Human Dimension: Experiences in Policy Research* (New Brunswick, NJ: Rutgers University Press).

Caporaso, J.A., Hermann, C.F., and Kegley, C.W. (1987), 'The Comparative Study of Foreign Policy: Perspectives on the Future', *International Studies Notes*, 13: 32–46.

Carbonell, J.G. (1978), 'Politics: Automated Ideological Reasoning', *Cognitive Science*, 2: 27–51.

Cardoso, F.H (2008), 'New Paths: Globalization in a Historical Perspective', *International Journal of Communication*, 2, 379–95.

Cardoso, F.H and Faletto, E. (1969), *Dependency and Development in Latin America* (Siglo Veintiuno Editores).

Carlsnaes, W. (1986), *Ideology and Foreign Policy: Problems of Comparative Conceptualisation* (Oxford: Oxford University Press).

Carlsnaes, W. (1992), 'The Agency–Structure Problem in Foreign Policy Analysis', *International Studies Quarterly*, 36: 245–70.

Carlsnaes, W. (2002), 'Foreign Policy', in W. Carlsnaes, T. Risse, and B.A. Simmons (eds), *Handbook of International Relations* (London: Sage), 331–49.

Carlsnaes, W. and Guzzini, S. (eds) (2011), *Foreign Policy Analysis*, Vols 1–5 (London: Sage).

Carlsnaes, W., Risse, T., and Simmons, B.A. (eds) (2002), *Handbook of International Relations* (London: Sage).

Carlsnaes, W., Risse, T., and Simmons, B.A. (eds) (2012), *Handbook of International Relations* (2nd edn) (London: Sage).

Carr, E.H. (1964), *The Twenty Years' Crisis* (2nd edn) (London: Macmillan).

Carruthers, S.L. (2000), *The Media at War: Communication and Conflict in the Twentieth Century* (London: Macmillan).

Caspary, W.R. (1970), 'The Mood Theory: A Study of Public Opinion and Foreign Policy', *American Political Science Review*, 64: 536–47.

Cass, L. (2008), 'A Climate of Obstinacy: Symbolic Politics in Australian and Canadian Policy', *Cambridge Review of International Affairs*, 21: 465–82.

Chakraborty, C. and Nunnenkamp, P. (2006), 'Economic Reforms, Foreign Direct Investment and its Economic Effects in India', Kiel Working Paper 1272, March (Kiel Institute for the World Economy).

Chan, S. (1984), 'Mirror, Mirror on the Wall . . . : Are Freer Countries More Pacific?', *Journal of Conflict Resolution*, 28: 617–48.

Chayes, A. and Chayes, A.H. (1995), *The New Sovereignty: Compliance with International Regulatory Agreements* (Cambridge, MA: Harvard University Press).

Checkel, J.T. (1997), *Ideas and International Political Change: Soviet/Russian Behavior and the End of the Cold War* (New Haven, CT: Yale University Press).

Checkel, J.T. (1998), 'The Constructivist Turn in International Relations Theory', *World Politics*, 50: 324–48.

Checkel, J.T. (2001), 'Why Comply? Social Learning and European Identity Change', *International Organization*, 55: 553–88.

Checkel, J.T. (2003), 'Going Native in Europe? Theorizing Social Interaction in European Institutions', *Comparative Political Studies* 36: 209–31.

Checkel, J.T. (2007a), 'Constructivism and EU Politics', in K.E. Joergensen, M. Pollack, and B. Rosamond (eds), *Handbook of European Union Politics* (London: Sage Publications), 57–76.

Checkel, J.T. (ed.) (2007b), *International Institutions and Socialization in Europe* (Cambridge: Cambridge University Press).

Checkel, J.T. (2007c), 'Process Tracing', in A. Klotz (ed.), *Qualitative Methods in International Relations* (New York: Palgrave Macmillan).

Chittick, W.O. (1970), *State Department, Press, and Pressure Groups: A Role Analysis* (New York: Wiley Interscience).

Christopher, W. (1982), 'Ceasefire between the Branches: A Compact in Foreign Affairs', *Foreign Affairs*, 60: 989–1005.

CIA Special National Intelligence Estimate, 'Major Consequences of Certain U.S. Courses of Action on Cuba', SNIE 11-19-62, 20 October 1962, in CIA History Staff (1992), *CIA Documents on the Cuban Missile Crisis 1962* (Washington, DC: CIA).

Clemens, W. (1982), 'The Superpowers and the Third World', in C. Kegley and P. McGowan (eds), *Foreign Policy: USA/USSR* (Beverly Hills: Sage).

Clinton, W. (1994), Address to the United Nations General Assembly, 26 September

Cluster Munition Coalition (2007), Key Facts (www.stopclustermunitions.org/dokumenti/dokument.asp).

Cluster Munition Coalition (2007), November Bulletin (www.stopclustermunitions.org/news.asp?id=45).

Cochrane, E. (1998), The Egyptian Staff Solution: Operational Art and Planning for the 1973 Arab–Israeli War (Newport, RI: Naval War College).

Cohen, B. (1963), *The Press and Foreign Policy* (Princeton, NJ: Princeton University Press).

Cohen, B. (1973), *The Public's Impact on Foreign Policy* (Boston, MA: Little, Brown).

Cohen, J. (2005), 'The Vulcanization of the Human Brain: A Neural Perspective on Interactions Between Cognition and Emotion', *Journal of Economic Perspectives*, 19: 3–24.

Cohen, S. (2001), *India: Emerging Power* (Washington, DC: Brookings Institution).

Cold War International History Project, documents of the Cuban Missile Crisis, translated by the Centre for Science and International Affairs, University of Harvard.

Collins, A. (ed.) (2007), *Contemporary Security Studies* (Oxford: Oxford University Press).

Commission of the European Communities (2000), 'Green Paper: Towards a European Strategy for Security of Energy Supply', Brussels, 29 November, COM, 769 final.

Commission on Intervention and State Sovereignty (2001), *The Responsibility to Protect* (Ottawa: International Development Research Center).

Constantinou, C. (1995), 'NATO's Caps: European Security and the Future of the North Atlantic Alliance', *Alternatives*, 20: 147–64.

Converse, P. (1964), 'The Nature of Belief Systems in Mass Publics', in D.E. Apter (ed.), *Ideology and Discontent* (New York: Free Press).

Cooley, A. and Ron, J. (2002), 'The NGO Scramble: Organizational Insecurity and the Political Economy of Transnational Action', *International Security*, 27: 5–39.

Cooper, A. (2005), 'Stretching the Model of "Coalitions of the Willing", working paper 1 (Waterloo: Centre for International Governance Innovation).

Cooper, A., Higgott, R., and Nossal, K. (1993), *Relocating Middle Powers: Australia and Canada in a Changing World Order* (Melbourne: Melbourne University Press).

Cooper, R.N., Kaiser, K., and Kosaka, M. (1978), 'Towards a Renovated International System' (Triangle Paper 14), in *Trilateral Commission Task Force Reports 9–14* (New York: New York University Press).

Copeland, D. (1996), 'Economic Interdependence and War: A Theory of Trade Expectations', *International Security*, 20: 5–41.

Cordesman, A. and Wagner, A. (1990), *The Lessons of Modern War*. Vol. I: *The Arab–Israeli Conflicts, 1973–1989* (Boulder, CO: Westview Press).

Coronakis, B. (2006), 'Military Secrets for Energy', *New Europe*, 7 January.

Cortright, D. and Lopez G. (2002), *Smart Sanctions: Targeting Economic Statecraft* (New York: Rowman and Littlefield).

Cortwright, D. and Lopez, G. (eds) (2000), *The Sanctions Decade: Assessing UN Strategies in the 1990s* (Boulder, CO: Lynne Rienner).

Cottam, M.L. (1986), *Foreign Policy Decision-Making: The Influence of Cognition* (Boulder, CO: Westview Press).

Cottam, M.L., and Shih, C. (eds) (1992), *Contending Dramas: A Cognitive Approach to International Organizations* (New York: Praeger).

Cottam, R. (1977), *Foreign Policy Motivation: A General Theory and a Case Study* (Pittsburgh, PA: University of Pittsburgh Press).

Cox, R. (1994), 'Global Restructuring: Making Sense of the Changing International Political Economy', in R. Stubbs and G.R.D. Underhill (eds), *Political Economy and the Changing Global Order* (Basingstoke: Macmillan).

Crawford, N. (2000), 'The Passion of World Politics: Propositions on Emotion and Emotional Relationships', *International Security*, 24: 116–56.

Crawford, N. (2002), *Argument and Change in World Politics: Ethics, Decolonization and Humanitarian Intervention* (Cambridge: Cambridge University Press).

Crawford, N. (2009), 'Human Nature and World Politics', *International Relations*, 23: 271–88.

Cronin, B. (1999), *Community under Anarchy: Transnational Identity and the Evolution of Cooperation* (New York: Columbia University Press).

Curtis, M. (2003), *Web of Deceit: Britain's Real Role in the World* (London: Vintage).

Cushman, D. and King, S. (1985), 'National and Organizational Culture in Conflict Resolution', in W. Gudykunst, L. Stewert, and S. Ting-Toomey (eds), *Communication, Culture, and Organizational Process* (Beverly Hills: Sage), 114–33.

Cutler, L.N. (1985), 'The Right to Intervene', *Foreign Affairs*, 64: 96–112.

Daalder, I. and Lindsay, J. (2003), *America Unbound: The Bush Revolution in Foreign Policy* (Washington, DC: Brookings Institution).

Dahl, R. (ed.) (1973), *Regimes and Oppositions* (New Haven, CT: Yale University Press).

Dallin, A. (1969), *Soviet Foreign Policy and Domestic Politics: A Framework for Analysis* (New York: Russian Institute, School of International Affairs, Columbia University).

Damasio, A.R. (1994), *Descartes' Error: Emotion, Reason, and the Human Brain* (New York: Putnam).

Damasio, A. (2005), 'Brain Trust', *Nature*, 435: 571–2.

Davis, P. (2000), *The Art of Economic Persuasion: Positive Incentives and German Economic Diplomacy* (Ann Arbor, MI: University of Michigan Press).

Davis Cross, M.K. (2007), *The European Diplomatic Corps: Diplomats and International Cooperation from Westphalia to Maastricht* (NY: Palgrave Macmillan).

Dawes, R. (1998), 'Behavioral Decision Making and Judgment', in D.T. Gilbert, S.T. Fiske, and G. Lindzey (eds), *The Handbook of Social Psychology*, Vol.1 (4th edn) (New York: McGraw-Hill), 497–548.

De Rivera, J. (1968), *The Psychological Dimension of Foreign Policy* (Columbus, OH: C.E. Merrill).

De Tocqueville, A. (1945), *Democracy in America*, Vol. I (New York: Vintage).

De Waal, A. (1997), *Famine Crimes: Politics and the Disaster Relief Industry in Africa* (Oxford: James Currey).

Deitelhoff, N. (2006), *Ueberzeugung in der Politik: Grundzuege einer Diskurstheorie internationalen Regierens* (Frankfurt am Main: Suhrkamp Verlag).

Der Derian, J. (1987), *On Diplomacy: A Genealogy of Western Estrangement* (Oxford: Basil Blackwell).

d'Estournelles de Constant, P.H.B.B. (1914) 'Introduction', in *Report of the International Commission to Inquire into the Causes and Conduct of the Balkan Wars* (Washington, DC: Carnegie Endowment for International Peace), 1–19.

Deudney, D. and Ikenberry, J. (1991/92), 'The International Sources of Soviet Change', *International Security*, 16: 74–118.

Deutsch, K. (1957), *Political Community and the North Atlantic Area: International Organization in the Light of Historical Experience* (Princeton, NJ: Princeton University Press).

Deutsch, K.W., Edinger, L.J., Macridis, R.C., and Merritt, R.L. (1967), *France, Germany, and the Western Allliance* (New York: Charles Scribner's Sons).

Dishon, D. (1978), 'Sadat's Arab Adversaries', *Jerusalem Quarterly*, Summer: 12–15.

Dixon, W.J. (1993), 'Democracy and the Management of International Conflict', *Journal of Conflict Resolution*, 37: 42–68.

Dobrynin, A. (1995), *In Confidence* (New York: Random House).

Dodds, K. and Atkinson, D. (2000), *Geopolitical Traditions: A Century of Geopolitical Thought* (London: Routledge).

Doig, A. (2005), '45 minutes of infamy? Hutton, Blair and the Invasion of Iraq', *Parliamentary Affairs*, 58: 109–23.

Domke, D. (2004), *God Willing? Political Fundamentalism in the White House, the War on Terror and the Echoing Press* (London: Pluto Press).

Donnelly, J. (2000), *Realism and International Relations* (Cambridge: Cambridge University Press).

Downer, A. (2002) 'Advancing the National Interest: Australia's Foreign Policy Challenge', speech at the National Press Club, Canberra, 7 May (http://www.foreignminister.gov.au/speeches/2002/020507_fa_whitepaper.html).

Doty, R.L. (1993), 'Foreign Policy as Social Construction: A Post-Positivist Analysis of US Counterinsurgency Policy in the Philippines', *International Studies Quarterly*, 37: 297–320.

Doty, R.L. (1996), *Imperial Encounters* (Minneapolis, MN: University of Minnesota Press).

Dowty, A. (2005), *Israel/Palestine* (Cambridge: Polity Press).

Doxey, M. (1996), *International Sanctions in Contemporary Perspective* (Basingstoke: Palgrave Macmillan).

Doyle, M. (1983a), 'Kant, Liberal Legacies, and Foreign Affairs: Part 1', *Philosophy and Public Affairs*, 12: 205–35.

Doyle, M. (1983b), 'Kant, Liberal Legacies, and Foreign Affairs: Part 2', *Philosophy and Public Affairs*, 12: 323–53.

Doyle, M. (1997), *Ways of War and Peace* (New York: W.W. Norton).

Doyle, M. (2009), 'A Few Words on Mill, Walzer and Nonintervention', *Ethics and International Affairs*, 23: 349–69.

Doyle, T. and Kellow, A (1995), *Environmental Politics and Policy Making in Australia* (London: Macmillan).

Drezner, D. (2009), 'Bad Debts: Assening China's Financial Influence in Great Power Politics', *International Security*, 34: 7–45.

Drolet, J. (2007), 'The Visible Hand of Neo-conservative Capitalism', *Millennium*, 35: 245–78.

Duchêne, F. (1973), 'The European Community and the Uncertainty of Interdependence', in M. Kohnstamm and W. Hager (eds), *A Nation Writ Large? Foreign Policy Problems Before the European Community* (Basingstoke: Macmillan).

Dunn, J. (1984), 'The Concept of Trust in the Politics of John Locke', in R. Rorty, J.B. Schneewind, and Q. Skinner (eds), *Philosophy in History: Essay on the Historiography of Philosophy* (New York: Cambridge University Press).

Dunne, T. (1995), 'The Social Construction of International Society', *European Journal of International Relations*, 1: 367–89.

Dunne, T. (2004), ' "When the Shooting Starts": Atlanticism in British Security Strategy', *International Affairs*, 80: 893–909.

Dunne, T. (2007), ' "The Rules of the Game are Changing": Human Rights in Crisis After 9/11', *International Politics*, 44: 269–86.

Dunne, T. (2008), 'Good Citizen Europe', *International Affairs*, 84: 13–25.

Dunne, T. and Koivisto, M. (2010), 'Crisis, What Crisis? Liberal Internationalism and World Order', *Millenium*, 38: 615–40.

Dunne, T. and Wheeler, N. (eds) (1999), *Human Rights in Global Politics* (Cambridge: Cambridge University Press).

Dunne, T., and Schmidt, B. (2011), 'Realism', in J. Baylis, S. Smith, and P. Owens (eds), *The Globalization of World Politics* (5th edn) (Oxford: Oxford University Press), 84–99.

Dupont, A. and Pearman, G. (2006). 'Heating up the Planet: Climate Change and Security', Lowy Institute Paper 12 (Sydney: Lowy Institute).

East, M.A. (1978), 'National Attributes and Foreign Policy', in M.A. East, S.A. Salmore, and C.F. Hermann (eds), *Why Nations Act* (Beverly Hills: Sage), 143–60.

East, M.A., and Hermann, C.F. (1974), 'Do Nation-types Account for Foreign Policy Behavior?', in J. N. Rosenau (ed.), *Comparing Foreign Policies* (New York: John Wiley), 269–303.

East, M.A., Salmore, S.A., and Hermann, C.F. (1978) (eds), *Why Nations Act* (Beverly Hills: Sage).

Economist (2007), 'A bear at the throat', 14 April: 37–9.

Edkins, J. (2003), *Trauma and the Memory of Politics* (Cambridge: Cambridge University Press).

Edwards, G. (2008), 'The Construction of Ambiguity and the Limits of Attraction: Europe and its Neighbourhood Policy', *European Integration*, 30: 45–62.

Ehrman, J. (1995), *The Rise of Neoconservatism: Intellectuals and Foreign Affairs 1945-1994* (New Haven, CT: Yale University Press), 173–92.

Einstein, A., and Infeld, L. (1938), *The Evolution of Physics* (New York: Simon & Schuster).

El-Gamasy, M.A.G. (1989), *The October War: Memoirs of Field Marshal El-Gamasy of Egypt* (Cairo: International Press). Translation of *Mudhakkarat al-Gamasi: Harb Uktubar 1973* (Cairo: American University of Cairo Press).

Elman, C. (1996), 'Cause, Effect, and Consistency: A Response to Kenneth Waltz', *Security Studies*, 6: 58–61.

Elster, J. (1986), 'Introduction', in J. Elster (ed.), *Rational Choice* (New York: New York University Press), 1–33.

Emesson, M. (2011), 'Dignity, Democracies and Dynasties-in the wake of the revolt on the Arab street', *CEPS* (Brussels: Centre for European Policy Studies).

Emerson, M. (2007), 'Editorial: EU–Russia post-Samara', *CEPS European Neighbourhood Watch*, 27: 1 (Brussels: Centre for European Policy Studies).

Enloe, C. (1989), *Bananas, Beaches and Bases: Making Feminist Sense of International Politics* (London: Pandora).

Entman, R. (1991), 'Framing US Coverage of International News: Contrasts in Narratives of the KAL and Iran Air Incidents', *Journal of Communication*, 41: 6–27.

Entman, R. (2004), *Projections of Power: Framing News, Public Opinion and US Foreign Policy* (Chicago, IL: University of Chicago Press).

Epstein, C. (2011), 'Who Speaks? Discourse, the Subject and the Study of Identity in International Politics', *European Journal of International Relations*, 17: 327–50.

Epstein, R.A. and Sedelmeier, U. (2009), *International Influence Beyond Conditionality: Postcommunist Europe after EU Enlargement* (London: Routledge).

Etheredge, L. (1978), *A World of Men: The Private Sources of American Foreign Policy* (Cambridge: MIT Press).

Etheredge, L. (1985), *Can Governments Learn? American Foreign Policy and Central American Revolutions* (New York: Pergamon Press).

Europa Handbook (1985) (London: Europa Publications).

European Commission (2001), 'Making a Success of Enlargement: Strategy Paper 2001 and Report of the European Commission on the Progress Towards Accession by Each of the Candidate Countries', Brussels, 13 November.

European Council (1993), Copenhagen, Presidency Conclusions, 22–23 June (www.europa.eu/european_council/conclusions/index).

European Council (1997), Luxembourg, Presidency Conclusions, 12–13 December, (www.europa.eu/european_council/conclusions/index).

European Council (2002), Copenhagen, Presidency Conclusions, 12–13 December (www.europa.eu/european_council/conclusions/index).

Evangelista, M. (1999), *Unarmed Forces: The Transnational Movement to End the Cold War* (Ithaca, NY: Cornell University Press).

Evans, P. Jacobson, H., and Putnam, R. (eds) (1993), *Double-edged Diplomacy: International Bargaining and Domestic Politics* (Berkeley, CA: University of California Press).

Evans, P., Rueschmeyer, D., and Skocpol, T. (1985), *Bringing the State Back In* (Cambridge: Cambridge University Press).

Falkowski, L.S. (ed.) (1979), *Psychological Models in International Politics* (Boulder, CO: Westview Press).

Farrell, R.B. (1966), *Approaches to Comparative and International Politics* (Evanston, IL: Northwestern University Press).

Fawcett, L. and Hurrell, A. (eds) (1995), *Regionalism in World Politics: Regional Organizations and International Order* (New York: Oxford University Press).

Finn, J. *et al.* (1995), *Freedom in the World 1994–1995* (New York: Freedom House).

Finnemore, M. (1996), *National Interests in International Society* (Ithaca, NY: Cornell University Press).

Finnemore, M., and Sikkink, K. (1998), 'International Norm Dynamics and Political Change', *International Organization*, 52: 887–917.

Fiske, S., and Taylor, S. (1984), *Social Cognition* (Reading, MA.: Addison-Wesley).

Flemes, D. (2007), 'Emerging Middle Powers' Soft Balancing Strategy. State and Perspectives of the IBSA Dialogue Forum', GIGA Working Paper 57 (Hamburg: German Institute of Global and Area Studies).

Flockhart, T. (2006), 'Complex Socialization: A Framework for the Study of State Socialization', *European Journal of International Relations*, 12: 89–118.

Flockhart, T. (2011), 'NATO and the (Re)Constitution of Roles', in S. Harnisch, C. Frank, and H.W. Maull (eds), *Role Theory in International Relations: Approaches and Analyses* (London: Routledge).

Foot, R. (2000), *Rights Beyond Borders: the Global Community and the Struggle over Human Rights in China* (Oxford: Oxford University Press).

Foot, R. (2011), 'The Responsibility to Protect (R2P) and its Evolution: Beijing's Influence on Norm Creation in Humanitarian Areas', *St Antony's International Review*, 6: 47–66.

Foreign Affairs Committee (2003), *The Decision to Go to War in Iraq*, Vol. 1 (http://www.fas.org/irp/threat/ukiraq0703.pdf).

Fossum, J.E. and Trenz, H. (2005), 'The EU's Fledgling Society: From Deafening Silence to Critical Voice in European Constitution Making', paper presented at the ARENA Research Seminar, ARENA Centre for European Studies, University of Oslo, 4 October.

Foucault, M. (1974), *The Archeology of Knowledge* (London: Tavistock Publications).

Foucault, M. (1984), 'Nietzsche, Genealogy, History', in P. Rabinow (ed.), *The Foucault Reader: An Introduction to Foucault's Thought* (Harmondsworth: Penguin), 76–100.

Foyle, D. (1999), *Counting the Public In: Presidents, Public Opinion and Foreign Policy* (New York: Columbia University Press).

Franck, T. (1996), *Fairness in International Law and Institutions* (Cambridge: Cambridge University Press).

Franck, T. (2003), 'Agora: What Happens Now? The United Nations after Iraq', *American Journal of International Law*, 97: 607–20.

Freedman, L. (2004), 'War in Iraq: Selling the Threat', *Survival*, 46: 7–50.

Freedom House (2007), 'Freedom in the World: Selected Data from Freedom House's Annual Global Survey of Political Rights and Civil Liberties'. (http://www.freedomhouse.org/uploads/press_release/fiw07_charts.pdf)

Frontline (co-production with the BBC and Silverbridge Productions Ltd) (2004), 'Interview with Anthony Lake', interview conducted on 15 December 2003, PBS Documentary: *Ghosts of Rwanda*, broadcast on 1 April 2004 (http://www.pbs.org/wgbh/pages/frontline/shows/ghosts/interviews/lake.html).

Fukuyama, F. (1989), 'End of History', *National Interest*, 16: 3–18.

Fukuyama, F. (2006), *After the Neocons: America at the Crossroads* (London: Profile Books).

Fuller, W.C., (1992), *Strategy and Power in Russia: 1600–1914* (New York: Free Press).

Fursenko, A. and Naftali, T. (1997), *'One Hell of a Gamble': Khrushchev, Castro and Kennedy 1958–1964* (New York: W.W. Norton).

Gaddis, J.L. (1982), *Strategies of Containment: A Critical Appraisal of Postwar American National Security Policy* (New York: Oxford University Press).

Gaenslen, F. (1989), 'On the Consequences of Consensual Decision Making: "Rational Choice" in Comparative Perspective', University of Vermont.

Gaenslen, F. (1992), 'Decision Making Groups', in E. Singer and V.M. Hudson (eds), *Political Psychology and Foreign Policy* (Boulder, CO: Westview Press), 165–94.

Galbraith, P. (2006), *The End of Iraq: How American Incompetence Created a War Without End* (New York: Simon & Schuster).

Garnaut, R. (2008), *The Garnaut Climate Change Review* (Cambridge: Cambridge University Press).

Garrison, J. (ed.) (2003), 'Foreign Policy Analysis in 20/20', *International Studies Review*, 5: 156–63.

Garrison, J.A. (2010), 'Small Group Effects on Foreign Policy Decision Making', in R.A. Denemark (ed.), *The International Studies Encyclopedia* (Oxford: Blackwell; Blackwell Reference Online).

Garvin, J.L., and Amery, J. (1935), *Life of Joseph Chamberlain* (London: Macmillan).

Gastil, R. (1985), 'The comparative survey of freedom', *Freedom at Issue*, 82: 3–10.

Gault, J. (2004), 'EU energy security and the periphery', in R. Dannreuther (ed.), *European Union Foreign and Security Policy: Towards a Neighbourhood Strategy* (London: Routledge).

Gauthier, A. and de Sousa, S.J. (2006), 'Brazil in Haiti: Debate over Peacekeeping Mission', FRIDE Comment, November (http://www.fride.org/publication/430/brazil-in-haiti:-debate-over-the-peacekeeping-mission).

George, A.L. (1969), 'The "Operational Code": A Neglected Approach to the Study of Political Leaders and Decision-making', *International Studies Quarterly*, 13: 190–222.

George, A.L. (1979), 'Case Studies and Theory Development: The Method of Structured Focused Comparison', in P.G. Lauren (ed.), *Diplomacy: New Approaches in History, Theory, and Policy* (New York: Free Press), 43–68.

George, A.L. (1993), *Bridging the Gap: Theory and Practice in Foreign Policy* (Washington, DC: US Institute for Peace).

George, A.L. (1994), 'The Two Cultures of Academia and Policy-Making: Bridging the Gap', *Political Psychology*, 15: 143–71.

George, A. and Simons, W.E. (1994) (eds), *The Limits of Coercive Diplomacy* (2nd edn) (Boulder, CO: Westview Press).

George, A.L. and Smoke, R. (1974), *Deterrence in American Foreign Policy: Theory and Practice* (New York: Columbia University Press).

George, A. and Smoke, R. (1989), 'Deterrence and Foreign Policy', *World Politics*, 41: 170–82.

Gerner, D.J. (1992), 'Foreign Policy Analysis: Exhilarating Eclecticism, Intriguing Enigmas', *International Studies Notes*, 17: 4–19.

Gerner, D.J., Schrodt, P.A., Francisco, R.A., and Weddle, J. (1994), 'Machine Coding of Events Data Using Regional and International Sources', *International Studies Quarterly*, 38: 91–120.

Gheciu, A. (2005), 'Security Institutions as Agents of Socialization? NATO and the New Europe', *International Organization*, 59: 973–1012.

Giacalone, R. (2011), 'Is There a New FPA in Latin America?', research paper presented at the International Studies Association Annual Conference, 'Global Governance: Political Authority in Transition', Montreal, Canada, 16–19 March 2011.

Giddens, A. (1991), *Modernity and Self-Identity: Self and Society in the Late Modern Age* (Stanford, CA: Stanford University Press).

Gilbert, M. (2007), 'The Terrible 20th Century: Canada's offer of a way forward can help prevent past horrors', *The Globe and Mail*, 31 January.

Gilpin, R. (1975), *US Power and the Multinational Corporation* (New York: Basic Books).

Gilpin, R. (1996), 'No One Loves a Political Realist', *Security Studies*, 5: 3–26.

Glad, B. (1989), 'Personality, Political, and Group Process Variables in Foreign Policy Decision-Making: Jimmy Carter's Handling of the Iranian Hostage Crisis', *International Political Science Review*, 10: 35–61.

Glimcher, P.W. (2002), 'Decisions, Decisions, Decisions: Choosing a Biological Science of Choice', *Neuron*, 36: 323–32.

Goldman, M. (2005), From Comrade to Citizen: The Struggle for Political Rights in China (Cambridge, MA: Harvard University Press).

Goldsmith, P. (2002), 'Downing Street Memo to Tony Blair' (London: Office of the Prime Minister).

Goldsmith, P. (2003), 'Iraq: The Legal Case'. Advice on the legality of the war given by the Attorney General on 7 March. *Guardian Unlimited*, 25 April 2007.

Goldsworthy, V. (1998), *Inventing Ruritania: The Imperialism of the Imagination* (New Haven, CT: Yale University Press).

Golich, V. (2000), 'The ABCs of Case Teaching', *International Studies Perspectives*, 1: 11–29.

Gooch, G.P., and Temperley, H. (eds) (1928), *British Documents on the Origins of the War, 1898–1914*, Vol.3 (London: HMSO).

Gordon, C. and Arian, A. (2001), 'Threat and Decision Making', *Journal of Conflict Resolution*, 45, 196–215.

Gorst, I. (2004), 'The Energy Dimension in Russian Global Strategy: Russian Pipeline Strategies: Business Versus Politics', working paper, James A. Baker III Institute for Public Policy of Rice University.

Gourevitch, P. (2002), 'Domestic Politics and International Relations', in W. Carlsnaes, T. Risse, and B. Simmons (eds), *Handbook of International Relations* (London: Sage), 309–28.

Gowing, N. (1994), 'Real-time Coverage of Armed Conflicts and Diplomatic Crises: Does it Pressure or Distort Foreign Policy Decisions?', working paper, Joan Shorenstein Barone Center on the Press, Politics and Public Policy, Harvard University.

Grabbe, H. (2004), 'Big Bang that Began With a Whimper', *E!Sharp*, May (www.cer.org.uk/enlargement).

Grabbe, H. (2006), The EU's Transformative Power: Europeanization through Conditionality in Central and Eastern Europe (Basingstoke: Palgrave Macmillan).

Graber, D.A. (1968), Public Opinion, the President, and Foreign Policy: Four Case Studies from the Formative Years (New York: Holt, Rinehart, and Winston).

Grattan, M. (2008), 'Australia to speak up in the world: PM', *The Age*, 27 March.

Gray, C. (1982), *Strategic Studies and Public Policy* (Lexington, KY: University of Kentucky Press).

Gregory, D.U. (1989), 'Foreword', in J. Der Derian and M.J. Shapiro (eds), *International/Intertextual Relations: Postmodern Readings of World Politics* (Lexington, MA: Lexington Books), xiii–xxi.

Gribkov, A. (1994) 'The View from Moscow and Havana', in A. Gribkov and W. Smith (eds), *Operation Anadyr: U.S. and Soviet Generals Recount the Cuban Missile Crisis* (Chicago, IL: Edition q).

Gribkov A., and Smith, W. (eds) (1994), *Operation Anadyr: U.S. and Soviet Generals Recount the Cuban Missile Crisis* (Chicago, IL: Edition q).

Grieco, J. (1988), 'Anarchy and the Limits of Cooperation', *International Organization*, 42: 485–507.

Gries, P.H. (2004), *China's New Nationalism* (Berkeley, CA.: University of California Press).

Gratius, S. (2007) 'Brasil en las Américas: ¿Una potencia regional pacificadora?', working paper no. 35, Fundación para las Relaciones Internacionales y el Diálogo Exterior (FRIDE), Madrid.

Gromyko, A. (1989), 'The Caribbean Crisis: On Glasnost Now and Secrecy Then', *Izvestia*, April 15.

Gromyko, A. (1995), *Cold War International History Project Bulletin*, translated by the Centre for Science and International Affairs, Harvard University.

Guetzkow, H. (1963), 'A Use of Simulation in the Study of Inter-nation Relations', in *Simulation in International Relations* (Englewood Cliffs, NJ: Prentice Hall).

Guguinou, J. (1993), French Ambassador to the UK, speech delivered on behalf of Alain Lamassoure, Minister for European Affairs, 'Maastricht: success or failure?', 26 October (London: Chatham House Library).

Güth, W., Schmittberger, R., and Schwarze, B. (1982), 'An Experimental Analysis of Ultimatum Bargaining', *Journal of Economic Behavior and Organization*, 3: 367–88.

Gutmann, A. (1980), *Liberal Equality* (Cambridge: Cambridge University Press).

Gutmann, A. and Thompson, D. (2005) (eds), *Ethics and Politics: Cases and Comments* (4th edn) (Belmont, CA: Wadsworth).

Guzzini, S. (1998), *Realism in International Relations and International Political Economy* (London: Routledge).

Guzzini, S. (2000), 'A Reconstruction of Constructivism in International Relations', *European Journal of International Relations*, 6: 147–82.

Hadfield, A. and Amkhan, A. (2012). 'Russia with Cold Feat: The Energy Charter Treaty and the Eu-Russia Relations', *International Journal of Energy Security and Environmental Research*, Inaugural Special Issue.

Hadfield, A. and Hudson, V.M. (2011). 'Bridging the Trans-Atlantic FPA Divide by Breaking a Methodological Impasse: Neo-Classical Realism and Behavioural IR', research paper presented at the International Studies Association Annual Conference, 'Global Governance: Political Authority in Transition', Montreal, Canada, 16–19 March.

Hagan, J.D. (1987), 'Regimes, Political Oppositions, and the Comparative Analysis of Foreign Policy', in C.F.

Hermann, C.W. Kegley, and J.N. Rosenau (eds), *New Directions in the Study of Foreign Policy* (Boston, MA: Allen & Unwin), 339–65.

Hagan, J.D. (1993), *Political Opposition and Foreign Policy in Comparative Perspective* (Boulder, CO: Westview Press).

Hagan, J.D. (1994), 'Regimes, Political Systems, and War', paper presented at the 35th Annual Conference of the International Studies Association, Washington, DC, 28 March–1 April.

Hagan, J. (2000), 'Teaching International Relations Theory Through Foreign Policy Cases', in J.S. Lantis, L.M. Kuzma, and J. Boehrer (eds), *The New International Studies Classroom: Active Teaching, Active Learning* (Boulder, CO: Lynne Reinner Publishers).

Haggard, S. and Moravcsik, A. (1993), 'The Political Economy of Financial Assistance to Eastern Europe, 1989–1991', in R.O. Keohane, J.S. Nye, and S. Hoffmann (eds), *After the Cold War* (Cambridge, MA: Harvard University Press), 246–85.

Hallin, D. (1986), *The Uncensored War* (Berkeley, CA: University of California Press).

Halper, S. and Clarke, J. (2004), *American Alone: The Neo-Conservatives and the Global Order* (Cambridge: Cambridge University Press).

Halperin, M. (1974), *Bureaucratic Politics and Foreign Policy* (Washington, DC: Brookings Institution).

Halperin, M.H. and Kanter, A. (1973) (eds), *Readings in American Foreign Policy: A Bureaucratic Perspective* (Boston, MA: Little, Brown).

Hamilton, C. (2001), *Running from the Storm* (Sydney: UNSW Press).

Handel, M. (1977), 'The Yom Kippur War and the Inevitability of Surprise', *International Studies Quarterly*, 21: 461–502.

Hanrieder, W. (1971), *Comparative Foreign Policy* (New York: MacKay).

Hansen, L. (2002), 'Sustaining Sovereignty: The Danish Approach to Europe', in L. Hansen and O. Wæver (eds), *European Integration and National Identity: The Challenge of the Nordic States* (London: Routledge), 50–87.

Hansen, L. (2006), *Security as Practice: Discourse Analysis and the Bosnian War* (London: Routledge).

Hansen, L. and Wæver, O. (eds) (2002), *European Integration and National Identity: The Challenge of the Nordic States* (London: Routledge).

Hart, P.T. (1990), *Groupthink in Government* (Amsterdam: Swets and Zeitlinger).

Hart, P.T., Stern, E.K., and Sundelius, B. (eds) (1997), *Beyond Groupthink: Political Group Dynamics and Foreign Policy-making* (Ann Arbor, MI: University of Michigan Press).

Hay, C. (1995), 'Structure and Agency', in D. Marsh and G. Stoker (eds), *Theory and Methods in Political Science* (London: Macmillan).

Hay, C. (2002), *Political Analysis: A Critical Introduction* (Basingstoke: Palgrave).

Held, D., and Archibugi, D. (1995), *Cosmopolitan Democracy: An Agenda for a New World Order* (Cambridge, MA: Polity Press).

Heller, M. (2000), 'Continuity and Change in Israeli Security Policy', Adelphi Paper 335, International Institute for Strategic Studies, London.

Hellman, D. (1969), *Japanese Foreign Policy and Domestic Politics* (Berkeley, CA: University of California Press).

Herek, G.M., Janis, I.L., and Huth, P. (1987), 'Decision Making During International Crises: Is Quality of Process Related to Outcome?', *Journal of Conflict Resolution*, 312: 203–26.

Herek, G.M., Janis, I.L., and Huth, P. (1989), 'Quality of Decision Making During the Cuban Missile Crisis: Major Errors in Welch's Reassessment', *Journal of Conflict Resolution*, 333: 446–59.

Herman, E. and Chomsky, N. (1988), *Manufacturing Consent: The Political Economy of the Mass Media* (New York: Pantheon).

Hermann, C.F. (1978), 'Decision Structure and Process Influences on Foreign Policy', in M.A. East, S.A. Salmore, and C.F. Hermann (eds), *Why Nations Act* (Beverly Hills, CA: Sage), 69–102.

Hermann, C.F. (1978), 'Foreign Policy Behaviour: That Which is to be Explained', in M.A. East, S.A. Salmore,and C.F. Hermann (eds), *Why Nations Act* (Beverly Hills, CA: Sage), 25–47.

Hermann, C.F. and Peacock, G. (1987), 'The Evolution and Future of Theoretical Research in the Comparative Study of Foreign Policy', in C.F. Hermann, C.W. Kegley, and J.N. Rosenau (eds), *New Directions in the Study of Foreign Policy* (Boston, MA: Allen & Unwin), 13–32.

Hermann, C.F., Kegley, C.W., and Rosenau, J.N. (eds) (1987), *New Directions in the Study of Foreign Policy* (Boston, MA: Allen & Unwin).

Hermann, M.G. (1970), 'Explaining Foreign Policy Behavior Using the Personal Characteristics of Political Leaders', *International Studies Quarterly*, 24: 7–46.

Hermann, M.G. (1978), 'Effects of Personal Characteristics of Leaders on Foreign Policy', in M.A. East, S.A. Salmore, and C.F. Hermann (eds), *Why Nations Act* (Beverly Hills, CA: Sage).

Hermann, M.G. and Kegley, C.W. (1994), 'Rethinking Democracy and International Peace', paper presented at the annual meeting of the American Political Science Association, New York, 1–4 September.

Hermann, M.G. and Kegley, C.W. (1995), 'Do Decision-makers Matter in Understanding Why Democracies Don't Fight One Another?' paper presented at the annual meeting of the International Studies Association, Chicago, IL, 21–25 February.

Hermann, M.G., and Milburn, T.W. (eds) (1977), *A Psychological Examination of Political Leaders* (New York: Free Press).

Hermann, M.G. and Preston, T. (1998), 'Presidents, Leadership Style, and the Advisory Process', in E.R. Wittkopf and J.M. McCormick (eds), *Domestic Sources of American Foreign Policy* (New York: Rowman & Littlefield).

Hermann, M.G., Hermann, C.F., and Hagan, J.D. (1987), 'How Decision Units Shape Foreign Policy Behavior', in C.F. Hermann, C.W. Kegley, and J.N. Rosenau (eds), *New Directions in the Study of Foreign Policy* (Boston, MA: Allen & Unwin), 309–38.

Herrmann, R. (1985), *Perceptions and Behavior in Soviet Foreign Policy* (Pittsburgh, PA: University of Pittsburgh Press).

Herrmann, R. (1986), 'The Power of Perceptions in Foreign Policy Decision Making: Do Views of the Soviet Union Determine the Policy Choices of American Leaders?' *American Journal of Political Science*, 30: 841–75.

Herrmann, R. (1993), 'The Construction of Images in International Relations Theory: American, Russian, and Islamic World Views', paper presented at the 34th annual conference of the International Studies Association, Acapulco, Mexico, 23–27 March.

Herz, M. (2011), 'Brazil: Major Power in the Making?', in T.J. Volgy, R. Corbetta, K.A. Grant, and R.G. Baird (eds), *Major Powers and the Quest for Status in International Politics: Global and Regional Perspectives* (New York: Palgrave MacMillan).

Hess, R. (1963), 'The Socialization of Attitudes Toward Political Authority: Some Cross-national Comparisons', *International Social Science Journal*, 15: 542–59.

Heuer, R. (1999), *The Psychology of Intelligence Analysis* (Washington DC: Government Printing Office).

Heymann, P. (1973), 'The Problem of Coordination: Bargaining and Rules', *Harvard Law Review*, 86: 797–877.

Hill, C. (2001), 'The EU's capacity for conflict prevention', *European Foreign Affairs Review*, 6: 315–33.

Hill, C. (2003), *The Changing Politics of Foreign Policy* (Basingstoke: Palgrave Macmillan).

Hill, C. (2007), 'Bringing War Home: Making Foreign Policy in Multicultural Societies', *International Relations*, 21: 259–83.

Hillion, C. (2010), *The Creeping Nationalisation of the EU Enlargment Policy. SIEPS Report No. 6* (Stockholm: Swedish Institute for European Policy Studies).

Hilsman, R. (1967), *To Move a Nation* (New York: Doubleday).

Hilsum, L. (2006), 'The Death of Israel's Dreams', *New Statesman*, 14 August (http://www.newstatesman.com/200608140018).

Hilton, S. (1985) 'The Argentine Factor in Twentieth Century Brazilian Foreign Policy Strategy', *Political Science Quarterly*, 100: 27–51.

Hines, N. and Charter, D. (2009), 'Hoax EU Sculpture by David Cerny Sparks Diplomatic Spat', *Times Online*, 14 January (http://www.timesonline.co.uk/tol/news/world/europe/article5517736.ece) (accessed 6 September 2011).

Hirsch, F. (1977), *The Social Limits to Growth* (Cambridge, MA: Harvard University Press).

Hirsch, F. and Doyle, M. (1977), 'Politicization in the World Economy' in F. Hirsch, M.W. Doyle, and E.L. Morse (eds), *Alternatives to Monetary Disorder* (New York: McGraw-Hill).

Hirschman, A. (1980) [1945], *National Power and the Structure of Foreign Trade* (Berkeley, CA: University of California Press).

Hirschman, A.O. (1982), 'Rival Interpretations of Market Society: Civilizing, Destructive or Feeble', *Journal of Economic Literature*, 20: 1463–84.

Hirst, M., Soares de Lima, M.R., and Pinheiro, L. (2010), 'A política externa brasileira en tempos de novos horizontes', *Nueva Sociedad* (Special Portuguese Edition), December: 22–41.

Hirt, E.R. and Sherman, S.J. (1985), 'The Role of Prior Knowledge in Explaining Hypothetical Events', *Journal of Experimental and Social Psychology*, 21: 519–43.

Hobbes, T. (1962) [1660]. *Leviathan* (London: Collier).

Hobbes, T. (1972) [1651], in M. Oakeshott (ed.), *Leviathan* (London: Collier).

Hodge, J. (2004), 'A Global Power Shift in the Making: Is the US ready?', *Foreign Affairs*, 83: 2–7.

Hoffmann, M.J. (2010), 'Norms and Social Constructivism in International Relations', in R.A. Denemark (ed.), *The International Studies Encyclopedia* (Oxford: Blackwell; Blackwell Reference Online).

Hoffmann, S. (1961), 'International Systems and International Law', in *The State of War: Essays on the Theory and Practice of International Politics* (New York: Praeger).

Hoffmann S. (1966), 'Obstinate or Obsolete? The Fate of the Nation State and the Case of Western Europe', *Daedalus*, 95: 862–915.

Hogarth, R. and Goldstein, W. (eds) (1996), *Judgment and Decision Making: An Interdisciplinary Reader* (Cambridge: Cambridge University Press).

Holbrooke, R. (1998), *To End a War* (New York: Random House).

Holland, H. (1984), *Managing Diplomacy* (Stanford, CA: Hoover Institution Press).

Hollis, M. and Smith, S. (1991), *Explaining and Understanding International Relations* (Oxford: Clarendon Press).

Holmes, S. (1979), 'Aristippus in and out of Athens', *American Political Science Review*, 73: 113–28.

Holsti, K.J. (1982), *Why Nations Realign* (London: Allen & Unwin).

Holsti, K.J. (1970), 'National Role Conceptions in the Study of Foreign Policy', *International Studies Quarterly*, 14: 233–309.

Holsti, K.J. (2004), *Taming the Sovereigns: Institutional Change in International Politics* (Cambridge: Cambridge University Press).

Holsti, O.R. (1977), *The 'Operational Code' as An Approach to the Analysis of Belief Systems* (Durham, NC: Duke University Press).

Holsti, O. (1989), 'Crisis Decision Making', in P. Tetlock, J. Husbands, R. Jervis, P. Stern, and C. Tilly (eds), *Behavior, Society, and Nuclear War*, Vol. I (New York: Oxford University Press), 8–84.

Holsti, O.R. and Rosenau, J.N. (1979), 'Vietnam, Consensus, and the Belief Systems of American Leaders', *World Politics*, 32: 1–56.

Holsti, O.R. (1992), 'Public Opinion and Foreign Policy: Challenges to the Almond–Lippman Consensus', *International Studies Quarterly*, 36: 439–66.

Holsti, O., North, R., and Brody, R. (1968), 'Perception and Action in the 1914 Crisis', in J.D. Singer (ed.), *Quantitative International Politics: Insights and Evidence* (New York: Free Press), 123–58.

Holzgrefe, J.L., and Keohane, R.O. (2003) (eds), *Humanitarian Intervention: Ethical, Legal, and Political Dilemmas* (Cambridge: Cambridge University Press).

Hooghe, L. and Marks, G. (2008), 'A Post-Functionalist Theory of European Integration: From Permissive Consensus to Constraining Dissensus', *British Journal of Political Science*, 39: 1–23.

Hopf, T. (1998), 'The Promise of Constructivism in International Relations Theory', *International Security*, 23: 171–200.

Hopf, T. (2002), *Social Construction of International Politics: Identities and Foreign Policies, Moscow, 1955 and 1999* (Ithaca, NY: Cornell University Press).

Houghton, D.P. (2007), 'Reinvigorating the Study of Foreign Policy Decision-Making: Toward a Constructivist Approach', *Foreign Policy Analysis*, 3: 24–45.

Hudson, V. M. (2005), 'Foreign Policy Analysis: Actor-Specific Theory and the Ground of International Relations', *Foreign Policy Analysis*, 1: 1–30.

Hudson, V.M. (2007), *Foreign Policy Analysis: Classic and Contemporary Theory* (Lanham, MD: Rowman & Littlefield).

Hudson, V. (2008), 'The History and Evolution of Foreign Policy Analysis', in S. Smith, A. Hadfield, and T. Dunne (eds), *Foreign Policy: Theories, Actors, Cases* (Oxford: Oxford University Press), 11–29.

Hufbauer, G.C., Schott, J., and Elliott, K.A. (1990), *Economic Sanctions Reconsidered: History and Current Policy* (Washington, DC: Institute for International Economics).

Hufbauer, G.C., Schott, J., Elliot, K.A., and Oegg, B. (2007), *Economic Sanctions Reconsidered* (3rd edn) (Washington, DC: Peterson Institute for International Economics).

Hughes, B.B. (1978), *The Domestic Context of American Foreign Policy* (San Francisco, CA: W.H. Freeman).

Hume, D. (1963) [1741–1742], *Essays: Moral, Political, and Literary* (London: Oxford University Press).

Huntington, S.P. (1960), 'Strategic Planning and the Political Process', *Foreign Affairs*, 38/2: 285–299.

Huntington, S.P. (1981a), *American Politics: The Promise of Disharmony* (Cambridge, MA: Harvard University Press).

Huntington, S.P (1981b), 'Human Rights and American Power', *Commentary*, 72: 37–43.

Hurrell, A. (1995), 'Explaining the Resurgence of Regionalism in World Politics', *Review of International Studies* 21: 331–58.

Hurrell, A. (2008), 'Lula's Brazil: A Rising Power, but Going Where?' *Current History*, 107: 51–7.

Hurrell, A. (2010), 'Cardoso e o Mundo', in H. Martins and M.A. D'Incao (eds), *Democracia, Crisis e Reforma. Estudos Sobre a Era Fernando Henrique Cardoso* (São Paulo: Editora Paz e Terra), 437–99.

Hurd, D. (1990), 'Europe: A Living Force', Speech at the La Fondation des Sciences Politiques, Paris, 24 April (London Press Service).

Hutchison, E. and Bleiker, R. (2008), 'Emotional Reconciliation: Reconstituting Identity and Community after Trauma', *European Journal of Social Theory*, 11: 385–403.

Hutton, D. and Connors, L. (1999), *A History of the Australian Environment Movement* (Cambridge: Cambridge University Press).

Hutton, W. (2001), 'If Europe Takes on Too Much We Will All Lose', *Observer*, 9 December.

Hyam, R. (1976), *Britain's Imperial Century: 1815–1914* (London: Batsford).

Hyde-Price, A. (1996), *The International Politics of East Central Europe* (Manchester: Manchester University Press).

Hyde-Price, A. (2000), *Germany and European Order: Enlarging NATO and the EU* (Manchester: Manchester University Press).

Hyde-Price, A. (2006), 'Normative Power Europe: A Realist Critique', *Journal of European Public Policy*, 13: 217–34.

Hymans, J.E.C. (2006), *The Psychology of Nuclear Proliferation: Identity, Emotions, and Foreign Policy* (Cambridge: Cambridge University Press).

Ignatieff, M. (2002), 'Is the Human Rights Era Ending?' *New York Times*, 5 February.

Ikenberry, G.J. (2001). *After Victory* (Princeton, NJ: Princeton University Press).

Imam, S. (1986), *Man Yamluk Misr [Who Owns Egypt?]* (Cairo: Dar al-Mustaqbal).

International Campaign to Ban Landmines (2006, 2005, 2004, 2003), *Landmine Monitor Report* (http://www.icbl.org/lm/).

International Campaign to Ban Landmines, States Parties (www.icbl.org/treaty/members).

International Commission of Intervention and State Sovereignty (2001), *Report: The Responsibility to Protect* (www.iciss.ca/report-en.asp).

International Criminal Court (http://www.icc-cpi.int/home.html).

IPCC (2007), *Climate Change 2007: Impacts, Adaptation and Vulnerability* (Cambridge: Cambridge University Press.

Ismail, F. (2009), 'Reflections on the WTO July 2008 Collapse: Lessons for Developing Country Coalitions', in A. Narlikar and B. Vickers (eds), *Leadership and Change in the Multilateral Trading System* (Leiden: Martinus Nijhoff).

Iyengar, S. and Kinder, D.R. (1987), *News That Matters: Television and American Public Opinion* (Chicago, IL: University of Chicago Press).

Iyengar, S., and Simon, A. (1994), 'News Coverage of the Gulf Crisis and Public Opinion: A Study of Agenda-Setting, Priming and Framing', in W.L. Bennett and D.P.L. Paletz (eds), *Taken by Storm: The Media, Public Opinion and US Foreign Policy in the Gulf War* (Chicago, IL: University of Chicago Press).

Jackson, R. (2005), *Writing Terrorism* (Manchester: Manchester University Press).

Jaguaribe, H. (1979), 'Autonomía periférica y hegemonía céntrica', *Estudios Internacionales*, 46: 91–130.

Janis, I.L. (1982), *Groupthink: Psychological Studies of Policy Decisions and Fiascos* (2nd edn) (Boston, MA: Houghton Mifflin).

Jenkins, R. (1999), *Democratic Politics and Economic Reform in India* (Cambridge: Cambridge University Press).

Jentleson, B. (2000), 'Economic Sanctions and Post-Cold War Conflicts: Challenges for Theory and Policy', in P. Stern and D. Druckman (eds), *International Conflict Resolution after the Cold War* (Washington, DC: National Academy Press).

Jervis, R. (1976), *Perception and Misperception in International Politics* (Princeton, NJ: Princeton University Press).

Jervis, R. (1986), 'Representativeness in Foreign Policy Judgments', *Political Psychology*, 7: 483–505.

Jervis, R. (2006), 'Reports, Politics, and Intelligence Failures: The Case of Iraq', *Journal of Strategic Studies*, 29: 3–52.

Jervis, R., Lebow, R.N., and Stein, J.G. (eds) (1985), *Psychology and Deterrence* (Baltimore, MD: Johns Hopkins University Press).

Johnson, L.K. (1977), 'Operational Codes and the Prediction of Leadership Behavior: Frank Church at Mid-Career', in M.G. Hermann (ed.), *A Psychological Examination of Political Leaders* (New York: Free Press).

Johnston, A.I. (2001), 'Treating International Institutions as Social Environments', *International Studies Quarterly*, 45: 487–516.

Johnston, A.I. (2007), *Social States: China in International Institutions, 1980–2000* (Princeton, NJ: Princeton University Press).

Jones, B. (2010), *Failing Intelligence: The True Story of How We Were Fooled into Going to War with Iraq* (Colorado Springs, CO: Dialogue).

Jones, C.M. (2010), 'Bureaucratic Politics and Organizational Process Models', in R.A. Denemark (ed.), *The International Studies Encyclopedia* (Oxford: Blackwell; Blackwell Reference Online).

Kaarbo, J. (1993), 'Power and Influence in Foreign Policy Decision-Making: The Role of Junior Parties in Coalition Cabinets in Comparative Perspective', paper presented at the annual meeting of the International Studies Association, Acapulco, Mexico, 23–27 March.

Kagan, R. (2003), *Of Paradise and Power: Europe and America in the New World Order* (New York: Knopf).

Kahler, M. (ed.) (1997), *Liberalization and Foreign Policy* (New York: Columbia University Press).

Kahler, M. (1998), 'Rationality in International Relations', *International Organization*, 52: 919–41.

Kahneman, D. and Tversky, A. (1979), 'Prospect Theory: An Analysis of Decision under Risk', *Econometrica*, 47: 263–91.

Kahneman, D. and Tversky, A. (eds) (2000), *Choices, Values, and Frames* (Cambridge: Cambridge University Press).

Kahneman, D., Slovic, P., and Tversky, A. (1982), *Judgment Under Uncertainty: Heuristics and Biases* (New York: Cambridge University Press).

Kalathil, S. and Boas, T.C. (2003), *Open Networks, Closed Regimes: The Impact of the Internet on Authoritarian Rule* (Washington, DC: Carnegie Endowment for International Peace).

Kalicki, J.H. and Goldwyn, D.A. (2005), *Energy and Security: Toward a New Foreign Policy Strategy* (Washington, DC: Woodrow Wilson Centre Press and Baltimore, MD: Johns Hopkins University Press).

Kampfner, J. (2004), *Blair's Wars: A Liberal Imperialist in Action* (London: Free Press).

Kant, I. (1970) [1795], 'Perpetual Peace', in H. Reiss and H.B. Nisbet (eds), *Kant's Political Writings* (Cambridge: Cambridge University Press).

Kaplan, M. (1957), *System and Process in International Politics* (New York: John Wiley).

Kaplan, M. (1972), 'Variants on Six Models of the International System', in J.N. Rosenau (ed.), *International Politics and Foreign Policy* (Glencoe, IL: Free Press of Glencoe), 291–303.

Karawan, I. (2005) 'Foreign policy restructuring: Egypt's disengagement from the Arab-Israeli conflict revisited', *Cambridge Review of International Affairs*, 18: 325–38.

Katzenstein, P. (1985), *Small States in World Markets: Industrial Policy in Europe* (Ithaca, NY: Cornell University Press).

Katzenstein, P. (ed.) (1996), *The Culture of National Security: Norms and Identity in World Politics* (New York: Columbia University Press).

Kaufman, S. (2001), *Modern Hatreds: The Symbolic Politics of Ethnic War* (Ithaca, NY: Cornell University Press).

Kaufmann, C. (2004), 'Threat Inflation and the Failure of the Marketplace of Ideas: The Selling of the Iraq War', *International Security*, 29: 5–48.

Kean, J., and McGowan, P. (1973), 'National Attributes and Foreign Policy Participation: A Path Analysis', in P. McGowan (ed.), *Sage International Yearbook of Foreign Policy Studies*, Vol. 1 (Beverly Hills, CA: Sage), 219–52.

Keck, M. and Sikkink, K. (1998), *Activists beyond Borders: Advocacy Networks in International Politics* (Ithaca, NY: Cornell University Press).

Kegley, C.W. (1980), *The Comparative Study of Foreign Policy: Paradigm Lost?*, Institute of International Studies Essay Series 10 (Columbia, SC: University of South Carolina).

Kennan, G.F. (1993), 'Somalia, Through a Glass Darkly', *New York Times*, 30 September.

Kennedy, P. (1988), *The Rise and Fall of the Great Powers: Economic Change and Military Conflict from 1500 to 2000* (London: Unwin Hyman).

Kennedy, R.F. (1969), *Thirteen Days: A Memoir of the Cuban Missile Crisis* (New York: W.W. Norton).

Kent, A. (1993), *Between Freedom and Subsistence: China and Human Rights* (Oxford: Oxford University Press).

Keohane, R.O. (1993), 'Institutional Theory and the Realist Challenge After the Cold War', in D.A. Baldwin (ed.), *Neorealism and Neoliberalism: The Contemporary Debate* (New York: Columbia University Press), 269–300.

Keohane, R.O., and Nye, J.S. (1998), 'Power and Interdependence in the Information Age', *Foreign Affairs*, 77: 81–94.

Keohane, R.O. and Nye, J. (2000), *Power and Interdependence* (3rd edn) (New York: Longman).

Keukeleire, S. and MacNaughtan, J. (2008), *The Foreign Policy of the European Union* (Basingstoke: Palgrave Macmillan).

Khong, Y.F. (1992), *Analogies at War: Korean, Munich, Dien Bien Phu, and the Vietnam Decisions of 1965* (Princeton, NJ: Princeton University Press).

Khrushchev to Castro, 30 October 1962, in released correspondence at the John F. Kennedy Library, President's Office Files.

Khrushchev, N. (1970), *Khrushchev Remembers: The Last Testament* (transl. S. Talbott) (Boston, MA: Little, Brown).

Kindleberger, C. (1973), *The World in Depression, 1929–1939* (Berkeley, CA: University of California Press).

Kirkpatrick, J. (1979), 'Dictatorships and Double Standards', *Commentary*, 68: 34–45.

Kirshner, J. (1995), *Currency and Coercion: The Political Economy of International Monetary Power* (Princeton, NJ: Princeton University Press).

Kissinger, H. (1957), *Nuclear Weapons and Foreign Policy* (New York: Harper & Brothers).

Kleine-Ahlbrandt, S. and Small, A. (2008), 'China's New Dictatorship Diplomacy', *Foreign Affairs*, 87: 38–56.

Klepak, H. and Neill, D. (2000), 'Are There Lessons for India and Pakistan from the Argentine–Brazilian Nuclear Policy?' Document prepared for the International Security Research and Outreach Programme, International Security Bureau, Department of Foreign Affairs and International Trade, Government of Canada.

Klotz, A. and Lynch, C. (2007), *Strategies for Research in Constructivist International Relations* (New York: M.E. Sharpe).

Kock, K. (1969), *International Trade Policy and the GATT, 1947–1967* (Stockholm: Amqvist & Wiksell).

Koehler, J. (1996), 'The Base-Rate Fallacy Reconsidered: Descriptive, Normative, and Methodological Challenges', *Behavioral and Brain Sciences*, 19: 1–53.

Kohli, A. (2004), *State-Directed Development: Political Power and Industrialization in the Global Periphery* (Cambridge: Cambridge University Press).

Korany, B. (1986) (ed.), *How Foreign Policy Decisions are Made in the Third World* (Boulder, CO: Westview Press).

Kosachev, K. (2006), in N. Popescu (ed.), *Russia's Soft Power Ambitions*, CEPS Policy Brief No. 115 (Brussels: Centre for European Policy Studies).

Kowert, P.A. (2010), 'Foreign Policy and the Social Construction of State Identity', in R.A. Denemark (ed.), *The International Studies Encyclopedia* (Oxford: Blackwell; Blackwell Reference Online).

Kramer, M. (1996–97), 'The "lessons" of the Cuban Missile crisis for Warsaw Pact Nuclear Operations', *Cold War International History Project Electronic Bulletin*, Spring: 59.

Krasner, S.D. (1971), 'Are Bureaucracies Important? (Or Allison Wonderland)', *Foreign Policy*, 7: 159–79.

Krasner, S.D. (1976), 'State Power and the Structure of International Trade', *World Politics*, 28: 317–47.

Kristol, I. (2004), 'The Neoconservative Persuasion: What It Was, and What It Is', in I. Stelzer (ed.), *Neoconservatism* (London: Atlantic Books), 33–7.

Kristol, W. (2004), 'Postscript—June 2004: "Neoconservatism Remains the Bedrock of U.S. Foreign Policy" ', in I. Stelzer (ed.), *Neoconservatism* (London: Atlantic Books), 75–7.

Kristol, W. and Kagan, R. (1996), 'Toward a Neo-Reaganite Foreign Policy', *Foreign Affairs*, 75: 18–32.

Kristol, W. and Kagan, R. (2004), 'National Interest and Global Responsibility', in I. Stelzer (ed.), *Neoconservatism* (London: Atlantic Books), 57–74.

Kruglanski, A.W., and Webster, D. M. (1996), 'Motivated Closing of the Mind: "Seizing" and "Freezing" ', *Psychological Review*, 103: 263–8.

Laclau, E. and Mouffe, C. (1985), *Hegemony and Socialist Strategy: Towards a Radical Democratic Politics* (London: Verso).

Lafer, C. (2001), *A Identidade Internacional do Brasil e a Política Externa Brasileira* (São Paulo: Editoria Perspectiva).

Lamborn, A. (1991), *The Price of Power: Risk and Foreign Policy in Britain, France and Germany* (London: Unwin Hyman).

Lamborn, A.C., and Mumme, S.P. (1989), *Statecraft, Domestic Politics, and Foreign Policy Making: The El Chamizal Dispute* (Boulder, CO: Westview Press).

Lampton, D.M. (with the assistance of Y. Sai-cheung) (1986), *Paths to Power: Elite Mobility in Contemporary China. Michigan Monographs in Chinese Studies Vol. 55* (Ann Arbor, MI: University of Michigan Press).

Lamy, S.L. (2001), *The Dutch in Srebrenica: A Noble Mission Fails. Pew Case Studies in International Affairs, Case 241* (Washington, DC: GUISD).

Larsen, H. (1997), *Foreign Policy and Discourse Analysis: France, Britain and Europe* (London: Routledge/LSE).

Larsen, H. (2009), 'A Distinct FPA for Europe? Towards a Comprehensive Framework for Analysing the Foreign Policy of EU Member States', *European Journal of International Relations*, 15: 537–66.

Larson, D.L. (1986), *The 'Cuban Crisis' of 1962: Selected Documents, Chronology and Bibliography* (2nd edn) (Lanham, MD: University Press of America).

Larson, D.W. (1985), *Origins of Containment: A Psychological Explanation* (Princeton, NJ: Princeton University Press).

Larson, D.W. (1993), 'Reagan, Bush, and Gorbachev: Changing Images and Building Trust', paper presented at the annual meeting of the International Studies Association, Acapulco, Mexico, 23–27 March.

Lasswell, H.D. (1930), *Psychology and Politics* (Chicago, IL: University of Chicago Press).

Lasswell, H.D. (1948), *Power and Personality* (New York: W.W. Norton).

Lau, B. and Glimcher, P.W. (2005), 'Dynamic Response-by-Response Models of Matching Behavior in Rhesus Monkeys', *Journal of the Experimental Analysis of Behavior*, 84: 555–79.

Lawler, P. (2004). 'The Good State: In Praise of 'Classical' Internationalism', *Review of International Studies*, 31: 427–99.

Lawrence, R. (2000), *The Politics of Force* (Berkeley, CA: University of California Press).

Le Billon, P. (2004), 'The Geopolitical Economy of Resource Wars', *Geopolitics*, 9: 1–28.

Leana, C.R. (1975), 'A Partial Test of Janis' Groupthink Model: Effects of Group Cohesiveness and Leader Behavior on Defective Decision-Making', *Journal of Management*, 111: 5–17.

Lebow, R.N. and Stein, J.G. (1990), 'Deterrence: The Elusive Dependent Variable', *World Politics*, 42: 336–69.

Lebow, R.N. and Stein, J.G. (1994), *We All Lost the Cold War* (Princeton, NJ: Princeton University Press).

LeDoux, J. (1996), *The Emotional Brain: The Mysterious Underpinnings of Emotional Life* (New York: Simon & Schuster).

Leffler, M. (2004a), 'National Security', in M. Hogan and T. Paterson (eds), *Explaining the History of American Foreign Relations* (2nd edn) (Cambridge: Cambridge University Press).

Leffler, M. (2004b), 'Bush's Foreign Policy', *Foreign Policy*, 144: 22–8.

Leites, N. (1951), *The Operational Code of the Politburo* (New York: McGraw-Hill).

Leung, K. (1987), 'Some Determinants of Reactions to Procedural Models for Conflict Resolution: A Cross-National Study', *Journal of Personality and Social Psychology*, 53: 898–908.

Levy, J. (1988), 'Domestic Politics and War', *Journal of Interdisciplinary History*, 18: 653–74.

Levy, J. (1994), 'Learning and Foreign Policy: Sweeping a Conceptual Minefield', *International Organization*, 48: 279–312.

Levy, J., and Vakili, L. (1989), 'External Scapegoating by Authoritarian Regimes: Argentina in the Falklands/Malvinas Case', paper presented at the annual meeting of the American Political Science Association, Atlanta, 31 August–3 September.

Lewis, J. (2005), 'The Janus Face of Brussels: Socialization and Everyday Decision Making in the European Union', *International Organization*, 59: 937–72.

Liberman, P. (1999–2000), 'The offense–defense balance, interdependence, and war, *Security Studies*, 9: 59–91.

Lichtblau, E. (2006), '2002 Memo Doubted Uranium Sale Claim', *New York Times*, January 18.

Linklater, A. (1998), *The Transformation of the Political Community* (London: Polity Press).

Lippmann, W. (1943), *U.S. Foreign Policy: Shield of the Republic* (Boston, MA: Little, Brown).

Lippmann, W. (1955), *Essays in the Public Philosophy* (Boston, MA: Little, Brown).

Lipset, S.M. (1966), 'The President, the Polls, and Vietnam', *Transaction*, 3: 19–24.

Livingston, S. (1997), 'Clarifying the CNN effect: An Examination of Media Effects According to Type of Military Intervention', research paper R-18, Joan Shorenstein Barone Center on the Press, Politics and Public Policy, Harvard University.

Livingston, S. and Riley, J. (1999), 'Television Pictures in Multilateral Policy Decision Making: An Examination of the Decision to Intervene in Eastern Zaire in 1996', presented at the British International Studies Annual Conference, University of Manchester, 21–23 December 1999.

Lobell, S.E., Ripsman N.M., and Taliaferro, J. (eds) (2009), *Neoclassical Realism, the State, and Foreign Policy* (Cambridge: Cambridge University Press).

Lochery, N. (2004), *Why Blame Israel?* (Cambridge: Icon Books).

Locke, J. (1988) [1689], 'Second Treatise', in P. Laslett (ed.), *Two Treatises of Government* (New York: Cambridge University Press).

Losman, D. (1979), *International Economic Sanctions: The Cases of Cuba, Israel, and Rhodesia* (Albuquerque, NM: University of New Mexico Press).

Löwenheim, O. and Heimann, G. (2008). 'Revenge in International Politics', *Security Studies*, 17: 685–724.

Lowi, T. (1963), 'Bases in Spain' in H. Stein (ed.), *American Civil-Military Decisions: A Book of Case Studies* (Tuscaloosa, AL: University of Alabama Press).

Lynn, L. (1999), *Teaching and Learning with Cases* (Chappaqua, NY: Seven Bridges Press and London: Chatham House).

McAuliffe, M.S. (ed.) (1992), *CIA Documents on the Cuban Missile Crisis* (Washington, DC: CIA History Staff).

McCauley, C. (1989), 'The Nature of Social Influence in Groupthink: Compliance and Internalization', *Journal of Personality and Social Psychology*, 572: 250–60.

McCombs, M.E., and Shaw, D.L. (1972), 'The Agenda-Setting Function of the Press', *Public Opinion Quarterly*, 36: 176–87.

McDonald, M. (2005), 'Fair Weather Friend? Australia's Approach to Global Climate Change', *Australian Journal of Politics and History*, 51: 216–34.

McDonald, M. (2011), *Security, the Environment and Emancipation* (London: Routledge).

McGowan, P. and Shapiro, H.B. (1973), *The Comparative Study of Foreign Policy: A Survey of Scientific Findings* (Beverly Hills, CA: Sage).

McKee, R. (2003), 'Storytelling That Moves People: A Conversation with Screenwriting Coach Robert McKee', *Harvard Business Review*, June 5–8.

McMillan, S. (1997), 'Interdependence and Conflict', *Mershon International Studies Review*, 41 (Suppl.): 33–58.

McSweeney, B. (1999), *Security, Identity and Interests: A Sociology of International Relations* (Cambridge: Cambridge University Press).

Magnus, P. (1954), *Gladstone: A Biography* (New York: E.P. Dutton).

Mahapatra, R. (2006), 'Governments Express Dismay at WTO Talks Collapse', *International Business Times*, 25 July.

Mandlebaum, M. and Schneider, W. (1979), 'The New Internationalisms', in K.A. Oye, D. Rothchild, and R.J. Lieber (eds), *Eagle Entangled: US Foreign Policy in a Complex World* (New York: John Wiley).

Mann, J. (2004), *Rise of the Vulcans: The History of Bush's War Cabinet* (London: Viking).

Manners, I. (2002), 'Normative power Europe: A contradiction in terms?', *Journal of Common Market Studies*, 40: 235–58.

Manners, I. and Whitman, R. (eds) (2000), *The Foreign Policies of European Union Member States* (Manchester: Manchester University Press).

Mansfield, E. (1994), *Power, Trade, and War* (Princeton, NJ: Princeton University Press).

Mansfield, E., and Snyder, J. (1995), 'Democratization and the Danger of War', *International Security*, 20: 5–38.

Mansfield, P. (1971), *The British in Egypt* (London: Weidenfeld & Nicolson).

Matthews, J., Thurbon, E., and Weiss, L. (2007), *National Insecurity: The Howard Government's Betrayal of Australia* (Sydney: Allen & Unwin).

Maull, H. (2005), 'Europe and the New Balance of Global Order', *International Affairs*, 81: 775–99.

Maoz, Z. and Russett, B. (1993), 'Normative and Structural Causes of the Democratic Peace, 1946–86', *American Political Science Review*, 87: 624–38.

Maran, M. (2001), WT/MIN(01)/ST/10, 10 November 2001, India (www.wto.org).

March, J.G and Olsen, J.P. (1989), *Rediscovering Institutions: The Organizational Basis of Politics* (New York: Free Press)

March, J.G. and Olsen, J.P. (1998), 'The Institutional Dynamics of International Political Orders', *International Organization*, 52: 943–969.

March, J.G. and Simon, H. (1981), 'Decision-Making Theory', in O. Grusky and G.A. Miller (eds), *The Sociology of Organizations: Basic Studies* (2nd edn) (New York: Free Press).

Margolis, M. and Mauser, G.A. (1989) (eds), *Manipulating Public Opinion* (Pacific Grove, CA: Brooks Cole).

Martin, L. (1992), *Coercive Economic Cooperation: Explaining Multilateral Economic Sanctions* (Princeton,NJ: Princeton University Press).

Mastanduno, M. (1992), *Economic Containment: CoCom and the Politics of East–West Trade* (Ithaca, NY: Cornell University Press).

Mastanduno, M. (1999–2000), 'Economic Statecraft, Interdependence, and National Security: Agendas for Research', *Security Studies*, 9: 288–316.

Mastanduno, M., Lake, D., and Ikenberry, J. (1989), 'Toward a Realist Theory of State Action', *International Studies Quarterly*, 33: 457–74.

May, E. and Zelikow, P. (1997), *The Kennedy Tapes: Inside the White House During the Cuban Missile Crisis* (Cambridge: Cambridge University Press).

Mazarr, M. (2007), 'The Iraq War and Agenda Setting', *Foreign Policy Analysis*, 3: 1–23.

Mearsheimer, J.J. (1990), 'Back to the Future: Instability in Europe After the Cold War', *International Security*, 15: 5–56.

Mearsheimer, J.J. (1994–95) 'The False Promise of International Institutions', *International Security*, 19: 5–49.

Mearsheimer, J.J. (1995), 'Back to the Future: Instability in Europe After the Cold War', in M.E. Brown, S.M. Lynn-Jones, and S.E. Miller (eds), *The Perils of Anarchy: Contemporary Realism and International Security* (Cambridge, MA: MIT Press), 78–129.

Mearsheimer, J.J. (2001), *The Tragedy of Great Power Politics* (New York: W.W. Norton).

Mearsheimer, J.J. and Walt, S.M. (2003), 'An Unnecessary War', *Foreign Policy*, 134: 50–60.

Mearsheimer, J.J, and Walt, S. (2006), 'The Israel Lobby and US Foreign Policy', *Middle East Policy*, 13: 29–87.

Mellegren, D. (2007), '46 Countries to Pursue Treaty on Cluster Bombs', *Washington Post*, 23 February.

Mercer, J. (2005), 'Rationality and Psychology in International Politics', *International Organization*, 59: 77–106.

Mercer, J. (2010), 'Emotional Beliefs', *International Organization*, 64: 1–31.

Merelman, R.M. (1969), 'The Development of Political Ideology: A Framework for the Analysis of Political Socialization', *American Political Science Review*, 69: 21–31.

Merelman, R.M. (1986), 'Revitalizing Political Socialization', in M.G. Hermann (ed.), *Political Psychology* (San Francisco, CA: Jossey-Bass), 279–319.

Merle, M. (1987), *The Sociology of International Relations* (transl. D. Parkin) (Leamington Spa: Berg).

Merritt, R.L. and Zinnes, D.A. (1991), 'Democracies and War', in A. Inkeles (ed.), *On Measuring Democracy* (New Brunswick, NJ: Transaction), 207–34.

Meyer, C. (2005), *DC Confidential: The Controversial Memoirs of Britain's Ambassador to the US at the Time of 9/11 and the Iraq War* (London: Weidenfeld & Nicolson).

Mill, J.S. (1973) [1859], 'A Few Words on Nonintervention', in G. Himmelfarb (ed.), *Essays on Politics and Culture* (Gloucester, MA: Peter Smith).

Milliken, J. (1999a), 'The Study of Discourse in International Relations: A Critique of Research and Methods', *European Journal of International Relations*, 5: 225–54.

Milliken, J. (1999b), 'Intervention and Identity: Reconstructing the War in Korea', in J. Weldes, M. Laffey, and H. Gusterson (eds), *Cultures of Insecurity: States, Communities, and the Production of Danger* (Minneapolis, MN: University of Minnesota Press), 91–117.

Milton-Edwards, B., and Hinchcliffe, P. (2004), *Conflicts in the Middle East* (2nd edn) (London: Routledge).

Mintz, A. (2007). 'Why Behavioral IR?' *International Studies Review*, 9: 157–62.

Mintz, A. and Derouen, K., Jr (2010), *Understanding Foreign Policy Decision Making* (Cambridge: Cambridge University Press).

Mitter, R. (2004), *A Bitter Revolution: China's Struggle with the Modern World* (Oxford: Oxford University Press).

Mitterrand, F. (1991), Allocution à l'Occasion de la Séance de Cloture des Assises de la Confédération Européenne, Prague, 14 June, Politique Etrangère de la France: Textes et Documents.

Moaz, Z. and Astorino, A. (1992), 'Waging War, Waging Peace: Decision-Making and Bargaining in the Arab–Israeli Conflict, 1970–1973', *International Studies Quarterly*, 36: 373–99.

Mohan, C.R. (2003), *Crossing the Rubicon: The Shaping of India's Foreign Policy* (New Delhi: Viking).

Monaghan A., and Montanaro-Jankovski, L. (2006), 'EU–Russia Energy Relations: The Need for Active Engagement', EPC Issue Paper No. 45, European Policy Centre.

Moravcsik, A. (1997), 'Taking Preferences Seriously: A Liberal Theory of International Politics', *International Organization*, 51: 513–53.

Moreira, A (2009), *Consejo Sudamericano de Defensa: Hacia una Integración Regional en Defensa* (http://www.resdal.org/csd/documento-de-debate-angela-moreira.pdf).

Morgan, T.C. (1992), 'Democracy and War: Reflections on the Literature', *International Interactions*, 18: 197–203.

Morgenthau, H. (1954), *Politics Among Nations: The Struggle for Power and Peace* (3rd edn) (Chicago, IL: University of Chicago Press).

Motokawa, T. (1989), 'Sushi Science and Hamburger Science', *Perspectives in Biology and Medicine*, 32: 489–504.

Moulton, H.G., and Pasvolsky, L. (1932), *War Debts and World Prosperity* (Washington, DC: Brookings Institution).

Mueller, H., and Risse-Kappen, T. (1993), 'From the Outside In and from the Inside Out: International Relations, Domestic Politics and Foreign Policy', in D. Skidmore and V. Hudson (eds), *The Limits of State Autonomy: Societal Groups and Foreign Policy Formulation* (Boulder, CO: Westview Press).

Mueller, J.E. (1973), *War, Presidents, and Public Opinion* (New York: John Wiley).

Mueller, J.E. (1989), *Retreat from Doomsday: The Obsolescence of Major War* (New York: Basic Books).

Mueller, J. and Mueller, K. (1999), 'Sanctions of Mass Destruction', *Foreign Affairs*, 78: 43–53.

Munton, D. (1976), 'Comparative Foreign Policy: Fads, Fantasies, Orthodoxies, and Perversities', in J.N. Rosenau (ed.), *In Search of Global Patterns* (New York: Free Press).

Muravchik, J. (1991), *Exporting Democracy: Fulfilling America's Destiny* (Washington, DC: AEI Press).

Muravchik, J. (2004), 'The Neoconservative Cabal', in I. Stelzer (ed.), *Neoconservatism* (London: Atlantic Books), 243–57.

Murphy. E. (2005), 'Zionism and the Arab–Israeli Conflict', in Y.M. Choueiri (ed.), *A Companion to the History of the Middle East* (Oxford: Blackwell), 269–90.

Narlikar, A. (2003), *International Trade and Developing Countries: Bargaining Coalitions in the GATT and WTO* (London: Routledge).

Narlikar, A. (2006), 'Fairness in International Trade Negotiations: Developing Countries in the GATT and WTO', *World Economy*, 29: 1005–29.

Narlikar, A. (2009), 'A Theory of Bargaining Coalitions', in A. Narlikar and B. Vickers (eds), *Leadership and Change in the Multilateral Trading System* (Leiden: Martinus Nijhoff).

Narlikar, A. and Hurrell, A. (2012), *Pathways to Power: Brazil and India in International Regimes*, to be published.

Narlikar, A. and Odell, J. (2006), 'The Strict Distributive Strategy for a Bargaining Coalition: The Like Minded Group in the World Trade Organization', in J. Odell (ed.), *Negotiating Trade: Developing Countries in the WTO and NAFTA* (Cambridge: Cambridge University Press).

Narlikar, A. and van Houten, P. (2010), 'Know thy Enemy: Uncertainty and Deadlock in the WTO,' in Amrita Narlikar (ed.) *Deadlocks in Multilateral Negotiations: Causes and Solutions* (Cambridge: Cambridge University Press).

Narlikar, A. and van Houten, P. (2006), 'Breaking Deadlocks: Signaling Mechanisms in North-South Negotiations', paper presented at the International Studies Association Convention, San Diego, 22–25 March.

Nath, K. (2005), WT/MIN(05)/ST/17, 14 December, India (www.wto.org).

Nathan, A. and Link, P. (eds) (2001), *The Tiananmen Papers: The Chinese Leadership's Decision to Use Force Against Their Own People* (London: Little, Brown).

Neack, L. (2003), *The New Foreign Policy: U.S. and Comparative Foreign Policy in the 21st Century* (Lanham, MD: Rowman & Littlefield).

Neack, L., Hey, J.A., and Haney, P.J. (1995), *Foreign Policy Analysis: Continuity and Change in Its Second Generation* (Englewood Cliffs, NJ: Prentice Hall).

Neumann, I.B. (1996), 'Collective Identity Formation: Self and Other in International Relations', *European Journal of International Relations*, 2: 139–74.

Neumann, I.B. (1999), *Uses of the Other: 'The East' in European Identity Formation* (Minneapolis, MN: University of Minnesota Press).

Neumann, I.B. (2002), 'Returning Practices to the Linguistic Turn: The Case of Diplomacy', *Millennium*, 31: 627–51.

Neustadt, R.E. (1960), *Presidential Power: The Politics of Leadership* (New York: John Wiley).

Neustadt, R.E. (1970), *Alliance Politics* (New York: Columbia University Press).

Neustadt, R.E. (1990), *Presidential Power and the Modern Presidents: The Politics of Leadership from Roosevelt to Reagan* (5th edn) (New York: Free Press).

Neustadt, R. and May, E. (1986), *Thinking in Time: The Uses of History for Decision-Makers* (New York: Free Press).

New York Review of Books (2009), 'China's Charter 08', 15 January: 54–56 (with postscript by Perry Link).

New York Times (2006), 'Rice's Counselor Gives Advice Others May Not Want to Hear', 28 October.

New York Times (2010), 'Winning, Losing and War', 28 August.

New York Times (2011), 'Obama Takes Hard Line with Libya After Shift by Clinton', 18 March.

Newnham, R. (2002), *Deutsche Mark Diplomacy: Positive Economic Sanctions in German–Russian Relations* (State College, PA: Penn State University Press).

Niblett, R. and Wallace, W. (eds) (2001), *Rethinking European Order: West European Responses, 1989–97* (London: Palgrave).

Nincic, M. (1992), *Democracy and Foreign Policy* (New York: Columbia University Press).

Nincic, M. (2011), *The Logic of Positive Engagement* (Ithaca, NY: Cornell University Press).

Nisbett, R. and Ross, L. (1980), *Human Inference: Strategies and Shortcomings of Social Judgment* (Englewood Cliffs, NJ: Prentice Hall).

Nixon, R. (1978), *The Memoirs* (New York: Grosset & Dunlap).

Nordlinger, E. (1995), *Isolationism Reconfigured* (Princeton,NJ: Princeton University Press).

Nozick, R. (1974), *Anarchy, State and Utopia* (New York: Basic Books).

Nye, J.S. (1971), *Peace in Parts: Integration and Conflict in Regional Organization* (Boston, MA: Little, Brown).

Nye, J.S. (2004), *Soft Power: The Means to Success in World Politics* (New York: Public Affairs Books).

Nye, J.S. (2008), *The Powers to Lead* (Oxford: Oxford University Press).

Nye, J.S. and Owens, W.A. (1996), 'America's Information Edge', *Foreign Affairs*, 75: 20–36.

Nzomo, M. (1999), 'The Foreign Policy of Tanzania: from Cold War to post-Cold War', in S. Wright (ed.), *African Foreign Policies* (Boulder, CO: Westview Press).

Obama, B.H. (2009). 'Nobel Peace Prize Lecture, 10 December 2009'. Available online at: http://www.nobelprize.org/nobel_prizes/peace/laureates/2009/obama-lecture_en.html

Oberthur, S. and Ott, H.(1999), *The Kyoto Protocol: International Climate Policy for the 21st Century* (Berlin: Springer).

Ochsner, K.N. and Gross, J.J. (2005), 'The Cognitive Control of Emotion', *Trends in Cognitive Science*, 9: 242–9.

Ogata, S. (1977), 'The Business Community and Japanese Foreign Policy', in R.A. Scalapino (ed.), *The Foreign Policy of Modern Japan* (Berkeley, CA: University of California Press), 175–203.

Olsen, J.P. (2002), 'The Many Faces of Europeanization', *Journal of Common Market Studies*, 40: 921–52.

Omand, D. (2010), *Securing the State* (London: Hurst).

O'Neal, J. and Russett, B. (1997), 'The Classical Liberals were Right', *International Studies Quarterly*, 41: 267–94.

O'Neal, J., O'Neal, F., Maoz, Z., and Russett, B. (1996), 'The Liberal Peace: Interdependence, Democracy and International Conflict, 1950–1985', *Journal of Peace Research*, 33: 11–28.

Onuf, N.G. (1989), *World of Our Making: Rules and Rule in Social Theory and International Relations* (Columbia, SC: University of South Carolina Press).

Oslo Conference on Cluster Munitions Declaration, 23 February 2007 (www.stopclustermunitions.org/news.asp?id=52).

Overbye, D. (2007), 'Free Will: Now You Have It, Now You Don't', *New York Times*, 2 January: D1.

Owen, D. (1995), *Balkan Odyssey* (New York: Harcourt Brace).

Owen, J. (1996), 'How liberalism produces democratic peace', in M.E. Brown, S.M. Lynn-Jones, and S.E. Miller (eds), *Debating the Democratic Peace* (Cambridge, MA: MIT Press), 116–54.

Packenham, R.A. (1973), *Liberal America and the Third World* (Princeton, NJ: Princeton University Press).

Paige, G. (1959), *The Korean Decision* (Evanston, IL: Northwestern University Press).

Paige, G. (1968), *The Korean Decision, June 24–30, 1950* (New York: Free Press).

Paine, T. (1995) [1791], *Rights of Man* (New York: Oxford University Press).

Panksepp, J. (1998), *Affective Neuroscience: The Foundations of Human and Animal Emotions* (New York: Oxford University Press).

Papadikis, E. (2002), 'Global Environmental Diplomacy: Australia's Stances on Global Warming', *Australian Journal of International Affairs*, 56: 265–77.

Pape, R. (1997), 'Why Economic Sanctions Do Not Work', *International Security*, 22: 90–136.

Pape, R. (2005), 'Soft Balancing Against the United States', *International Security* 30:7–45.

Pappe, I. (2004), *A History of Modern Palestine: One Land, Two Peoples* (Cambridge: Cambridge University Press).

Pappe, I. (2006), *The Ethnic Cleansing of Palestine* (Oxford: Oneworld).

Parmar, I. and Cox, M. (eds) (2010), *Soft Power and US Foreign Policy: Theoretical, Historical and Contemporary Perspectives* (London: Routledge).

Paterson, T. (ed.) (1978), *Major Problems in American Foreign Policy*, Vols I and II (Lexington, MA: D.C. Heath).

Payne, J. (1986), 'Marxism and Militarism', *Polity*, 19: 270–89.

PBS Online News Hour, Presidential Debate, 12 October 2000 (www.pbs.org/newshour/bb/politics/july-dec00/for-policy-10-12.html)

Peace Journalism (2007), '46 Nations Call For Ban on Cluster Bombs', 24 February.

Pearse, G. (2007), *High and Dry: John Howard, Climate Change and the Selling of Australia's Future* (Melbourne: Penguin).

Pei, M. (1995), ' "Creeping Democratization" in China', *Journal of Democracy*, 6: 65–79.

People's Republic of China (2005), 'Position Paper of the People's Republic of China on the United Nations Reforms', 9 June 2005 (http://www.china.org.cn/english/government/131308.htm).

Petito, F. and Hatzopoulos, P. (2004), *Religion in International Relations: The Return from Exile* (Basingstoke: Palgrave Macmillan).

Phillips, N. (2003), 'The Rise and Fall of Open Regionalism? Comparative Reflections on Regional Governance in the Southern Cone of Latin America', *Third World Quarterly*, 24: 217–34.

Philo, G. (1993), 'From Buerk to Band Aid: The Media and the 1984 Ethiopian Famine', in J. Eldridge (ed.), *Getting the Message: News, Truth and Power* (London: Routledge), 104–25.

Pictet, J. (1979), *Fundamental Principles of the Red Cross* (Geneva: International Committee of the Red Cross).

Piebalgs, A. (2006), Speaking notes welcoming the agreement between Gazprom and Naftogaz, Joint Press Conference, Brussels, 4 January.

Pinheiro, L. (2004), *Política Externa Brasileira, 1889–2002* (Rio de Janeiro: Zahar).

Pollack, K. (2002), *The Threatening Storm: The Case for Invading Iraq* (New York: Random House).

Pollack, K. (2007), Interview by Tim Dunne and Gareth Stansfield, Washington, DC, 6 June.

Popescu, N. (2006), *Russia's Soft Power Ambitions, CEPS Policy Brief No. 115* (Brussels: Centre for European Policy Studies) (http://www.ceps./be).

Popescu, N. and Wilson, A. (2011), *Turning Presence into Power: Lessons from the Eastern Neighbourhood, European Council on Foreign Relations Policy Brief* (www.ecfr.eu).

Posen, B. and Van Evera, S. (1980), 'Overarming and Underwhelming', *Foreign Policy*, 40: 99–118.

Post, J. (1990), 'Saddam Hussein of Iraq: A Political Psychology Profile', *Political Psychology*, 12: 279–89.

Pouliot, V. (2004), 'The Essence of Constructivism', *Journal of International Relations and Development*, 7, 319–36.

Pouliot, V. (2008), 'The Logic of Practicality: A Theory of Practice of Security Communities', *International Organization*, 62, 257–88.

Powell, G.B. (1982), *Contemporary Democracies* (Cambridge, MA: MIT Press).

Press Release (2006), US Mission to the UN, Geneva, 24 July (http://geneva.usmission.gov/Press2006/0724Doha.html).

Price, R. (1998), 'Reversing the Gunsights: Transnational Civil Society Targets Land Mines', *International Organization*, 52: 613–44.

Project for the New American Century (1998), Letter to President Clinton on Iraq, 16 January (www.newamericancentury.org/iraqclintonletter.htm).

Przeworski, A. (1995), *Sustainable Democracy* (with the Group on East–South Systems Transformations) (New York: Cambridge University Press).

Putnam, R. (1988), 'Diplomacy and Domestic Politics: The Logic of Two-Level Games', *International Organization*, 43: 427–60.

Pye, L. (1986), 'Political Psychology in Asia', in M.G. Hermann (ed.), *Political Psychology* (San Francisco, CA: Jossey-Bass), 467–86.

Pye, L.W. and Verba, S. (eds) (1965), *Political Culture and Political Development* (Princeton, NJ: Princeton University Press).

Qian, Q. (2005), *Ten Episodes in China's Diplomacy* (New York: Harper Collins).

Quattrone, G. and Tversky, A (1988), 'Contrasting Rational and Psychological Analyses of Political Choice', *American Political Science Review*, 82: 719–36.

Quester, G. (1980), 'Consensus Lost', *Foreign Policy*, 40: 18–32.

Rahigh-Aghsan, A. (2011), 'Turkey's EU Quest and Political Cleavages under AKP', *Review of European Studies*, 3: 43–53.

Rawls, J. (1971), *A Theory of Justice* (Cambridge, MA: Harvard University Press).

Rawls, J. (1999), *The Law of Peoples* (Cambridge, MA: Harvard University Press).

Ray, J.L. (1993), 'Wars between Democracies: Rare or Nonexistent?', *International Interactions*, 18: 251–76.

Redick, J.R., Carasales, J.C. and Wrobel, P.S. (1994) 'Nuclear Rapproachement: Argentina, Brazil and the Non-Proliferation Regime', *Washington Quarterly*, 18: 107–22.

Reisman, M. (1984), 'Coercion and Self Determination: Construing Charter Article 2(4)', *American Journal of International Law*, 78: 642–5.

Reiter, D. and Stam, A. (2003), 'Identifying the Culprit: Democracy, Dictatorship and Dispute Settlement', *American Political Science Review*, 97: 333–7.

Renouvin, P. and Duroselle, J.B. (1968), *Introduction to the History of International Relations* (London: Pall Mall Press).

Renshon, S.A. (ed.) (1977), *Handbook of Political Socialization: Theory and Research* (New York: Free Press).

Rhodes, E. (1994), 'Do Bureaucratic Politics Matter? Some Disconfirming Findings from the Case of the US Navy', *World Politics*, 47: 1–41.

Richardson, N.R., and Kegley, C. W. (1980), 'Trade Dependence and Foreign Policy Compliance: A Longitudinal Analysis', *International Studies Quarterly*, 24: 191–222.

Richter, J.G. (1994), *Khrushchev's Double Bind: International Pressures and Domestic Coalition Politics* (Baltimore, MD: Johns Hopkins University Press).

Rilling, J.K., Gutman, D.A., Zeh, T.R., Pagnoni, G., Berns, G., and Kilts, C.D. (2002), 'A Neural Basis for Social Cooperation', *Neuron*, 35: 395–405.

Ripley, B. (1989), 'Kennedy, Johnson, and Groupthink: A Theoretical Reassessment', paper presented at the annual meeting of the American Political Science Association, Atlanta, 31 August–3 September.

Risse, T. (2000), "Let's Argue!" Communicative Action in World Politics', *International Organization*, 54: 1–39.

Risse, T. (2003), 'Beyond Iraq: Challenges to the Transatlantic Security Community', *German–American Dialogue Working Paper Series* (Washington, DC: American Institute for Contemporary German Studies).

Risse, T. (2004), 'Social Constructivism Meets Globalization', unpublished mimeo, 19 August, Otto Suhr Institute of Political Science, Free University Berlin.

Risse, T. and Sikkink, K. (1999), 'The Socialization of International Human Rights Norms into Domestic Practices: Introduction', in T. Risse, S.C. Ropp, and K. Sikkink (eds), *The Power of Human Rights: International Norms and Domestic Change* (Cambridge: Cambridge University Press).

Risse, T., Ropp, S., and Sikkink, K. (eds) (1999), *The Power of Human Rights: International Norms and Domestic Change* (Cambridge: Cambridge University Press).

Risse-Kappen, T. (1991), 'Public Opinion, Domestic Structure and Foreign Policy in Liberal Democracies', *World Politics*, 43: 479–512.

Risse-Kappen, T. (1996), 'Collective Identity in a Democratic Community: The Case of NATO', in P.J. Katzenstein (ed), *The Culture of National Security: Norms and Identity in World Politics* (New York: Columbia University Press), 357–99.

Rittberger, V. (ed.) (2001), *German Foreign Policy Since Unification: Theories and Case Studies* (Manchester: Manchester University Press).

Rivarola Puntigliano, A. (2008), 'Going Global: An Organizational Study of Brazilian Foreign Policy', *Revista Brasileira de Política Internacional*, 51: 28–52.

Robinson, P. (2002), *The CNN Effect: The Myth of News, Foreign Policy and Intervention* (London: Routledge).

Robinson, P. (ed.) (2011), 'The CNN Effect Revisited', Special issue, *Media, War and Conflict*, 4: 3–95.

Robinson, P., Goddard, P., Parry, K., Murray, C., and Taylor, P.M. (2010), *Pockets of Resistance: British News Media, War and Theory in the 2003 Invasion of Iraq* (Manchester: Manchester University Press).

Robyn, D. (1986), *What Makes A Good Case?* (Cambridge, MA.: Kennedy School of Government Case Program at Harvard).

Rootes, C. (2008), 'The First Climate Change Election? The Australian General Election of 24 November 2007', *Environmental Politics*, 17: 473–80.

Rootes, C. (2011), 'Denied, Deferred, Triumphant? Climate Change, Carbon Trading and the Greens in the Australian Federal Election of 21 August 2010', *Environmental Politics*, 20: 410–17.

Rosati, J.A. (1995), 'A Cognitive Approach to the Study of Foreign Policy', in L. Neack, J.A.K. Hey, and P.J. Haney (eds), *Foreign Policy Analysis: Continuity and Change in its Second Generation* (Englewood Cliffs, NJ: Prentice Hall), 49–70.

Rose, D. (2007), 'Iraq: Neo Culpa', *Vanity Fair*, (www. vanityfair.com/politics/features/2007/01/ neocons200701)

Rose, G. (1998), 'Neoclassical Realism and Theories of Foreign Policy', *World Politics*, 51: 144–172.

Rosecrance, R.N. (1963), *Action and Reaction in World Politics: International Systems in Perspective* (Boston, MA: Little, Brown).

Rosenau, J.N. (1963), *Calculated Control as a Unifying Concept in the Study of International Politics and Foreign Policy*, Research Monograph No. 15, Center of International Studies, Princeton University.

Rosenau, J.N. (1966), 'Pre-Theories and Theories of Foreign Policy', in R.B. Farrell (ed.), *Approaches to Comparative and International Politics* (Evanston, IL: Northwestern University Press), 27–92.

Rosenau, J.N. (1974), (ed.), *Comparing Foreign Policies: Theories, Findings, and Methods* (New York: John Wiley).

Rosenau, J.N. (2003), *Distant Proximities: Dynamics Beyond Globalization* (Princeton, NJ: Princeton University Press).

Ross, A.A.G. (2006), 'Coming in from the Cold. Constructivism and Emotions', *European Journal of International Relations* 12: 197–222.

Rousseau, D., (2005), *Democracy and War* (Stanford, CA: Stanford University Press).

Rowe, D. (1999–2000), 'Economic Sanctions Do Work: Economic Statecraft and the Oil Embargo of Rhodesia', *Security Studies*, 9: 254–87.

Ruggie, J.G. (1998), 'What Makes the World Hang Together? Neo-Utilitarianism and the Social Constructivist Challenge', *International Organization*, 52: 855–85.

Ruggie, J.G. (ed.) (1993), *Multilateralism Matters: The Theory and Praxis of an Institutional Form* (New York: Columbia University Press).

Rühe, V. (1994), 'Germany's Responsibility in and for Europe', Konrad Adenauer Stiftung, St Antony's College), Oxford.

Rummel, R.J. (1972), *The Dimensions of Nations* (Beverly Hills, CA: Sage).

Rummel, R.J. (1977), *Understanding Conflict and War* (Beverly Hills, CA: Sage).

Rummel, R.J. (1979), *National Attributes and Behavior* (Beverly Hills, CA: Sage).

Rummel, R.J. (1983), 'Libertarianism and International Violence', *Journal of Conflict Resolution*, 27: 27–71.

Runciman, D. (2006), *The Politics of Good Intentions* (Princeton,NJ: Princeton University Press).

Rupert, M. (2007), 'Marxism and Critical Theory', in T. Dunne, M. Kurki, and S. Smith (eds), *International Relations Theories: Discipline and Diversity* (Oxford: Oxford University Press).

Russett, B.M. (1993a), 'Can a Democractic Peace be Built?', *International Interactions*, 18: 277–82.

Russett, B.M. (1993b), *Grasping the Democratic Peace: Principles for a Post-Cold War World* (Princeton, NJ: Princeton University Press).

Saich, T. (2004), *Governance and Politics of China* (2nd edn) (Basingstoke: Macmillan).

Salmore, B.G. and Salmore, S.A. (1978), 'Political Regimes and Foreign Policy', in M.A. East, S.A. Salmore, and C.F. Hermann (eds), *Why Nations Act* (Beverly Hills, CA: Sage), 103–22.

Sampson, M. (1987), 'Cultural Influences on Foreign Policy', in C.F. Hermann, C.W. Kegley, and J.N. Rosenau (eds), *New Directions in the Study of Foreign Policy* (Boston, MA: Allen & Unwin), 384–408.

Saurette, P. (2006), 'You Dissin Me? Humiliation and Post-9/11 Global Politics', *Review of International Studies*, 32: 495–522.

Schachter, O. (1984), 'The Legality of Pro-democratic Intervention', *American Journal of International Law*, 78: 645–50.

Schilling, W.R., Hammond, P.Y., and Snyder, G.H. (1962), *Strategy, Politics, and Defense Budgets* (New York: Columbia University Press).

Schimmelfennig, F. (2003), *The EU, NATO and the Integration of Europe: Rules and Rhetoric* (Cambridge: Cambridge University Press).

Schimmelfennig, F. (2011), 'EU Membership Negotiations with Turkey: Entrapped Again', in DC Thomas (ed.), *Making EU Foreign Policy: National Preferences, European Norms and Common Policies* (Basingstoke: Palgrave Macmillan).

Schlesinger, A. (1965), *A Thousand Days: John F. Kennedy in the White House* (Boston, MA: Houghton Mifflin).

Schmidt, B. (2005), 'Competing Realist Conceptions of Power', *Millennium*, 33: 523–49.

Schoultz, L. (1981), *Human Rights and United States Policy toward Latin America* (Princeton, NJ: Princeton University Press).

Schrodt, P.A. (1995), 'Event Data in Foreign Policy Analysis', in L. Neack, J.A.K. Hey, and P.J. Haney (eds) *Foreign Policy Analysis: Continuity and Change in Its Second Generation* (Englewood Cliffs, NJ: Prentice-Hall), 145–66.

Schumacher, M. (1990), *Keeping the Cold War: Dick Cheney and the Department of Defense* (Cambridge, MA.: Kennedy School of Government, Harvard University).

Schumpeter, J. (1955), *Imperialism and Social Classes* (New York: Meridian).

Schwab, S. (2011), 'After Doha: Why the Negotiations Are Doomed, and What We Should Do About It', *Foreign Affairs*, 90: 96–103.

Schwartz, T. (1991), *America's Germany: John J. McCloy and the Federal Republic of Germany* (Cambridge, MA: Harvard University Press).

Schwellnus, G. (2006), 'Dynamics of Norm-Construction and Norm-Resonance in the Context of EU Enlargement: Minority Rights in Poland', Ph.D. thesis, Faculty of Legal, Social and Educational Sciences, Queen's University Belfast.

Sedelmeier, U. (2005a), 'Eastern Enlargement: Towards a European EU?', in H. Wallace, W. Wallace, and M. Pollack (eds), *Policy-Making in the European Union* (5th edn) (Oxford: Oxford University Press).

Sedelmeier, U. (2005b), *Constructing the Path to Eastern Enlargement: The Uneven Policy Impact of EU Identity* (Manchester: Manchester University Press).

Sedelmeier, U. (2010), 'Enlargement: From Rules for Accession to a Policy Towards Europe', in H. Wallace, M. Pollack, and A.R. Young (eds), *Policy-Making in the European Union* (6th edn) (Oxford: Oxford University Press).

Seib, P. (2008), *The Al Jazeera Effect: How the New Global Media Are Reshaping World Politics* (Washington, DC: Potomac).

Seldon, A. (2005), *Blair* (London: Free Press).

Semmel, A.K. (1982), 'Small Group Dynamics in Foreign Policy-Making', in G.W. Hopple (ed.), *Biopolitics, Political Psychology, and International Politics* (New York: St. Martin's Press), 94–113.

Semmel, A.K., and Minix, D. (1979), 'Small Group Dynamics and Foreign Policy Decision-Making: An Experimental Approach', in L.S. Falkowski (ed.), *Psychological Models in International Politics* (Boulder, CO: Westview Press), 251–87.

Sen, J. (2003), 'Lessons Not Learned: India's Trade Policymaking Process from Uruguay to Doha', working paper, Globalization and Poverty, London, August (http://www.gapresearch.org/governance/Sen-LessNotLearned-AUG031.pdf) (accessed 15 April 2007).

Sestanovich, S. (1988), 'Gorbachev's Foreign Policy: a Diplomacy of Decline?', *Problems of Communism*, 37: 1–15.

Shapiro, M.J. (1988), *The Politics of Representation: Writing Practices in Biography, Photography and Policy Analysis* (Madison, WI: University of Wisconsin Press).

Shapiro, M. and Bonham, M. (1973), 'Cognitive Process and Foreign Policy Decision-Making', *International Studies Quarterly*, 17: 147–74.

Shaw, M. (1996), *Civil Society and Media in Global Crises* (London: St Martin's Press).

Shea, J. (2010), 'NATO at Sixty—and Beyond', in G. Aybet and R. Moore (eds), *NATO in Search of a Vision* (Washington, DC: Georgetown University Press).

Shih, C.Y. (1993), *China's Just World: The Morality of Chinese Foreign Policy* (Boulder, CO: Lynne Rienner).

Shlaim, A. (1996), 'The Middle East: The Origins of Arab-Israeli Wars', in N. Woods (ed.), *Explaining International Relations Since 1945* (Oxford: Oxford University Press), 219–40.

Shlaim, A. (2000), *The Iron Wall: Israel and the Arab World* (New York: W. W. Norton).

Shue, H. (2011), 'Face Reality? After You!—A Call for Leadership on Climate Change', *Ethics and International Affairs*, 25: 17–26.

Simms, B. (2001), *Unfinest Hour: Britain and the Destruction of Bosnia* (London: Allen Lane)

Simon, H. (1985), 'Human Nature in Politics: The Dialogue of Psychology with Political Science', *American Political Science Review*, 79: 293–304.

Simon, L. and Stephen, J. (1981), *El Salvador Land Reform 1980–1981* (Boston, MA: Oxfam-America).

Singer, E. and Hudson, V.M. (1992) (eds), *Political Psychology and Foreign Policy* (Boulder, CO: Westview Press).

Singer, J.D. (1961), 'The Level-of-Analysis Problem in International Relations', *World Politics*, 14: 77–92.

Singer, J.D., Bremer, S., and Stuckey, J. (1972), 'Capability Distribution, Uncertainty, and Major Power War, 1820–1965', in B.M. Russett (ed.), *Peace, War, and Numbers* (Beverly Hills, CA: Sage).

Sjursen, H. (ed.) (2006a), *Questioning EU Enlargement: Europe in Search of Identity* (London: Routledge).

Sjursen, H. (2006b), 'What Kind of Power? European Foreign Policy in Perspective', Special issue, *Journal of European Public Policy*, 13(2).

Skidmore, D. and Hudson, V.M. (eds) (1993), *The Limits of State Autonomy: Societal Groups and Foreign Policy Formulation* (Boulder, CO: Westview Press).

Skinner, R. (2006), *Strategies for Greater Energy Security and Resource Security* (Oxford: Oxford Institute for Energy Studies) (http://www.oxfordenergy.org/).

Skowronek, S. (2006), 'The Reassociation of Ideas and Persons: Racism, Liberalism and the American Political Tradition', *American Political Science Review*, 100: 385–401.

Smith, C. (2005), 'The Arab–Israeli Conflict', in L. Fawcett (ed.), *International Relations of the Middle East* (Oxford: Oxford University Press), 217–39.

Smith, C. (2010), *Palestine and the Arab–Israeli Conflict: A History with Documents* (7th edn) (New York: Palgrave Macmillan).

Smith, K. (2004), *The Making of EU Foreign Policy: The Case of Eastern Europe* (Basingstoke: Palgrave MacMillan).

Smith, K. (2005), 'Enlargement and European Order', in C. Hill and M. Smith (eds), *International Relations and the European Union* (Oxford: Oxford University Press).

Smith, K. (2006), *Security Implications of Russian Energy Policies, CEPS Policy Brief No. 90* (Brussels: Centre for European Policy Studies).

Smith, S. (1987), 'CFP: A Theoretical Critique', *International Studies Notes*, 13: 47–8.

Smith, S. (1991), 'Foreign Policy Analysis and the Study of British Foreign Policy', in L. Freedman and M. Clarke (eds), *Britain in the World* (Cambridge: Cambridge University Press).

Smith, S. (1995), 'The Self-Images of a Discipline: A Genealogy of International Relations Theory', in K. Booth and S. Smith (eds), *International Relations Theory Today* (Cambridge: Polity Press.

Smith, S., Hadfield, A., and Dunne, T. (2008), 'Introduction', in S. Smith, A. Hadfield, and T. Dunne (eds), *Foreign Policy: Theories, Actors, Cases* (Oxford: Oxford University Press), 1–8.

Smith, T. (1994), *America's Mission* (Princeton, NJ: Princeton University Press).

Snare, C. (1992), 'Applying Personality Theory to Foreign Policy Behavior: Evaluating Three Methods of Assessment', in E. Singer and V.M. Hudson (eds), *Political Psychology and Foreign Policy* (Boulder, CO: Westview Press), 103–34.

Snyder, R. (2005), 'Bridging the Realist/Constructivist Divide: The Case of the Counterrevolution in Soviet Foreign Policy at the End of the Cold War', *Foreign Policy Analysis*, 1: 55–71.

Snyder, R.C., Bruck, H.W., and Sapin, B. (1954), *Decision-Making as an Approach to the Study of International*

Politics, Foreign Policy Analysis Project Series No. 3 (Princeton, NJ: Princeton University Press).

Snyder, R.C., Bruck, H.W., and Sapin, B. (1963) (eds), *Foreign Policy Decision-Making: An Approach to the Study of International Politics* (Glencoe, IL: Free Press).

Snyder, R.C., Bruck, H.W., and Sapin, B. (2002) (eds), *Foreign Policy Decision-Making (Revisited)* (New York: Palgrave Macmillan).

Snyder, R and Paige, G. (1958), *The United States Decision to Resist Aggression in Korea: The Application of an Analytical Scheme* (Glencoe, IL: Free Press).

Soares de Lima, M.R. (2008), 'Brazil Rising', *Internationale Politik*, 9: 62–7.

Soares de Lima, M.R. and Hirst, M. (2006), 'Brazil as an Intermediate State and Regional Power: Action, Choice and Responsibilities', *International Affairs*, 82: 21–40.

Soccor, V. (2006), 'Russia Bans Georgian, Moldovan Wines and Other Products', *Eurasia Daily Monitor*, 3/60, 28 March (www.http://jamestown.org).

Sorensen, T. (1965), *Kennedy* (New York: Harper & Row).

Sorj, B. and Fausto, S. (2011), 'El Papel de Brasil en América del Sur: Estrategias y Percepciones Mutuas', working paper no. 1, Plataforma Democrática.

Souza Costa Barros, A. (1983), 'Política Exterior Brasileña y el Mito del Barón', *Foro Internacional*, 24: 1–20.

Sprecher, C. and DeRouen, K. (2005), 'The Domestic Determinants of Foreign Policy Behavior in Middle East Enduring Rivals, 1948–1998', *Foreign Policy Analysis*, 1: 121–41.

Sprout, H. and Sprout, M. (1956), *Man–Milieu Relationship Hypotheses in the Context of International Politics* (Princeton, NJ: Princeton University Press).

Sprout, H. and Sprout, M. (1957), 'Environment Factors in the Study of International Politics', *Journal of Conflict Resolution*, 1: 309–28.

Sprout, H. and Sprout, M. (1965), *The Ecological Perspective on Human Affairs: with Special Reference to International Politics* (Princeton, NJ: Princeton University Press).

Stansfield, G. (2005), 'Political Life and the Military', in Y.M. (Choueiri (ed.), *Companion to the History of the Middle East* (Oxford: Blackwell), 355–71.

Steel, R. (1969), 'Interview with Robert Kennedy', *New York Review of Books*, 13 March: 22.

Stein, A.A. (2008), 'Neoliberal Institutionalism', in C. Reus-Smit and D. Snidal (eds), *The Oxford Handbook of International Relations* (Oxford: Oxford University Press), 201–21.

Stein, J.D. and Lang, E. (2007), *The Unexpected War: Canada in Kandahar* (Toronto: Penguin).

Stein, J.G. (1985), 'Calculation, Miscalculation, and Conventional Deterrence. I: The View from Cairo', in R. Jervis, R.N. Lebow and J.G. Stein (eds), *Psychology and Deterrence* (Baltimore, MD: Johns Hopkins University Press), 34–59.

Stein, J.G.(1994). 'Political Learning by Doing: Gorbachev as a Uncommitted Thinker and a Motivated Learner', *International Organization*, 48: 155–83.

Stein, J.G. (1996), 'Deterrence and Learning in an Enduring Rivalry: Egypt and Israel, 1948–73', *Journal of Strategic Studies*, 6: 104–52.

Stein, K. (1999), *Heroic Diplomacy: Sadat, Kissinger, Carter, Begin, and the Quest for Arab–Israeli Peace* (London: Routledge).

Stelzer, I. (ed.) (2004), *Neoconservatism* (London: Atlantic Books).

Stern, J. (2006), 'The Russian–Ukrainian Gas Crisis of January 2006', Oxford Institute for Energy Studies (http://www.oxfordenergy.org/).

Stern, N. (2006), *The Economics of Climate Change: The Stern Review* (Cambridge: Cambridge University Press).

Stevenson, H. (2009), 'Cheating on Climate Change? Australia's Challenge to Global Warming Norms', *Australian Journal of International Affairs*, 63: 165–86.

Stewart, L. (1977), 'Birth Order and Political Leadership', in M.G. Hermann (ed.), *A Psychological Examination of Political Leaders* (New York: Free Press), 206–36.

Stewart, P.D., Hermann, M.G., and Hermann, C.F. (1989), 'Modeling the 1973 Soviet Decision to Support Egypt', *American Political Science Review*, 83: 35–59.

Stiglitz, J. (2002), *Globalization and its Discontents* (New York: W.W. Norton).

Strange, S. (1988) *States and Markets* (London: Pinter).

Streit, C. (1938), *Union Now: A Proposal for a Federal Union of the Leading Democracies* (New York: Harper & Brothers).

Stuart, D.T. (2008), 'Foreign-Policy Decision-Making', in C. Reus-Smit and D. Snidal (eds), *The Oxford Handbook of International Relations* (Oxford: Oxford University Press), 576–93.

Stuart, D. and Starr, H. (1982), 'Inherent Bad Faith Reconsidered: Dulles, Kennedy, and Kissinger', *Political Psychology*, 3: 1–33.

Suedfeld, P. and Tetlock, P. (1977), 'Integrative Complexity of Communications in International Crisis', *Journal of Conflict Resolution*, 21:169–84.

Suettinger, R. L. (2003), *Beyond Tiananmen: the Politics of US–China Relations 1989–2000* (Washington, DC: Brookings Institution).

Suskind, R. (2006), *The One Percent Doctrine* (New York: Simon & Schuster).

Swidler, A. (2001), 'What Anchors Cultural Practices', in T.R. Schatzki, K. Knorr-Cetina, and E.V. Savigny (eds), *The Practice Turn in Contemporary Theory* (London: Routledge).

Sylvest, C. (2009), *British Liberal Internationalism: Making Progress?* (Manchester: Manchester University Press).

TACIS Home Page, Europa Website: http://ec.europa.eu/external_relations/ceeca/tacis.

Taliaferro, J.W. (2010), 'Prospect Theory and Foreign Policy Analysis', in R.A. Denemark (ed.), *The International Studies Encyclopedia* (Oxford: Blackwell; Blackwell Reference Online).

Taliaferro, J.W., Lobell, S.E., and Ripsman, N.M. (2009), 'Introduction: Neoclassical Realism, the State, and Foreign Policy', in S.E. Lobell, N.M. Ripsman, and J.W. Taliaferro (eds), *Neoclassical Realism, the State, and Foreign Policy* (Cambridge: Cambridge University Press), 1–41.

Taylor, C. (1964), *The Explanation of Behaviour* (London: Routledge & Kegan Paul).

Tesón, F. (2003), 'The Liberal Case for Humanitarian Intervention', in J.L. Holzgrefe and R. Keohane (eds), *Humanitarian Intervention: Ethical, Legal, and Political Dilemmas* (New York: Cambridge University Press), 93–129.

Tetlock, P.E. (1979), 'Identifying Victims of Groupthink from Public Statements of Decision Makers', *Journal of Personality and Social Psychology*, 37: 1314–24.

Tetlock, P.E. (1998a), 'Social Psychology and World Politics', in D.T. Gilbert, S.T. Fiske, and G. Lindzey (eds), *Handbook of Social Psychology* (4th edn) (New York: McGraw-Hill).

Tetlock, P.E. (1998b), 'Close-call Counterfactuals and Belief System Defenses: I Was Not Almost Wrong but I was Almost Right', *Journal of Personality and Social Psychology*, 75: 639–52.

Tetlock, P.E. (2006), *Expert Political Judgment: How Good is It? How Can we Know?* (Princeton, NJ: Princeton University Press).

Tetlock, P.E., and Breslauer, G. (eds) (1991), *Learning in US and Soviet Foreign Policy* (Boulder, CO: Westview).

Thies, C.G. (2010), 'Role Theory and Foreign Policy', in R.A. Denemark (ed.), *The International Studies Encyclopedia* (Oxford: Blackwell; Blackwell Reference Online).

Third World Network information service, 10 November 2005 (http://www.twnside.org.sg/title2/twninfo297.htm).

Third World Network information service, 25 July 2006 (http://www.twnside.org.sg/title2/twninfo454.htm).

Tickner, J.A. (1992), *Gender in International Relations: Feminist Perspectives on Achieving Global Security* (New York: Columbia University Press).

Tickner, J.A. (2004), 'Feminist Responses to International Security Studies', *Peace Review*, 16: 43–8.

Tignor, R. (1966), *Modernization and British Colonial Rule in Egypt* (Princeton, NJ: Princeton University Press).

Timesonline (2005), 'The Secret Downing Street Memo', 1 May 2005 (www.timesonline.co.uk/printFriendly/0,,1-523-1593607-523,00.html).

Timesonline (2008), 'The Three Trillion Dollar War, Op. Ed. by J. Stiglitz and L. Bilmes, 23 February 2008 (www.timesonline.co.uk/tol/comment/columnists/guest_contributors/article3419840.ece) (accessed 23 August 2011).

Timoshenko, Y. (2007), 'Containing Russia', *Foreign Affairs*, 86: 69–82.

Titscher, S., Meyer, M., Wodak, R., and Vetter, E. (2000), *Methods of Text and Discourse Analysis* (London: Sage).

Toje, A. (2011), 'The European Union as a Small Power', *Journal of Common Market Studies*, 49: 43–60.

Todorova, M. (1997), *Imagining the Balkans* (Oxford: Oxford University Press).

Tovias, A. and Ugur, M. (2004), 'Can the EU Anchor Policy Reforms in Third Countries', *European Politics*, 5: 395–418.

Tranter, B. (2011), 'Political Divisions Over Climate Change and Environmental Issues in Australia', *Environmental Politics*, 20: 78–96.

Treaty Establishing a Constitution for Europe (2004), *Official Journal of the European Union*, C310, Vol.47, 16 December (http://eur-lex.europa.eu/JOHtml.do?uri=OJ:C:2004:310:SOM:EN:HTML).

Tversky, A. and Kahneman, D. (1973), 'Availability: A Heuristic for Judging Frequency and Probability', *Cognitive Psychology*, 5: 207–32.

Tversky, A. and Kahneman, D. (1983), 'Extensional Versus Intuitive Reasoning: The Conjunction Fallacy in Probability Judgment', *Psychological Review*, 90: 293–315.

Tversky, A. and Kahneman, D. (1992), 'Advances in Prospect Theory: Cumulative Representation of Uncertainty', *Journal of Risk and Uncertainty*, 5. 297–323.

UK Government (2002), *Iraq's Weapons of Mass Destruction—The Assessment of the British Government* (London: the Stationery Office), 1–50.

UNDP (1993), *Human Development Report 1993* (Oxford: Oxford University Press).

UNDP (1994), *Human Development Report 1994: New Dimensions of Human Security* (New York: Oxford University Press).

United Nations (2005), *World Summit Outcome Document, UNGA Res 60/1*, 24 October 2005 (http://www.unhcr.org/refworld/docid/44168a910.html).

US Congress, House Appropriations Committee, Subcommittee on Department of Defense Appropriations, *Hearings*, 88th Congress, 1st Session, 1963.

US Congress, Senate Armed Services Committee, Preparedness Investigating Subcommittee, *Interim Report on Cuban Military Buildup*, 88th Congress, 1st Session, 1963.

US Department of Defense, *Special Cuba Briefing*, 6 February 1963.

US Intelligence Board (1962), 'The Military Buildup in Cuba', Special National Intelligence Estimate 85-3-62, 19 September 1962, in CIA History Staff (1992), *CIA Documents on the Cuban Missile Crisis 1962* (CIA: Washington, DC).

US Department of State (1996), *Foreign Relations of the United States 1961–1963: Cuban Missile Crisis and Aftermath*, Vol. 11 (Washington, DC: US Government Printing Office).

US Senate (1953), Hearings Before the Committee on Foreign Relations on the Nomination of John Foster Dulles, Secretary of State Designate, 15 January, 83rd Congress, 1st Session (Washington, DC: US Government Printing Office).

Vachudova, M. (2005), *Europe Undivided: Democracy, Leverage, and Integration After Communism* (Oxford: Oxford University Press).

Van Belle, D. (1993), 'Domestic Imperatives and Rational Models of Foreign Policy Decision Making', in D. Skidmore and V.M. Hudson (eds), *The Limits of State Autonomy: Societal Groups and Foreign Policy Formulation* (Boulder, CO: Westview Press), 151–83.

Vasquez, J.A. and Elman, C. (eds) (2003), *Realism and the Balancing of Power: A New Debate* (Saddle River, NJ: Prentice-Hall).

Védrine, H. (2001), Interview on the Le Grand Jury RTL–Le Monde–LCI television programme, Paris, 9 September (www.ambafrance-uk.org).

Verba, S. and Brody, R.A. (1970), 'Participation, Policy Preferences, and the War in Vietnam', *Public Opinion Quarterly*, 34: 325–32.

Verba, S., Brody, R.A., Parker, E.B., *et al.* (1967), 'Public Opinion and the War in Vietnam', *American Political Science Review*, 61: 317–33.

Verbeek, B. (2003), *Decision-Making in Great Britain During the Suez Crisis* (Aldershot: Ashgate).

Verheugen, G. (1999), 'Enlargement: Speed and Quality', Speech in The Hague, 4 November.

Verheugen, G. (2001), 'Debate on EU Enlargement in the European Parliament', Strasbourg, 4 September.

Vertzberger, Y. (1990), *The World in Their Minds: Information Processing, Cognition, and Perception in Foreign Policy Decision-Making* (Stanford, CA: Stanford University Press).

Vigevani, T. and Cepaluni, G. (2007), 'Lula's Foreign Policy and the Quest for Autonomy through Diversification', *Third World Quarterly*, 28: 1309–26.

Volkmer, I. (1999), *News in the Global Sphere* (Luton: University of Luton Press).

von Winterfeldt, D. and Edwards, E. (1986), *Decision Analysis and Behavioral Research* (New York: Cambridge University Press).

Voss, J. and Dorsey, E. (1992), 'Perception and International Relations: An Overview', in E. Singer and V.M. Hudson (eds), *Political Psychology and Foreign Policy* (Boulder, CO: Westview Press), 3–30.

Voss, J., Wolfe, C.R., Lawrence, J., and Engle, R. (1991), 'From Representation to Decision: An Analysis of Problem Solving in International Relations', in R. Sternberg and P. Frensch (eds), *Complex Problem Solving: Principle and Mechanisms* (Hillsdale, NJ: Erlbaum).

Wade, R. (1992), 'East Asia's Economic Success', *World Politics*, 44: 270–320.

Wæver, O. (1996), European Security Identities', Journal of Common Market Studies, 34: 103–32.

Wæver, O. (1998), 'Explaining Europe by Decoding Discourses', in A. Wivel (ed.), *Explaining European Integration* (Copenhagen: Copenhagen Political Studies Press).

Wæver, O. (2002), 'Identity, Communities and Foreign Policy: Discourse Analysis as Foreign Policy Theory', in L. Hansen and O. Wæver (eds), *European Integration and National Identity: The Challenge of the Nordic States* (London: Routledge), 20–49.

Wæver, O. (2004), 'Discursive Approaches', in T. Diez and A. Wiener (eds), *European Integration Theory* (Oxford: Oxford University Press), 197–216.

Walker, R.B.J. (1986), 'Culture, Discourse, Insecurity', *Alternatives*, 11: 485–504.

Walker, R.B.J. (1987), 'Realism, Change and International Political Theory', *International Studies Quarterly*, 31: 65–86.

Walker, R.B.J. (1990), 'Security, Sovereignty, and the Challenge of World Politics', *Alternatives*, 15: 3–27.

Walker, R.B.J. (1993), *Inside/Outside: International Relations as Political Theory* (Cambridge: Cambridge University Press).

Walker, R.B.J. (ed.) (2006), 'Special Section. Theorizing the Liberty–Security Relation: Sovereignty, Liberalism and Exceptionalism', *Security Dialogue*, 37: 7–82.

Walker, S.G. (1977), 'The Interface Betwen Beliefs and Behavior: Henry A. Kissinger's Operational Code and the Vietnam War', *Journal of Conflict Resolution*, 21: 129–68.

Walker, S.G. (ed.) (1987), *Role Theory and Foreign Policy Analysis* (Durham, NC: Duke University Press).

Walker, S.G., Malici, A., and Schafer, M. (2011). *Rethinking Foreign Policy Analysis: States, Leaders, and the Microfoundations of Behavioral International Relations* (New York: Routledge).

Wallace, W. (1990), *The Transformation of Western Europe* (London: Pinter).

Walt, S.M. (1991), 'The Renaissance of Security Studies', *International Studies Quarterly*, 35: 211–39.

Walt, S. (1992), 'Revolution and War', *World Politics*, 44: 321–68.

Walt, S. (1998), 'International Relations: One World, Many Theories', *Foreign Policy*, 110, 29–46.

Walt, S.M. (2002), 'The Enduring Relevance of the Realist Tradition', in I. Katznelson and H.V. Milner (eds), *Political Science: The State of the Discipline* (New York: W.W. Norton).

Walt, S. (2005), *Taming American Power: The Global Response to US Primacy* (London: W.W. Norton).

Waltz, K.N. (1959), *Man, the State, and War* (New York: Columbia University Press).

Waltz, K.N. (1979), *Theory of International Politics* (Reading, MA: Addison Wesley).

Waltz, K.N. (1988), 'The Origins of War in Neorealist Theory', in R. Rotberg and T. Rabb (eds), *The Origin and Prevention of Major Wars* (Cambridge: Cambridge University Press).

Waltz, K.N. (1993) 'The Emerging Structure of International Politics', *International Security*, 18, 44–79.

Waltz, K.N. (1996), 'International Politics is not Foreign Policy', *Security Studies*, 6: 54–7.

Walzer, M. (1977/1992), *Just and Unjust Wars: A Moral Argument with Historical Illustrations* (New York: Basic Books).

Wasserman, B. (1960), 'The Failure of Intelligence Prediction', *Political Studies*, 8: 156–69.

Weber, C. (1995), *Simulating Sovereignty: Intervention, the State and Symbolic Exchange* (Cambridge: Cambridge University Press).

Weede, E. (1984), 'Democracy and War Involvement', *Journal of Conflict Resolution*, 28: 649–64.

Weldes, J. (1999), *Constructing National Interests: The United States and the Cuban Missile Crisis* (Minneapolis, MN: University of Minnesota Press).

Weldes, J., Laffey, M., Gusterson, H., and Duvall, R. (eds) (1999), *Cultures of Insecurity* (Minneapolis, MN: University of Minnesota Press).

Wendt, A. (1987), 'The Agent–Structure Problem in International Relations', *International Organization*, 41: 335–70.

Wendt, A. (1992), 'Anarchy Is What States Make of It: The Social Construction of Power Politics', *International Organization*, 46: 395–421.

Wendt, A. (1995), 'Constructing International Politics', *International Security*, 20: 71–81.

Wendt, A. (1998), 'Constitution and Causation in International Relations', *Review of International Studies* 24: 101–18.

Wendt, A. (1999), *Social Theory of International Politics* (Cambridge: Cambridge University Press).

Wheeler, N. (1997), 'Humanitarian Intervention and World Politics', in J. Baylis and S. Smith (eds), *The Globalisation of World Politics: An Introduction to International Relations* (Oxford: Oxford University Press).

Wheeler, N.J. (2000), *Saving Strangers: Humanitarian Intervention in International Society* (Oxford: Oxford University Press).

Wheeler, N. and Booth, K. (1992), 'The Security Dilemma', in J. Baylis and N.J. Rennger (eds), *Dilemmas of World Politics* (Oxford: Oxford University Press).

Wheeler, N.J. and Dunne, T. (2004), 'Moral Britannia? Evaluating the Ethical Dimension in Labour's Foreign Policy', Foreign Policy Centre paper (http://fpc.org.uk/fsblob/233.pdf).

White, B. (2001), *Understanding European Foreign Policy* (Basingstoke: Palgrave Macmillan).

White House (2002), The President's State of the Union Address (www.whitehouse.gov/news/releases/2002/01/print/20020129-11.html) (accessed 31/3/2007).

Whitman, R. and Juncos, A. (2009), 'The Lisbon Treaty and the Foreign, Security and Defence Policy: Reforms, Implementation and the Consequences of (Non-)Ratification', *European Foreign Affairs Review*, 14: 25–46.

Whitman, R. and Wolff, S. (eds.) (2010), *The European Neighbourhood Policy in Perspective: Context, Implementation and Impact* (Basingstoke: Palgrave Macmillan).

Wight, C. (2006), *Agents, Structures and International Relations: Politics and Ontology* (Cambridge: Cambridge University Press).

Wilkenfeld, J., Hopple, G.W., Rossa, P.J., and Andriole, S.J. (1980), *Foreign Policy Behavior: The Interstate Behavior Analysis Model* (Beverly Hills, CA: Sage).

Williams, P. (2005), *British Foreign Policy Under New Labour 1997–2005* (Basingstoke: Palgrave Macmillan).

Wilson, D. and Purushothaman, R. (2003), 'Dreaming with the BRICs', Global Economics Paper No. 99, Goldman Sachs, 1 October.

Wilson, W. (1924), *The Messages and Papers of Woodrow Wilson* (ed. A. Shaw) (New York: Review of Reviews).

Winkielman, P. and Berridge, K.C. (2004), 'Unconscious Emotion', *Current Directions in Psychological Science*, 13: 120–3.

Winter, D.G. (1973), *The Power Motive* (New York: Free Press).

Winter, D.G., Hermann, M.G., Weintraub, W., and Walker, S.G. (1991), 'The Personalities of Bush and Gorbachev Measured at a Distance: Procedures, Portraits, and Policy', *Political Psychology*, 12: 215–45.

Wish, N. (1980), 'Foreign Policy Makers and Their National Role Conceptions', *International Studies Quarterly*, 24: 532–43.

Wivel, A. (2005), 'Explaining Why State X Made a Certain Move Last Tuesday: The Promise and Limitations of Realist Foreign Policy Analysis', *Journal of International Relations and Development*, 8: 355–80.

Wohlforth, W.C. (1993), *The Elusive Balance: Power and Perceptions During the Cold War* (Ithaca, NY: Cornell University Press).

Wohlforth, W.C. (1999), 'The Stability of a Unipolar World', *International Security*, 21: 1–36.

Wohlstetter, A. (1959), 'The Delicate Balance of Terror', *Foreign Affairs*, 37: 221–34.

Wohlstetter, R. (1962), *Pearl Harbor: Warning and Decision* (Stanford, CA: Stanford University Press).

Wolfers, A. (1952), 'National Security as an Ambiguous Symbol', *Political Science Quarterly*, 4: 481–502.

Wolfsfeld, G. (1997), *The Media and Political Conflict* (Cambridge: Cambridge University Press).

Woodward, B. (2002), *Bush at War* (New York: Simon & Schuster).

Woodward, B. (2004), *Plan of Attack* (New York: Simon & Schuster).

Woodward, B. (2006), *State of Denial* (New York: Simon & Schuster).

Wright, L. (1998), 'Greenhouse: Libs Secret Backdown', *Canberra Times*, 26 September: 1.

WT/GC/W/442, Proposal for a Framework Agreement on Special and Differential Treatment, 19 September 2001.

Yankelovich, D. (1979), 'Farewell to "President Knows Best"', *Foreign Affairs*, 57: 670–93.

Yergin, D. (1991), *The Prize: The Epic Quest for Oil, Money and Power* (London: Simon & Schuster).

Zacher, M. and Matthew, R. (1995), 'Liberal International Theory: Common Threads Divergent Strands', in C. Kegley (ed.), *Controversies in International Relations Theory* (New York: St Martin's Press), 107–40.

Zajonc, R.B. (1980), 'Feeling and Thinking: Preferences Need no Inferences', *American Psychologist*, 35: 151–75.

Zajonc, R.B. (1984), 'On the Primacy of Affect', *American Psychologist*, 39: 117–23.

Zajonc, R.B. (1998), 'Emotions', in D Gilbert, S.T. Fiske, and G. Lindzey, *The Handbook of Social Psychology* (4th edn), Vol. I (New York: Oxford University Press), 591–632.

Zeev, M. and Abdolali, N. (1989), 'Regime Types and International Conflict, 1816–1976', *Journal of Conflict Resolution*, 33: 3–35.

Zelikow, P. and Rice, C. (1995), *Germany Unified and Europe Transformed* (Cambridge, MA: Harvard University Press).

Zhang, Q. (2011), 'Towards an Integrated Theory of Chinese Foreign Policy', research paper presented at the International Studies Association Annual Conference, 'Global Governance: Political Authority in Transition', Montreal, Canada, 16–19 March 2011.

Zinn, H. (1996), *A People's History of the United States from 1492 to the Present* (2nd edn) (Harlow: Pearson Education).

Zolberg, A. (1969), *One Party Government in the Ivory Coast* (Princeton, NJ: Princeton University Press).

Zuern, M. (2002), 'From Interdependence to Globalization', in W. Carlsnaes, T. Risse, and B. Simmons (eds), *Handbook of International Relations* (London: Sage), 235–54.

Zuern, M. and Checkel, J.T. (2005), 'Getting Socialized to Build Bridges: Constructivism and Rationalism, Europe and the Nation State', *International Organization*, 59: 1045–79.

Zweig, D. (1991), 'Sino-American Relations and Human Rights: June 4 and the Changing Nature of a Bilateral Relationship' in W.T. Tow (ed.), *Building Sino-American Relations: An Analysis for the 1990s* (New York: Paragon House).

Index